Paul Parker

Formula 1

IN CAMERA 1960–69

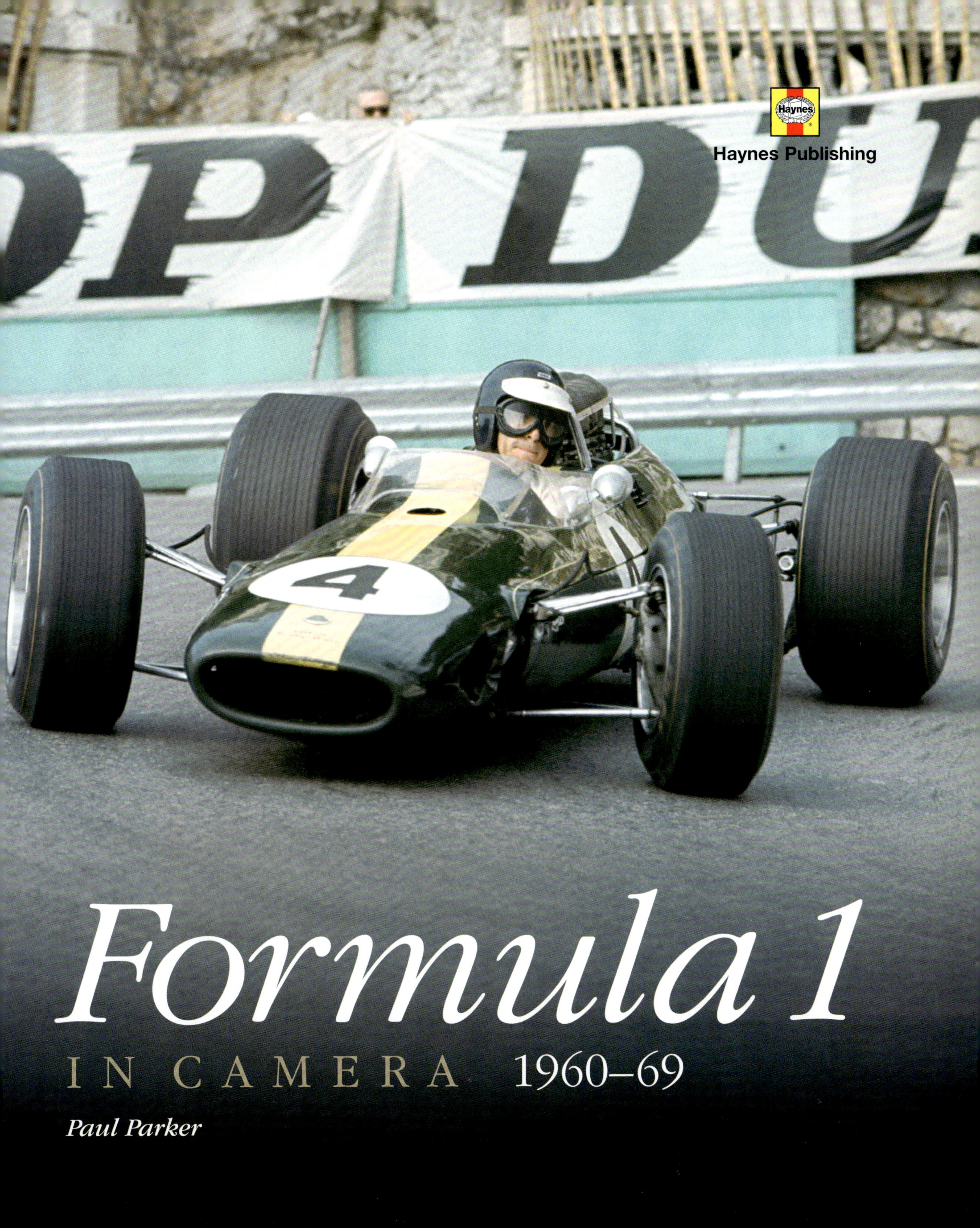

Haynes Publishing

Formula 1

IN CAMERA 1960–69

Paul Parker

First published in June 2006

A catalogue record for this book is available from the British Library

ISBN 1 84425 218 3

Library of Congress catalog card no. 2005935266

Haynes North America Inc., 861 Lawrence Drive,
Newbury Park, California 91320, USA.

Published by Haynes Publishing,
Sparkford, Yeovil, Somerset BA22 7JJ, UK.
Tel: 01963 442030 Fax: 01963 440001
Int. tel: +44 1963 442030
Int. fax: +44 1963 440001
E-mail: sales@haynes.co.uk
Website: www.haynes.co.uk

Printed and bound in Britain by J. H. Haynes & Co. Ltd,
Sparkford, Yeovil, Somerset BA22 7JJ

Photograph credits
All photographs supplied by LAT Photographic apart from the following:

Ferret Fotographic: pages 8/9, 10 top, 11 top (and back cover), 20, 21, 26, 27, 28 top, 36, 58, 63 bottom, 67, 78 bottom, 80, 87 bottom, 101 top, 129 bottom, 155 top, 156 top, 212 bottom

Grand Prix Library: pages 12, 13, 14, 15, 16, 17, 18, 19, 53 bottom, 99 top, 144 bottom,

Michael Cooper Archive: pages 84/85, 141 bottom, 142, 202 bottom

Sutton Motorsport Images: pages 8/9, 10 bottom, 23 bottom, 28 bottom, 37, 38 top, 39, 40 bottom, 48, 71, 88 bottom, 108 bottom, 130 bottom, 162 top, 163 top

CONTENTS

AUTHOR'S INTRODUCTION

I suppose this book could be described in the modern idiom as a 'prequel', following on from my earlier effort *F1 in Camera 1970–79* and Quentin Spurring's *F1 in Camera 1980–89.*

During the 1960s some continental racing still took place on public roads, and even purpose built circuits had scenery and an aesthetic appeal that is now long gone. It extended to the drivers whose individual style and appearance was plainly visible, helped by the relatively low cockpit sides, open face helmets, goggles or visors and the archetypal string back driving gloves. The exclusivity and fenced off mentality of modern F1 was a long way into the future. Enthusiasts, small boys and grannies et al could mingle with the great and the good in race paddocks for a modest sum.

By 1969 wings, wide tyres, commercial sponsorship, the Bell Star full face helmet, fire resistant driver's suits and gauntlets rather than gloves had begun to dilute the human aspect, at least from the spectator's viewpoint. Nevertheless a high level of public accessibility was still possible.

In a decade of change there were three different F1 formulae within seven seasons, 2500cc in 1960, 1500cc during 1961–65 and 3000cc from 1966 onwards.

After the demise of the 1954–60 2.5-litre F1, the much maligned 1.5-litre formula actually produced some heroic racing and was relatively safe although it suffered the worst F1 accident in history at Monza in 1961. The cars were easier to handle than their predecessors and had better brakes, but were not as fast in a straight line. Their pace was bound up in carrying speed into and through the corners and the advent of the wider Dunlop R7 tyres in 1964 greatly enhanced the effect. The downside was that the machines were too tame and the better drivers could have handled much more power. However, because the performance envelope was so narrow it took considerable skill and finesse to extract the best from the cars.

Another aspect of the period was the ability of lesser drivers to chop and change around the teams; see the 1961 listings as a perfect example (note that the Teams, Drivers and Results tabulations are for World Championship events only). Certain Grands Prix of this era attracted local 'aces' whose championship participation was limited to their home race. Others would cherry pick their races of choice and ignore the rest, often for financial reasons.

Grid numbers varied enormously and whilst Monaco was limited to 16 starters, 32 cars raced at Monza in 1961, the highest number ever for a World Championship GP. This also highlights the enormous diversity of entrants that is the very antithesis of the modern closed shop era. However, it should be admitted that during the late 1960s numbers could dwindle alarmingly, only 13 F1 cars starting in the 1968 Spanish, 1969 French and 1969 German GPs.

When engine swept volumes doubled in 1966 (imagine doing that today) F1 immediately became much more dangerous. Some of the cars had questionable structural integrity and were effectively crude Molotov cocktails on wheels. At the end of the decade, advances in tyres, grip, handling, power and braking had transformed everything and certain venues were now very marginal where safety was concerned.

For the classic road circuits the problems were just beginning. The Belgian GP on the daunting 8.76-mile Spa-Francorchamps circuit was not run in 1969 due to financial problems and its last F1 hurrah would be 1970. In Germany, the awesome Nürburgring survived in a mildly sanitised version although increasingly unsuitable for ever quicker cars.

During this decade the established non-championship F1 races went into decline. For example, there were 20 such events in 1962, nine in England alone including the last ever F1 race at Crystal Palace, the others shared between South Africa, France, Belgium, Germany, Italy, Sicily, Sweden, Denmark and Mexico. Possibly the plethora of such events was due to there being no active F2 class for the first three seasons of the 1.5-litre F1. Once the 1-litre F2 became established in 1964, these pre-season warm-ups and fillers began to diminish in number.

Inevitably the passage of time has robbed us not only of many participants of this long-ago era but also some of its colour photographic material. Furthermore, colour was used sparingly due to cost, and professional photographers of any given period concentrate on the front runners rather than the also rans.

Additionally, despite sifting through mountains of material, I could find no decent colour images of the 1960s equivalent of a Balestre or a Moseley or indeed many of the team owners, managers and one B. C. Ecclestone who handled Jochen Rindt's affairs.

Another problem was the access restrictions placed upon visiting photographers at Monza until 1965/66 that were not applied to locals, as the late Michael Cooper told me a few years ago. However I did manage to unearth some Ferrari gems from the 1960 race.

So here we go again and to misquote the Lone Ranger television trailer, "Back to those thrilling days of yesteryear".

Paul Parker
Spring 2006

1960

'BLACK JACK' IS BACK

The first season of the new decade was the seventh and last of the 2.5-litre Formula 1. Cooper, which had proved its mid-engine concept in 1959, continued to dominate and Jack Brabham clinched a second consecutive title with a string of five Grand Prix victories using its new 'low-line' T53. Brabham's team mate, Bruce McLaren, won the first round in Argentina and, with a series of 2nd and 3rd places, was the runner-up in the World Championship.

The season was marred by tragedy. In May, Harry Schell died in a practice crash at Silverstone at the wheel of the Yeoman Credit team's Cooper. In June, Stirling Moss and Mike Taylor both suffered serious injuries during practice at Spa when their Lotus 18s had mechanical failures; during the race, Alan Stacey and rising star Chris Bristow both lost their lives. Moss's injuries kept him out of the French and British Grands Prix, but he made an astonishingly rapid recovery and was back in the cockpit for the race in Portugal. Earlier in the year, Moss had given Lotus its maiden Grand Prix victory, at Monaco, and ended the season by winning the US Grand Prix at Riverside. He also won the Gold Cup at Oulton Park.

Following an impressive debut in the Argentine Grand Prix, Team Lotus works driver Innes Ireland brilliantly won the non-championship races at Goodwood and Silverstone with Colin Chapman's new Lotus 18. Later, he added the Lombank Trophy at Snetterton. Lotus also ran Jim Clark in both Formula Junior and Formula 1 (in which he made his debut at Zandvoort) and occasionally motorcycle champion John Surtees, who was more impressive than his team mates, finishing 2nd in the British Grand Prix and leading the Portuguese Grand Prix.

At BRM, Graham Hill was increasingly competitive with the mid-engined P48 and led the British Grand Prix until failing brakes caused him to crash. Otherwise, apart from a 3rd place in Holland, chronic unreliability spoiled his season. His team mates, Dan Gurney and Jo Bonnier, also suffered, in particular Gurney, who was smitten by a brake failure at Zandvoort and crashed, killing a spectator.

Ferrari's front-engined Dino 246 was still competitive at Spa, Reims and Monza, where Phil Hill won after the British teams had boycotted the Italian Grand Prix on safety grounds, due to the use of the bumpy, high-speed banked section of the Autodromo Nazionale. Aston Martin and Scarab also operated front-engined cars, as did Vanwall, which briefly returned. A modified Vanwall was raced at Goodwood at Easter and subsequently formed the basis of a 'lowline' hybrid, driven without success at Reims by Tony Brooks. Brooks's regular drive was with the Yeoman Credit team, but the deaths of Schell and Bristow cast a lengthening shadow over his career.

The grids otherwise comprised a varied collection, including Maserati powered Coopers. This was the final season in which the Indianapolis 500 counted towards the Formula 1 World Championship, and Jim Rathmann duly scored eight points to finish 8th in the Drivers' table.

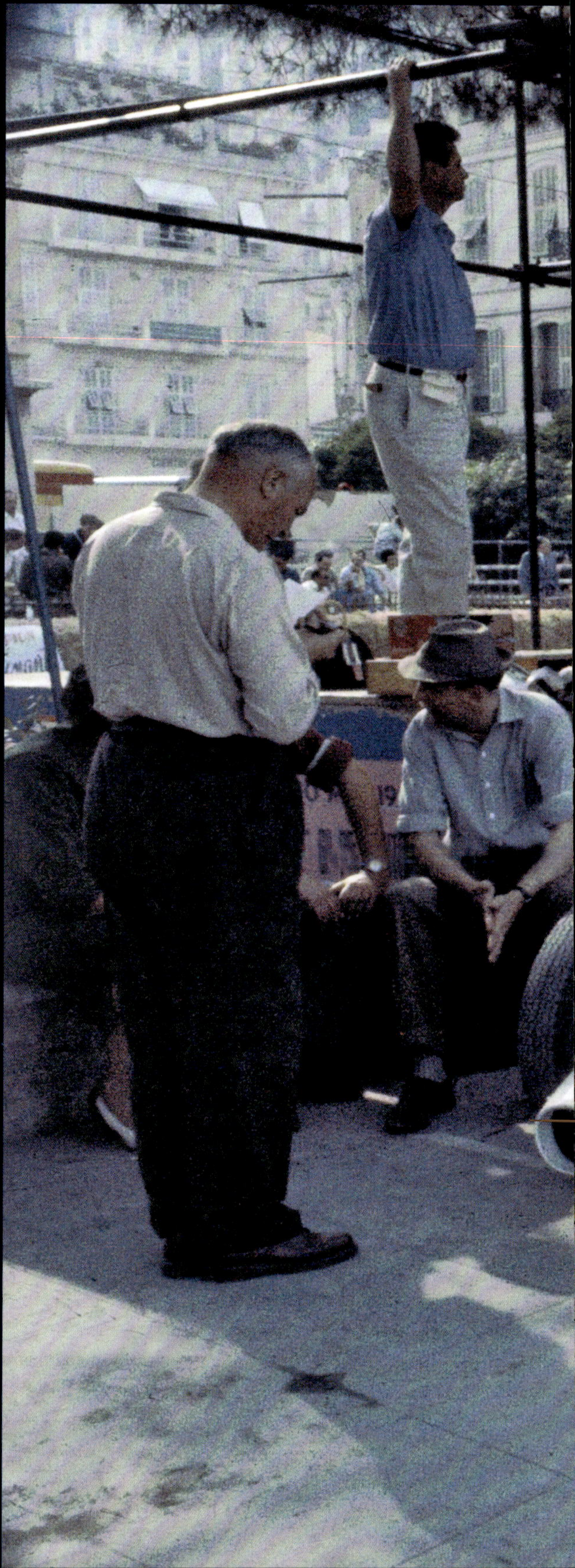

Lance Reventlow's Scarab is shaded from the sun in the original Monaco pits. Directly behind the car are future Ferrari ace Lorenzo Bandini and famous photographer Louis Klemantaski. Neither this car nor Chuck Daigh's qualified for the race. Stirling Moss tried Lance's machine during qualifying and recorded a lap-time of 1m 45.1s (a competitive Formula Junior time, but nearly nine seconds slower than his pole position in Rob Walker's Lotus at 1:36.3).

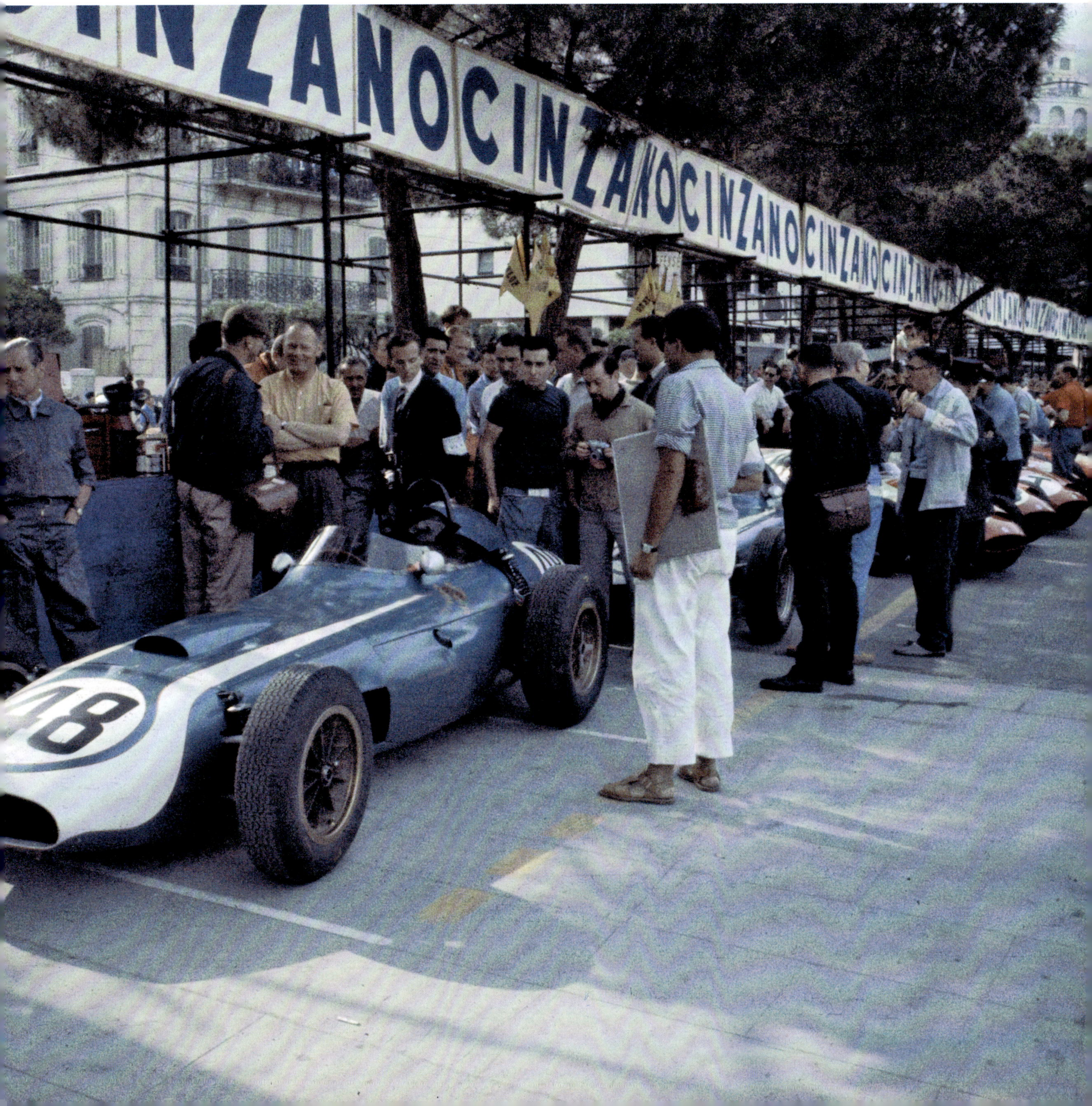

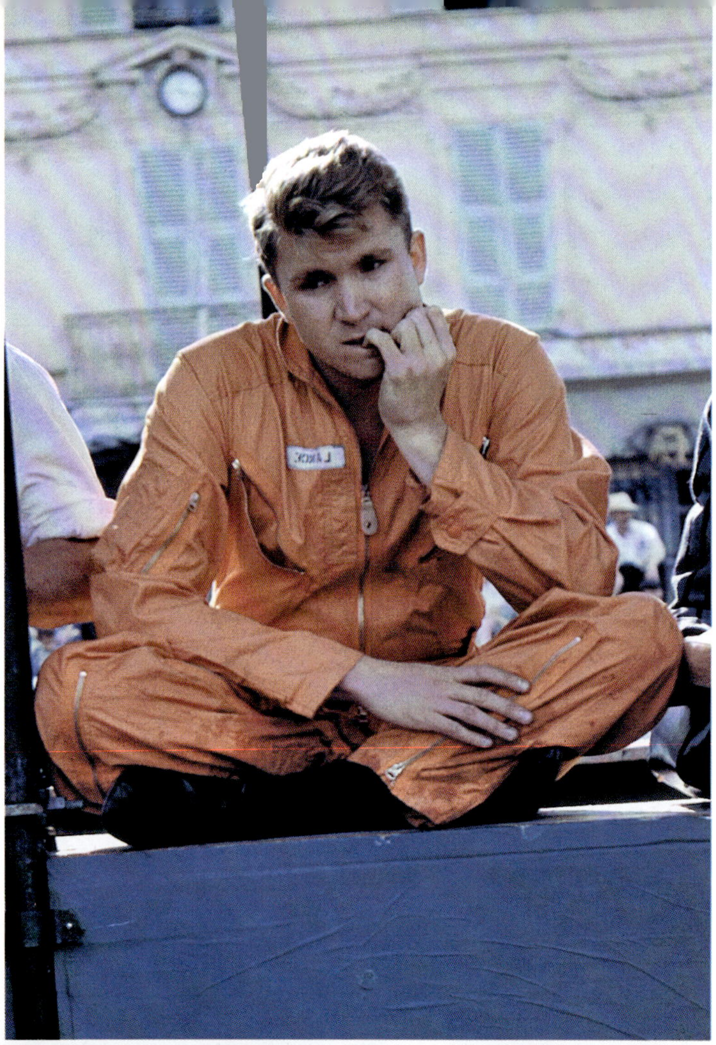

Count Lance von Haugwitz-Hardenberg-Reventlow (aka Lance Reventlow) has bitten off more than he can chew, and the realisation appears to have dawned as he nibbles his nails reflectively on the Monaco pit counter. The only son of American socialite and Woolworth heiress Barbara Hutton with Danish nobleman Curt von Haugwitz-Hardenberg-Reventlow, he had ventured to Europe in 1957 to race a Maserati and a Cooper. The foray into Formula 1 was brave but mistimed. Reventlow briefly returned to American racing with Chevy-powered sports-racing Scarabs before selling his workshops to Carroll Shelby. He was killed in a light aircraft accident near Aspen, Colorado, in 1972, aged 36.

Lance Reventlow failed to qualify his Scarab amid the grassy sand dunes of Zandvoort, but a lap-time described as "hooey" by Reventlow was credited to team mate Chuck Daigh (an obviously optimistic 1m 36.6s, on the pace of all three Ferraris). However, a disagreement over starting money resulted in another non-show for the hapless American team. Two weeks later, both Scarabs qualified at Spa, but they retired with engine failures.

Bruce McLaren spun his Cooper T53 Climax (F2-5-60) during Monaco practice and was lucky not to hit anything. Despite starting 11th on the grid, he finished 2nd in the race behind Stirling Moss and set the fastest lap. This was his second season as a Cooper works driver and he was famous for being the youngest driver ever to win a World Championship Grand Prix, at Sebring in 1959, aged 22 years and 104 days. He then won the opening 1960 race in Argentina and ended the year as Championship runner-up to team mate Jack Brabham.

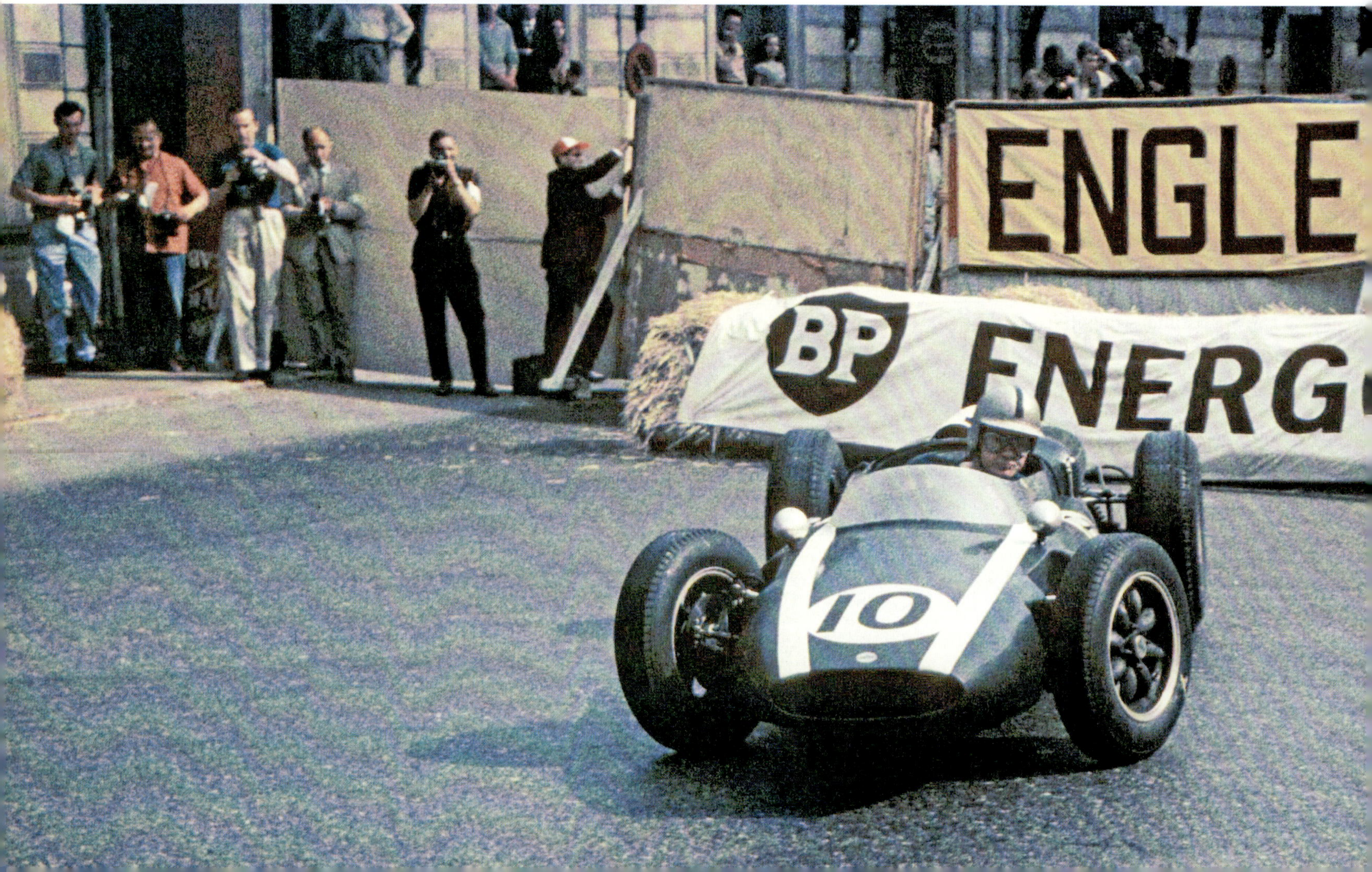

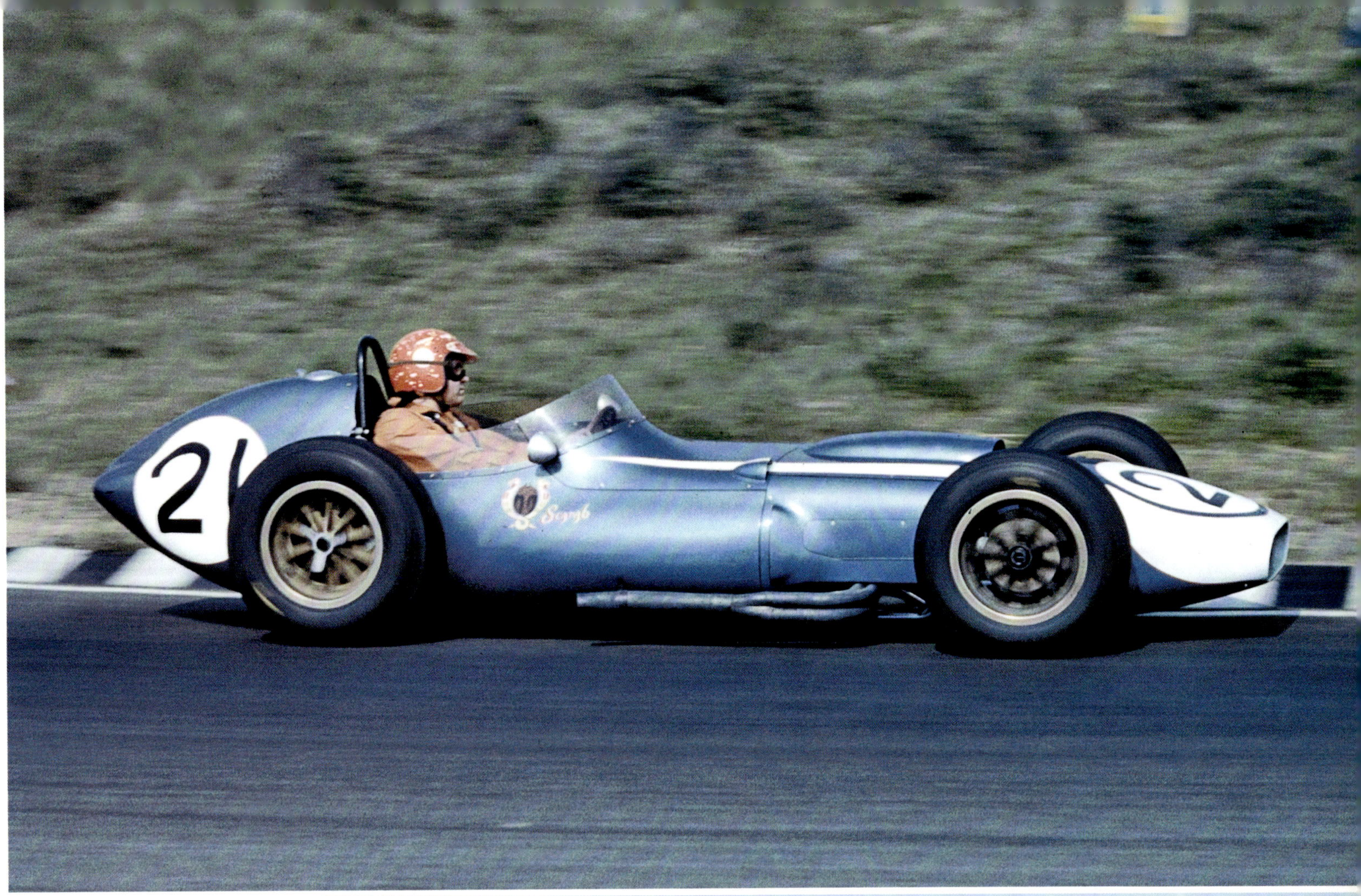

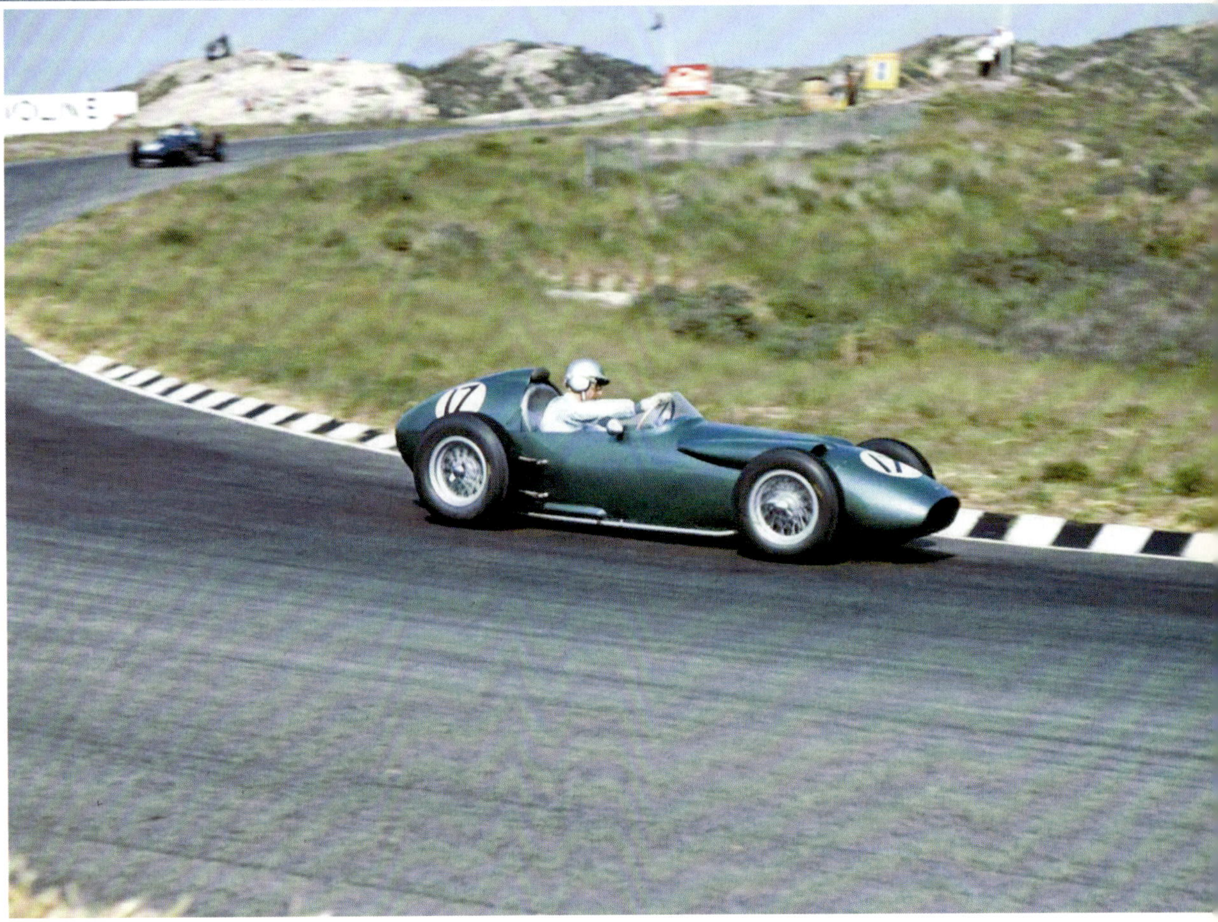

Four front-engined Formula 1 designs were still active during 1960, but only Ferrari was racing one with meaningful intentions. Aston Martin's one-year-old DBR4/250 project was already outmoded although development had trimmed the weight and width and added a Maserati transaxle and independent rear suspension. The handsome, straight-six cars, driven by Roy Salvadori and Maurice Trintignant, appeared only at Zandvoort, where Salvadori (pictured) did not start due to a start money dispute, and at Silverstone, where both started, Trintignant's being one of two wholly new DBR5s. David Brown then withdrew his company from Formula 1 and both DBR5s were broken up.

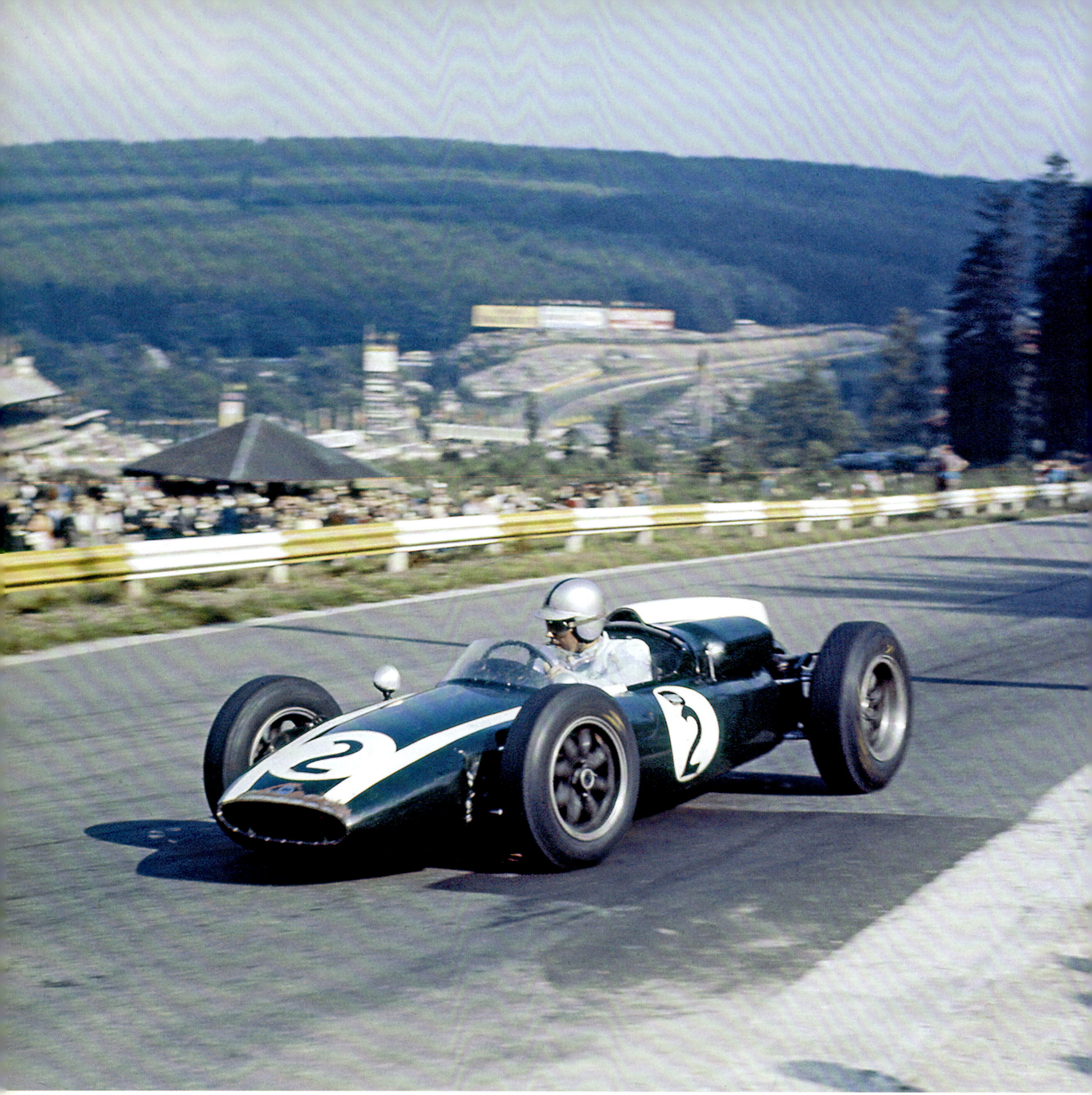

↑ Jack Brabham races his pockmarked Cooper T53 Climax (F2-8-60) towards the second of five consecutive Formula 1 victories, in the Belgian Grand Prix at Spa. Following the Moss and Taylor practice accidents there were two fatalities in this race: Chris Bristow, dicing with Willy Mairesse's Ferrari, overturned his Yeoman Credit team Cooper in the high-speed Burnenville curve and was decapitated, and later Alan Stacey was hit in the face by a bird, and his Lotus 18 crashed and caught fire. A leader article in *Autosport* referred to the rivalry between Spa, Reims and Monza, and noted: "Grand Prix racing does not need special tracks, and Belgium, France and Italy should abandon this rather senseless competition for the doubtful honour of possessing the fastest circuit in Europe."

Although Vanwall withdrew from racing in January 1959, its 270bhp four-cylinder racing engines were used in developing the range of mainstream Vandervell automotive bearings. Tony Brooks raced the old 1957–58 'VW5' chassis, heavily modified at the Easter Monday Goodwood, then lowered and renumbered 'VW11' for the French Grand Prix. This rare photograph, taken in the Reims garage, shows the drilled inboard rear disc brakes and the Colotti five-speed gearbox and independent rear suspension that replaced the original de Dion layout. Note the substantial fuel tanks, mounted either side of the scuttle, that supplemented a tail-mounted cell (absent here). A startline bump led to an early retirement at Reims, and the final exit of the Vanwall marque in F1.

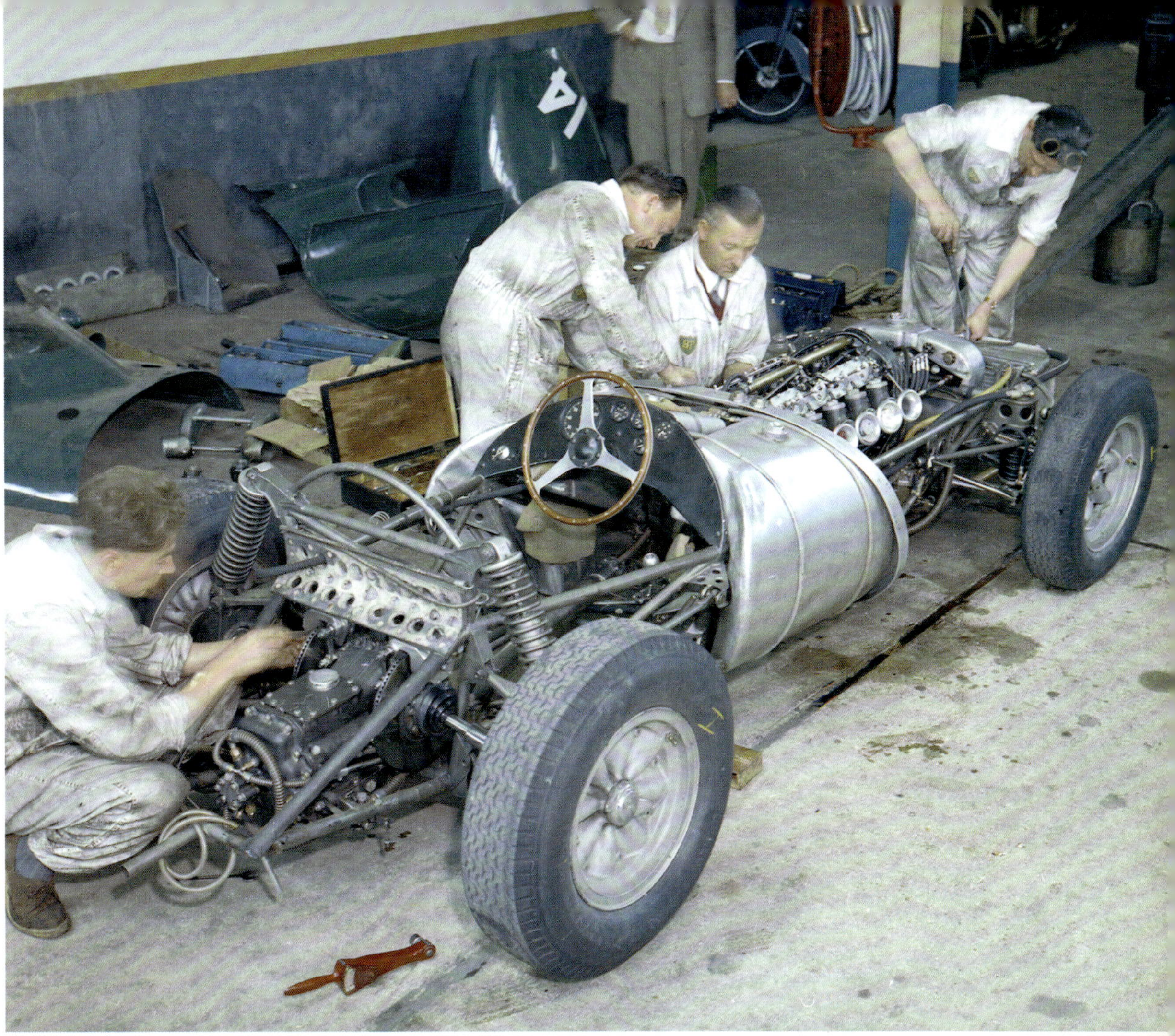

When full, the tail-mounted fuel tank of the Ferrari Dino 246 must have made for interesting handling, although the big pannier tanks were intended to reduce the effects of the progressive weight loss on front:rear balance. This long-wheelbase chassis was driven at Reims by Wolfgang von Trips, and ran as high as second before its transmission failed. The third-generation Fantuzzi-bodied Dino, with all-independent coilspring and wishbone suspension, worked well on high-speed circuits with the quad-cam V6, producing 275bhp at 8500rpm, tuned for torque rather than all-out power.

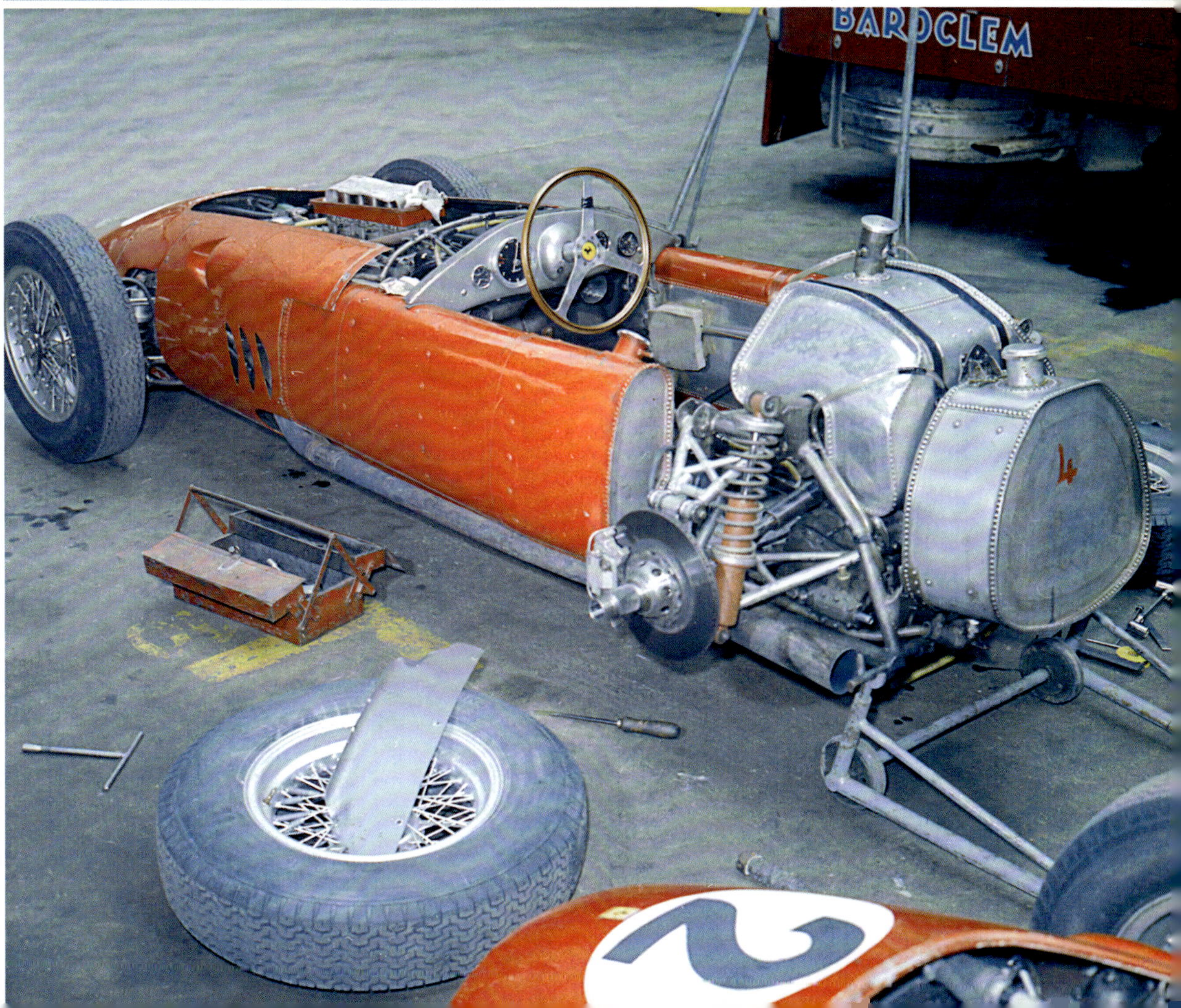

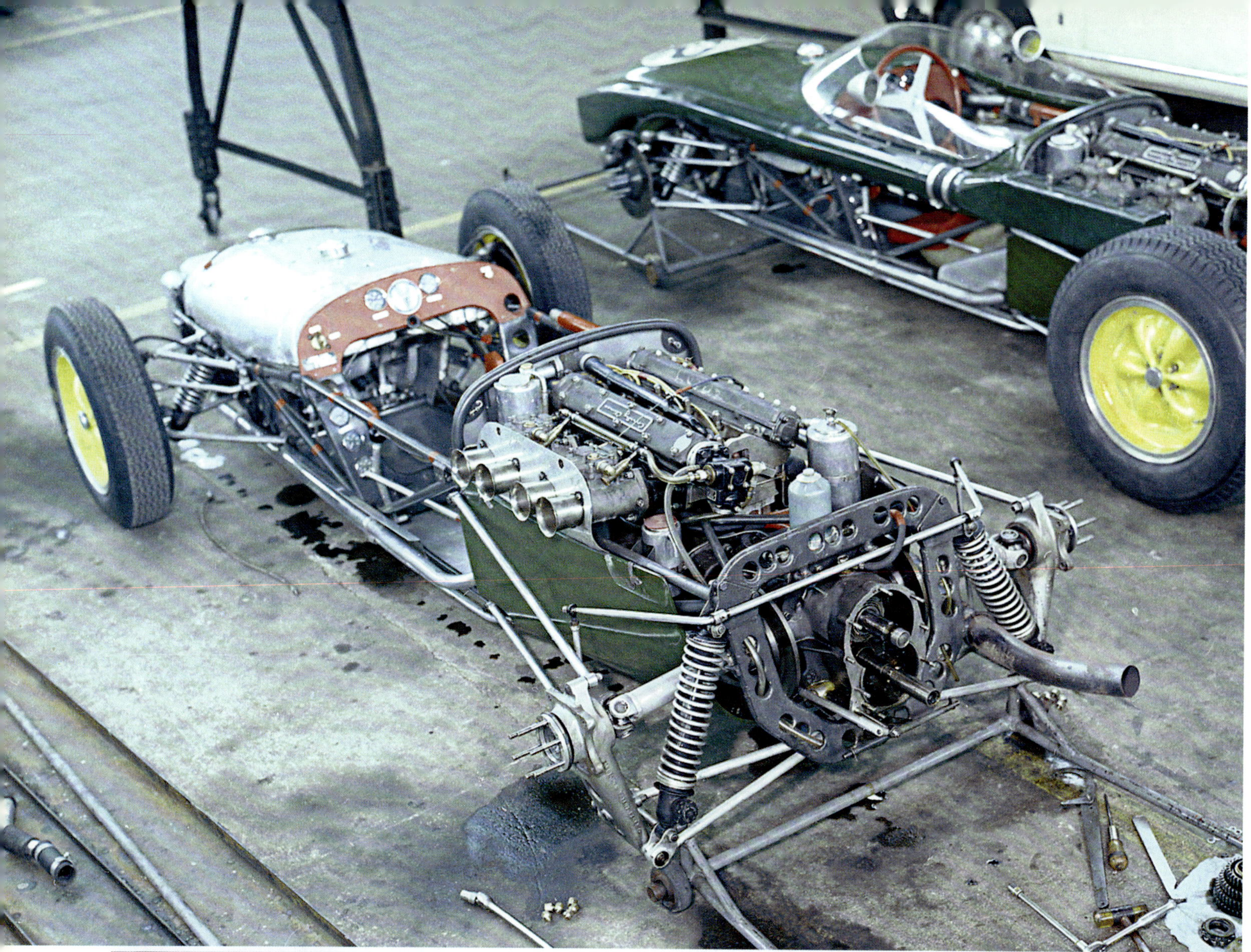

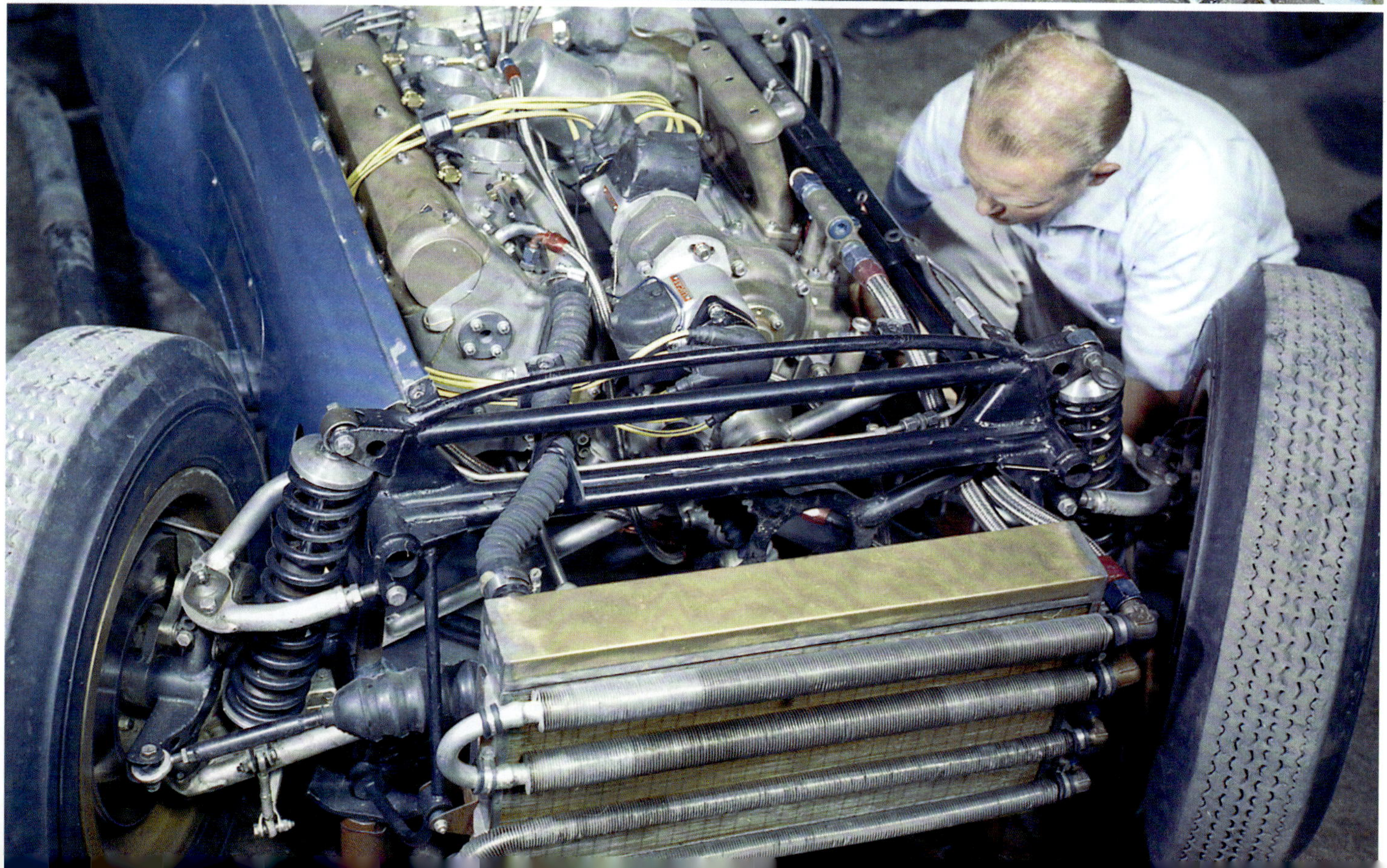

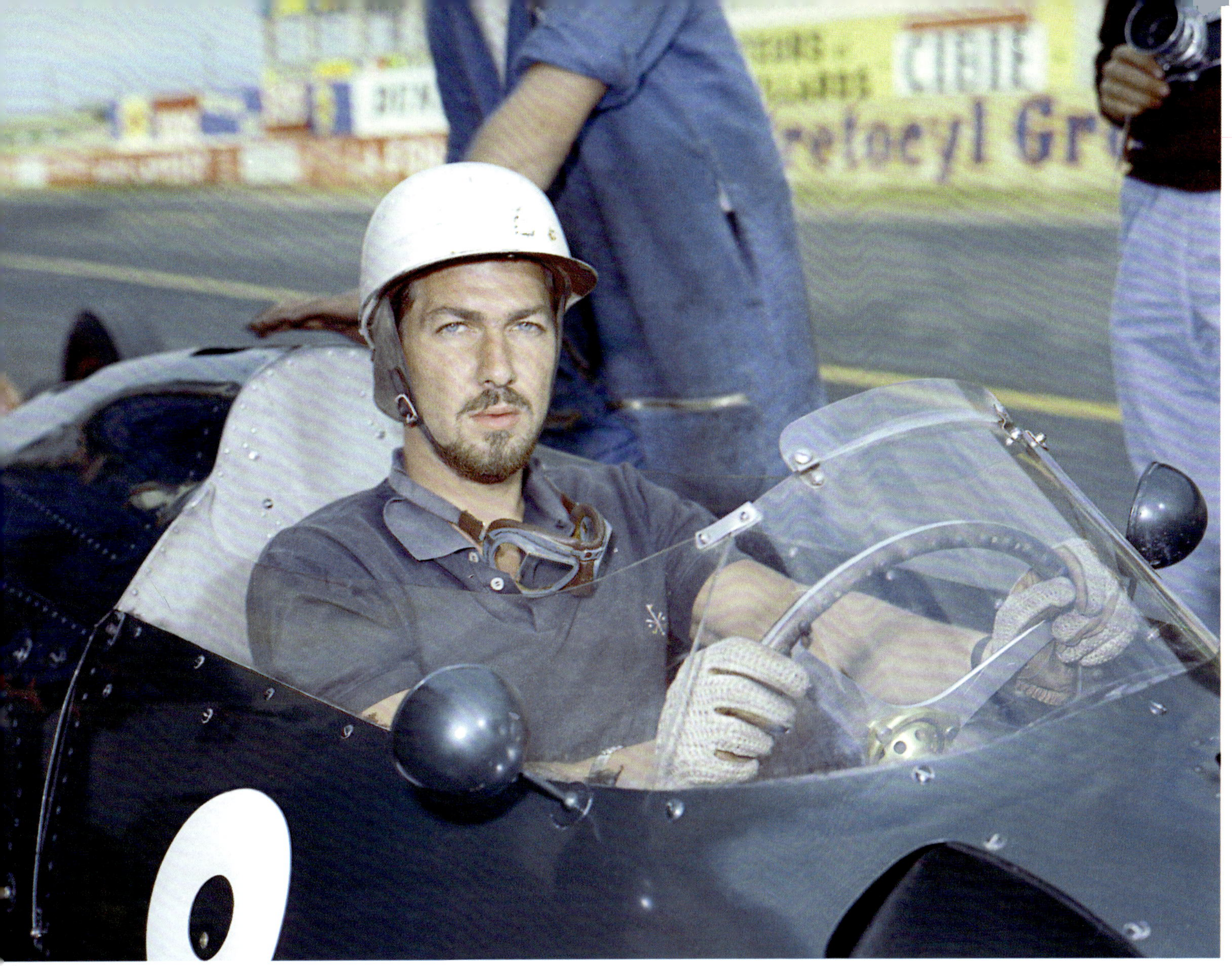

This posed portrait of handsome, 30-year-old Swede Jo Bonnier at Reims in his BRM P48 (484) encapsulates perfectly the period equipment and garb. The lightweight Herbert Johnson polo helmet, Lewis Mk8 motorcycle goggles, stringback gloves and short-sleeved Aertex shirt are typical. Note also the absence of any harness and the added Perspex lip on the top of the screen. Bonnier's main claim to fame was achieving BRM's maiden Grand Prix victory, at Zandvoort in 1959. Thereafter his single-seater performances were inconsistent, although he continued in Formula 1 for many years. He was more successful in sports car racing with Porsche, Ferrari, Lola and other cars, but crashed fatally at Le Mans in 1972.

A Lotus 18 (also available in FJ and F2 guise) reveals the new order in Formula 1. Tiny and very light, Colin Chapman's design looked simple but was actually more sophisticated than the front-engined dinosaurs, with a fully triangulated chassis frame and all-round independent wishbone suspension. The Coventry Climax FPF engine produced 240bhp at 6750rpm and 212lb ft torque – good enough in the dynamically superior Cooper and Lotus chassis to see off the more powerful opposition. The Lotus carried 22-gallons of fuel in a front tank placed over the driver's legs, visible here, and a 9.5-gallon cell behind and to the right of the seat. The fuel mass was kept within the wheelbase but hitting anything head-on was not recommended…

Chuck Daigh works on the Scarab, with its rock-hard Goodyear sports car tyres, at Reims. Neither car qualified (Richie Ginther tried Reventlow's machine) and were withdrawn from the race. Thereafter a chastened Reventlow returned to California and, apart from entering Daigh in the US Grand Prix and two British Intercontinental formula races in 1961, these machines were seen no more in four-cylinder form. The offset of the Offenhauser-based but underpowered, 230bhp engine, which featured desmodromic valve actuation and Hilborn-Travers fuel-injection, is well illustrated here, as is the extraordinary amount of steering lock on offer.

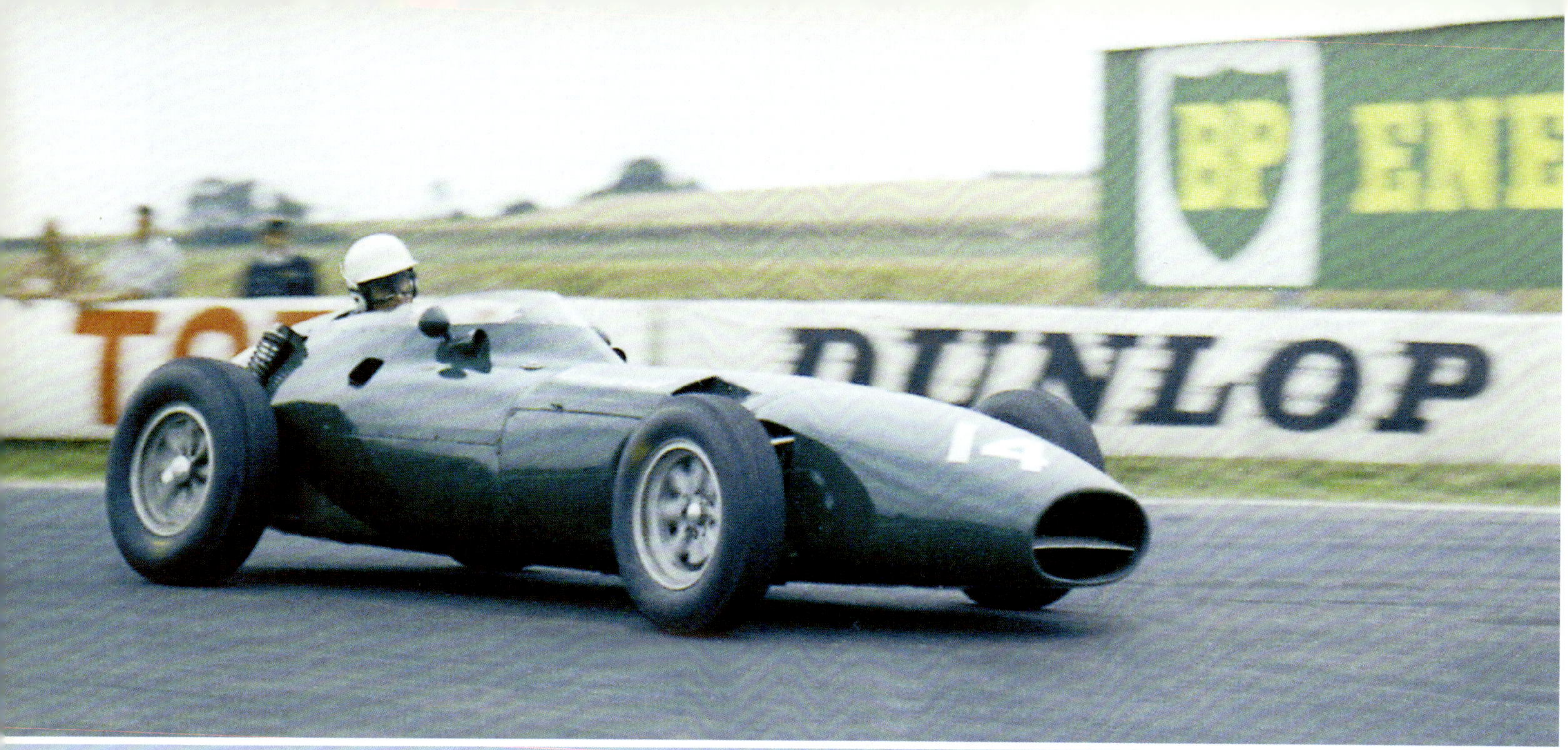
BP
DUNLOP
14

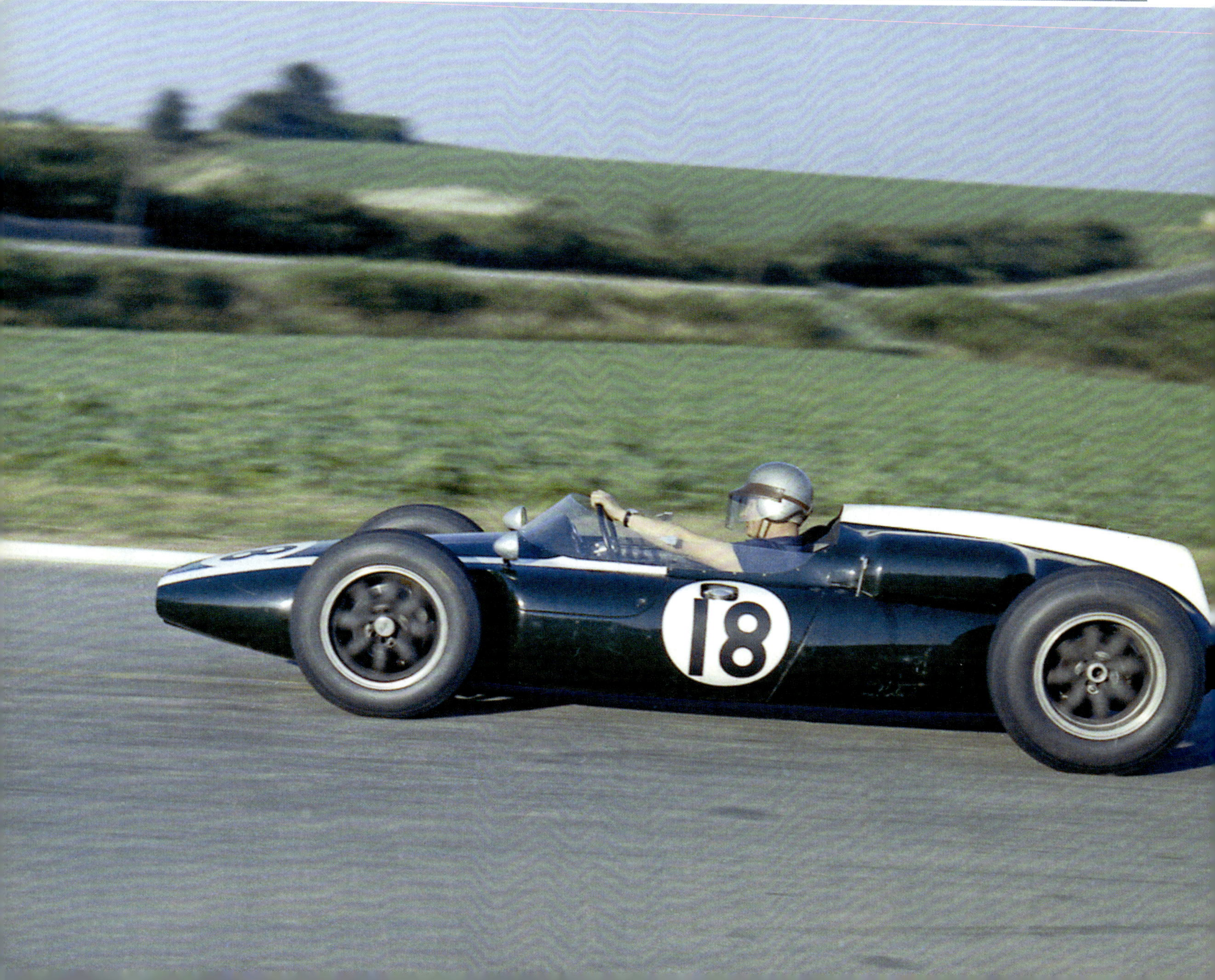
18

Tony Brooks was the supreme master of high-speed circuits like Reims and Spa, but even his skills could not make the redesigned Vanwall perform: in its 1958 guise, chassis 'VW5' recorded a lap-time of 2m 23.4s in his hands at Reims, and two years on 'VW11' managed 2:23.3 despite the advantage of better tyres, a reduced frontal area and the other supposed improvements. Note the amount of roll and the attitude of the wheels as he negotiates Thillois. The front wheels are similar to the Minilite alloys that would become so popular in racing later in the decade and beyond.

Bruce McLaren, the young team mate of Jack Brabham at Cooper Cars, lines up his T53 (F2-5-60) for the Muizon corner during practice at Reims. The Kiwi qualified on the fourth row but finished 3rd behind Brabham and Olivier Gendebien in the Yeoman Credit team's Cooper. McLaren, who had won the 1959 Formula 1 finale at Sebring, finished the 1960 season as the runner-up to his team leader in the World Championship.

No mistaking Betty's cardigan as Jack Brabham tries his best to smile at the camera in the long shadows of evening practice at Reims. He qualified on the pole and secured the third of five consecutive Grand Prix wins with the 'low-line' Cooper T53 Climax (F2-8-60) *en route* to his successful World Championship defence. The combination of the quick, well-sorted and reliable T53 and one of the best drivers of the day was unbeatable in 1960, the more so following Stirling Moss's incapacitation after Spa.

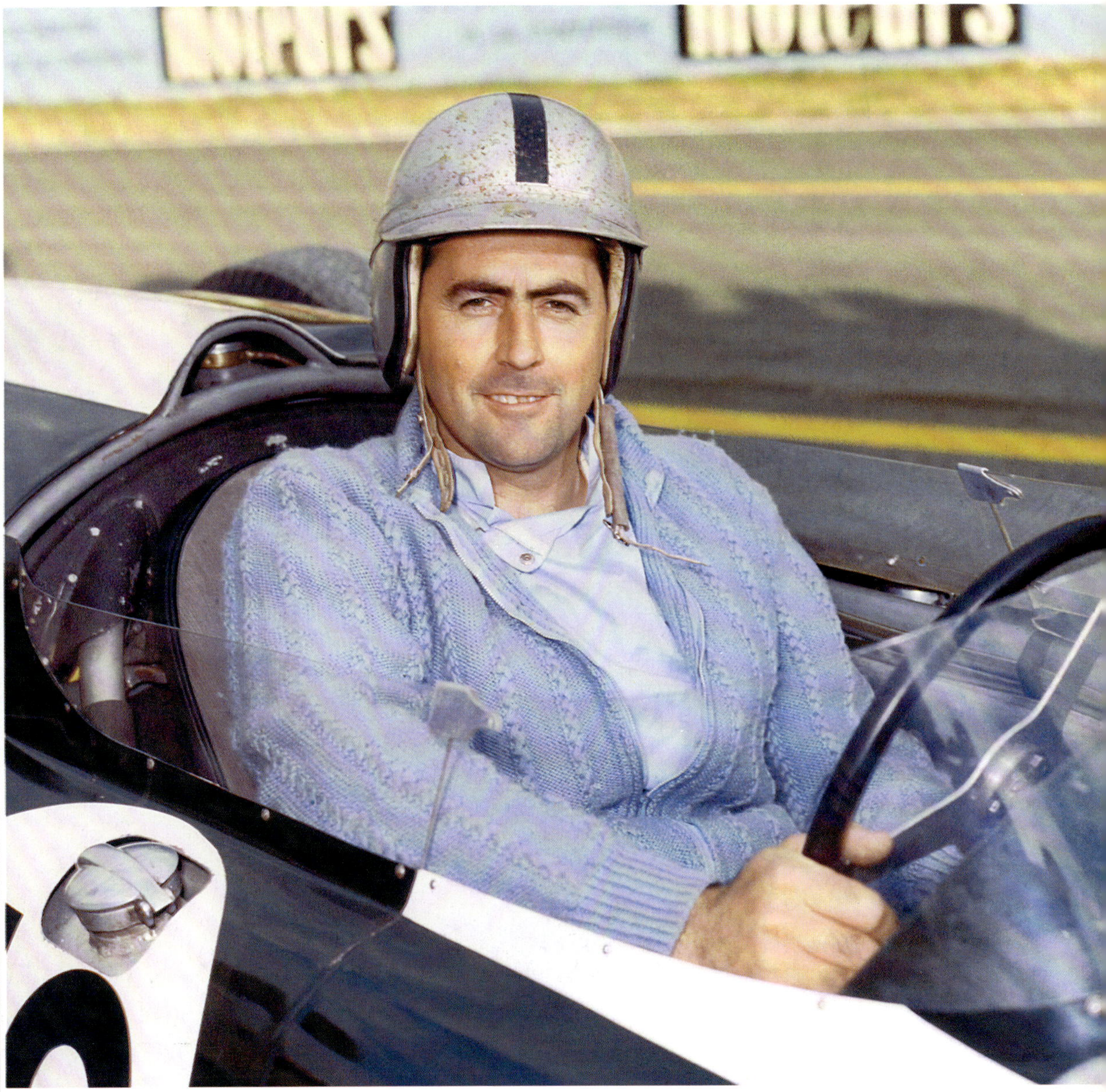

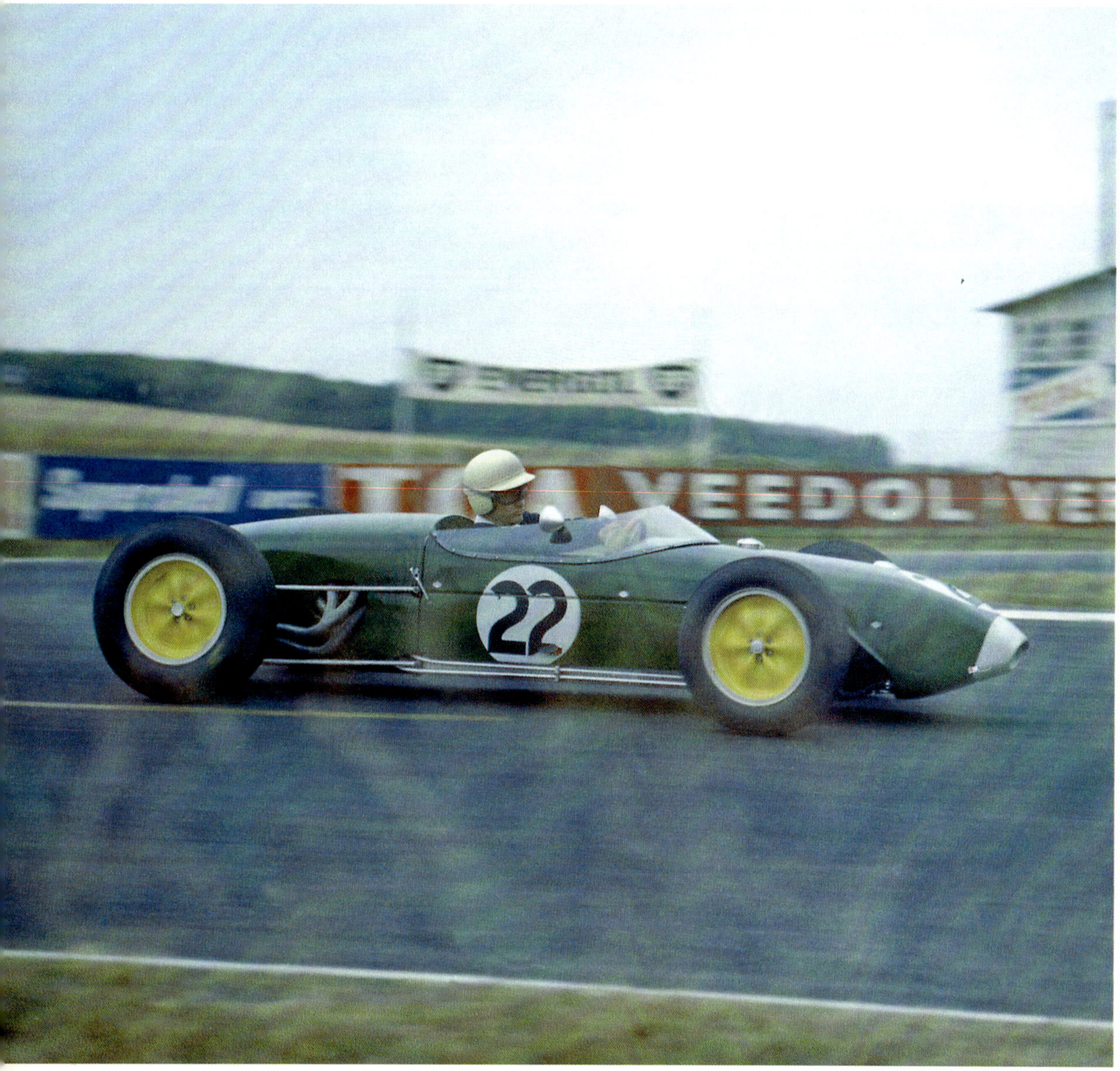

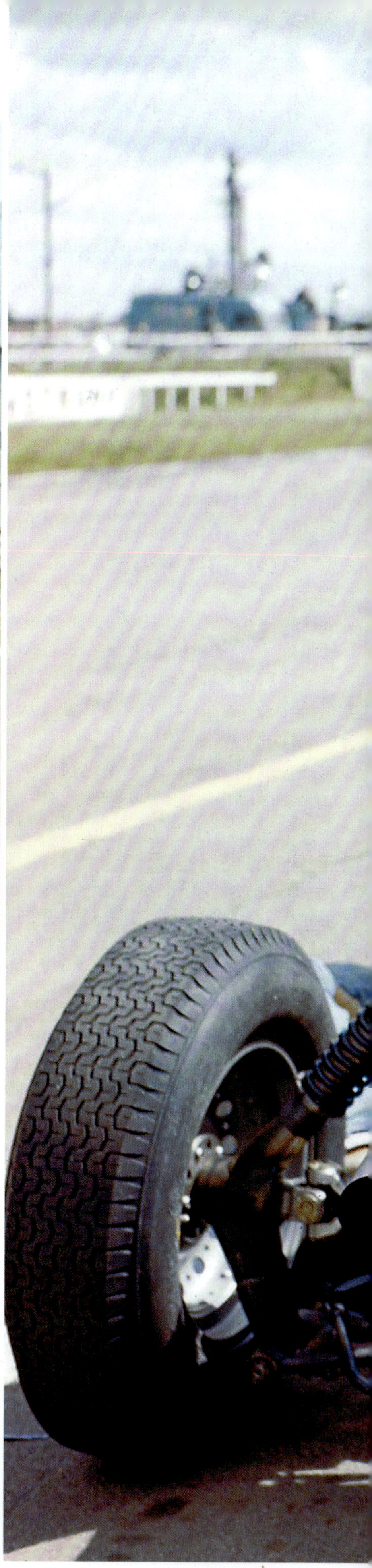

Scotsman Ron Flockhart is best known for his 1956 and 1957 Le Mans victories with D-type Jaguars, but he was also a competent single-seater racer. Here at Reims, he drove the third works Lotus 18 Climax (374) to 6th place and, later in the year, he raced a works Cooper in the US Grand Prix at Riverside. Flockhart died in April 1962 when his WW2 Mustang fighter plane broke up in mid-air near Melbourne during preparation for a London–Sydney record attempt.

Dan Gurney with a BRM P48 (486) during practice for the British Grand Prix at Silverstone, in his second season of Formula 1. Gurney was not happy at BRM, where his laid-back manner did not sit well with the management. In addition, he was badly upset by a crash at Zandvoort, caused by a hydraulic pipe detaching from the single 'cheesecutter' brake disc on the back of the gearbox (visible here), which killed a boy standing in a prohibited area. The BRM discs were cast and slotted, rather than drilled, after designer Tony Rudd had copied the idea from the Berlin Metro railway. The four-cylinder BRM engine, carried over from the P25 produced 275bhp. Gurney was delayed in this race by gear selection problems, an example of BRM's abysmal reliability during 1960.

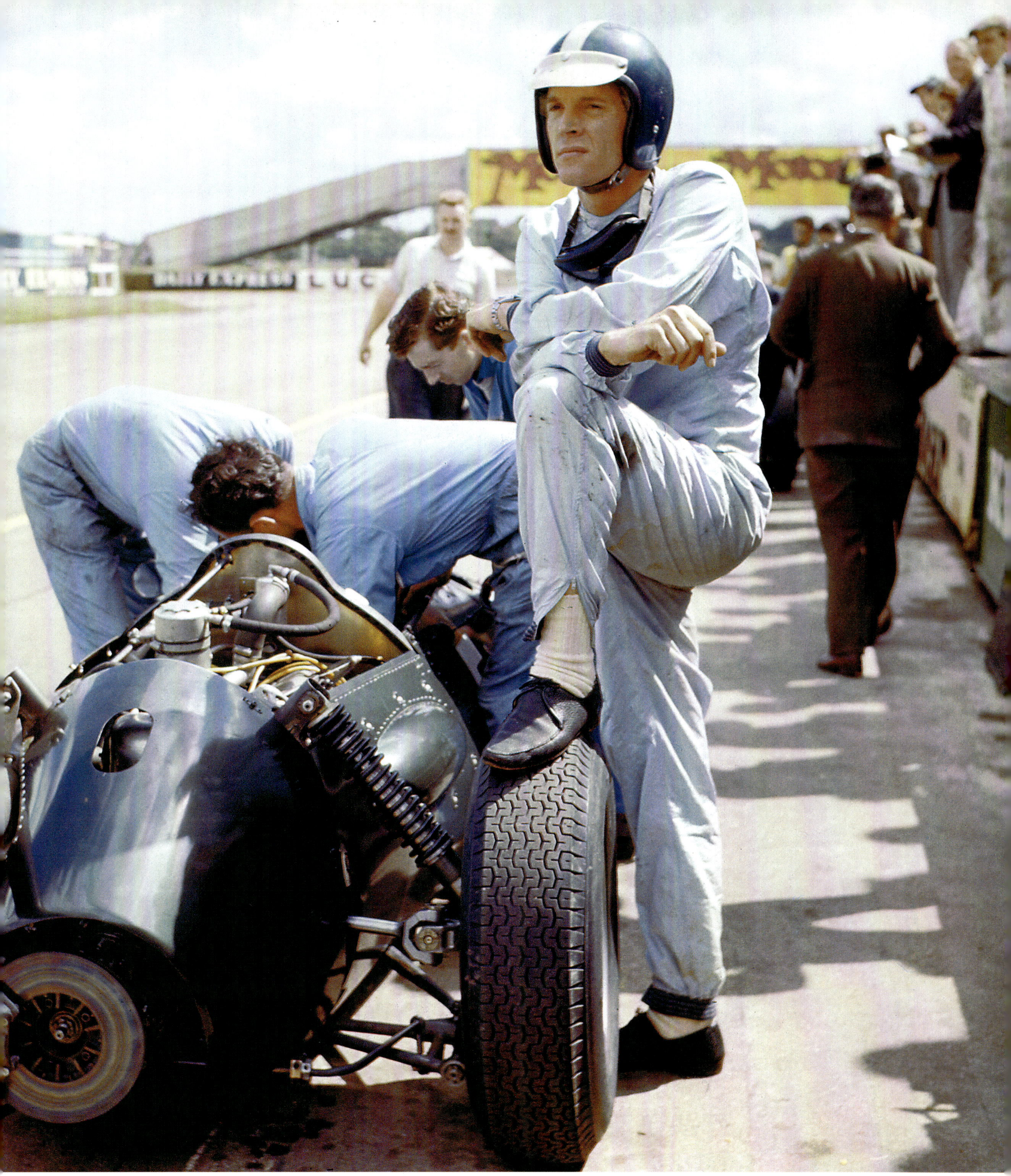

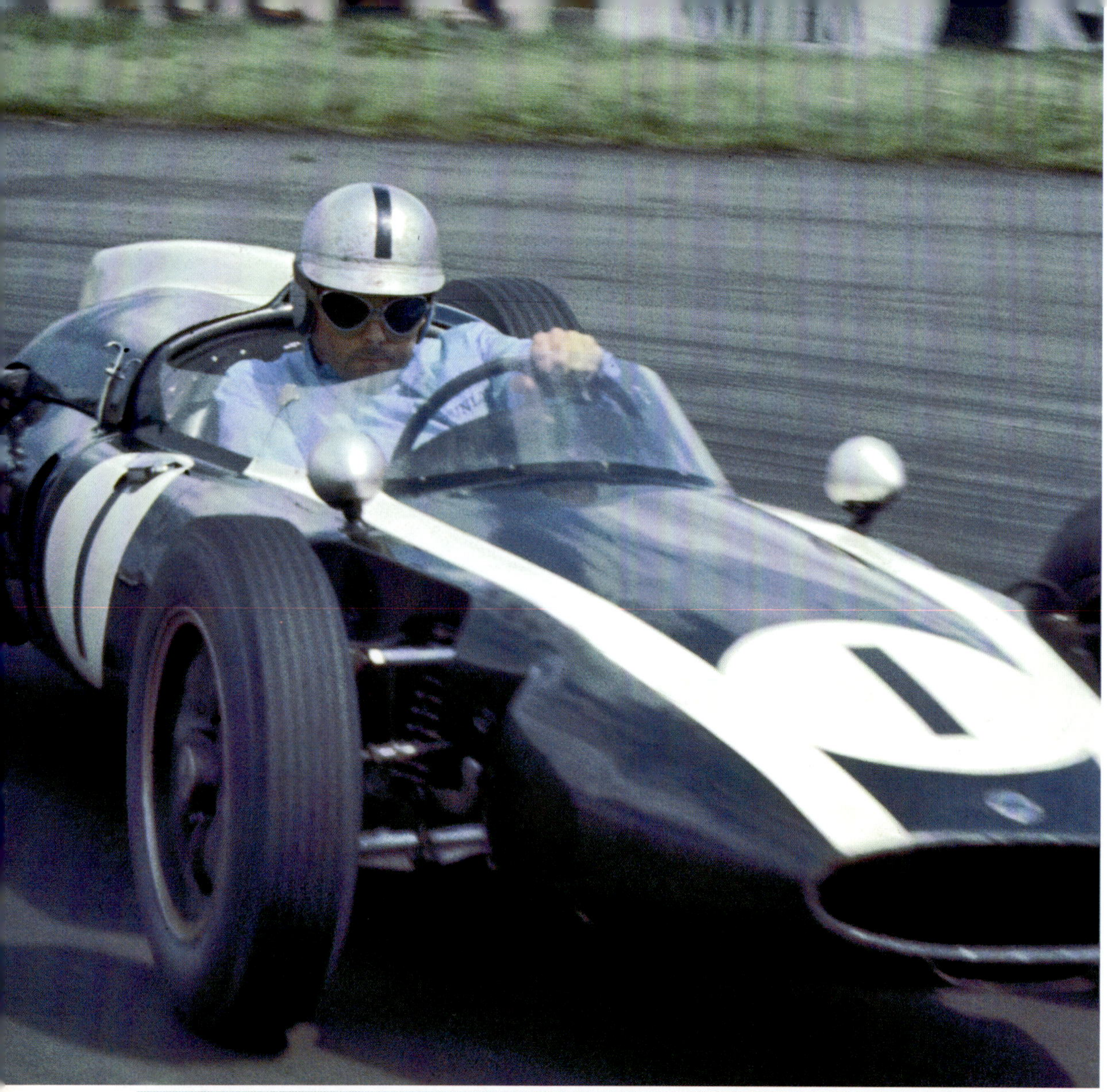

A close-up of Jack Brabham, head-down in typically determined pose, during practice for the British Grand Prix with chassis F2-8-60. The new 'low-line' Cooper T53 used a state-of-the-art suspension system with wishbones and coil springs in place of the transverse leaf spring layout of 1959. Brabham, who had already won the Belgian, Dutch and French Grands Prix, started from the pole here at Silverstone, but was caught and passed by Graham Hill's BRM who then spun off at Copse. The back-to-back World Championships by 'Black Jack' were the apogee of Cooper's racing career and they were never to repeat the sustained triumphs of 1959 and 1960.

Wolfgang von Trips demonstrates chronic understeer with his Ferrari Dino 0005 at Silverstone. Despite this wayward handling, Trips was quicker in the race than his team mate and putative superior, Phil Hill, finishing 4 seconds ahead in a twice lapped 6th place.

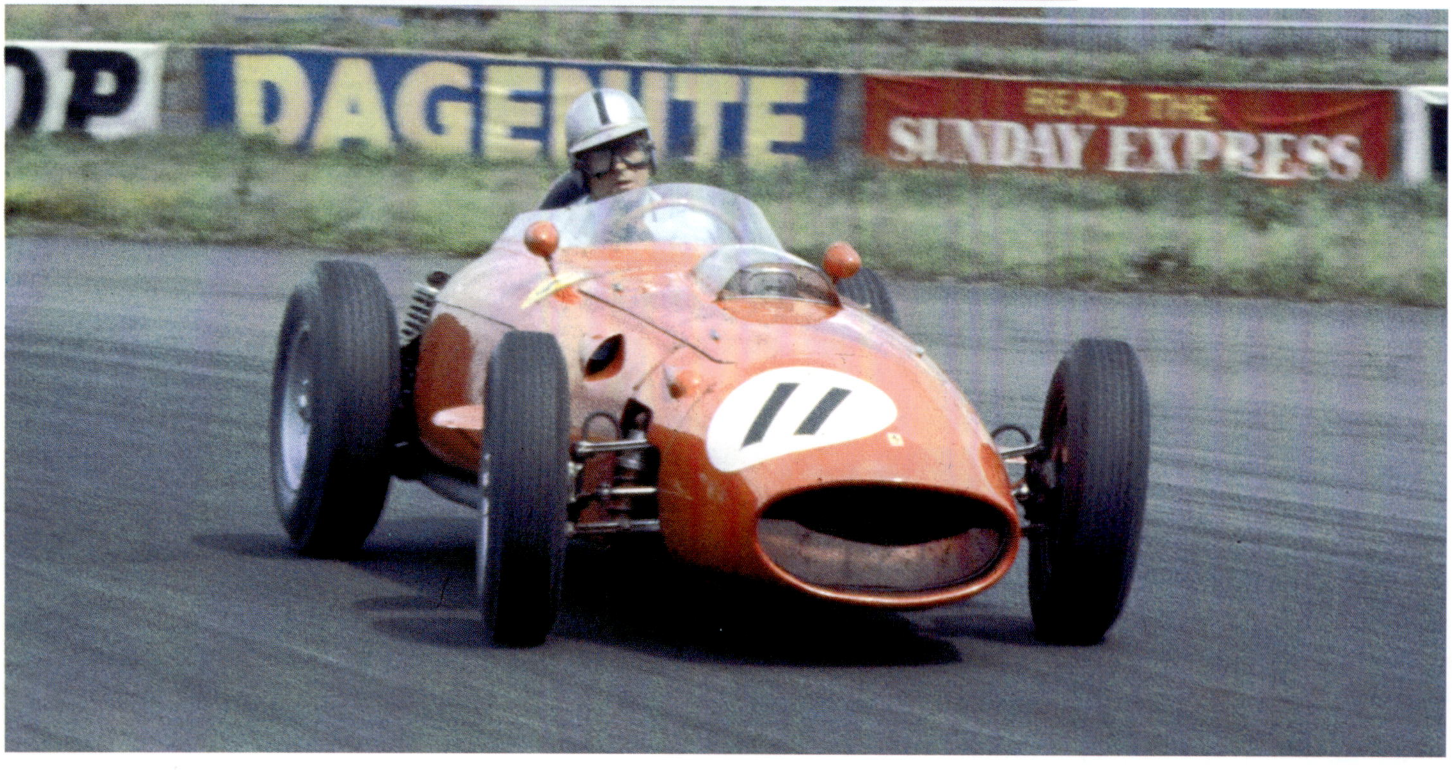

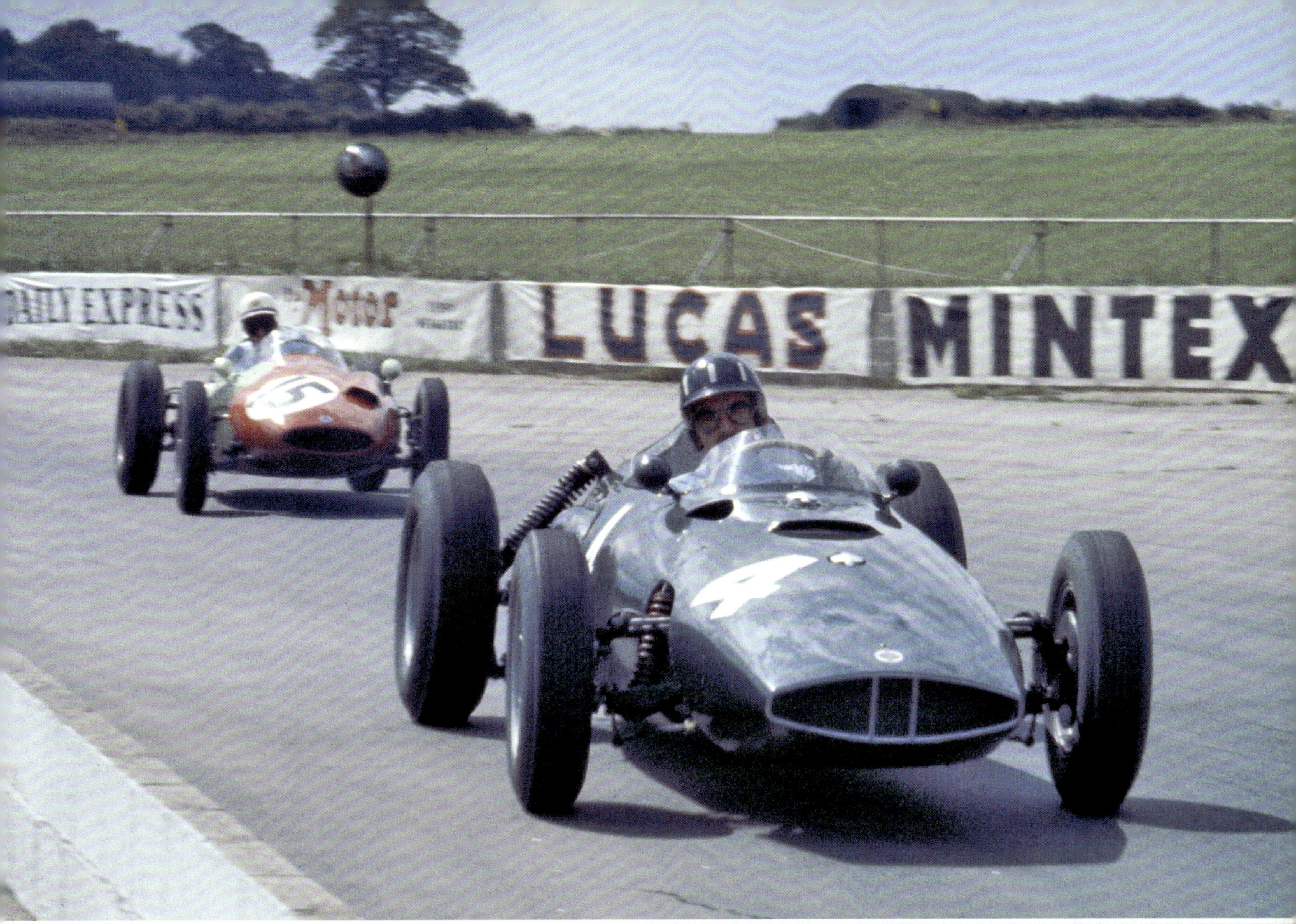

⇑ BRM's management style and chief designer Peter Berthon's reluctance to listen to the drivers' complaints led to the resignation of new team manager Bertie Bradnack. Thereafter the P48 was gradually sorted out by Tony Rudd, who was put in charge of development by team owner Alfred Owen after Zandvoort. Graham Hill stalled on the line at Silverstone and was hit by Tony Brooks's Yeoman Credit Cooper. Push-started 30 seconds behind the rest, Hill sliced through the field and eventually passed race leader Jack Brabham on lap 54. Coming up to lap the Ferraris at Copse on lap 72 in his P48 (485), Hill was caught out by an increasingly long brake pedal travel, and spun into the bank. Following is Henry Taylor in the other Yeoman Credit Cooper.

⇒ Innes Ireland at the same corner in the works Lotus 18 (374), sporting a sleeker nose that had first appeared at Reims. The engine was canted over to expose the Weber carburettors to the airflow provided by the trunking on the left side of the nose. After winning the International Trophy at Silverstone in May, Ireland must have thought he could do it again, but he was outpaced by his novice team mate, John Surtees, and had to be content with 3rd place.

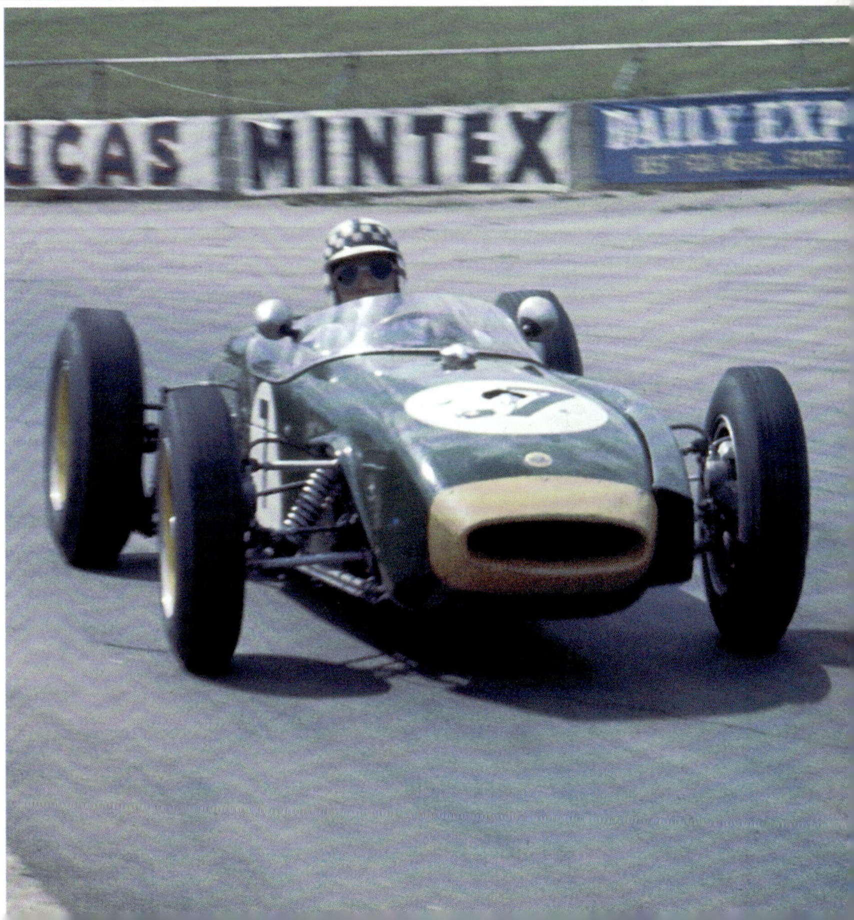

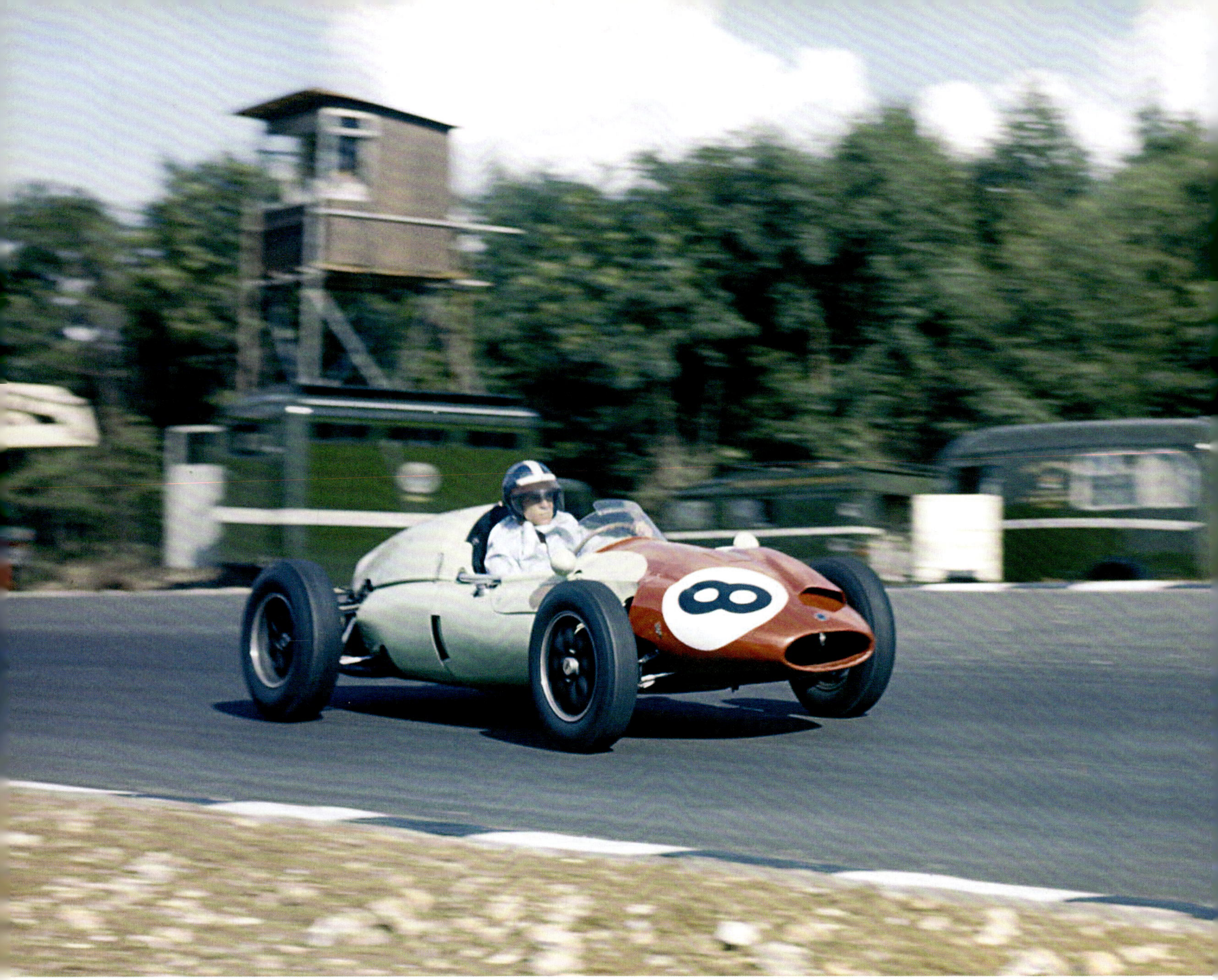

Yeoman Credit Racing, run by Ken Gregory and Alfred Moss, was a regular Formula 1 player during 1960, using 1959 Cooper T51s. The team employed six drivers in total (Tony Brooks, Harry Schell, Chris Bristow, Olivier Gendebien, Henry Taylor and Bruce Halford). This is Halford, who was a Torquay hotelier, sometime Maserati 250F privateer and accomplished sports car racer, who finished 8th in both the French Grand Prix and the Silver City Trophy here at Brands Hatch in the T51 (F2-1-59). He briefly returned decades later to historic racing, and died in December 2001.

Phil Hill races onto the main straight of the newly lengthened (2.65 miles) Brands Hatch during the Silver City Trophy on August 1960 in the Ferrari 246 Dino 0004. Despite starting from the fifth row Hill raced to 4th place, a fantastic effort in an uncompetitive car. The old passenger bridge that spanned the track past South Bank can be seen in the background.

John Surtees started from pole position and led the Portuguese Grand Prix in a works Lotus 18, setting fastest lap. However, petrol was leaking into the cockpit and, on lap 35, Surtees's foot slipped off the brake pedal and he hit a kerb at the Lidador corner, bursting the radiator. At this very early point in his motor racing career, while he was still racing motorcycles, Surtees was more than a match for Jimmy Clark. Earlier in the year, he had won his first race in Ken Tyrrell's FJ Cooper, and had bought a Formula 2 version before being asked to drive for Lotus by the astute Colin Chapman. Oporto was only his third Grand Prix and he had already finished 2nd at Silverstone.

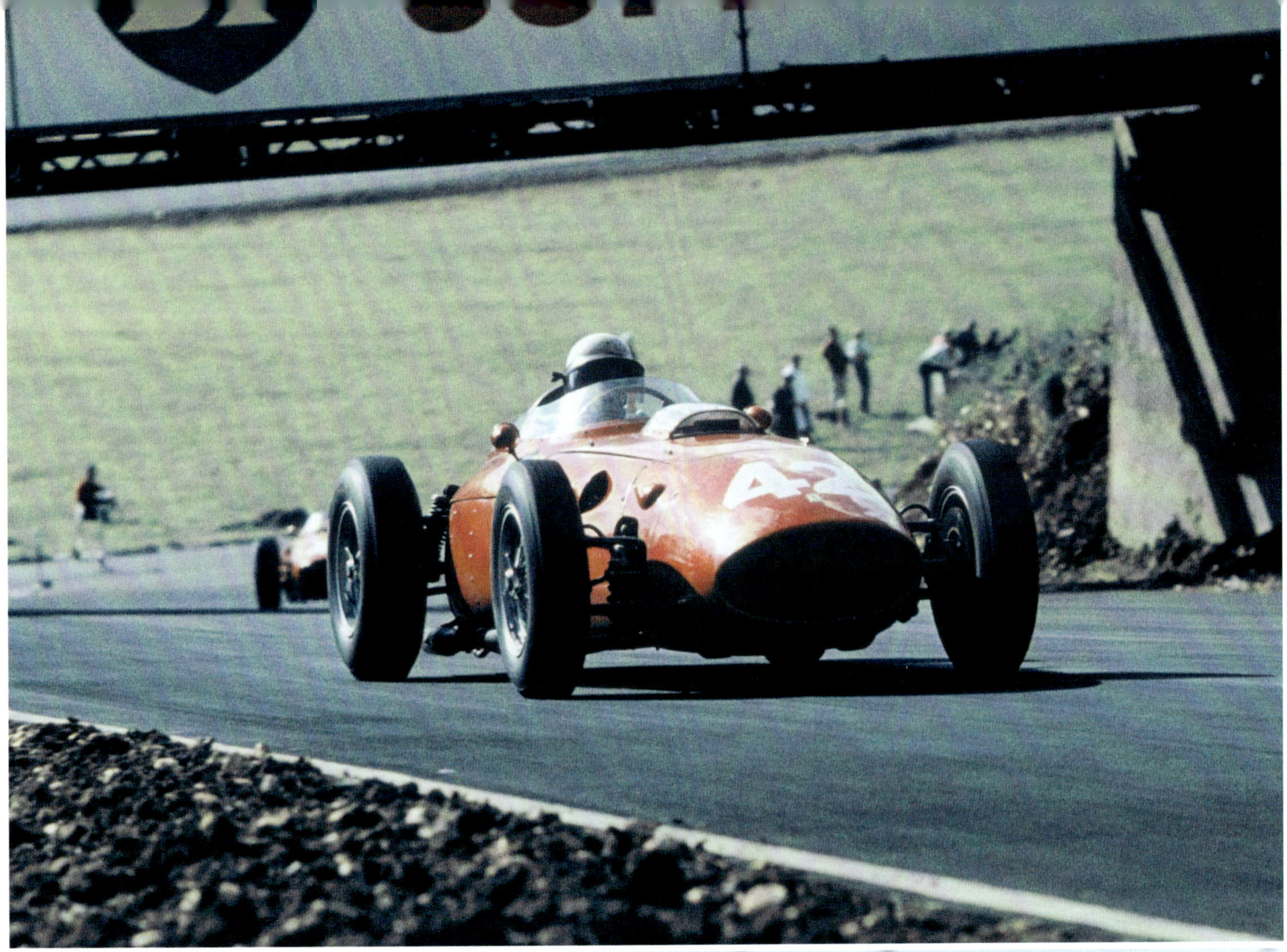

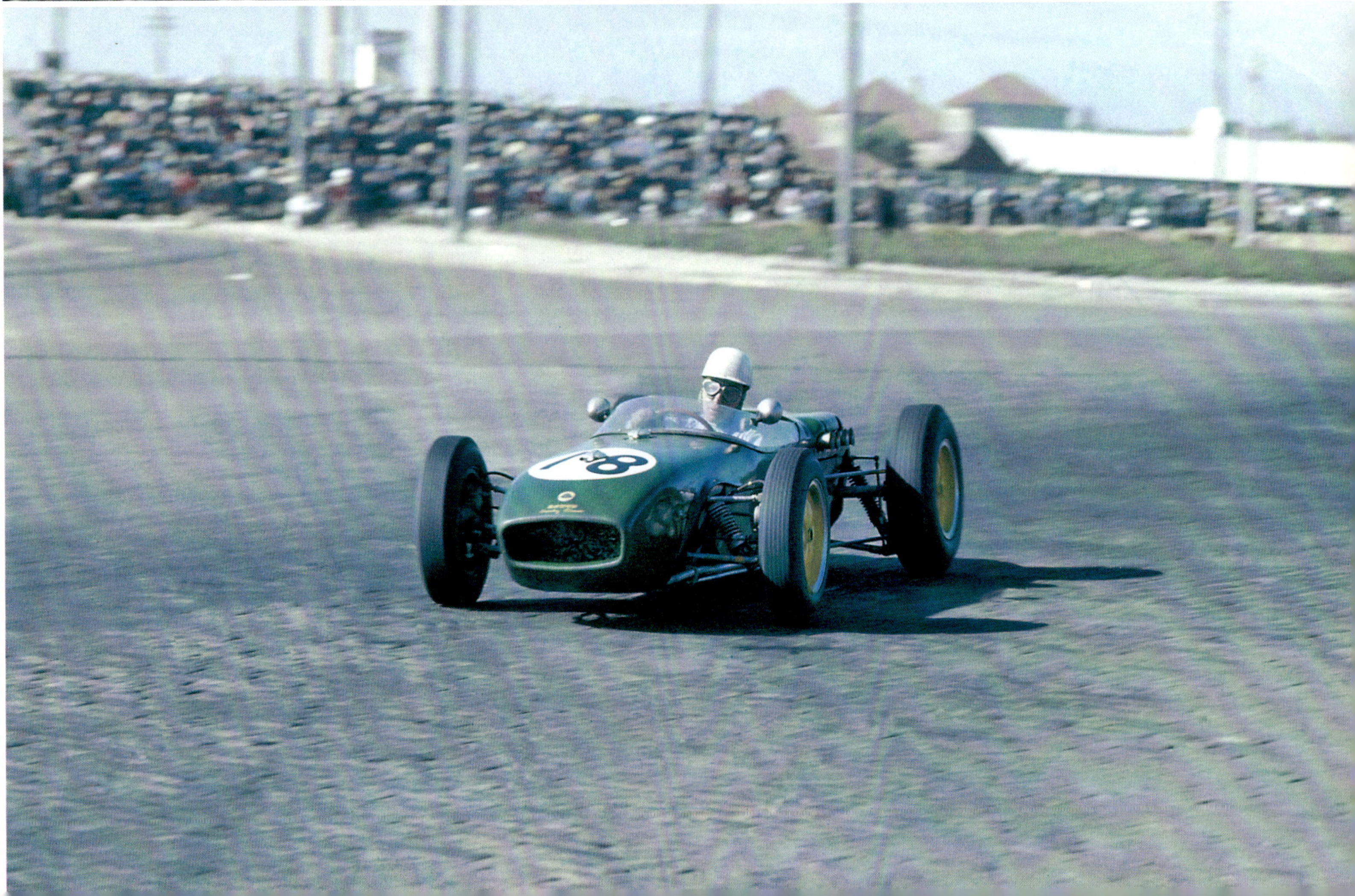

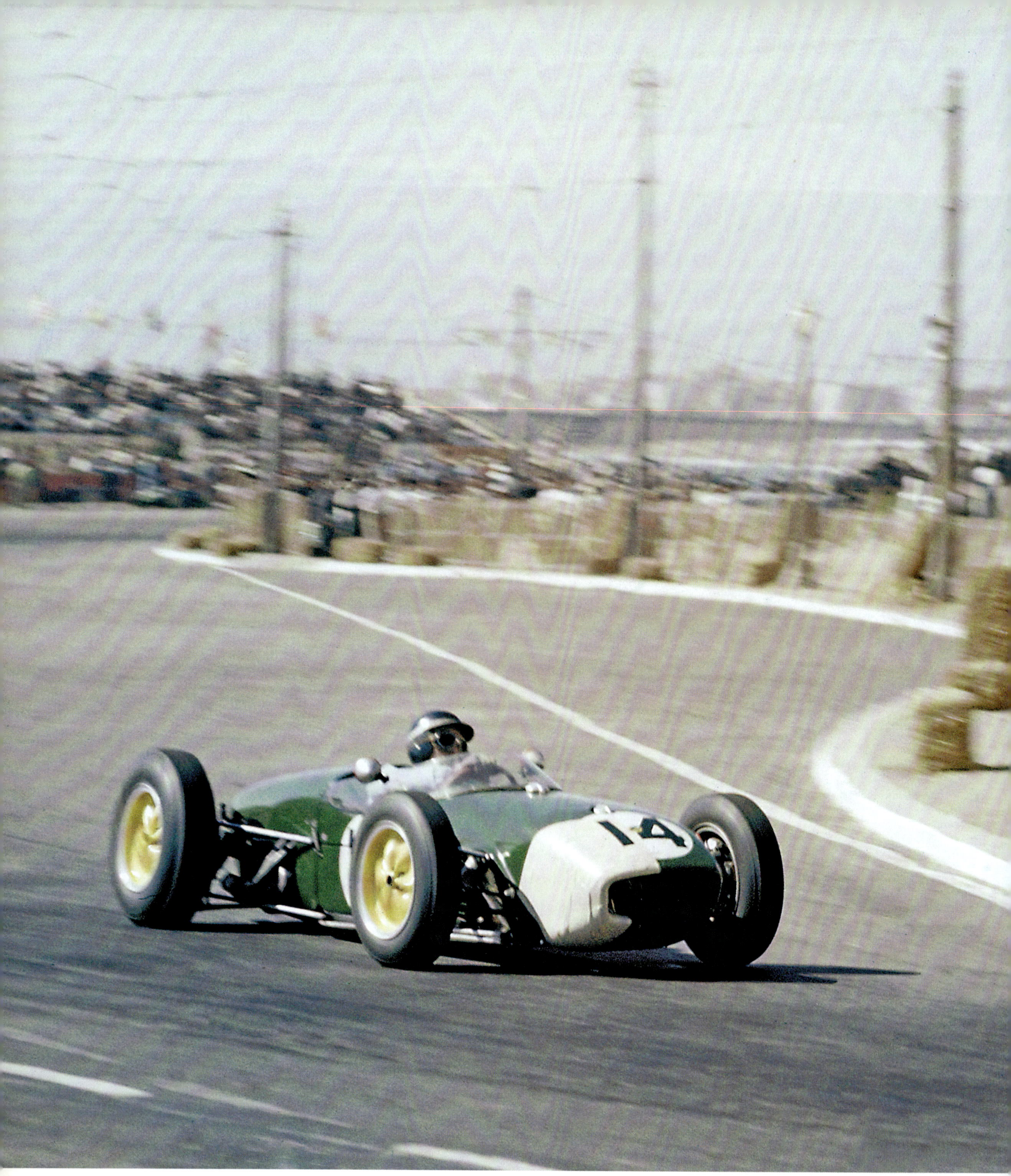
14

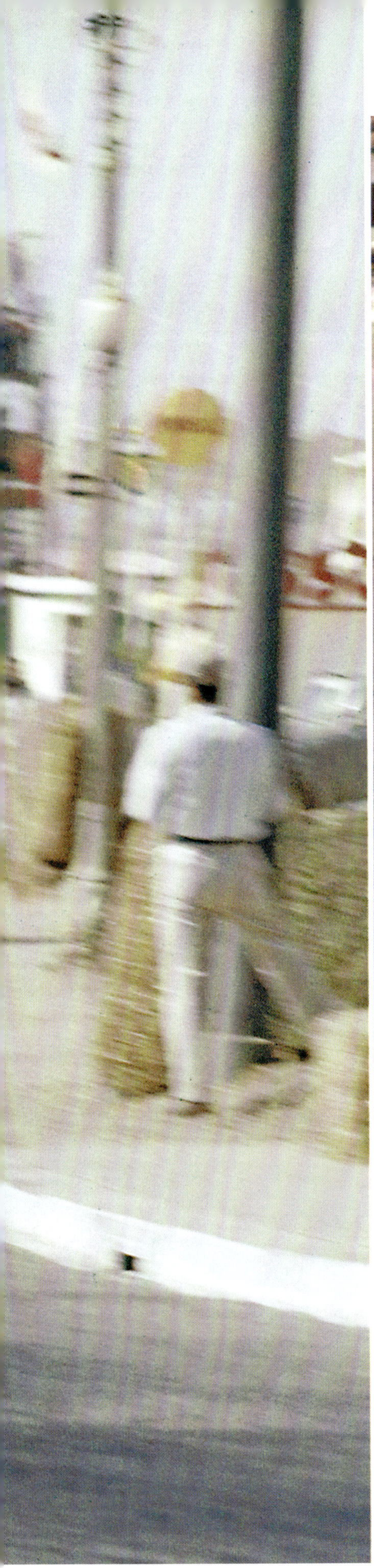

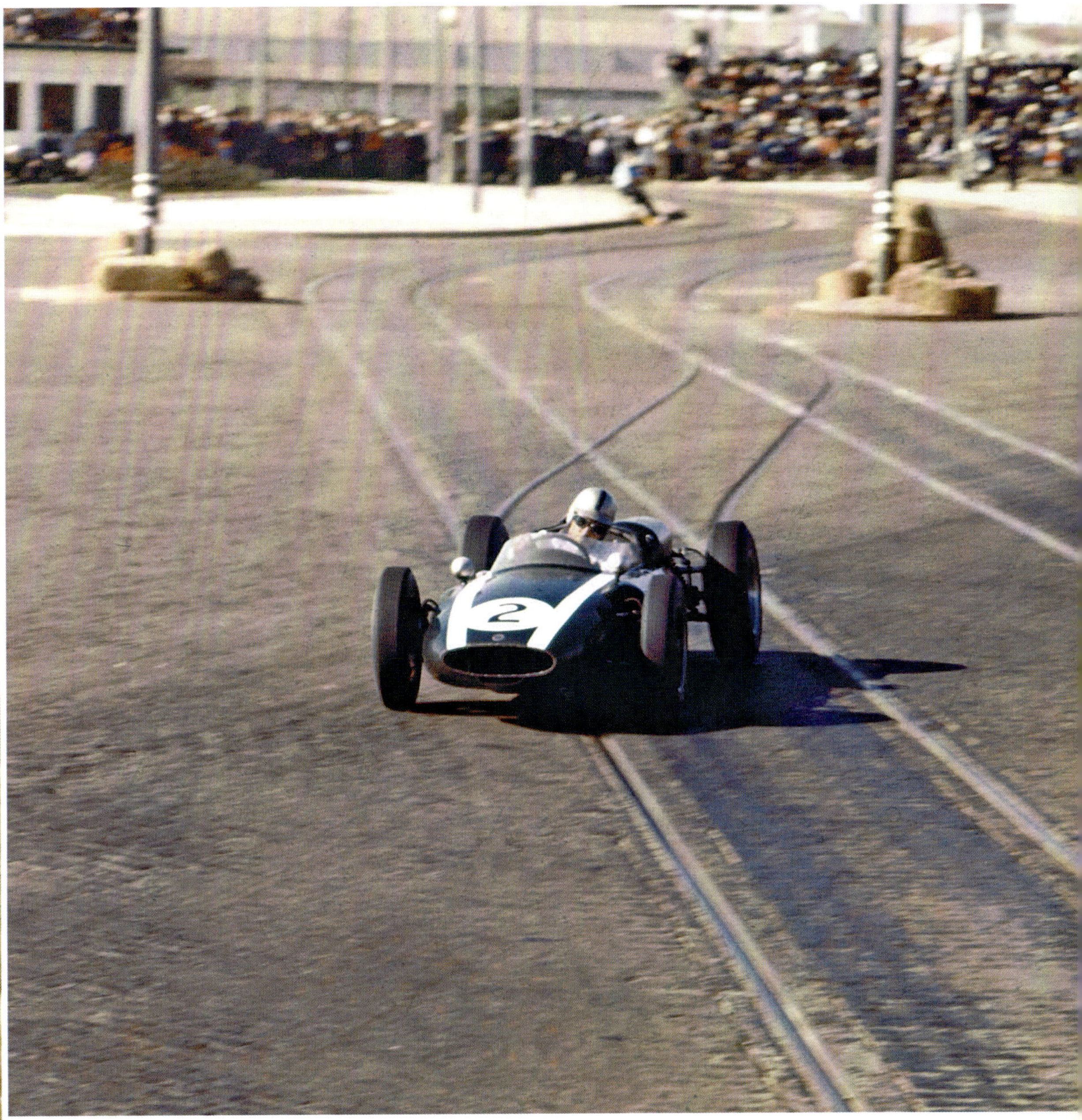

Jack Brabham on his way to winning his fifth consecutive Grand Prix of the season at Oporto in his regular Cooper T53 (F2-8-60), finishing almost a minute ahead of Bruce McLaren's similar car. Note the tramlines and the huge expanse of roadway, surely the widest ever used for a World Championship Grand Prix.

Slightly further into the same curve at Oporto, Jim Clark races his battered Lotus 18 towards 3rd place, the nosecone held together with duct tape. Some 45 years later, Team Lotus mechanic Jim Endruweit recalled welding up the badly damaged chassis, which had made heavy contact with some straw bales during the second practice session. On the grid, Colin Chapman asked Endruweit whether the car would stay in one piece, and received no confident reply. Chapman turned to Clark and told him to take it easy and avoid the other runners! Against the odds, Clark's supremely gentle touch – a skill many of his contemporaries lacked – got the car to the finish.

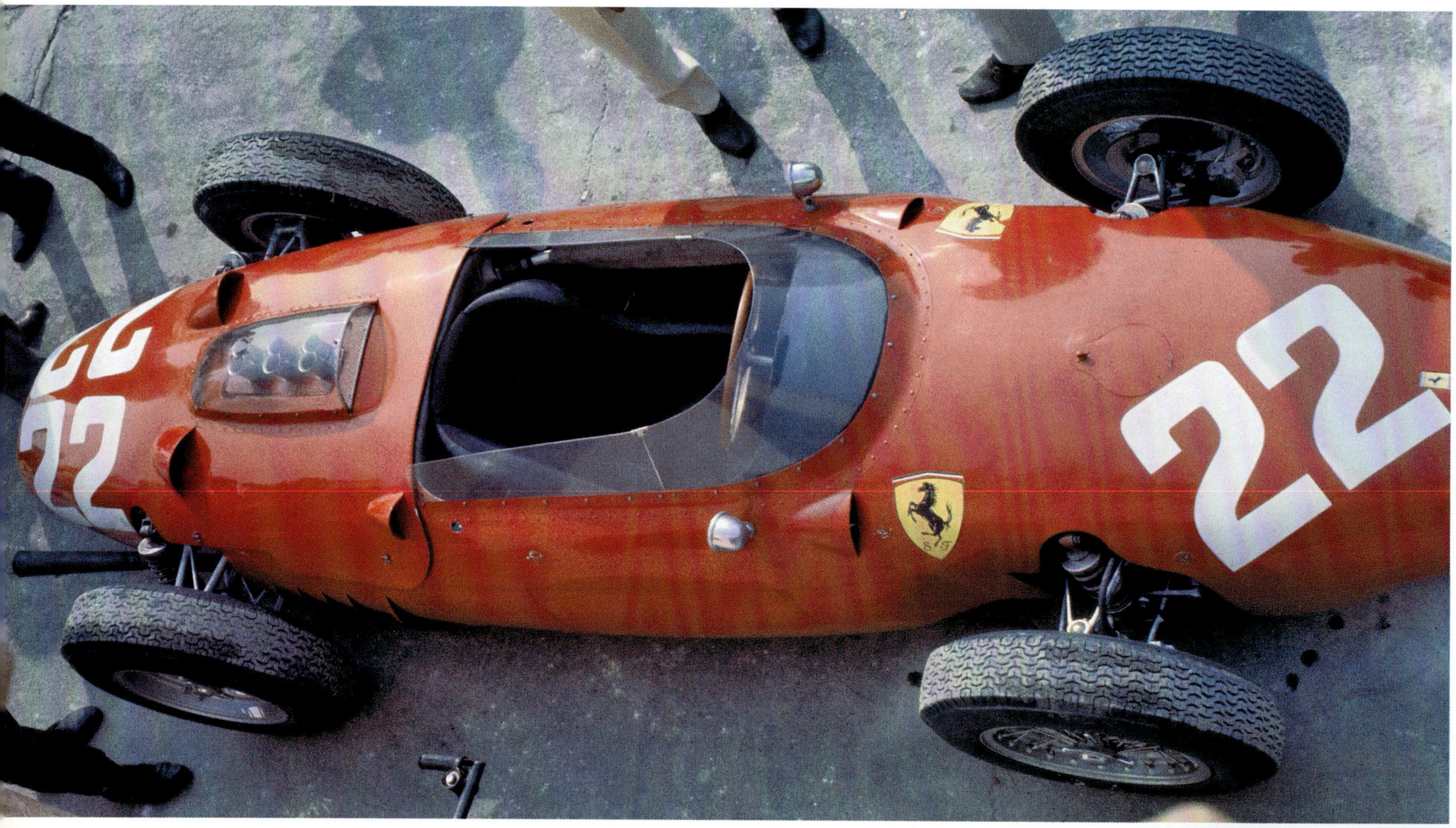

Scuderia Ferrari prepared for the forthcoming 1.5-litre Formula 1 by running a modified mid-engined Dino Formula 2 car at Monaco, during practice at Zandvoort, Solitude and here at Monza, where it was driven by Wolfgang von Trips to 5th place in the Italian Grand Prix. The car's 65-degree V6 engine developed about 170bhp, installed in a big-tube spaceframe chassis with all-independent suspension.

Too many cooks spoil the broth: Richie Ginther (left) seems bemused, Carlo Chiti (in blue cap) unconvinced, Enzo Ferrari (in grey cap) concerned, and Phil Hill (hand on chin) visibly disenchanted by the whole affair. Just another day in paradise – or, rather, practice at Monza. Against expectations, apparently, Hill did win the Italian Grand Prix, securing the last F1 World Championship victory by a front-engined car.

This is the notorious Monza banking that caused the British teams to withdraw their entries from the Italian Grand Prix on safety grounds (although, 12 months later, they turned up with the equally fragile 1.5-litre cars). Richie Ginther, clad in a short-sleeved shirt, hammers round the concrete bowl in the Ferrari Dino (which may or may not be chassis 0003 due to historical confusions) on his way to 2nd place.

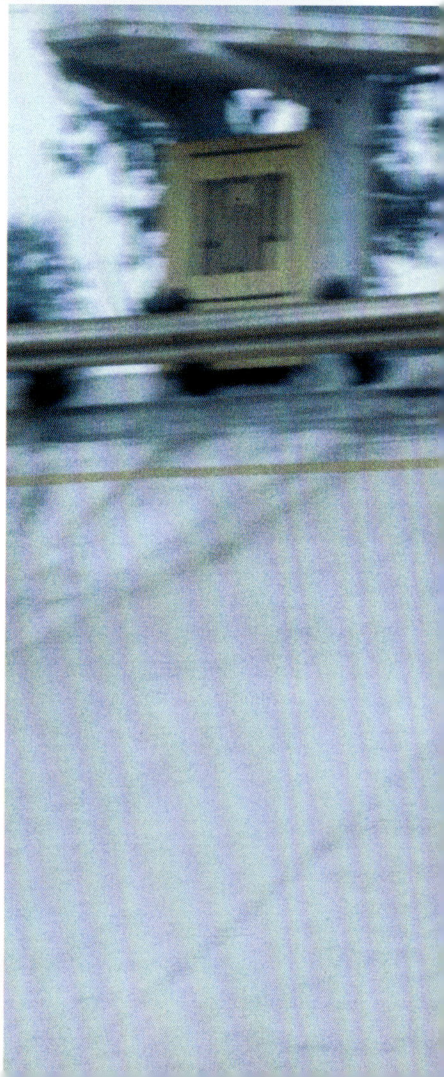

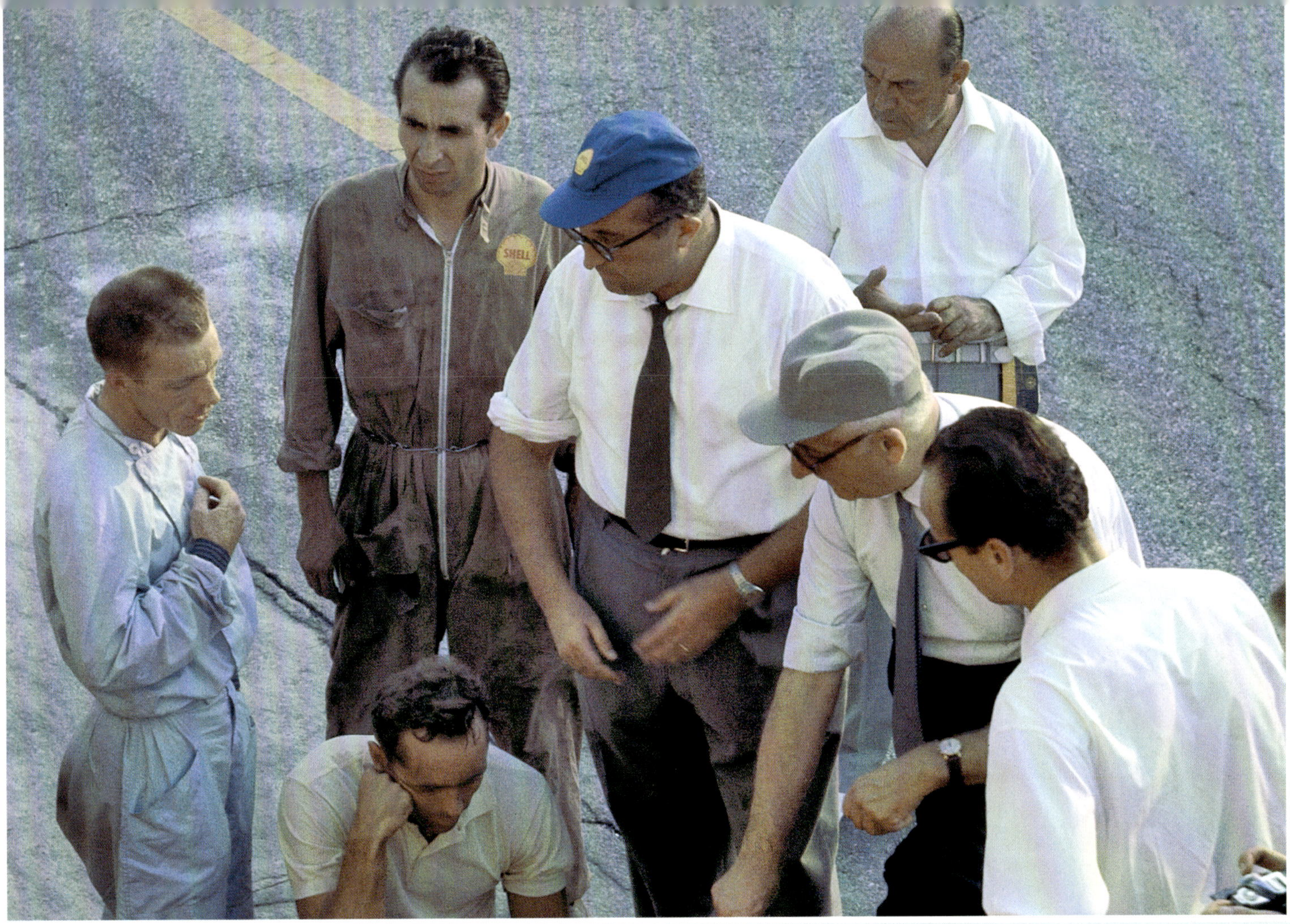
SHELL

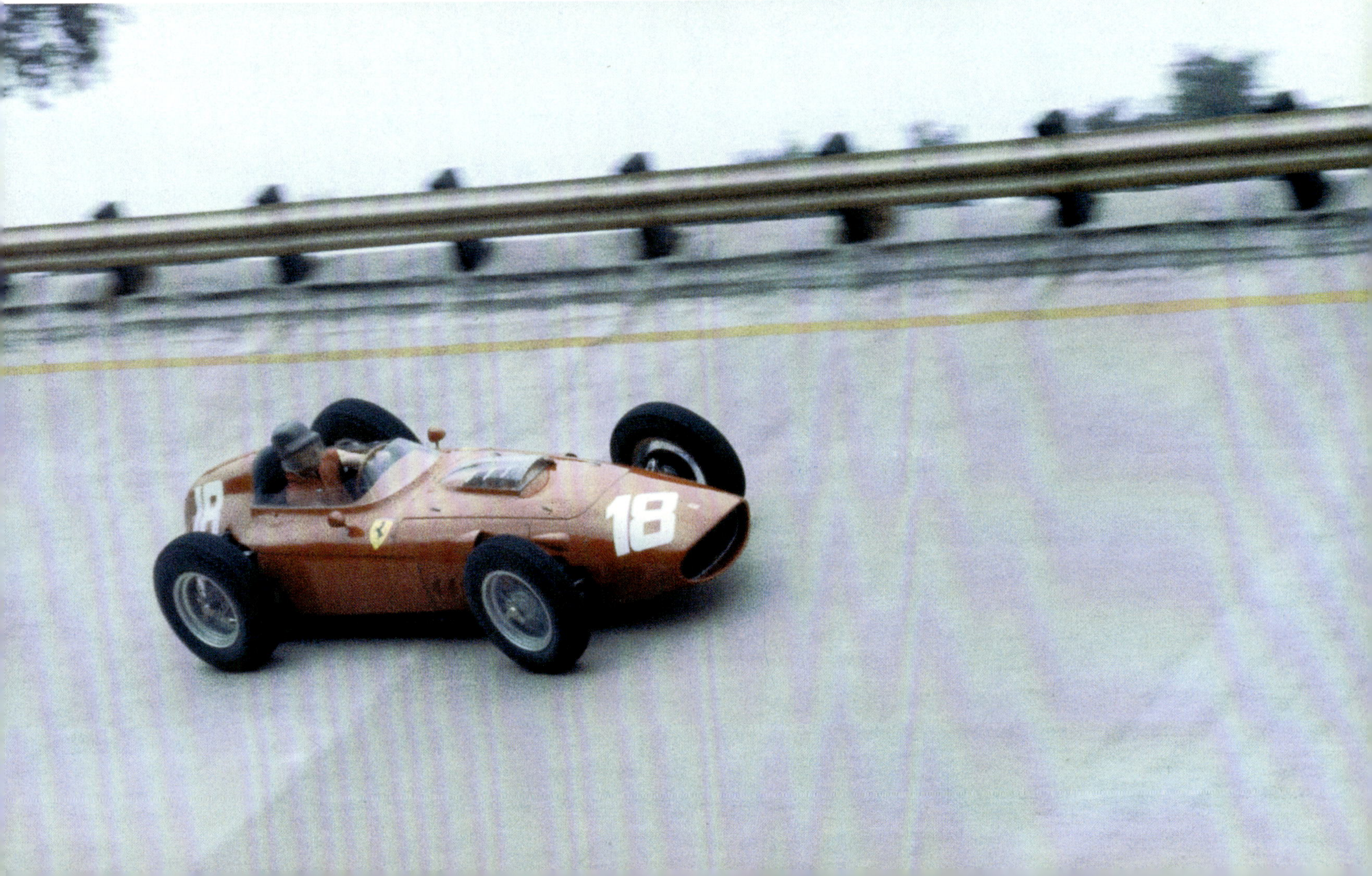
18

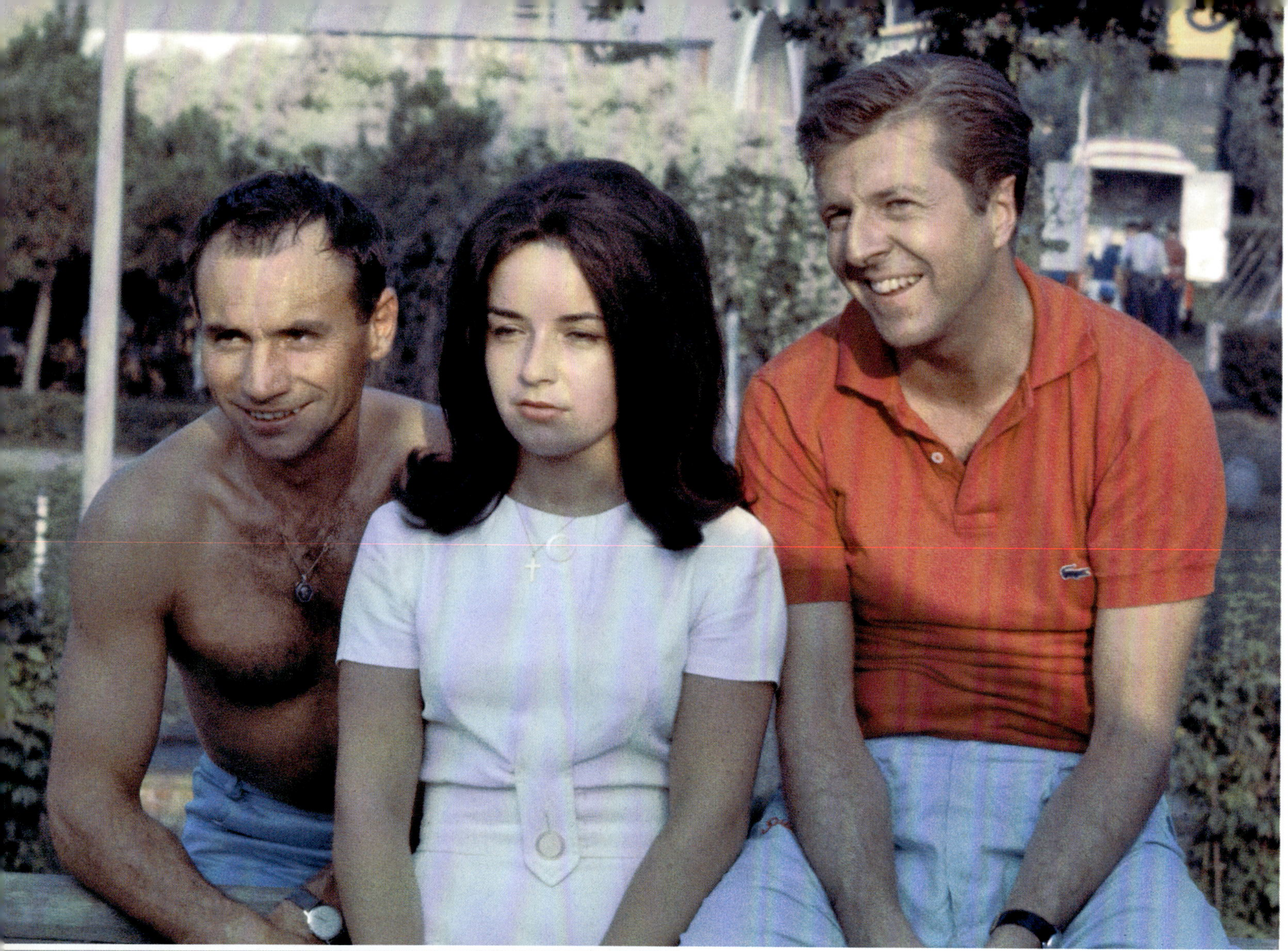

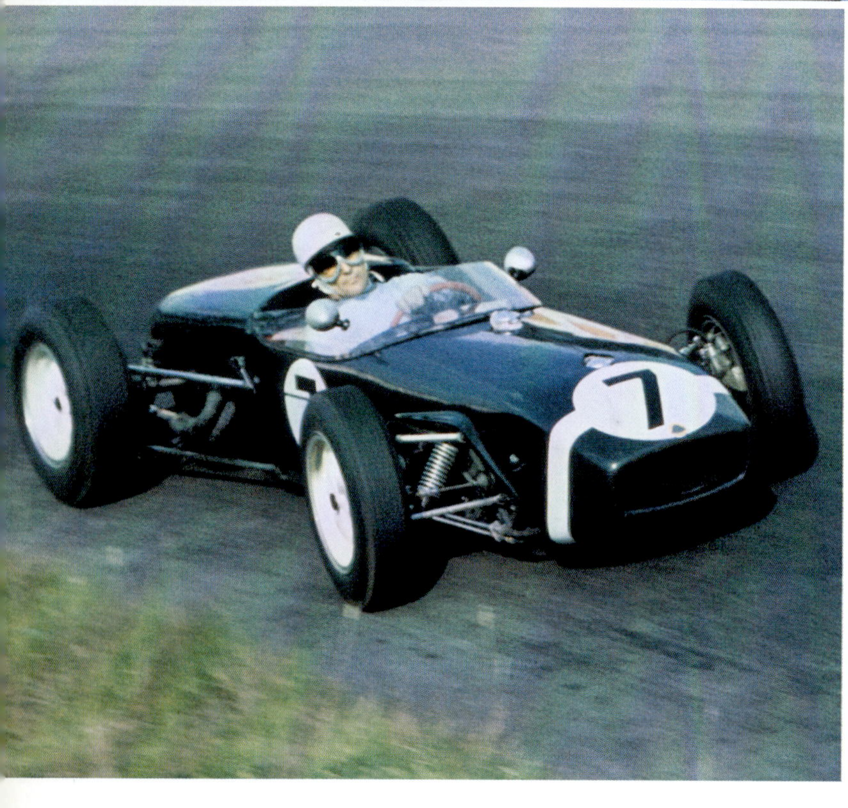

Happier faces here: a pretty girl enjoys the late afternoon sun at Monza with Ferrari team mates Willy Mairesse, *sans blouson*, and German aristocrat Graf Berghe Wolfgang von Trips, in a Lacoste shirt. This scene does not have a happy ending. 'Taffy' von Trips, also known colloquially as 'von Crash' died the following year at Monza in an horrific accident after colliding with Jim Clark's Lotus. Mairesse committed suicide in an Ostend hotel room in 1969, his racing career ended by an accident at Le Mans in 1968 that had left him with brain damage and deep depression.

Stirling Moss returned to Formula 1 at Oporto after breaking both legs and his nose, and crushing three spinal vertebrae, in a crash at Spa on 18 June. Yet within a month he was cycling around the hospital grounds, and was discharged on 19 July. Less than three weeks later he was winning at Karlskoga in a Lotus 19. With a new Lotus 18 to replace the Spa wreck he battled with Surtees for the lead of the Portuguese Grand Prix, but encountered an engine problem and locking brakes that caused him to spin and stall. He was then disqualified for push starting the car against the traffic! Moss missed Monza due to the British boycott but won the International Gold Cup at Oulton Park (seen here) three weeks later in the Rob Walker Lotus 18 (906) from Jack Brabham and Graham Hill and completed his comeback by winning the final Grand Prix of the season at Riverside.

1960 Teams, drivers and results

Cooper Car Co – Cooper T51 and T53 Climax
Jack Brabham (AUS) (WORLD CHAMPION, used T51 for Argentine GP only)
Bruce McLaren (NZ) (Used T51 for Argentine GP only)
Ron Flockhart (GB) (US GP only)
Lance Reventlow (USA) (T51 British GP practice only)
Chuck Daigh (USA) (T51 British GP only, shared with Reventlow but raced by Daigh)

Team Lotus – Lotus 16 Climax and 18 Climax
Innes Ireland (GB)
Jim Clark (GB) (Debut Dutch GP)
Alan Stacey (GB) (Used 16 in Argentine GP, fatal crash Belgian GP)
John Surtees (GB) (Debut Monaco GP, then British, Portugese and US GPs only)
Ron Flockhart (GB) (French GP only)
Rodriguez Larreta (RA) (Argentine GP only in 16)

Owen Racing Organisation – BRM P25 and P48
Graham Hill (GB) (Used P25 for Argentine GP)
Dan Gurney (USA) (Missed Argentine GP)
Jo Bonnier (S) (Used P25 for Argentine GP)

SEFAC Ferrari – Ferrari Dino 246
Phil Hill (USA)
Wolfgang von Trips (D) (Used rear-engined prototype 1.5 Dino at Italian GP)
Cliff Allison (GB) (Argentine GP only, dns Monaco GP after practice crash)
Richie Ginther (USA) (Monaco using rear-engined prototype, Dutch, and Italian GPs only)
Willy Mairesse (B) (Belgian, French and Italian GPs only)
Froilan Gonzalez (RA) (Argentine GP only)

Yeoman Credit Racing Team – Cooper T51 Climax
Tony Brooks (GB) (Drove Vanwall at French GP)
Harry Schell (F/USA) (Fatal crash Silverstone International Trophy practice)
Chris Bristow (GB) (Fatal crash Belgian GP)
Olivier Gendebien (B) (Belgian, French, British, Portuguese and US GPs only)
Henry Taylor (GB) (Dutch, French, British, Portuguese [dns practice accident], and US GPs only)
Bruce Halford (GB) (French GP only)

Reventlow Automobiles Inc – Scarab
Chuck Daigh (USA) (Monaco dnq, Dutch dns, Belgian, French dns and US GPs only)
Lance Reventlow (USA) (Monaco dnq, Dutch dns and Belgian GPs only)
Richie Ginther (USA) (French GP only dns)

R. R. C. Walker Racing Team – Cooper T51 Climax and Lotus 18 Climax
Stirling Moss (GB) (Raced Cooper in Argentine and took over Trintignant's similar car when his retired, dns Belgian GP after practice crash in Lotus, missed French and British GPs)
Maurice Trintignant (F) (Argentine GP only, car taken over by Moss in race)

Vandervell Products – Vanwall VW11 'Lowline'
Tony Brooks (GB) (French GP only)

David Brown Corporation – Aston Martin DBR4/250 and DBR5/250
Roy Salvadori (GB) (Dutch dns [starting money dispute] and British GPs only)
Maurice Trintignant (F) (British GP only)

Porsche System Engineering – Porsche 718 F4 (F2 car)
Hans Herrmann (D) (Italian GP only)
Edgar Barth (D) (Italian GP only. Entered by Dr. Ing. F. Porsche KG)

Scuderia Centro Sud – Cooper T51 Maserati
Masten Gregory (USA) (Monaco dnq, Dutch dns [starting money dispute], French, British and Portuguese GPs only)
Carlos Menditéguy (RA) (Argentine GP only, his final F1 race)
Roberto Bonomi (RA) (Argentine GP only)
Maurice Trintignant (F) (Monaco, Dutch, French and US GPs only)
Ian Burgess (GB) (Monaco dnq, French, British and US GPs only)
Mario de Cabral (P) (Portuguese GP only)
Wolfgang von Trips (D) (US GP only)
Alfonse Thiele (I/USA) (Italian GP only)

Scuderia Eugenio Castellotti – Cooper T51 Ferrari Super Squalo and Cooper T51 Maserati
Gino Munaron (I) (Monaco dnq, French, British and Italian GPs only)
Giulio Cabianca (I) (Italian GP only)
Giorgio Scarlatti (I) (Monaco dnq and Italian GPs only)

High Efficiency Motors (C. T. Atkins) – Cooper T51 Climax
Roy Salvadori (GB) (Monaco and US GPs only)
Jack Fairman (GB) (British GP only)

Gilbey Engineering Co Ltd – Cooper T45 Maserati
Keith Greene (GB) (British GP only)

J B Naylor – JBW-Maserati
Brian Naylor (GB) (Monaco dnq, British, Italian and US GPs only)

Robert Bodle Ltd – Lotus 16 Climax
David Piper (GB) (French dns and British GPs only)

Equipe Nationale Belge – Cooper T45 Climax
Lucien Bianchi (B) (Belgian GP only)

Fred Tuck Cars – Cooper T45 Climax
Bruce Halford (GB) (Monaco GP only, dnq)
Lucien Bianchi (B) (French and British GPs only)

Scuderia Colonia – Cooper T43 Climax (F2 car)
Piero Drogo (I) (Italian GP only)

Wolfgang Seidel – Cooper T45 Climax (F2 car)
Wolfgang Seidel (D) (Italian GP only)

Arthur Owen – Cooper T45 Climax
Arthur Owen (GB) (Italian GP only)

Equipe Prideaux/Dick Gibson – Cooper T43 Climax (F2 car)
Vic Wilson (GB) (Italian GP only)

Fred Armbruster – Cooper T45 Ferrari 625LM
Pete Lovely (USA) (US GP only)

Joe Lubin – Maserati 250F (Final World Championship appearance of 250F)
Bob Drake (USA) (US GP only)

Ecurie Bleue – Cooper T51 Climax
Harry Schell (F/USA) (Argentine GP only)

Camoradi International – Porsche RSK F4 Sports and Behra-Porsche F4 (F2 car)
Masten Gregory (USA) (Argentine GP only)
Fred Gamble (USA) (Italian GP only)

Giorgio Scarlatti (Scuderia Centro Sud) – Maserati 250F
Giorgio Scarlatti (I) (Argentine GP only)

Gino Munaron (Scuderia Centro Sud) – Maserati 250F
Gino Munaron (I) (Argentine GP only)

Nasif Estéfano (Scuderia Centro Sud) – Maserati 250F
Nasif Estéfano (RA) (Argentine GP only)

Ettore Chimeri (Escuderia Sorocaima) – Maserati 250F
Ettore Chimeri (YV) (Argentine GP only)

Antonio Creus – Maserati 250F
Antonio Creus (E) (Argentine GP only)

WORLD CHAMPIONSHIP VENUES AND WINNERS
(Nine rounds plus Indianapolis)

Argentine GP	Buenos Aires	Bruce McLaren
Monaco GP	Monte Carlo	Stirling Moss
Indianapolis 500	Indianapolis	Jim Rathmann
Dutch GP	Zandvoort	Jack Brabham
Belgian GP	Spa-Francorchamps	Jack Brabham
French GP	Reims	Jack Brabham
British GP	Silverstone	Jack Brabham
Portuguese GP	Oporto	Jack Brabham
Italian GP	Monza	Phil Hill
United States GP	Riverside	Stirling Moss

DRIVERS' CHAMPIONSHIP (including Indianapolis 500)
Points: 8-6-4-3-2-1, fastest lap 1 point. Best 6 scores

1	Jack Brabham (AUS)	Cooper	43
2	Bruce McLaren (NZ)	Cooper	34
3	Stirling Moss (GB)	Cooper/Lotus	19
4	Innes Ireland (GB)	Lotus	18
5	Phil Hill (USA)	Ferrari/Cooper	16
6	Olivier Gendebien (B)	Cooper	10
7	Wolfgang von Trips	Ferrari/Cooper	10
8	Jim Rathmann (USA)	Ken-Paul Spl	8
9	Richie Ginther (USA)	Ferrari	8
10	Jim Clark (GB)	Lotus	8
11	Tony Brooks (GB)	Cooper/Vanwall	7
12	Cliff Allison (GB)	Ferrari	6
13	Rodger Ward (USA)	Leader Card 500	6
14	John Surtees (GB)	Lotus	6
15	Paul Goldsmith (USA)	Demler Special	4
16	Graham Hill (GB)	BRM	4
17	Willy Mairesse (B)	Ferrari	4
18	Jo Bonnier (S)	BRM	4
19	Carlos Menditéguy	Cooper	3
20	Don Branson (USA)	Bob Estes Spl	3
21	Henry Taylor (GB)	Cooper	3
22	Giulio Cabianca (I)	Cooper	3
23	Johnny Thomson (USA)	Adams Qtr Horse Spl	2
24	Eddie Johnson (USA)	Jim Robbins Spl	1
25	Lucien Bianchi (B)	Cooper	1
26	Ron Flockhart (GB)	Lotus/Cooper	1
27	Hans Herrmann (D)	Porsche	1

No points awarded for 3rd place in Argentine GP (shared drive Trintignant/Moss)

CONSTRUCTORS' CHAMPIONSHIP (excluding Indianapolis 500)
Points: 8-6-4-3-2-1, (awarded only to best-placed finisher). Best 6 scores

1	Cooper-Climax	48
2	Lotus-Climax	34
3	Ferrari	26
4	BRM	8
5	Cooper-Maserati	3
6	Cooper-Castellotti (Ferrari)	3

1961

FORZA FERRARI!

At the Royal Automobile Club in London on 29 October 1958, Formula 1 people assembled to celebrate the achievements of the new World Champion, Mike Hawthorn, and the winning Constructor, Tony Vandervell. The president of the FIA's Commission Sportive Internationale, Auguste Pérouse, chose this occasion to reveal that, starting in 1961, Formula 1 cars would be powered by engines with a maximum swept volume of 1500cc, and would weigh a minimum of 500kg. The announcement received very vocal disapproval by many of those present.

The various nations represented on the CSI each had one vote, but only Britain and Italy were actively involved in Formula 1. Both had wished to retain the 2.5-litre Formula 1, established in 1954. However, France (a non-competing country) had proposed a 1.5-litre limit and had been supported by Germany, Monaco, Belgium and Holland. The motion was passed. The British constructors had since tried but failed to change the minds of the bureaucrats. The *Autosport* of 25 March 1960 reported: "The Society of Motor Manufacturers & Traders, comprising constructors, accessory and component makers, with full support from the major oil companies, are resolved not to support this formula…"

As part of the British dissent, a 3-litre 'Intercontinental' formula was briefly activated, but it soon disappeared. The new Formula 1 went ahead, although the British contingent did persuade the governing body to lower the minimum weight (to 450kg).

As a result of the FIA's decision, and British intransigence that cost a whole year of engine development, Ferrari was handed a head-start in the new Formula 1. The British teams relied on the underpowered, four-cylinder Coventry Climax FPF until new, purpose-designed V8 engines were developed by Climax and BRM. However, Stirling Moss had two wins with Rob Walker's Lotus at the Monaco and German Grands Prix while, in the absence of the Ferraris, Innes Ireland won the US Grand Prix for Team Lotus (the first Grand Prix victory for the works team, but it did not save his drive). Otherwise the British teams had a very thin year, including outgoing champions Cooper, with Jimmy Clark's 3rd place at Zandvoort for Lotus standing out.

Ferrari won all the remaining Grands Prix and the championship, with Phil Hill, but lost Wolfgang von Trips in a tragic Monza accident that also killed 14 spectators – the worst disaster in Formula 1 history. Consequently Ferrari did not attend the US Grand Prix, fearing adverse publicity despite having delivered the first American World Champion.

Porsche had a fluctuating season, three 2nd places by Dan Gurney accounting for most of its points. Of the many other private and part-time entrants, little needs to be said, but mention of the four-wheel-drive Ferguson P99 should be made. It was raced at the British Grand Prix without success, but then Moss won his final Oulton Park Gold Cup with it in September 1961.

The 21 non-championship Formula 1 races in Britain, Europe and South Africa were largely the preserve of British drivers, with Moss, Clark, Ireland, John Surtees and Roy Salvadori all winning one or more races.

↓ Pre-season non-championship races, such as the Gran Premio di Siracusa in Sicily, were regular features of the period. The 1961 race delivered a debut Formula 1 victory for a phenomenon named Giancarlo Baghetti, who won his first three races in this Ferrari Dino 156 (almost certainly the 1960 prototype 0008 rebodied and developed) entered by the Federazione Italiana Scuderie Automobilistiche, a consortium of Italian teams. He started on the front row and defeated Dan Gurney's Porsche 718 (following here) and the rest of a high-class field. The result came as a real shock: this was not a works car, and was equipped with the older 65-degree V6 engine. Baghetti would deliver more surprises. As for Syracuse, just look at the spectators. Photographer's pass? No need.

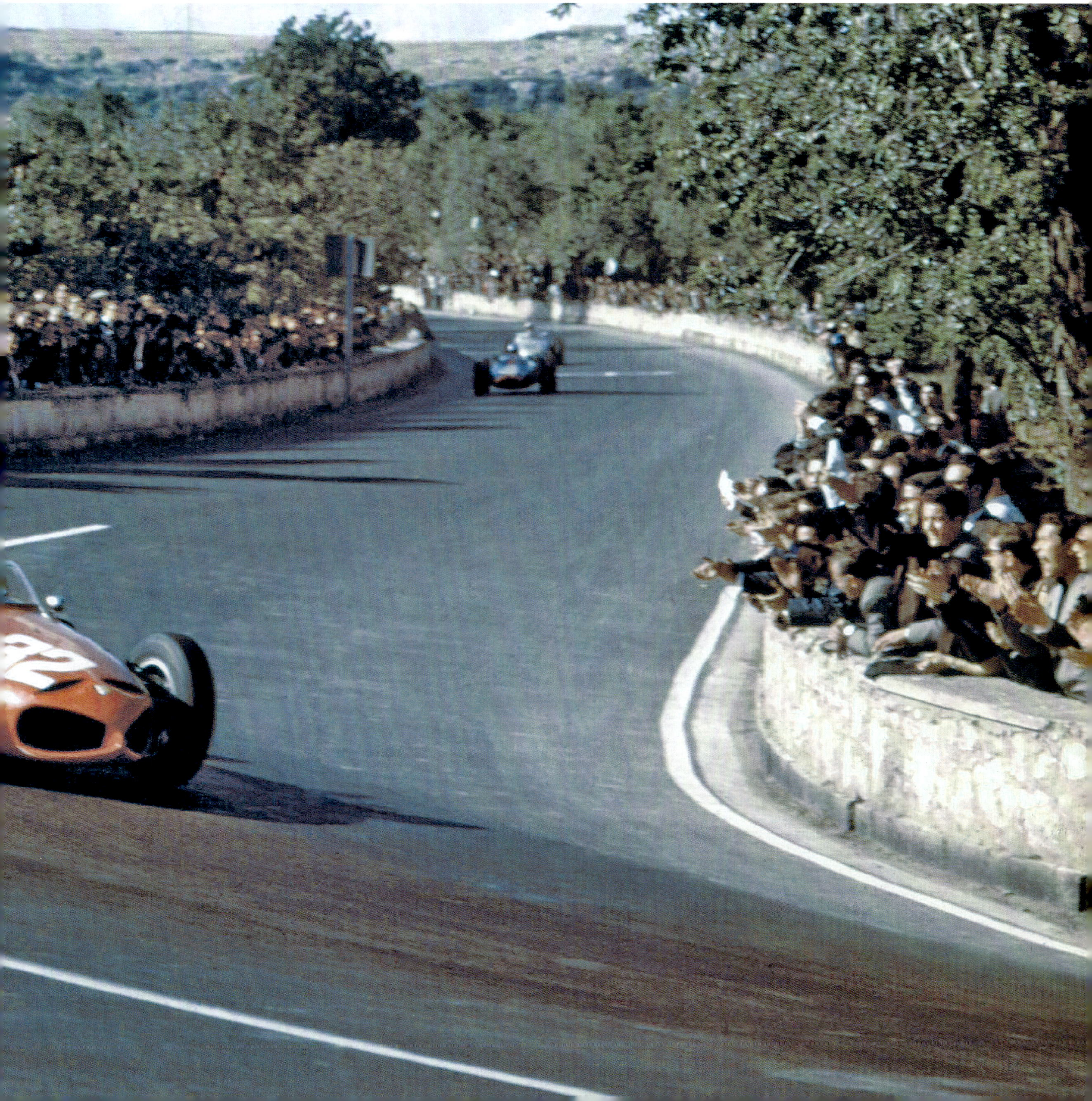

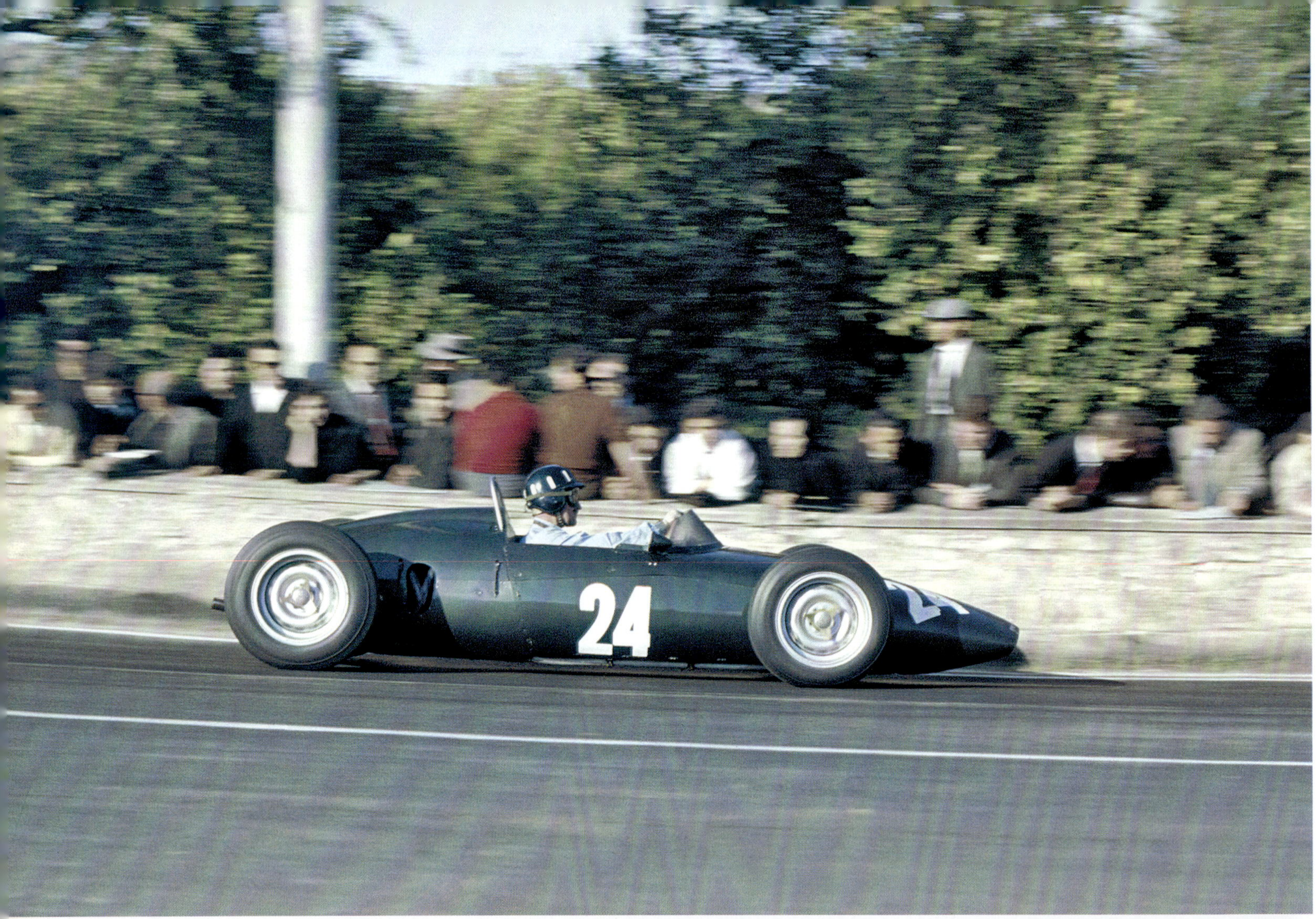
24

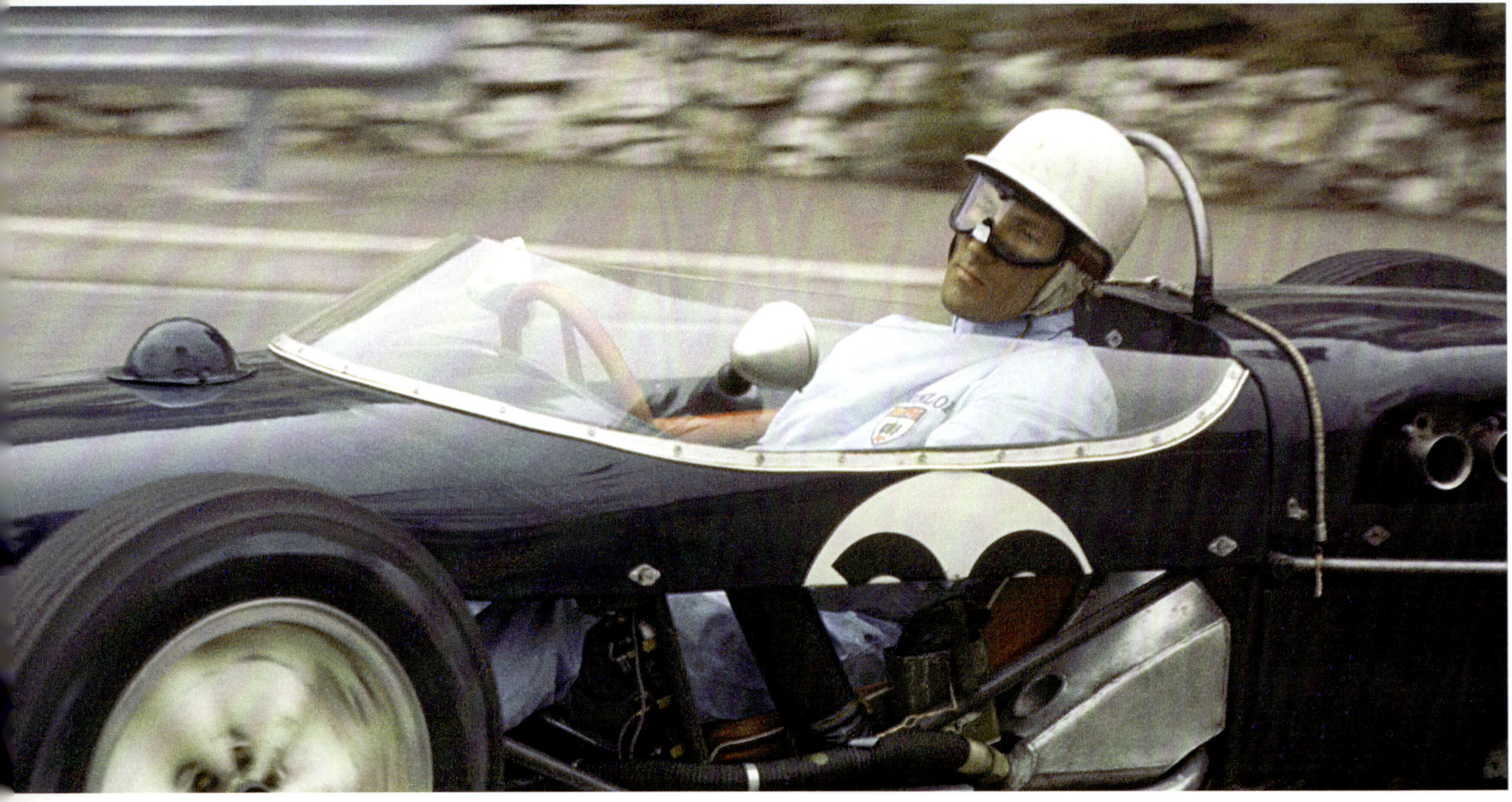

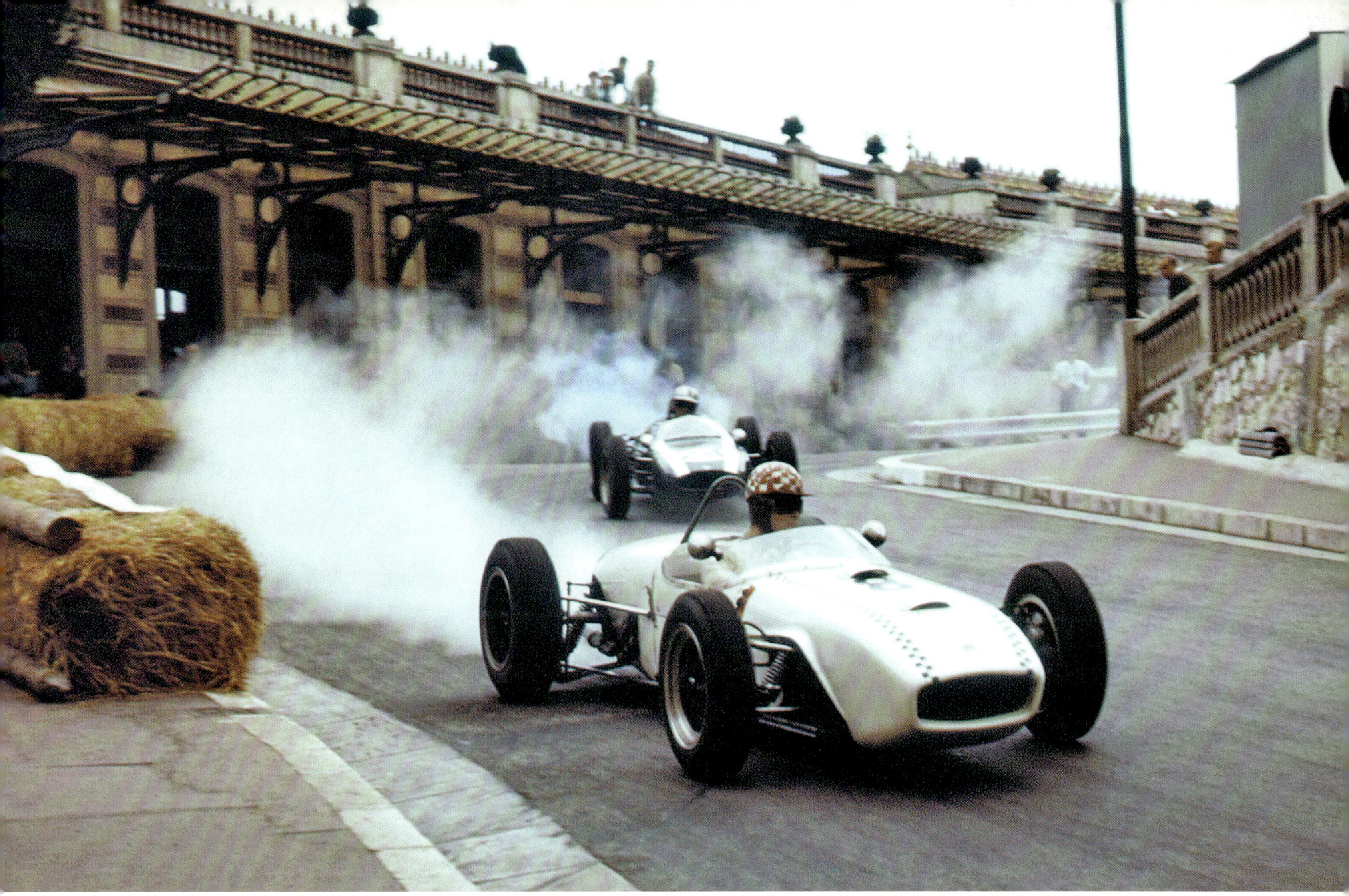

↑ Michael May's Scuderia Colonia Lotus 18 (914), followed by Jack Brabham's Cooper, is about to depart the Monaco Grand Prix with a split gearbox oil pipe. This car was owned and raced on occasion by sports car driver Wolfgang Seidel. At Monaco, only 16 cars were allowed to start and ten works entries plus Rob Walker team drivers Moss and Trintignant were guaranteed the maximum £1000 start money, while the remaining four were paid £500 apiece. Swiss born May was an engineer who fitted a wing to his Porsche 550 at the 1956 Nürburgring 1000km but it was mounted too far forward to be effective. He retired following a practice crash before the 1961 German Grand Prix, thereafter concentrating on fuel-injection development for Porsche and later Ferrari.

↖ BRM did not have its V8 ready for the start of the new formula, and Dan Gurney and Jo Bonnier departed to Porsche, but Graham Hill stayed put. Hill started his Climax engined BRM 48/57 (571) from the second row and spent almost all the race battling with Jack Brabham's Cooper. With four laps to go, running fourth, he over-revved the engine and was ultimately unclassified. The new BRM was 70kg overweight, an undesirable situation with only 145–150bhp available from the Mk2 Climax FPF engine.

← One of Stirling Moss's finest drives came at Monaco, where he won for a third time after a race-long battle with Ferrari's Phil Hill and Richie Ginther. The side panels of Rob Walker's Lotus 18 (912) have been removed to allow some airflow into the cockpit on a muggy day; chief mechanic Alf Francis had also welded up a cracked chassis tube on the grid, after wrapping the full fuel tank with wet towels! The photograph reveals the lack of driver protection, the purely cosmetic rollover bar, the vulnerable fuel pipe, part of an auxiliary fuel tank behind the seat, bungee cords strapped across the engine cover and hooked around the rear radius arms, and a spare pair of goggles wedged inside a tin between the seat and the tubular framework. Moss is entering the Station hairpin, a picture of symmetry and harmony that belies the fact that this race was run at a record-breaking speed, with the fastest lap (shared by Moss and Ginther) almost three seconds quicker than Stirling's pole.

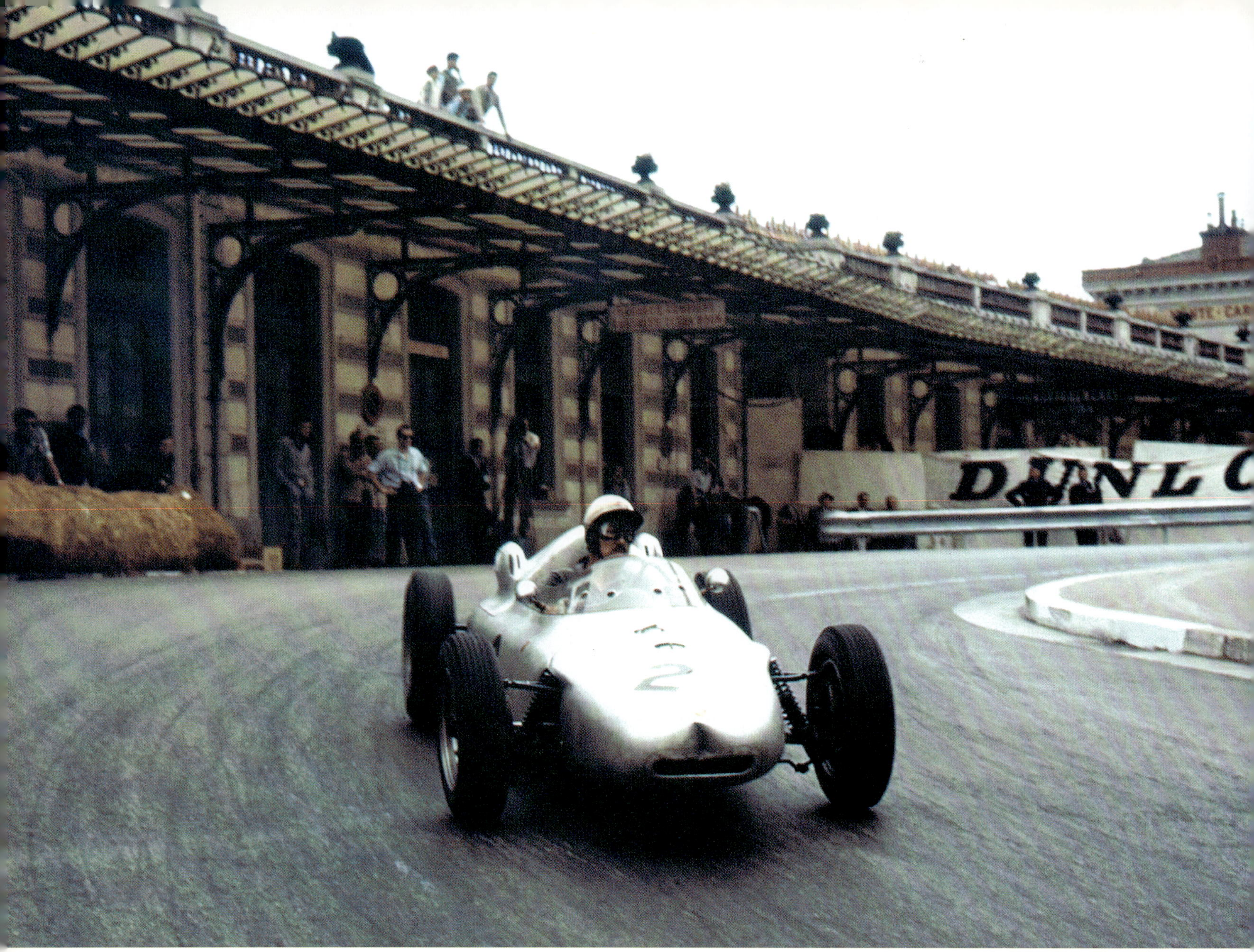

Intrepid spectators on the Monaco station roof have a fine view of Jo Bonnier briefly running his Porsche 787-01 in second place, before retiring due to a fuel vapour lock in the new Kugelfischer fuel-injection system. This was a prototype long-wheelbase version of the 718, meant to accommodate the forthcoming flat-eight. Bonnier used a four-speed gearbox while the other older 718 Porsches had five-speed transmissions. Dan Gurney finished 5th here, scoring Porsche's first ever World Championship points.

Cliff Allison returned to Formula 1 in 1961 with UDT Laystall's Lotus 18 (915). Starting on the penultimate row, he finished 8th. Allison joined Lotus in 1955 and graduated with the team to Grand Prix racing in 1958, where he outperformed Graham Hill and might have won the Belgian Grand Prix if it had lasted one more lap. He moved to Ferrari in 1959 and a victory with Phil Hill in the Buenos Aires 1000km sports car race early in 1960 was followed by a 2nd place in the Argentine Grand Prix before a nasty shunt at Monaco ended his season. Allison's talent was unfulfilled: he was competing with team mate Henry Taylor for a drive at the 1961 Belgian Grand Prix when he crashed and suffered severe leg injuries that prompted him to retire. He died in April 2005.

Pictured at the exact same spot, exiting Portier and approaching the old tunnel that passed under the railway line, Wolfgang von Trips races his Ferrari 156 Dino (0003) in the 1961 Monaco Grand Prix. He was classified 4th, two laps behind the winner, after an ignition failure in the older, 65-degree V6 (only Richie Ginther had the newer, 120-degree engine for the race). The abbreviated screen is a typical Monaco modification, although the trademark 'shark nose' must have been a liability around here.

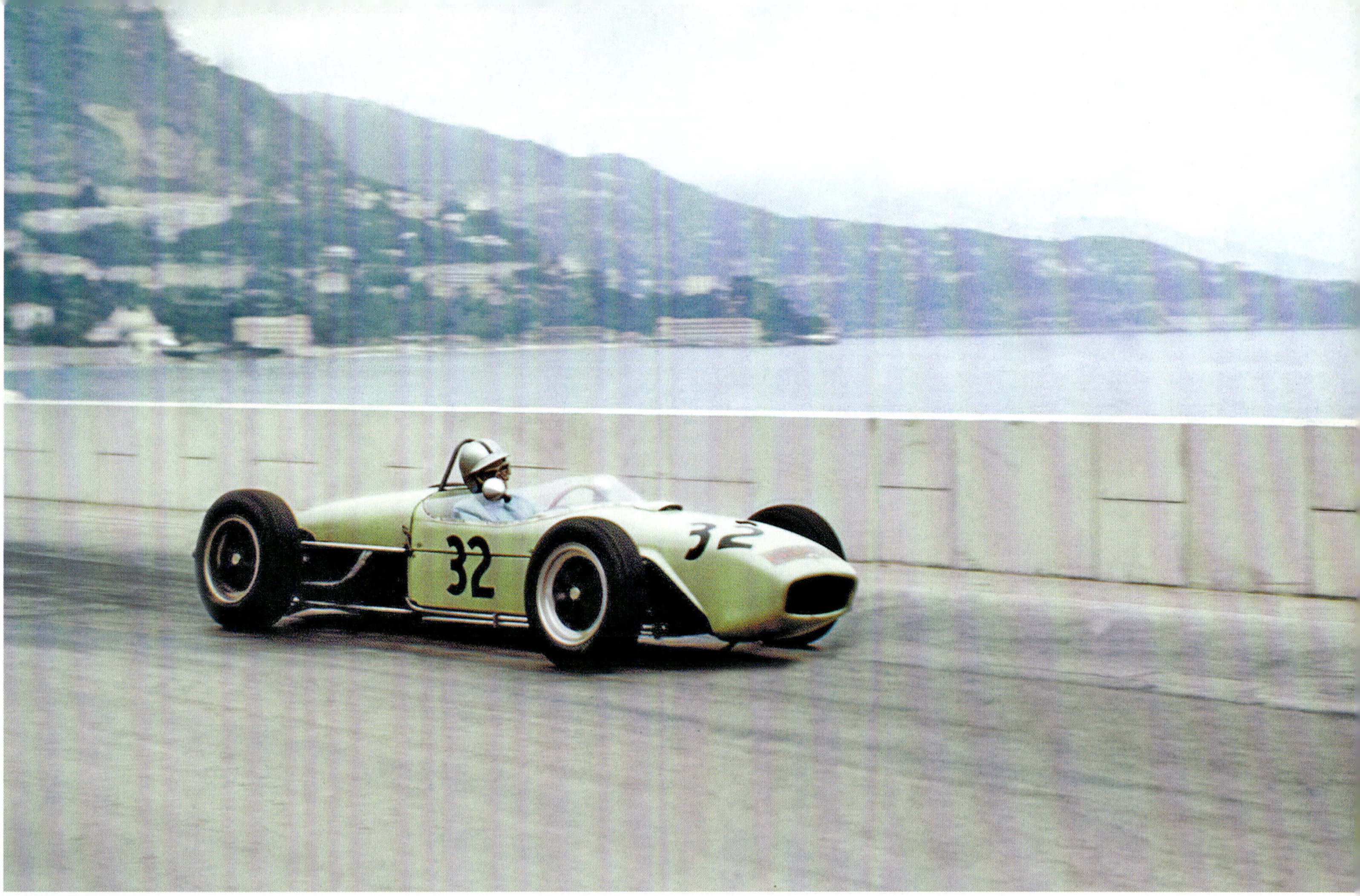
32
32

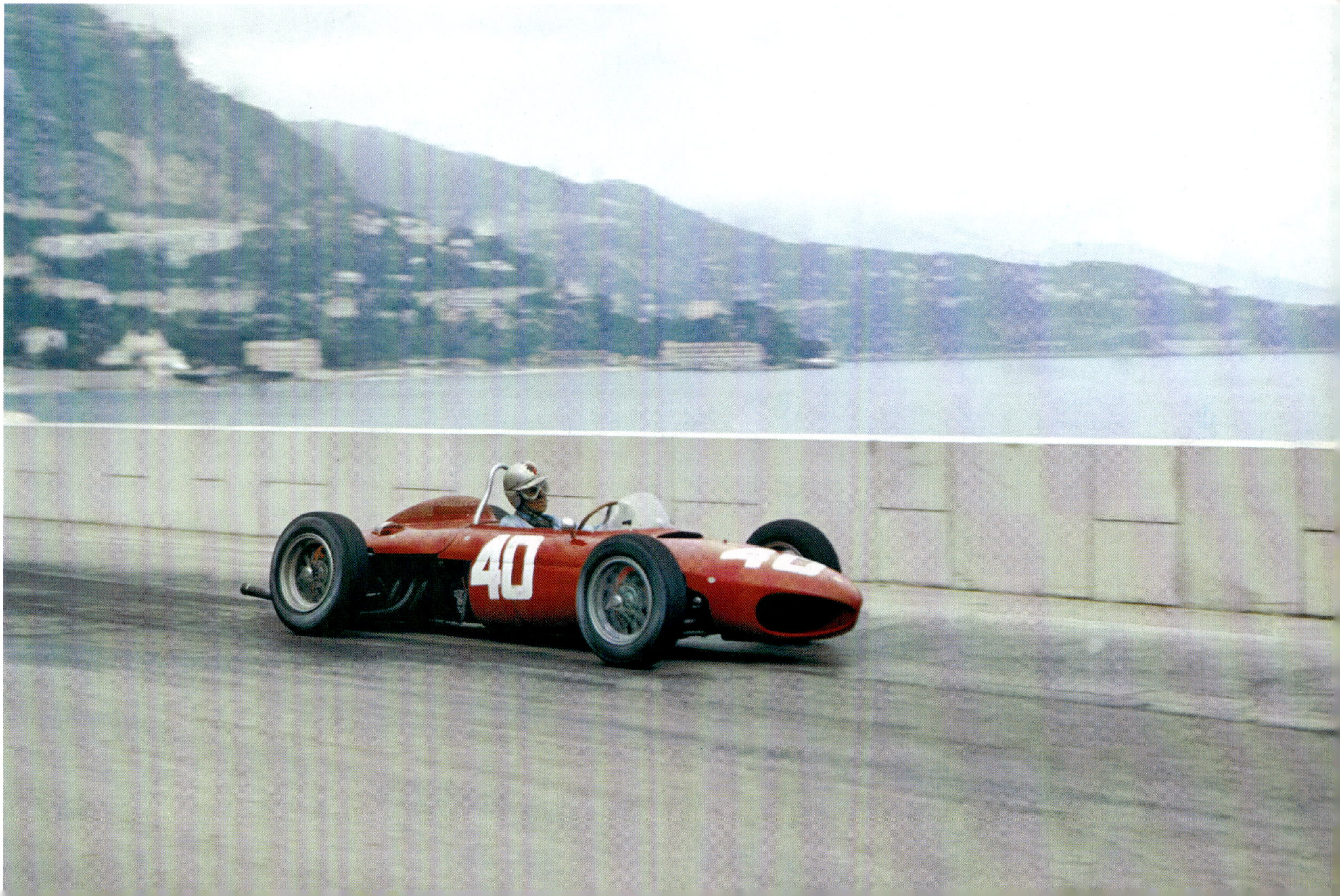
40

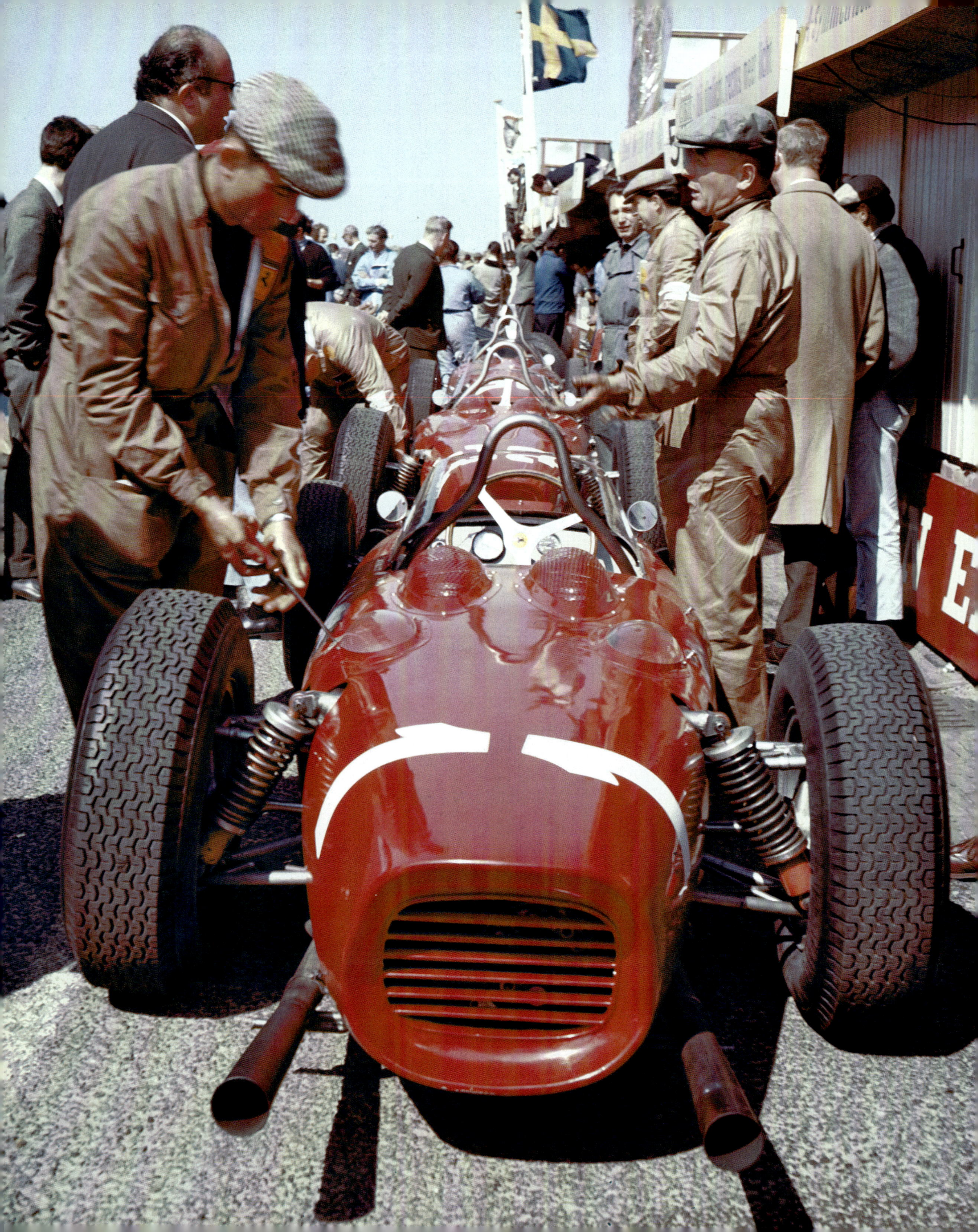

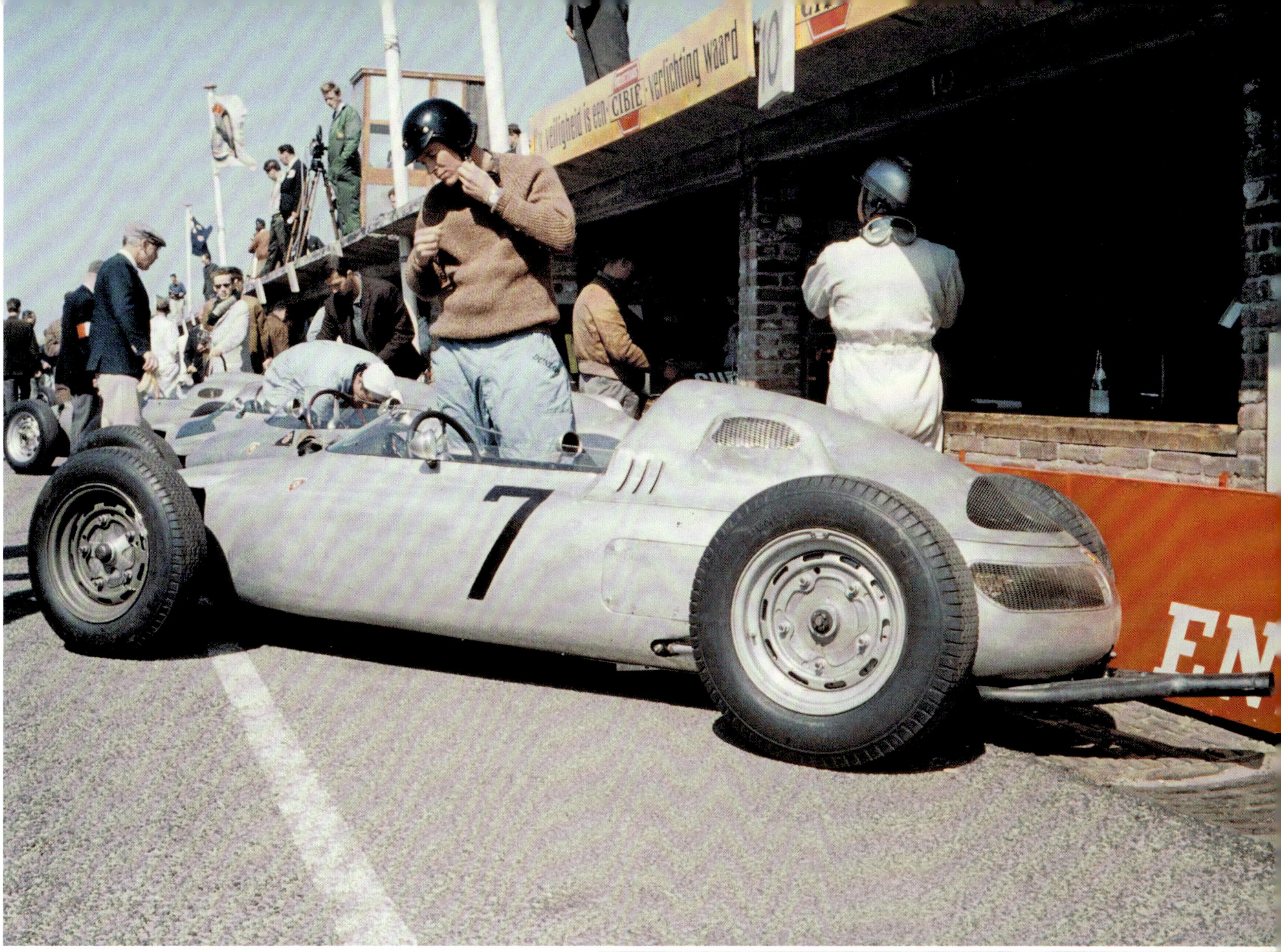

↑ Dan Gurney in a substantial looking pullover and the new Porsche 787 with its very long exhaust in the Zandvoort pits at the Dutch Grand Prix. Team mate Hans Herrmann is to the right, back to camera. The three ill-handling 787s were a big letdown and finished 10th (Gurney), 11th (Bonnier) and 15th (Herrmann). Ferry Porsche ordered the 787 to be discarded (although one was entered for Edgar Barth at Solitude) and the team reverted to the older, shorter wheelbase, Weber-carburetted 718s.

← A mechanic secures the engine cover of Phil Hill's Ferrari 156 Dino in the Zandvoort pits. Behind him can just be seen the team's engineering chief, Carlo Chiti. This is the later, 120-degree V6 engined car, distinguishable from the 65-degree model by the twin blisters on the engine cover. With a claimed 190bhp, the Ferraris had a big power advantage over the four-cylinder cars but the Dino chassis, with built-in negative camber front and rear (visible here), were less effective. Hill followed team mate von Trips across the line after spending much of the race battling with Clark's Lotus 21.

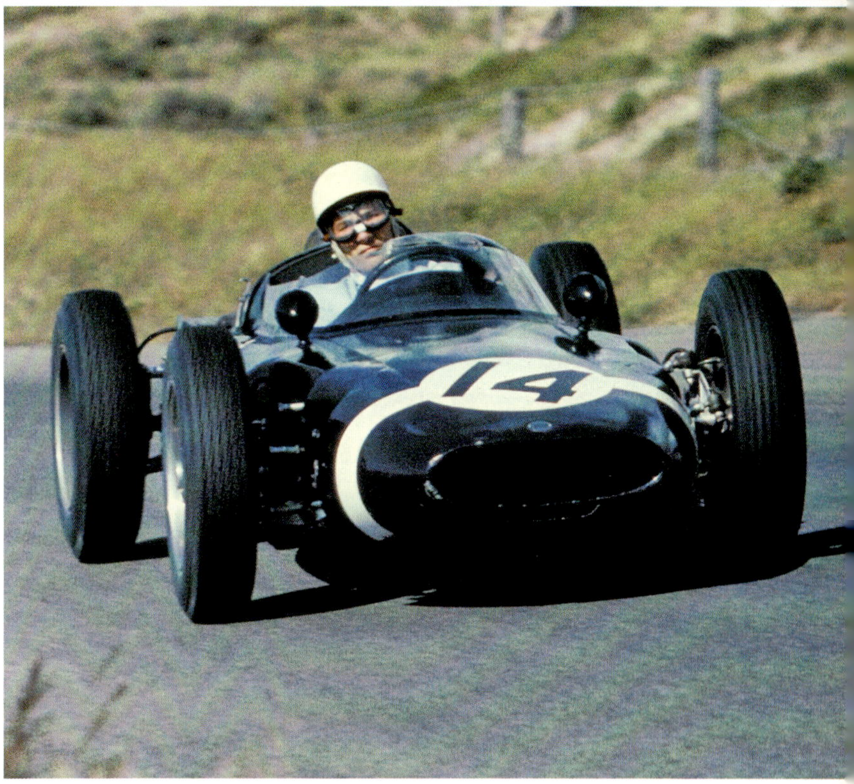

→ Stirling tried Rob Walker's Cooper T53 (F1-7-61) during practice for the Dutch Grand Prix but ultimately chose to use the Monaco winning Lotus 18. Imagine the paroxysms of bureaucratic paranoia this would generate today if a team wanted to substitute a different make of car for one of their entries.

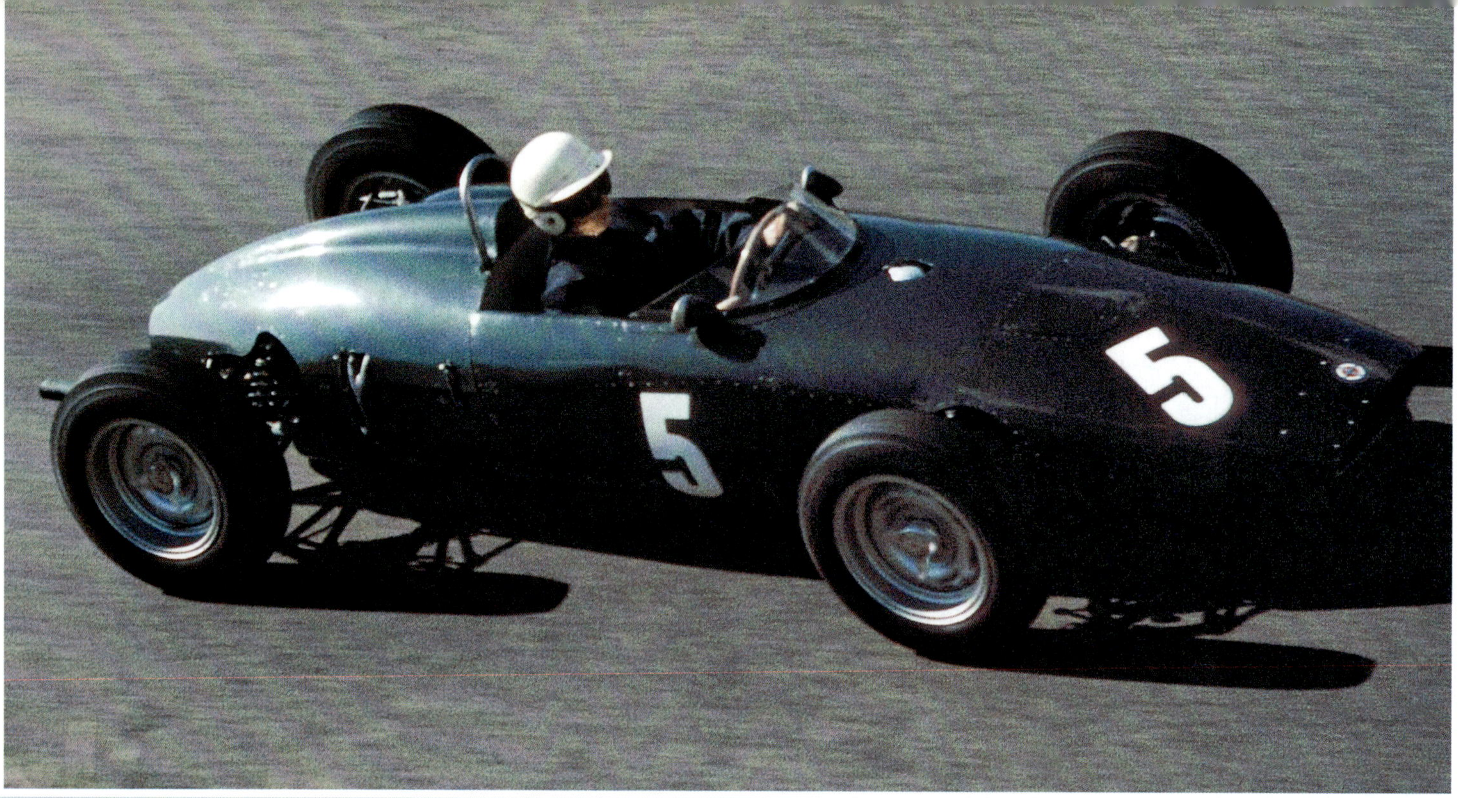
5

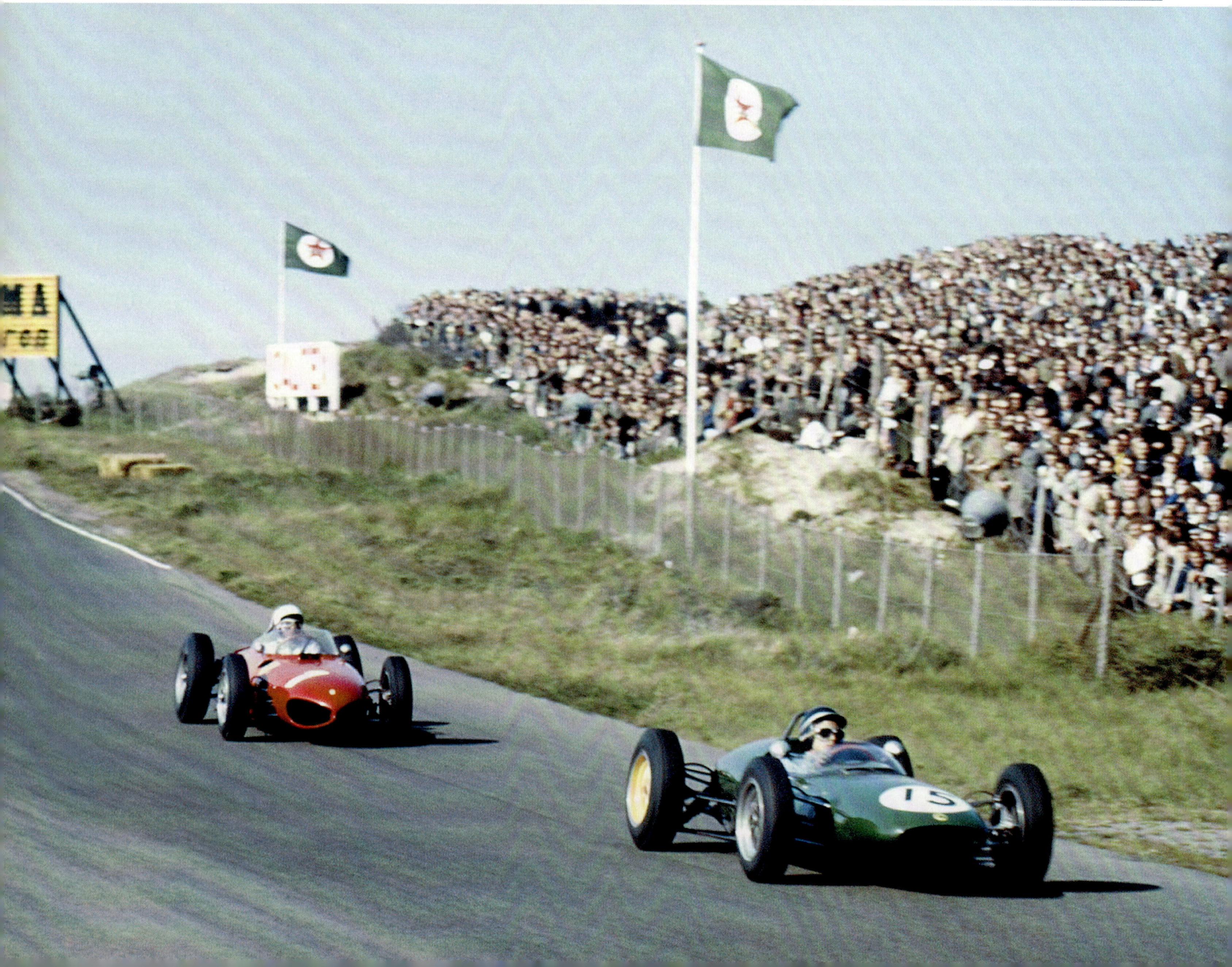
15

Tony Brooks spent the final year of his motor racing career playing second fiddle to Graham Hill at BRM, although he was arguably the better driver. More aware than most of the extreme vulnerability of his contemporaries and self, he put survival and his family life first. At Zandvoort he finished 9th in the overweight, underpowered P48/57 (572) behind team mate Hill.

Here is the new Lotus 21 chassis 930, with which Jimmy Clark outpaced the older Lotus 18 of Stirling Moss, leading Hill's Ferrari until the American finally got by and setting the fastest lap of the Dutch Grand Prix on his way to 3rd place. As usual, BRM's Tony Rudd was timing the cars in sections around the track, and he discovered that the svelte Lotus was faster down the straights than the Ferrari.

The works Ferraris of Richie Ginther, Phil Hill and Wolfgang von Trips in the pits at Spa. Once again the extraordinary (by modern standards) public accessibility of the period is obvious here, including what looks like a Belgian boy scout and a very young girl, a nostalgic rebuke to latter day restrictions.

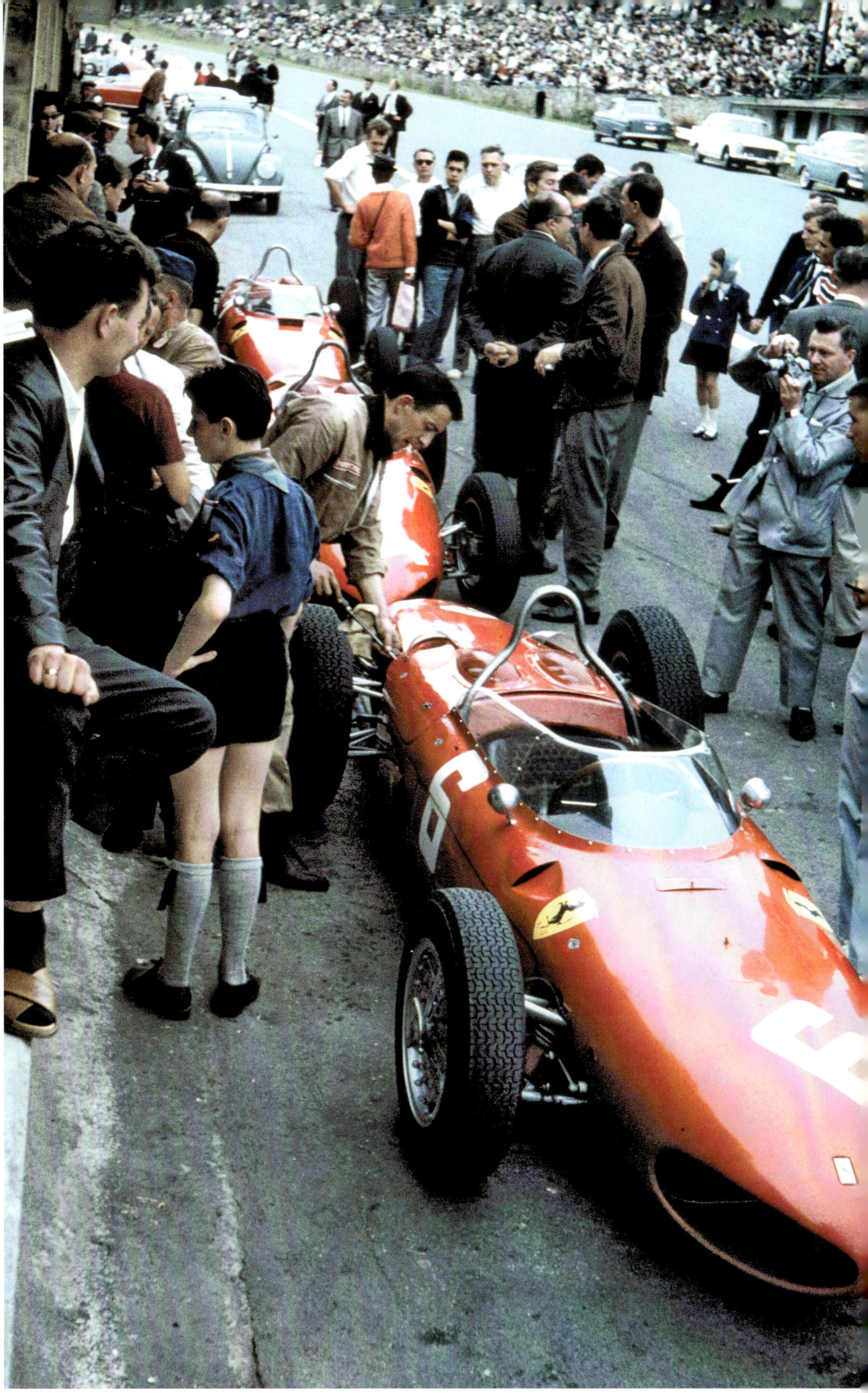

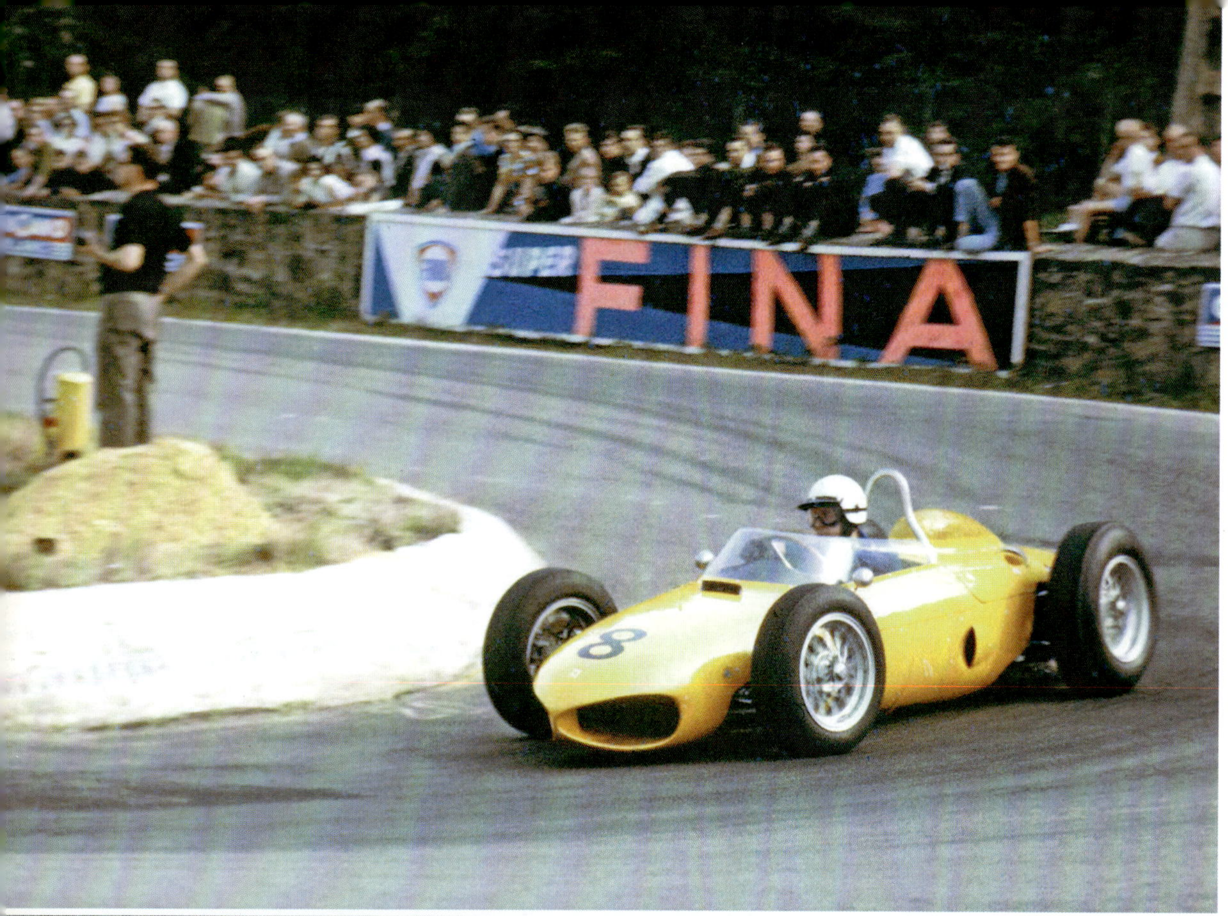

1961 was the second time that Olivier Gendebien had raced a works-loaned Ferrari at Spa, painted in Belgium's national racing colour for Equipe Nationale Belge. He drove a Dino 246 in 1958 and this time, at the wheel of a Dino 156 (0003) with the less potent 65-degree V6, he contested the lead strongly with Phil Hill. Gendebien eventually dropped back when oil started to leak onto his rear tyres, but survived to finish 4th behind the three works cars. A former WW2 paratrooper, Gendebien was a Belgian aristocrat, four-times Le Mans winner for Ferrari and one of the greatest sports and GT drivers of his era. He retired after his final Le Mans victory in 1962 and died in 1998.

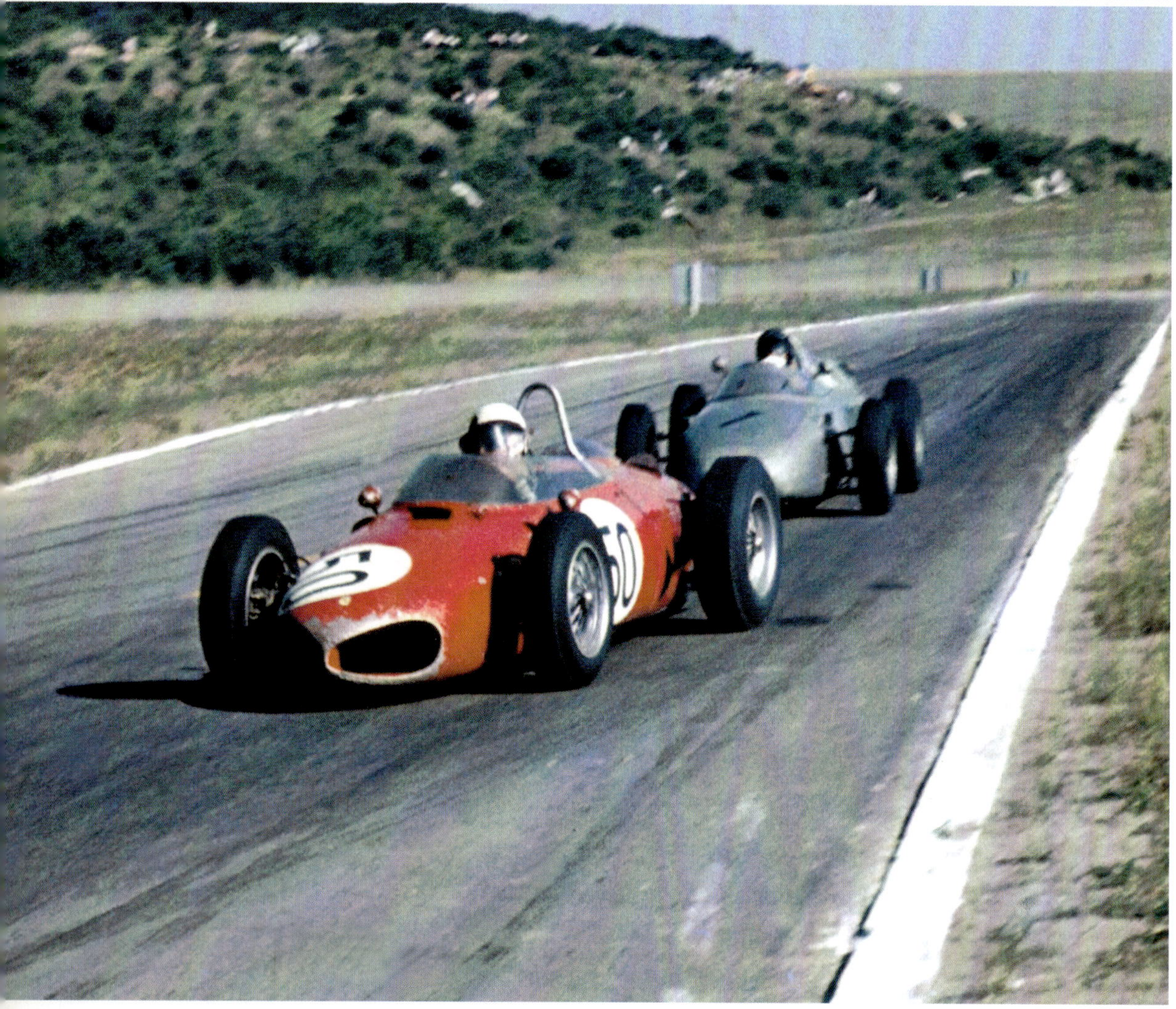

Two weeks after Spa, the extraordinary hat-trick performed by Giancarlo Baghetti – victories in his first three Formula 1 races with a privately entered Ferrari Dino 156 – climaxed like a giant firework at Reims in the French Grand Prix. The works Ferraris were all in trouble and Baghetti fought a long, hard, slipstreaming battle with the Porsches of Jo Bonnier and Dan Gurney (following) before winning his first ever World Championship Grand Prix from Gurney by a tenth of a second. Perhaps inevitably, this was the absolute zenith of Baghetti's career: he never again got anywhere near the prize money in F1.

⇒ Innes Ireland presses on at Thillois to finish 4th with the Lotus 21 chassis 933 at Reims some nine seconds adrift of team mate Clark in the sister car. Three weeks later he won a do or die battle at Solitude against Gurney's Porsche and in October the US GP at Watkins Glen. Nevertheless, he lost his seat at Lotus, discovering the unpleasant truth at the London Motor Show that Chapman favoured a younger Trevor Taylor.

⇓ This wonderfully atmospheric shot of Richie Ginther captures the broiling sun, melted tar and stone-blasted cars that so defined Reims. None of the works Ferraris survived the French Grand Prix. Ginther's 156 (0001) was halted by failing oil pressure with 12 laps to go.

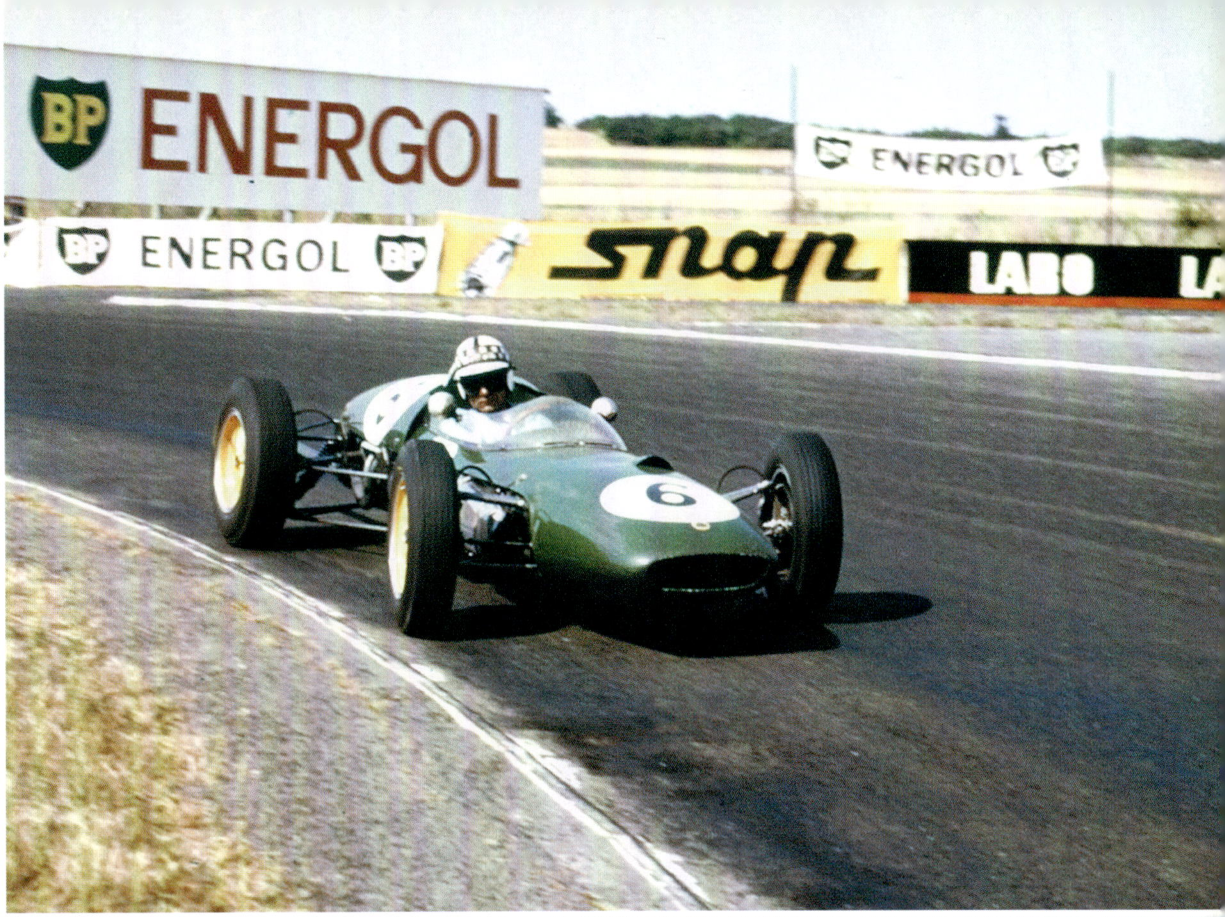

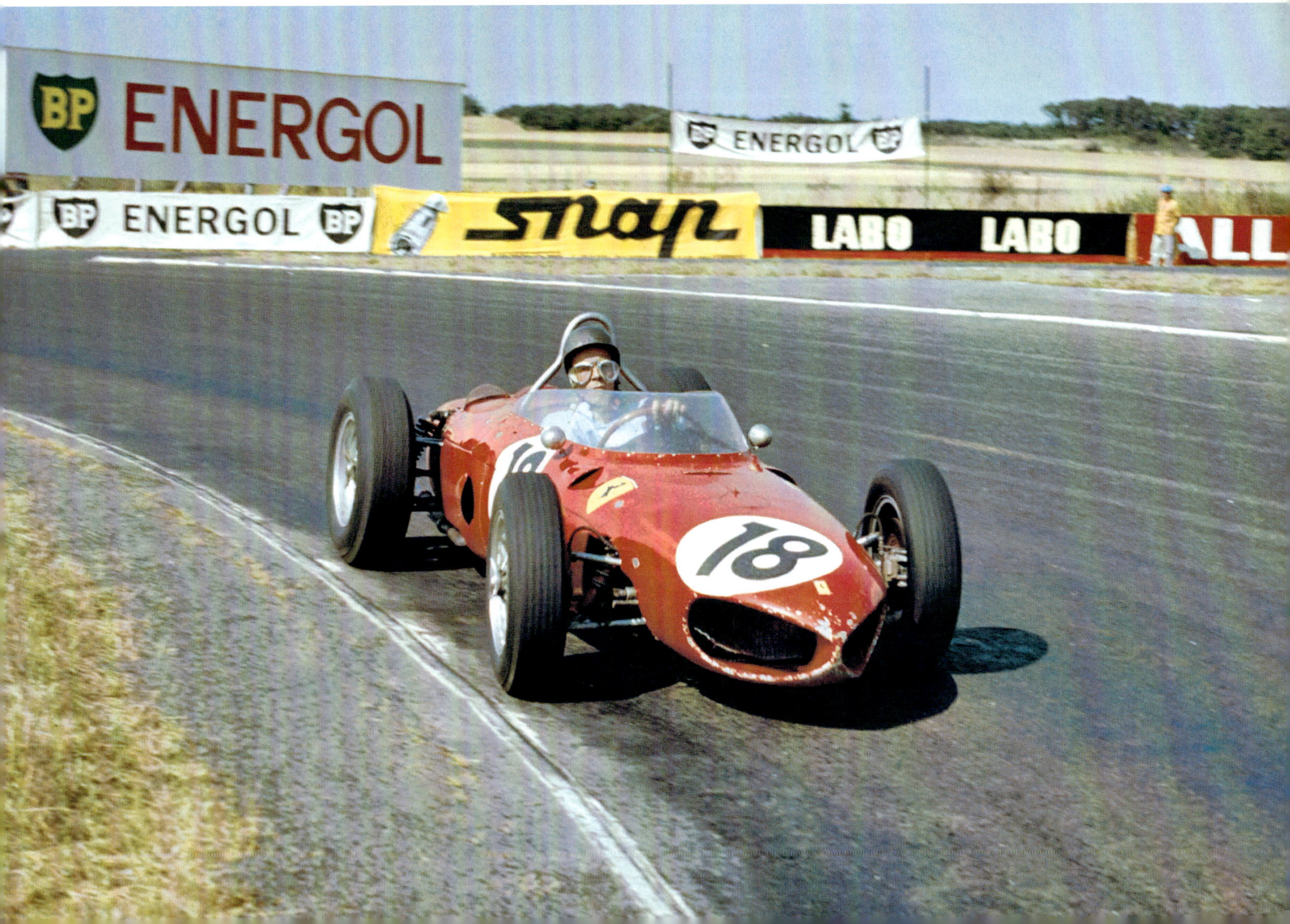

This picture, taken from the Dunlop footbridge some way beyond the start, gives an accurate impression of the flat-out 'blind' that was the 5.159-mile Reims road circuit. The three works Ferraris led away but they all failed, although the Prancing Horse still galloped home thanks to Giancarlo Baghetti. The ultra high speeds possible at Reims were rather wasted on the 1.5-litre cars, most of which would struggle to better 150/155mph. Meanwhile, six years after the Le Mans tragedy the pits are totally exposed to cars racing by at top speed; it is a major miracle that such complacency was not more frequently punished. Note the huge crowd and the obviously blistering heat of a typical Reims French Grand Prix.

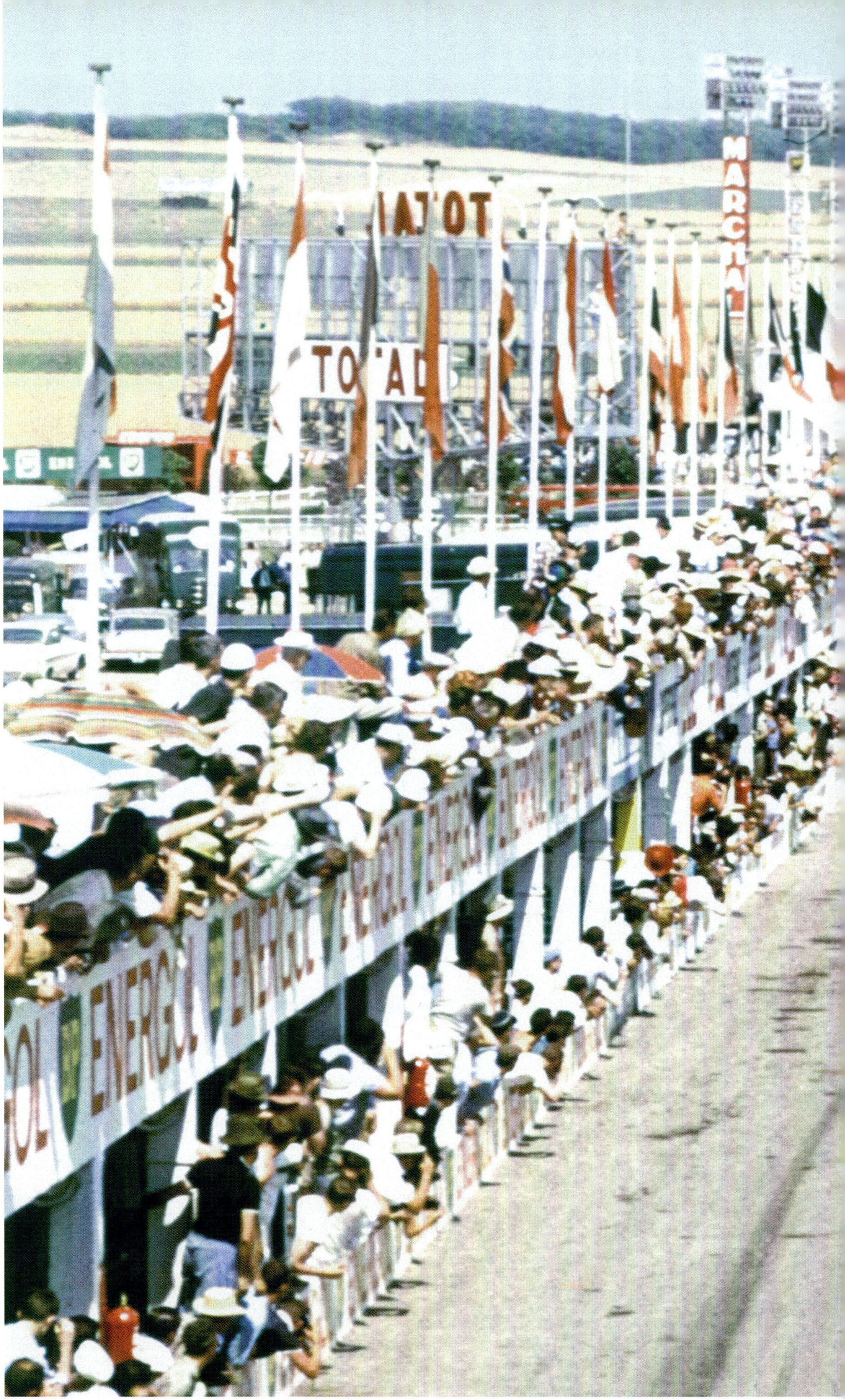

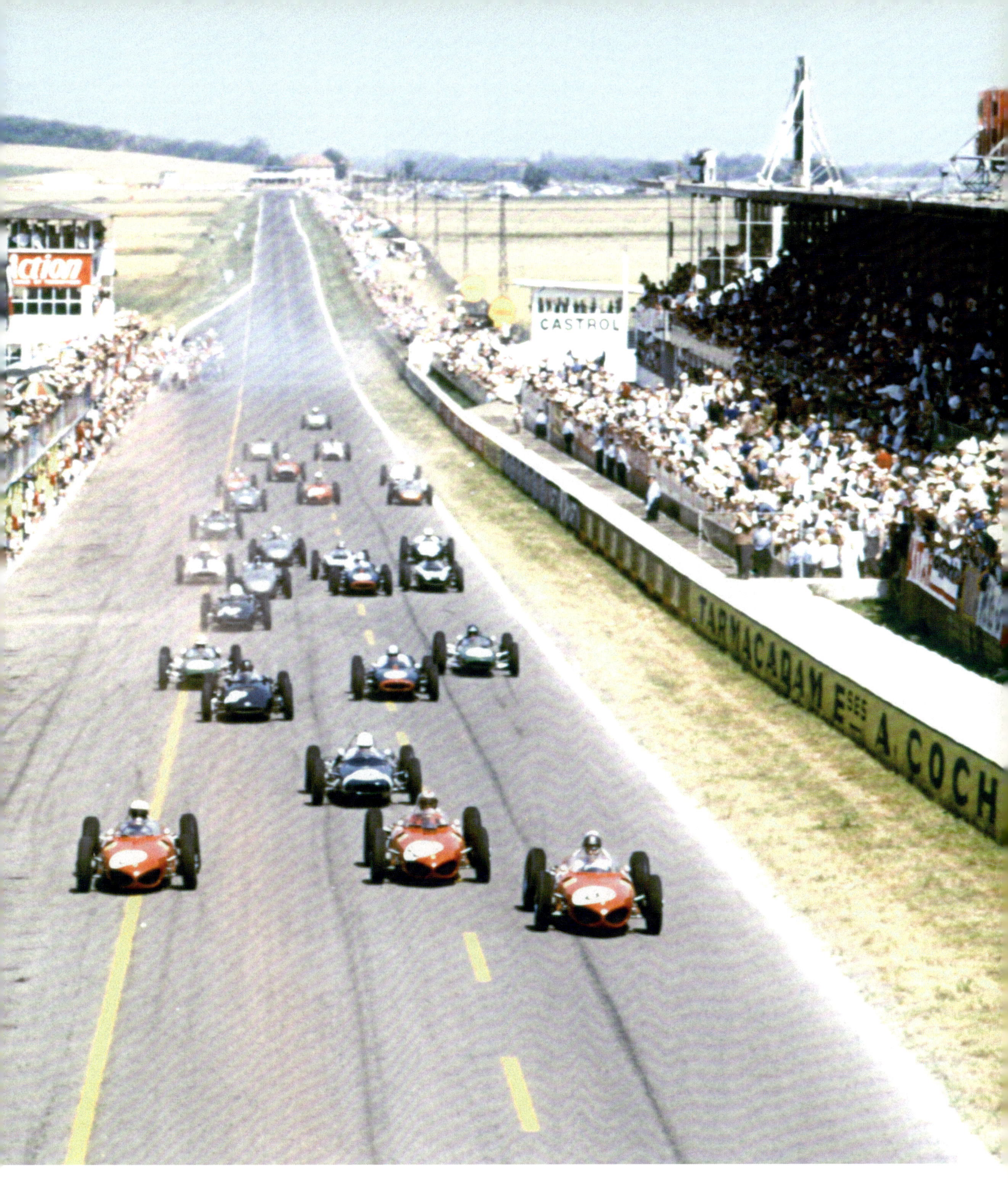
CASTROL
TARMACADAM

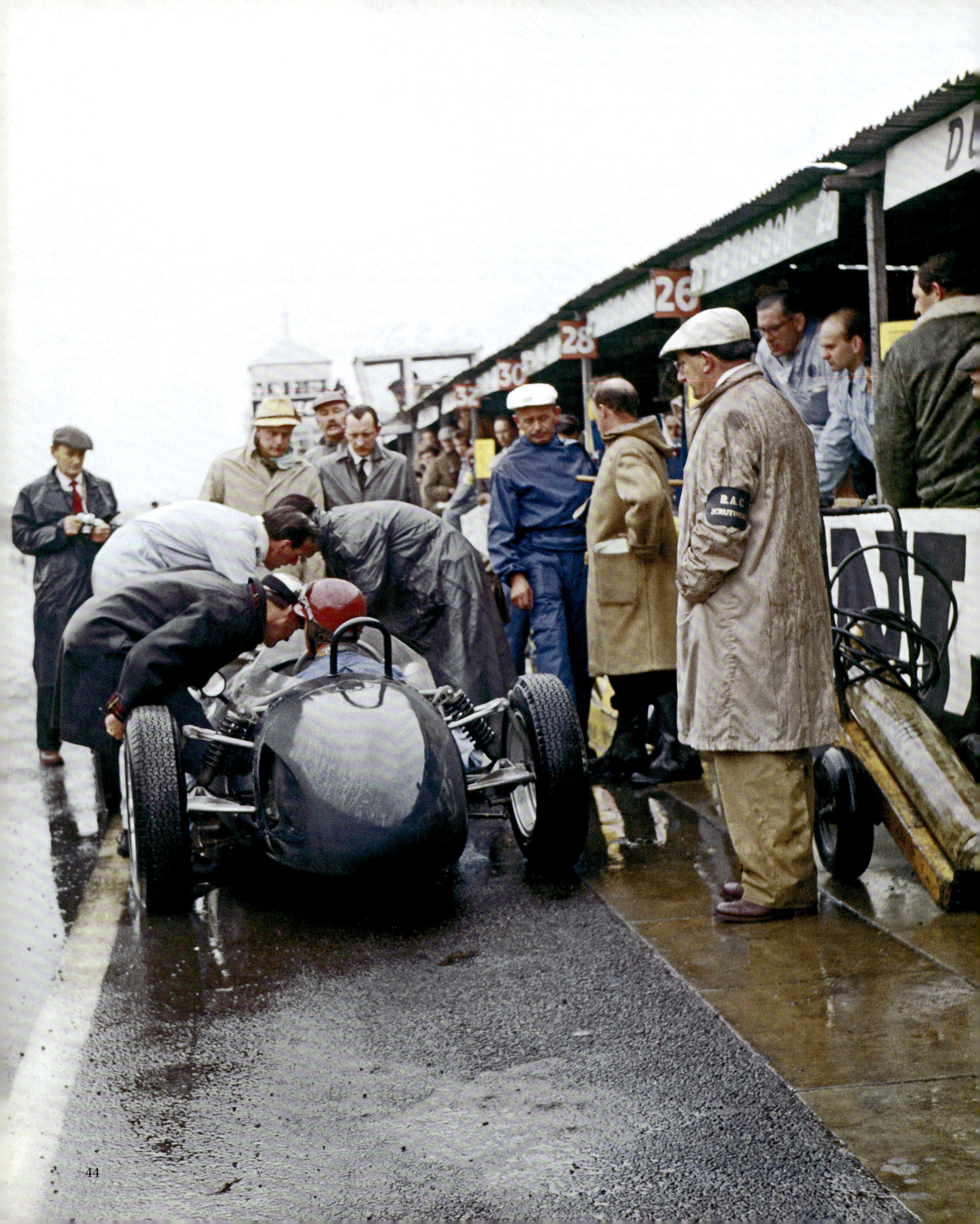
26
28
30
32

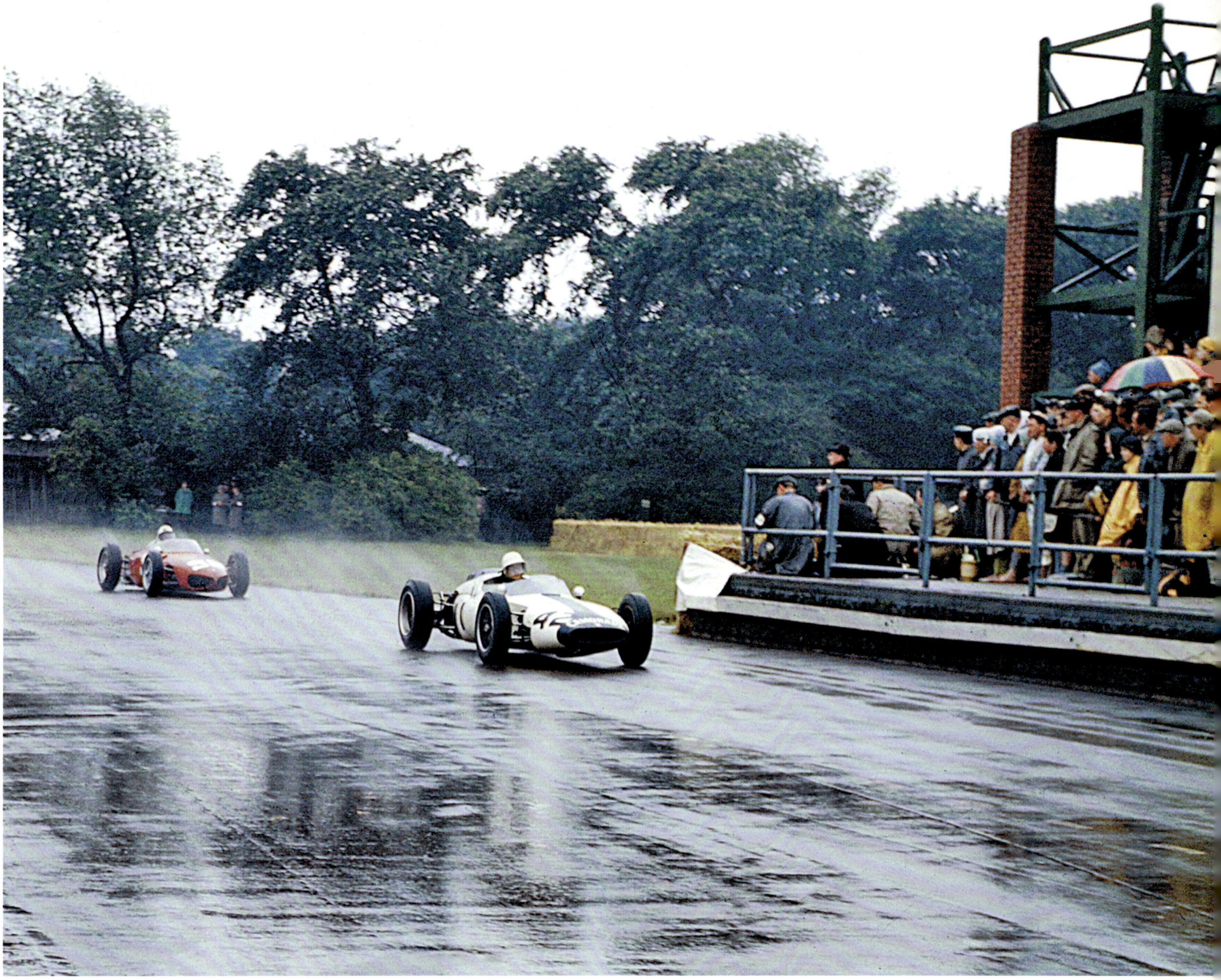

One of the short-lived Formula 1 entrants of the period was Camoradi International, owned by Lloyd 'Lucky' Casner and best remembered for its successes with 'birdcage' Maserati sports-racing cars. Here the team's Cooper T53 (F1-3-61), driven by Masten Gregory, leads Baghetti's Ferrari out of Tatts corner at Aintree and past the pits. Gregory finished 11th but Baghetti wrecked the Ferrari. A former Cooper works driver and noted Lister Jaguar racer, Masten was famed for jumping out of crashing cars but survived his racing career. A lifelong smoker and reputed user of illegal substances he died after a heart attack in 1985, aged 53.

It is pouring with rain, the backdrop is grim, and no one is enjoying the British Grand Prix at Aintree, near Liverpool. The unique four-wheel-drive Ferguson P99 Climax FPF, entered by Rob Walker and driven by veteran Jack Fairman, has stopped with soaked electrics, to the consternation of chief mechanic Alf Francis (white cap). The head poking between the observers in front of the car is wearing the trademark deerstalker of John Bolster, the long-time BBC pit-lane commentator and technical editor of *Autosport* magazine. Fairman was push-started and was later called in to be replaced by Stirling Moss (in duffel coat talking to Francis), who had retired the team's Lotus 18/21. Moss began lapping quickly in the now healthy Ferguson, but the car was disqualified for the earlier push-start.

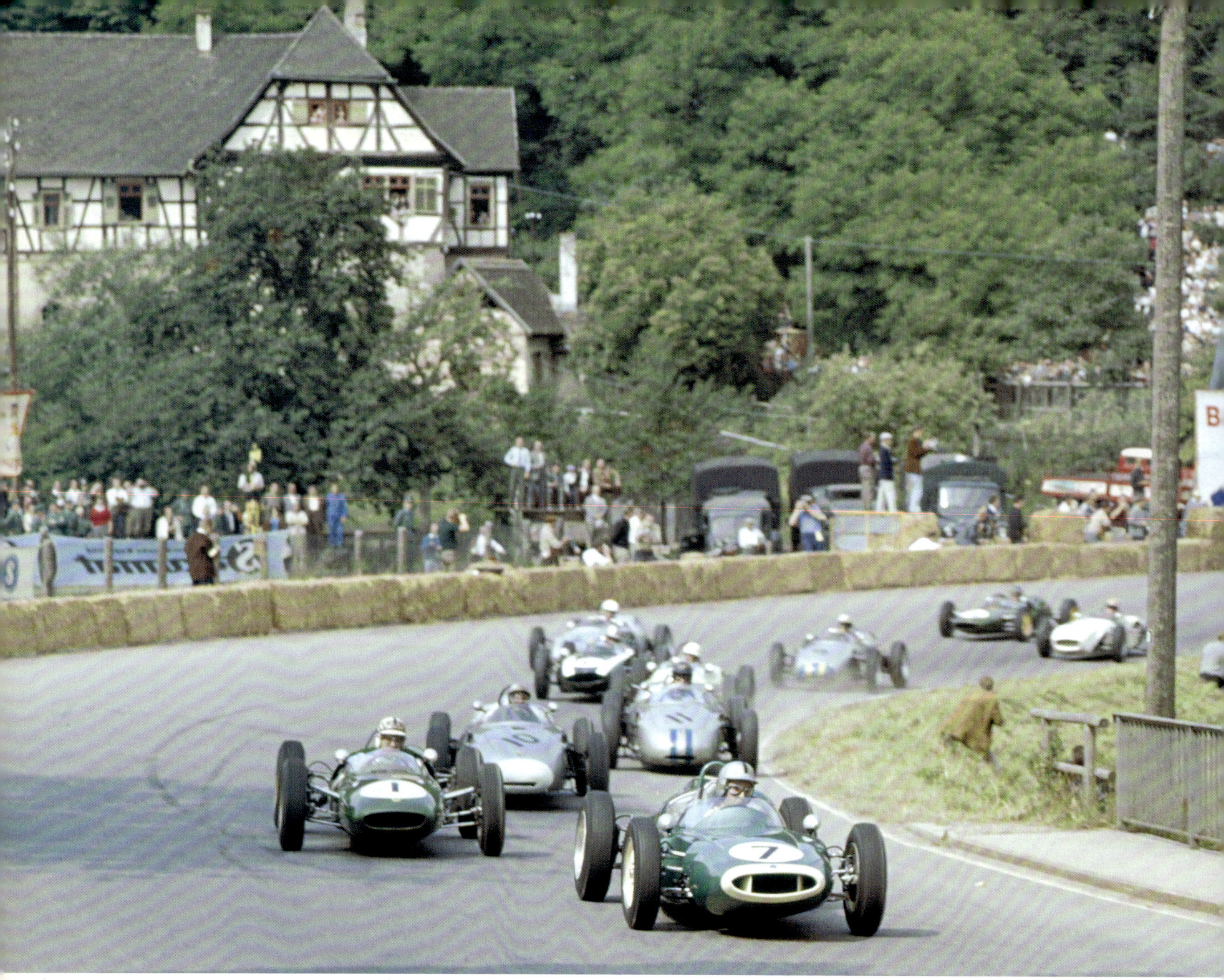

In between the British and German Grands Prix, the town of Solitude hosted a non-championship Formula 1 race on a 7.1-mile circuit on tree-lined public roads, first used in 1925. Here Bruce McLaren in Tommy Atkins's Cooper T53 heads Innes Ireland's race-winning Lotus 21, the Porsches of Hans Herrmann and Dan Gurney and the rest of the pack. Solitude, a few miles west of Stuttgart, lost its fixture in 1965 and was effectively replaced by Hockenheim.

Stirling Moss amid the arboreal splendour of the Eifel hills, practising for the German Grand Prix on the Nordschleife in Rob Walker's Lotus 18/21. Moss was impressed by Dunlop's new high-grip D12 rain tyres, but Dunlop's Vic Barlow refused to accept any responsibility for racing on them because they tended to wear excessively on drying roads. Having established an advantage in the early wet conditions, Moss sought out the damp patches to preserve his rapidly wearing rubber when the track began to dry. His innately smooth and sensitive style paid off and he won by 21.4 seconds. The Ferraris of Wolfgang von Trips and Phil Hill gave chase, the latter setting a new lap record (the first under nine minutes), but by then Moss was out of reach. It was the 100th World Championship Grand Prix and his last World Championship victory.

An interesting shot of Bruce McLaren *en route* to 4th place at Solitude with Tommy Atkins's Cooper T53 (FII-8-60). Note the lake on the left, the rudimentary guardrail and the bare-knuckle driving. The Coopers were less sophisticated than the latest cars from Lotus, but more forgiving to drive. Atkins ran McLaren, Roy Salvadori and Chris Amon during the early 1960s in a variety of cars, but sadly died in 1965.

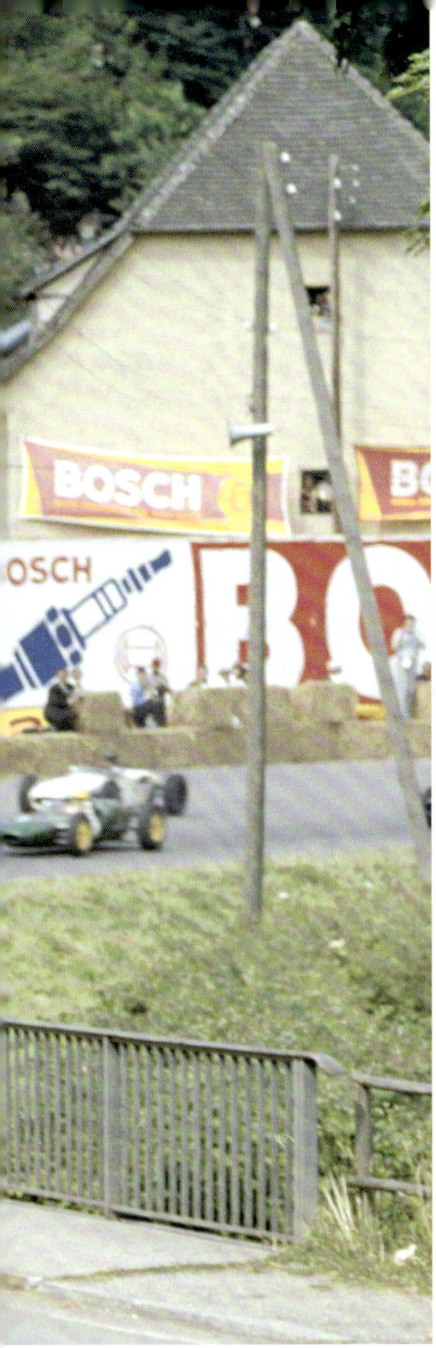
BOSCH

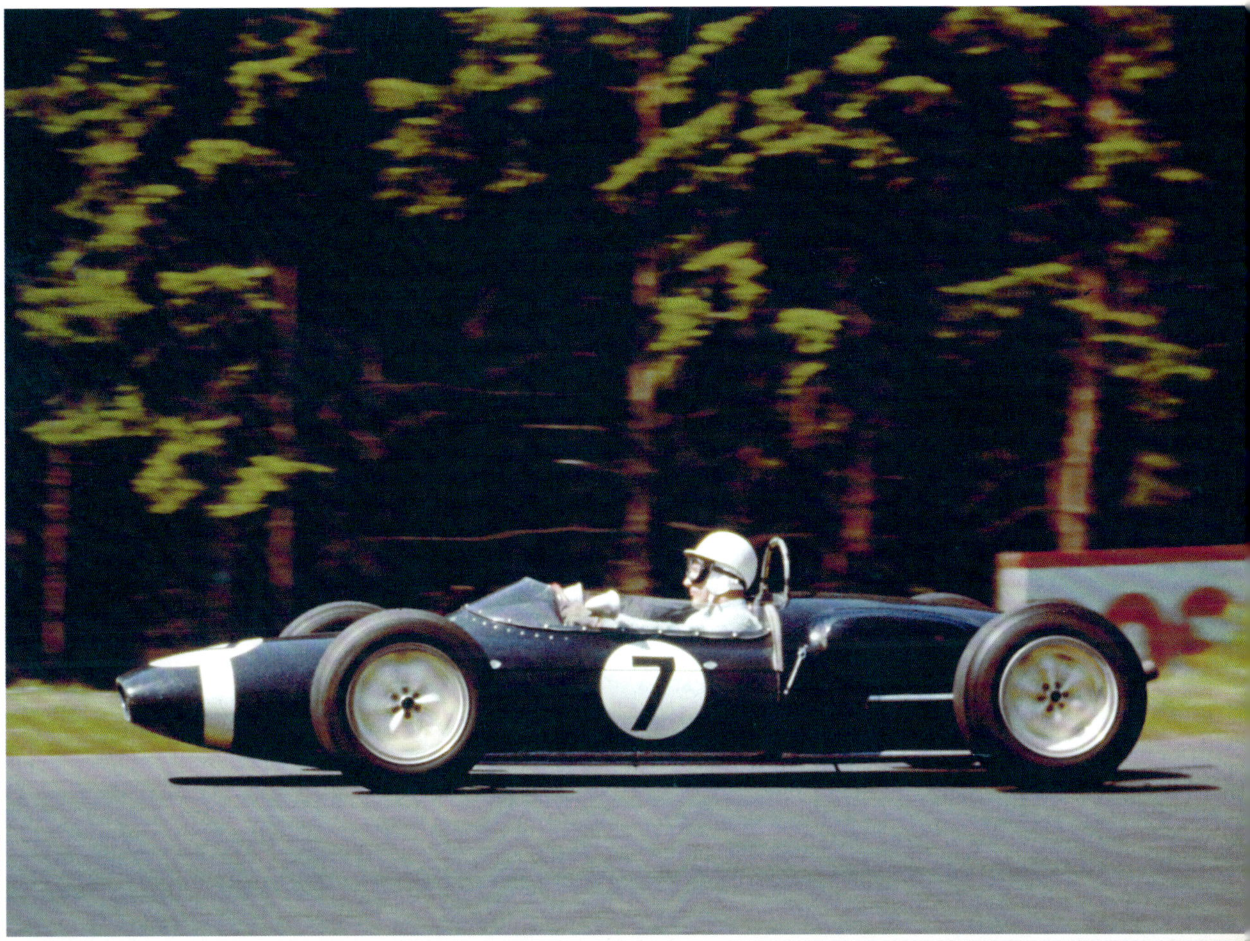
7

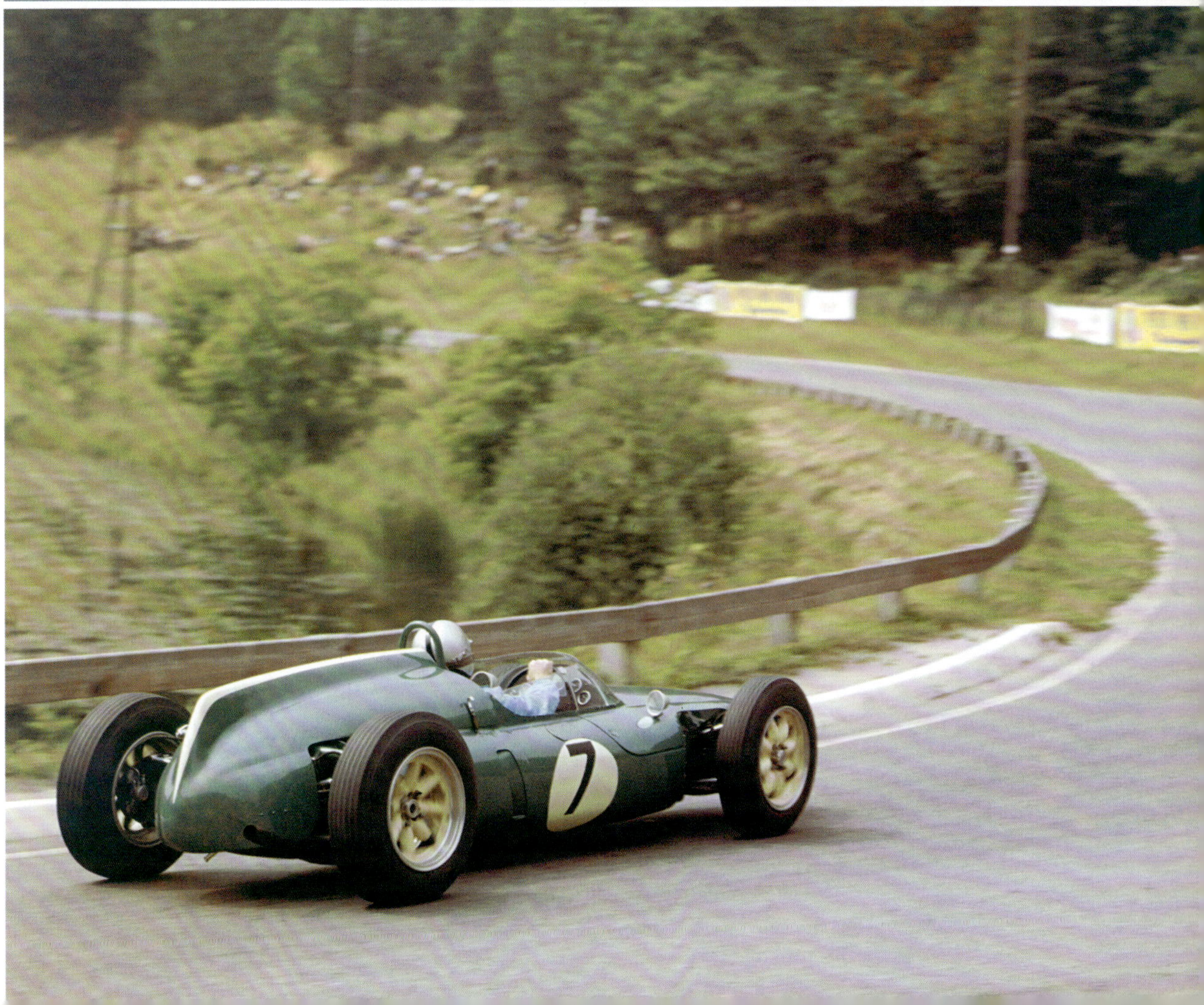
7

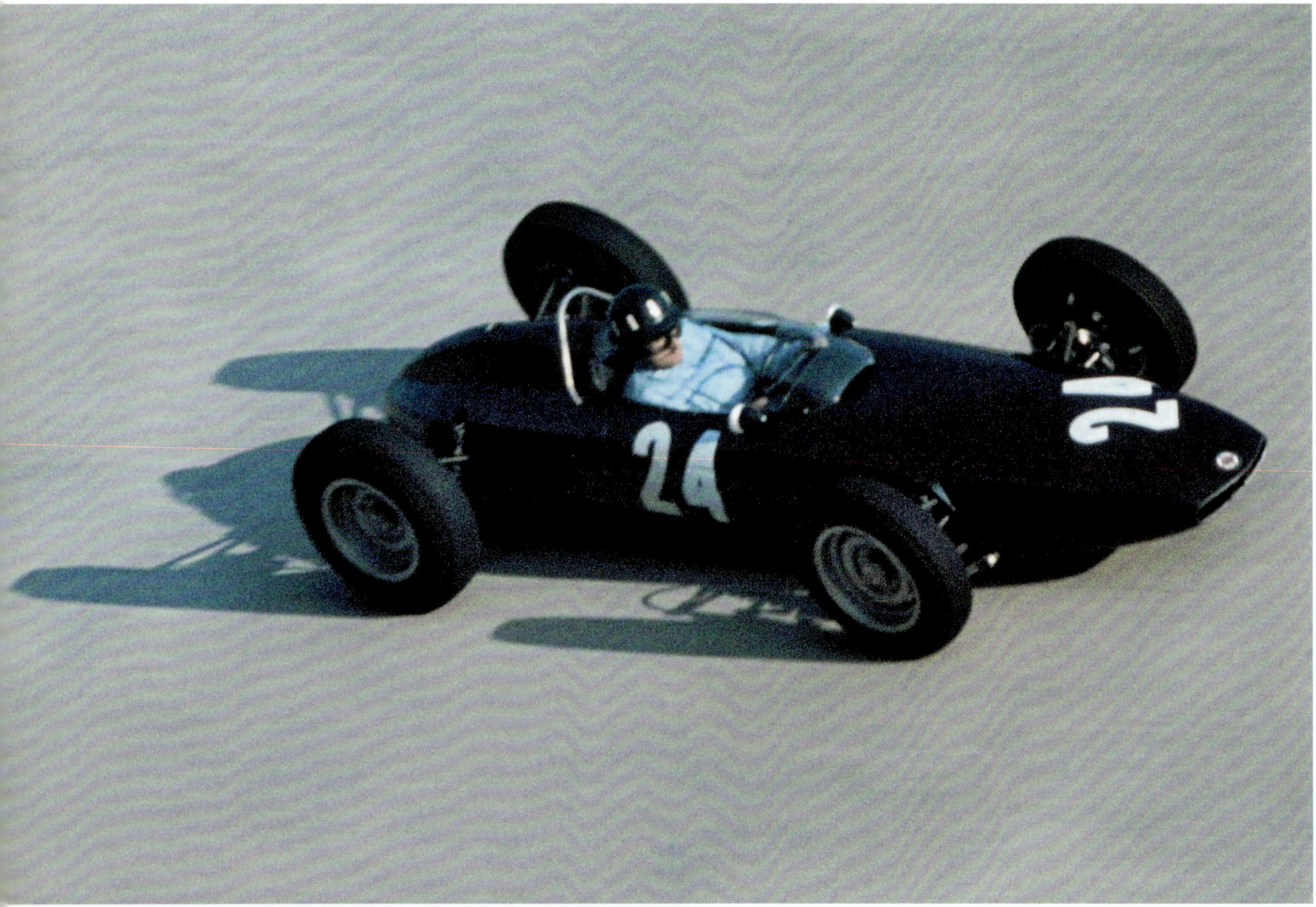

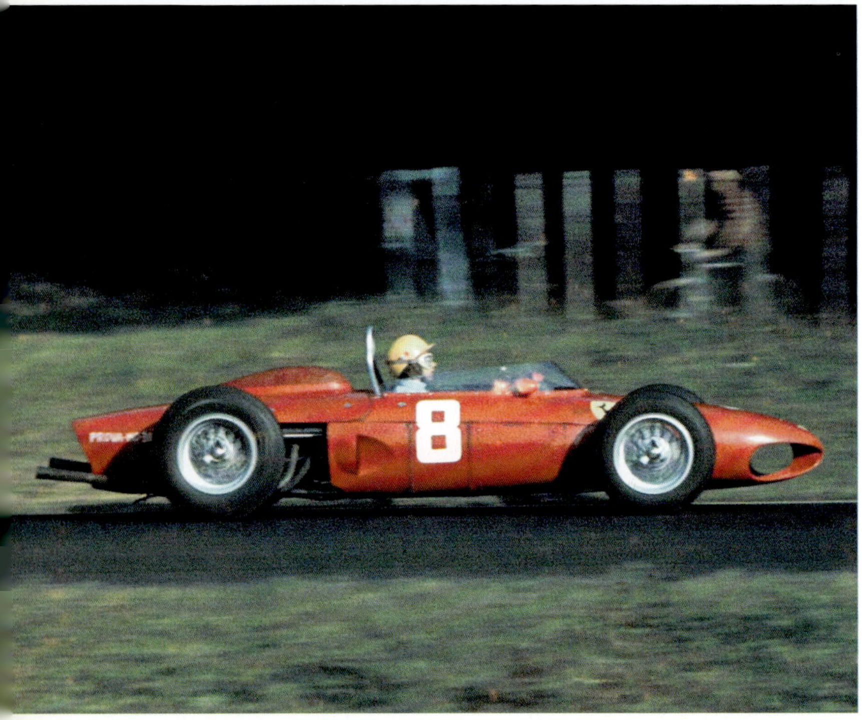

↑ Graham Hill tried the new V8 BRM during practice at the Italian Grand Prix, but it was decided not to race it as it was still suffering teething problems. This was the fourth and last time that the road/banked circuit combination was used for F1 and Hill thunders round the daunting and rough banking to set third quickest time.

← The incredibly quick 19-year-old Ricardo Rodriguez with his familiar yellow helmet, younger brother of Pedro, made his Grand Prix debut at Monza in the Ferrari Dino 156 0006. He made second fastest time in practice, but retired on lap 13 with fuel pump failure. Had Ricardo survived he would surely have become one of the era's greatest and fastest drivers, but his brief F1 career was largely spent with Ferrari where his talent was squandered. The race was overshadowed by the dreadful accident that killed World Champion elect Wolfgang von Trips who collided with Jim Clark on lap one and also claimed the lives of 14 spectators. Germany had to wait a further 33 years before they could claim a World Champion driver. Phil Hill was left to win the race and the 1961 World Championship.

1961 Teams, drivers and results

Cooper Car Co. – Cooper T55 Climax FPF
Jack Brabham (AUS)
Bruce McLaren (NZ)

Team Lotus – Lotus 18 Climax FPF and 21 Climax FPF
Innes Ireland (GB)
Jim Clark (GB)
Trevor Taylor (GB) (Dutch GP only in 18, his debut for Lotus in F1 as Ireland still unfit after Monaco practice crash)
Willy Mairesse (B) (French GP only)

Owen Racing Organisation – BRM P48/57 Climax FPF
Graham Hill (GB)
Tony Brooks (GB)

SEFAC Ferrari – Ferrari Dino 156 (65-degree and 120-degree V6s)
Phil Hill (USA) (WORLD CHAMPION, missed US GP, Ferrari not entered)
Wolfgang von Trips (D) (Fatal accident at Italian GP)
Richie Ginther (USA)
Olivier Gendebien (B) (Belgian GP only, entered under Equipe Nationale Belge in yellow national colours)
Willy Mairesse (B) (German GP only)
Ricardo Rodriguez (MEX) (Italian GP only)

Federazione Italiana Scuderie Automobilistiche/Scuderia Sant Ambroeus – Ferrari Dino 156 (65-degree V6)
Giancarlo Baghetti (I) (French, British and Italian GPs only. Won his World Championship debut race at Reims and also his first two non-championship races at Syracuse and Napoli)

Porsche System Engineering – Porsche 718 and 787
Dan Gurney (USA) (Used lwb 787 at Dutch GP, car then withdrawn from racing)
Jo Bonnier (S) (Used lwb 787 at Monaco and Dutch GPs, car then withdrawn from racing)
Hans Herrmann (D) (Monaco and German GPs only)

Ecurie Maarsbergen – Porsche 718
Carel de Beaufort (NL) (Did not race at Monaco and US GPs)
Hans Herrmann (D) (Dutch GP only)

R. R. C. Walker Racing Team – Cooper T53 Climax FPF/Lotus 18 Climax FPF , 18/21, 21 and Ferguson P99 Climax FPF
Stirling Moss (GB) (Took over Ferguson P99 in British GP from Jack Fairman and dsq, won Oulton Park Gold Cup in September. He also raced Ireland's works 21 in Walker colours at Monza)
Jack Fairman (GB) (British GP only, dsq)

Yeoman Credit Racing Team – Cooper T53 Climax FPF
John Surtees (GB)
Roy Salvadori (GB) (French, British, German, Italian and US GPs only)

UDT-Laystall Racing Team – Lotus 18 Climax FPF
Cliff Allison (GB) (Monaco GP only. Crashed and seriously injured during practice at Belgian GP leading to his retirement
Henry Taylor (GB) (dnq Monaco, dnp Belgian GP car crashed by Allison, and then British (injured in crash) and Italian GPs only. Retired from F1 after Italian GP)
Masten Gregory (USA) (Italian and US GPs only. Took over Gendebien's car in US GP)
Lucien Bianchi (B) French and British GPs only)
Olivier Gendebien (B) (US GP only, last F1 start)

Scuderia Colonia – Lotus 18 Climax FPF
Michael May (CH) (Monaco and French GPs only, dns German GP)
Wolfgang Seidel (D) (dns Belgian GP, British, German and Italian GPs only)

Scuderia Centro Sud – Cooper T51 Maserati and T53
Lorenzo Bandini (I) (Belgian, British, German and Italian GPs only)
Massimo Natili (I) (British GP only, dnq Italian GP)

Scuderia SSS Serenissima di Venezia – Cooper T51 Maserati, de Tomaso F1-001 Osca and de Tomaso F1-003 Alfa Romeo
Maurice Trintignant (F) (Practised Osca at French GP, but used Cooper in race)
Giorgio Scarlatti (I) (French GP only in de Tomaso with Osca engine)
Nino Vaccarella (I) (Italian GP only in de Tomaso with Alfa Romeo engine)

Scuderia Settecolli – de Tomaso F1-002 Osca
Roberto Lippi (I) (Italian GP only)

Isobele de Tomaso – de Tomaso F1-004 Alfa Romeo
Roberto Bussinello (Italian GP only)

Equipe Nationale Belge – Emeryson Climax FPF/Lotus 18 Climax FPF
Lucien Bianchi (B) (dnq Monaco and dns French GP in Emeryson, Belgian GP in Lotus only)
Willy Mairesse (B) (Belgian and French GPs only)
Olivier Gendebien (B) (Monaco only with Emeryson and dnq)

H & L Motors – Cooper T53 Climax FPF
Jack Lewis (GB) (Belgian, French, British, German and Italian GPs only)

Camoradi International – Cooper T53 Climax FPF and Lotus 18 Climax FPF
Masten Gregory (USA) (dnq Monaco and Dutch GPs, Belgian, French and British GPs only)
Ian Burgess (GB) (dns Dutch GP, dnq Belgian GP, French, British and German GPs only. All in Lotus except Cooper in German GP)

Tony Marsh – Lotus 18 Climax FPF
Tony Marsh (GB) (dns Belgian GP, British and German GPs only)

Bernard Collomb – Cooper T53 Climax FPF
Bernard Collomb (F) (French and German GPs only)

Tim Parnell – Lotus 18 Climax FPF
Tim Parnell (GB) (British and Italian GPs only)

Gerry Ashmore – Lotus 18 Climax FPF
Gerry Ashmore (GB) (British, German and Italian GPs only)

Louise Bryden-Brown – Lotus 18 Climax FPF
Tony Maggs (ZA) (British and German GPs only)

Gilbey Engineering Co Ltd – Gilbey Climax
Keith Greene (GB) (British GP only)

J. B. Naylor – JBW Climax
Brian Naylor (GB) (Italian GP only)

Fred Tuck – Cooper T45 Climax
Jack Fairman (GB) (Italian GP only)

Pescara Racing Club – Cooper T51 Maserati
Renato Pirocchi (I) (Italian GP only)

Prince Gaetano Starrabba – Lotus 18 Maserati 18
Prince Gaetano Starrabba (I) (Italian GP only)

'Hap' Sharp – Cooper T53 Climax FPF
'Hap' Sharp (USA) (US GP only)

John M. Wyatt III – Cooper T53 Climax FPF
Roger Penske (USA) (US GP only)

J. Wheeler Autosport – Lotus 18/21 Climax FPF
Peter Ryan (CDN) (US GP only)

Jim Hall – Lotus 18/21 Climax FPF
Jim Hall (USA) (US GP only)

J. Frank Harrison – Lotus 18 Climax FPF
Lloyd Ruby (USA) (US GP only)

Momo Corporation – Cooper T53 Climax FPF
Walt Hansgen (USA) (US GP only)

WORLD CHAMPIONSHIP VENUES AND WINNERS (Eight rounds)

Monaco GP	Monte Carlo	Stirling Moss
Dutch GP	Zandvoort	Wolfgang von Trips
Belgian GP	Spa-Francorchamps	Phil Hill
French GP	Reims	Giancarlo Baghetti
British GP	Aintree	Wolfgang von Trips
German GP	Nürburgring	Stirling Moss
Italian GP	Monza	Phil Hill
United States GP	Watkins Glen	Innes Ireland

DRIVERS' CHAMPIONSHIP

Points: 9-6-4-3-2-1. Best 5 scores

1	Phil Hill (USA)	Ferrari	34
2	Wolfgang von Trips (D)	Ferrari	33
3	Stirling Moss (GB)	Lotus	21
4	Dan Gurney (USA)	Porsche	21
5	Richie Ginther (USA)	Ferrari	16
6	Innes Ireland (GB)	Lotus	12
7	Jim Clark (GB)	Lotus	11
8	Bruce McLaren (NZ)	Cooper	11
9	Giancarlo Baghetti (I)	Ferrari	9
10	Tony Brooks (GB)	BRM	6
11	Jack Brabham (AUS)	Cooper	4
12	John Surtees (GB)	Cooper	4
13	Olivier Gendebien (B)	Ferrari/Lotus	3
14	Jack Lewis (GB)	Cooper	3
15	Jo Bonnier (S)	Porsche	3
16	Graham Hill (GB)	BRM	3
17	Roy Salvadori (GB)	Cooper	2

CONSTRUCTORS' CHAMPIONSHIP

Points: 9-6-4-3-2-1, (awarded only to best-placed finisher). Best 5 scores

1	Ferrari	40
2	Lotus-Climax	32
3	Porsche	22
4	Cooper-Climax	14
5	BRM-Climax	7

1962

BOURNE AGAIN

The British teams reasserted their previous dominance in 1962, as Ferrari failed to develop its advantage after the team's rampant internal politics led to a mass walk-out of top personnel, including chief engineer Carlo Chiti and team manager Romolo Tavoni. Lotus, Cooper, Lola and BRM enjoyed a significant chassis superiority, and the new V8 engines from Coventry Climax and BRM delivered the power.

Sadly, Stirling Moss crashed a UDT Laystall Lotus at Goodwood, suffering serious head injuries that ended his career. At Silverstone in May, the team entered a Ferrari that was to have been driven by Moss; Innes Ireland brought it home a lapped 4th, but thereafter raced the team's Lotus 24s.

Graham Hill and BRM excelled with the new V8 P57 and followed up a victory at Zandvoort with further wins in the German, Italian and South African Grands Prix, clinching the Drivers' Championship and the Constructors' Cup. Hill's new team mate, Richie Ginther, was eclipsed and had to suffer most of BRM's mechanical problems.

Jimmy Clark started the 1962 season with a new spaceframe Lotus 24, but was soon equipped with Colin Chapman's monocoque masterpiece, the 25. If it stayed in one piece, he usually won. After securing three Grands Prix, not to mention a fistful of non-championship wins, Clark lost the championship at the last race in South Africa when his Climax V8 broke down. Struggling in his wake was the unlucky Trevor Taylor, who survived a horrendous crash with Ferrari driver Willy Mairesse in the Belgian Grand Prix, and seemingly endless mechanical failures.

Cooper lost the services of Jack Brabham and began a gradual decline from which it never fully recovered. The team continued with Bruce McLaren and South African Tony Maggs, who drove well with an average car. After Clark and Hill had retired, McLaren won at Monaco, just beating a charging Phil Hill in Ferrari's best performance of the year. The New Zealander also won the non-championship Reims Grand Prix.

Porsche introduced its new flat-eight 804 and Dan Gurney won the French Grand Prix, also placing 3rd in Germany and 5th in America, but this was the end of Porsche's official Formula 1 aspirations. The other regular front-runner was John Surtees with a new Lola with which he posted two 2nd places, in Britain and Germany. Jack Brabham raced a 'customer' Lotus 24 until the German Grand Prix, where he debuted his own BT3. Typically the rest comprised privately entered cars built by Lotus, Cooper or Porsche.

Clark and Hill did most of the winning in the various non-championship Formula 1 events across Europe and in South Africa, with Surtees and Ireland (now with BRP) joining in. Ending a dreadful year for Rob Walker's team, Ricardo Rodriguez was killed in its Lotus 24 during practice for the Mexican Grand Prix, and then motorcycle ace Gary Hocking died in the replacement car during practice for the Natal Grand Prix three days before Christmas. The race was won by Trevor Taylor who for once finished ahead of Clark.

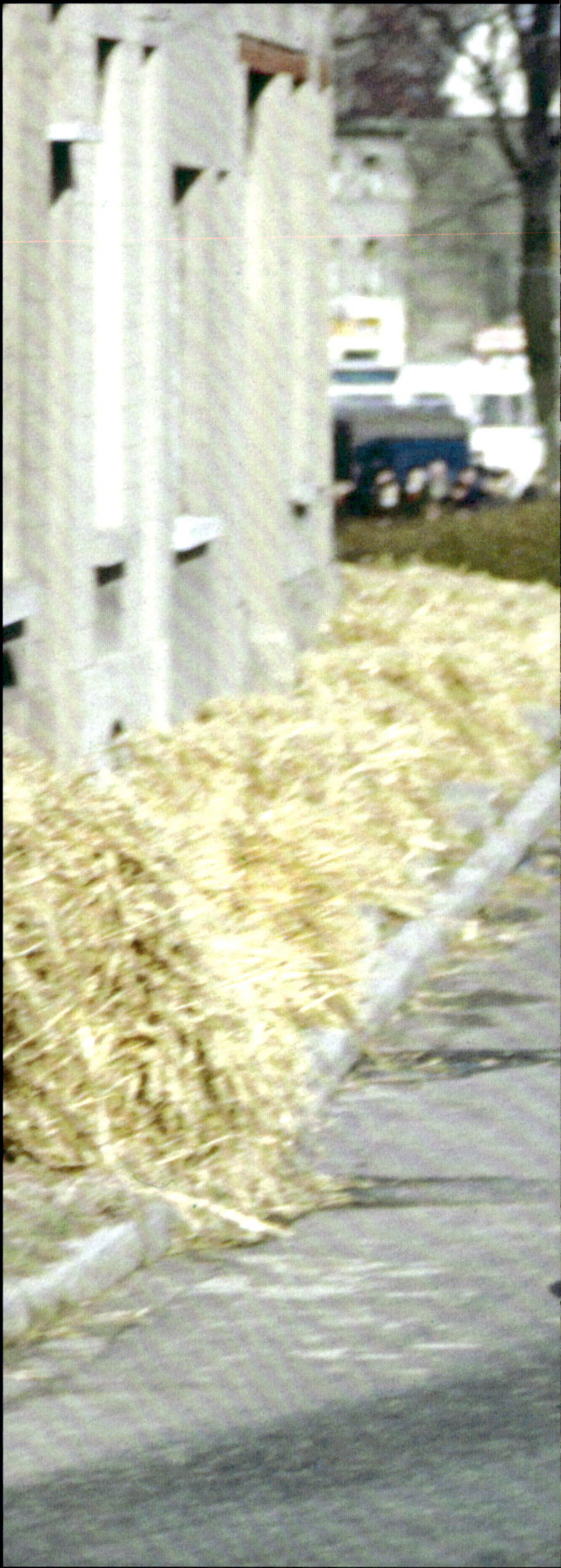

Fancy holding an F1 race? Simple on the continent. Just close down a few streets and public roads, adorn liberally with straw bales and hey presto! The IV Grand Prix de Bruxelles 1 April 1962 on the Heysel circuit, a location later to become infamous for the football crowd disaster of 1985. This is the Gilby of Keith Greene that finished 4th overall after the three heat event. Designer Len Terry remembers this as a good car, straight out of the box. Greene, whose father Sid owned Gilby Engineering who built and entered it, was better known as a sports car driver.

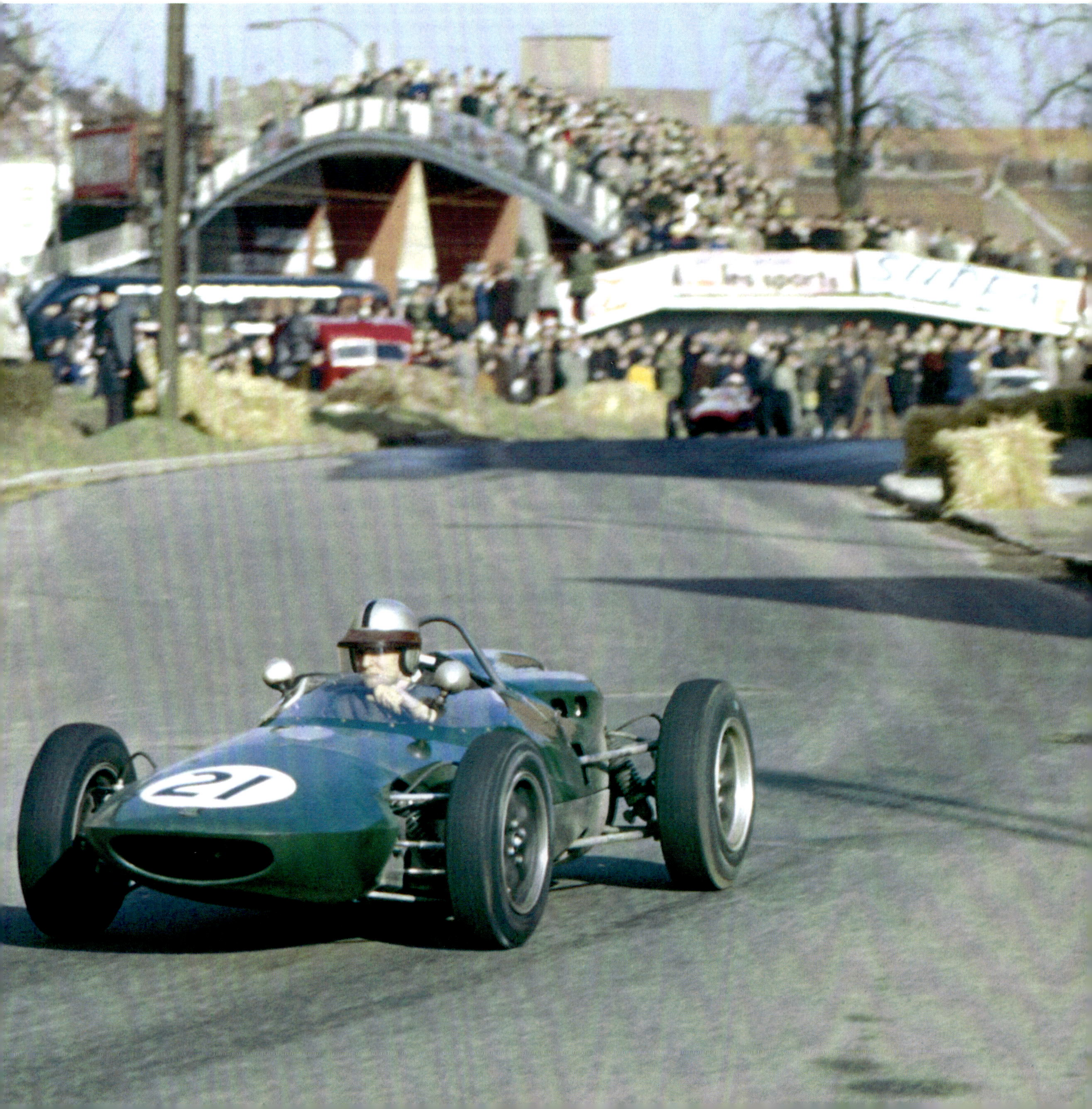

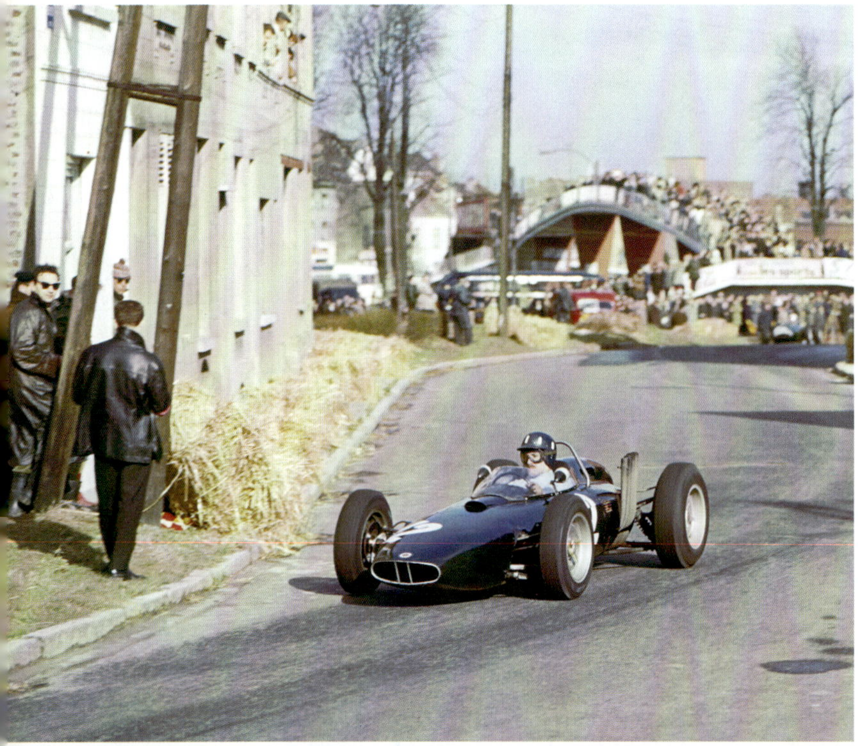

Graham Hill at the same spot in the V8 BRM P57 (5781), its exhaust stacks smoking. He won the first heat but was disqualified for a push-start in the second after his starter motor failed. Tony Rudd had been offered sole control of BRM's racing team at Sir Alfred Owen's command, displacing Raymond Mays and Peter Berthon. Owen, the head of Rubery-Owen group that funded BRM, had been under pressure from his brother to stop wasting money on the team. He had spent some £1 million on motor racing during the 1950s, a vast sum at a time when a front-running team cost less than £85,000 a season. Fortunately Sir Alfred's sister, Jean, who was married to Louis Stanley, persuaded Owen to give BRM one last chance. It was win or bust for 1962. Note the casual bystanders.

Multiple RAC British Hillclimb champion Tony Marsh was a motorsports polymath who competed in races, hillclimbs, sprints, trials and rallies. He drove in the 1957 and 1958 German Grands Prix and entered three Formula 1 championship races in 1961. For the 1962 season, Marsh bought this BRM P48/57 (573), BRM's 'customer' version of its new V8, and is about to be passed here by Willy Mairesse in the winning Ferrari Dino 156 (0006). Marsh considered the car to be unraceworthy and eventually instigated legal proceedings against BRM. A deal was struck and BRM settled with Marsh (and later with Jack Lewis, who had bought a similar car).

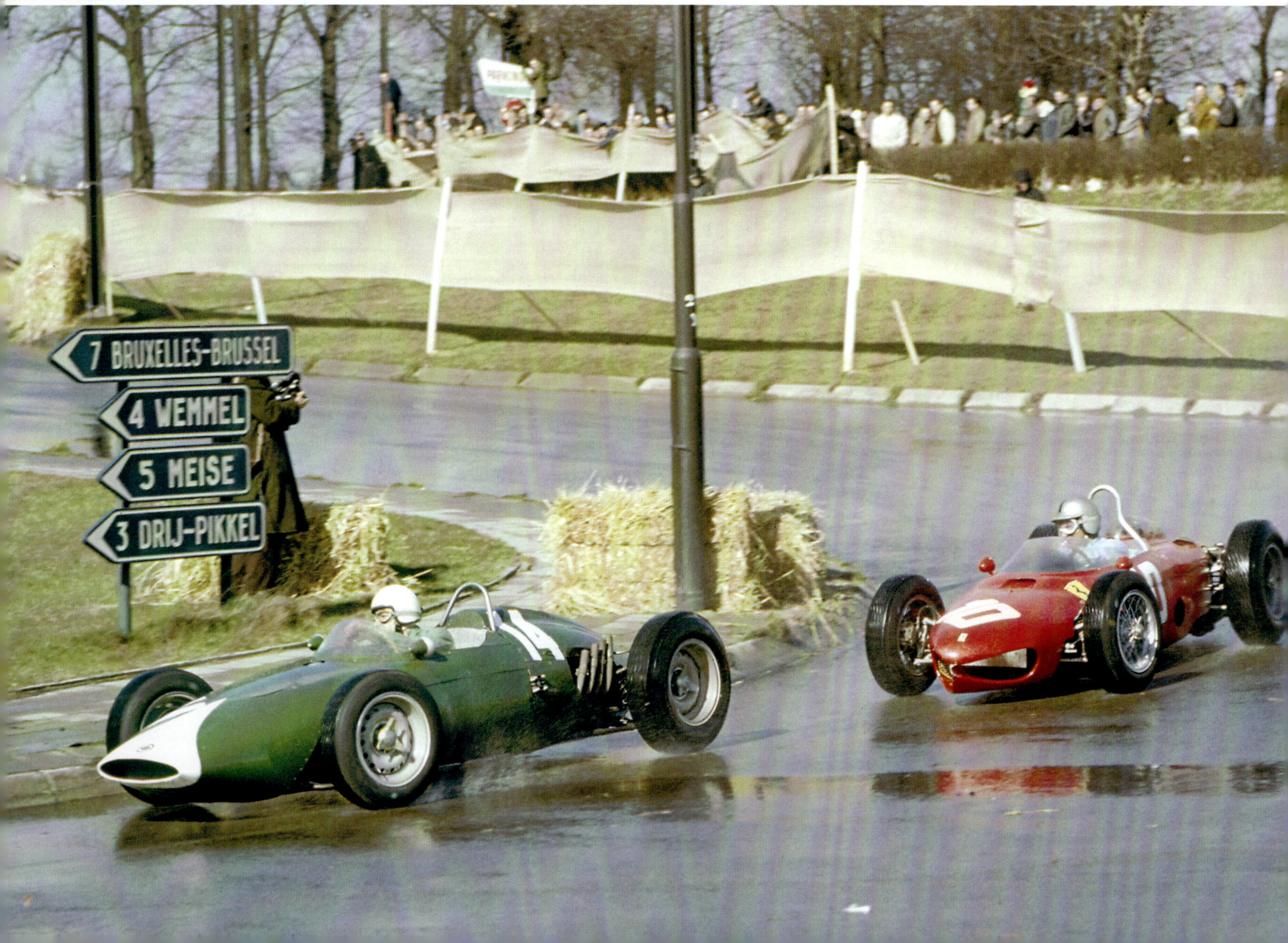

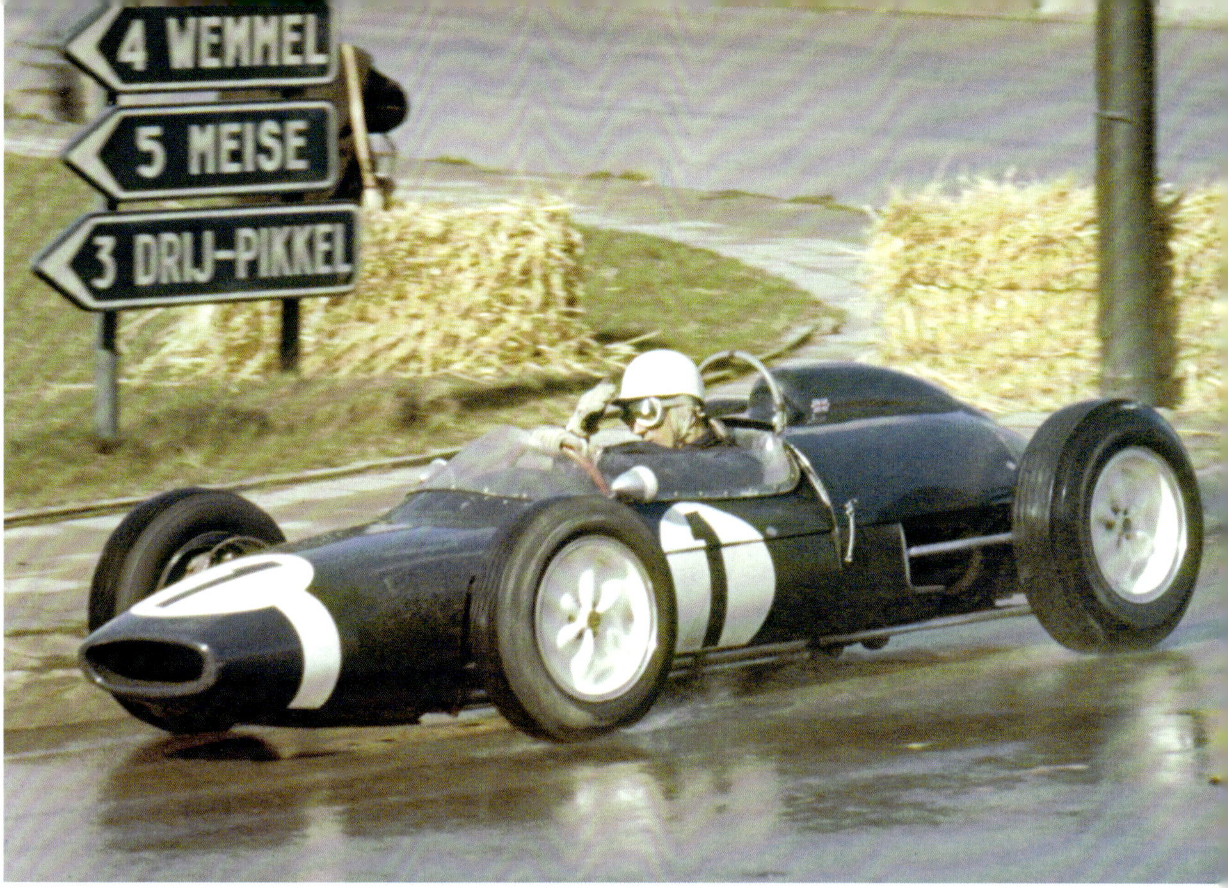

Stirling Moss shields his eyes from the afternoon sun in Heysel as he corners Rob Walker's Lotus 18/21 Climax V8 (906). He finished 2nd in the first heat after spinning off with a locked brake, but retired from the meeting during the second heat with deranged valve gear. The white-painted wheels suit the Rob Walker colour scheme rather well.

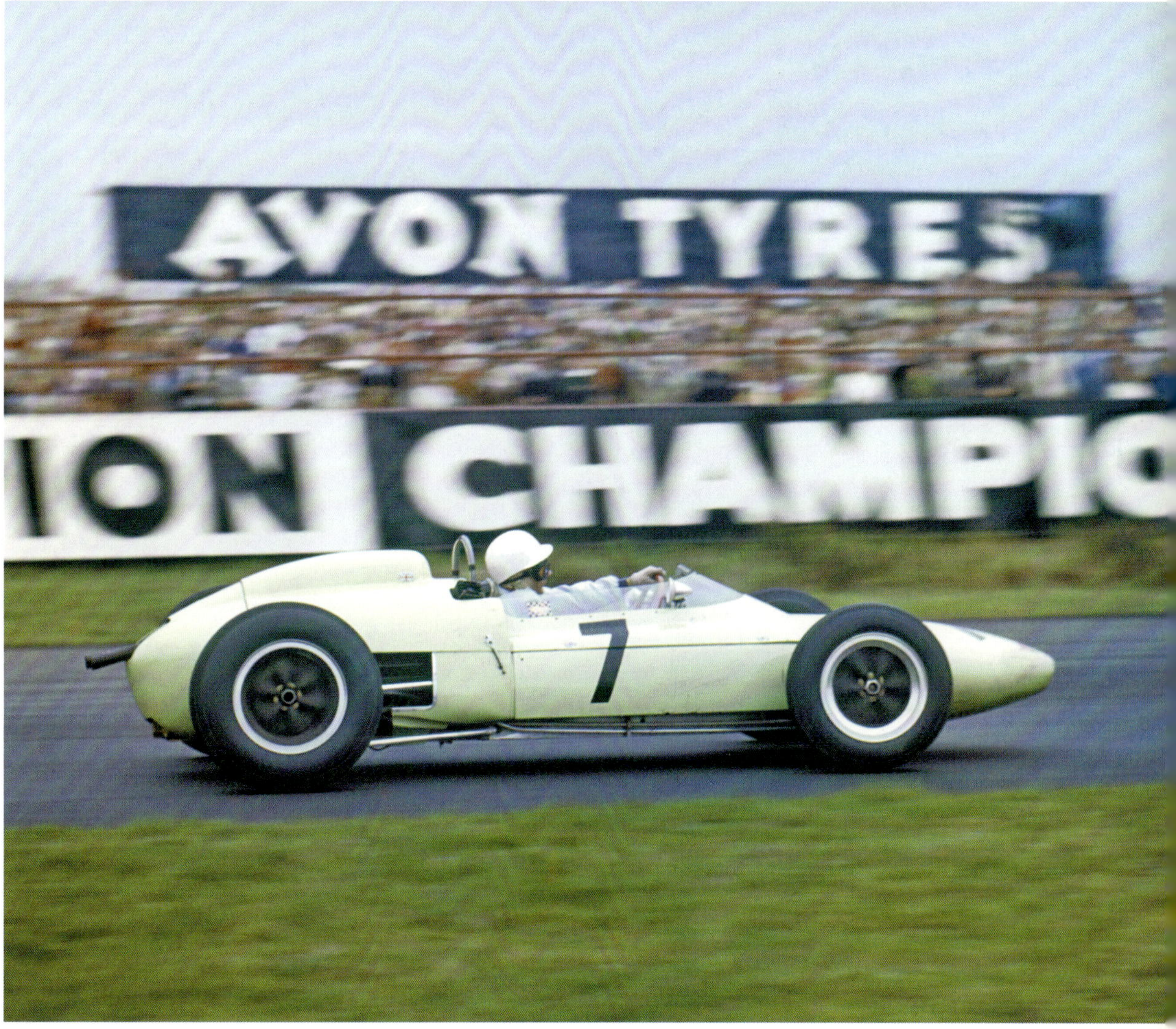

A poignant photograph of the era's greatest driver as he presses on to his fateful encounter with Graham Hill at Fordwater during the Glover Trophy race at Goodwood on Easter Monday. This is Rob Walker's Lotus 18/21 hybrid (906) that Stirling Moss had driven in Brussels, repainted and loaned to the UDT Laystall team for Snetterton and Goodwood. Moss's mother, Eileen, blamed Hill for the accident. It appears to have been caused by a misunderstanding over a hand signal that Hill used to acknowledge a blue flag (warning him that Moss was coming up fast, in fact to unlap himself after a pitstop). It seems possible that Stirling mistook Graham's wave to mean that he was to pass on the left, but then the BRM took its customary wider line approaching St Mary's and pushed the Lotus onto the grass and the final impact with the earth bank. A lap after the crash, Hill slowed down at the scene and shouted to photographer Michael Cooper: "Is he all right?"

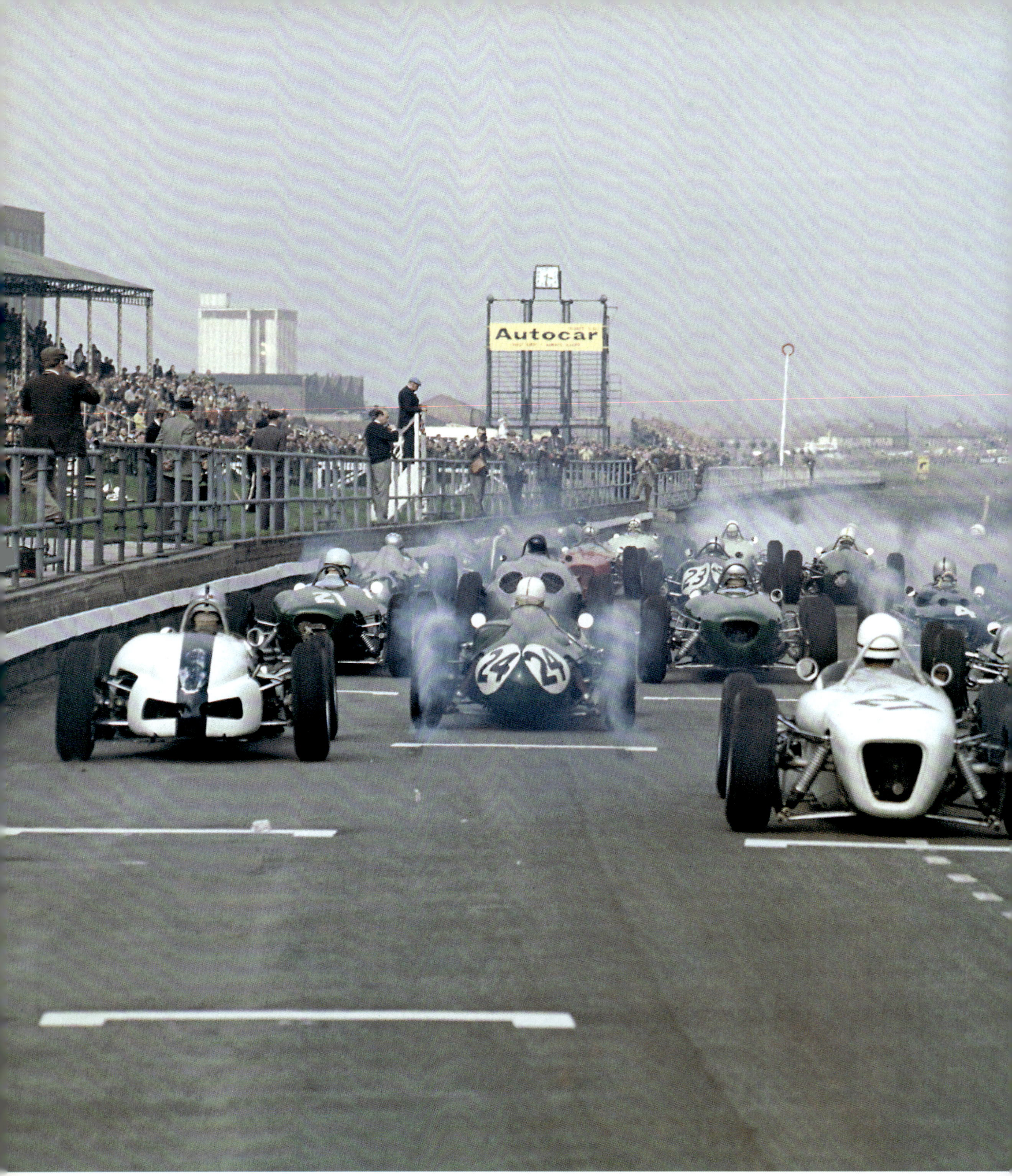
Autocar

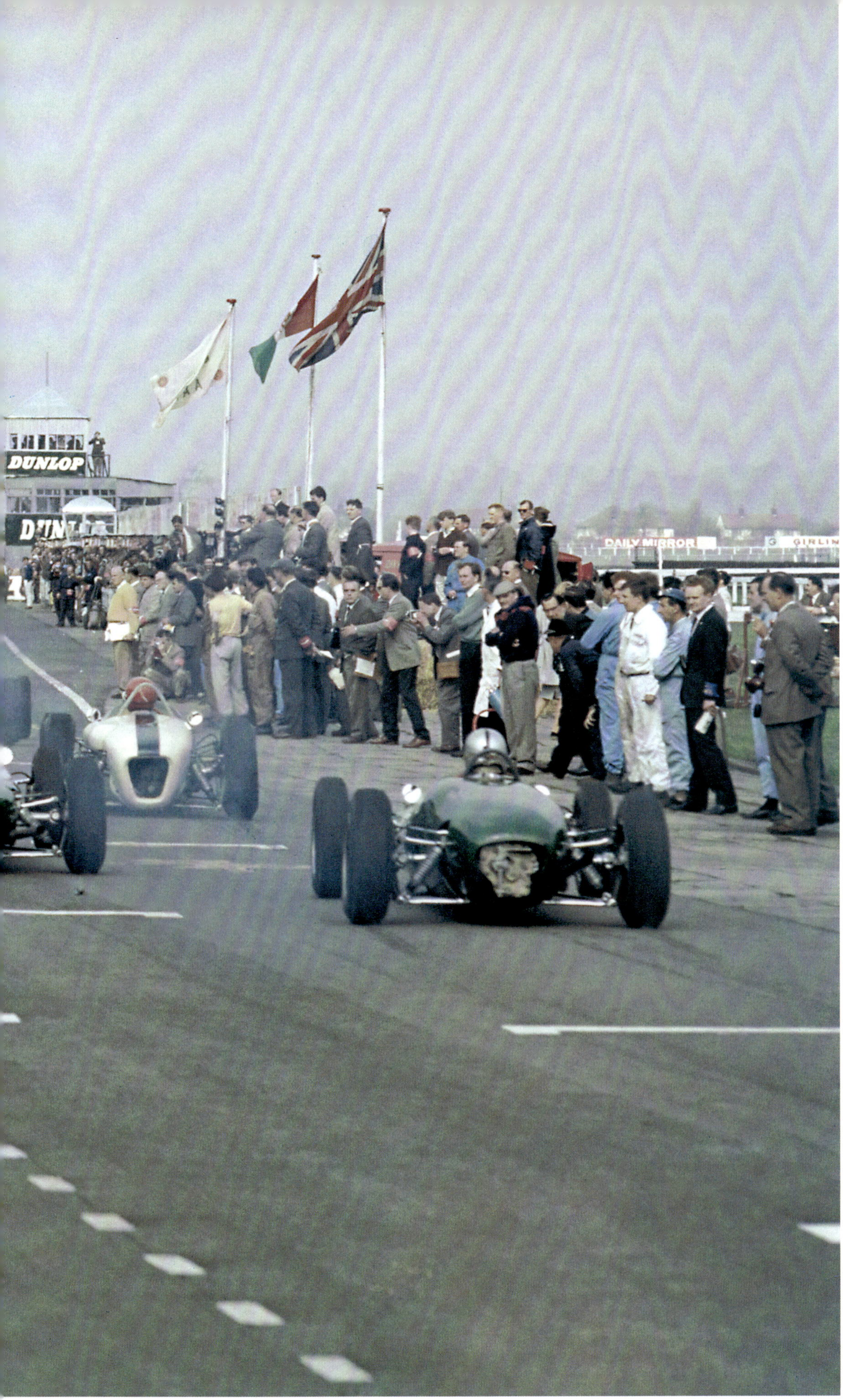

The start of the seventh Aintree 200 at the polite end of the grid. At the back is the Autosport Team Wolfgang Seidel Lotus 18 driven by Günther Seifert, and on the far left is the Cooper special of Ian Burgess, entered by Anglo American Equipe. At right is Jack Brabham (silver helmet and stripe) in a Lotus 21 and the cars on the row ahead of him are the Emeryson of Tony Settember and the works Lotus 24 of Trevor Taylor (yellow helmet). Also visible are Tim Parnell (No 21 Lotus 18/21), Roy Salvadori (No 4 Bowmaker Lola) and Keith Greene (No 23 Gilby). The race has started, rear tyres are smoking, and yet some of the unprotected bystanders on the right have turned their backs on the rear of the grid as it lets rip.

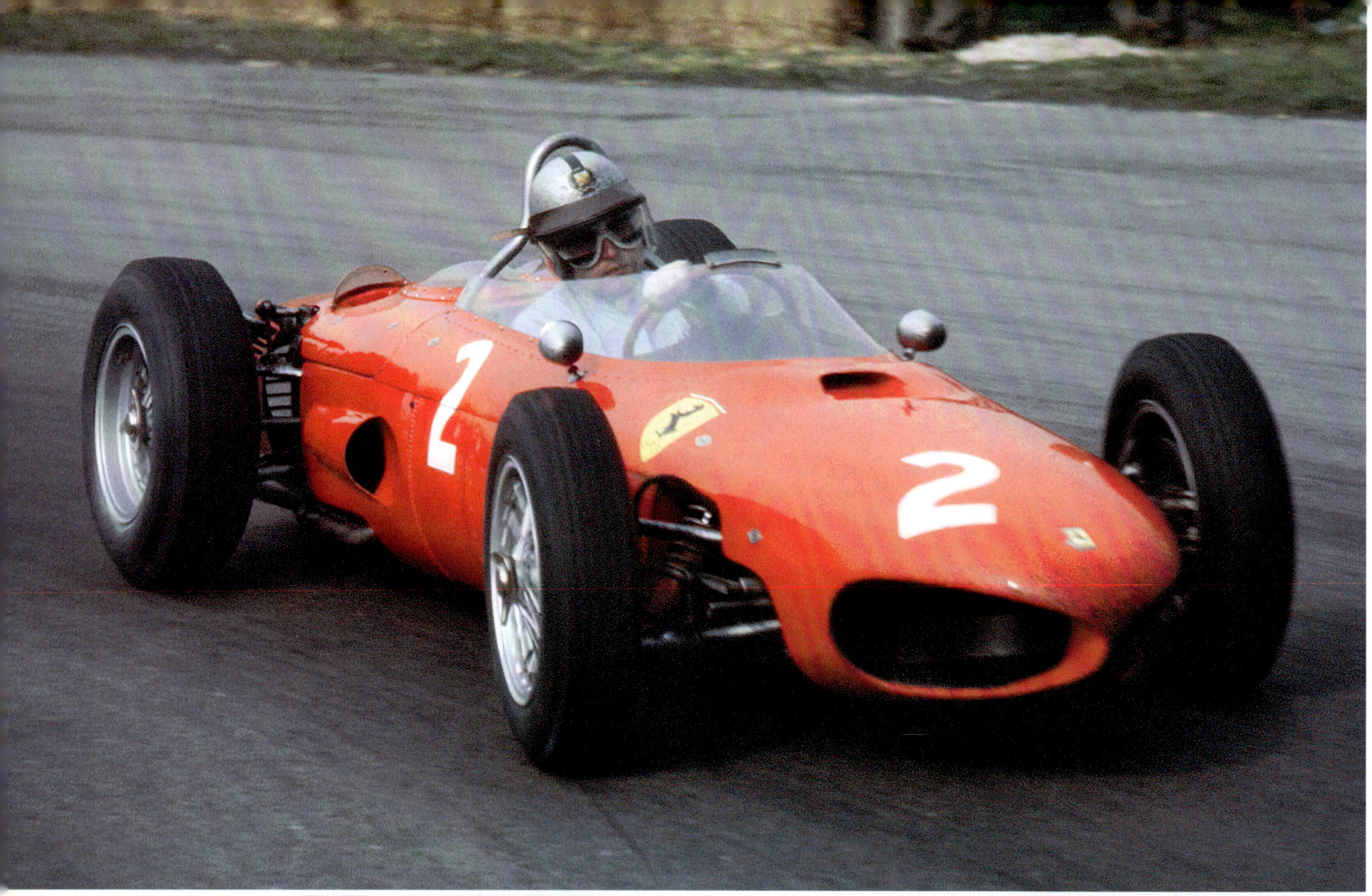
2

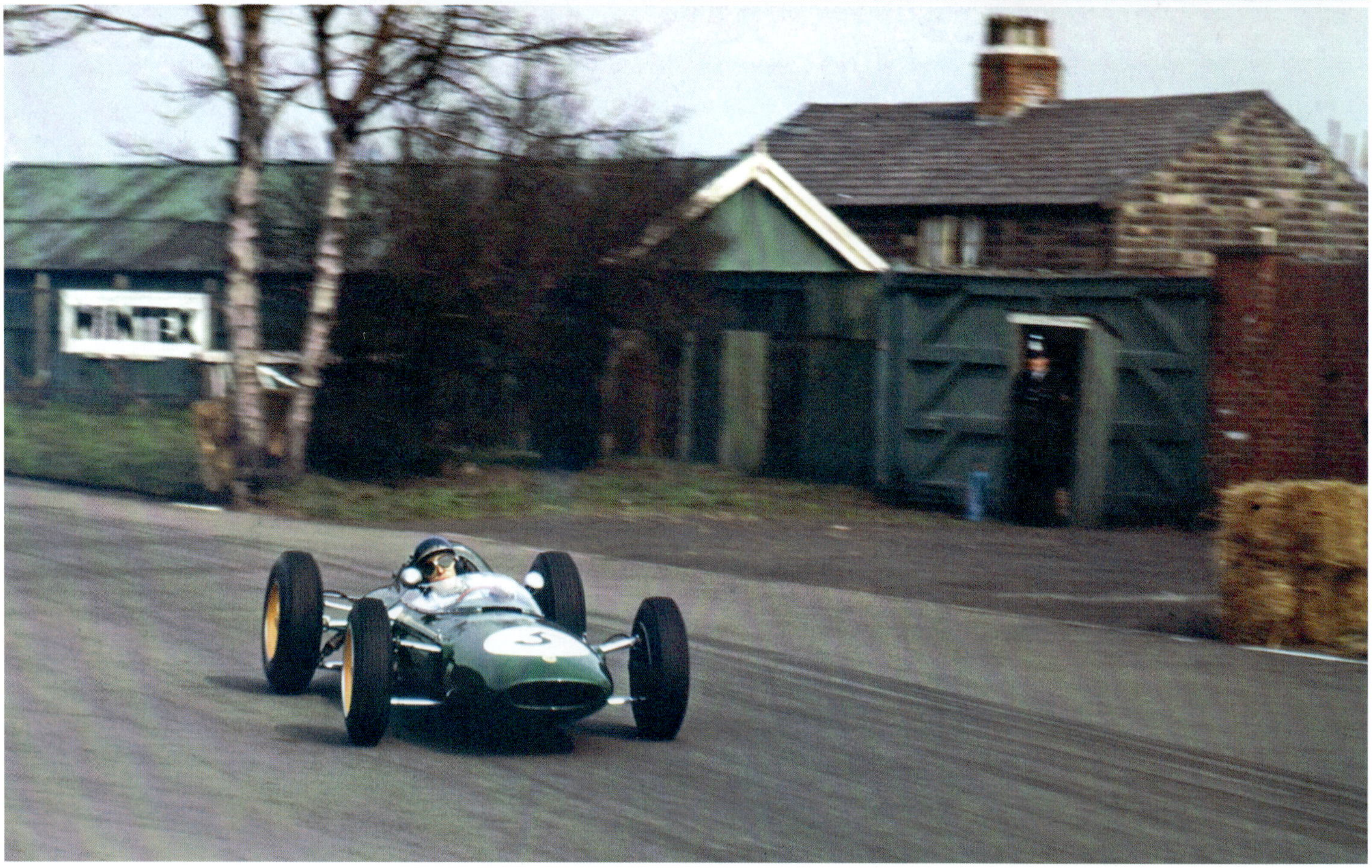

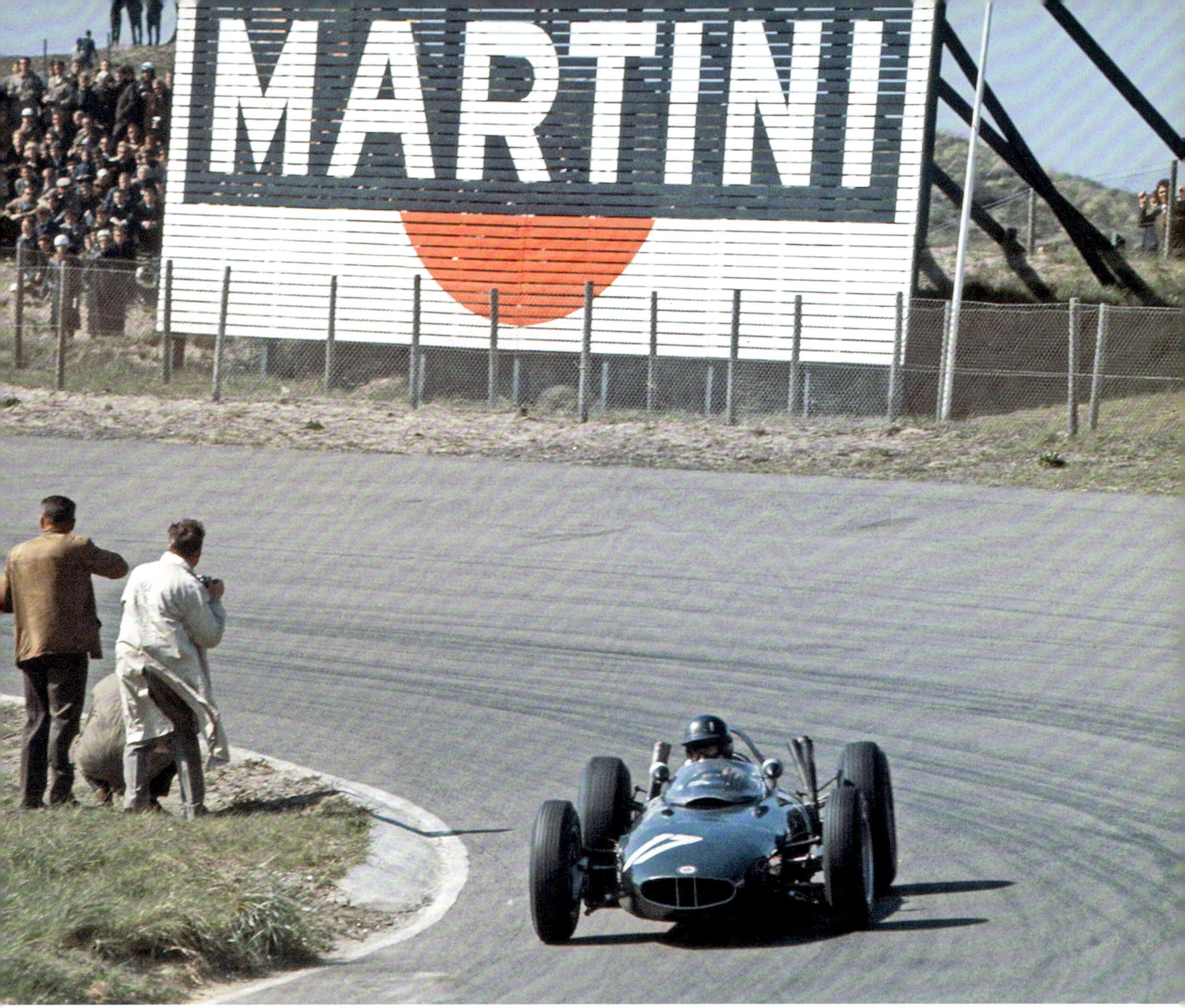

Having just beaten Jim Clark, literally on the line, to win the Silverstone International Trophy, Graham Hill won the Dutch Grand Prix at Zandvoort – the constructor's second race victory in the World Championship, three years on from its first at the same venue. His BRM P57 (5781) is still equipped with its stackpipe exhaust system, which is beginning to collapse. This was soon replaced by a more conventional and stable set-up. Immured as we have become to modern advertising and product placement, it is instructive to see, in this age of black-and-white TV when racing was rarely broadcast, the huge Martini billboard.

By 1962, Giancarlo Baghetti had become a works Ferrari driver. He is pictured during the Aintree 200 in pursuit of team leader Phil Hill, on his way to finishing less than a second behind the defending World Champion. This Ferrari 156 Dino (0001) is the car that was to have been driven by Stirling Moss at the Silverstone International Trophy but was raced instead by Innes Ireland.

Jim Clark at Melling Crossing on his way to a dominant victory in the Aintree 200 with a works Lotus 24 Climax V8 (948), more than half a minute ahead of Bruce McLaren's Cooper T55 Climax FPF. At the time, the 24 seemed like the real deal but better – much better – was on its way. This was the last spaceframe F1 Lotus.

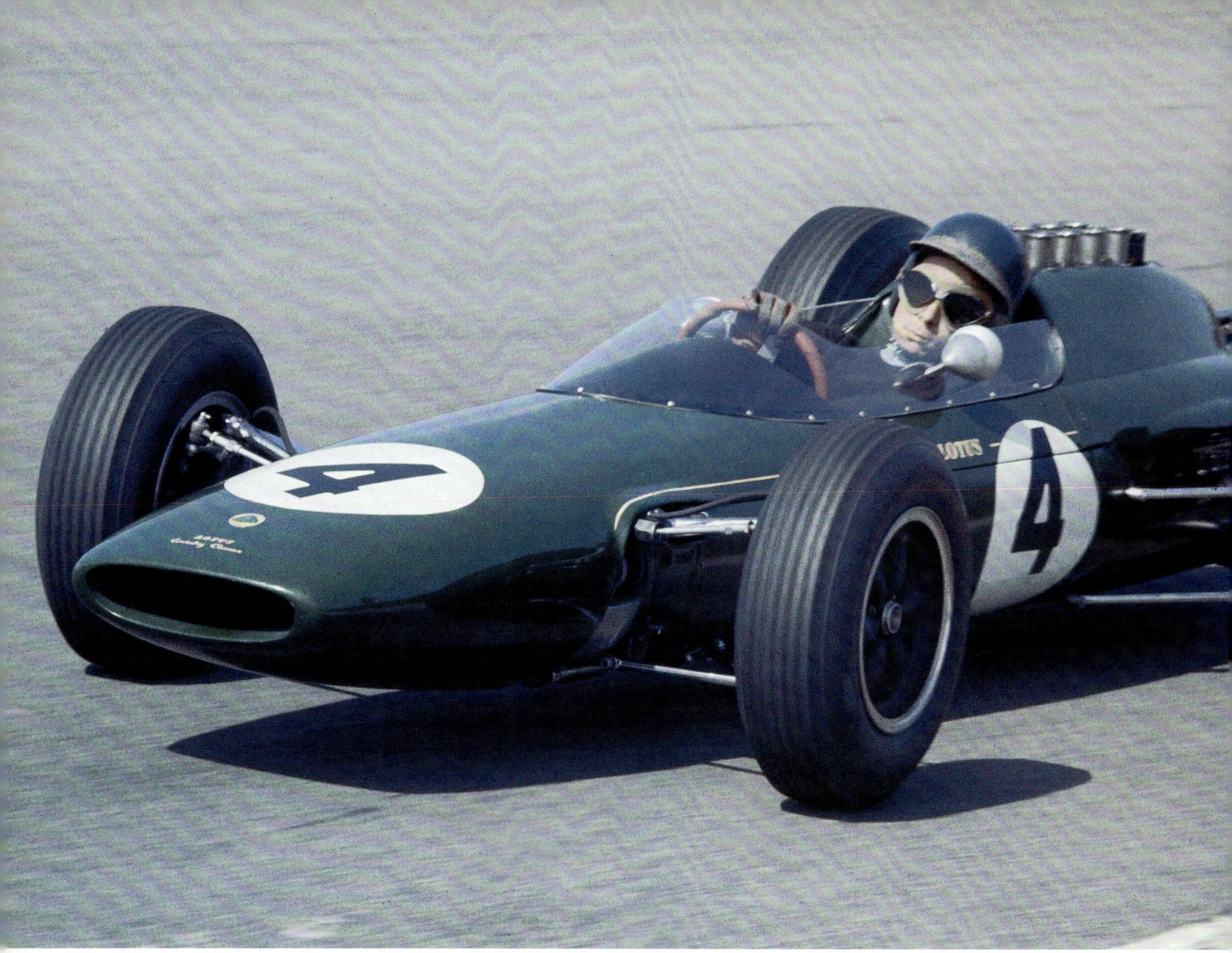

Zandvoort was the scene of the debut for Colin Chapman's monocoque masterpiece, the Lotus 25. Its aluminium sheet chassis tub carried the semi-stressed Coventry Climax FWMV ('featherweight multi-valve') V8, developing 185bhp at 8500rpm, and the whole ensemble weighed 452kg. Jim Clark, pictured during practice, started from the outside of the front row and led the Dutch Grand Prix for ten laps. The new Lotus was then hampered by a collapsing pedal box, and eventually finished 9th after a long stop for repairs. With Moss *hors de combat,* Clark had taken over the mantle of the maestro and it is noticeable how similar his composure and style are. Chapman described the Lotus 25 as: "Quite the cleanest and nicest looking car we've ever made." Customers who had bought the instantly obsolete type 24 and could not get the 25 were unimpressed.

Like Lotus, Cooper and Porsche chose Zandvoort to unveil their latest cars and this is Bruce McLaren in the new Cooper T60, built on a multi-tubular chassis frame and equipped with a new, six-speed Cooper-Knight transaxle on the back of the almost ubiquitous Coventry Climax FWMV V8. McLaren set the fastest race lap but was halted by a broken quill-shaft in the gearbox.

The now forgotten Jack Lewis, who had five Formula 1 starts during 1961 and 1962, had considerable talent and took 4th place in the 1961 Italian Grand Prix at Monza. For 1962, he bought one of the disappointing BRM P48/57 'customer' cars (finishing 3rd in the Pau Grand Prix) and continued with his Cooper T53 (F1-6-61), here at Zandvoort. The Welshman and his Ecurie Galloise team bowed out after the German Grand Prix, and Lewis spent the next 40 years farming sheep.

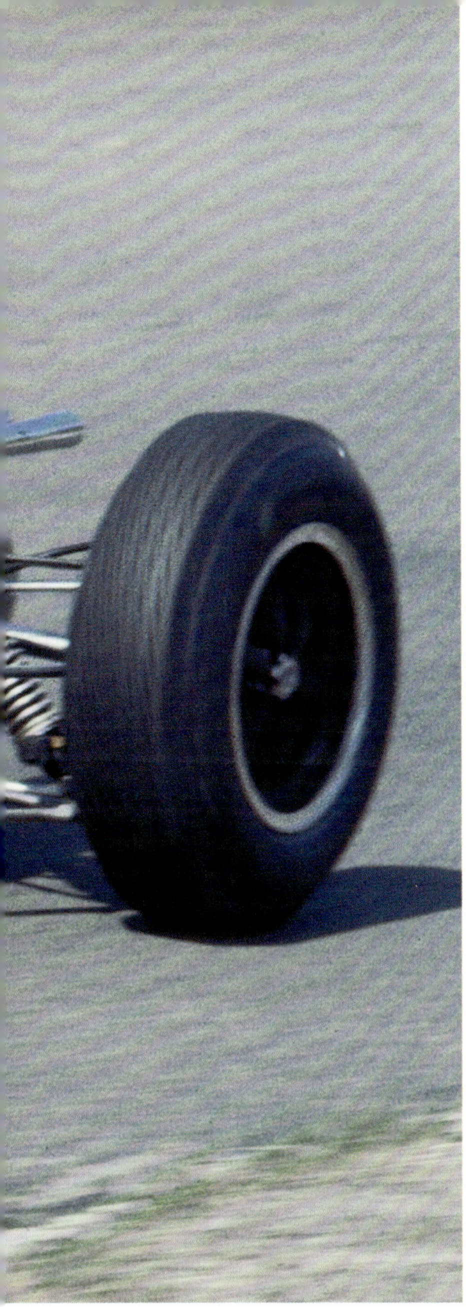

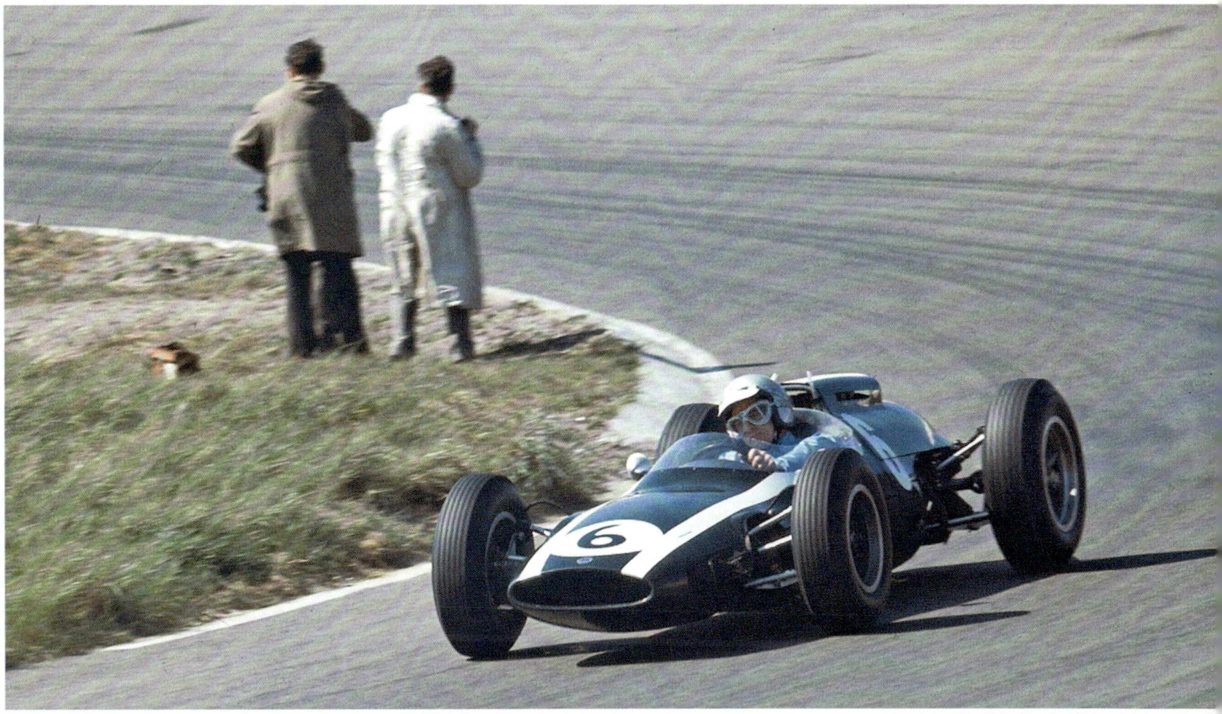

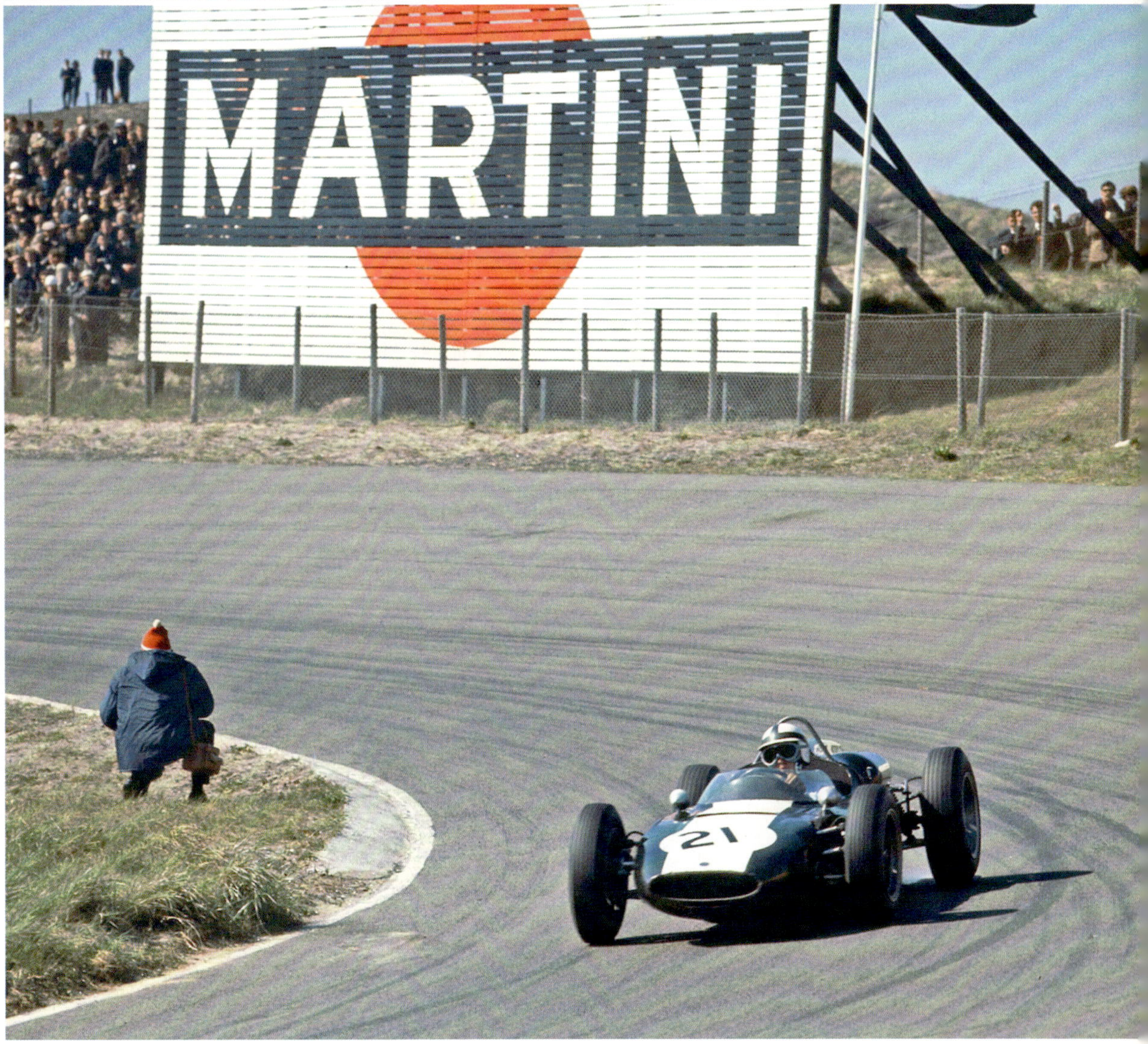
MARTINI
6
21

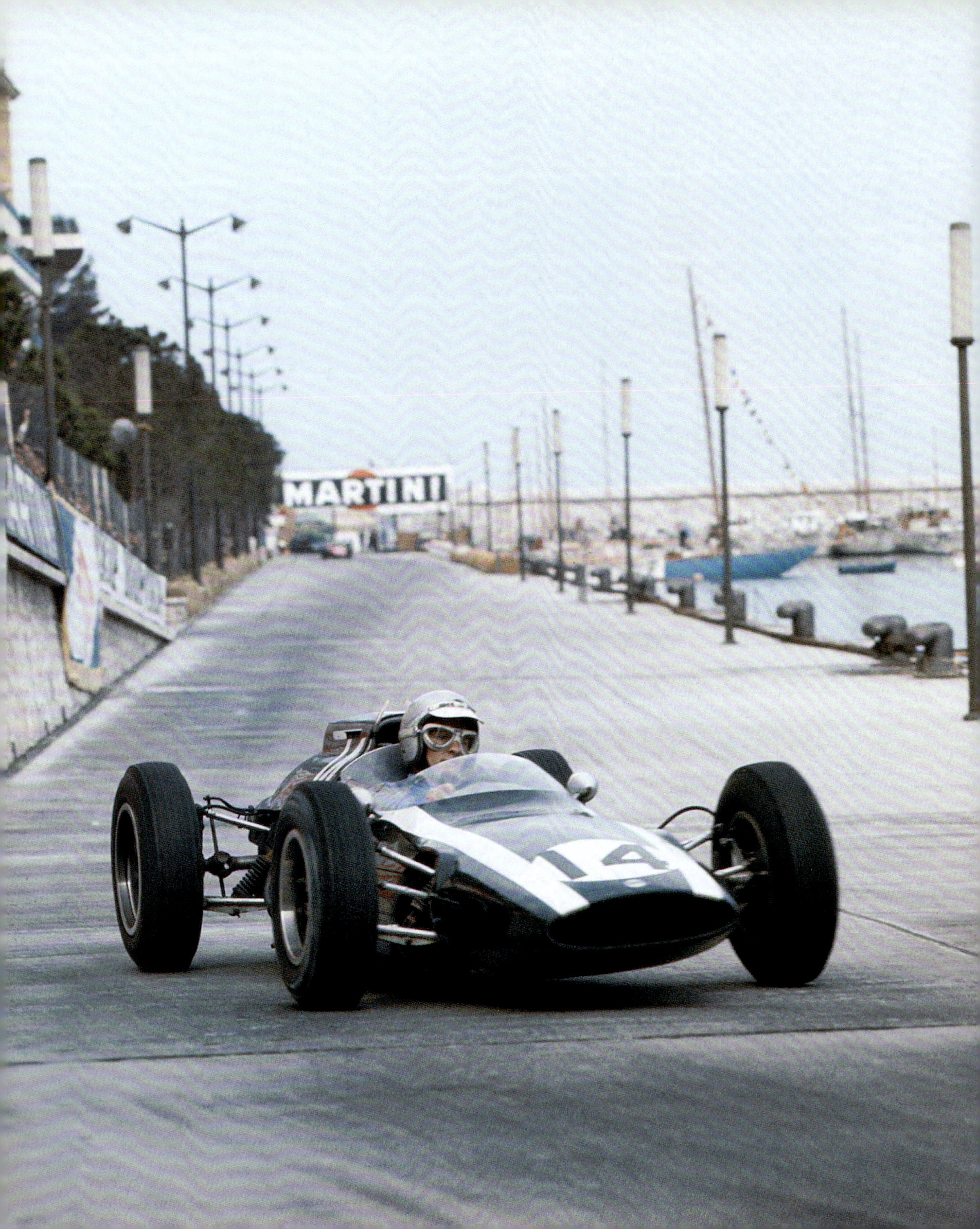
MARTINI
14

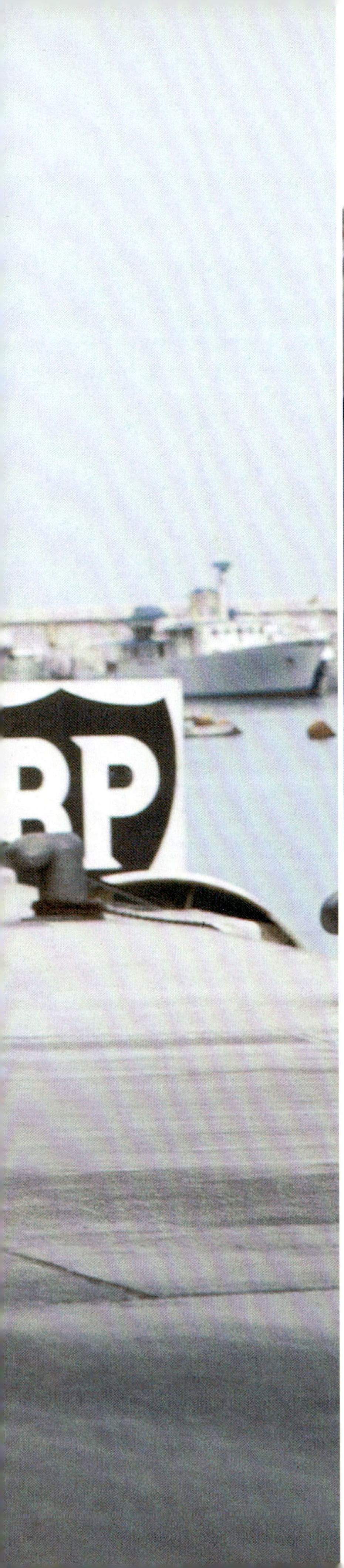

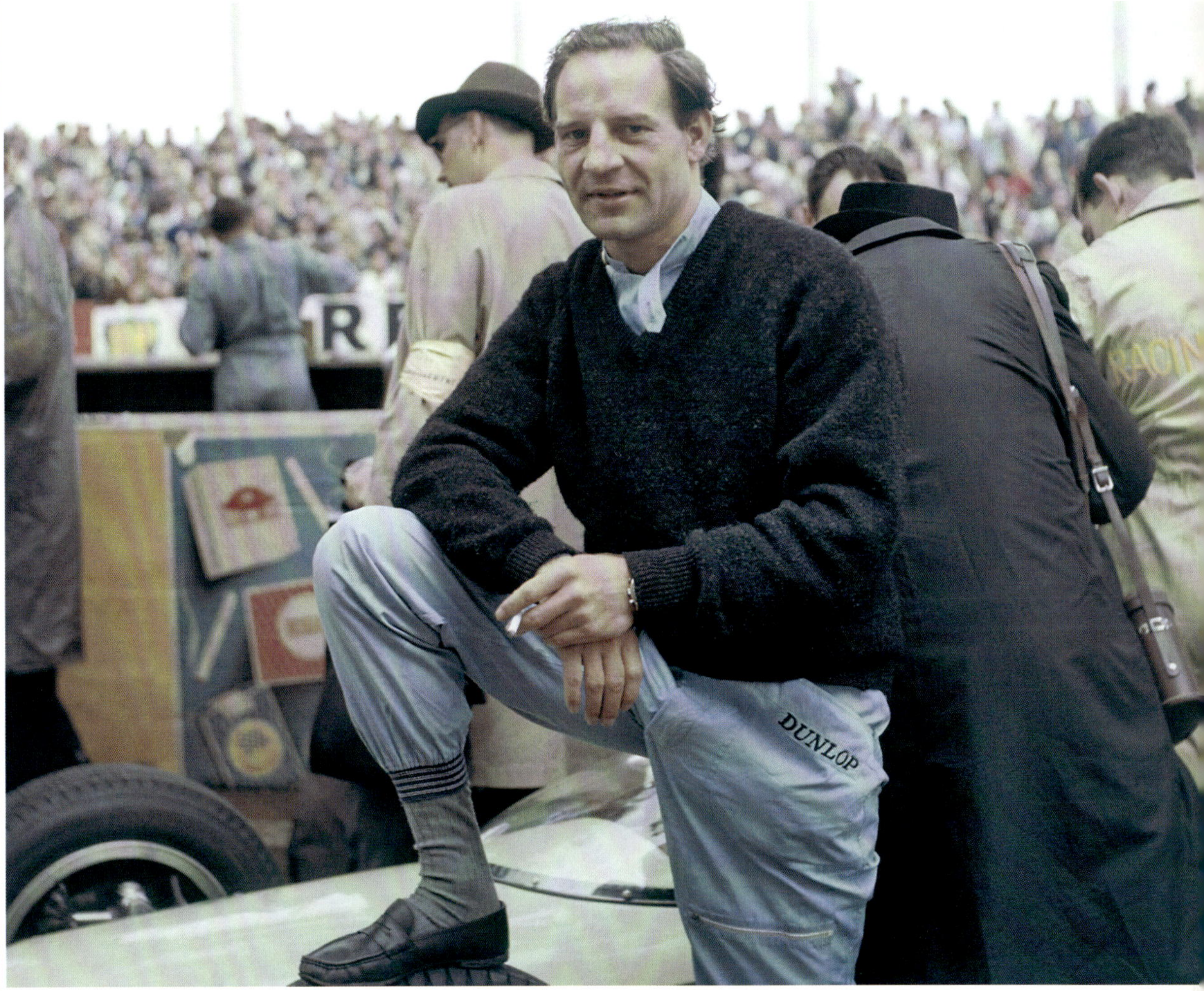

↑ Innes Ireland was one of the last of his kind, a professional racing driver with an amateur spirit. He was a brilliant sports and GT driver whose single-seater performances (after he had been sacked by Lotus) were blunted by second-string cars and his apparently infinite capacity for enjoying himself. Typically Ireland has a 'coffin nail' on the go at Monaco as he poses nonchalantly with the UDT Laystall team's Lotus 24 Climax V8 (943). The Dunlop cotton overalls and slip-on loafer-style shoes were almost *de rigueur* for the period. In the race, Ireland was involved in a first-corner contretemps caused by Willy Mairesse and, after restarting, retired with fuel pump failure. Eight days later, he won the last ever Formula 1 race at Crystal Palace with the team's BRM powered 24 (944). Ireland, who later became a racing journalist, succumbed to cancer in 1993.

← Bruce McLaren only won four Grands Prix during his career, and this is number three, at Monaco. The new Cooper T60 (F1-17-61) was competitive, but against the Lotus 25 and the BRM P57 it was second class. This is the classic Monaco shot with the Cooper just turning into Tabac with the old chicane in the background. Today there is a different road layout, but the bollards are still in situ. Monaco had yet to become the epitome of gratuitous wealth that now so defines it. Instead it was almost scruffy away from Casino Square and the Palace, still more *belle époque* than film set glamour. The more familiar scene with its multi-million dollar yachts, cruisers and liners occupying every available berth and harbour space lay in the future.

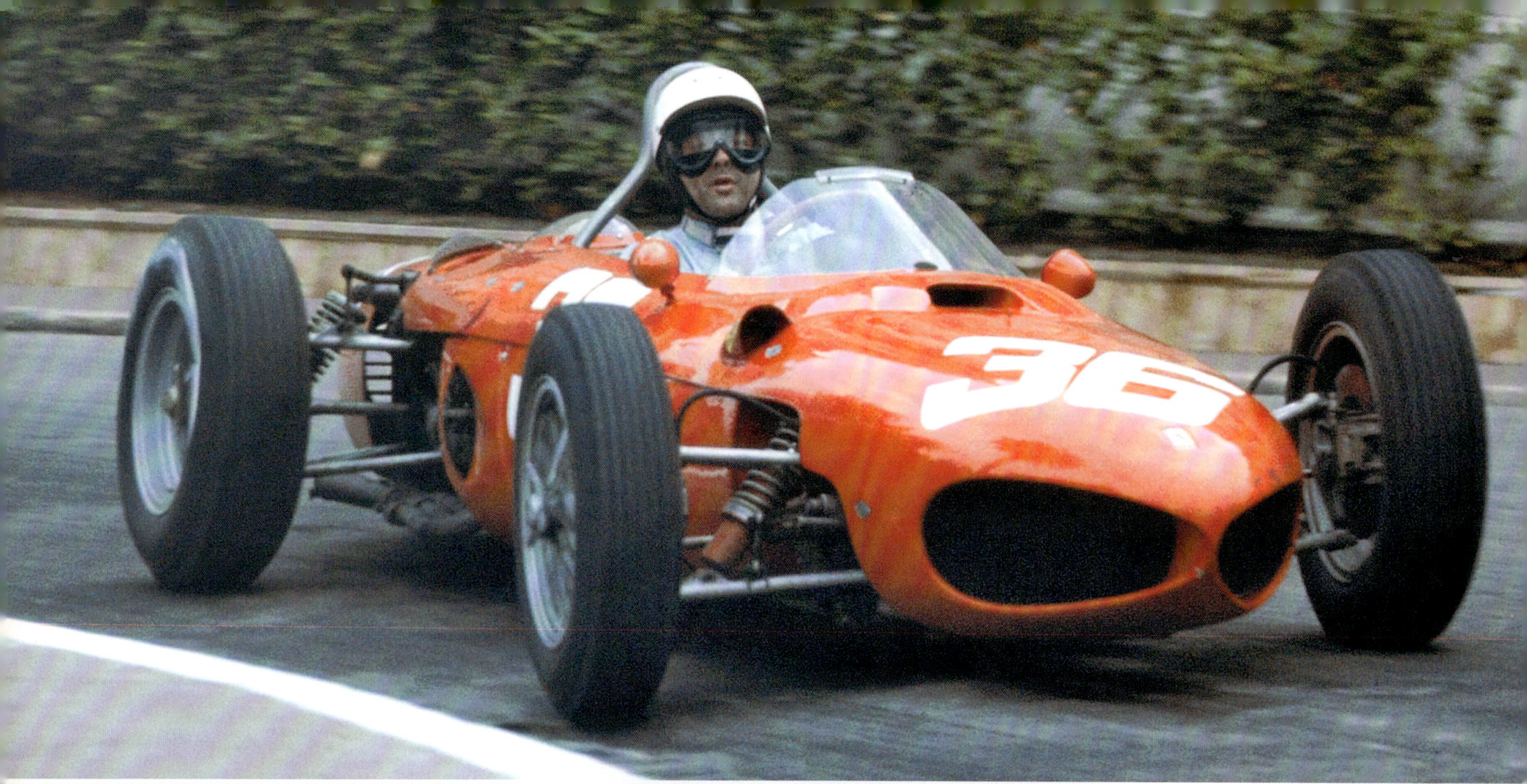

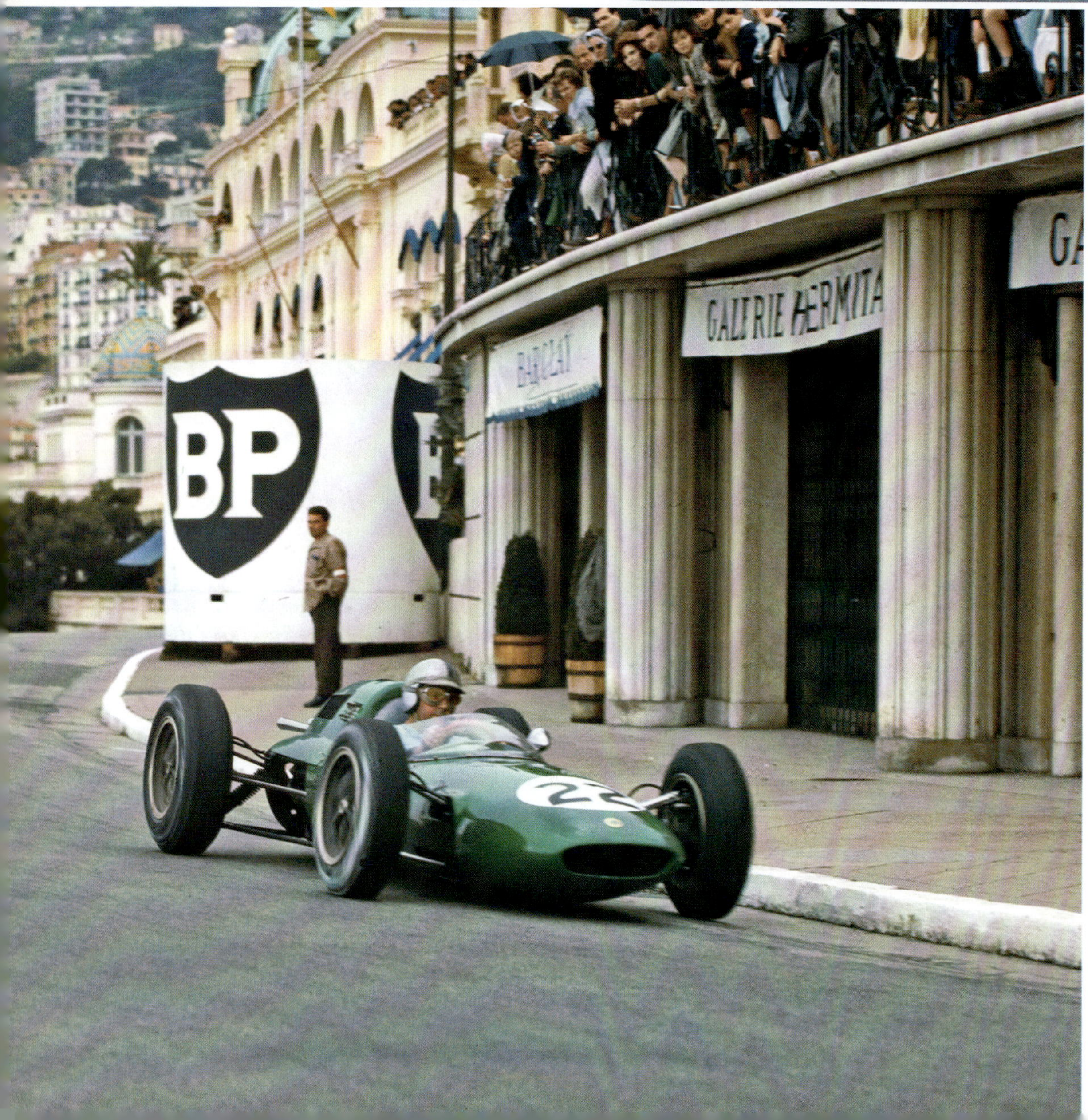

Casino Square, Monaco, and the increasingly antique-looking, wire-wheeled Ferrari Dino (0007) of Phil Hill presses on to finish an impressive 2nd, only 1.3sec behind winner Bruce McLaren. This was the best Ferrari performance of the entire season and emphasised Hill's capabilities on a driver's circuit with a relatively uncompetitive car. The unmarked right front tyre sidewall bears witness to his precise driving style, in contrast to Brabham's scuffed rubber as below.

After leaving Cooper and before his own Brabham BT3 was ready, Jack Brabham raced a Lotus 21 and then a new 24 (947). Here at Monaco, tucking in the 24 tight to the kerb at the top of the hill approaching Casino Square, Brabham was twice delayed by Willy Mairesse, who caused a first-corner incident and later spun his Ferrari at the Station Hairpin, blocking Brabham against the trackside wall. Ultimately, Brabham retired with a split radiator and bent front suspension after avoiding Phil Hill's Ferrari, which had half-spun in Casino Square. Not his day.

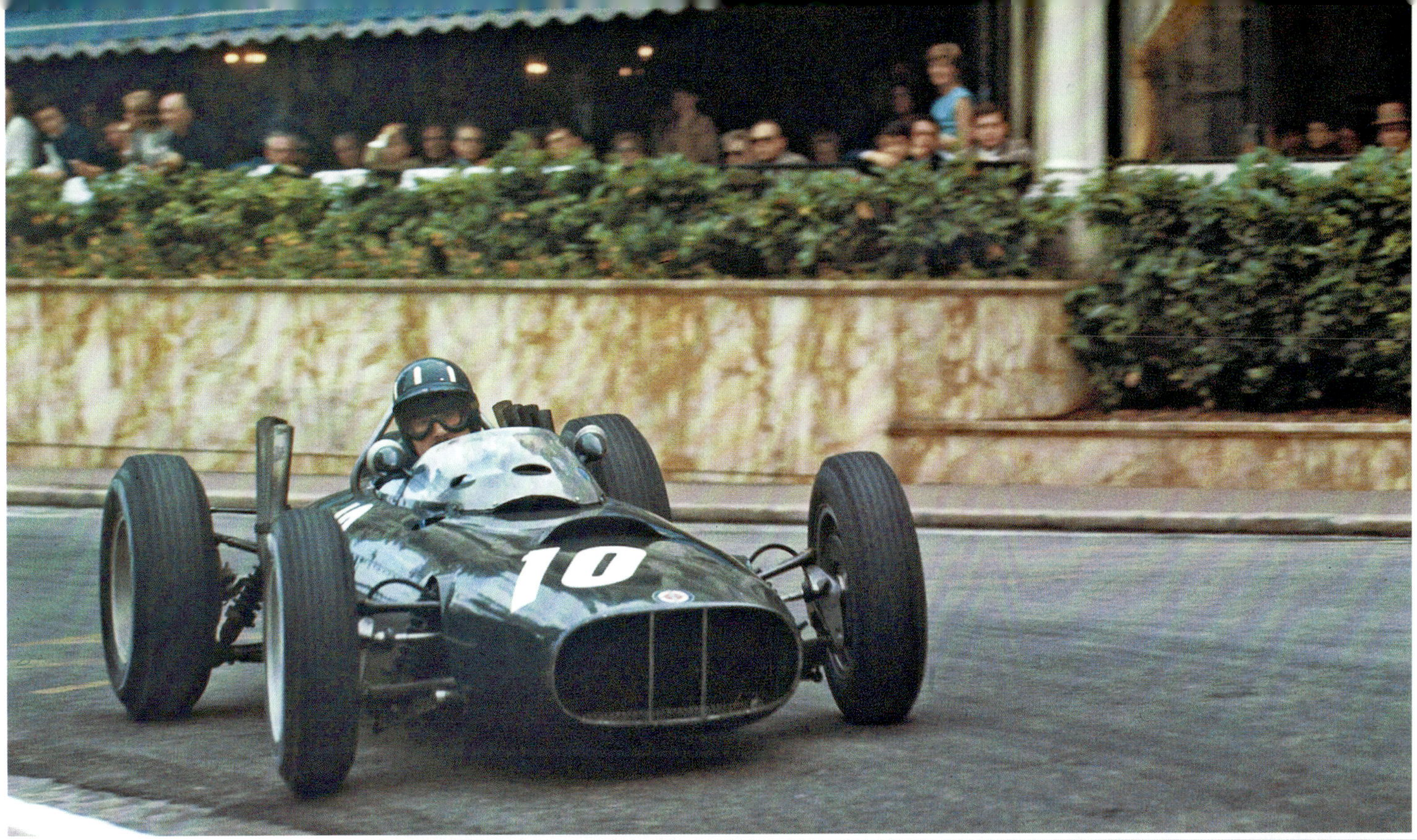

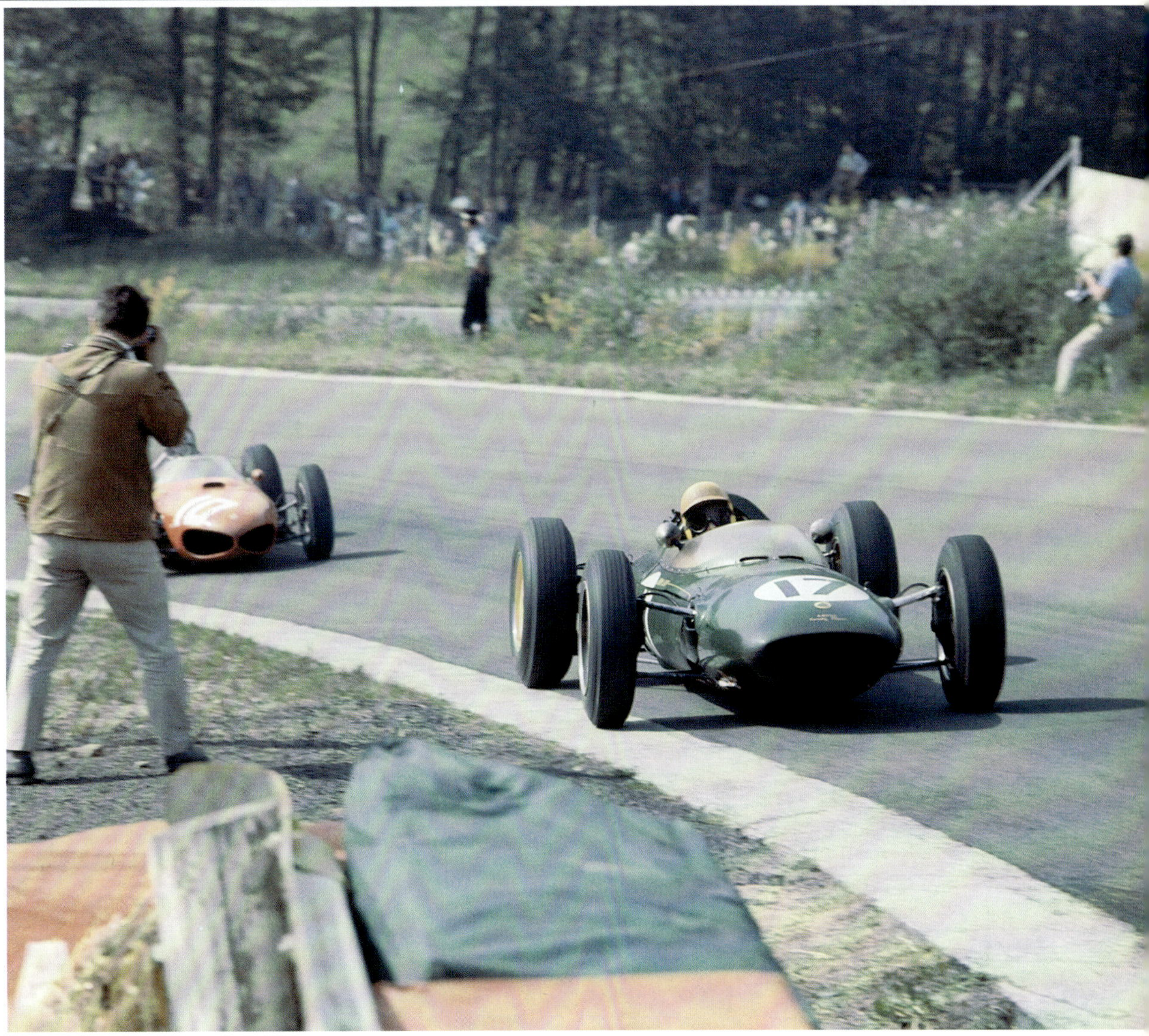

⇧ Graham Hill, his BRM P57 (5781) sporting the almost obligatory shortened Monaco nose, searches for the apex in Casino Square. He led for most of the race after a battle with Jim Clark's Lotus, only to suffer a seized engine on the 93rd of the 100 laps. All the oil had leaked out via the distributor drive due to a seal being fitted the wrong way round. Nevertheless he was classified 6th.

⇨ Trevor Taylor never stood a chance at Spa-Francorchamps once he had become embroiled with Willy Mairesse in a battle for 2nd place. Taylor started his Lotus 24 (948) from the front row and led 'Wild Willy' until lap 25 when, inevitably, the Ferrari hit the back of the Lotus approaching Blanchimont, causing both cars to crash. Fortunately Taylor was unhurt, despite knocking over a telegraph pole, while Mairesse escaped from the overturned, burning Ferrari. Jim Clark won the race convincingly from Graham Hill's misfiring BRM.

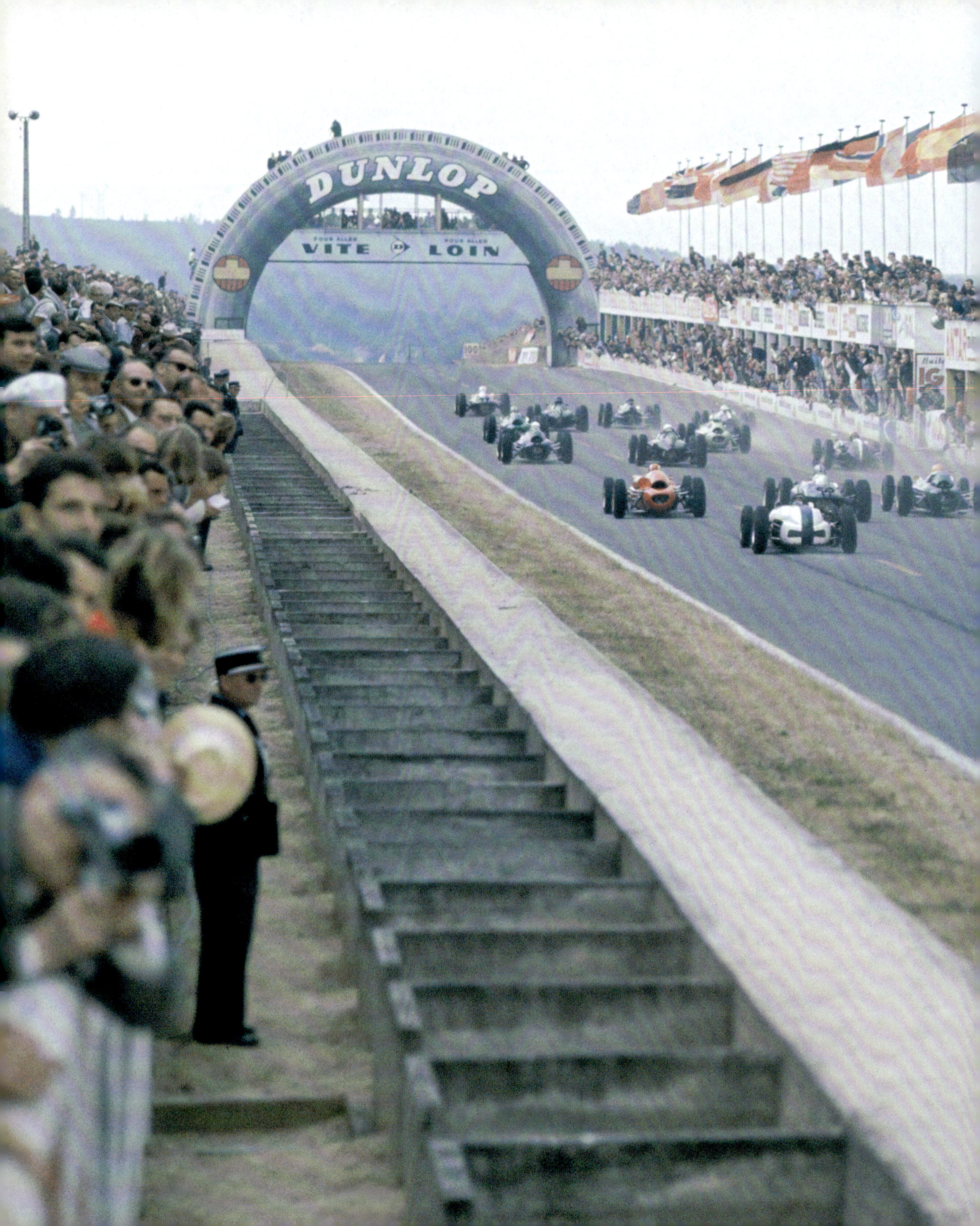
DUNLOP
VITE
LOIN

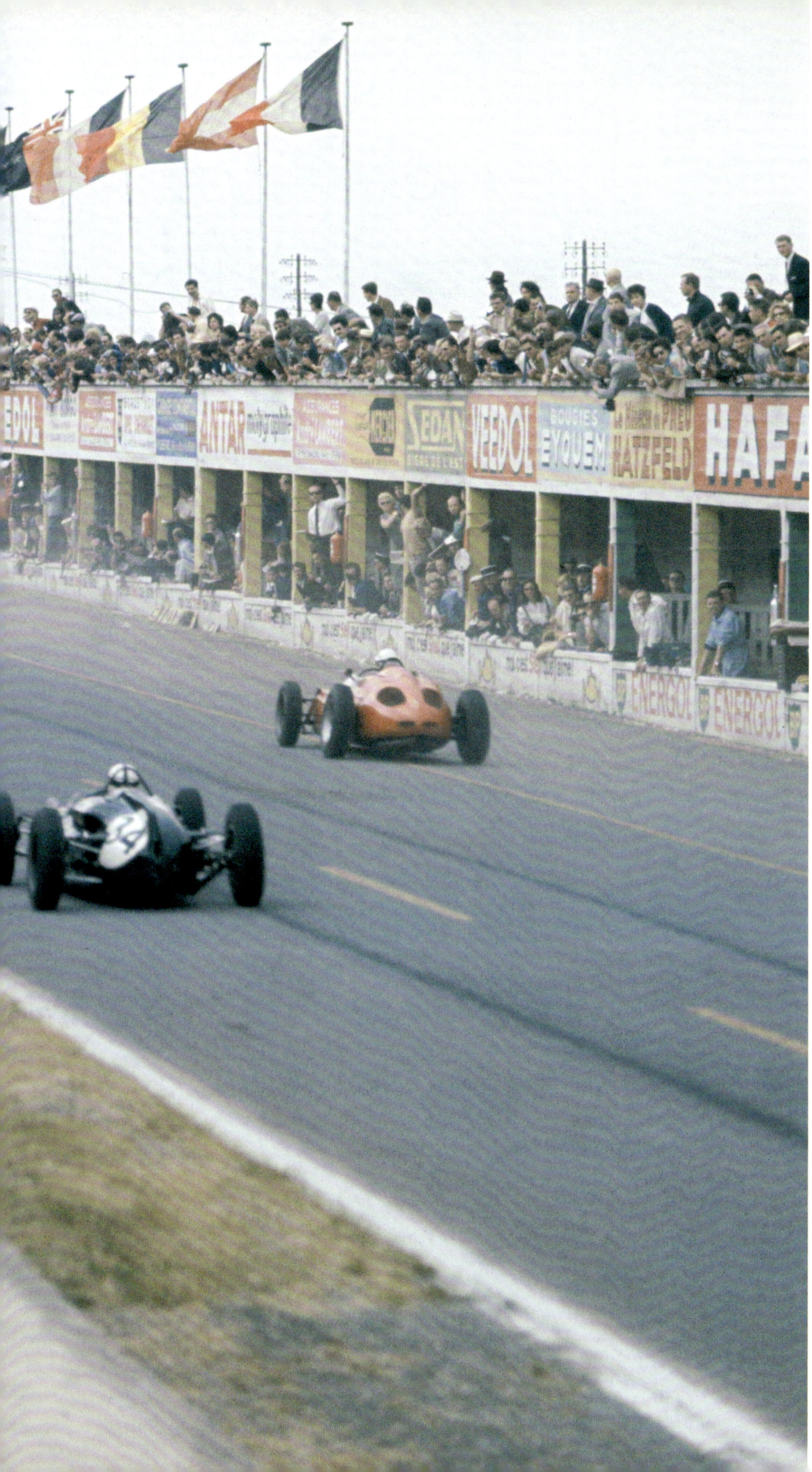

When the Grand Prix de l'ACF was relocated to Rouen for 1962, Reims held its own non-championship race that attracted all the notable teams bar Ferrari and Porsche. No 34 is Jack Lewis's Cooper T53 and the red Porsche 718 is driven by Jo Bonnier, subbing for the Scuderia SSS Republica di Venezia team (chassis 203). The national flags fluttering in the breeze and the Dunlop tyre bridge are very much redolent of the period.

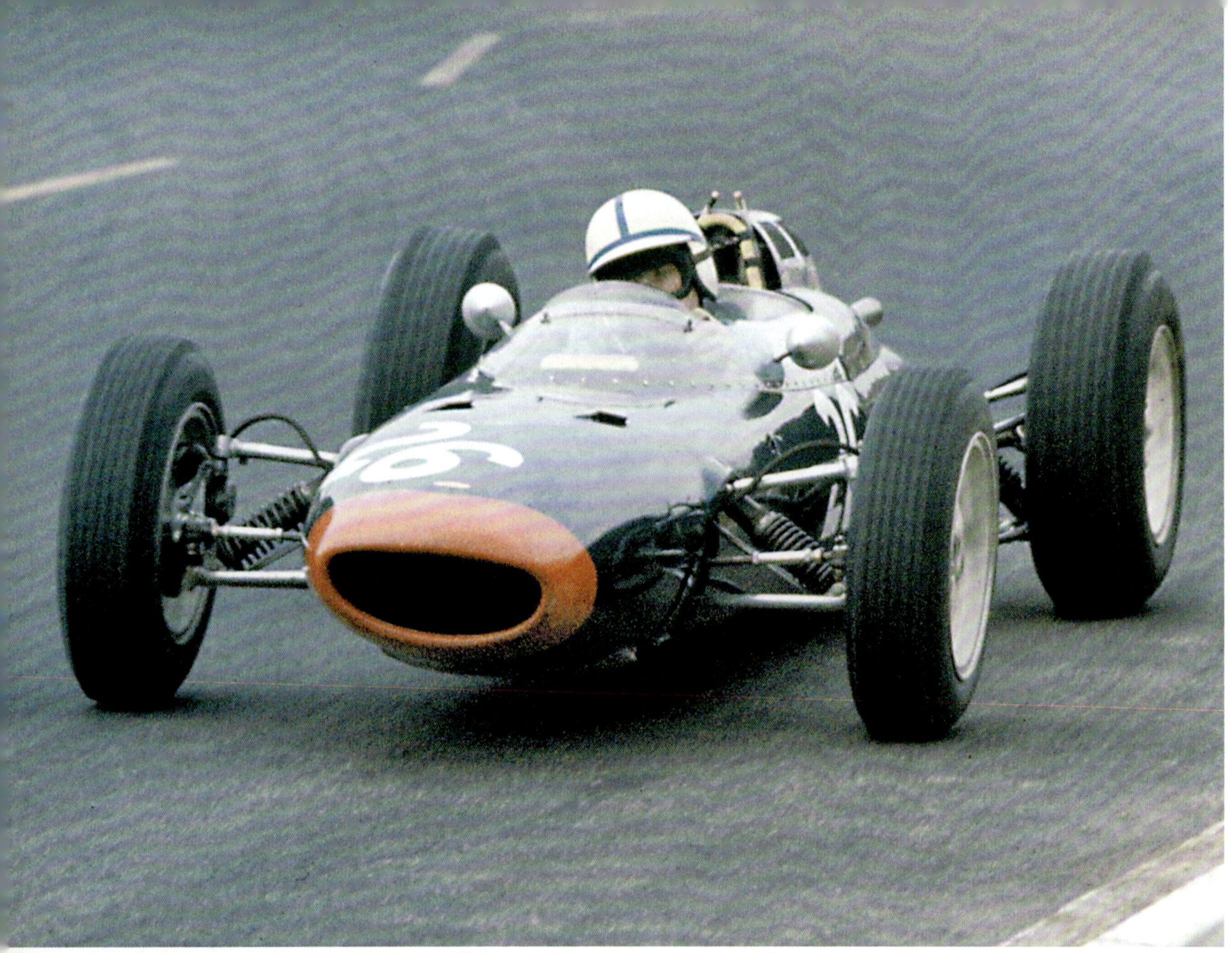

John Surtees convincingly led the first 25 laps at Reims with the Bowmaker Racing Team's Lola, pulling away even from Jim Clark's Lotus 25. Alas, Surtees suffered a broken valve spring and lost a certain victory.

With Surtees and Clark already retired, the race at Reims was left to McLaren, Hill and Brabham, seen here at Thillois, to fight it out. McLaren is driving Maggs's Spa T60, Hill 'old faithful' (5781) and Brabham his customer Lotus 24 (947) on opposite lock. Ultimately McLaren won by eight seconds from Hill whilst Brabham missed the pit signals to turn on his reserve fuel supply and ended up 4th behind Innes Ireland in the UDT Laystall Lotus 24. Afterwards he told his pit crew to throw the fuel funnel at him next time.

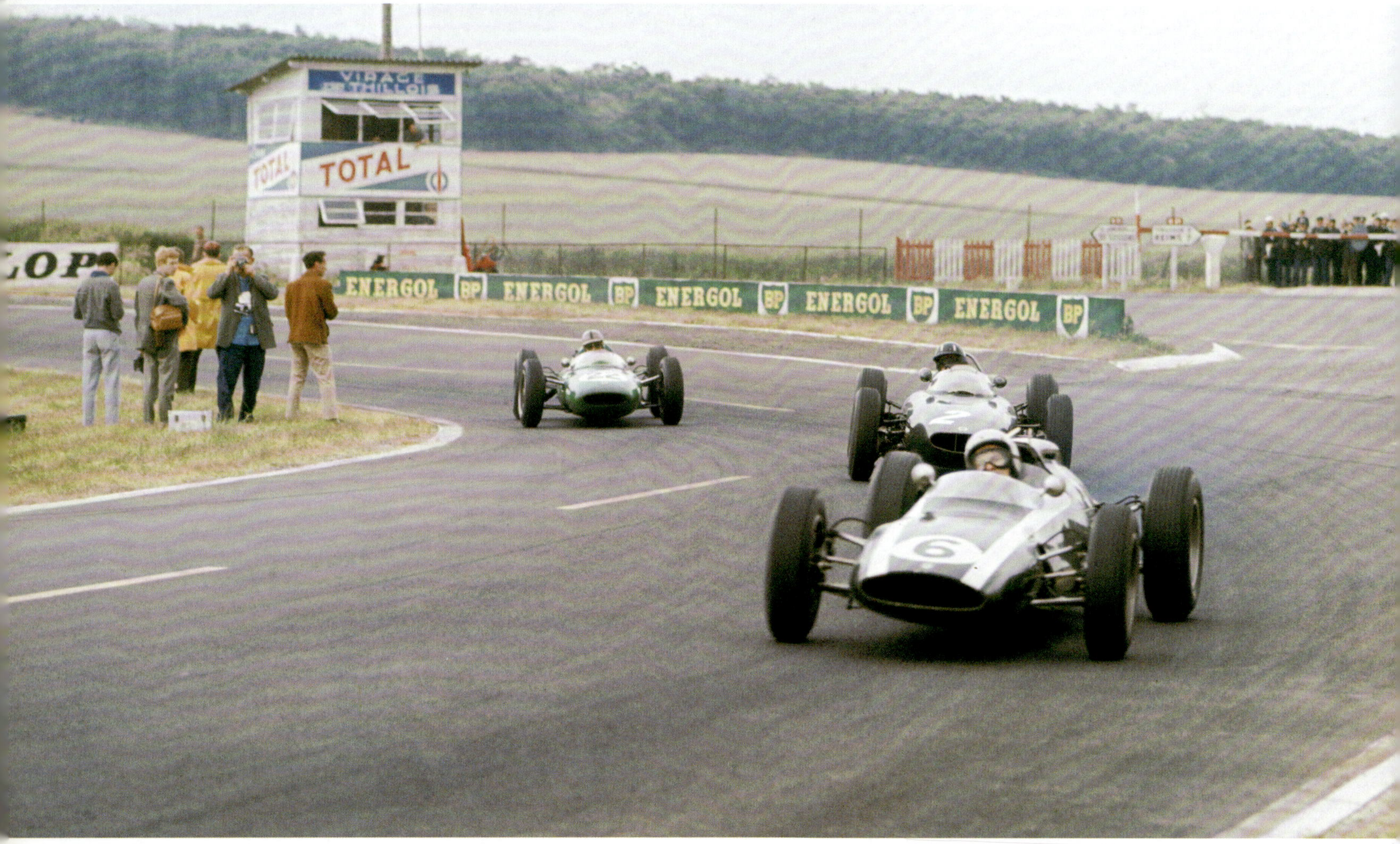

A series of shots taken at the Nouveau Monde hairpin during the French Grand Prix at Rouen-les-Essarts in July 1962:

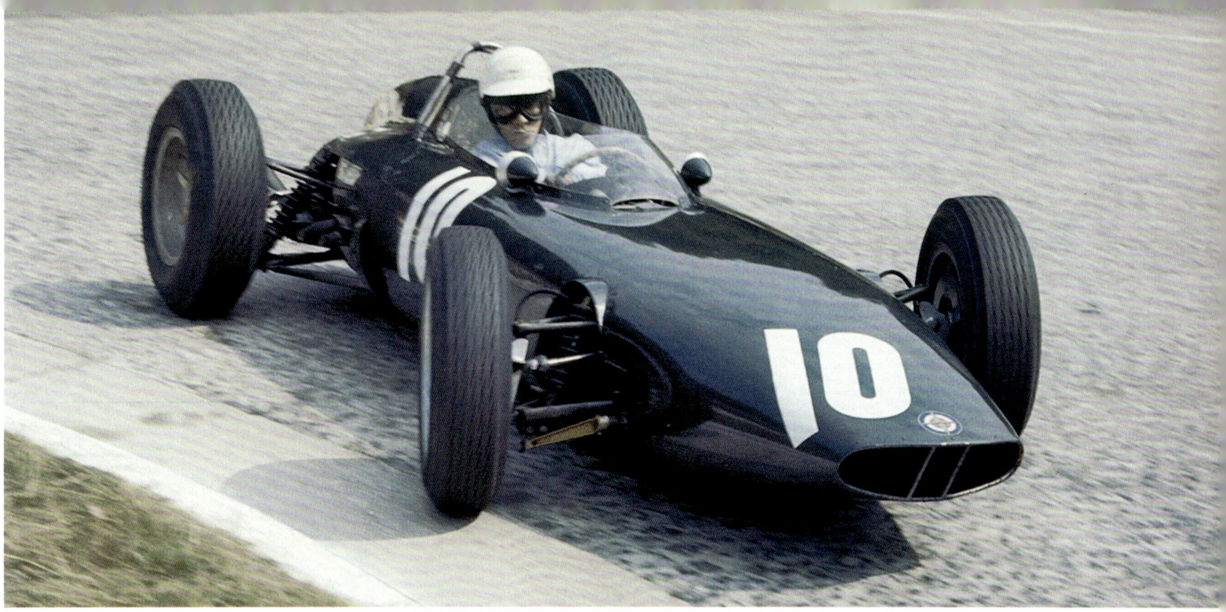

An aggressive Richie Ginther finished 3rd with this BRM P57 (5784) despite delays caused by a starter motor failure at the start and by a broken throttle cable near the end.

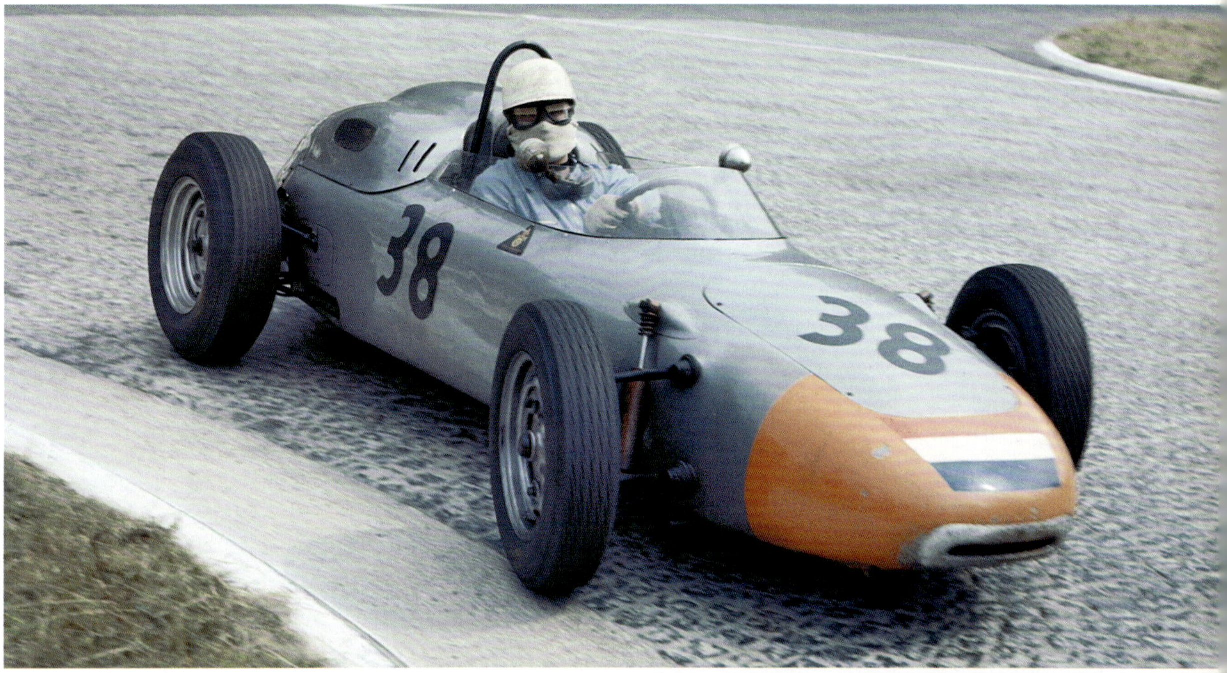

Carel de Beaufort wears facial protection in his 1959 Porsche 718 (201) on his way to 6th place. He was still racing this old car in 1964 when he was fatally injured during practice for the German Grand Prix.

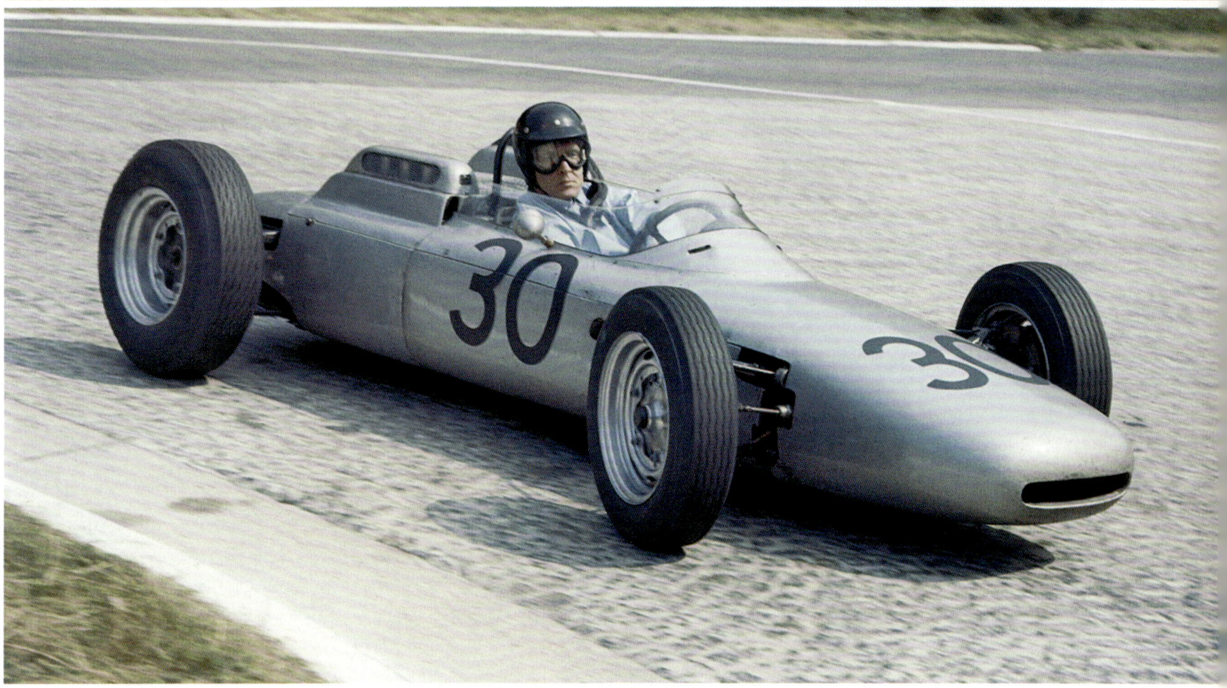

Race winner Dan Gurney's flat-eight Porsche 804 (01) seems unfinished in pristine silver, with no cosmetic adornments and wheels that look like they belong on a beach buggy. This was Porsche's only championship Grand Prix victory. The race should have been won by Graham Hill's BRM, but it was put off the track by Jack Lewis and then hampered by a malfunctioning throttle.

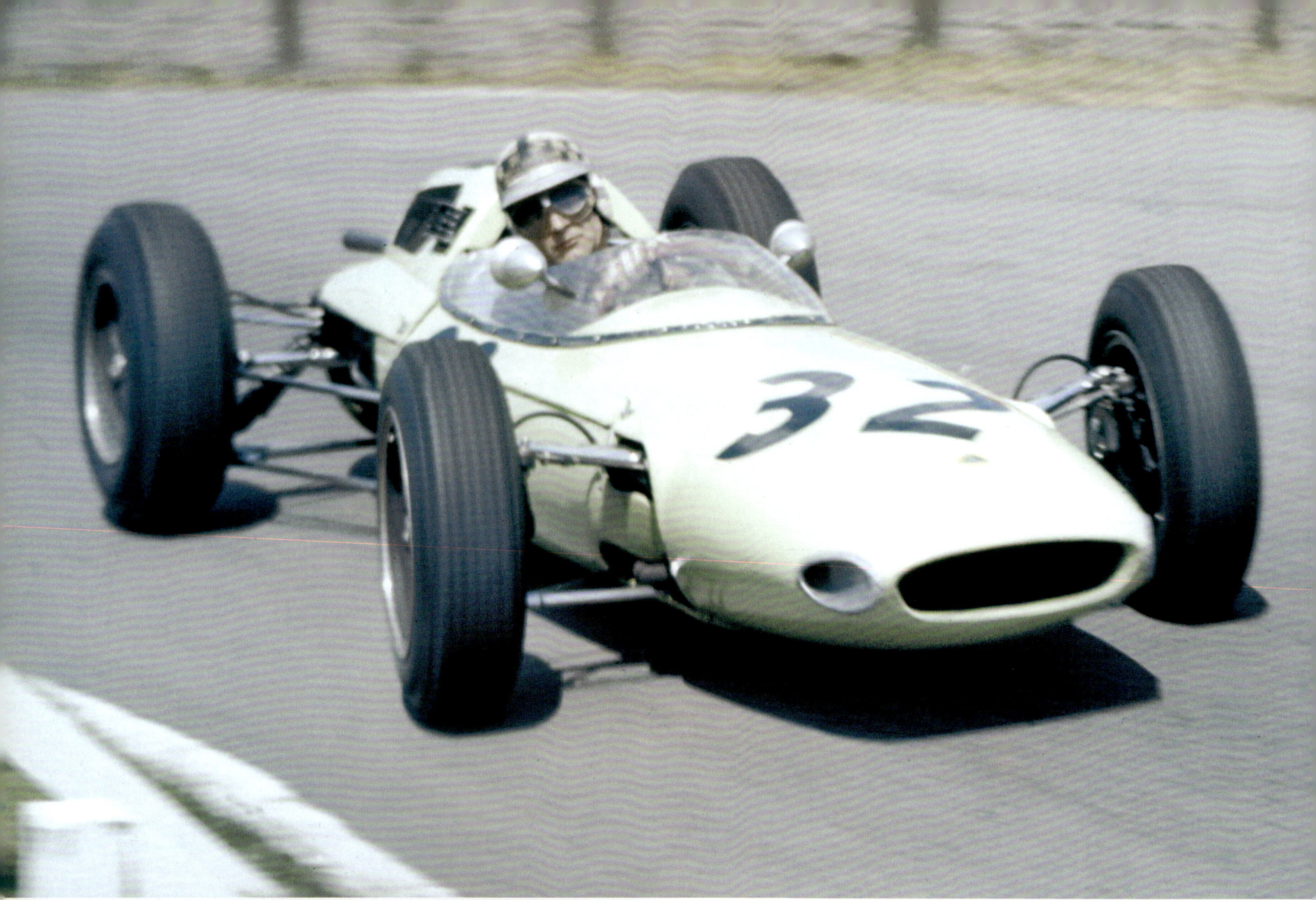

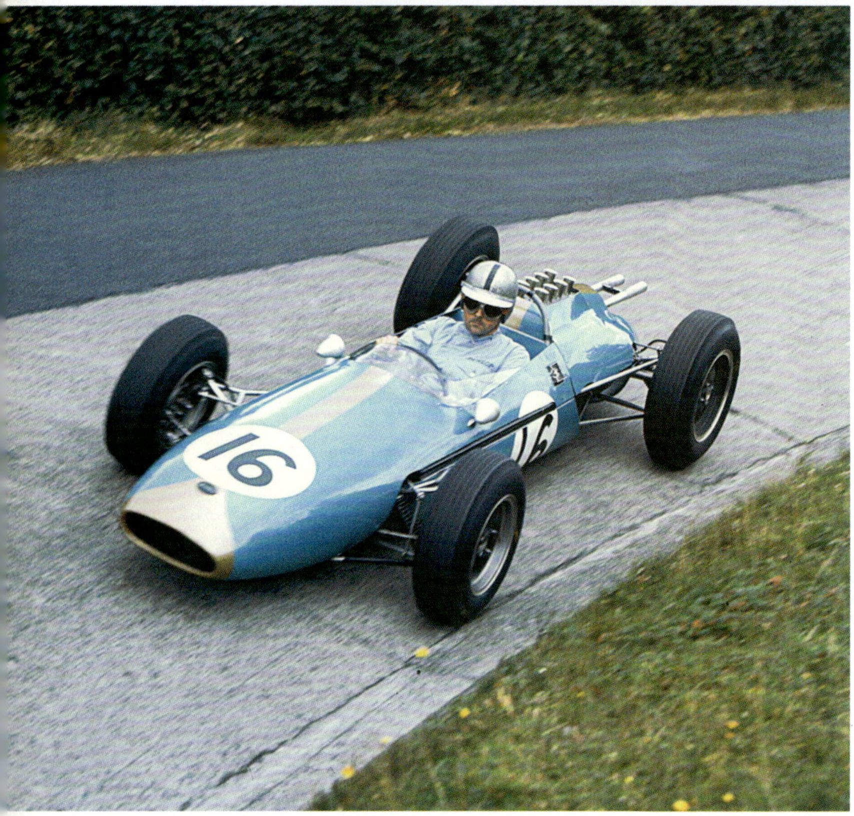

The British Grand Prix was run at Aintree for the second year running and here, at Tatts corner, the photogenic, press-on driving style of Innes Ireland is well illustrated. Driving the UDT Laystall team's Lotus 24 Climax (943), Ireland occupied the third slot on the front row of the grid, but lost many laps with a deranged gear selector that took 15 minutes to repair. The race was a walkover for Team Lotus and Jim Clark, who finished 50 seconds ahead of John Surtees (Lola). The rest, led by Bruce McLaren (Cooper) and an outpaced Graham Hill (BRM), were lapped.

Jack Brabham introduced his new Formula 1 car to the press the week before the German Grand Prix. Designated BT3 (BT1 and 2 were Formula Junior projects), it was designed by Ron Tauranac around a simple, multi-tubular spaceframe and powered by the Coventry Climax FWMV V8, driving through a six-speed Colotti transaxle. The pretty, turquoise-and-gold colour scheme was the original Motor Racing Developments livery and this was the last Brabham to wear it. The BT3 is pictured in the Karussel, making a modest debut on the Nürburgring before stopping with a malfunctioning throttle. Later in the season, Brabham finished 4th in the US Grand Prix, thus becoming the first driver ever to score World Championship points in a car of his own manufacture.

Graham Hill survived a 140 mph practice shunt in practice for the German GP after running over a camera that had fallen off de Beaufort's Porsche. BRM's new car was wrecked, so Hill used his regular P57 (5781) to win the wet German GP. He narrowly defeated Surtees (Lola) and Gurney (Porsche) whilst championship rival Jim Clark stalled at the start having forgotten to turn on his petrol pumps, eventually finishing 4th.

Veteran Roy Salvadori grapples with his Bowmaker Lola (BRGP43) during the German Grand Prix. This was the final season for 'Salvo' as a Grand Prix driver and he was overshadowed by the brilliance of his team mate, John Surtees. The winner of the 1959 Le Mans 24 Hours, Salvadori continued successfully to race saloon, GT and sports cars before finally retiring early in 1965. During 1966–67, he acted as the Formula 1 team manager of Cooper Cars.

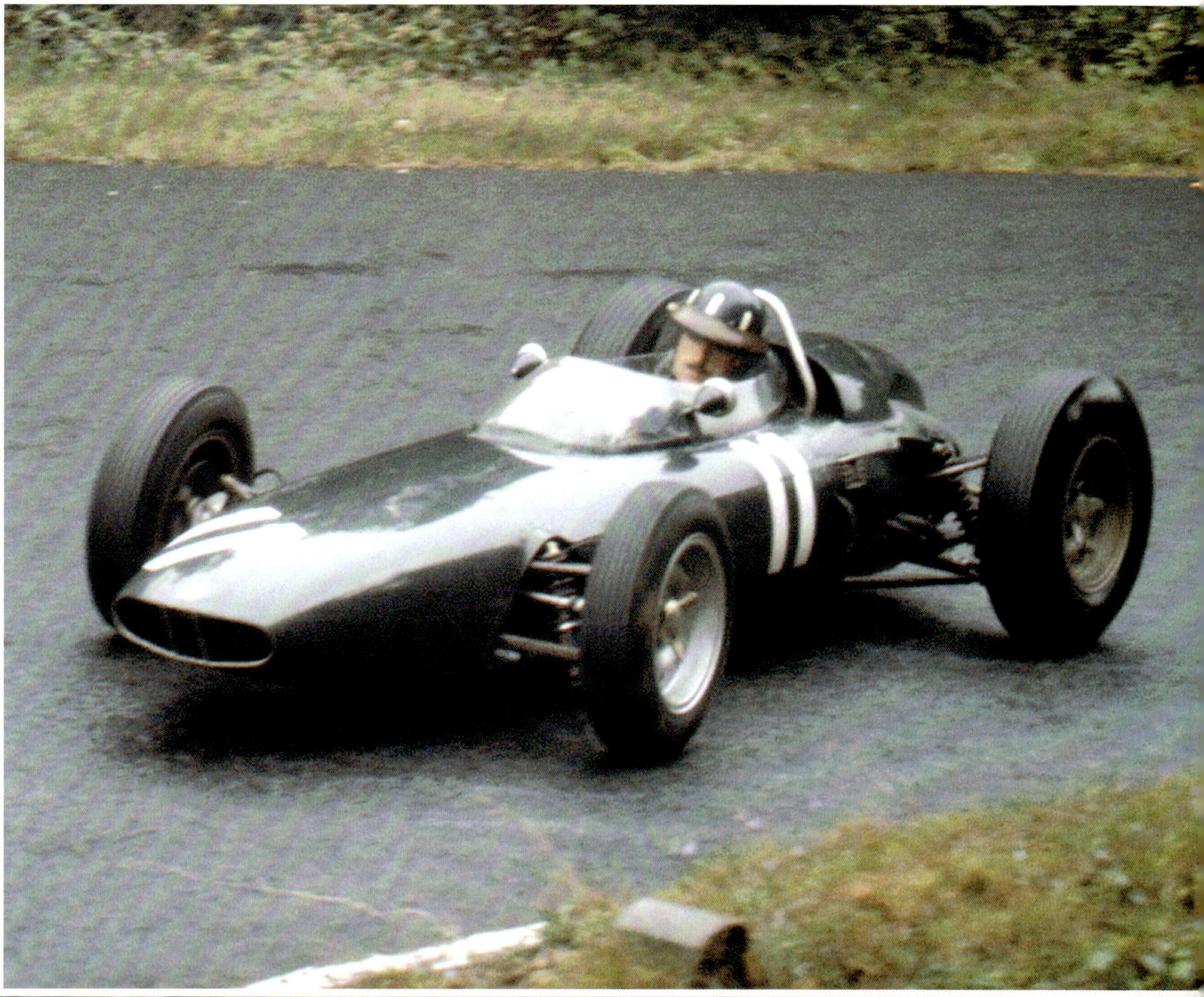

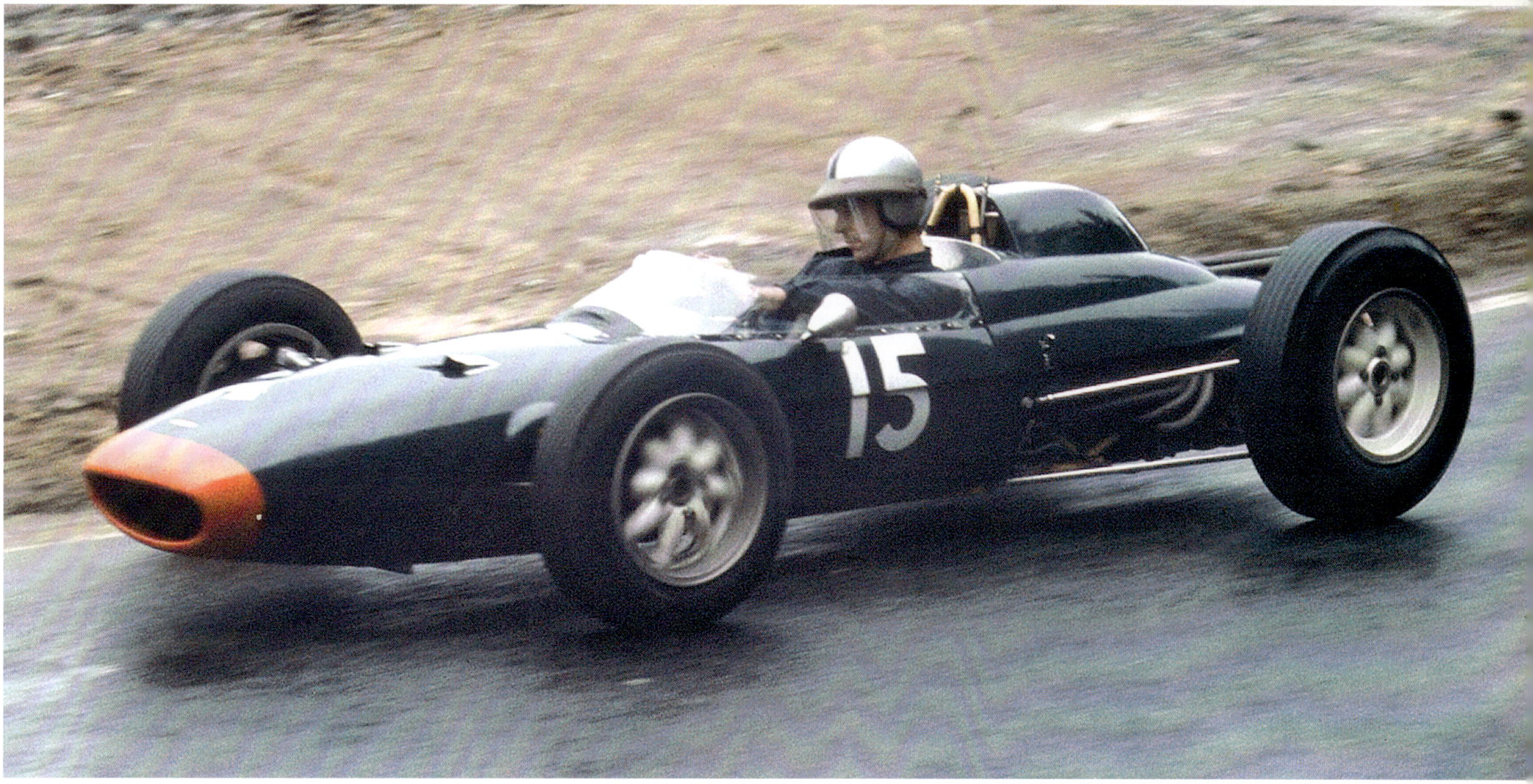

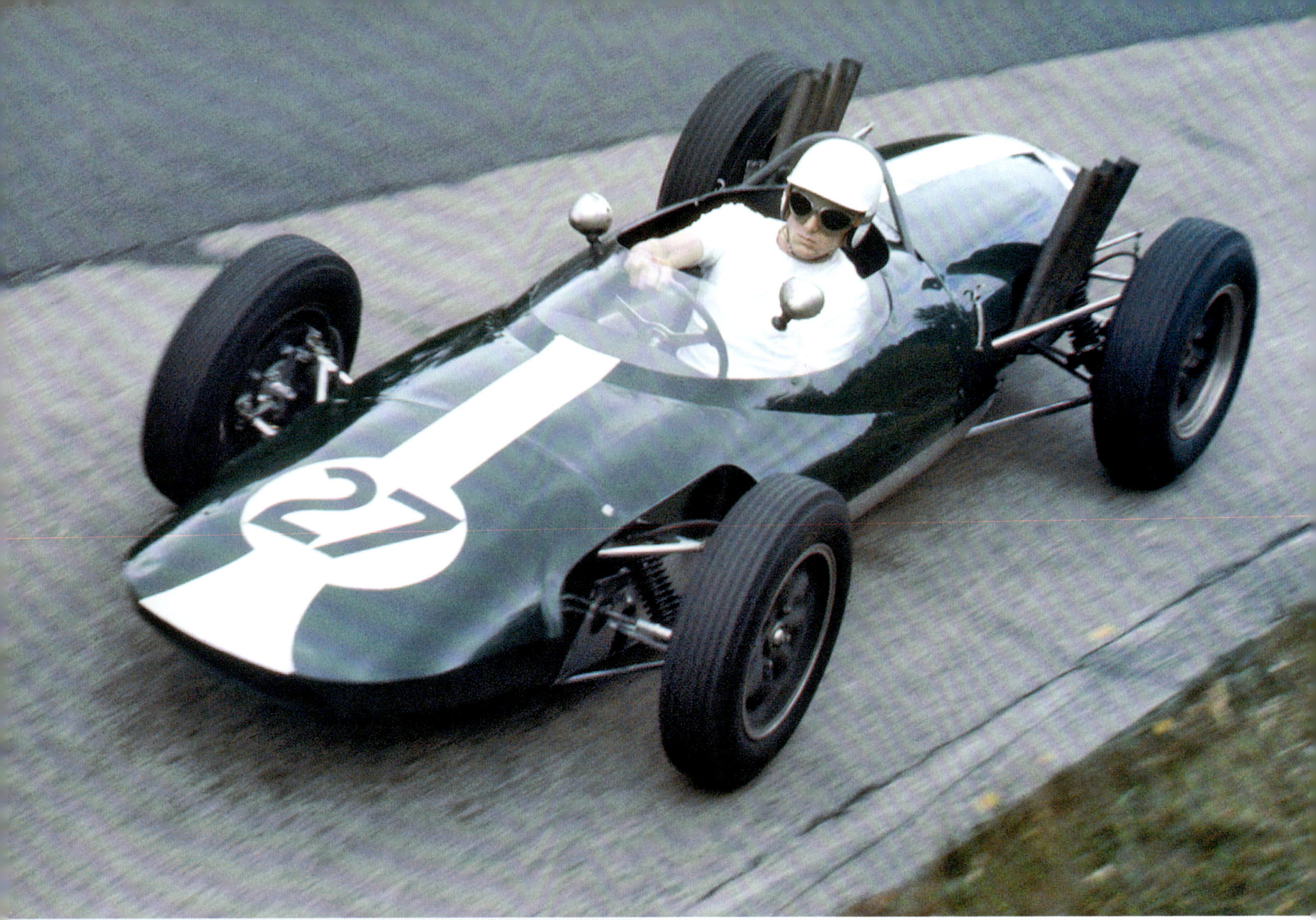

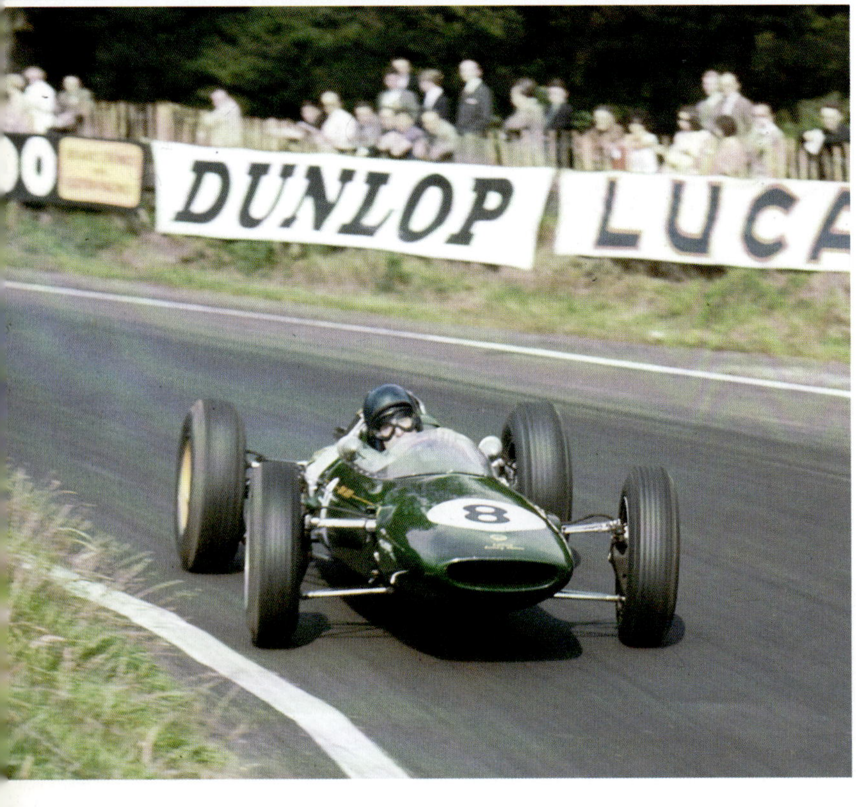

↑ Gilby Engineering fitted its Formula 1 car with a 'customer' BRM V8, still using the stackpipe exhaust system long since abandoned by the works team. Keith Greene drove it thus equipped in the German Grand Prix. The Gilby, which was retired on the seventh lap after a front suspension failure, could perform well in non-championship events but it struggled at Grand Prix level. Greene did not qualify for the Italian GP and this marked the end of his Formula 1 career. He returned to sports car racing and ultimately ended his racing activities in team management during the 1990s.

→ What looks like two Ferrari Dinos followed by a flat-eight Porsche enjoy the pre-chicane flat out blind on the old Monza circuit with the banked section just visible to the right. The heavily wooded, almost rural, appearance of the track typifies the period. BRM scored a 1–2 with Graham Hill leading home Richie Ginther.

← Two weeks before the Italian Grand Prix, Jim Clark led the Oulton Park Gold Cup from start to finish, beating Graham Hill's BRM by a massive 78 seconds. Clark's Lotus 25 (R2) is riding high on its haunches, an attitude that was familiar in the pre-spoiler days when Formula 1 cars had more air flowing underneath them than over the top.

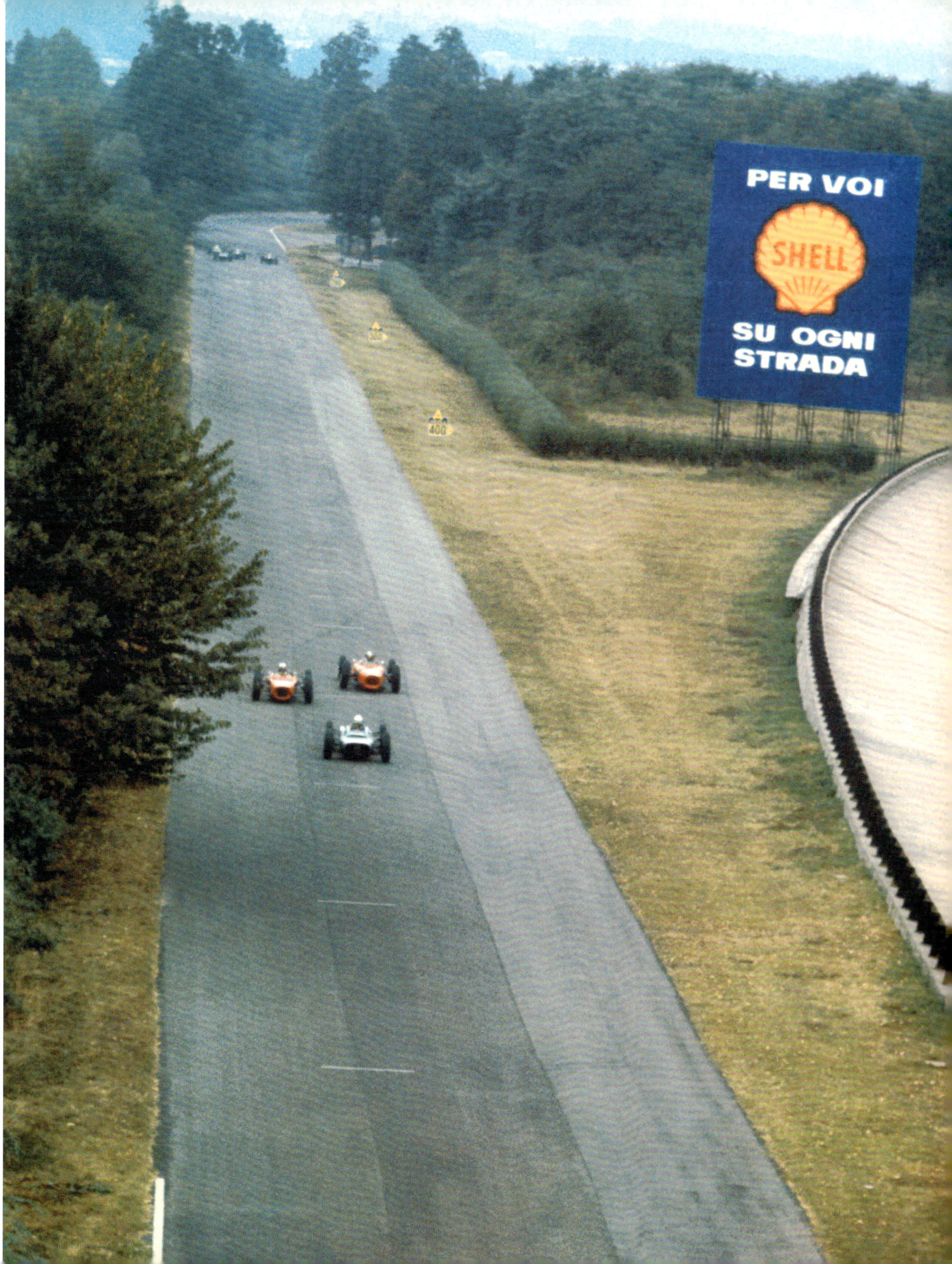
PER VOI
SHELL
SU OGNI
STRADA

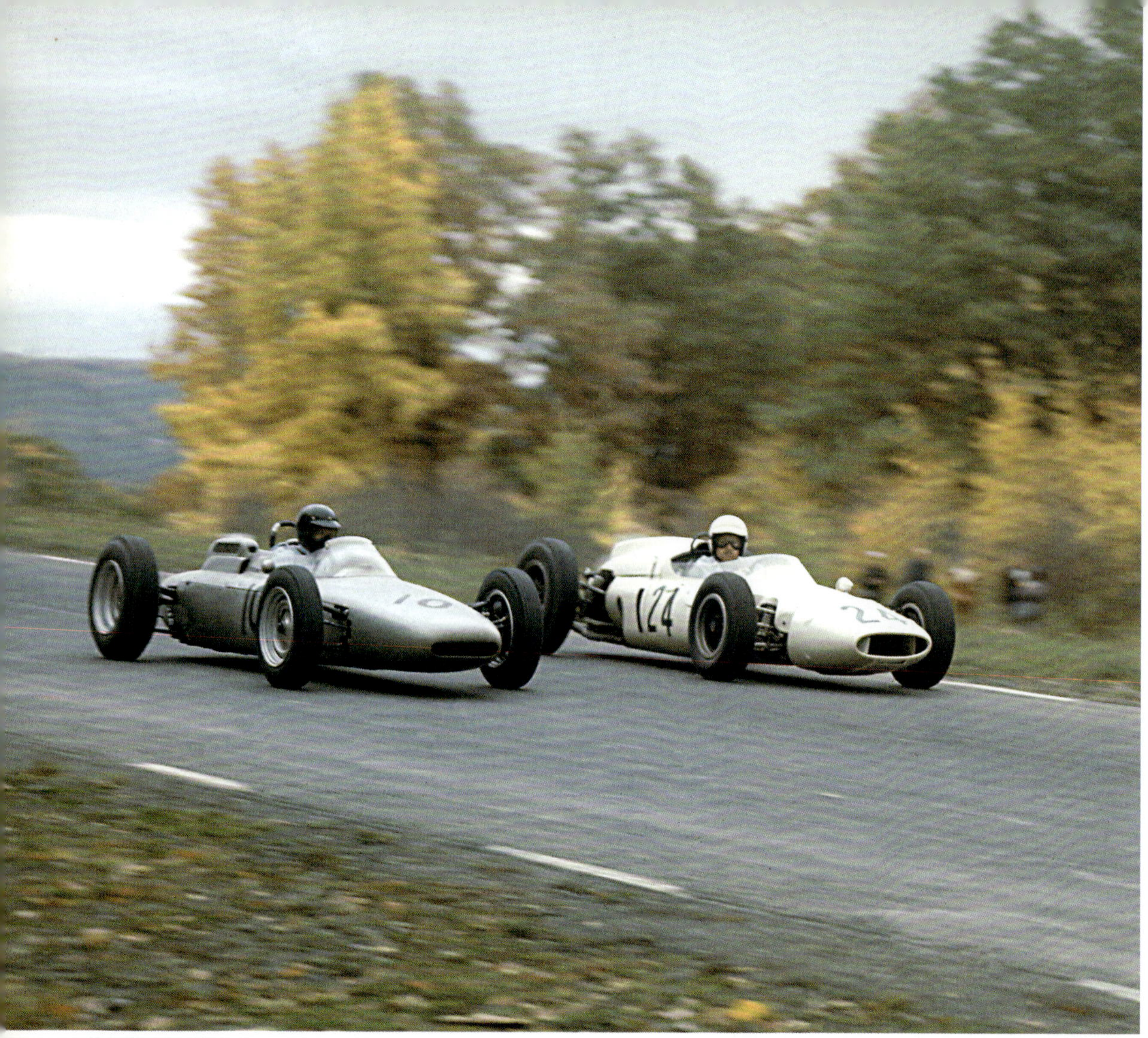

A golden autumn in New York state, and the final race for Porsche's Formula 1 team. After the Italian Grand Prix at Monza, won by Graham Hill from his BRM team mate, Richie Ginther, the status quo was restored when Jim Clark beat Hill to the flag in the US Grand Prix at Watkins Glen. Here Dan Gurney's Porsche 804 (03) races past Hap Sharp's Cooper T53 (F1-15-61) on its way to 5th place, one lap behind. Sharp who later raced Chaparrals successfully finished 11th.

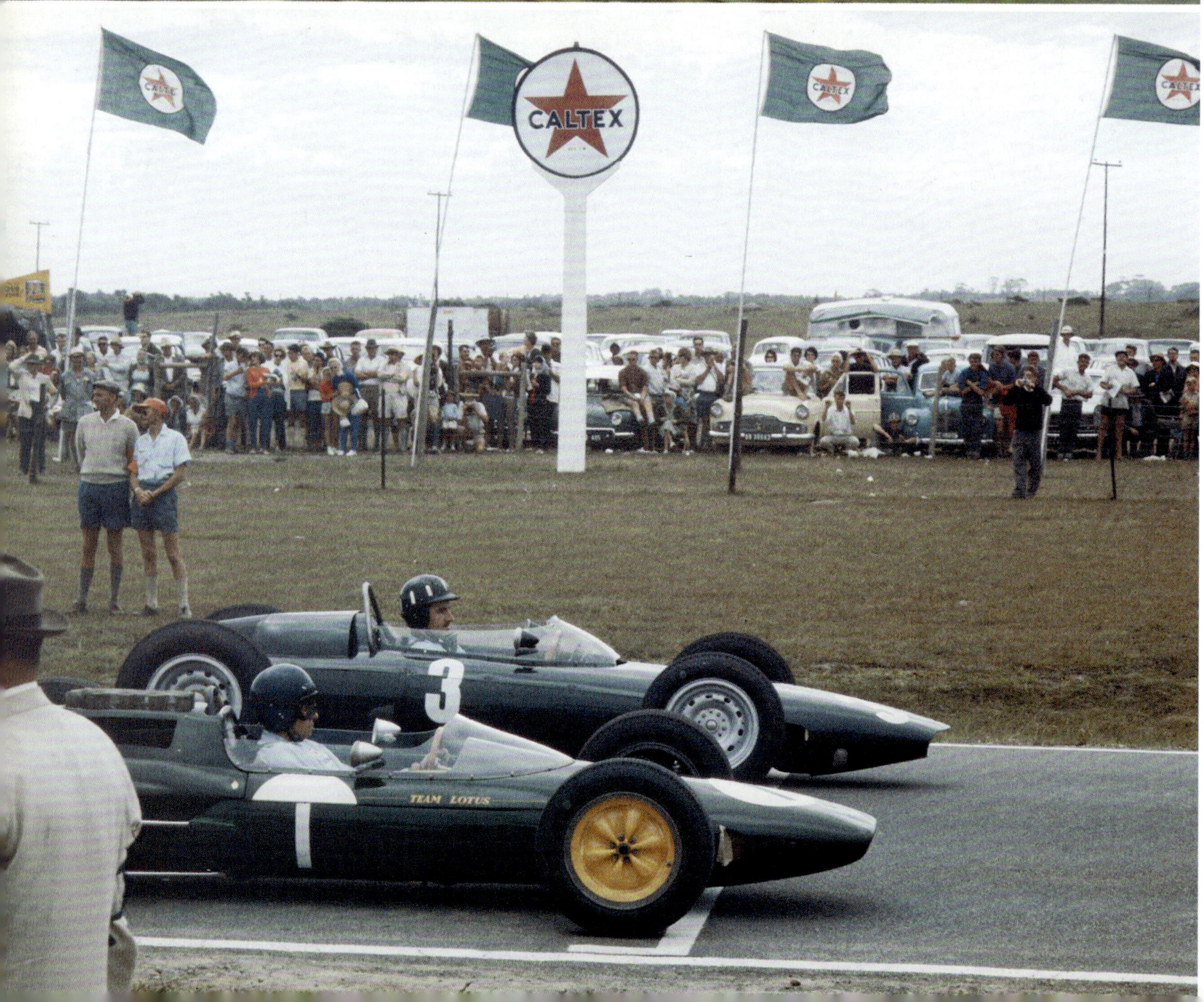

The East London circuit, the scene of the South African Grand Prix on 29 December 1962, was narrow even by the standards of the era. Jim Clark (nearer camera) is on pole position as he and Graham Hill await the start of the race which would settle the outcome of the championship. At bottom right can be seen Lotus mechanic Cedric Selzer. Clark's race-leading Lotus 25 was retired due to an engine oil leak, caused by a bolt falling out of the crankcase because it had not been secured with a locking washer. Hill won with the latest, sleeker, lighter BRM P57 (5785). Earlier in the year, team principal Tony Rudd had been told that BRM would be closed down unless there were at least two Grand Prix wins. Now it had won four, and had added the Drivers' title and the Constructors' Cup for good measure.

1962 Teams, drivers and results

Cooper Car Co – Cooper T55 Climax FPF and T60 Climax V8
Bruce McLaren (NZ)
Tony Maggs (ZA)
Tim Mayer (USA) (US GP only in T55)

Team Lotus – Lotus 24 Climax V8 and 25 Climax V8
Jim Clark (GB)
Trevor Taylor (GB)

Owen Racing Organisation – BRM P48/57 and P57
Graham Hill (GB) (WORLD CHAMPION)
Richie Ginther (USA)
Bruce Johnstone (ZA) (South African GP only in P48/57 ex-Jack Lewis on loan)

SEFAC Ferrari – Ferrari 156/61 and 156/62
Ferrari not entered at French (industrial action), US and South African GPs. Only one car entered at British GP (Hill)
Phil Hill (USA)
Giancarlo Baghetti (I) (Dutch, Belgian, German and Italian GPs only)
Ricardo Rodriguez (MEX) (Dutch, Monaco dns, Belgian, German and Italian GPs only. Fatally injured driving Rob Walker Lotus 24 during practice for non-championship Mexican GP in November 1962)
Lorenzo Bandini (I) (Monaco, German and Italian GPs only)
Willy Mairesse (B) (Monaco, Belgian and Italian GPs only)

Porsche System Engineering – Porsche 804
Dan Gurney (USA) (dns Belgian and South African GPs)
Jo Bonnier (S) (dns Belgian and South African GPs, raced 718 borrowed from Count Volpi's Scuderia SSS Republica di Venezia at Monaco)

Brabham Racing Organisation – Lotus 24 Climax V8 and Brabham BT3 Climax V8
Jack Brabham (AUS) (Used Lotus for Dutch, Monaco, Belgian and British GPs. Switched to Brabham thereafter but dns Italian GP due to inadequate starting money)

UDT-Laystall Racing Team – Lotus 18/21 Climax FPF, 24 Climax V8 and 24 BRM V8
Innes Ireland (GB) (dns German GP)
Masten Gregory (USA) (dns German and South African GPs)

Bowmaker Racing Team – Lola 4 Climax V8
John Surtees (GB)
Roy Salvadori (GB) (dns Belgian GP)

R. R. C. Walker Racing Team – Lotus 24 Climax V8
Maurice Trintignant (F) (dns Dutch GP, car not ready, dns British GP, car destroyed at French GP after being hit by Taylor's works Lotus)

Ecurie Maarsbergen – Porsche 718, 787 and Emeryson Climax FPF
Carel de Beaufort (NL) (dnq Monaco GP)
Ben Pon (NL) (Dutch GP only in works loaned 787)
Wolfgang Seidel (D) (Dutch GP only in Emeryson with entry obtained by de Beaufort who had bought back his Porsche 718-01 from Seidel for the Dutch GP)

Ecurie Galloise – Cooper T53 Climax FPF and BRM P48/57
Jack Lewis (GB) (Dutch, Monaco dnq in BRM, French, British and German GPs only)

Emeryson Cars – Lotus 18 Climax FPF and Emeryson 1004/1006 Climax FPF
John Campbell-Jones (GB) Belgian GP only in Lotus)
Tony Settember (USA) (British and Italian GPs only)

Equipe Nationale Belge – Lotus 18/21 Climax FPF and ENB Maserati
Lucien Bianchi (B) (Belgian and German GPs only)

Ecurie Nationale Suisse/Scuderia Filipinetti – Lotus 21 Climax FPF, 24 BRM V8 and Porsche 718
Jo Siffert (CH) (Practised but dns Monaco GP, Belgian, French, German and Italian [dnq] GPs only)
Heinz Schiller (CH) (German GP only in Lotus 24)
Heini Walter (CH) (German GP only in Porsche)

Anglo American Equipe – Aiden Cooper T53 Special Climax FPF
Ian Burgess (GB) (British and German GPs only, dnq Italian GP)

Autosport Team Wolfgang Seidel – Lotus 24 BRM V8
Wolfgang Seidel (D) British GP only, dnq German GP)
Tony Shelly (NZ) (dnq Italian GP)

Ecurie Excelsior – Lotus 18 Climax FPF
Jay Chamberlain (USA) (British GP only, dnq German and Italian GPs)

John Dalton – Lotus 18/21 Climax FPF
Tony Shelly (NZ) (British GP only, dnq German GP)
Keith Greene (GB) (Drove car in practice British GP, dns)

Scuderia SSS Republica di Venezia – Porsche 718, Lotus 18/21 Climax FPF and Lotus 24 Climax V8
Nino Vaccarella (I) (dnq Monaco Lotus 18/21, German GP Porsche 718 and Italian GP Lotus 24)

Gilby Engineering – Gilby BRM V8
Keith Greene (GB) (German GP only, dnq Italian GP)

Bernard Collomb – Cooper T53 Climax FPF
Bernard Collomb (F) (German GP only)

Dupont Team Zerex – Lotus 24 Climax V8 (Car on loan from UDT-Laystall)
Roger Penske (USA) (US GP only)

'Hap' Sharp – Cooper T53 Climax FPF
'Hap' Sharp (USA) (US GP only)

John Mecom – Lotus 24 Climax V8
Bob Schroeder (USA) (US GP only)

Ernest Pieterse – Lotus 21 Climax FPF
Ernest Pieterse (ZA) (South African GP only)

John Love – Cooper T55 Climax FPF
John Love (RSR) (South African GP only)

Neville Lederle – Lotus 21 Climax FPF
Neville Lederle (ZA) (South African GP only)

Otelle Nucci – LDS Mk2 Alfa Romeo
Doug Serrurier (ZA) (South African GP only)

Mike Harris – Cooper T53 Alfa Romeo
Mike Harris (ZA) (South African GP only)

WORLD CHAMPIONSHIP VENUES AND WINNERS (nine rounds)

Dutch GP	Zandvoort	Graham Hill
Monaco GP	Monte Carlo	Bruce McLaren
Belgian GP	Spa-Francorchamps	Jim Clark
French GP	Rouen-les Essart	Dan Gurney
British GP	Aintree	Jim Clark
German GP	Nürburgring	Graham Hill
Italian GP	Monza	Graham Hill
United States GP	Watkins Glen	Jim Clark
South African GP	East London	Graham Hill

DRIVERS' CHAMPIONSHIP
Points: 9-6-4-3-2-1. Best 5 scores

1	Graham Hill	BRM	42
2	Jim Clark	Lotus	30
3	Bruce McLaren	Cooper	27
4	John Surtees	Lola	19
5	Dan Gurney	Porsche	15
6	Phil Hill	Ferrari	14
7	Tony Maggs	Cooper	13
8	Richie Ginther	BRM	10
9	Jack Brabham	Lotus/Brabham	9
10	Trevor Taylor	Lotus	6
11	Giancarlo Baghetti	Ferrari	5
12	Lorenzo Bandini	Ferrari	4
13	Willy Mairesse	Ferrari	3
14	Jo Bonnier	Porsche	3
15	Innes Ireland	Lotus	2
16	Carel de Beaufort	Porsche	1
17	Masten Gregory	Lotus	1
18	Neville Lederle	Lotus	1

CONSTRUCTORS' CHAMPIONSHIP
Points: 9-6-4-3-2-1, (awarded only to best-placed finisher). Best 5 scores

1	BRM	42
2	Lotus-Climax	36
3	Cooper-Climax	29
4	Lola-Climax	19
5	Porsche	18
6	Ferrari	18
7	Brabham-Climax	6
8	Lotus-BRM	1

1963

SCOTTISH SUPREMACY

The 1963 Formula 1 World Championship was almost exclusively the domain of one man and one team, and was also notable for the fact that all ten races fell to British drivers. Seven Grands Prix were won by Jim Clark for Team Lotus, two by Graham Hill for British Racing Motors, and one by John Surtees for Scuderia Ferrari SEFAC. No one else really mattered.

Colin Chapman of Lotus retained both his 1962 drivers, as did BRM and Cooper, but Ferrari hired Surtees in a bid to restore its fortunes, and also finally produced a new car, although failing to deploy its new V8 engine. At Reims, BRM appeared with a new semi-monocoque car that would evolve into the P261 the following season. It was raced twice by Graham Hill, finishing 3rd in France but failing to endure at Monza. Richie Ginther had a good season in the second BRM, ending up 3rd overall with three 2nd places and in fact scoring championship points in every race bar one. One oddity this season was a decision by the Italian organisers to run the Monza race on the combined road and banked oval course, as in 1961, but a practice accident that befell privateer Bob Anderson persuaded them otherwise. For the record, Hill was 2.6sec quicker on this course than Ginther, his nearest challenger.

Porsche had departed, unconvinced of the merits of Formula 1 and alarmed at increasing costs, so Dan Gurney pitched up at Brabham to drive alongside 'Black Jack'. Unlike Lotus, Brabham endured bitter disappointment with its Coventry Climax V8s, the otherwise well prepared cars suffering many engine failures.

The Italian-built ATS cars, built by the group that had abruptly quit Ferrari in early 1962, were eagerly awaited but turned out to be a total disaster, permanently damaging the careers of Phil Hill and Giancarlo Baghetti. There were a couple of old, 1961-style Porsche 718/2s for Gerhard Mitter and Dutch aristocrat Carel Godin de Beaufort. Also present was the very smart but underdeveloped, American-funded Scirocco, a doomed project that was terminated after the Oulton Park Gold Cup in September. As ever, assorted cars built by Cooper, Lotus and Lola (including one such driven by future Ferrari ace Chris Amon) made up the grid.

Clark had by now become omnipotent, occupying the role once held by Stirling Moss, and he won as he pleased in Belgium, Holland, France, Britain, Italy, Mexico and South Africa. Hill was the runner-up in the championship and won in Monaco (the first of a hat-trick there) and at Watkins Glen. Surtees beat Clark on the Nürburgring, but only because the Scotsman's Lotus was misfiring.

At Brabham, Dan Gurney and Jack Brabham managed three 2nd places between them, while the Cooper team achieved two. There were 14 non-championship races and they were once again the preserve of the usual suspects, Clark and Hill winning several races apiece in Britain and Europe, and Brabham, Surtees, Anderson, Innes Ireland and Jo Siffert succeeding in one or more events.

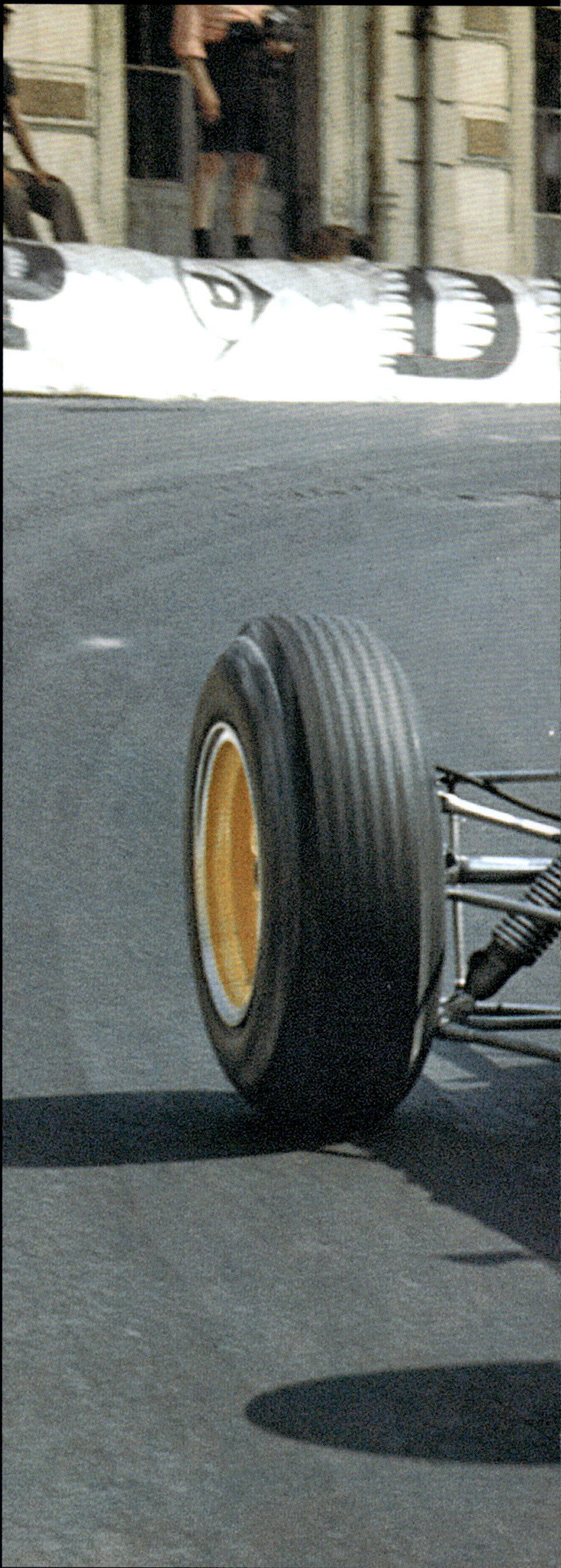

Colour co-ordinated: A lovely shot of Trevor Taylor's Lotus 25 (R5) as it exits the Station hairpin at Monaco, where he finished 6th. In contrast with Clark's almost metronomic consistency, Taylor's Team Lotus rides were characterised by every form of mechanical mishap and, all too frequently, major accidents not of his own making.

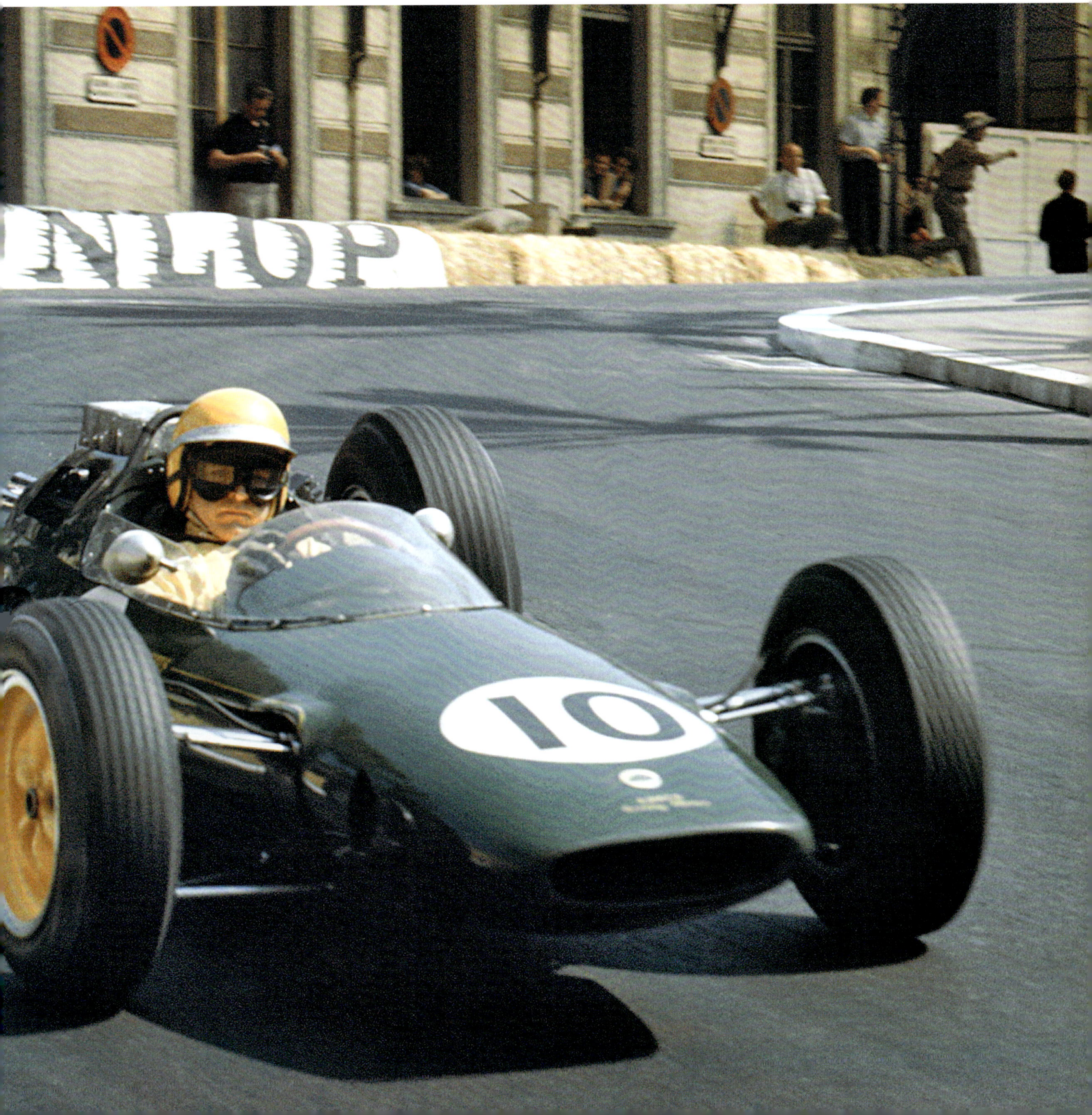

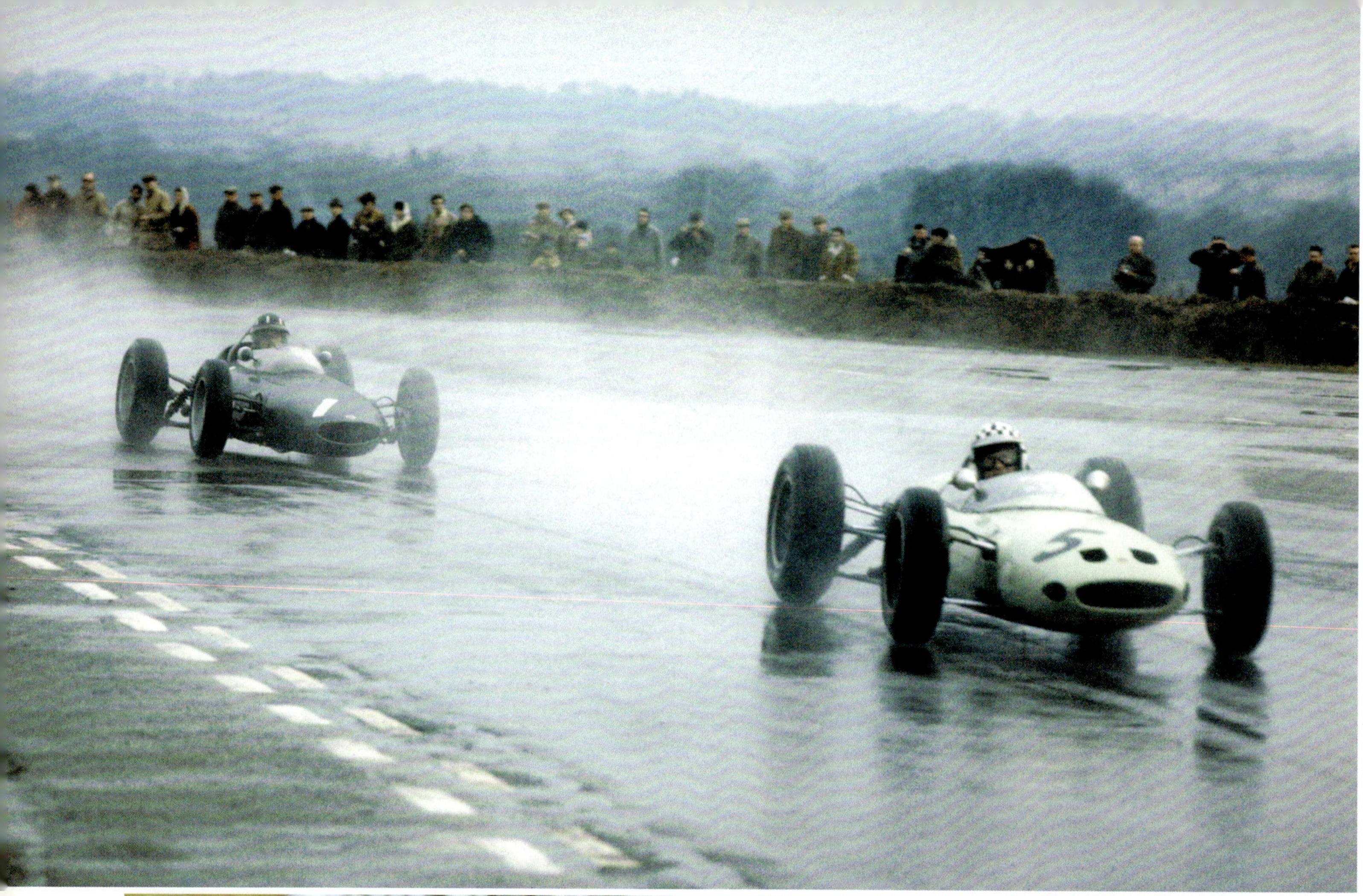

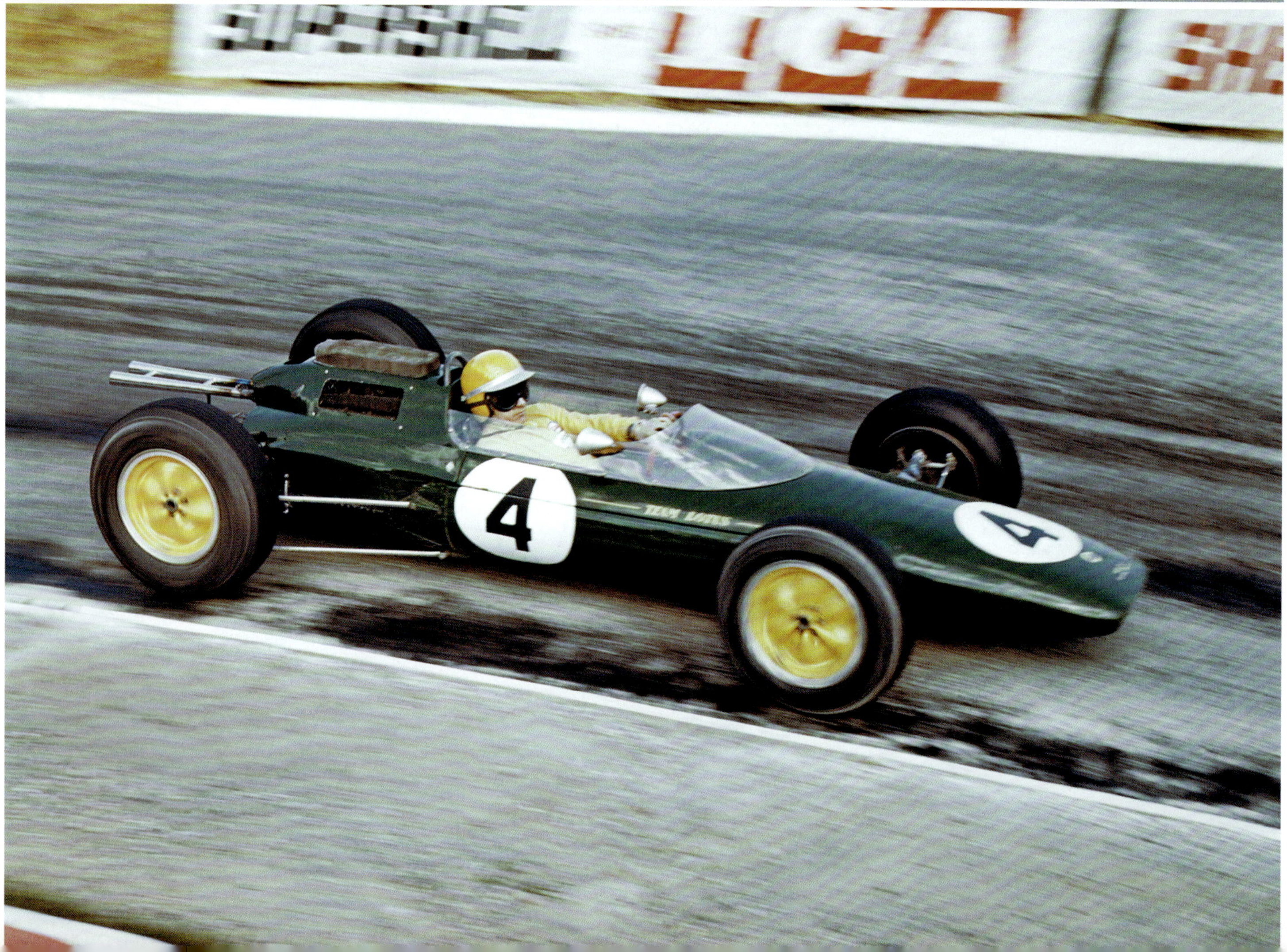

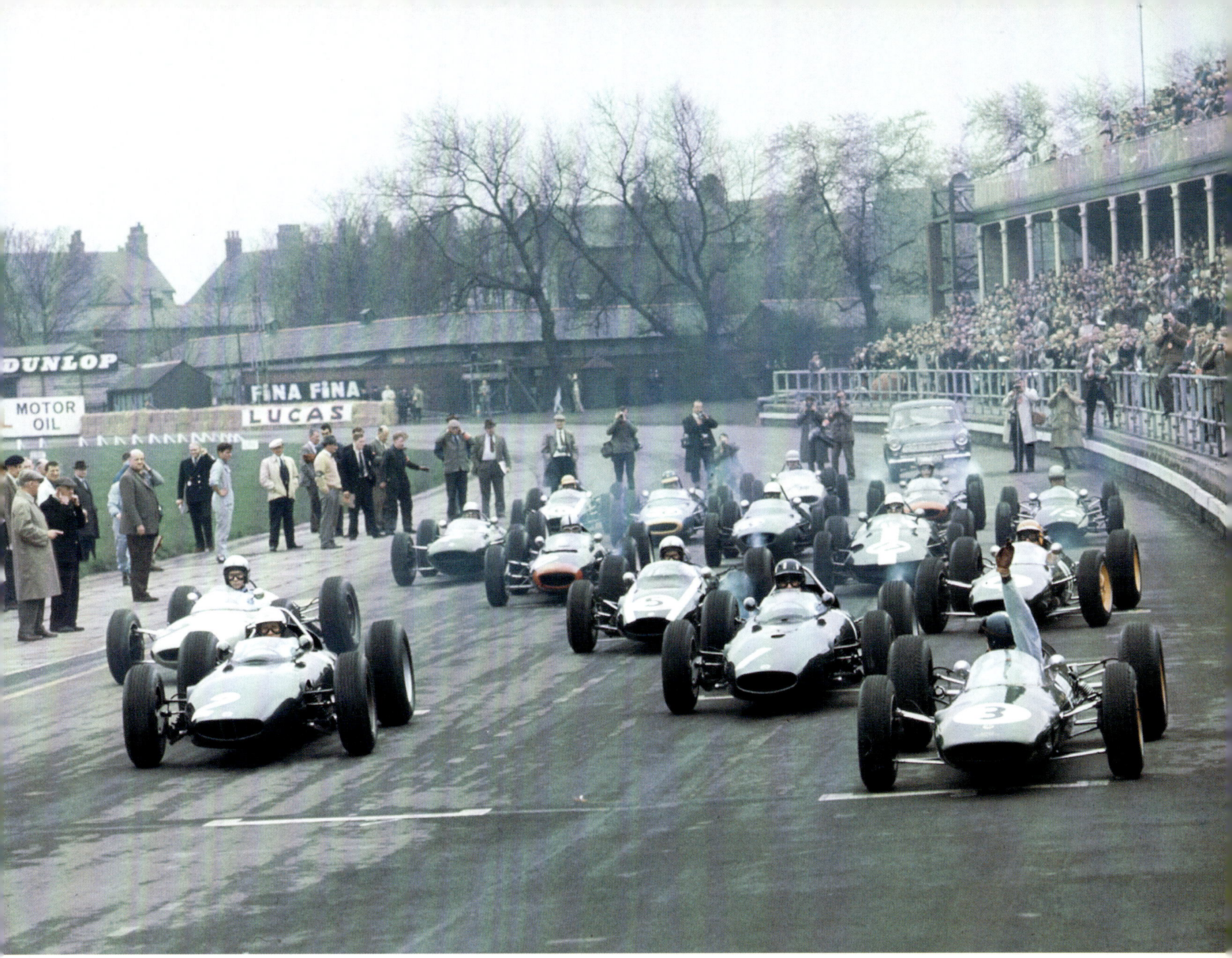

Please sir, I want to go! The naughtiest boy on the grid indicates that his Lotus 25 has a flat battery and cannot start the eighth Aintree 200 in late April. Jimmy Clark eventually got away over a lap adrift, and later Colin Chapman called in both cars, putting Clark in Trevor Taylor's sister car (seen here taking avoiding action). He then pulverised the lap record and finished 3rd behind Graham Hill (BRM P57) and Innes Ireland (Lotus 24) after 50 laps. Had the race been run over a full Grand Prix distance, Clark would have caught both of them. The empty space on the grid should have been occupied by Jack Brabham, but his engine had broken a piston. The photographers standing behind the grid are typical of the period, although not perhaps the Ford Cortina.

Formula 1 at Snetterton, Norfolk, and it is raining horizontally as Innes Ireland (BRP Lotus 24 BRM 944) tiptoes ahead of Graham Hill (BRM P57 5785). There were only ten starters and seven finishers, and Hill won a dismal race from Jim Clark (Lotus 25), with Ireland 3rd. The British Racing Partnership team was run by Ken Gregory and Alfred Moss, respectively Stirling's long-time manager and father. During 1961/62 they had been funded by United Dominion Trust (UDT Laystall) but they withdrew in 1963 as had the other finance houses Bowmaker and Yeoman Credit.

Trevor Taylor drove the Lotus 25 (R3) to finish a tenth of a second behind team leader Jim Clark in the 23rd Grand Prix de Pau in April. The 100-lap race lasted two hours and 47 minutes, a lifetime on this sinuous street circuit in south-west France, and the Lotus duo finished five laps clear of the rest. Despite the presence of Jo Bonnier, Jo Siffert and Maurice Trintignant, who all failed to finish, there was no effective competition. It must have been very boring to watch.

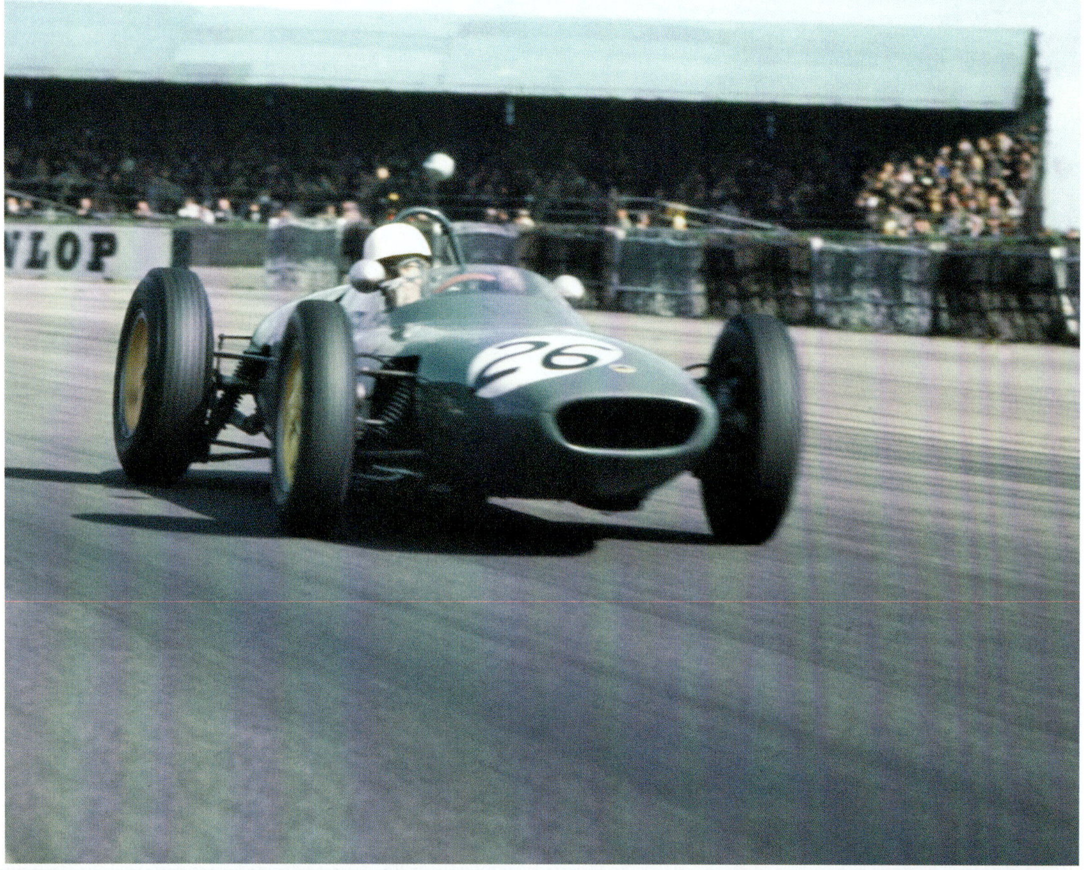

The International Trophy at Silverstone, like many such non-championship races of the time, tended to attract relatively unknown drivers. Here is Philip Robinson in the cockpit of an old Lotus 18/21 hybrid (904), entered by A. Robinson & Sons, that had started life in 1960 as a 'customer' car built by Lotus Components for Reg Parnell Racing. Robinson, who failed to finish here due to a broken crownwheel and pinion, also raced at Goodwood, Aintree and Solitude.

Jim Clark would surely have won all the 1963 Grands Prix but for niggling mechanical gremlins. At Monaco in the 25 (R4) he had gear selection problems after leading convincingly. This was not only due to his peerless driving skills but also the superiority of the 25 that put its power down better than its rivals and the stronger torque characteristics of the Climax FWMV compared to the BRM V8. This is Casino Square with the Hotel de Paris on the right and a collection of café furniture, bench and a metal sign casually occupying the centre pavement.

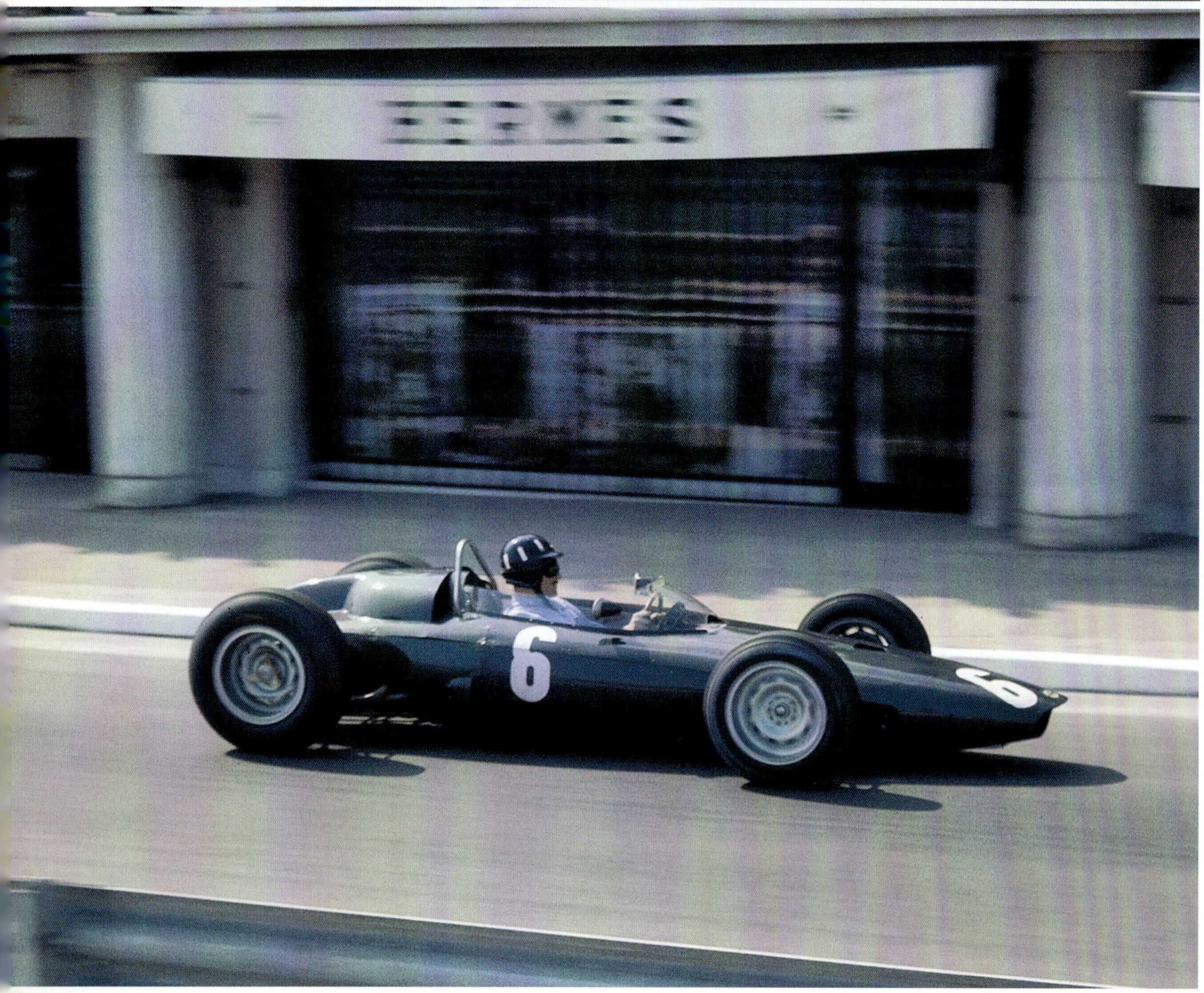

Graham Hill motors past the Hermes shop at the top of the hill leading into Casino Square. With BRM chassis 5785, known as the 'lightweight', he won the Monaco Grand Prix by 4.6 seconds ahead of team mate Richie Ginther – the first victory of a hat-trick sequence. However, Jim Clark had led for more than 60 laps but retired with gear selection problems

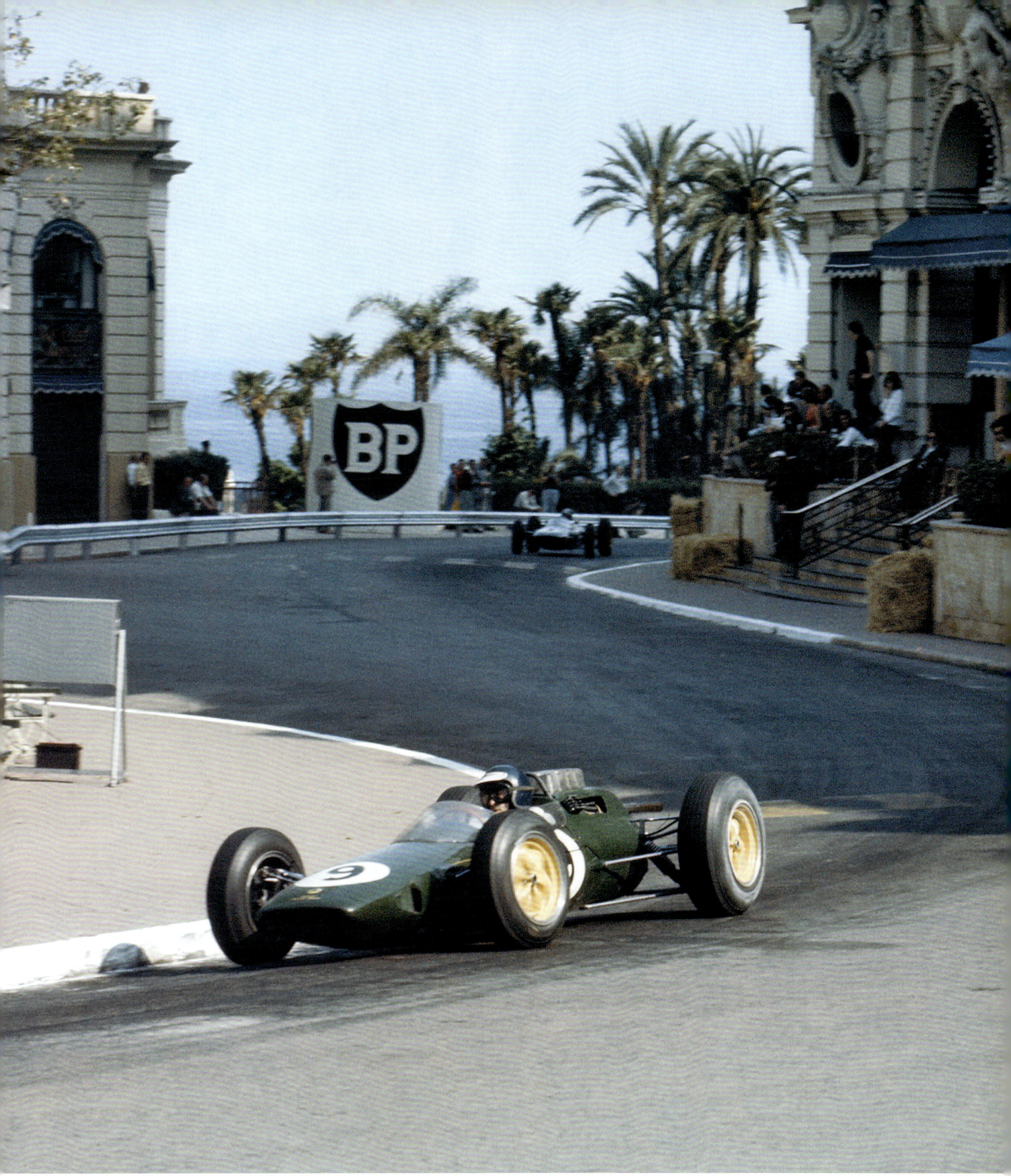
BP

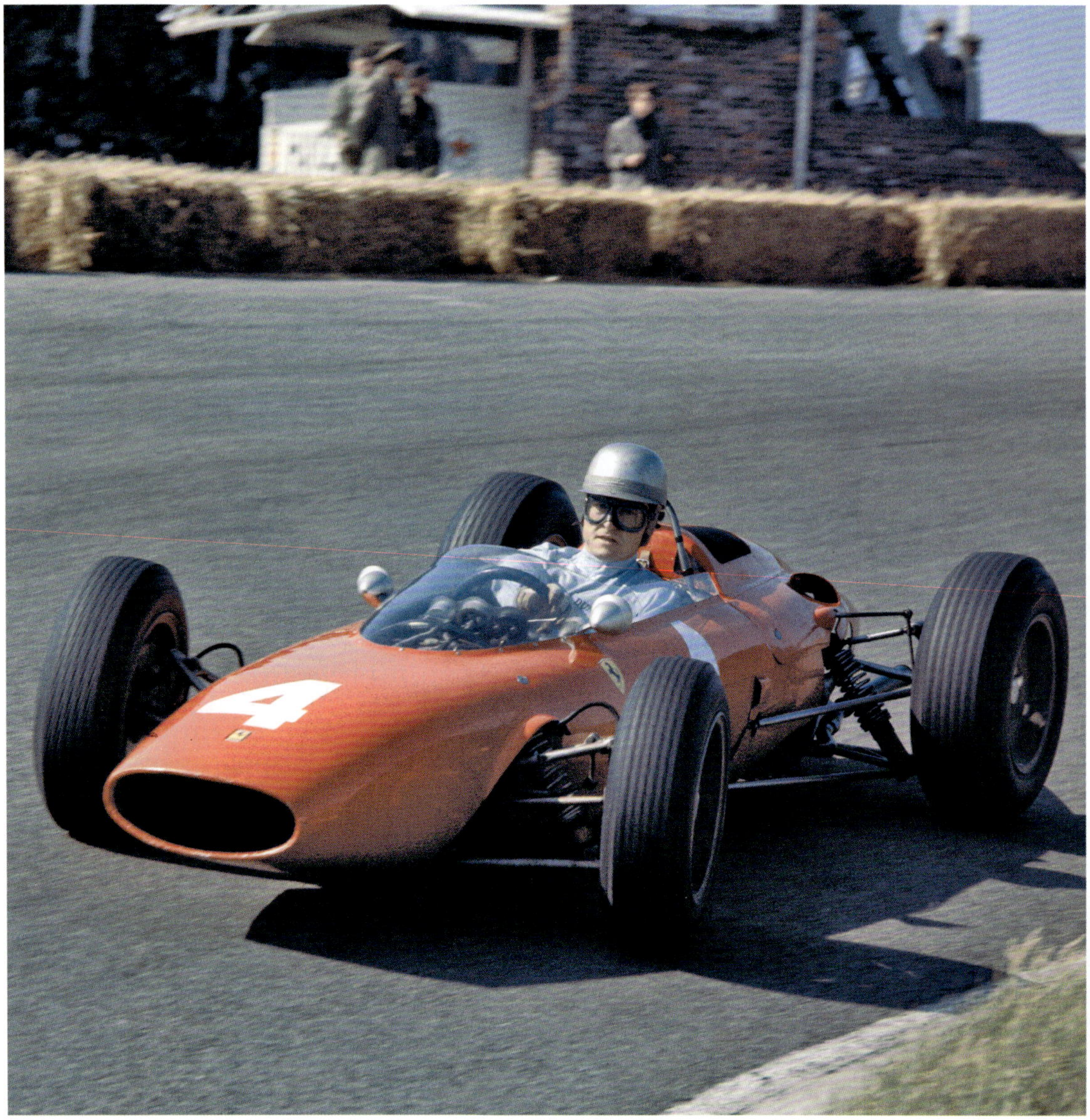

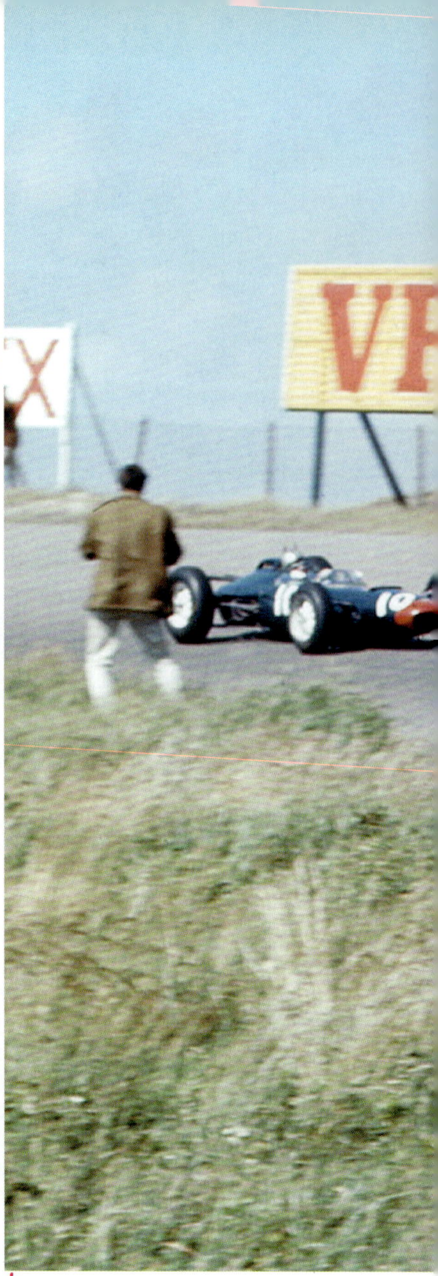

Ludovico Scarfiotti, nephew of Gianni Agnelli, chairman of Fiat, began racing in 1955. He made his F1 debut in 1963 for Ferrari at the Dutch GP, replacing the injured Mairesse who had sustained burns at Le Mans. He finished 6th in the Ferrari Dino 156 (0002), rebuilt after a Mairesse crash at Silverstone in May. Note the askew helmet, about as much use in an accident as a brown paper bag.

Richie Ginther (BRM P57 5784), Dan Gurney (Brabham BT7 F1-1-63), Jo Bonnier (Cooper T60 F1-18-61) and Chris Amon (Lola 4A BRGP 44) in formation at Zandvoort. Ginther finished 5th, his car using a new 6-speed gearbox, Gurney 2nd despite a pit stop, Bonnier 11th and Amon in only his third Grand Prix retired. Clark who had recently dominated the wet Belgian GP won by over a lap.

Out of the frying pan into the fire. Having endured a demoralising 1962 season Phil Hill and Giancarlo Baghetti decided to throw in their lot with the newly formed ATS (Automobili Turismo e Sport) team fronted by ex-Ferrari engineer Carlo Chiti and sporting director Romolo Tavoni. It was funded by Count Giovanni Volpi di Misurata founder of Scuderia Serinissima di Venezia. Sadly it terminally undermined their careers. The cars were underpowered, fragile and very badly designed (the frame had to be unwelded to get the 4-cam V8 engine out). It's hard to believe that the chief personnel were all ex-Ferrari having resigned on principle over the behaviour of Enzo's disagreeable and interfering wife Laura. At the Dutch GP both cars qualified poorly and retired early on (Hill is shown here in ATS 100 01).The rest of the year was no better and the team folded after the Mexican GP, although a much modified Alf Francis version designated Derrington-Francis-ATS ran unsuccessfully at Monza in 1964.

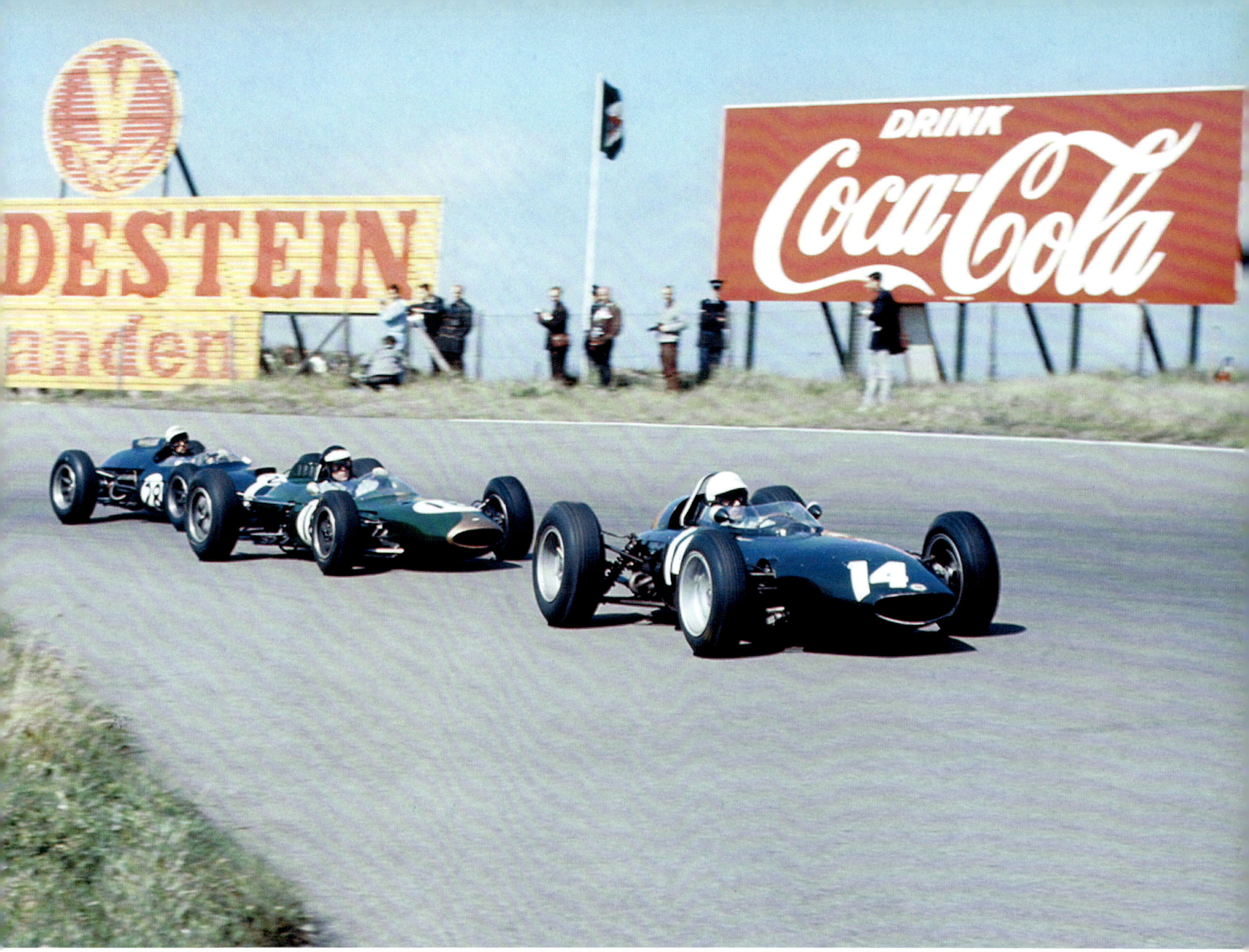
DESTEIN
anden
DRINK
Coca-Cola
14

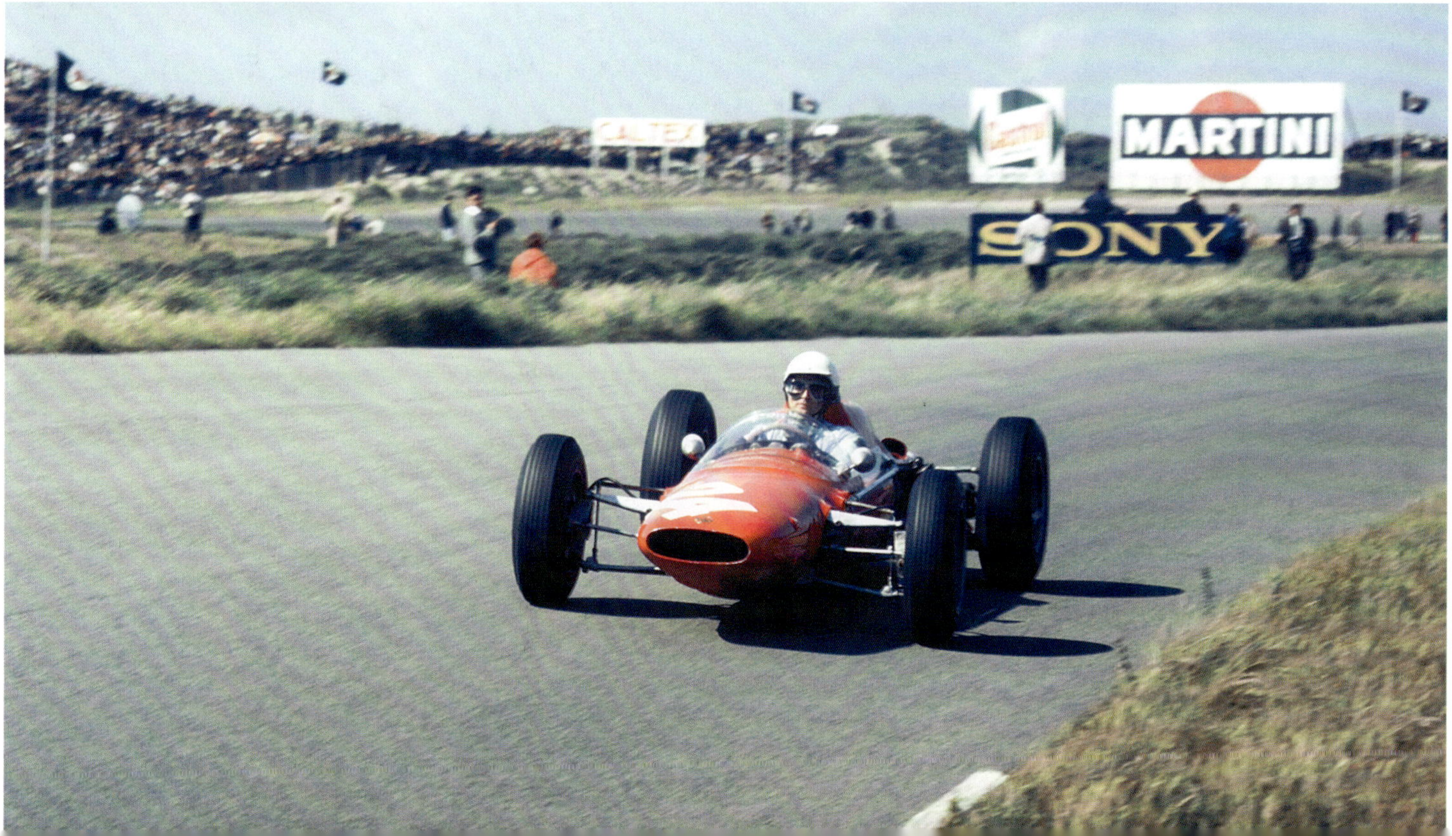
CALTEX
Castrol
MARTINI
SONY

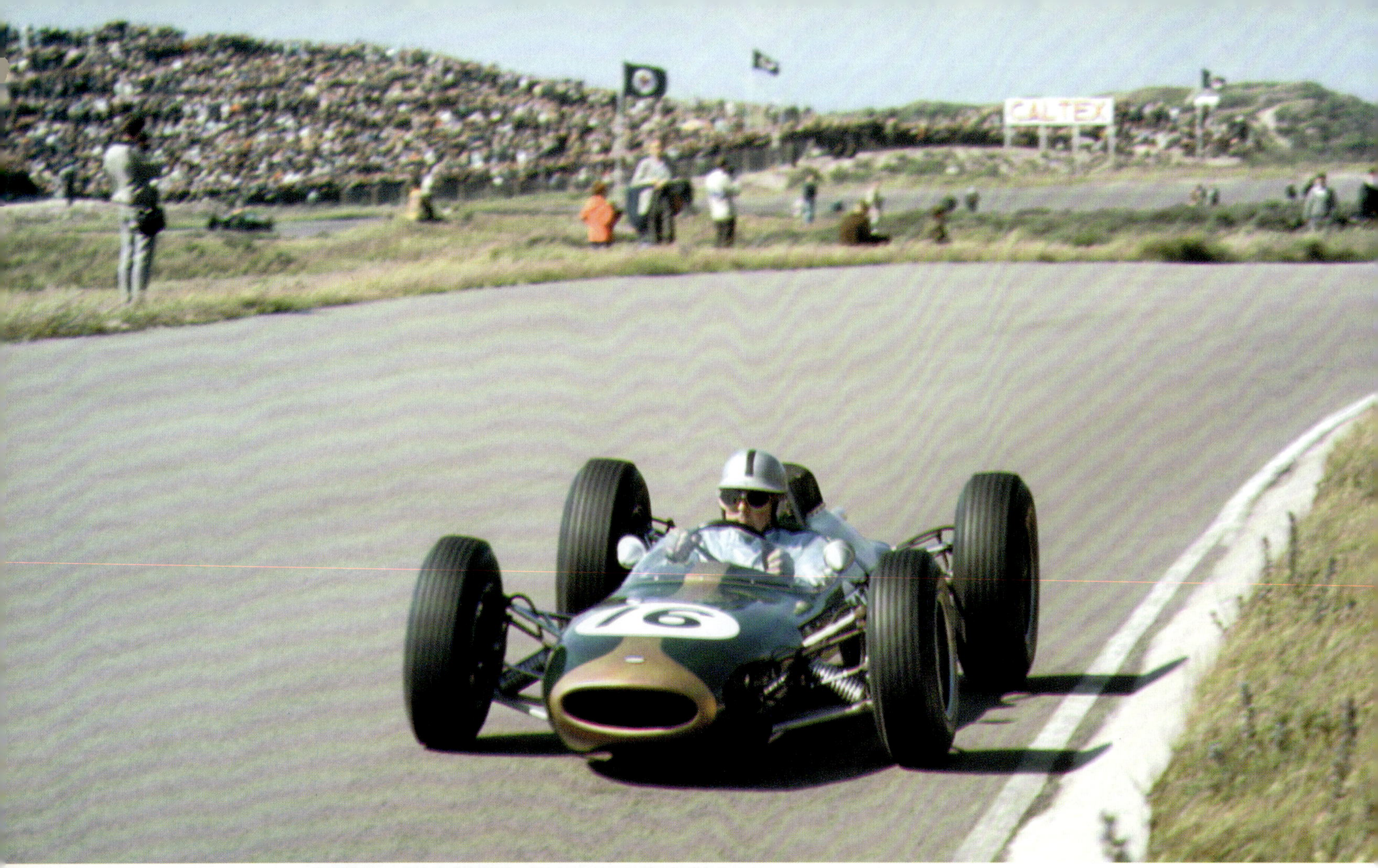

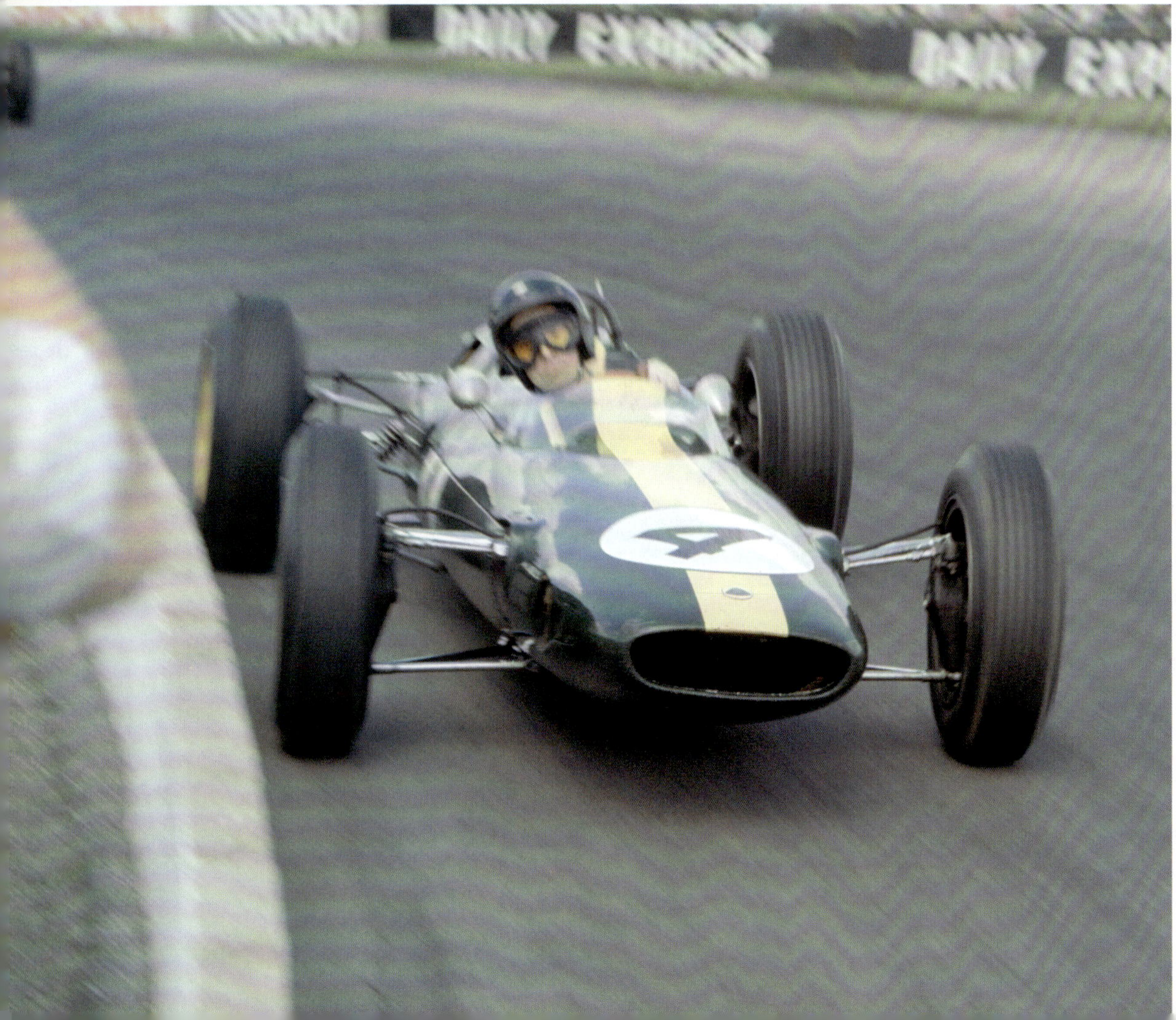

↑ Throw out the anchor! Look at the front suspension compression as Brabham hits those brakes hard in the Brabham BT7 Climax (F1-2-63), now finished in the familiar Australian dark green. Starting from row two at Zandvoort he held 2nd place, but a throttle return spring broke at wide open and he had to get back to the pits by alternatively turning the engine on and off. His progress became a series of violent lunges, running off the road twice and breaking the car's chassis.

← With Jim Clark winning the French GP at Reims, the rest of the players must have been getting desperate by the time the British GP at Silverstone (July 20 1963) arrived. Here Clark, in a blur of speed, does it again in his regular 25 (R4) winning by 25.8 seconds after easing off, although at one point he was 50 seconds ahead.

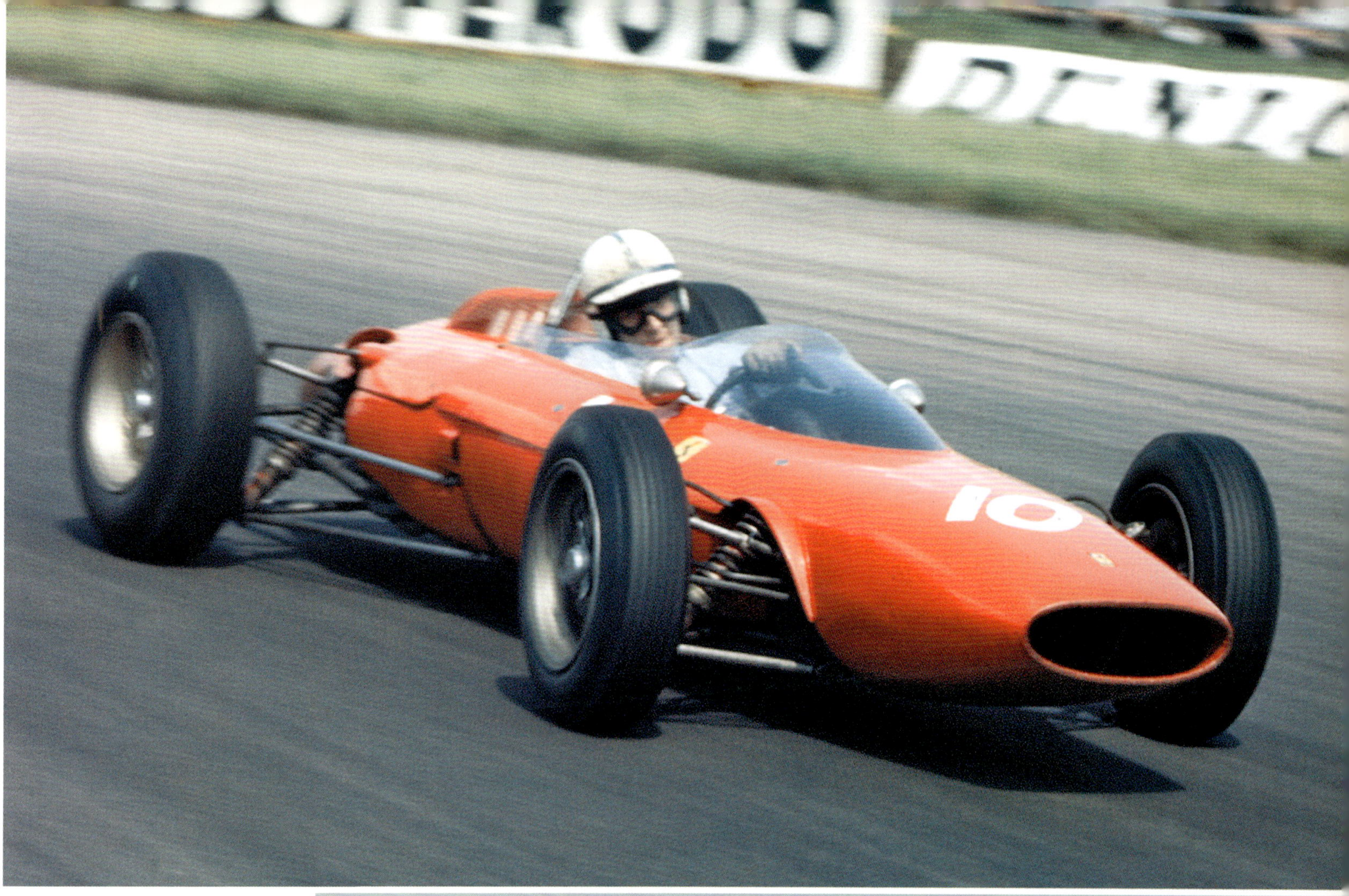

↑ John Surtees finished 2nd at Silverstone in the Ferrari Dino 156/63 0003, setting fastest race lap. Yet again Ferrari entered only a single car for the British GP and Surtees finished ahead of Hill whose BRM started to run out of fuel despite being brimmed at the start.

→ Instantly recognisable by his black helmet, Dan Gurney thunders over the Silverstone tarmac in his Brabham BT7 (F1-1-63). Gurney started second on the grid and, at first, raced second to Jim Clark, but his engine blew up. Jack Brabham's BT7 also expired, adding to the team's appalling record of Coventry Climax failures. Afterwards, Brabham's rev-counter telltale registered 9800rpm, Gurney's 9700: the engines were meant to be safe to 10,000.

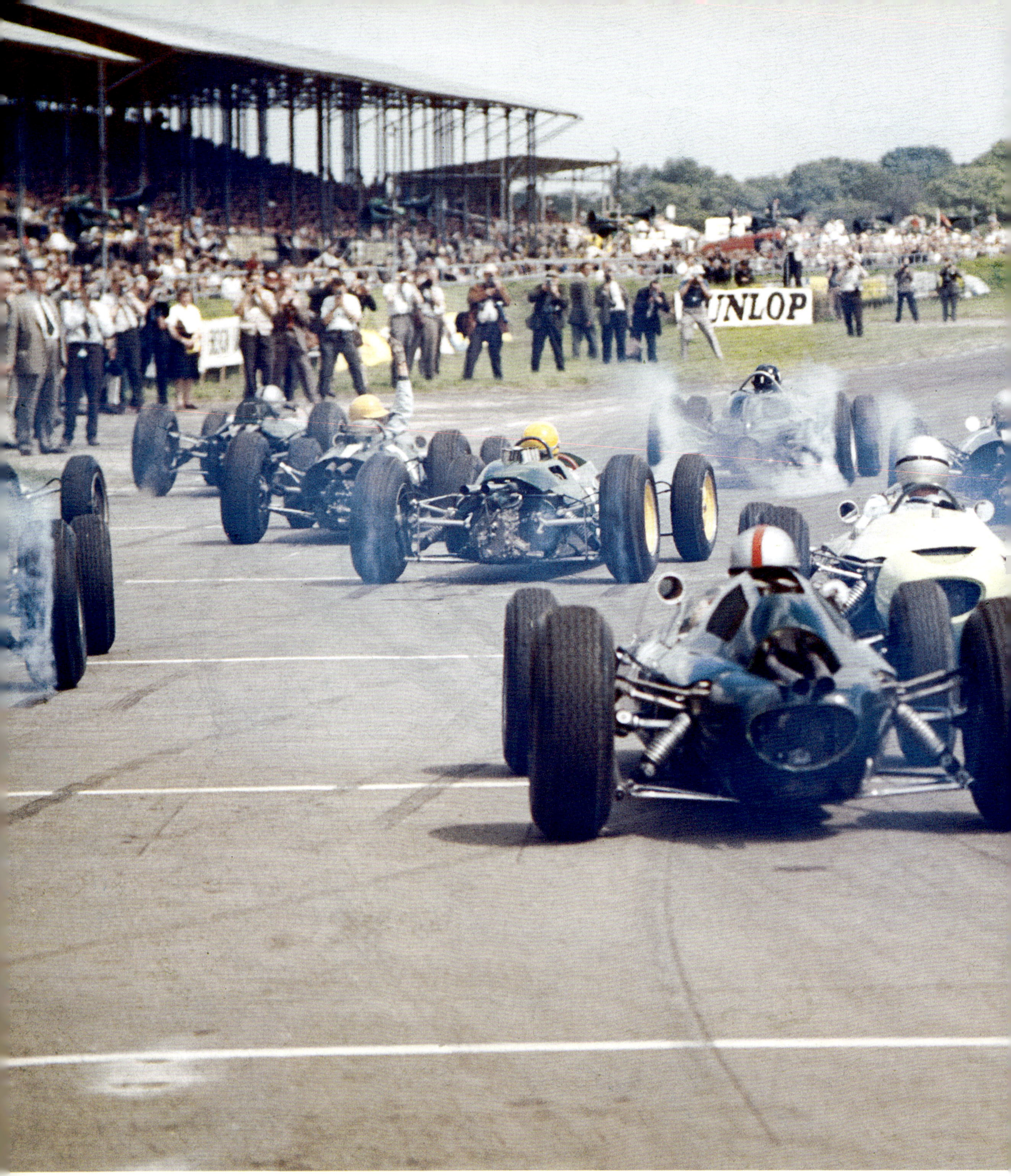
UNLOP

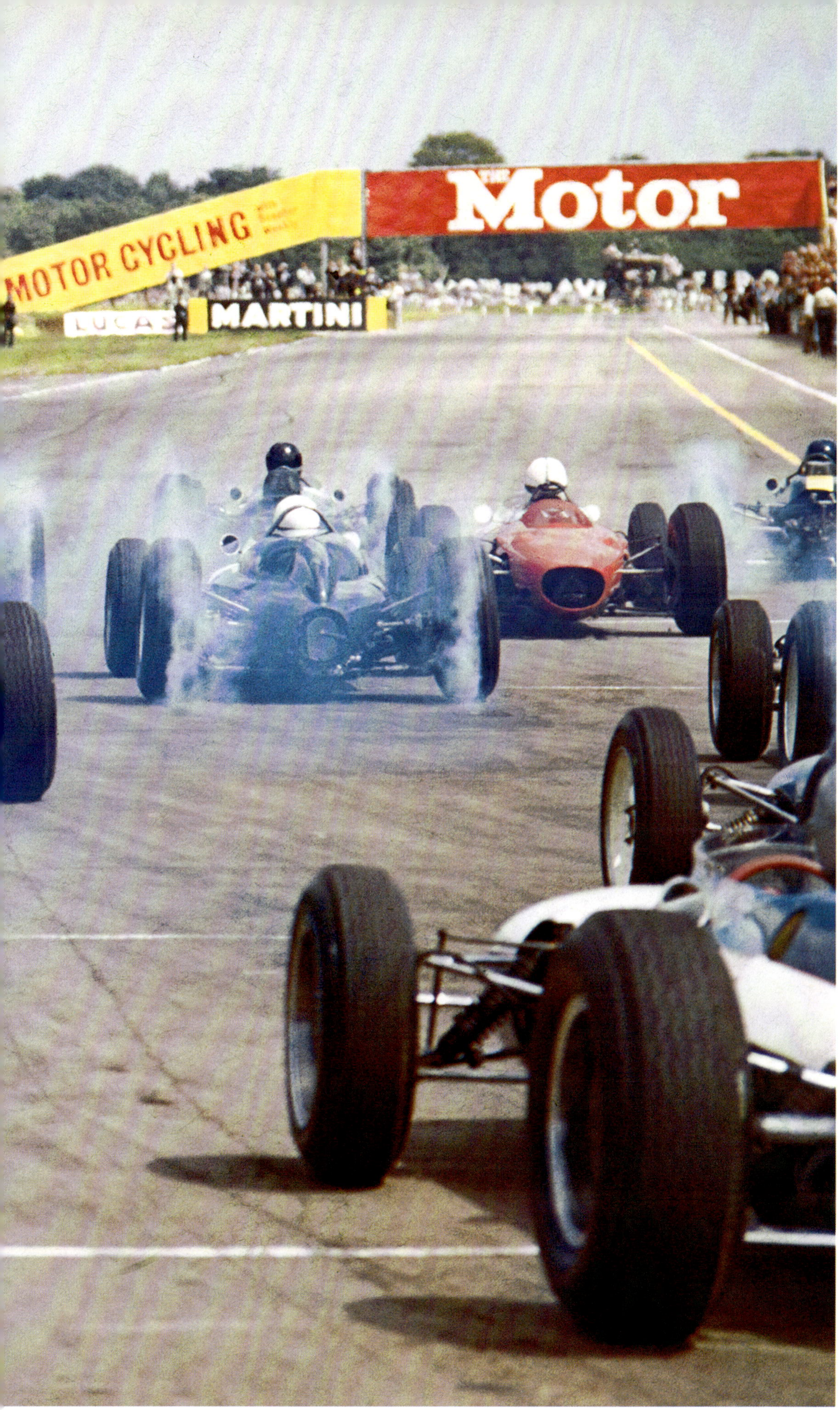

On no account show this Michael Cooper picture to the Health & Safety brigade. Sound, fury, spinning tyres and totally exposed persons. This then was motor racing and once again if you look carefully there are people walking away, backs turned on the action. On the left can be seen Tony Maggs (Cooper), arm up to indicate he has stalled whilst to his right is the other yellow helmet of Trevor Taylor (Lotus) taking avoiding action. At the front left Hill seems determined to set fire to his BRM's tyres whilst Clark on the right is similarly disposed. The car dead centre is Hailwood's Parnell Racing Lotus 24 (943, ex-UDT Laystall) whilst the partially obscured machine on the far right is Ian Burgess in one of the ill-fated Sciroccos.

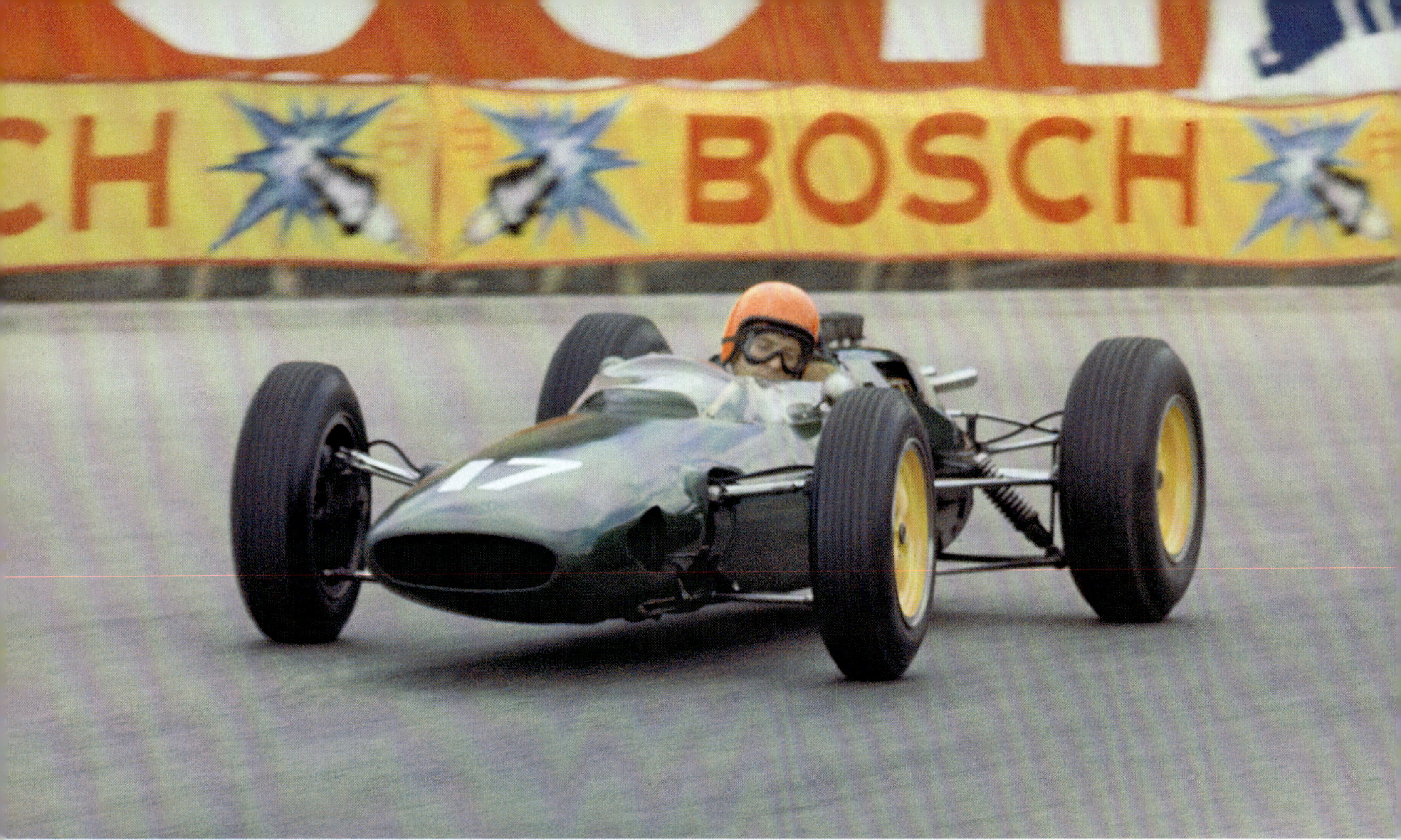

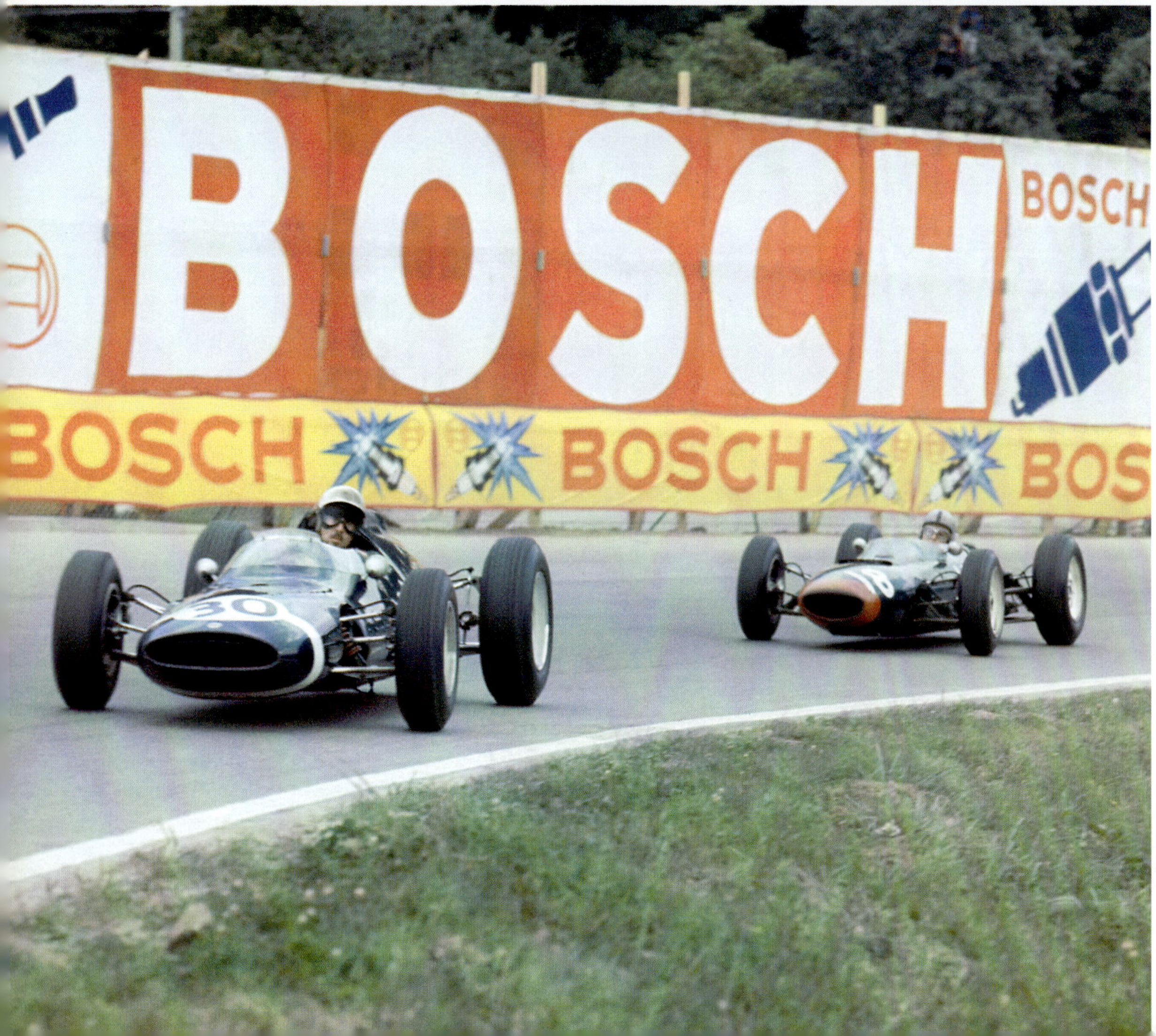

The non-championship Solitude race attracted a big field but *sans* BRM and Ferrari. Peter Arundell drove the Lotus 25 (R2) in his second F1 race (he had competed in the 1962 Reims race and practised but did not start in the 1963 French GP). Alas, the talented Arundell spent too long in Formula Junior where he reigned almost supreme with Lotus in 1962/3. He finished 2nd behind Jack Brabham after Clark suffered drive shaft failure at the start and Trevor Taylor retired.

Jo Bonnier's Rob Walker Cooper T60 (F1-18-61) displays a significant amount of body roll as he is chased by Chris Amon in the Parnell Racing Lola 4A (BRGP 44) at Solitude. Despite starting on the front row Bonnier faded to 9th whilst Amon's car ran its bearings after only six laps.

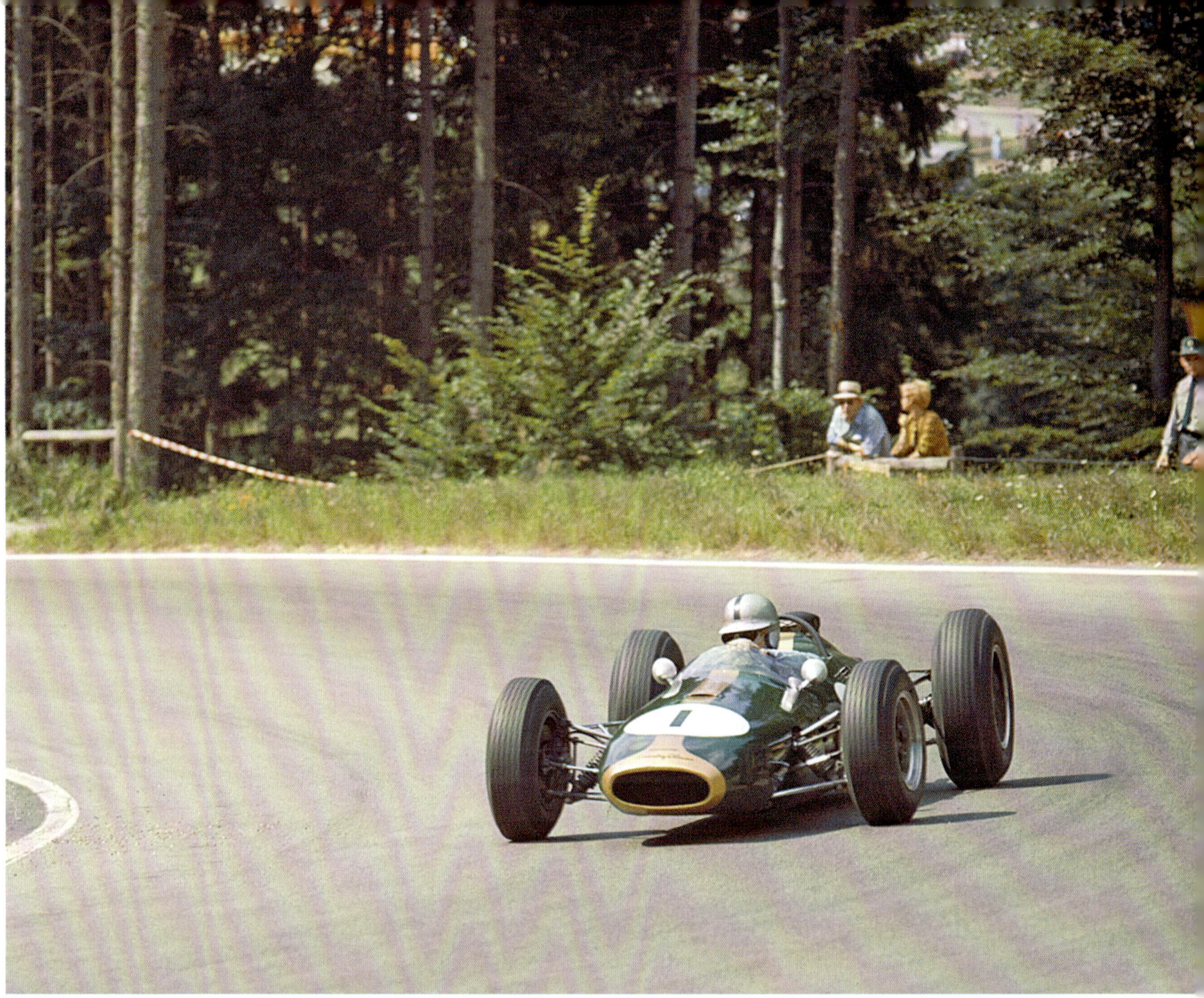

With both BT7s out of commission following the British GP, Jack Brabham entered the old BT3 for Solitude and promptly won. It was the team's first ever F1 victory, albeit in a non-championship race.

Looking almost as youthful as the autograph hunting schoolboy Jim Clark signs his name for a young admirer in the Solitude paddock.

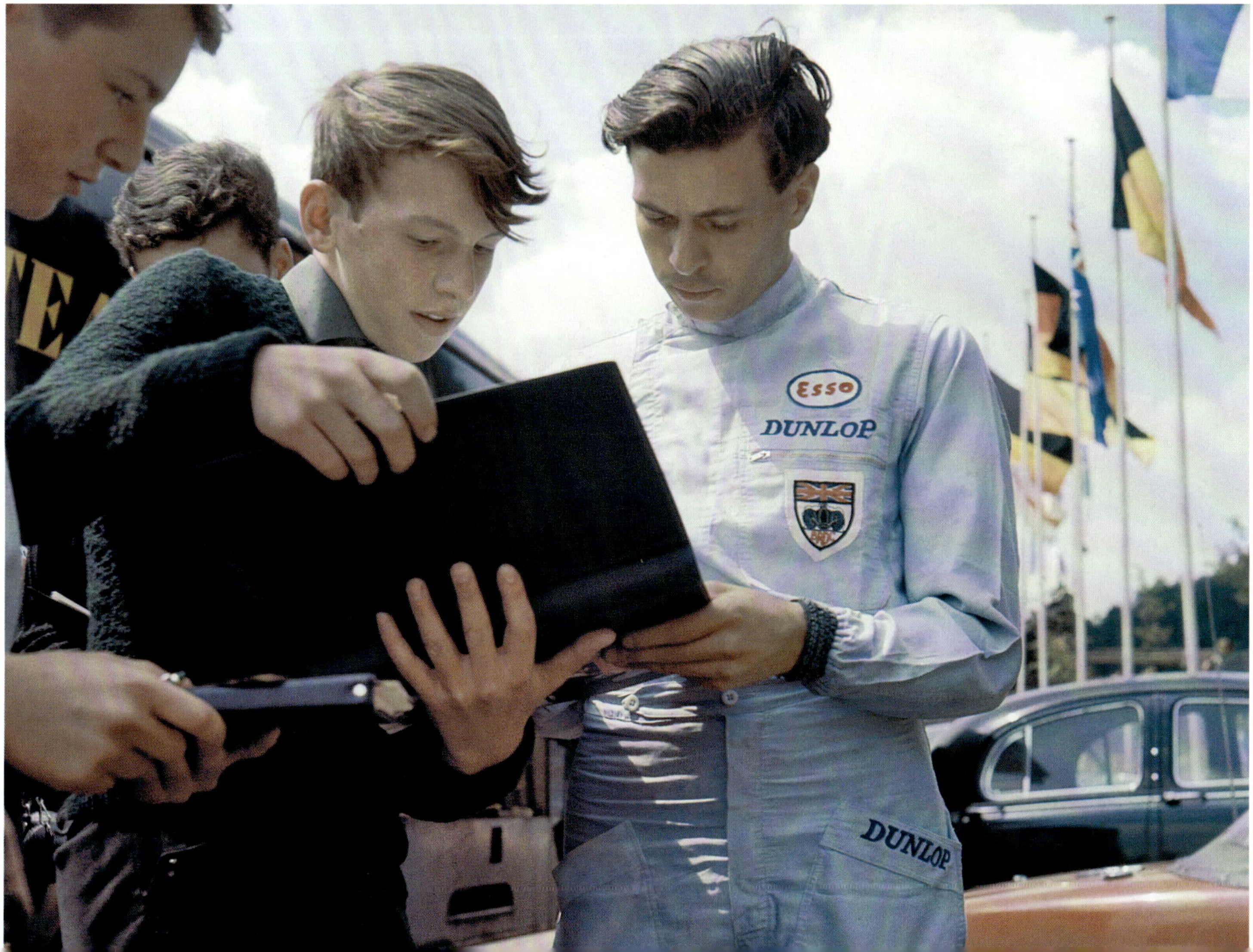

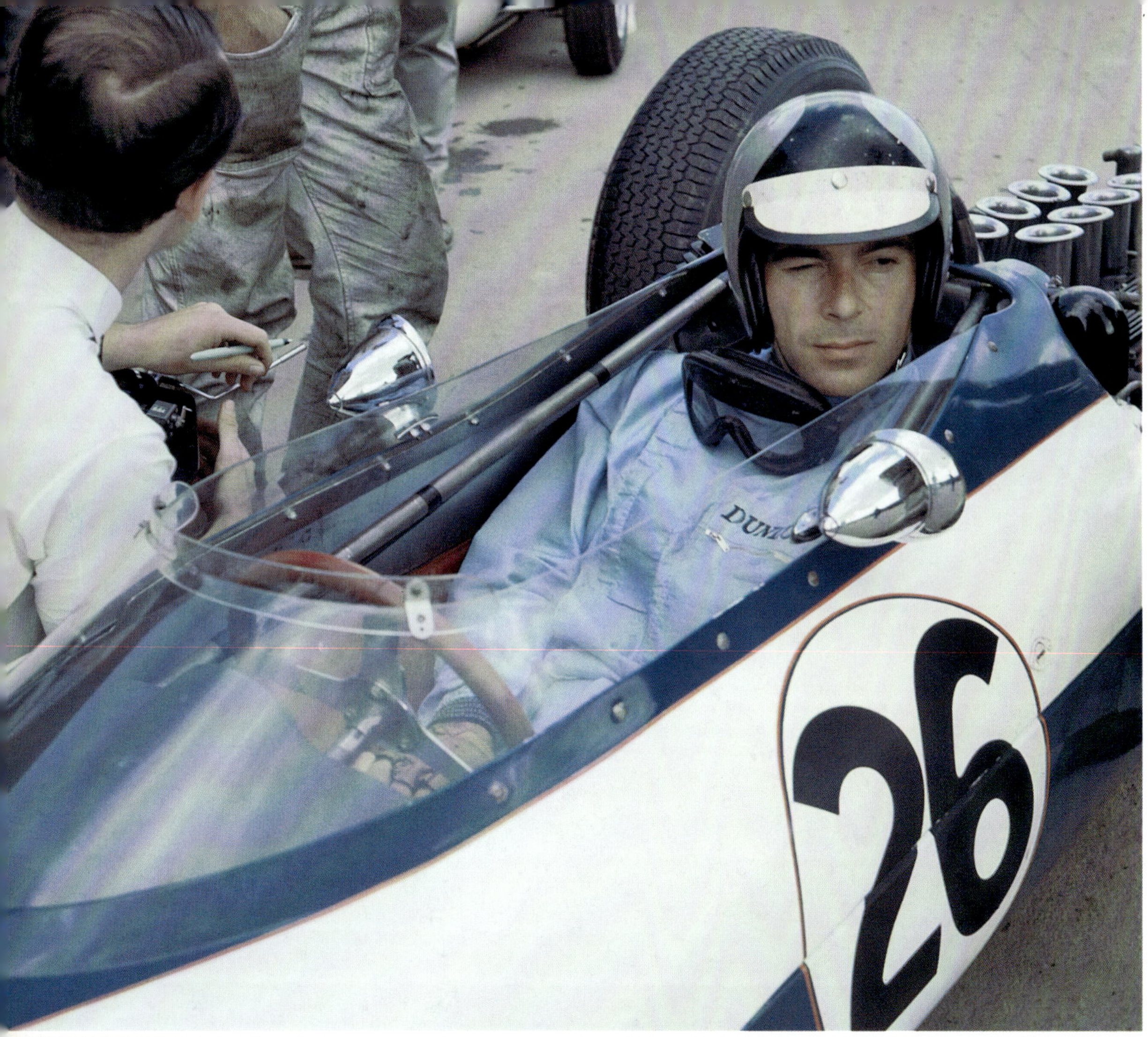

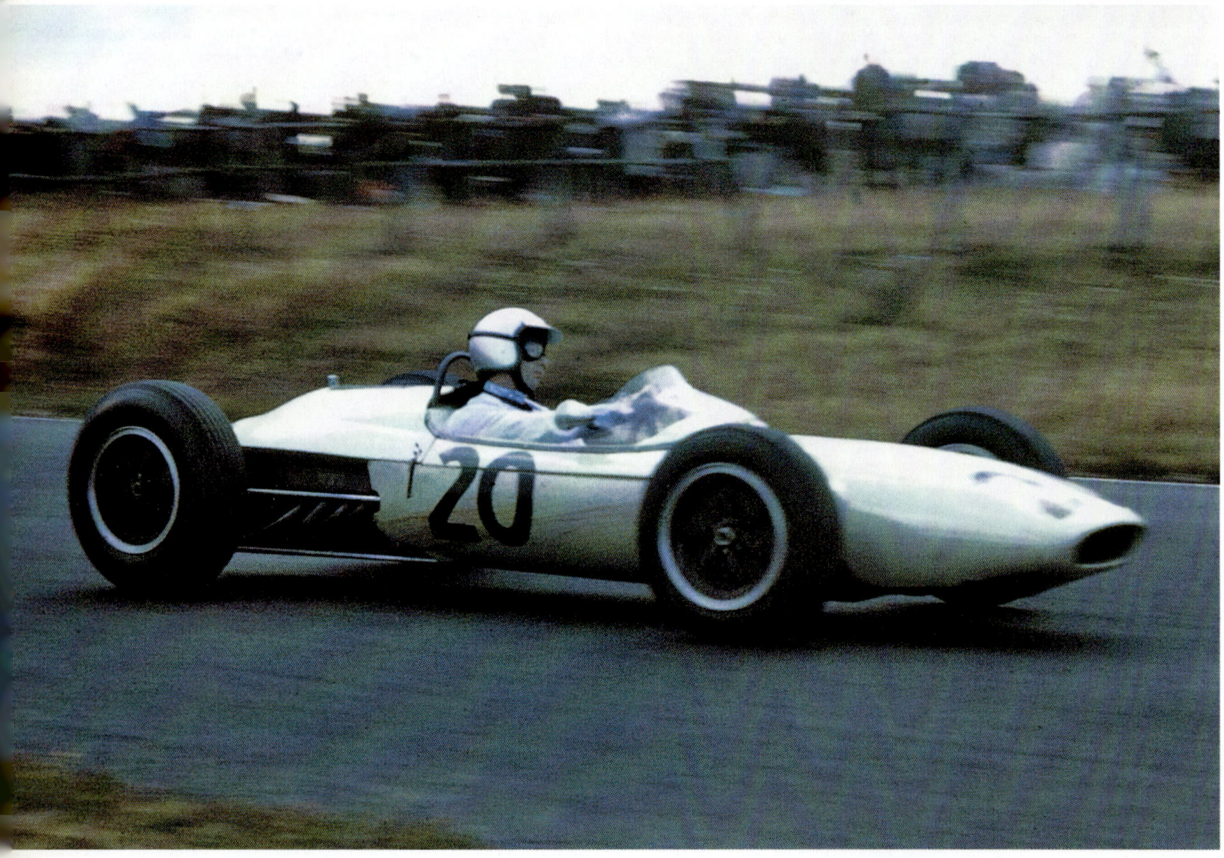

Tony Settember, Italian-American sports car racer was the guardian of his wealthy young friend Hugh Powell and persuaded him to finance his F1 career. Settember drove an Emeryson in the 1962 British and Italian GPs and then for 1963 a whole new team and cars based on the 1962 Emeryson were created, known as Scirocco Powell (Racing Cars) and using BRM V8 engines. The team was located behind a public house in Goldhawk Road, West London. Driven by Settember and Ian Burgess, they were never competitive, partly due to lack of development, and Hugh Powell withdrew after the Oulton Park Gold Cup in September. One car reappeared with a Climax V8 engine driven by André Pilette in 1964.

Graham Hill in his regular chassis 5785 won the US Grand Prix at Watkins Glen from team mate Richie Ginther, but only after John Surtees's Ferrari suffered an engine breakage near the end of the race. Jim Clark, who had just blitzed the Italian Grand Prix and the Oulton Park Gold Cup, was delayed at the start when a faulty fuel pressure pump caused a flat battery. Here Hill leads Ginther, Surtees and the rest on the first lap.

Tall man, small car. Jim Hall dwarfs the BRP team's Lotus 24 BRM (945) at the German Grand Prix that was won by John Surtees in the Ferrari Dino ahead of Clark's misfiring Lotus 25. Hall was very successful in American sports car racing, but his Formula 1 sorties were unconvincing, due to uncompetitive machinery and his unfamiliarity with the European circuits. Having raced in the 1961 and 1962 US Grands Prix, he undertook a full 1963 season with BRP, his best result a 5th here in Germany. He then quit Formula 1 and returned to Texas to build his innovative Chaparral sports-racing cars.

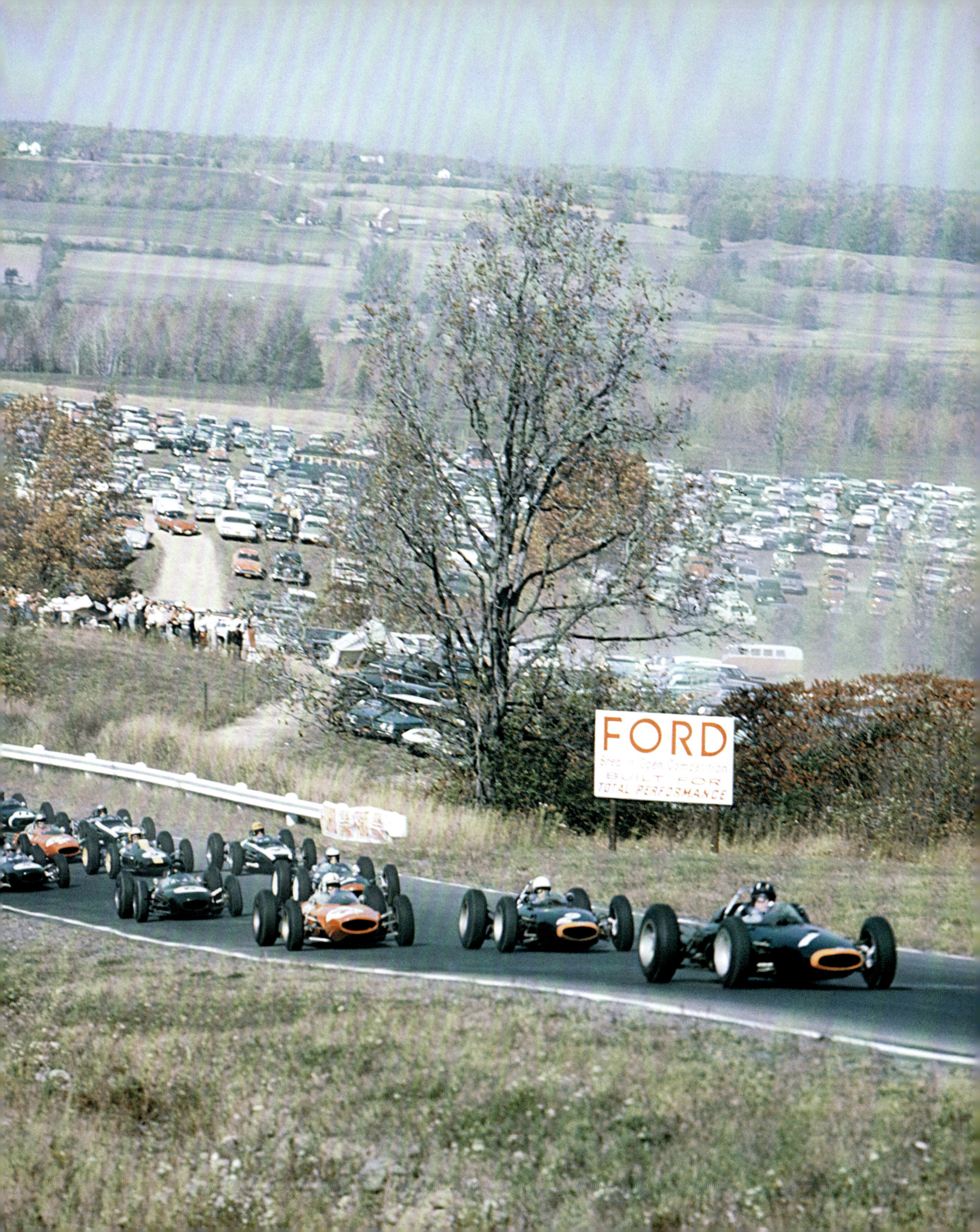
FORD
BUILT FOR
TOTAL PERFORMANCE

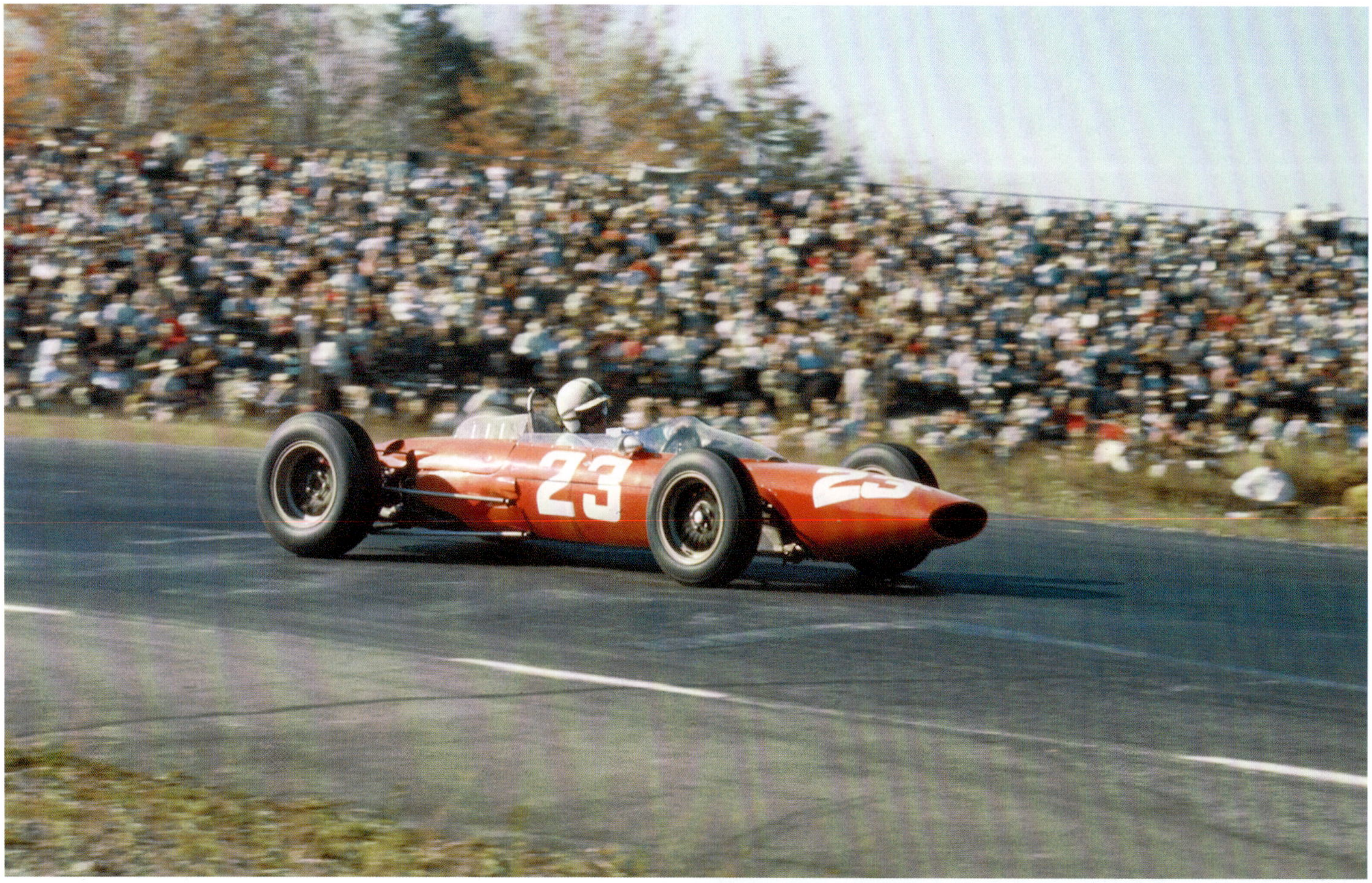

Only three of these Ferrari Dino 156/63s were built using the 120-degree V6 engine. This is chassis 0003 driven mainly by John Surtees and twice by Mairesse who crashed it in Germany. It was rebuilt as a spare car and used by Surtees at Watkins Glen. He was able to hold his own against everybody during the season bar the quicker Clark/Lotus 25 combination and won the German GP beating Clark's misfiring Lotus. At Watkins Glen he was on his way to victory until a broken valve spring spelt *finis* having spent nearly half the race dicing with Graham Hill.

Jim Clark won the Mexican GP by 101 seconds in the Lotus 25 (R4) from Brabham and Ginther. Total domination in F1 is nothing new. He leaves the line wreathed in tyre smoke alongside Surtees (Ferrari 156 Dino) who was disqualified for a push start on lap 19.

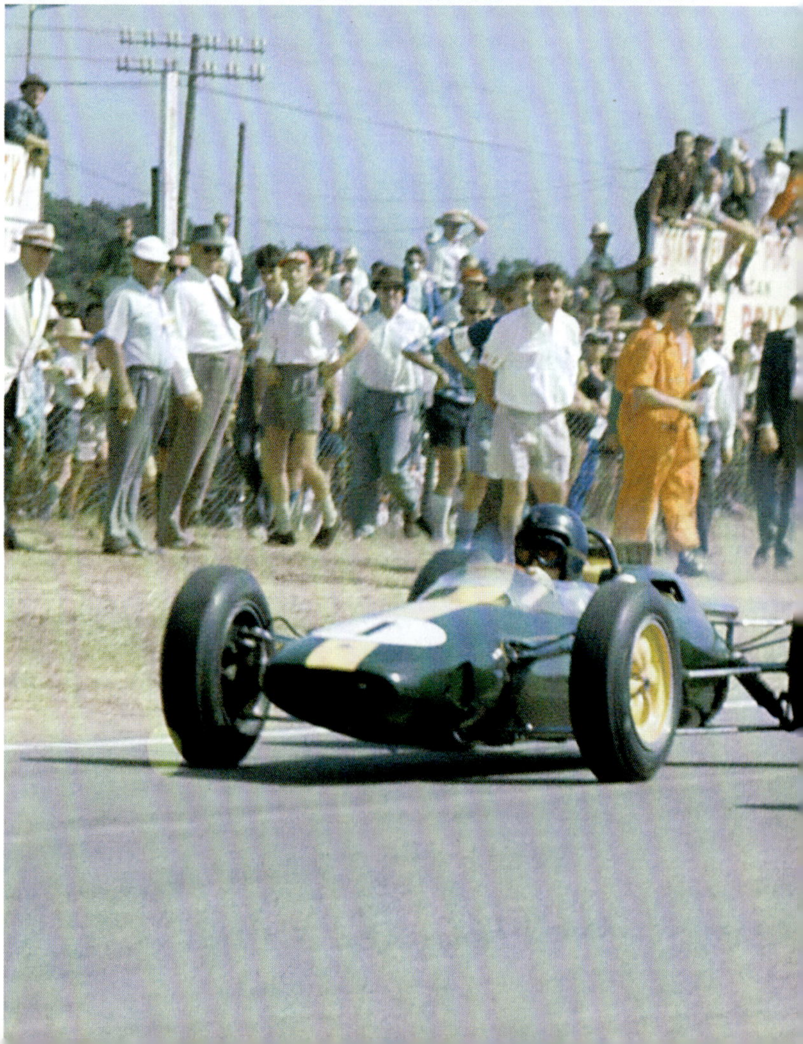

Having won the Mexican GP, the Scotsman turned up to take his seventh and final Grand Prix victory of the year in South Africa at East London. Sharing the front row with Clark's Lotus 25 (R4) are Brabham's BT7 (F1-2-63) and Gurney's BT7 (F1-1-63) whilst behind are the two monocoque 'Aero' Ferraris (first seen at Monza) of Surtees and Bandini. Gurney finished 2nd, the only driver not to be lapped, with Graham Hill's BRM 3rd.

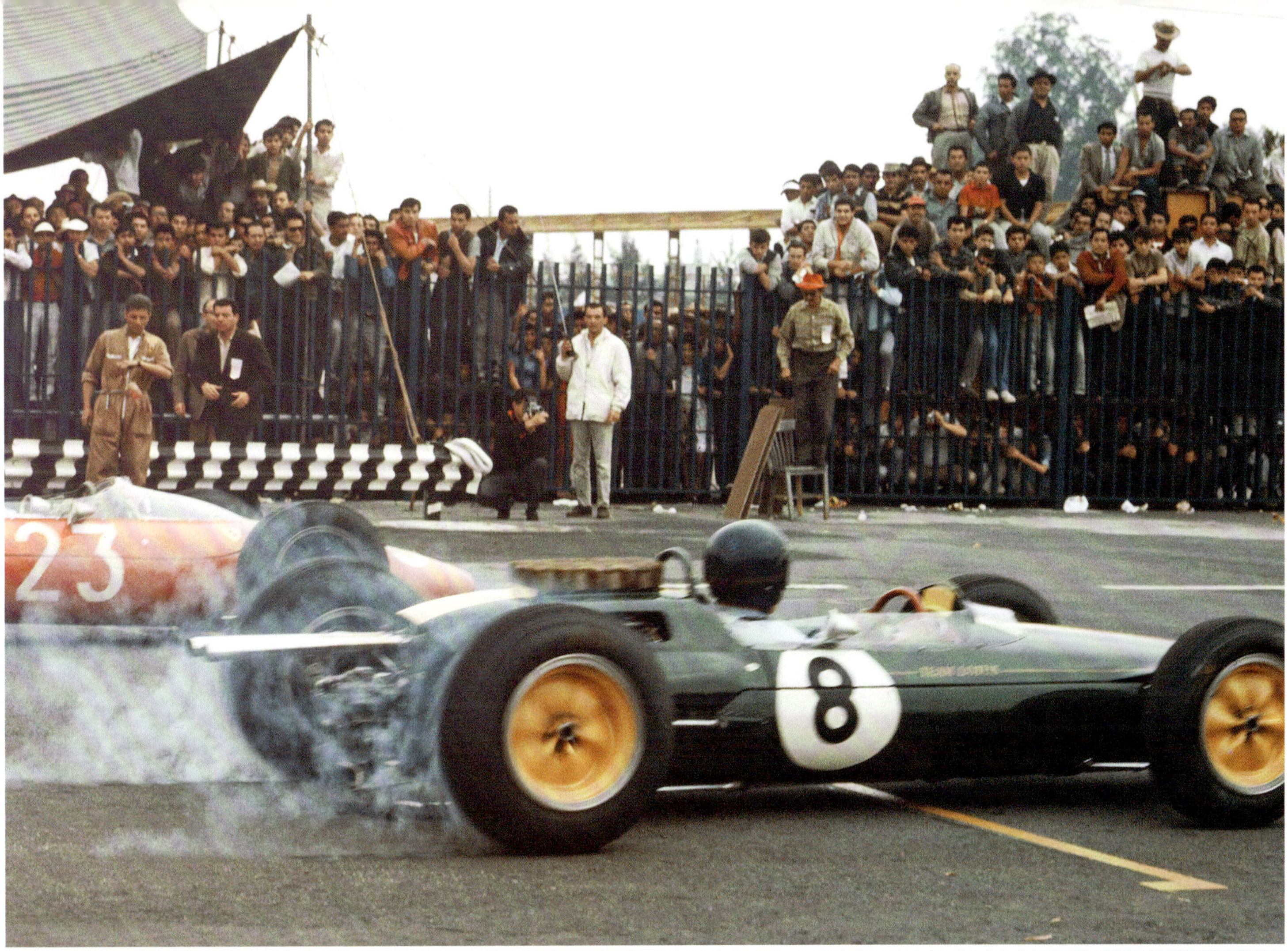

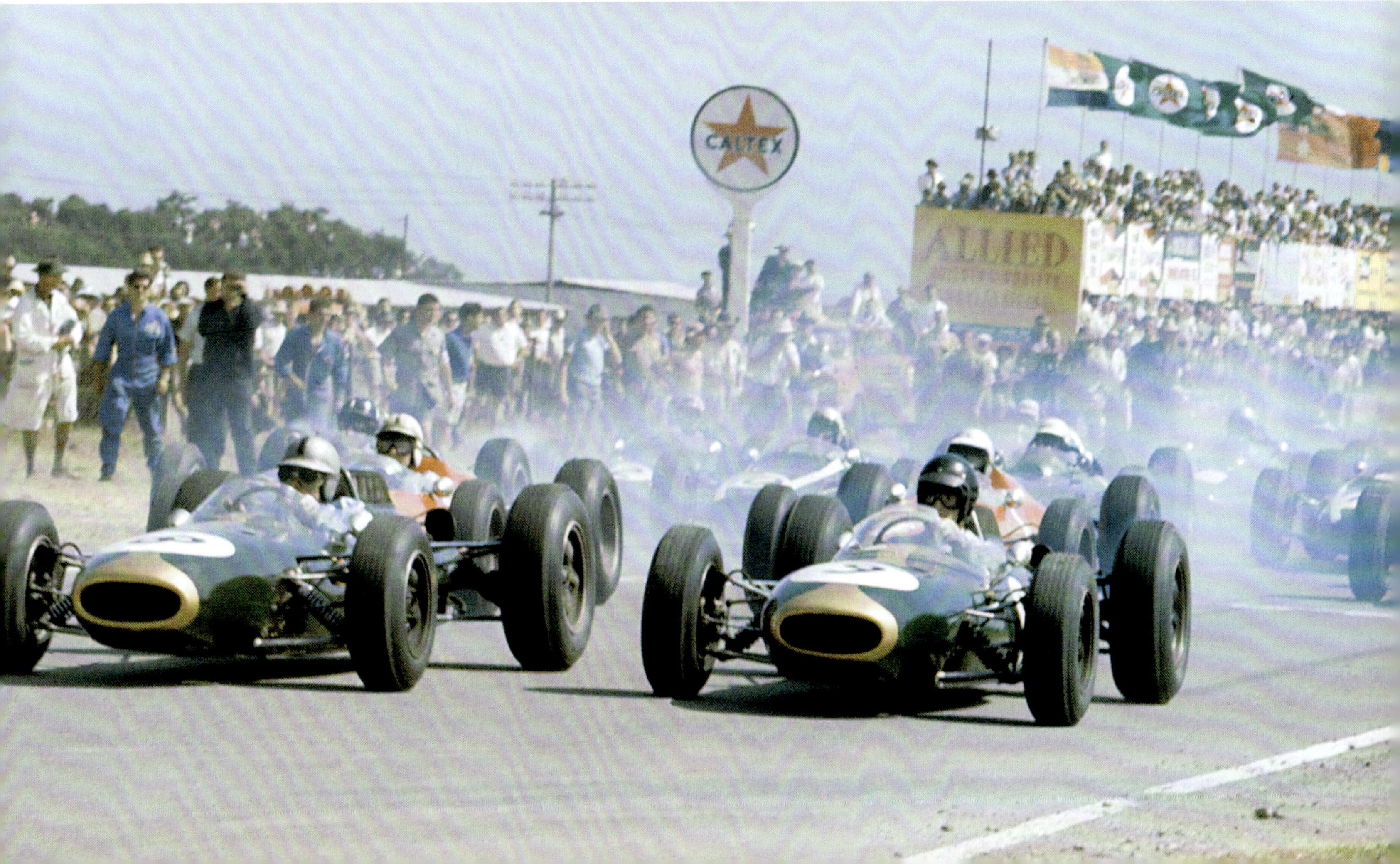
CALTEX
ALLIED

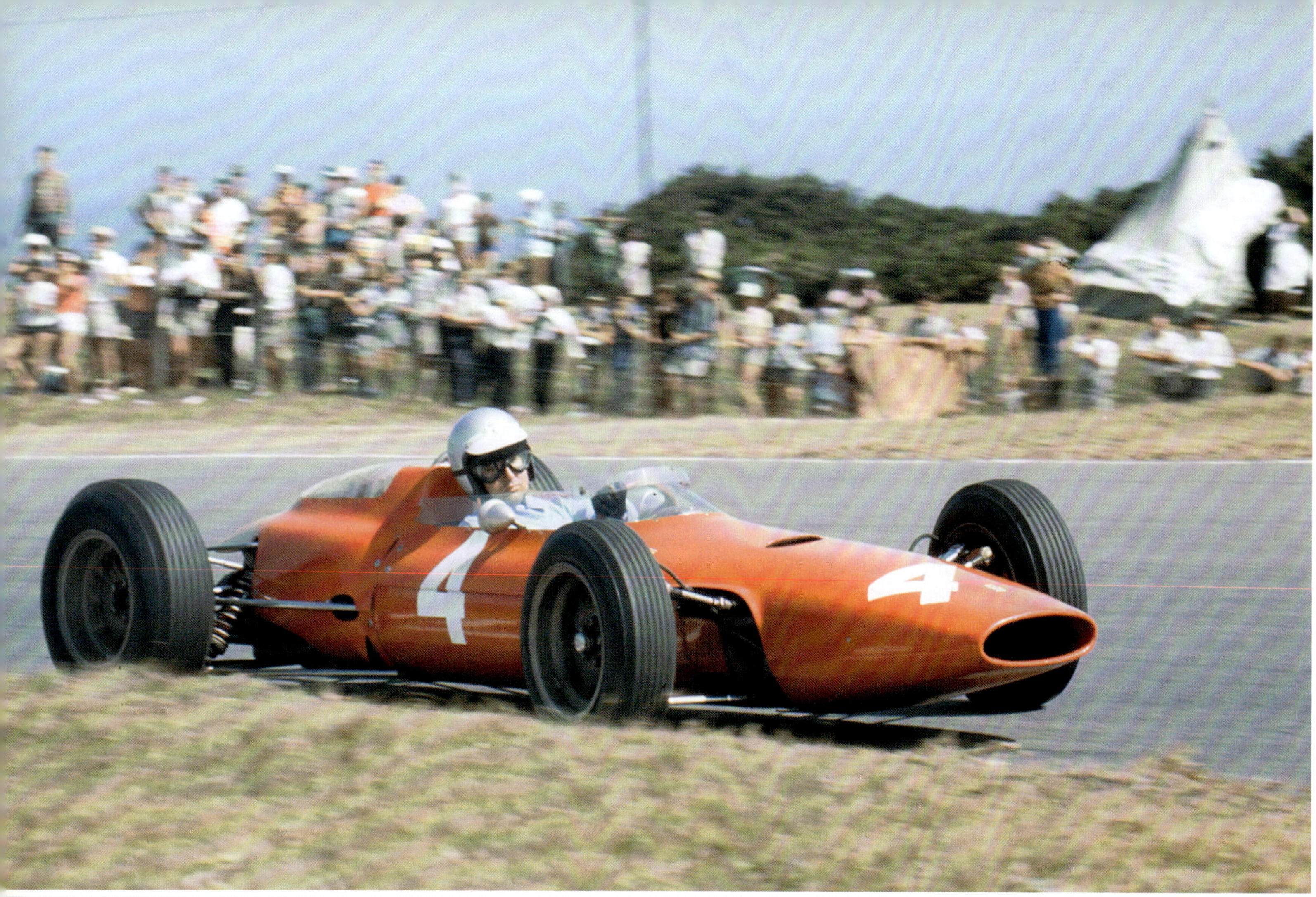

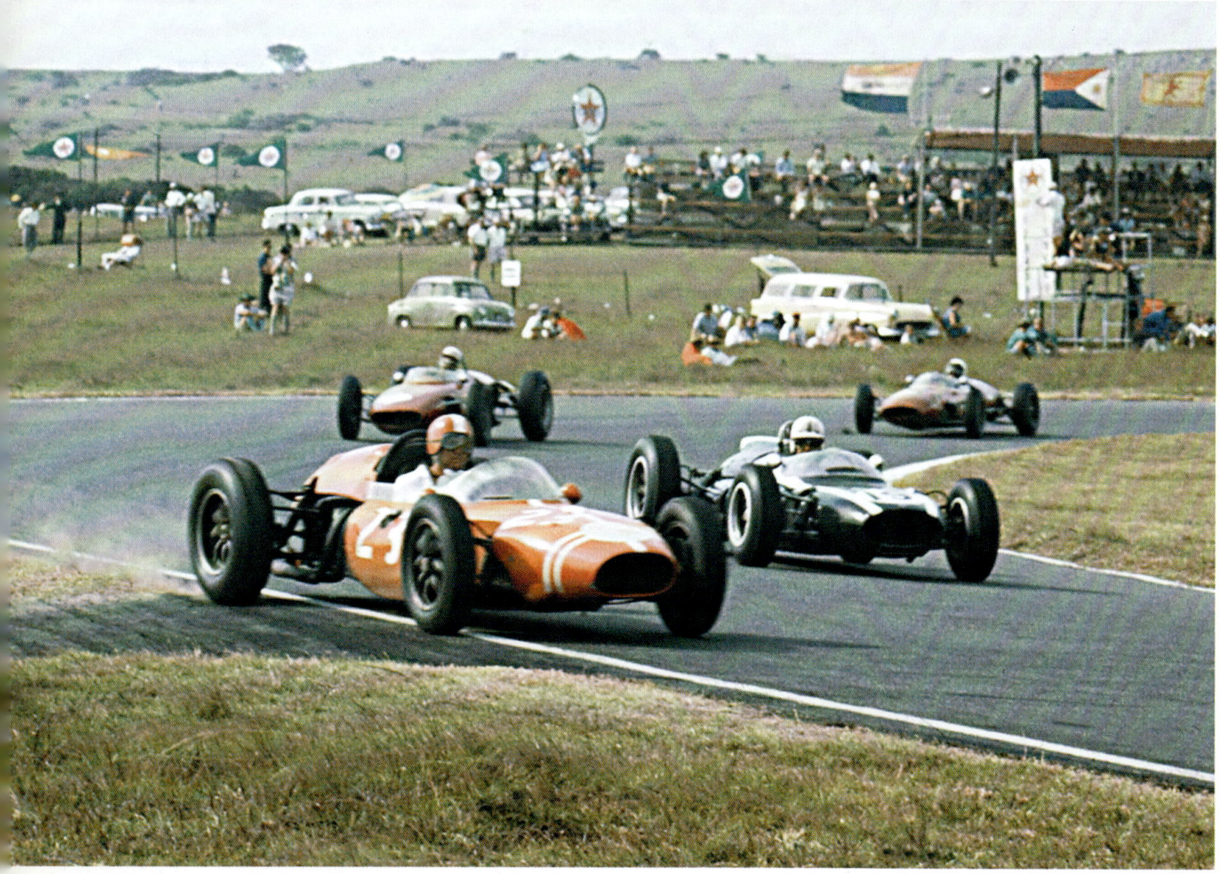

↑ Lorenzo Bandini enjoying his fourth Ferrari GP drive of the year in the new 'Aero' monocoque Ferrari 156 0004 (intended for the forthcoming V8 engine). He finished 5th whilst team leader Surtees suffered an engine blow-up.

← During practice for the South African GP, Trevor Blodyk runs wide in his ancient Scuderia Lupini Cooper-Maserati T51 (F2-16-60) and is overtaken by John Love's elderly Cooper T55 Climax (F1-11-61). South African Blodyk, an ex-speedway rider, came to Europe in 1965, racing in F3 where he was very impressive until a bad accident at Albi left him with serious injuries. After recovering from this, he raced on in F3 until early 1969 when he returned to South Africa. Sadly he died from a heart attack aged just 59 in 1995.

1963 Teams, drivers and results

Cooper Car Co – Cooper T66 Climax V8
Bruce McLaren (NZ)
Tony Maggs (RA)

Team Lotus – Lotus 25 Climax V8
Jim Clark (GB) (WORLD CHAMPION)
Trevor Taylor (GB) (Missed Italian GP due to injury)
Mike Spence (GB) (Italian GP only replacing Taylor)
Pedro Rodriguez (MEX) (US and Mexican GPs only)

Owen Racing Organisation – BRM P57 and P61
Graham Hill (GB)
Richie Ginther (USA)

Brabham Racing Organisation – Brabham BT3 and BT7 Climax V8 and Lotus 25 Climax V8
Jack Brabham (Used loaned Lotus 25 at Monaco due to engine shortage)
Dan Gurney

SEFAC Ferrari – Ferrari 156
John Surtees (GB)
Willy Mairesse (B) (Monaco, Belgian and German GPs only)
Lodovico Scarfiotti (I) (Dutch GP only, dns French GP due to accident)
Lorenzo Bandini (I) (Italian, US, Mexican and South African GPs only)

British Racing Partnership – Lotus 24 BRM V8 and BRP BRM V8
Innes Ireland (GB) (Missed US, Mexican and South African GPs due to injury)
Jim Hall (USA) (Missed South African GP, BRP did not enter)

R. R. C. Walker Racing Team – Cooper T60 Climax V8 and Cooper T66 Climax V8
Jo Bonnier

Reg Parnell (Racing) – Lola 4 Climax V8, Lola 4A Climax V8, Lotus 24 Climax V8 and Lotus 24 BRM V8
Maurice Trintignant (F) (Monaco and French GPs only)
Chris Amon (NZ) (Missed US and South African GPs)
Lucien Bianchi (B) (Belgian GP only)
Mike Hailwood (GB) (British and Italian GPs only)
Masten Gregory (USA) (British, US and Mexican GPs only)
Rodger Ward (USA) (US GP only)
'Hap' Sharp (USA) (US and Mexican GPs only)

Tim Parnell – Lotus 24 BRM V8 and Lola 4 Climax V8
Masten Gregory (USA) (French and Italian GPs only)
John Campbell-Jones (GB) (British GP only)

Siffert Racing Team – Lotus 24 BRM V8
Jo Siffert (CH) (Missed South African GP)

Scirocco Powell (Racing Cars) – Scirocco BRM V8
Tony Settember (USA) (Belgian, French, British and German GPs only, dnq Italian GP)
Ian Burgess (GB) (British and German GPs only)

Automobili Tourismo Sport – ATS 100
Phil Hill (USA) (Belgian, Dutch, French, Italian, US and Mexican GPs only)
Giancarlo Baghetti (I) (Belgian, Dutch, Italian, US and Mexican GPs only)

Ecurie Maarsbergen – Porsche 718
Carel de Beaufort (NL) (dns Monaco GP, not entered French GP)
Gerhard Mitter (D) (Dutch and German GPs only)

Ecurie Filipinetti – Lotus 24 BRM V8
Phil Hill (USA) (French GP only)

Scuderia Centro Sud – BRM P57 and Cooper T60 Climax V8
Lorenzo Bandini (I) (French, British and German GPs only)
Mario de Cabral (P) (German GP only and dnq Italian GP, in Cooper)
Maurice Trintignant (F) (Italian GP only in BRM)
Moises Solana (MEX) (Mexican GP only)

DW Racing Enterprises – Lola 4 Climax V8
Bob Anderson (GB) (British and Italian GPs only)

Ian Raby (Racing) – Gilby BRM V8
Ian Raby (GB) (British GP only, dnq German and Italian GPs)

Bernard Collomb – Lotus 24 Climax V8
Bernard Collomb (F) (Monaco GP excluded, German GP only)

Canadian Stebro Racing – Stebro 4 Ford
Peter Broeker (CDN) (US GP only)

Lawson Organisation – Lotus 21 Climax FPF
Ernest Pieterse (ZA) (South African GP only)

Otelle Nucci – LDS Mk2 Alfa Romeo and Alfa Romeo Special
Doug Serrurier (ZA) (South African GP only)
Piet de Klerk (ZA) (South African GP only)

John Love – Cooper T55 Climax FPF
John Love (RSR) (South African GP only)

Sam Tingle – LDS Mk1 Alfa Romeo
Sam Tingle (RSR) (South African GP only)

Ted Lanfear – Lotus 22 Ford
Brausch Niemann (ZA) (South African GP only)

David Prophet – Brabham BT6 Ford
David Prophet (GB) (South African GP only)

Scuderia Lupini – Cooper T51 Maserati
Trevor Blokdyk (ZA) (South African GP only

WORLD CHAMPIONSHIP VENUES AND WINNERS (ten rounds)

Monaco GP	Monte Carlo	Graham Hill
Belgian GP	Spa-Francorchamps	Jim Clark
Dutch GP	Zandvoort	Jim Clark
French GP	Reims	Jim Clark
British GP	Silverstone	Jim Clark
German GP	Nürburgring	John Surtees
Italian GP	Monza	Jim Clark
United States GP	Watkins Glen	Graham Hill
Mexican GP	Mexico City	Jim Clark
South African GP	East London	Jim Clark

DRIVERS' CHAMPIONSHIP
Points: 9-6-4-3-2-1. Best 6 scores

1	Jim Clark	Lotus	54
2	Graham Hill	BRM	29
3	Richie Ginther	BRM	29
4	John Surtees	Ferrari	22
5	Dan Gurney	Brabham	19
6	Bruce McLaren	Cooper	17
7	Jack Brabham	Brabham	14
8	Tony Maggs	Cooper	9
9	Innes Ireland	Lotus/BRP	6
10	Lorenzo Bandini	BRM/Ferrari	6
11	Jo Bonnier	Cooper	6
12	Gerhard Mitter	Porsche	3
13	Jim Hall	Lotus	3
14	Carel de Beaufort	Porsche	2
15	Trevor Taylor	Lotus	1
16	Lodovico Scarfiotti	Ferrari	1
17	Jo Siffert	Lotus	1

CONSTRUCTORS' CHAMPIONSHIP
Points: 9-6-4-3-2-1, (awarded only to best-placed finisher). Best 6 scores

1	Lotus-Climax	54
2	BRM	36
3	Brabham-Climax	28
4	Ferrari	26
5	Cooper-Climax	25
6	BRP-BRM	6
7	Porsche	5
8	Lotus-BRM	4

1964

MEXICAN STAND-OFF

During 1964 tyre development intensified. For years Dunlop had been supplying rubber better suited to long distance sports car racing rather than featherweight F1 cars. In 1963, Clark's Lotus had completed four Grands prix on one set of tyres! The new Dunlop R7 covers were noticeably wider and stickier than their R6 predecessors.

It was to be a surprising season with unlikely results and twists of fate right up to the last race in Mexico. BRM were now fielding the first generation of their full monocoque P261 and retained their driver line-up whilst Lotus kept the 25 and later produced a development version, the 33, that was used in tandem. Clark's position as *numero uno* was unchallenged, but Graham Hill's perceived position as the next best was under threat from the arguably more talented Surtees and Gurney.

Lotus dropped Trevor Taylor and employed Peter Arundell, but he was badly injured in a Reims F2 race and was replaced by Mike Spence. Tony Maggs left Cooper and his drive was taken by Phil Hill who endured a miserable time in his last full season in F1. Honda appeared at the German GP with their own F1 machine, the V12 RA271, but the car was slow and underdeveloped. Their choice of driver seemed somewhat inappropriate, American sports car racer Ronnie Bucknum, who not surprisingly struggled to be competitive at the German GP on the fearsome Nürburgring. During practice Count Carel Godin de Beaufort had a fatal accident in his old Porsche 718, thus ending the de Beaufort dynasty.

Hill won Monaco after Clark retired, a familiar scenario. At Spa Hill, Gurney and McLaren all ran out of fuel, leaving Clark to win from 4th place who then proceeded to run out of fuel after crossing the line! Clark won in Holland and again in the first British GP at Brands Hatch, being closely pursued by Hill, but had a poor late season although he was heading for the title in Mexico when his car retired. Gurney won the French GP for Brabham and the Mexican GP. They were still using their 1963 BT7, albeit updated.

Ferrari had a new type 158 V8 for Surtees, but Bandini spent the year chopping and changing between the old V6 motor, the V8 and even an all new flat-12. Nevertheless he won the Austrian GP with the V6 engine. Surtees took the German and Italian GPs and scored three 2nd places and a 4th to win the World Championship and Ferrari the Constructors' title, but only after Bandini accidentally rammed Hill in Mexico, otherwise the Englishman would have been champion. A new star was on the horizon, Jackie Stewart, who dominated F3 and tried an F1 Lotus at the British GP at Brands Hatch during the lunch break.

The four non-championship British F1 events were won by Ireland (Snetterton), Clark (Goodwood) and Brabham (Aintree and Silverstone). Abroad the races fell to Surtees (Syracuse), Clark (Solitude) and Siffert (Enna) who memorably beat Clark by one tenth of a second.

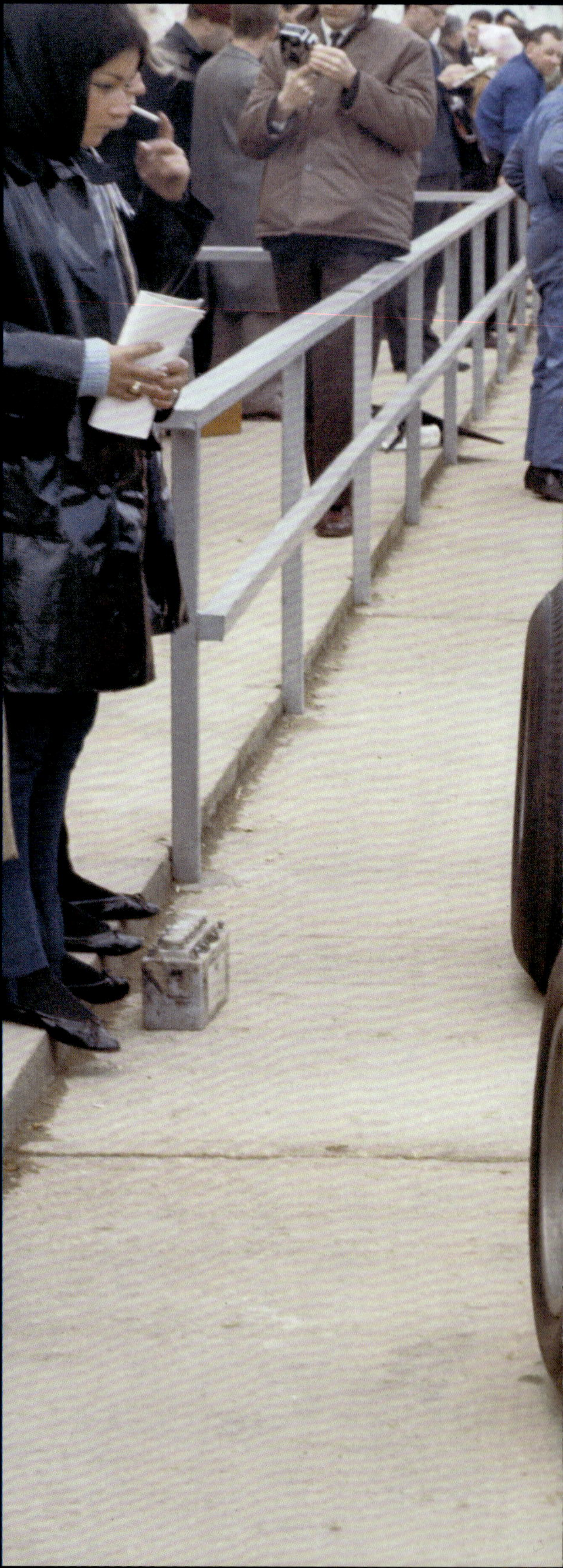

This is the 1962 works Cooper T60 (F1-18-61) at the Silverstone International Trophy in May 1964. It was entered by Fabré Urbain and driven by the Swiss Jean-Claude Rudaz who qualified 20th and finished 14th. Later that year it appeared at the Italian GP but failed to qualify. Rudaz is one of many now forgotten drivers who competed in F1, usually in the non-championship events of the period. Behind the Cooper is Jo Siffert's Lotus 24 BRM. The raised pit lane was a response to the fatality that occurred when a car spun out of Woodcote and into the unprotected pits during 1963, killing a bystander.

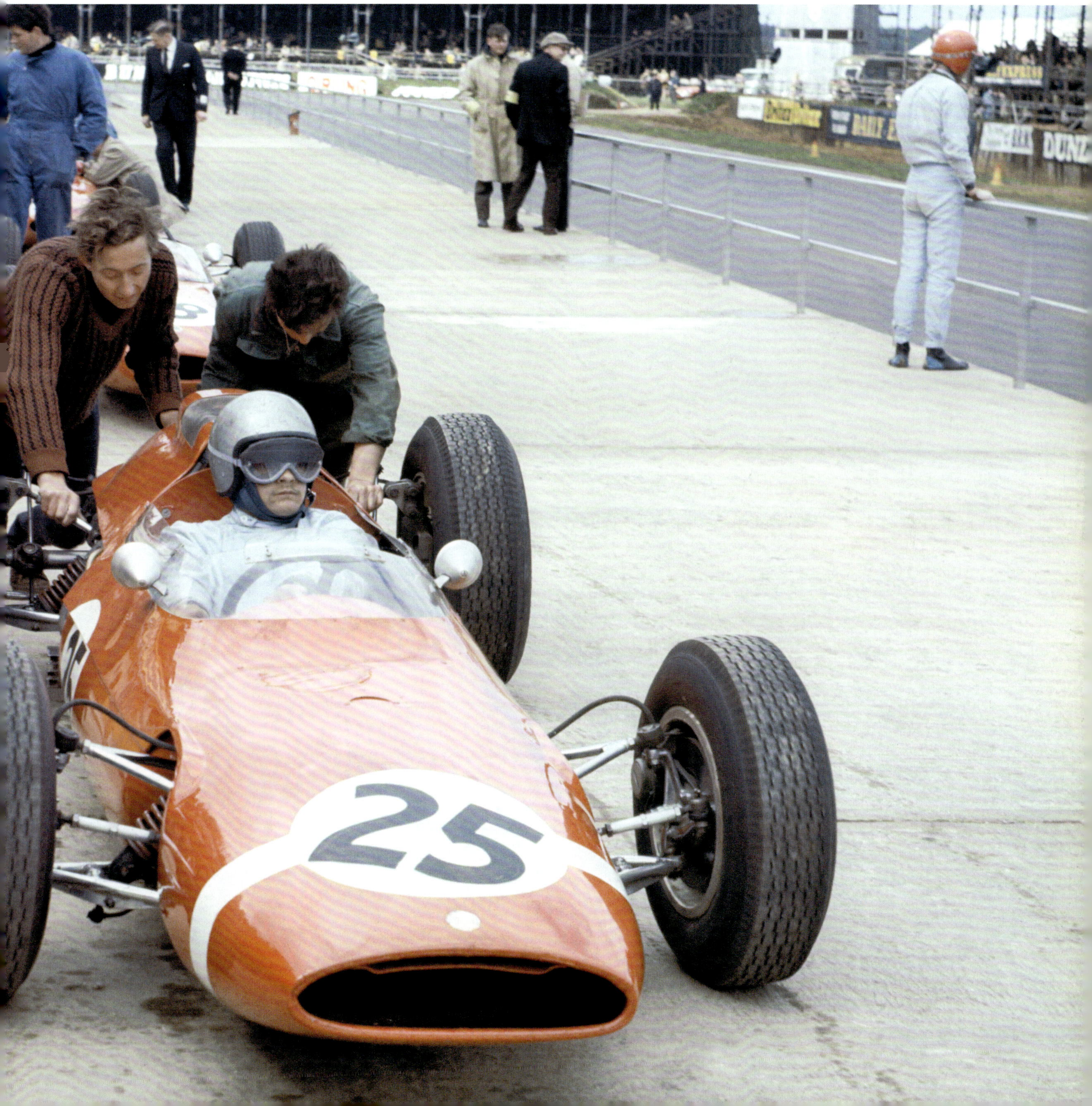

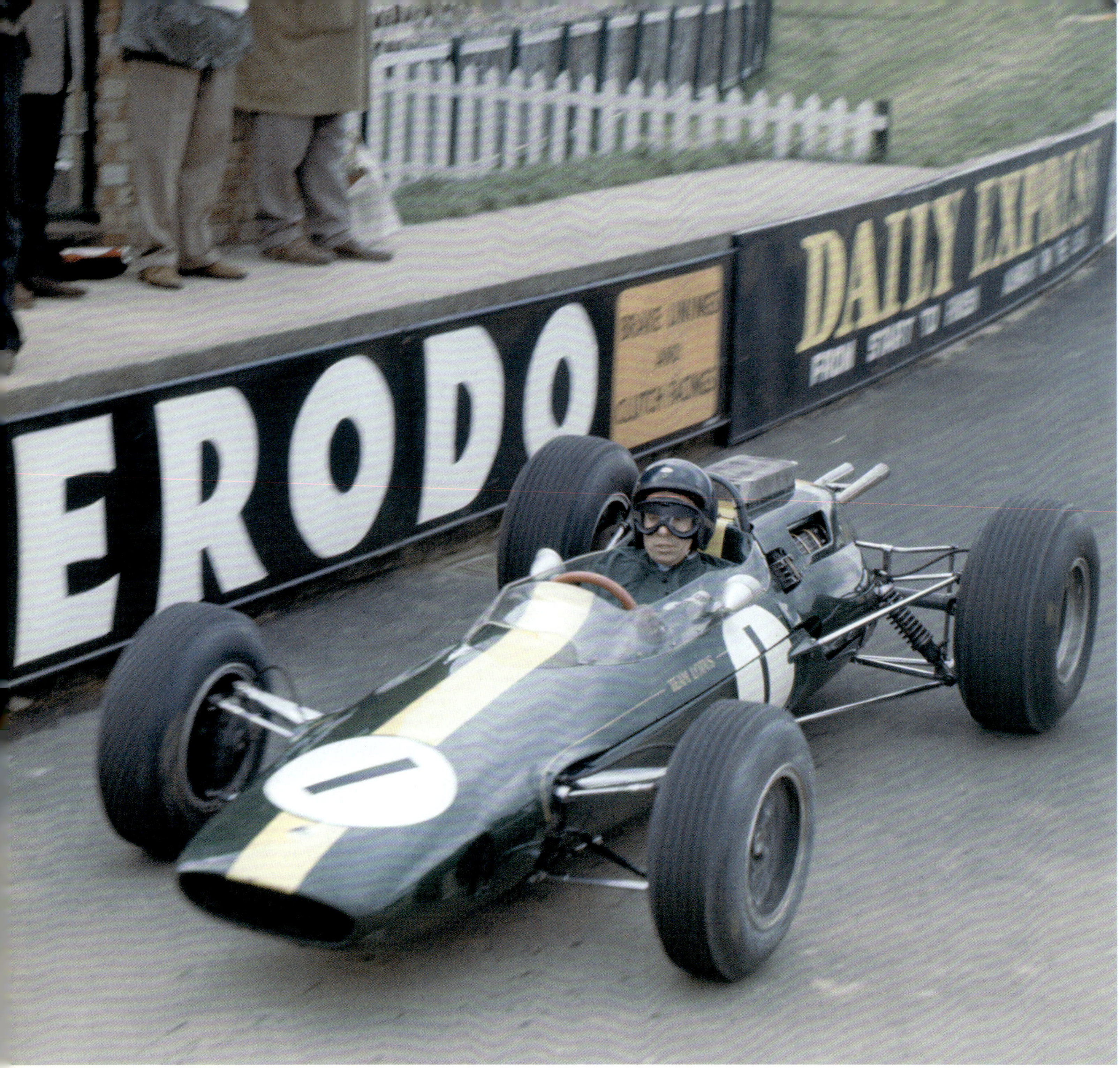

Jim Clark returns to the pits at Silverstone in his Lotus 25 (R6). It is wearing the new wider Dunlop R7 tyres and will start on the outside of the front row. He led the International Trophy for five laps but then suffered a seized engine. A thrilling race ensued with Jack Brabham just pipping Hill's BRM literally on the line by driving round the outside of Woodcote just as Hill had done to Clark two years earlier, and onto the grass verge after the flag.

Brabecue! Jo Bonnier only got as far as Copse when Rob Walker's brand new and still not fully painted Brabham BT11 (F1-4-64) caught fire. So 'Jo Bo' had to race Walker's old Cooper T66 and finished last. Not a good weekend, then.

Tony Maggs had left Cooper, his place taken by Phil Hill and pitched up at Scuderia Centro Sud to drive one of the 1962 BRM P57s (5784). Maggs finished 7th at the International Trophy at Silverstone, crashed in Holland but managed 6th in Germany and 4th in Austria, his last race for the team.

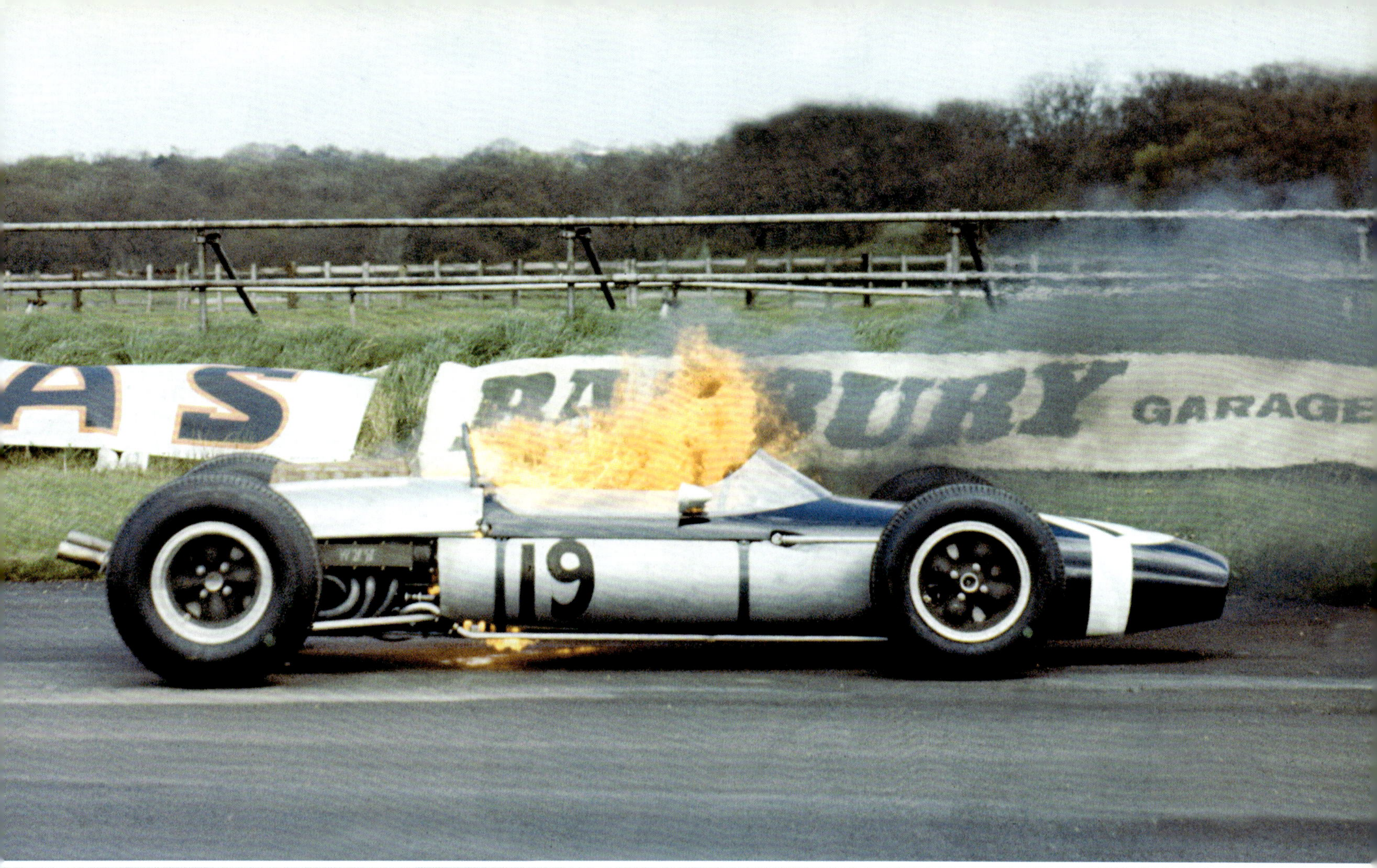
GARAGE
119

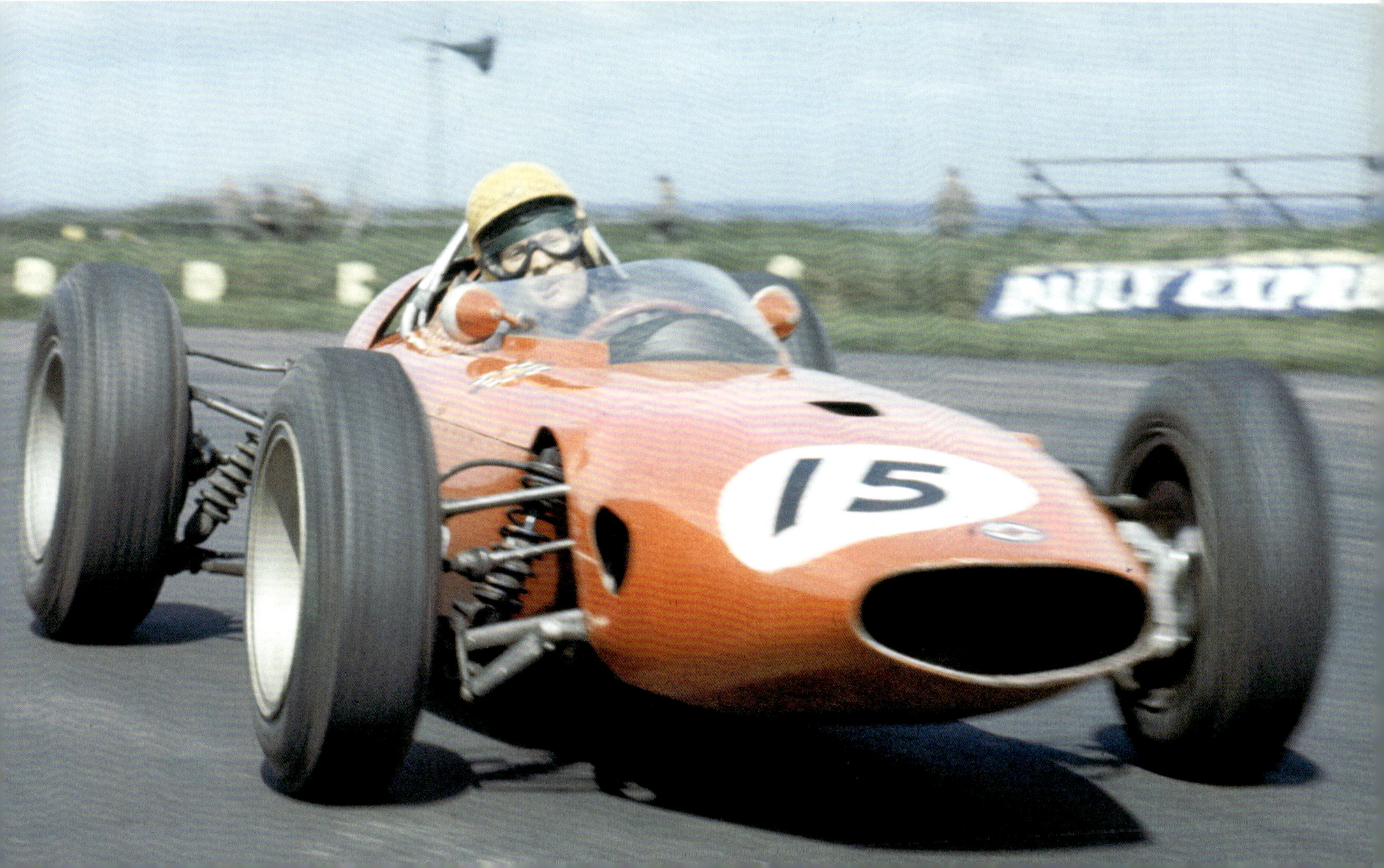
15

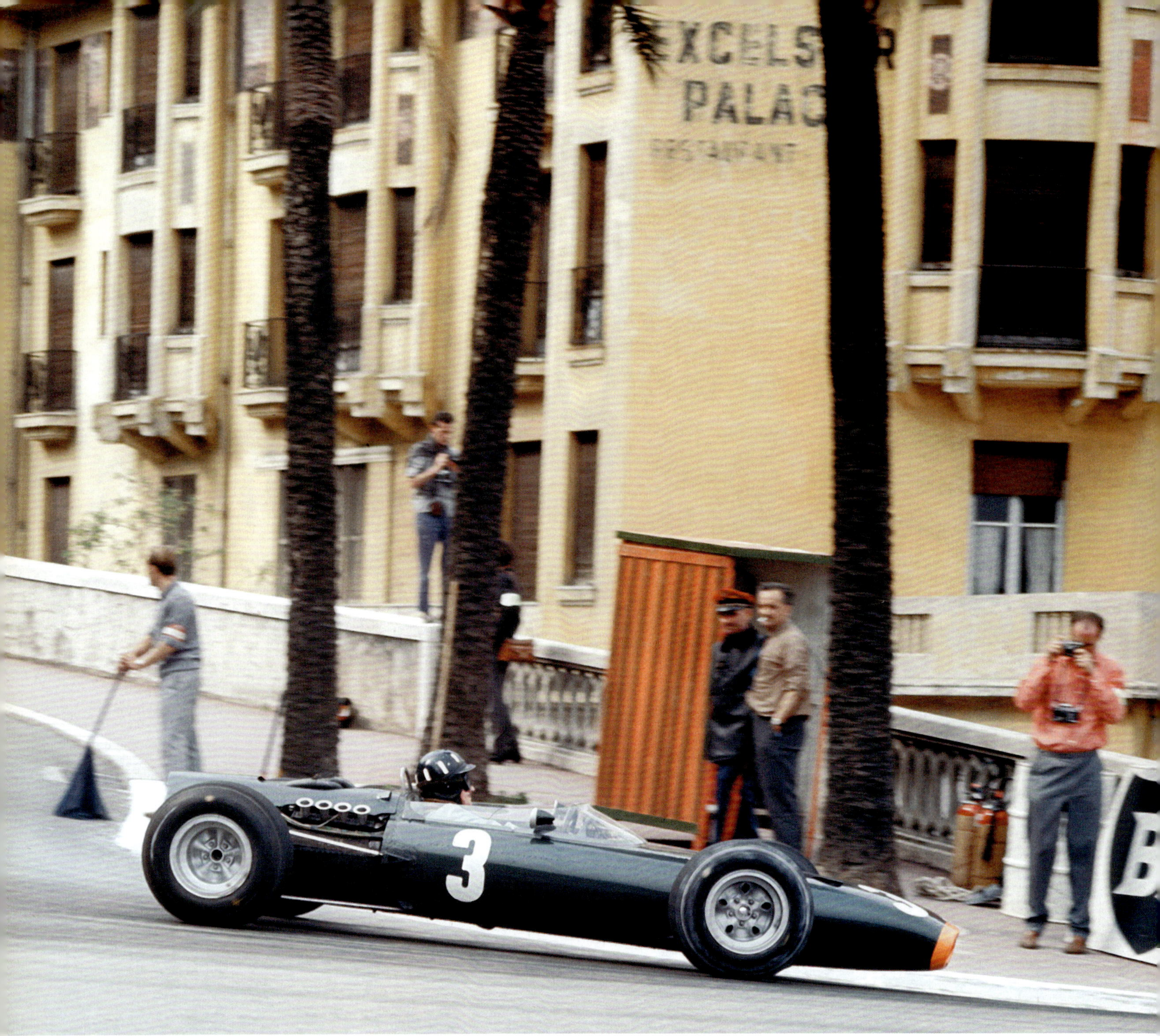

⇧ Monaco win number number two for Norman Graham Hill in the new monocoque BRM P261 (2614). He won at a record average speed and set a new lap record after Clark's Lotus and Gurney's Brabham broke down. The profile of the BRM is an almost perfect caricature of a cigar tube on wheels as it rounds the station hairpin.

⇗ Maurice Trintignant won the Monaco GP twice (1955 and 1958). His long Grand Prix career began in 1950 at Monaco and ended at Monza in 1964. A long standing Rob Walker driver, he bought the famous ex-Hill 'Old Faithful' BRM 5781 in 1964 from Scuderia Centro Sud, painting it French blue and sponsored by BP France, retiring here at Monaco. However he won the famous Mont Ventoux mountain hillclimb setting a course record and finished in 5th place in the German GP. The car was sold back to Centro Sud for 1965. 'Trint' retired from racing in 1965 and died in 2005.

⇨ After his totally dominant 1963 season Jim Clark suffered his usual Monaco luck despite leading with his 25 (R6), even with a broken rear anti-roll bar. He stopped to have it disconnected and rejoined in 3rd but suffered engine failure on lap 96.

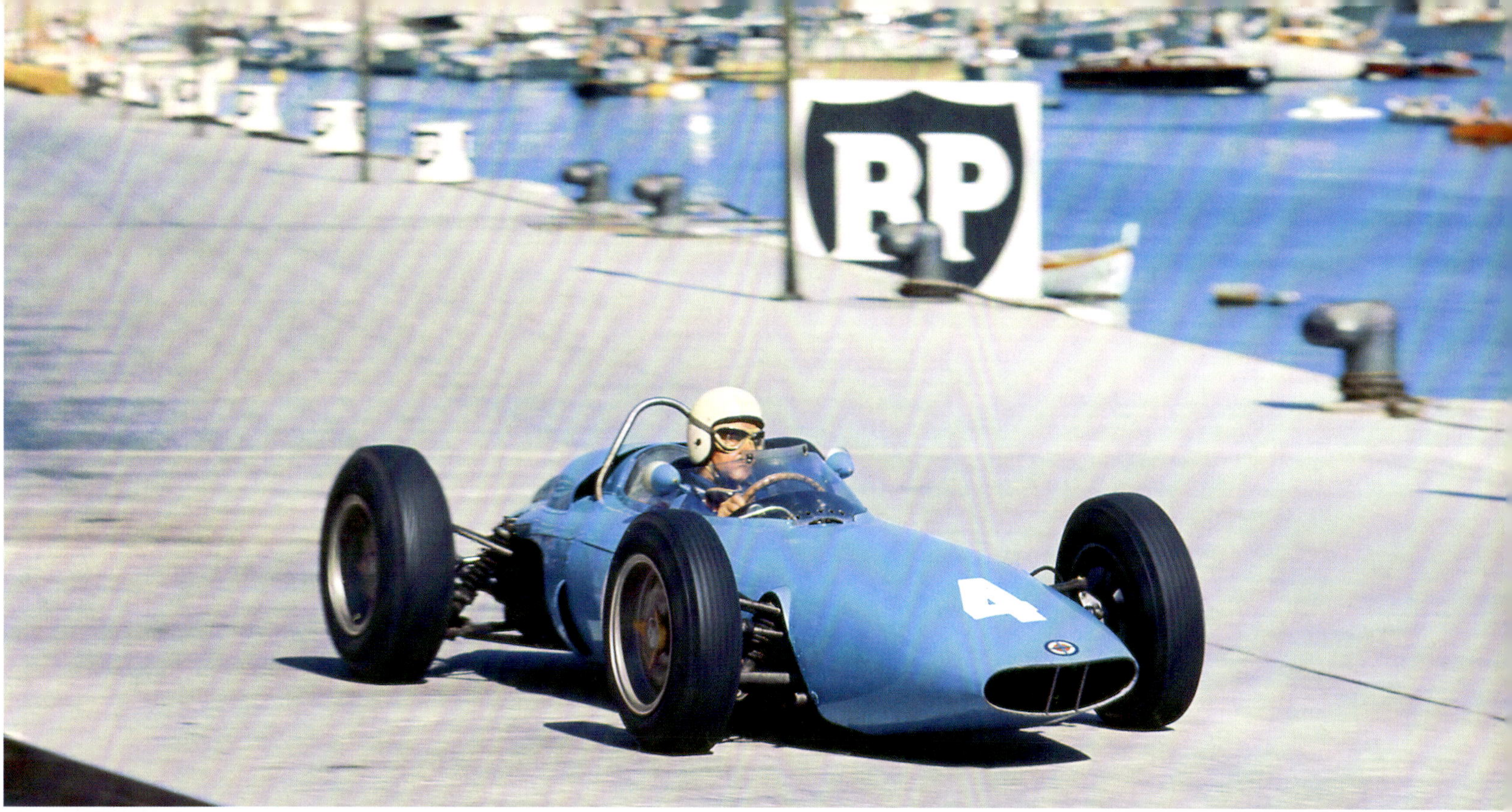
BP
4

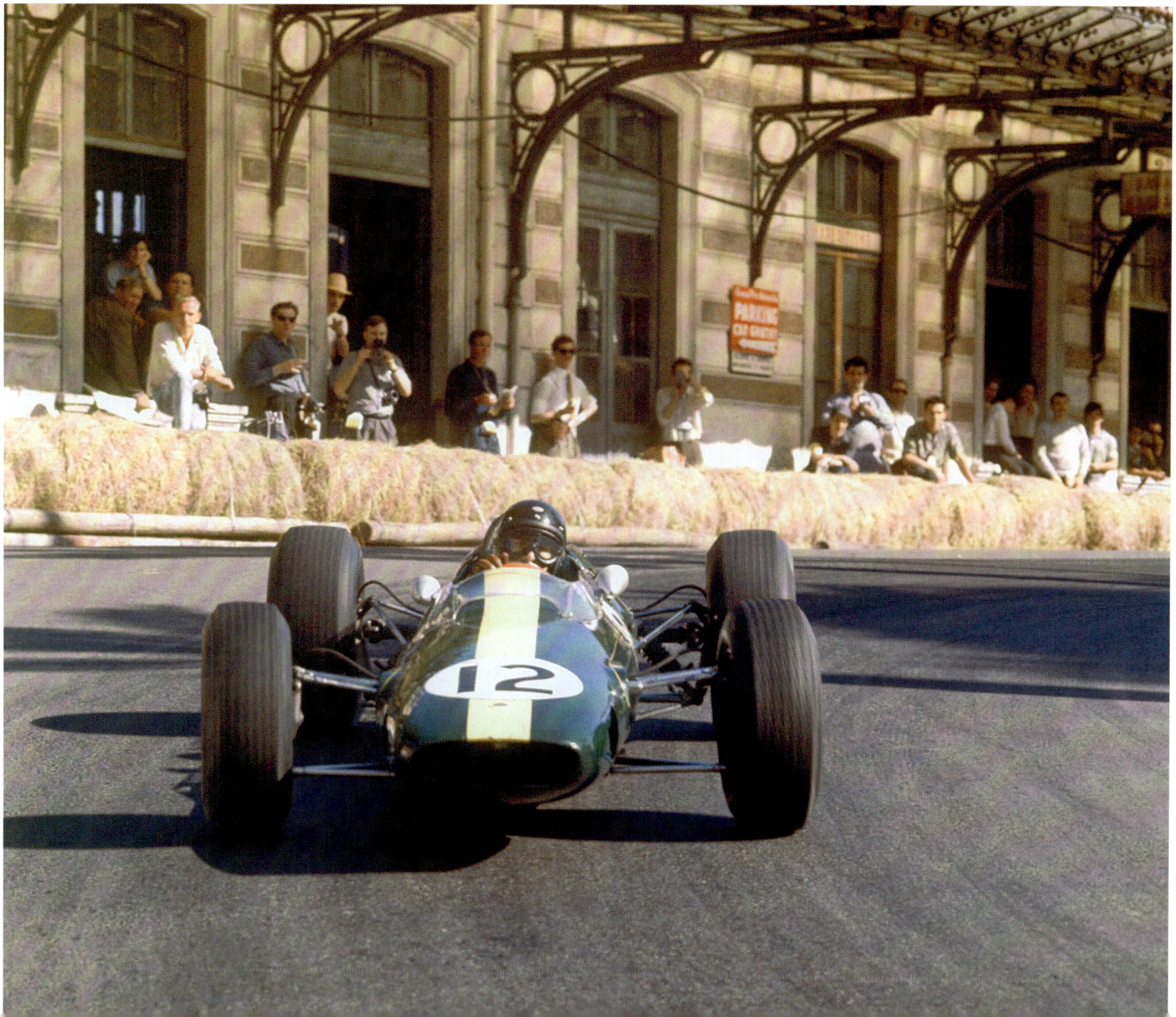
PARKING
12

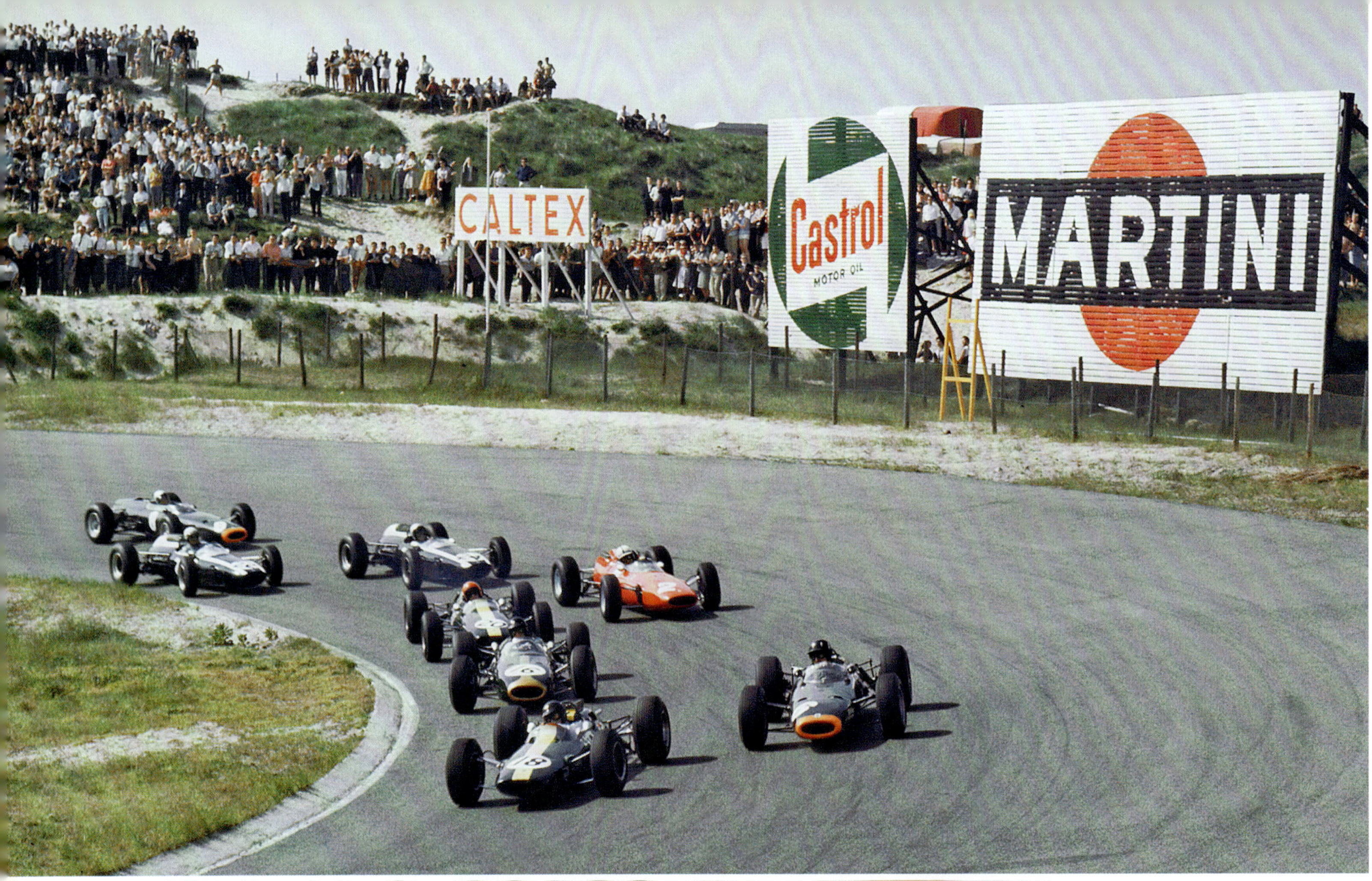

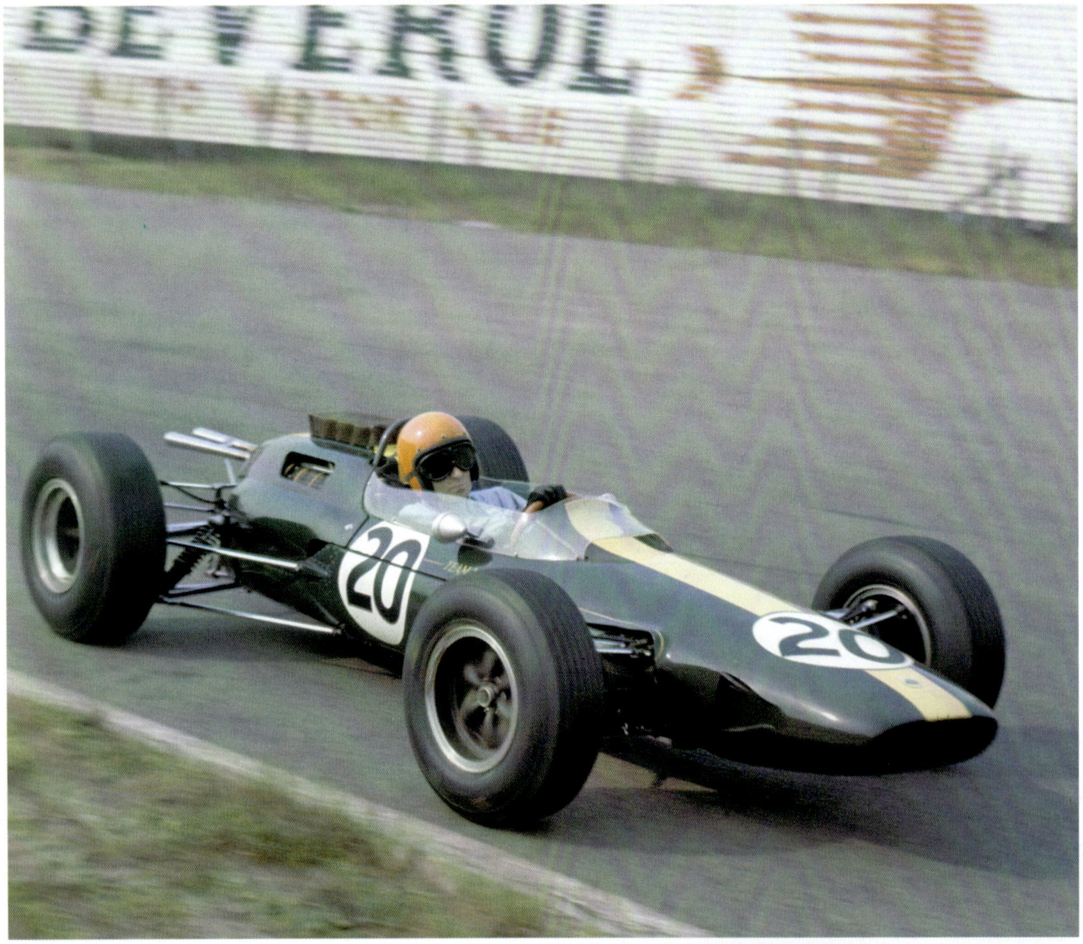

The opening lap of the Dutch GP at Zandvoort and as ever Jim Clark has taken control. He is accompanied by Hill's BRM on the outside and Gurney's Brabham astern, followed by Arundell's Lotus and the rest. The tiny toy like 1.5-litre cars occupy little space on the wide track; there was little reason to collide with anybody here unlike latter day F1 hooliganism.

Following his successful Monaco outing, Peter Arundell qualified 5th for the Dutch GP in the Lotus 25 (R4) now designated 25B by Lotus due to suspension modifications, new wheels, the latest gearbox and other updates. This action shot displays his sure touch as he applies a little opposite lock *en route* to another 3rd place. Following a 4th place at the French GP at Rouen, Arundell suffered very serious injuries in an accident at Reims that kept him out of F1 until 1966.

Absolute precision. A lovely shot of Gurney in full flow with maximum commitment during the Dutch GP in the Brabham BT7 (F1-3-63). He started from pole but Clark led from start to finish whilst Dan's steering wheel broke forcing him to retire on lap 23!

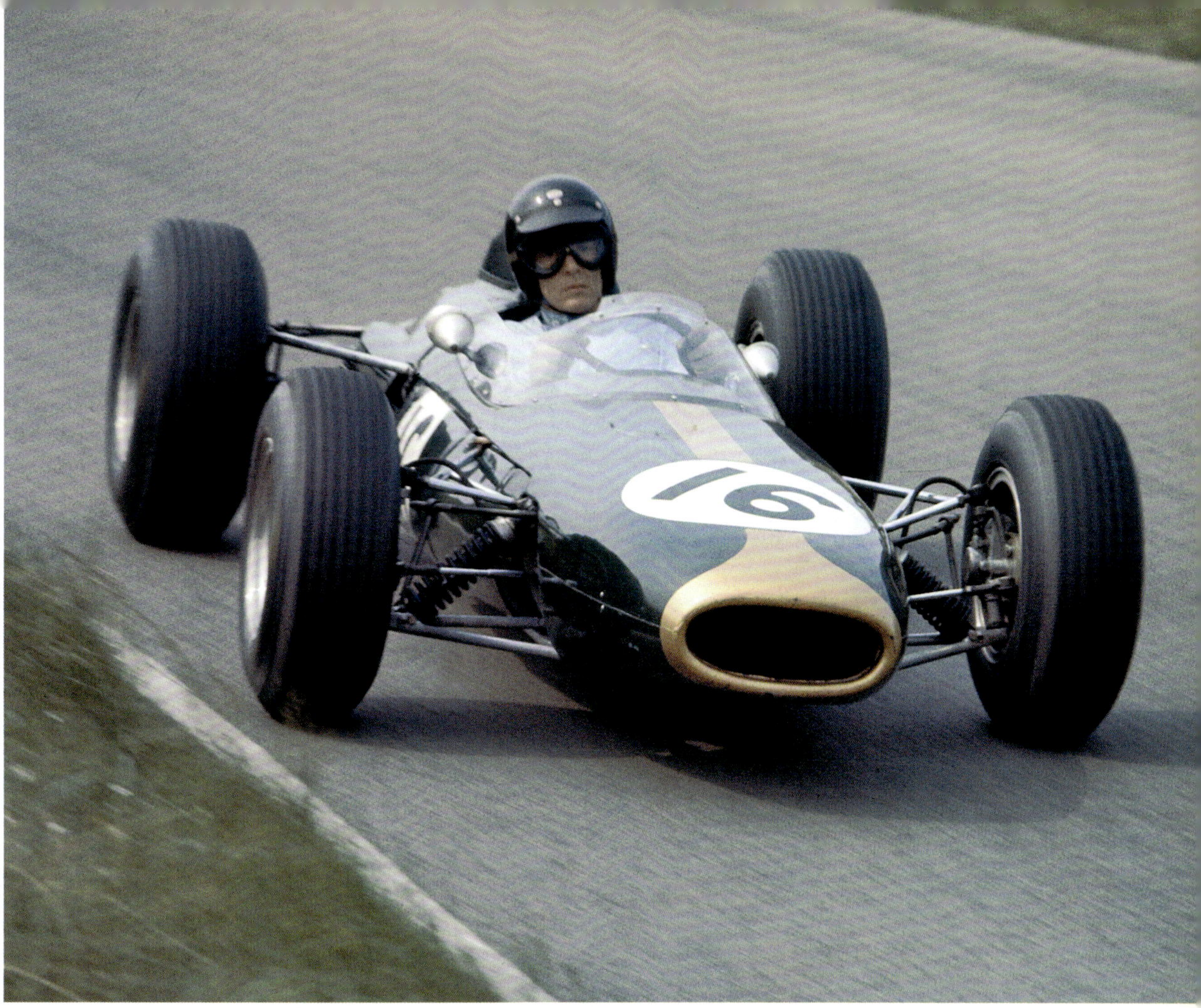

The current and former Ferrari number twos are nose to tail at Zandvoort. Lorenzo Bandini's Ferrari 158 (0002) has just passed Giancarlo Baghetti's Scuderia Centro Sud ex-works BRM P57 (5784). Bandini retired from the Dutch Grand Prix when the belt snapped in the fuel-injection pump drive. Baghetti soldiered on to finish 10th.

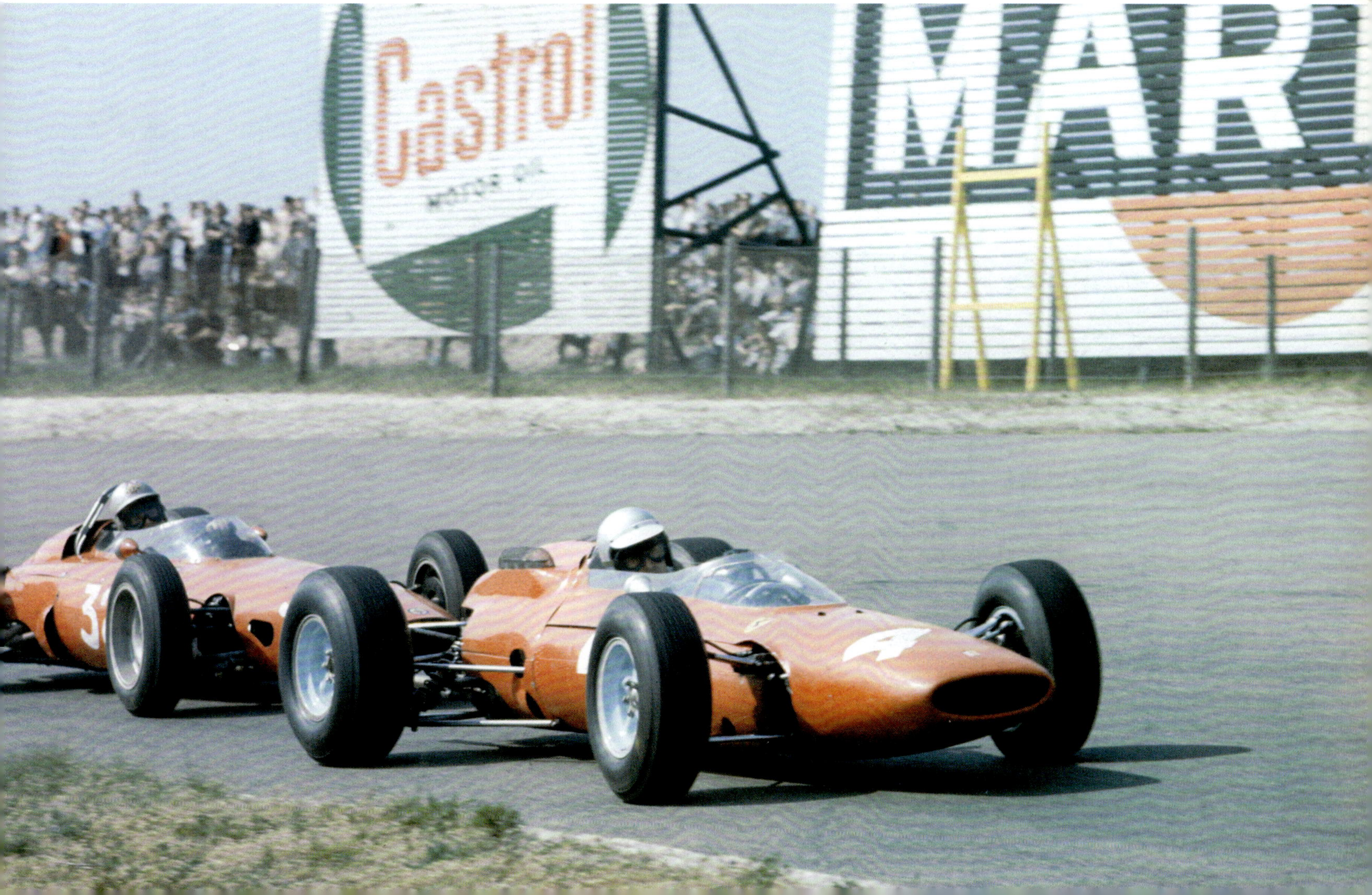

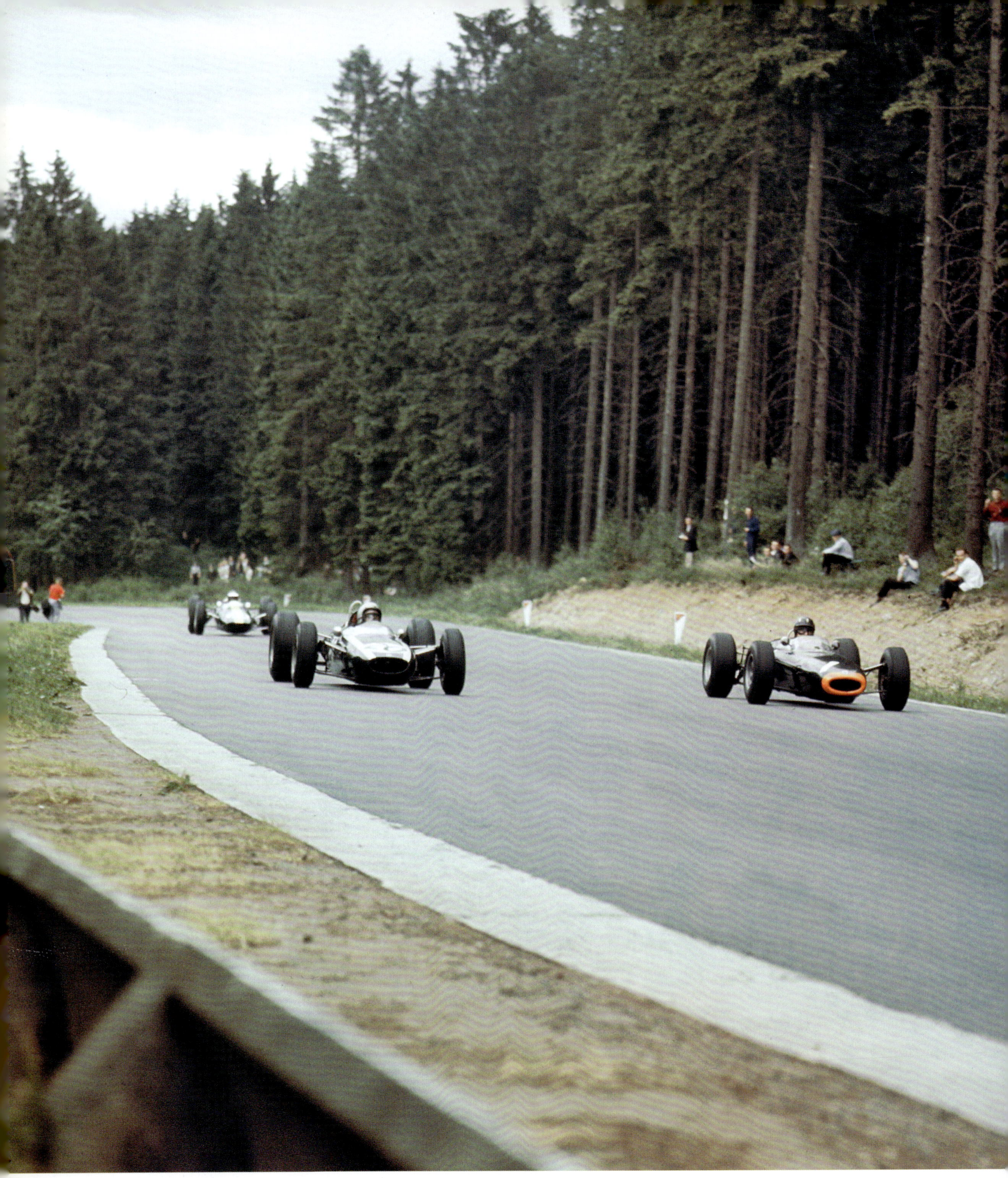

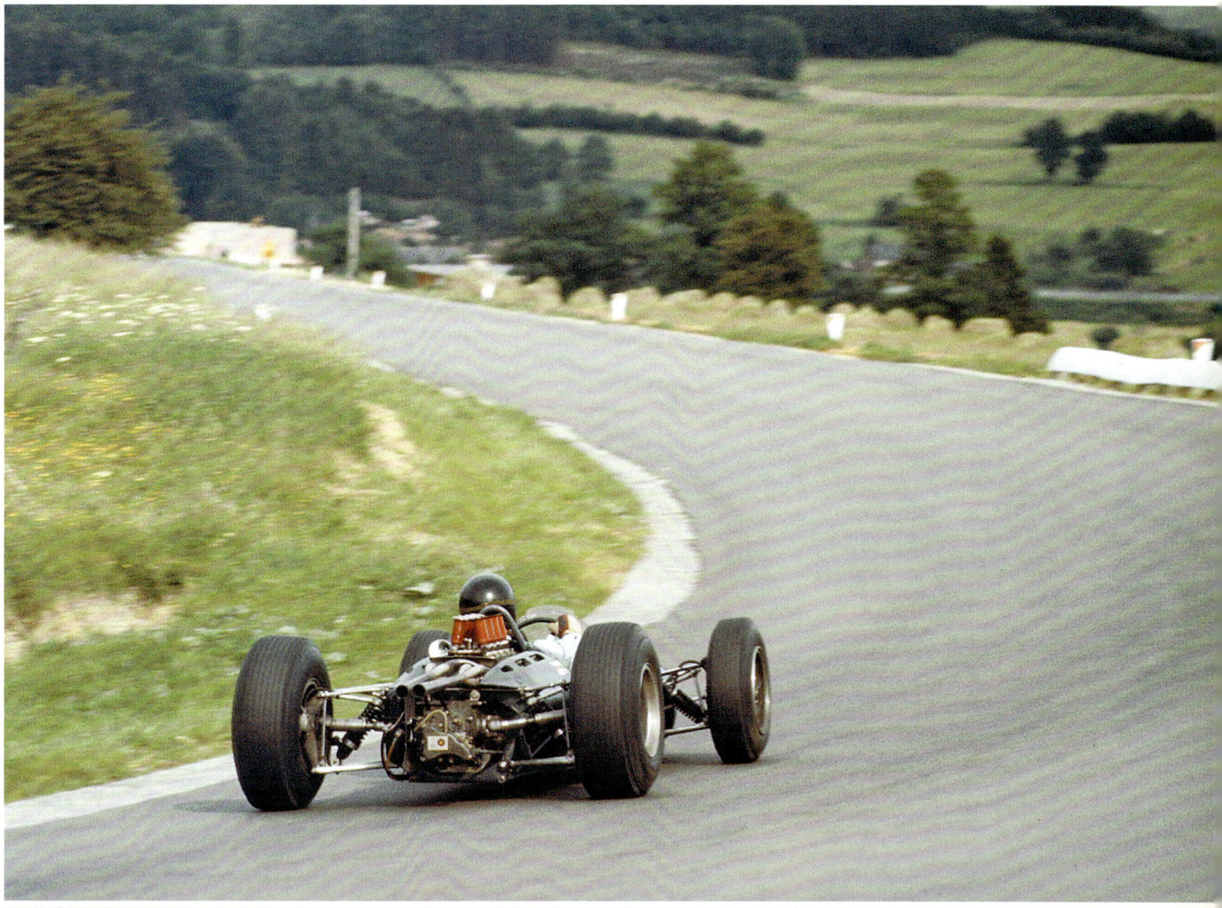

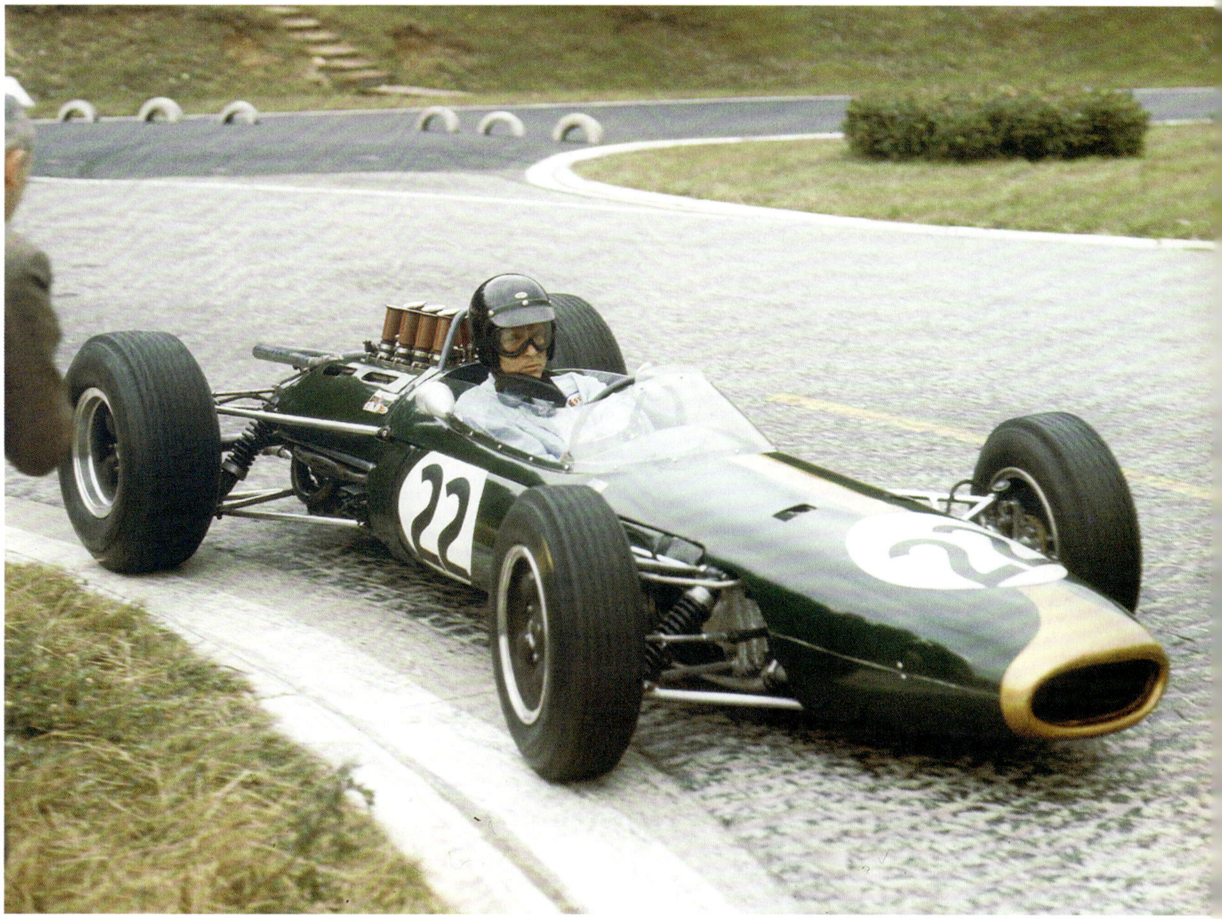

→ Dan Gurney was way faster than the rest at Spa-Francorchamps, but began to run out of fuel three laps before the finish. He pitted, but in those days Formula 1 cars were not meant to be refuelled during the races. When Graham Hill, Jim Clark and Bruce McLaren all roared past as the Brabham pit crew was struggling with fuel churns, Gurney took off again – only to run dry on the last lap at Stavelot. He was classified 4th. This is a typical mid-1960s Spa scene: anyone leaving the road here would probably have ended up somewhere in Germany…

← Behind Gurney, Hill, BRM (right), McLaren, Cooper (left) and Clark, Lotus, following, had a lively scrap. When Gurney pitted Hill took the lead and then Clark stopped for water, leaving Graham leading McLaren. However, on the fateful last lap Hill's BRM's Bendix fuel pump failed to pick up the remaining three gallons and he too effectively ran out of fuel. Then as McLaren approached La Source the Cooper's engine died and he coasted over the line having just been passed by Clark's Lotus that promptly ran out of fuel just beyond the finish! Sometimes Clark could not help but win.

→ Better luck thankfully at Rouen for Dan Gurney who presses on unchallenged in his Brabham BT7 (F1-3-63) at the French GP after Clark's demise. Following Spa, Brabham made sure that the fuel pumps would pick up to the last half gallon. This was the first World Championship victory for the Brabham Racing Organisation and they had a very good weekend at Rouen. The boss battled with Hill and Arundell, just losing 2nd to the BRM but setting fastest lap.

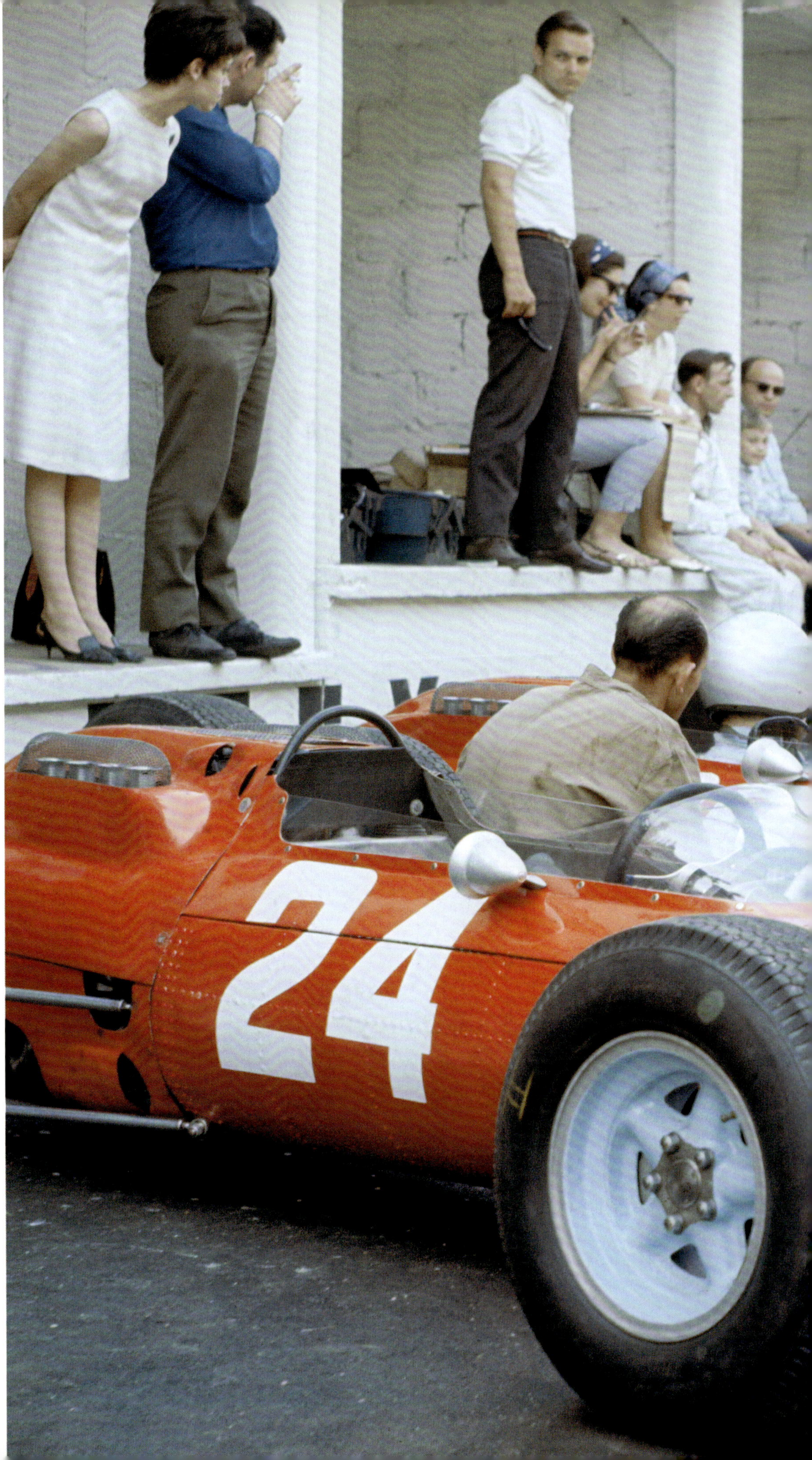

➡ In the red. Prancing horses at rest in the Rouen pits. Number 24 is the Surtees car 158 (0006) whilst Bandini seated in 0005 looks across at Mike Hailwood in the Reg Parnell Racing Lotus 25 BRM (R7). Beyond him is the sister car (R3) of Chris Amon. The Ferraris were quad-cam V8s and gave Surtees two GP wins, but at Rouen Il Grande John retired and Bandini finished 9th. The figure holding sunglasses standing on the pit counter behind Hailwood's car is Peter Revson whilst the control tower clock reads 6.10pm.

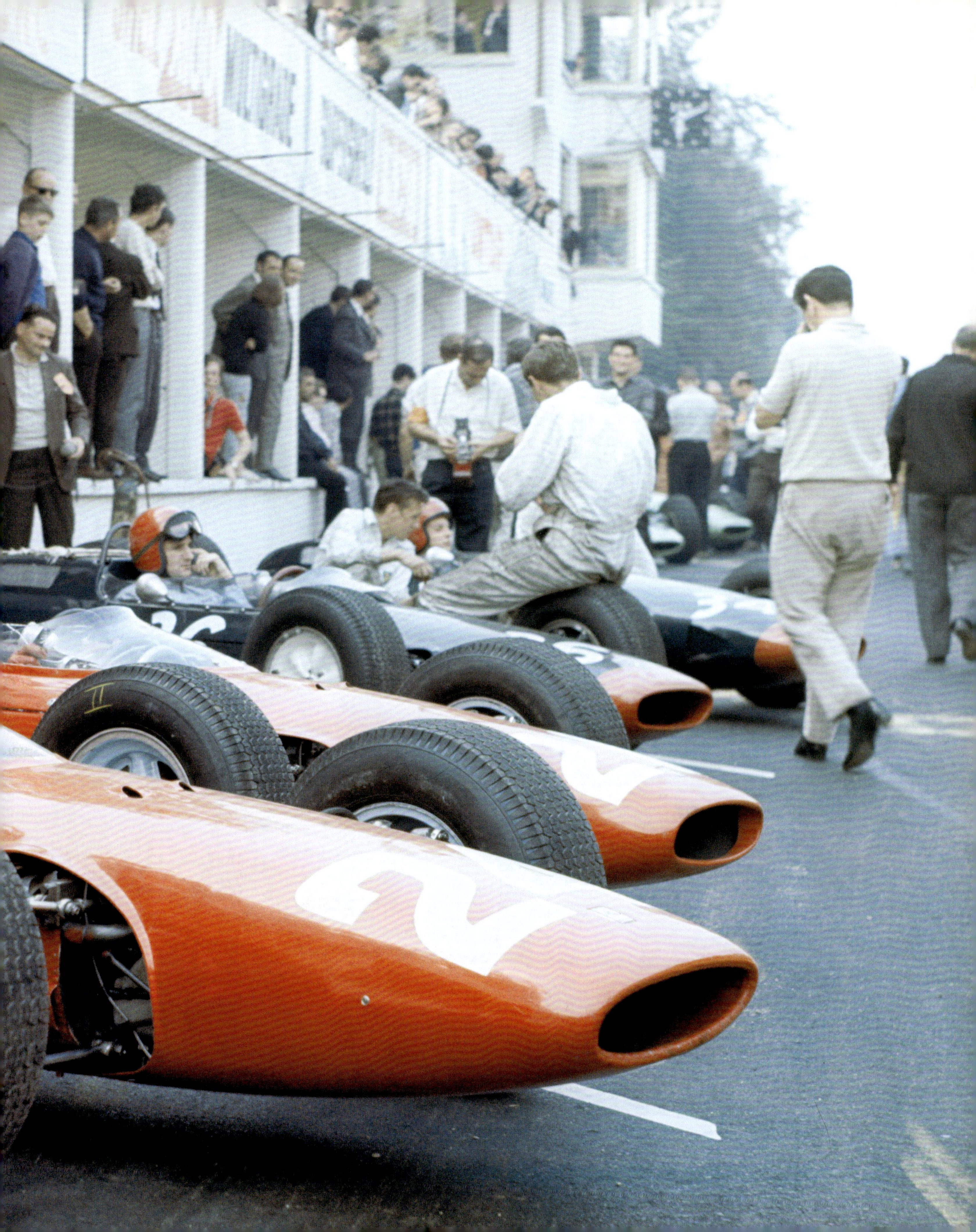

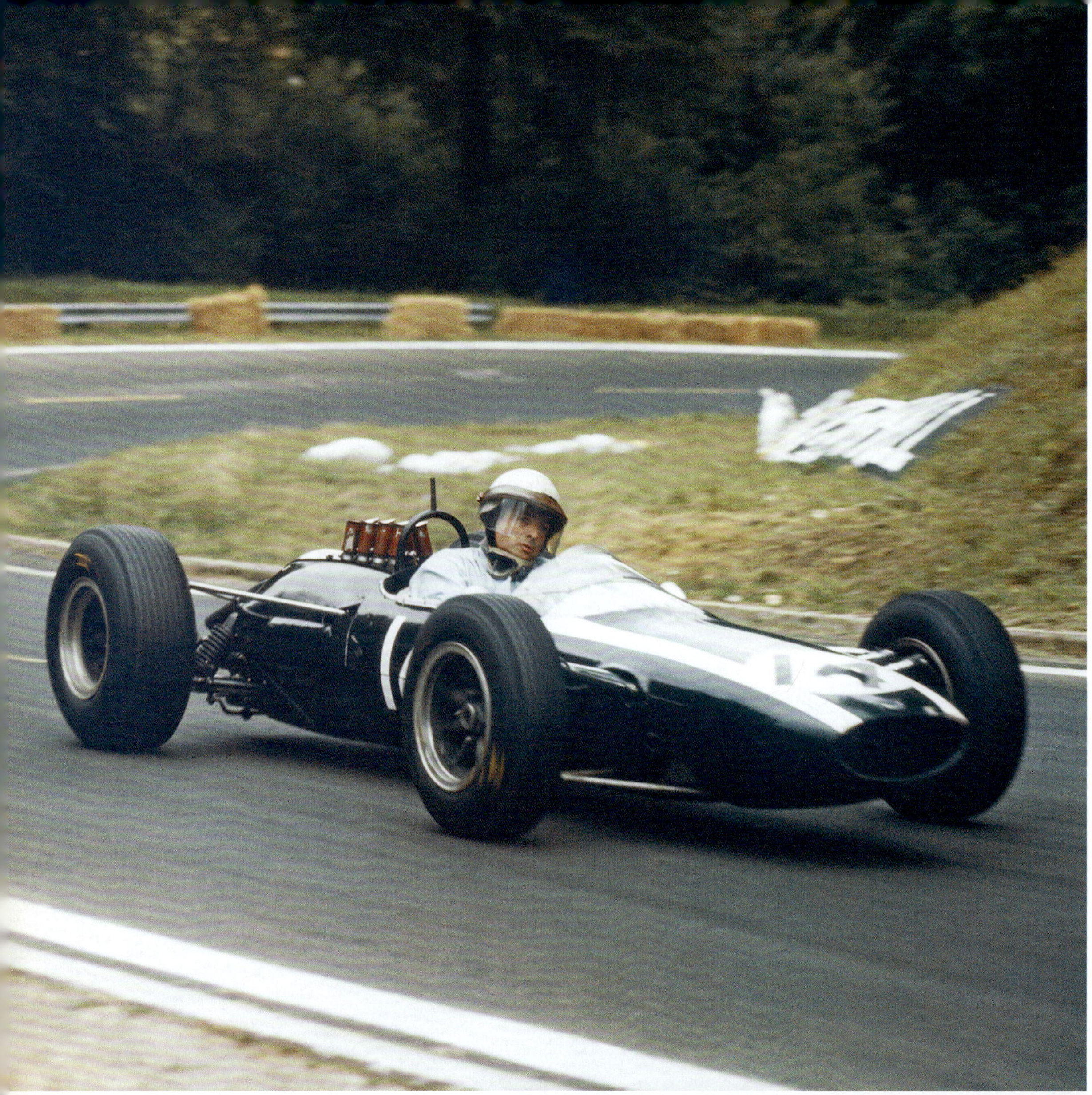

Poor Phil Hill was a very unhappy man at Cooper in 1964 following the ATS debacle of 1963. He had joined after American Timmy Meyer (younger brother of Teddy) was killed in the pre-season Tasman series. Hill complained about underpowered engines that explained his lacklustre performances but Cooper were inclined to blame him. However, it later transpired that a mechanic had been taping the outer throttle cable sleeve to a chassis tube instead of securing it properly, allowing it to flex. Consequently, Hill was not getting full throttle although when tested by hand at the engine end it seemed fine. He finished 7th in the Cooper T73 (F1-2-64).

Colin Chapman sold this Lotus 25 (R7) to Reg Parnell Racing and Mike Hailwood drove it at Rouen to 8th place. The BRM V8 powered 25s were rarely competitive in private hands, and did little justice to the talents of Hailwood, Chris Amon and others. These are the famous cobbles of the Nouveau Monde hairpin.

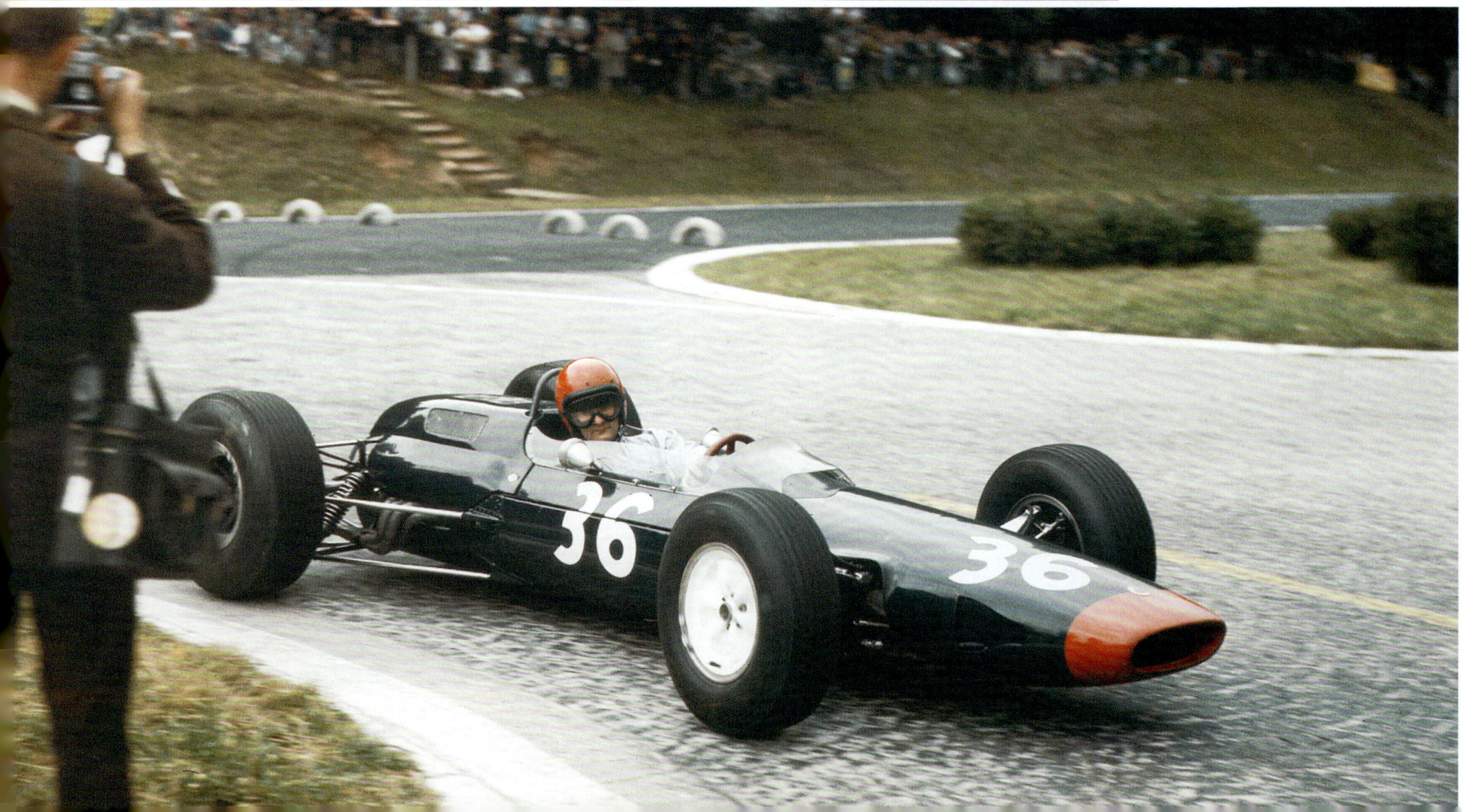

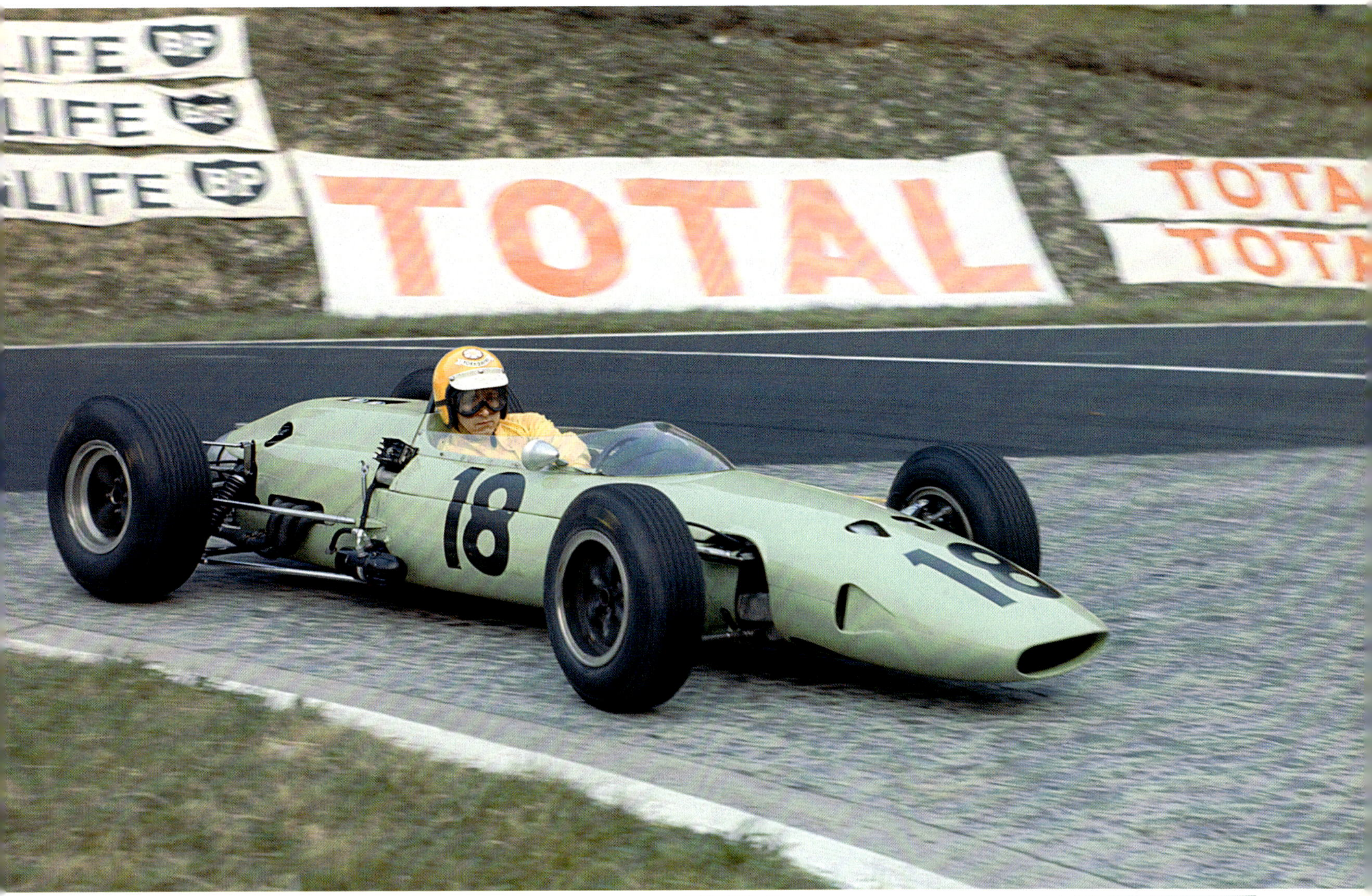

Another car that disappointed was the BRP that was loosely based on the Lotus 25. In 1962, BRP having paid Lotus handsomely for their tubular frame 24s were angered by the appearance of the monocoque 25 that was not available to customers. So Tony Robinson designed and built their own version using Lotus suspension. Innes Ireland competed in the original car in 1963 and a second was constructed for 1964. Innes won the wet *Daily Mirror* Trophy at Snetterton in March, but that was their best result. Here is Trevor Taylor in BRP-3-64 that crashed due to brake failure. Taylor survived no less than six Grand Prix shunts between 1962–64, most of them not his fault.

Californian Richie Ginther, friend of Phil Hill, sports car racer *par excellence* and brilliant test and development driver for Ferrari and BRM. He was often overshadowed by his team mates, inevitably playing a supporting role that did not do him justice. BRM engineer John Sismey remembers him as being very twitchy and sarcastic. By 1964, Tony Rudd was becoming concerned about Richie's lack of drive and his marriage was causing problems. This was his final year with BRM and at Brands Hatch for the British GP Richie finished an undistinguished 8th.

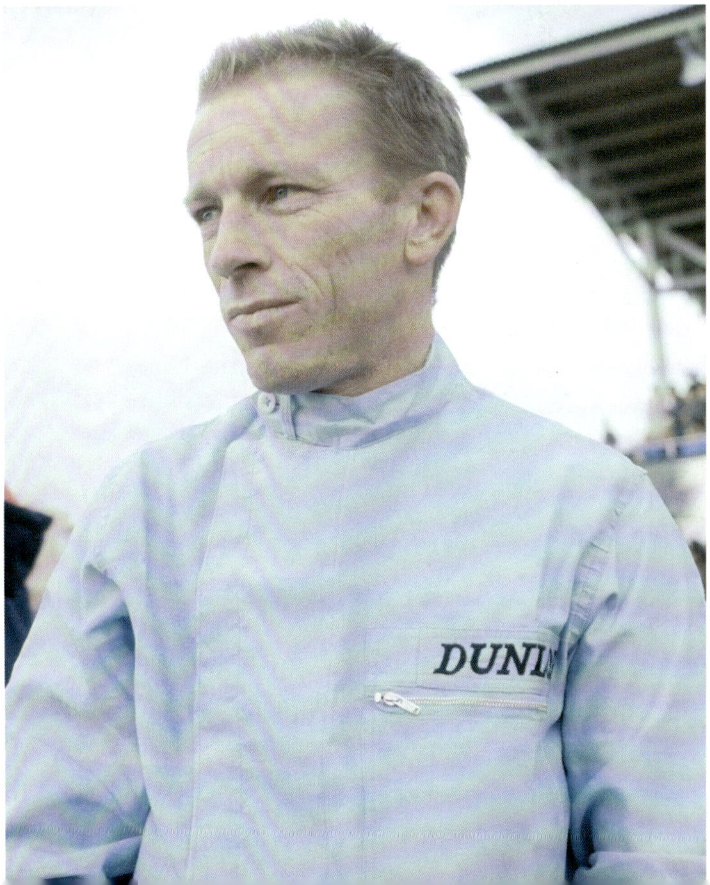

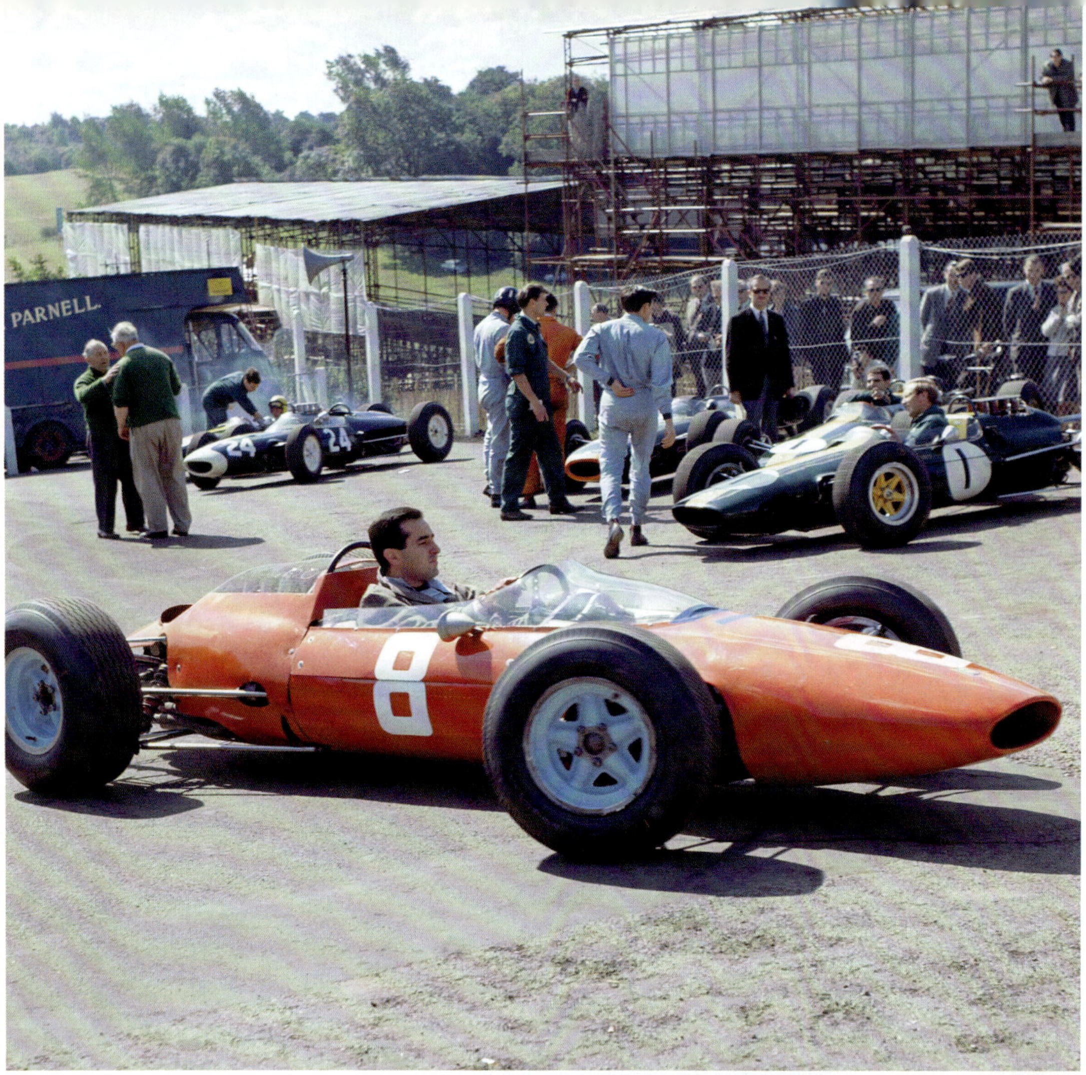

Lorenzo Bandini drives his Ferrari Dino 156 (0004) out of the paddock at Brands Hatch before a practice session for the British Grand Prix, behind the temporary grandstands on the outside of Paddock Hill Bend. Jim Clark strides to his car watched by Colin Chapman whilst a helmeted Graham Hill prepares to mount his BRM. The other car in shot is Peter Revson's Lotus 24 BRM with the Parnell Racing van behind. Clark and Hill finished 1st and 2nd in this race which, according to Tony Rudd, would have been won by Hill if he had taken full advantage of the slippery conditions, in which the BRM was superior. Bandini finished 5th and note the scruffy front wheel.

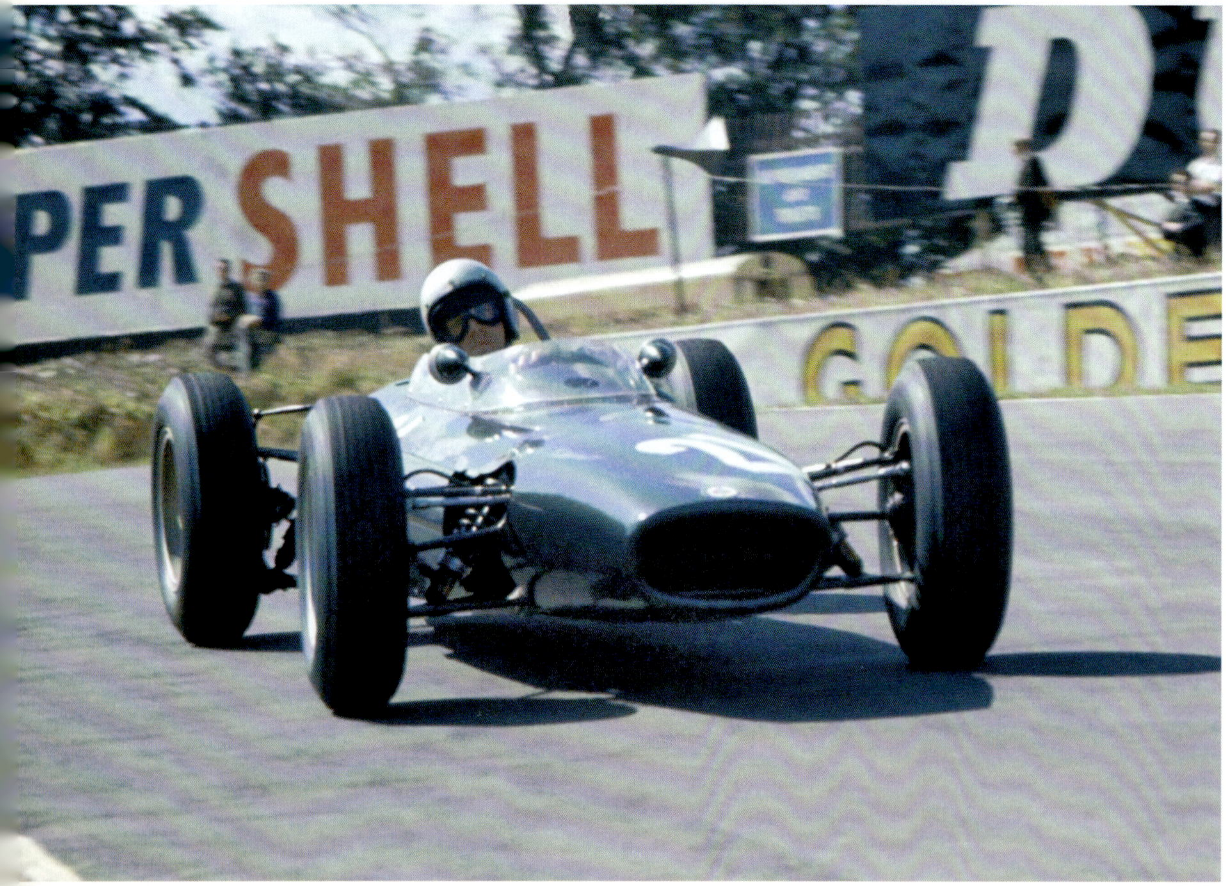

Richard Attwood in BRM's spaceframe 4wd P67 at Brands Hatch where it was the slowest car during Friday practice and was withdrawn from the race. When Ferguson stopped racing their 4wd P99 they offered the technology to anybody interested and BRM took it over, probably with the 3-litre F1 in mind. It was a hybrid machine using a spaceframe for ease of access to the 4wd system, built by Mike Pilbeam, but it was 150lb overweight, not a good idea with only 200bhp. BRM had no real intention of racing it. Ironically it was later resurrected by former Ferguson hillclimb champion Peter Westbury and Peter Lawson won the 1968 British Hillclimb Championship with the unique machine.

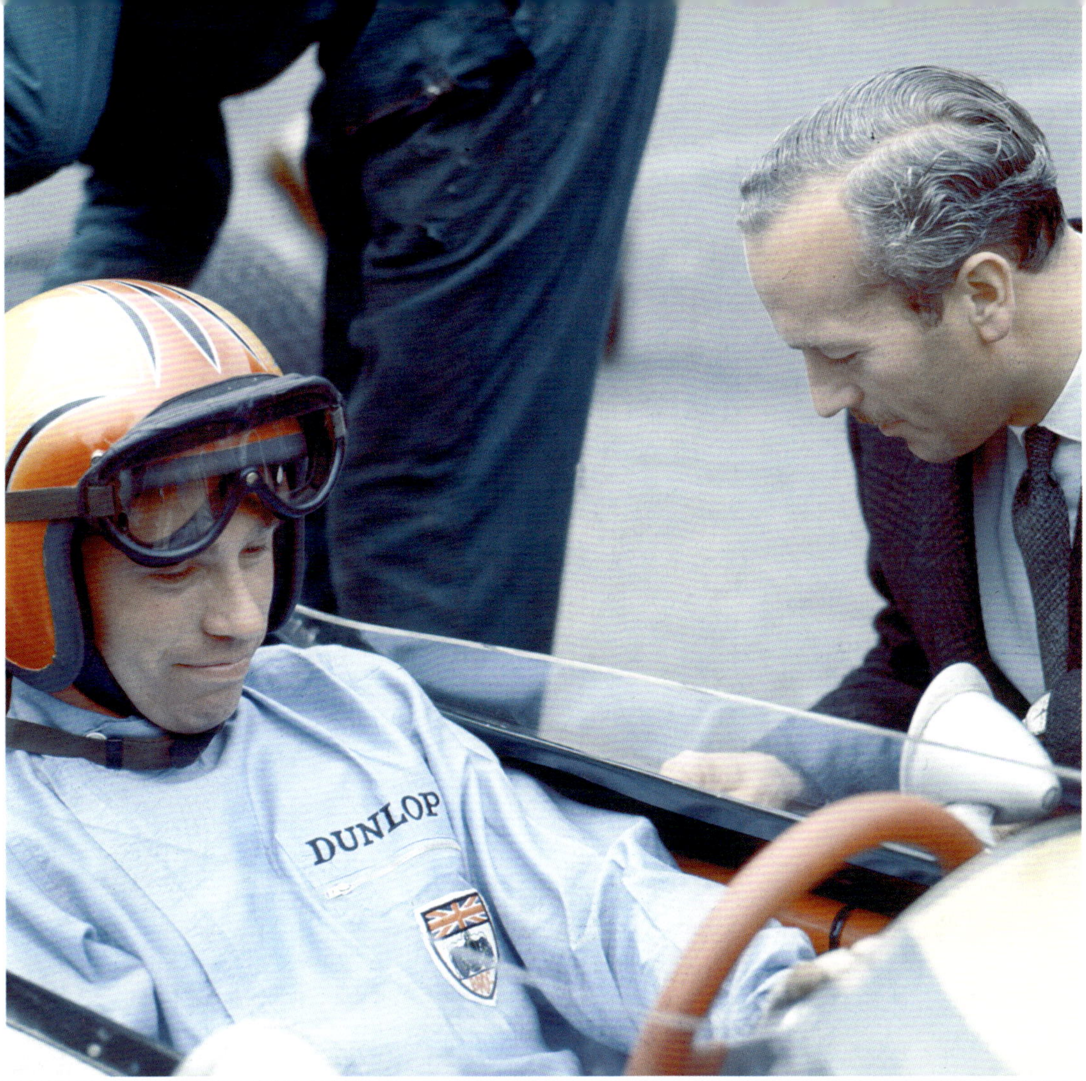

Mike Spence replaced the injured Peter Arundell at Team Lotus for the British Grand Prix and the rest of the season. Here Spence seems very pleased with himself while Colin Chapman fiddles with something on the side of the Lotus 25. While his team leader won the race, Spence started from mid-grid and finished 8th.

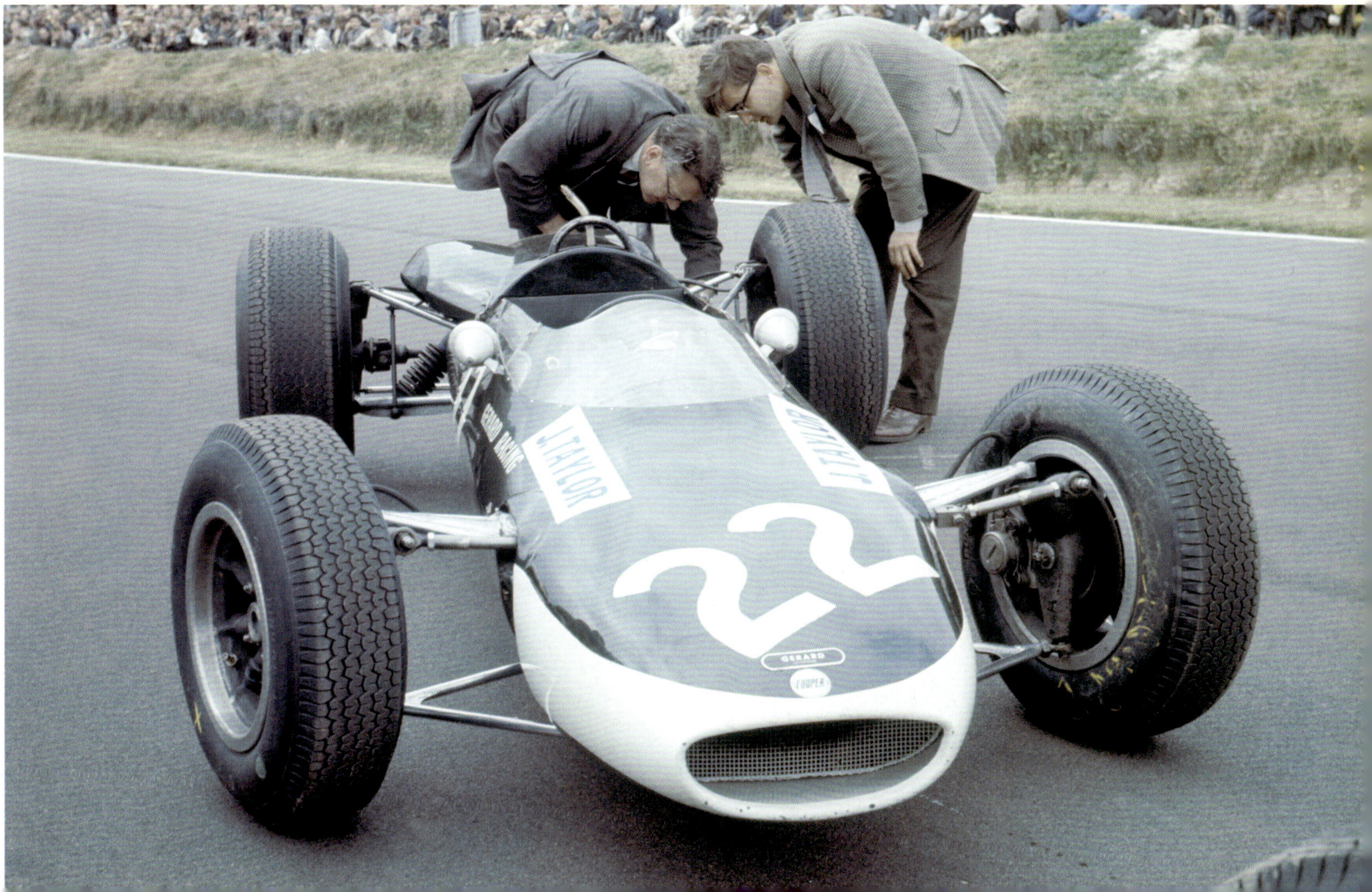

Bob Gerard was a famous postwar ERA driver turned entrant who ran F1 and F2 cars for a variety of drivers over the years. This much modified Cooper T59 began life as an FJ car (GR-13-62). In 1964, the promising John Taylor drove it with a Ford engine modified by the recently formed Cosworth concern and finished 5th at Aintree and Silverstone. Their one and only Grand Prix came at Brands Hatch where Taylor outqualified three pukka F1 cars but retired on lap 56. How relatively easy it was then to race in F1.

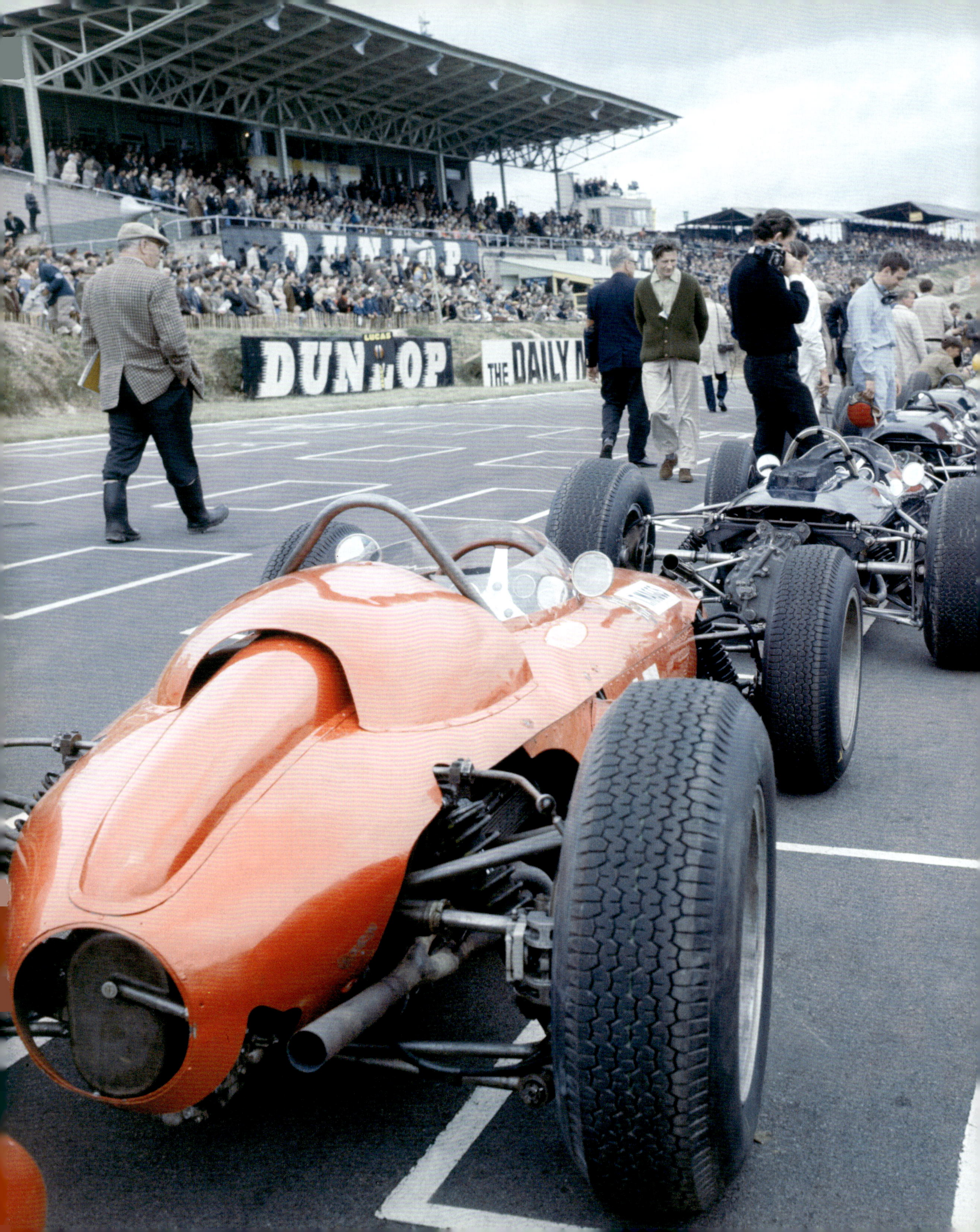
LUCAS
THE DAILY

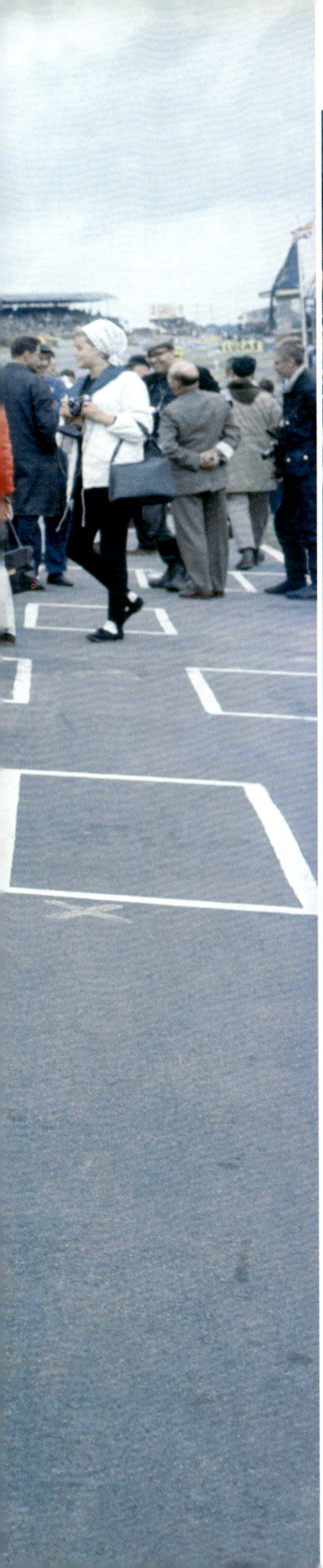

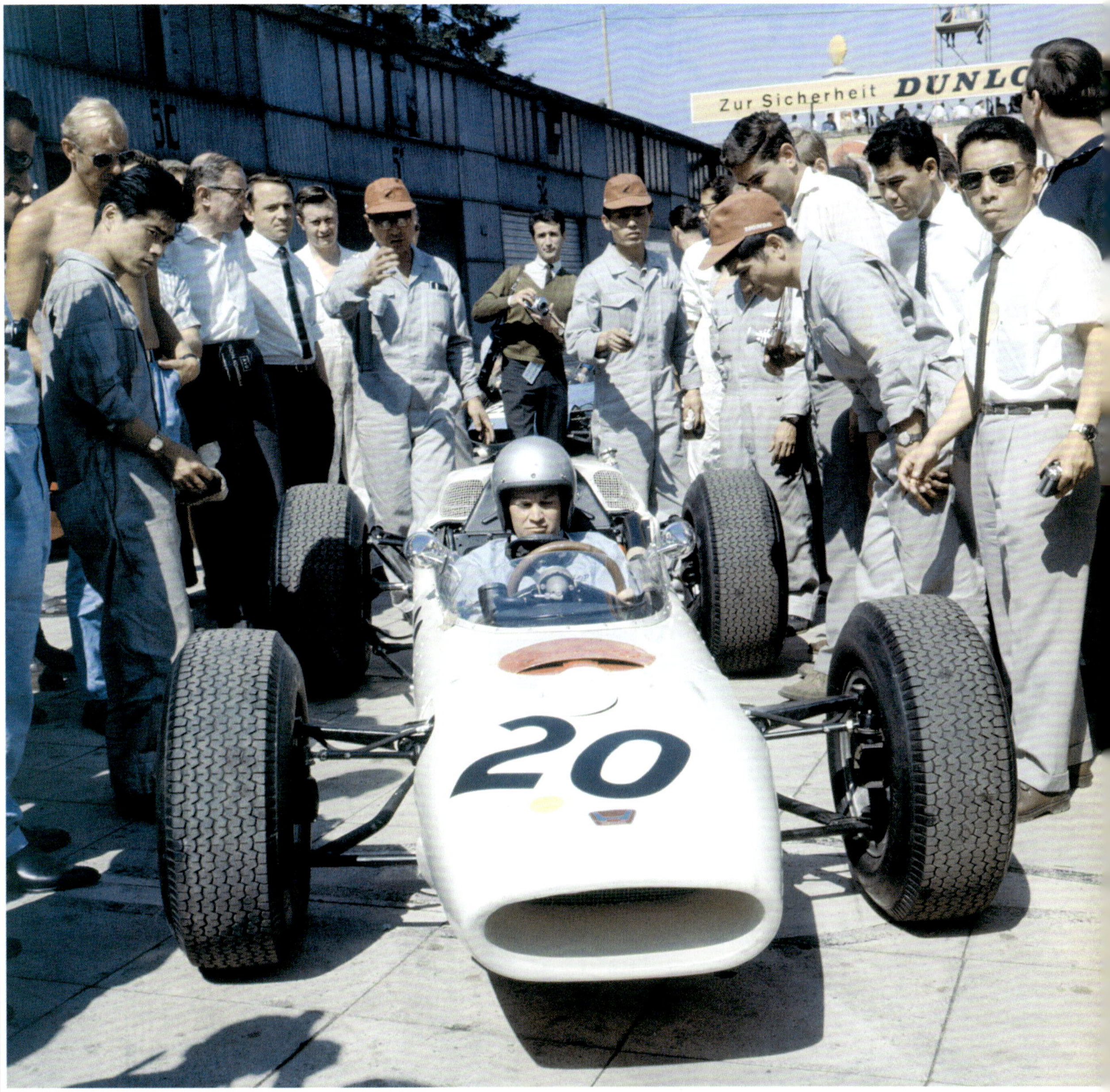

Honda entered the F1 arena at the 1964 German GP with a dumpy looking car designated RA271 that uniquely used a transverse-mounted 60-degree V12 engine. They had purchased a Cooper T53 in 1962 for exploratory purposes and ultimately built this monocoque car. It was driven by American sports car racer Ronnie Bucknum, a man with no single seater experience at all and who had never raced in Europe. This controversial decision was apparently based on the assumption that Bucknum's novice F1 status would not prejudice attitudes as to the car's performance that was being presented as an experimental venture. Bucknum qualified, albeit last, reached 11th but crashed out on lap 11 when the steering failed, not a bad effort for your F1 debut on a damp and daunting Nordschleife.

This is the grid line-up for the British GP at Brands Hatch (the first held here, the last being in 1986) and the car nearest is probably Tony Maggs' BRM P57 (5785). The entrant Scuderia Centro Sud was founded by Guglielmo 'Mimmo' Dei, an Alfa Romeo and Maserati dealer and distributor for central and southern Italy (hence Centro Sud), and his brother. They were largely funded courtesy of BP Italia, starting in F1 during the 1950s with Maserati 250Fs. For 1963 they bought Hill's 'Old Faithful' BRM P57 5781 and the Bourne rebuilt car, properly maintained and driven by Bandini was still competitive. However, by 1964 the cars were run on the proverbial shoestring and Bandini had returned to Ferrari. Patched and mended and with inadequate maintenance the BRMs were last raced at Monza in 1965 by which time they were completely worn out.

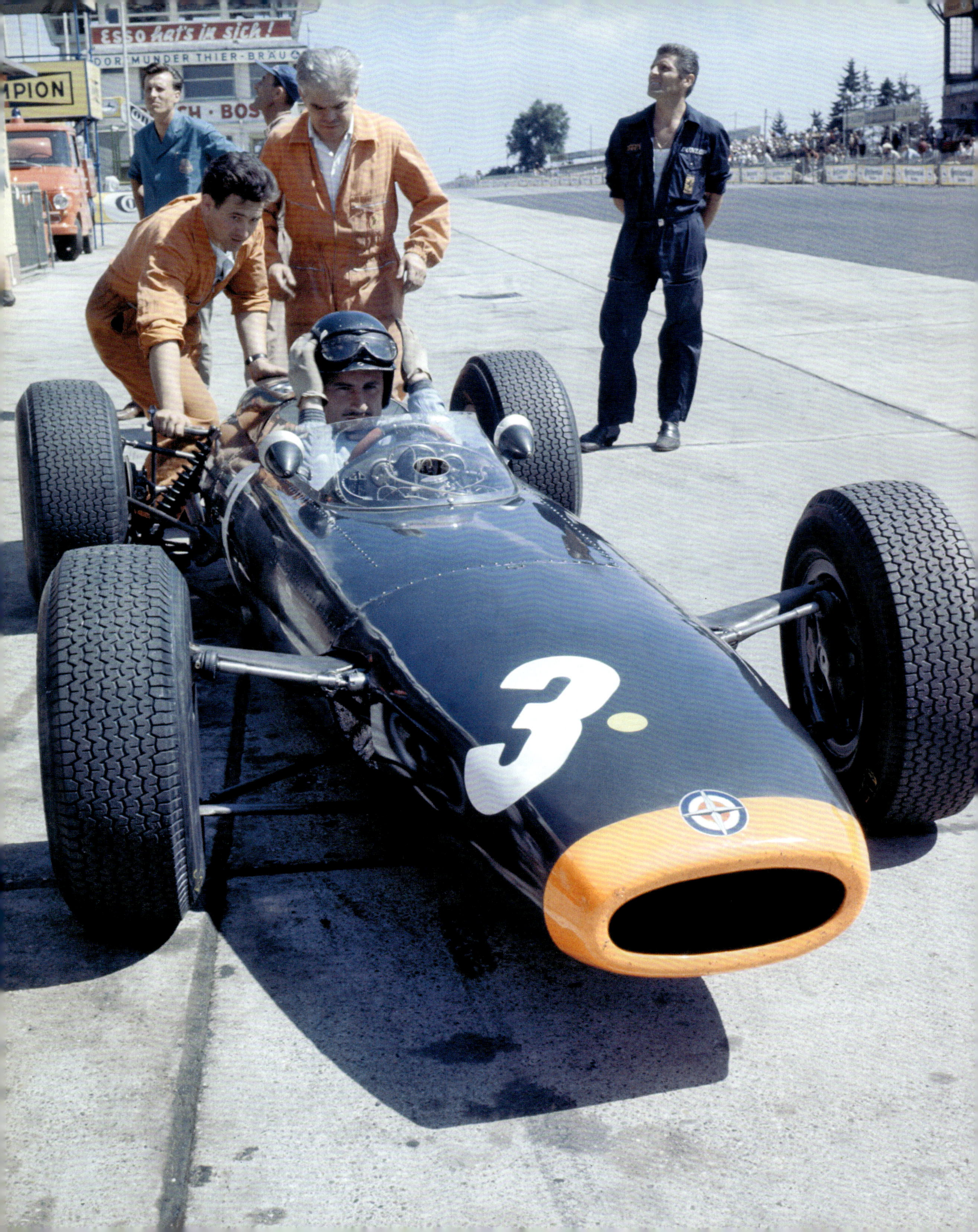
Esso hat's in sich!
3

BRM mechanic Alan Challis pushes Graham Hill's P261 (2614) along the wide concrete apron of the old Nürburgring pits while colleague Willy Southcott looks on. Both BRM drivers missed gears and broke tappets during practice necessitating engine changes. For once Hill was not on the front row, starting fifth but still finished 2nd behind Surtees' Ferrari despite a misfire caused by a broken ignition wire.

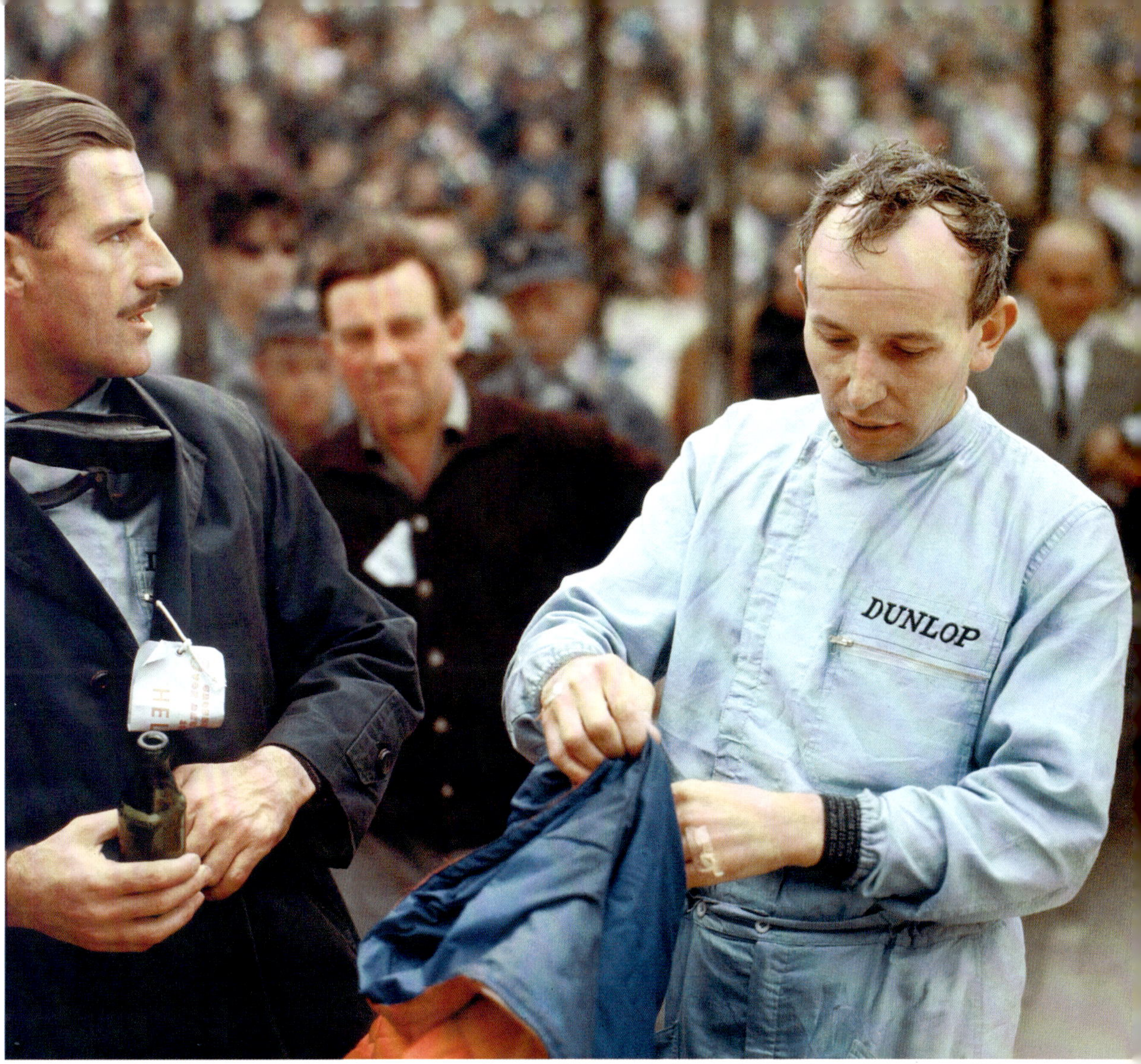

Runner up Graham Hill clutches a bottle whilst winner John Surtees is struggling with his jacket. The begrimed goggle marked faces bear witness to their vicissitudes during the German GP.

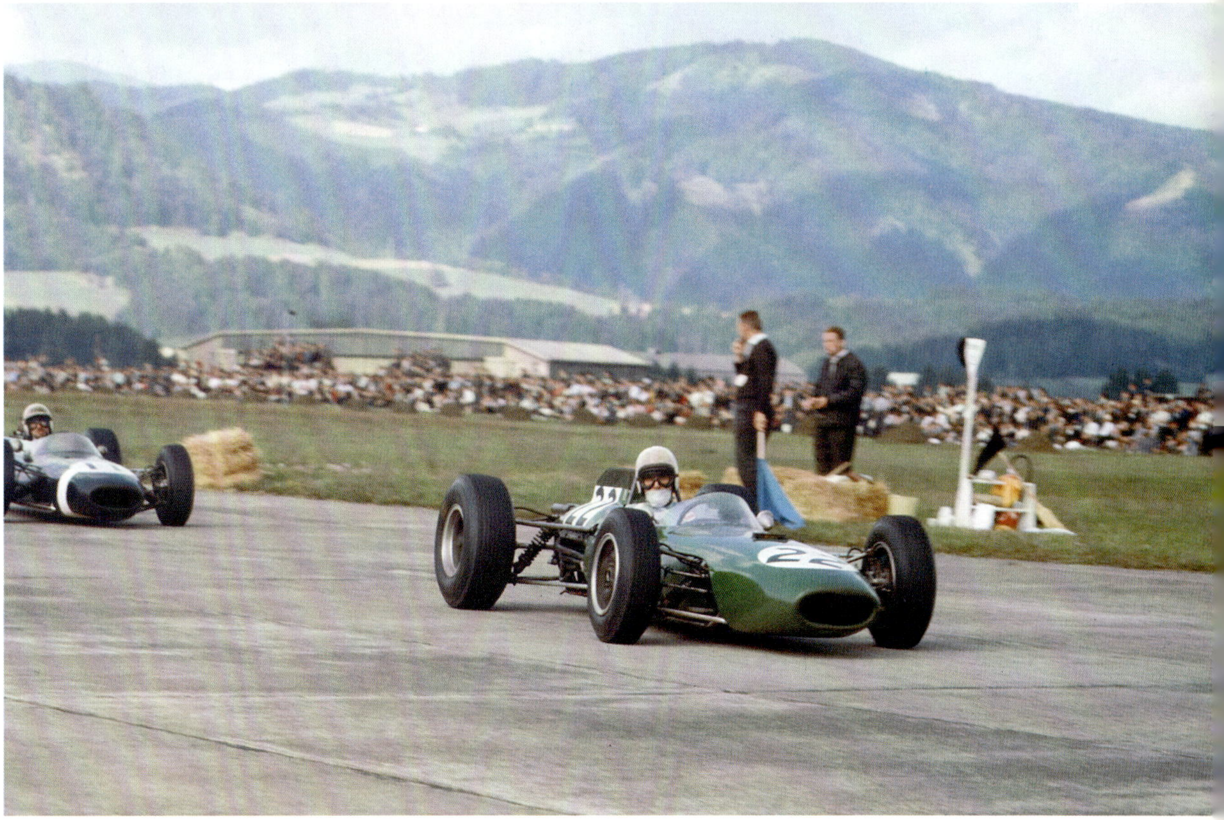

The high rate of attrition that struck most of the front runners in the Austrian GP at Zeltweg airport, helped Bob Anderson (followed here by Bonnier's Brabham) to finish 3rd in his Brabham BT11 (F1-5-64) behind winner Bandini's Ferrari Dino V6 (his only GP win) and Ginther's BRM. Anderson's virtually single handed efforts in his privately run car were worthy of the highest praise.

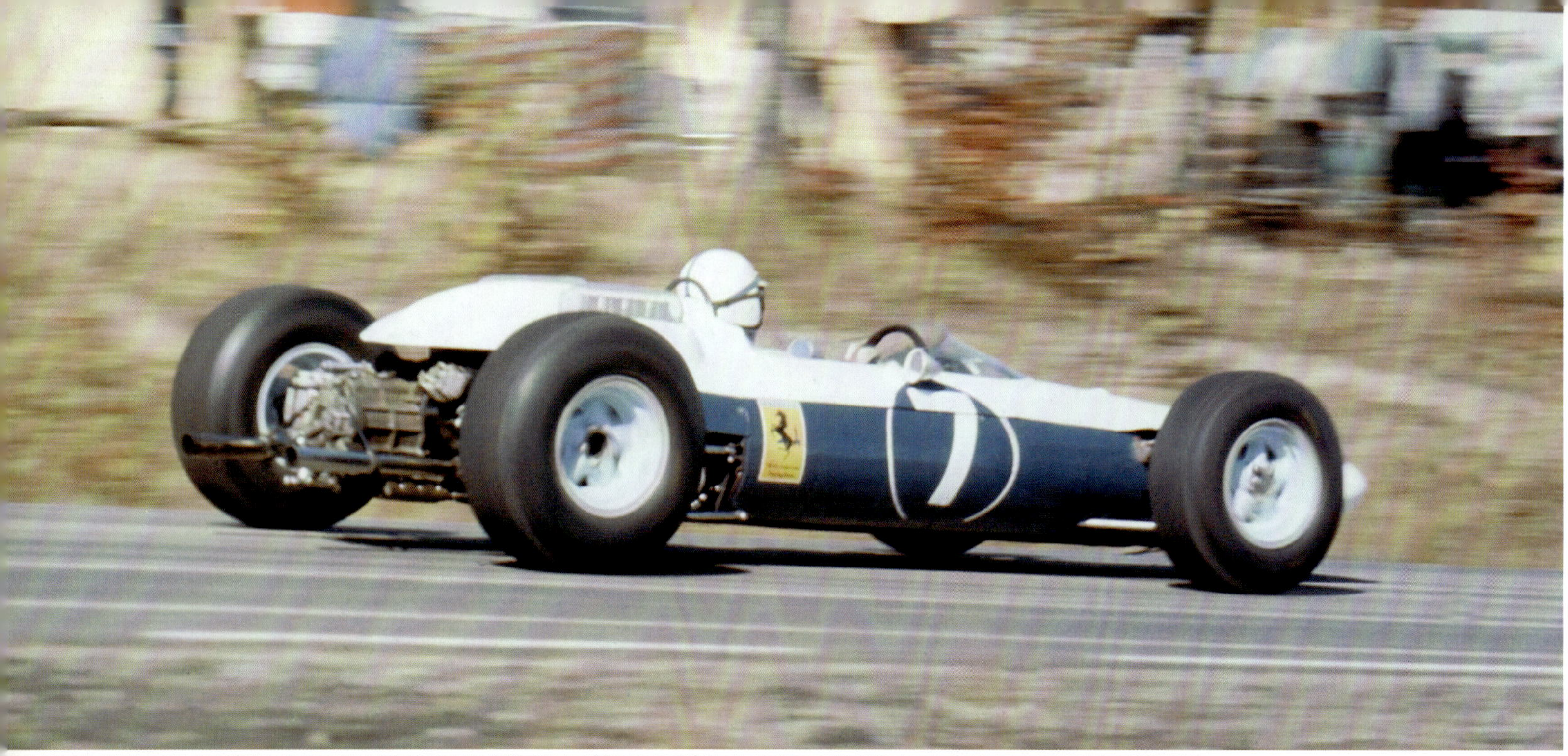

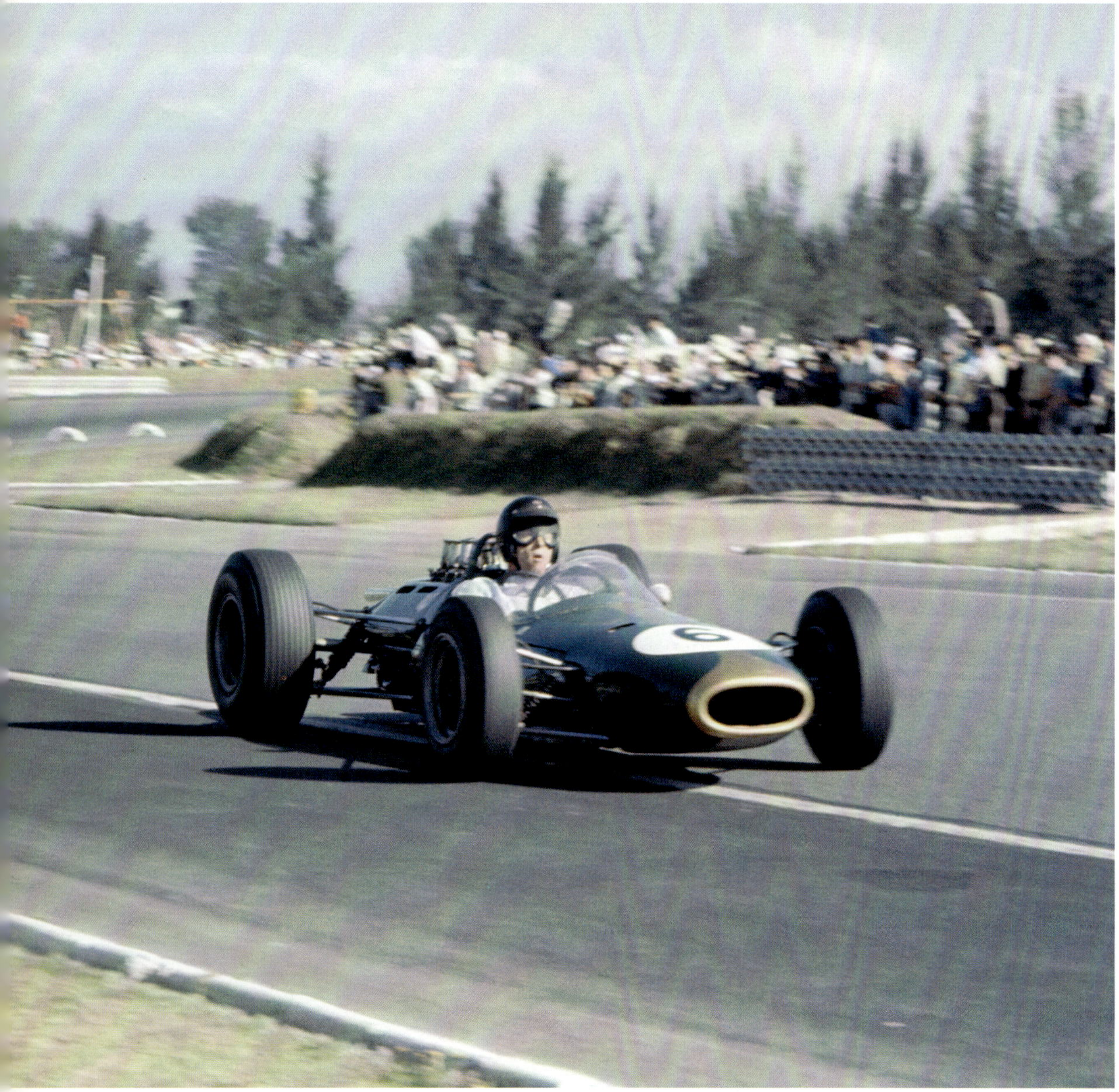

Having won convincingly at Monza, John Surtees in the Ferrari 158 (0005) heads for 2nd place in the US GP at Watkins Glen behind Graham Hill's BRM after spinning off whilst leading. The change of livery to North American Racing Team colours followed a spat involving Enzo Ferrari, the Italian authorities and the CSI, who had refused to accept the new prototype 250LM as a GT car. Ferrari declined to race in Italian red and Luigi Chinetti's NART organisation ostensibly handled the entries for the American and Mexican Grands Prix. In Mexico, Surtees became the World Champion after team mate Lorenzo Bandini had shunted Hill off the road and Jim Clark had retired.

Jim Clark led the Mexican GP until the last lap when his Lotus ran out of lubricant; luck had finally deserted him. Dan Gurney inherited the lead in his Brabham BT7 (F1-1-63), some compensation for losing the Belgian GP and the many engine failures that Brabham had suffered during 1964. Gurney only won one more Grand Prix after this, an extraordinary paucity of results for an extraordinary surplus of talent.

1964 Teams, drivers and results

Cooper Car Co – Cooper T66 Climax V8 and T73 Climax V8
Bruce McLaren (NZ) (Used older T66 at Monaco)
Phil Hill (USA) (Missed Italian GP)

Team Lotus – Lotus 25 Climax V8 and 33 Climax V8
Jim Clark (GB)
Peter Arundell (GB) (Monaco, Dutch, Belgian and French GPs only, badly injured at Reims F2 race and missed rest of the season)
Mike Spence (GB) (Replaced Arundell from British GP onwards)
Gerhard Mitter (D) (German GP only)
Walt Hansgen (USA) (US GP only)
Moises Solana (MEX) (Mexican GP only)

Owen Racing Organisation – BRM P261
Graham Hill (GB)
Richie Ginther (USA)

Brabham Racing Organisation – Brabham BT7 Climax V8
Jack Brabham (AUS)
Dan Gurney (USA)

SEFAC Ferrari – Ferrari 156, 158 and 1512
John Surtees (GB) (WORLD CHAMPION)
Lorenzo Bandini (I) (Used new 1512 flat 12 US GP only)
Lodovico Scarfiotti (I) (Italian GP only)

North American Racing Team – Ferrari 156
Pedro Rodriguez (MEX) (US GP only)

Honda R & D Co – Honda RA271
Ronnie Bucknum (USA) (German, Italian and US GPs only)

British Racing Partnership – BRP BRM V8
Trevor Taylor (GB) (Missed Dutch and German GPs)
Innes Ireland (GB) (dns Monaco GP practice crash, missed Dutch and German GPs)

R. R. C. Walker Racing Team – Cooper T66 Climax V8, Brabham BT11 Climax V8 and BT7 Climax V8
Jo Bonnier (S) (Missed French GP)
Edgar Barth (D) (German GP only in Cooper)
Jochen Rindt (A) (Austrian GP only)
Jo Siffert (CH) (US and Mexican GPs only)
'Hap' Sharp (USA) (US and Mexican GPs only)

Reg Parnell (Racing) – Lotus 25 BRM V8 and 24 BRM V8
Mike Hailwood (GB) (Missed Belgian GP due to illness, car driven by Revson)
Chris Amon (NZ) (Missed Italian GP no car available)
Peter Revson (USA) (dnq Monaco Gp, dsq Belgian GP, dns French GP car driven by Hailwood, British, German and Italian GPs only)

Ecurie Maarsbergen – Porsche 718
Carel de Beaufort (NL) (Dutch GP only, fatal crash practice German GP)

Scuderia Centro Sud – BRM P57
Giancarlo Baghetti (I) (Dutch, Belgian, British, German, Austrian and Italian GPs only)
Tony Maggs (RA) (dns Dutch GP practice crash, dns Belgian GP engine failure practice, British, German and Austrian GPs only)

DW Racing Enterprises – Brabham BT11 Climax V8
Bob Anderson (GB) (dns Belgian GP ignition problems, missed US and Mexican GPs)

Siffert Racing Team – Lotus 24 BRM V8 and Brabham BT11 BRM V8
Jo Siffert (CH) (Entered by Rob Walker for US and Mexican GPs)

Maurice Trintignant – BRM P57
Maurice Trintignant (F) (Monaco, French, German and Italian GPs only, dnq British GP)

Equipe Scirocco Belge – Scirocco Climax V8
André Pilette (B) (Belgian GP only, dnq German GP)

Gerard Racing – Cooper T59 Ford 4
John Taylor (GB) (British GP only)

John Willment Automobiles – Brabham BT10 Ford 4
Frank Gardner (AUS) (British GP only, starting line accident)

Ian Raby (Racing) – Brabham BT3 BRM V8
Ian Raby (GB) (British GP only, dnq Italian GP)

Derrington-Francis Racing Team – ATS 100
Mario de Cabral (P) (Italian GP only)

WORLD CHAMPIONSHIP VENUES AND WINNERS
(ten rounds)

Monaco GP	Monte Carlo	Graham Hill
Dutch GP	Zandvoort	Jim Clark
Belgian GP	Spa-Francorchamps	Jim Clark
French GP	Rouen-les Essarts	Dan Gurney
British GP	Brands Hatch	Jim Clark
German GP	Nürburgring	John Surtees
Austrian GP	Zeltweg	Lorenzo Bandini
Italian GP	Monza	John Surtees
United States GP	Watkins Glen	Graham Hill
Mexican GP	Mexico City	Dan Gurney

DRIVERS' CHAMPIONSHIP
Points: 9-6-4-3-2-1. Best 6 scores

1	John Surtees	Ferrari	40
2	Graham Hill	BRM	39
3	Jim Clark	Lotus	32
4	Lorenzo Bandini	Ferrari	23
5	Richie Ginther	BRM	23
6	Dan Gurney	Brabham	19
7	Bruce McLaren	Cooper	13
8	Peter Arundell	Lotus	11
9	Jack Brabham	Brabham	11
10	Jo Siffert	Lotus/Brabham	7
11	Bob Anderson	Brabham	5
12	Tony Maggs	BRM	4
13	Mike Spence	Lotus	4
14	Innes Ireland	BRP	4
15	Jo Bonnier	Cooper/Brabham	3
16	Chris Amon	Lotus	2
17	Maurice Trintignant	BRM	2
18	Walt Hansgen	Lotus	2
19	Mike Hailwood	Lotus	1
20	Phil Hill	Cooper	1
21	Trevor Taylor	BRP/Lotus	1
22	Pedro Rodriguez	Ferrari	1

CONSTRUCTORS' CHAMPIONSHIP
Points: 9-6-4-3-2-1, (awarded only to best-placed finisher). Best 6 scores

1	Ferrari	45
2	BRM	42
3	Lotus-Climax	37
4	Brabham-Climax	30
5	Cooper-Climax	16
6	Brabham-BRM	7
7	BRP-BRM	5
8	Lotus-BRM	3

1965

CLARK/CHAPMAN RULE, OK!

The last year of the 1.5-litre F1 and Jim Clark and Lotus regained their titles with Jimmy winning six races although he missed Monaco to race (and win) at Indianapolis. Graham Hill scored a hat trick at Monaco, beating strong Ferrari opposition from Surtees and Bandini. Hill also won the US GP and had three 2nds to finish runner-up again.

BRM signed up Jackie Stewart by outbidding Lotus, who impressed everybody by finishing 2nd in Belgium, France and Holland and won at Monza after Hill made a mistake. John Surtees endured a poor season with the V8 Ferrari and newer Flat-12 (first seen in 1964) and won no races, a sad state of affairs for a reigning World Champion. Lorenzo Bandini who finished 2nd at Monaco enjoyed better reliability and the cracks were widening 'twixt Surtees and Maranello. Dan Gurney and Jack Brabham were on the pace but again suffered reliability problems with their Coventry Climax engines, although Dan did achieve three 3rds and a brace of 2nds in the last five races of the championship. He also missed Monaco because like Clark he was racing in the Indy 500 and from here onwards the team fielded New Zealander Denny Hulme.

Cooper continued their gradual decline but held onto Bruce McLaren who was joined by 1964 F2 wunderkind Jochen Rindt. Having been surpassed by Lotus and Brabham the Surbiton team were now at the back of the queue for the best Coventry Climax engines. Richie Ginther left BRM to join Honda who retained Ronnie Bucknum. Their 1965 RA272 was very fast but unreliable and inconsistent. However, Ginther won the last GP of the year at Mexico and also the last race of the 1.5-litre formula. The rest of the grid included regulars Rob Walker, Reg Parnell (Racing) and DW Racing amongst others, none of whom excluding Rob Walker were very effective.

Aussie sports car racer Paul Hawkins, achieved unwanted notoriety by plunging into the harbour at Monaco thus emulating Ascari's 1955 effort in the Lancia D50. Scuderia Centro Sud continued to use their trio of ancient BRM P57s at a handful of European races, perhaps the oldest survivors of the existing formula still racing in World Championship events.

Leonard Lee of Coventry Climax shocked everybody on 17 October by announcing their intention to stop supplying racing engines. They had already abandoned any further development on their four-valve V8 engine in favour of a flat-16, but this was futile given the forthcoming 3-litre F1. Additionally the involvement with Jaguar's future V12 production engine was taking priority and prevented any chance of designing and building a new 3-litre racing engine.

The British non-championship events saw Spence win the Race of Champions at Brands Hatch after Clark crashed out under pressure from Gurney. However, the Scotsman won at Goodwood and in Sicily (Syracuse) but was once again beaten by Jo Siffert at Enna. Stewart defeated Surtees to win the International Trophy at Silverstone, his first ever F1 victory.

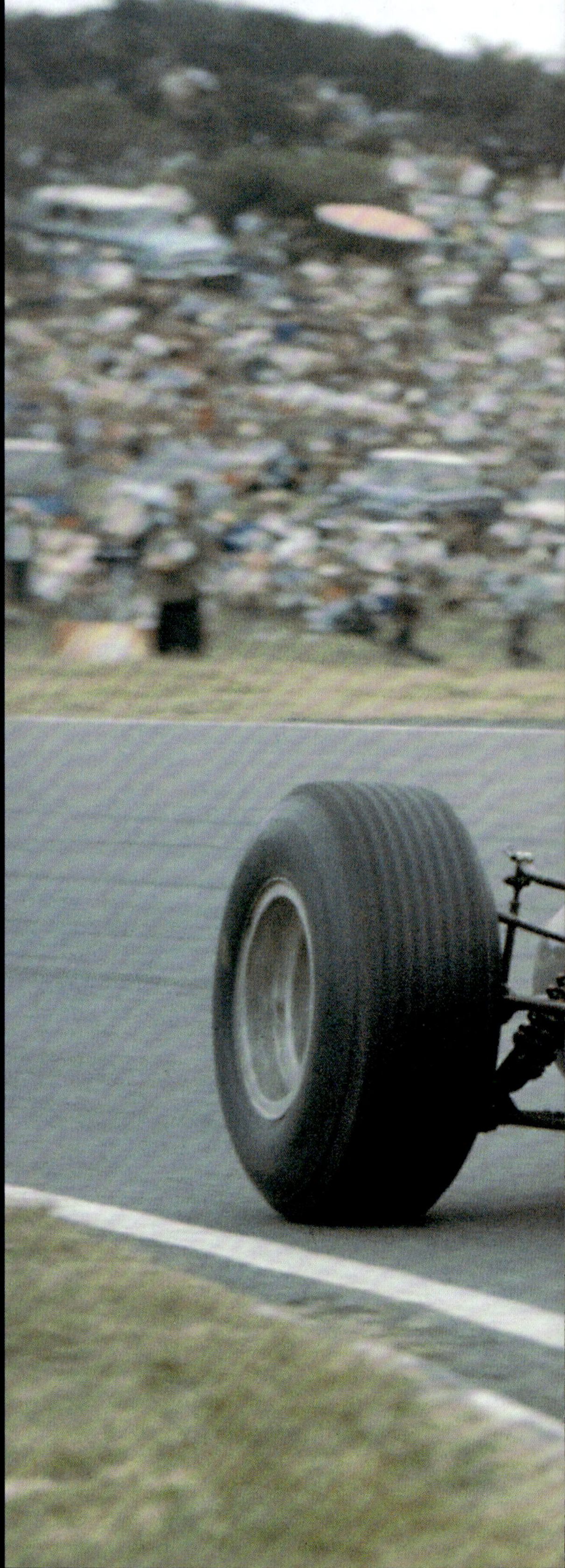

↓ Something rapid this way comes. Jackie Stewart's first championship Grand Prix came at East London, South Africa on New Year's Day 1965. He finished 6th to score a point in his debut despite a failing fuel pump. This is a new P261 (2617) that has a rather more bulbous snout than the usual shape.

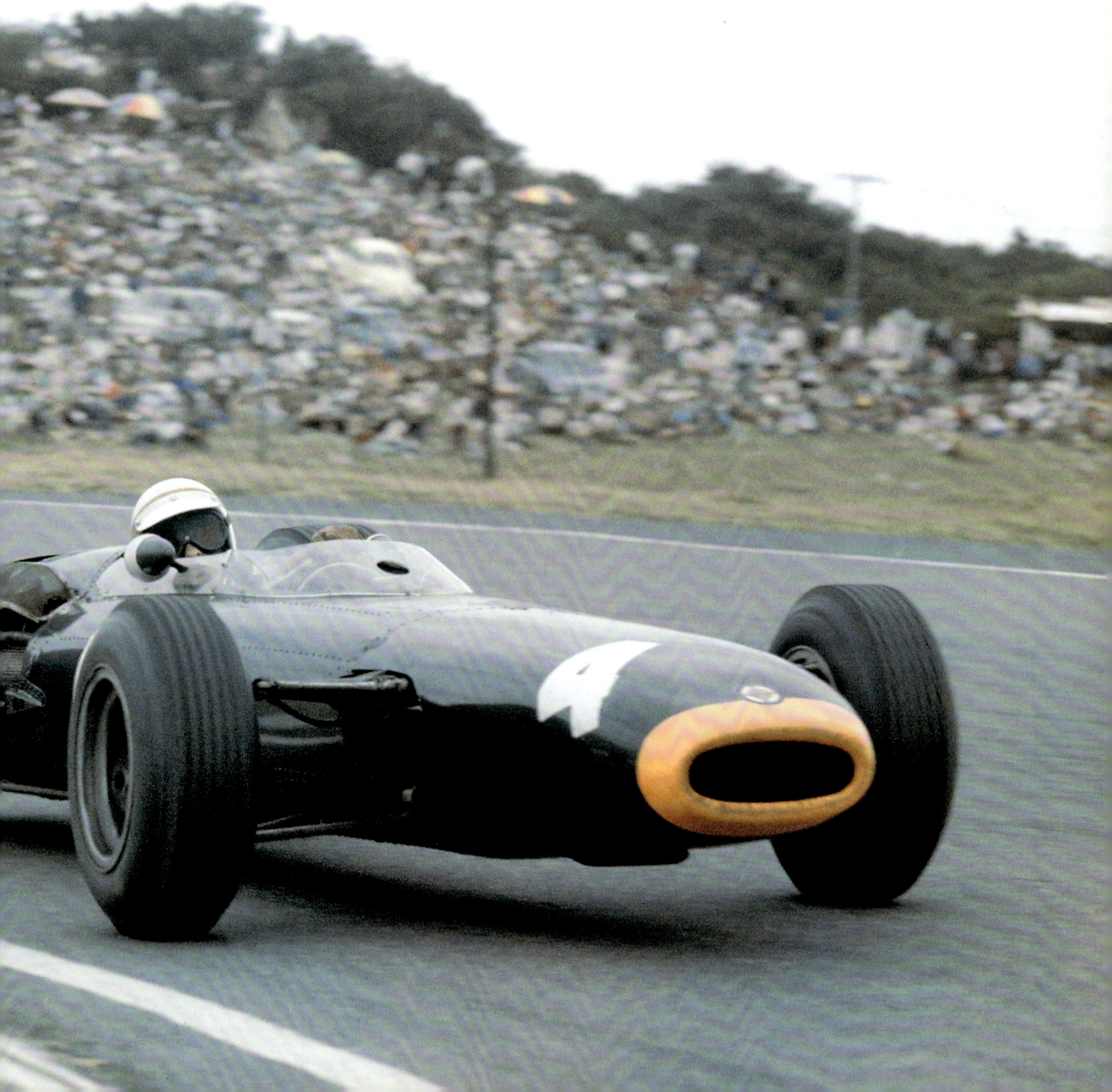

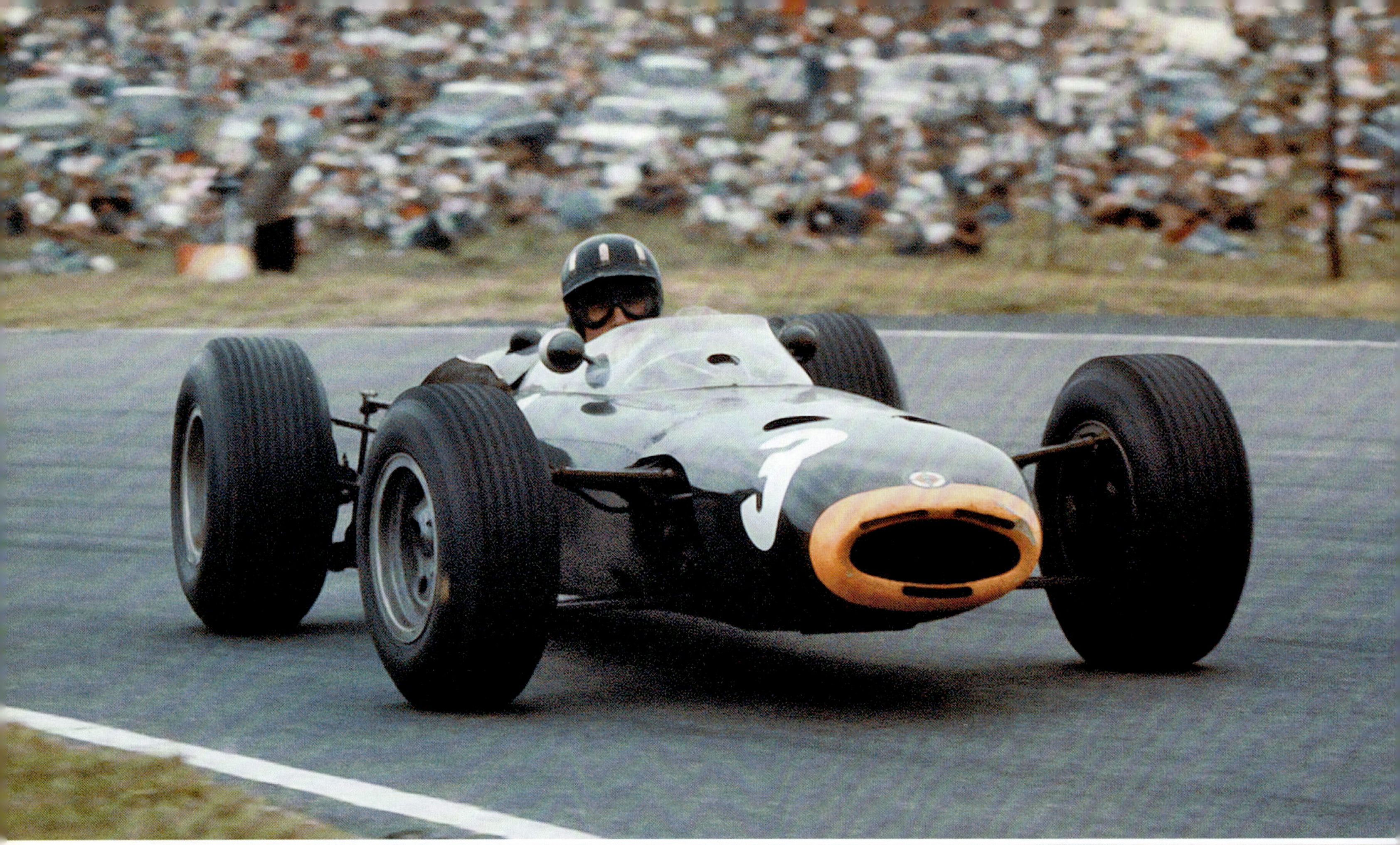
3

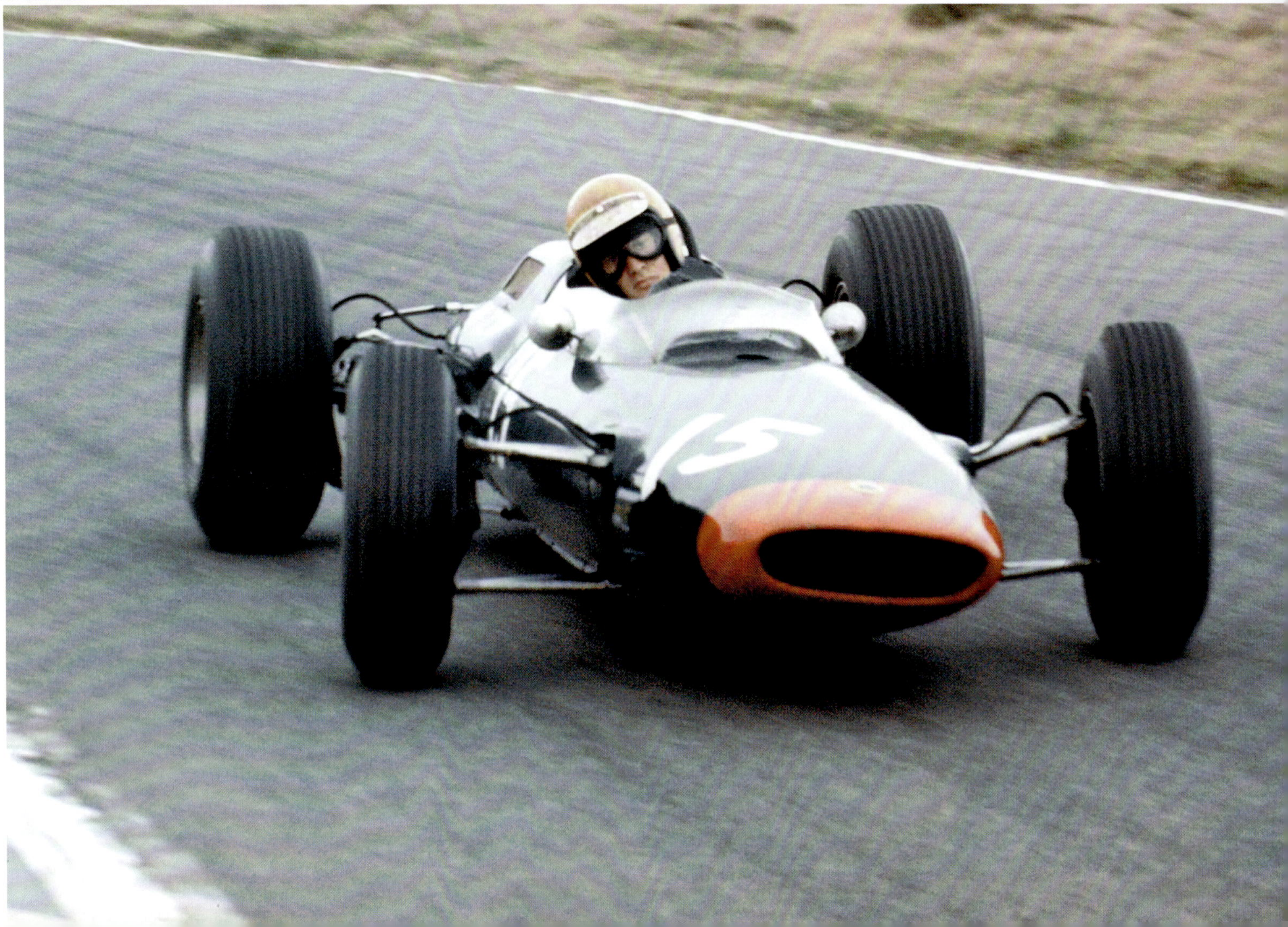
15

Compare Graham Hill's oversteering 2616 with the more conventional nose. Hill will finish 3rd behind John Surtees (Ferrari), both outpaced by Jim Clark's Lotus 33.

Tony Maggs in his final Grand Prix with the Reg Parnell Racing Lotus 25 (R4) BRM. He finished 11th, the old 25 displaying considerable understeer and body roll. After this he shared David Piper's Ferrari 250LM to finish 3rd at Sebring and scored a 2nd and two 4ths in an F2 Lola before crashing his Brabham in a local race at Pietermaritzburg. Tragically a small boy who was standing in a prohibited area was killed causing Maggs to retire from racing and return to farming.

Don't shoot until you can see the whites of their eyes. Jim Clark won the South African GP in the Lotus 33 (R10), leading from flag to flag with team mate Mike Spence in tow until he spun twice, dropping to 4th place. R10 will later be written off when Clark crashed at the Brands Hatch Race of Champions.

Frank Gardner in the John Willment Brabham BT11 BRM (F1-4-64) at East London. The team were inexperienced at this level and Gardner's abilities were wasted. He later competed in the Tasman series and F2 and one last GP at Monza in 1968 with a privately entered BRM that was not good enough to qualify. A man of great talent and versatility who sadly never raced a competitive F1 car, Frank Gardner instead triumphed in F5000 and saloon car categories achieving two championships in the former and several more in touring cars with Ford and Chevrolet into the 1970s.

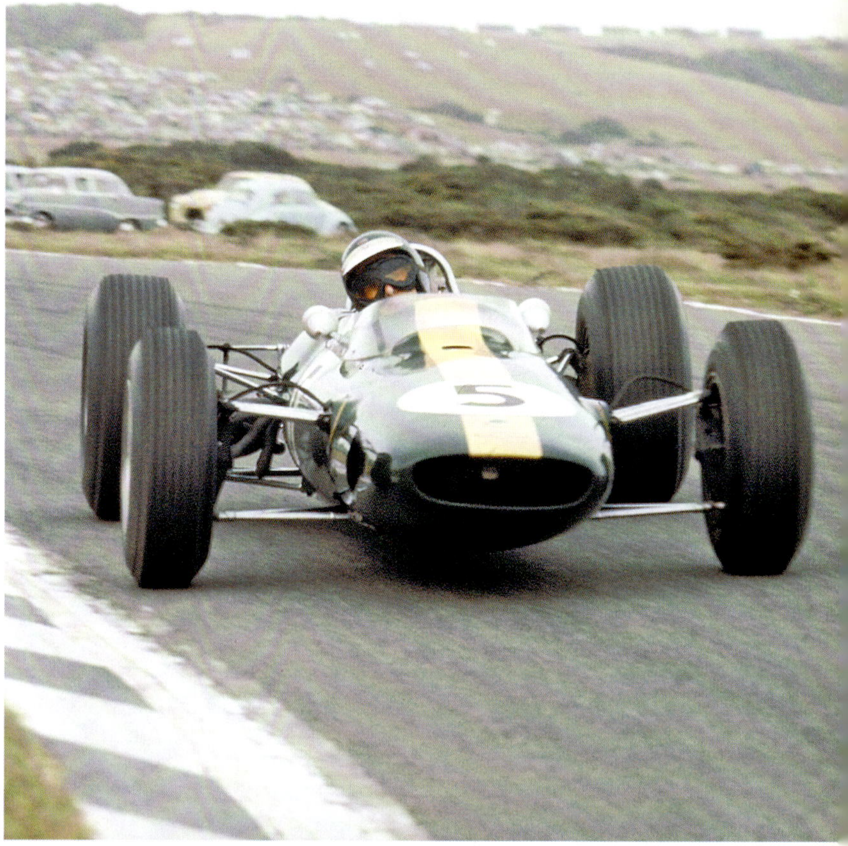

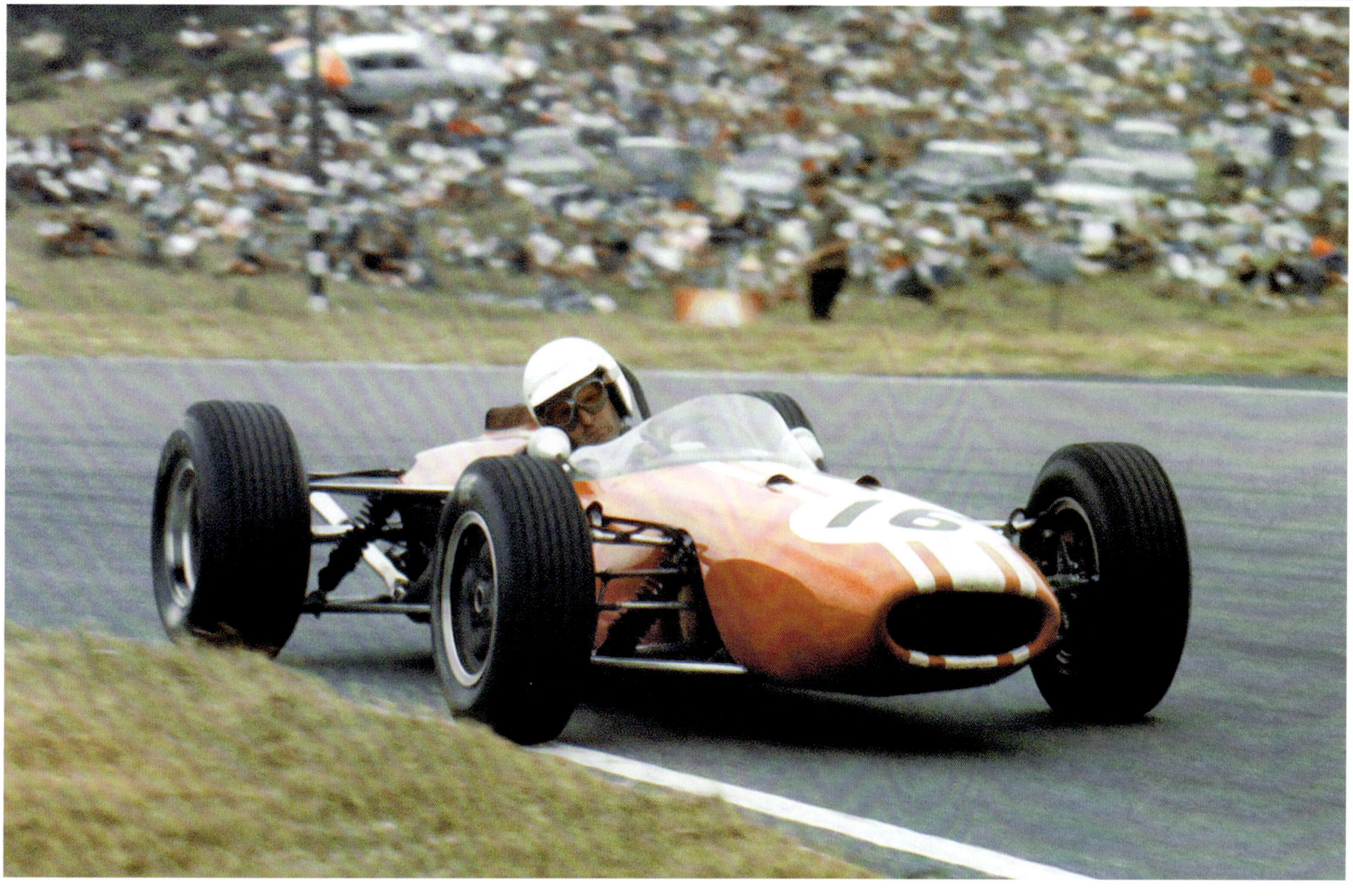

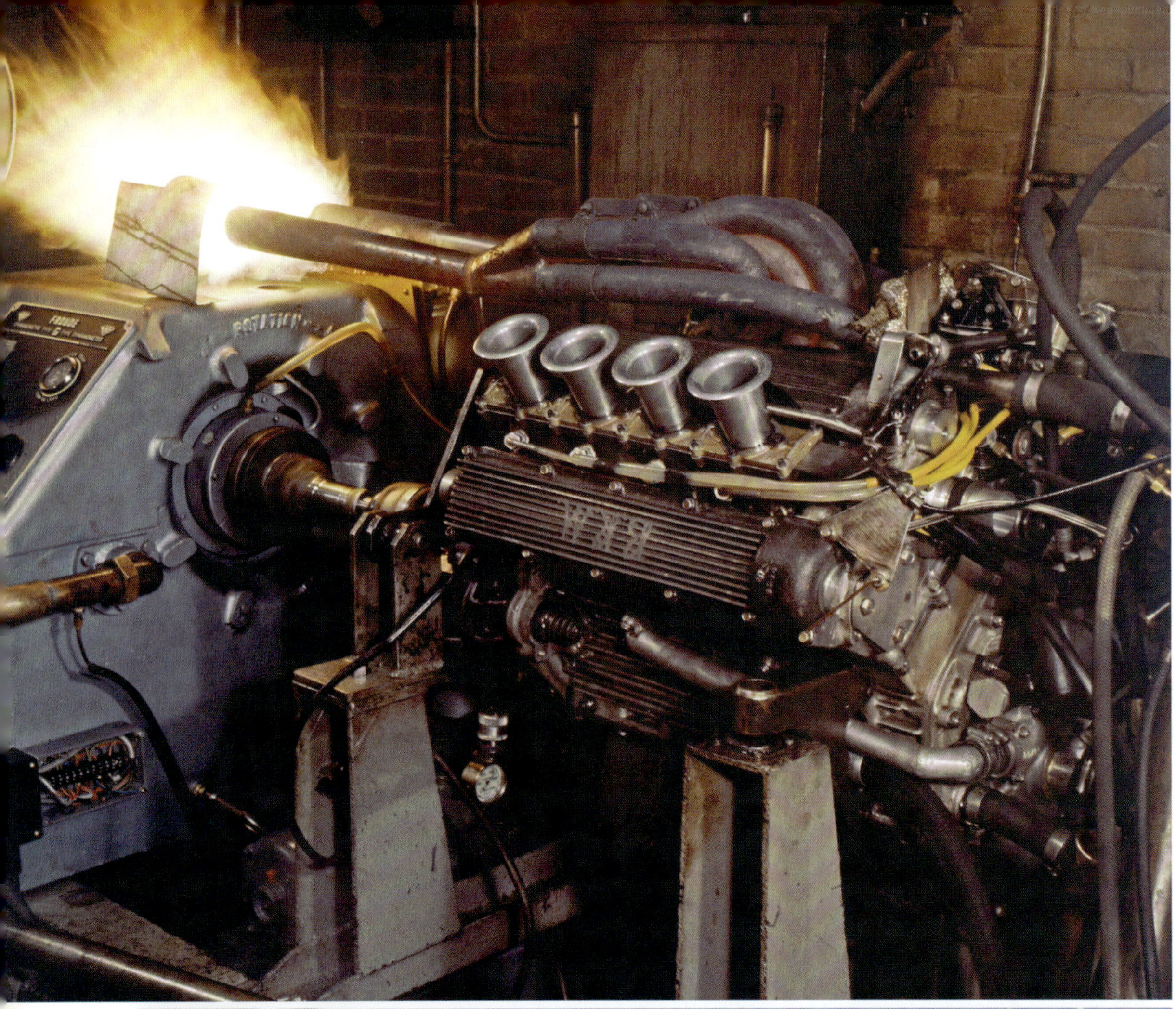

Come on baby, light my fire. BRM's wonderful 1498cc 90-degree V8 masterpiece on the BRM dynamometer at the engine testing sheds on Folkingham airfield in early 1965. Originally conceived by Peter Berthon with input from the multi-talented Amherst Villiers, engineered by Aubrey Woods and further developed by Tony Rudd it ultimately offered 222bhp @ 11,750rpm, 148bhp/litre. Very impressive for a naturally aspirated engine over 40 years ago.

Sparkling under a blue Sicilian sky, the simple elegant lines of the period racing car, unencumbered with the disfiguring commercial graffiti and ugly excrescences that will define the genre in future times. A bespectacled Mauro Forgheri and the Ferrari 158 (0005) of John Surtees at the XIV Gran Premio di Siracusa where he finished 2nd to Jim Clark's new Lotus 33 (R11).

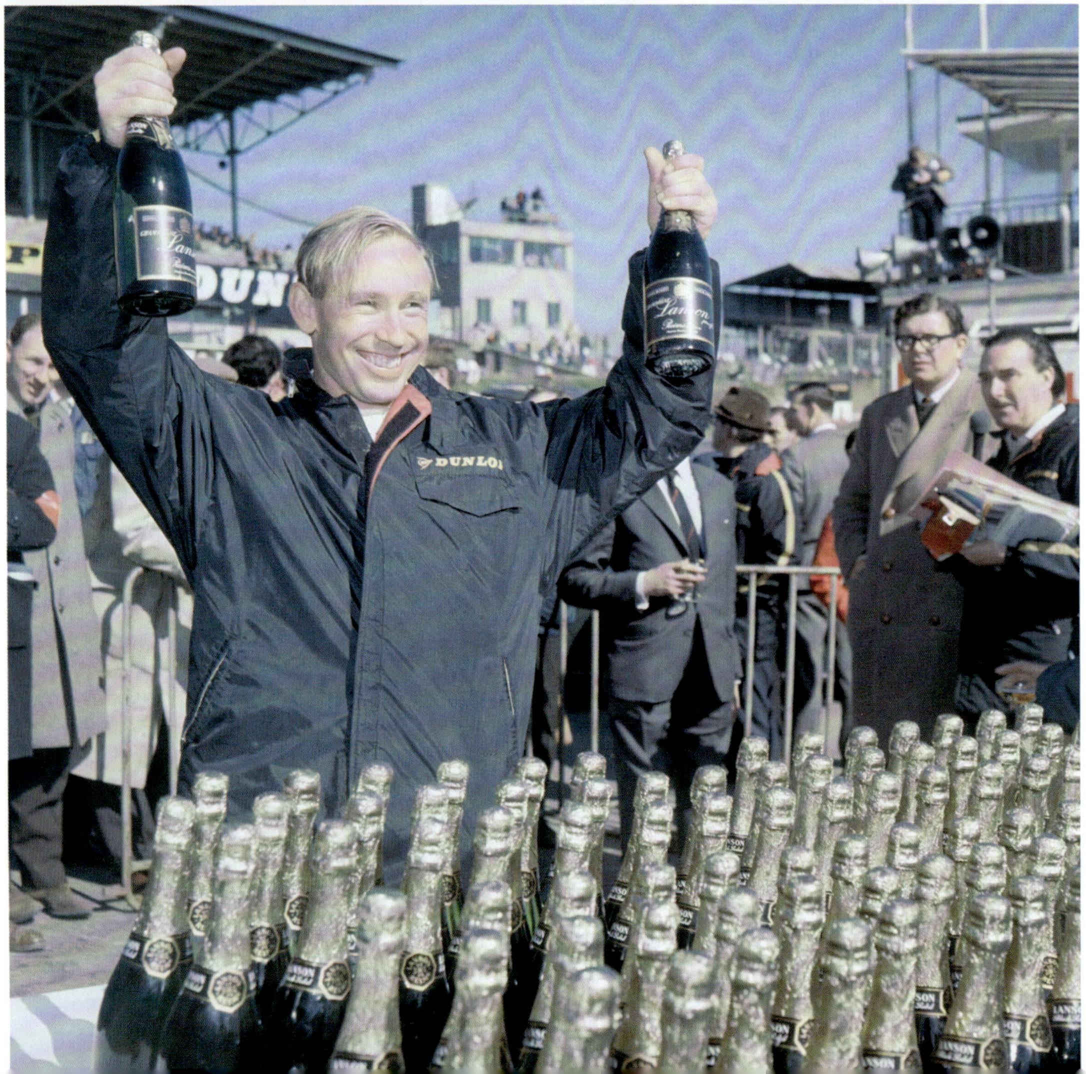

Mike Spence and 100 bottles of Lanson 'Black Label' champagne at Brands Hatch after the Race of Champions. The event was run in two heats and Spence's Lotus 33 finished 3rd in the first behind Jim Clark's sister car and Dan Gurney's Brabham. He then won the second heat after Clark had crashed out under pressure from Gurney, who had then himself retired. At right can be seen BRSCC secretary and clerk of the course Nick Syrett (in the overcoat), with race commentator Peter Scott-Russell.

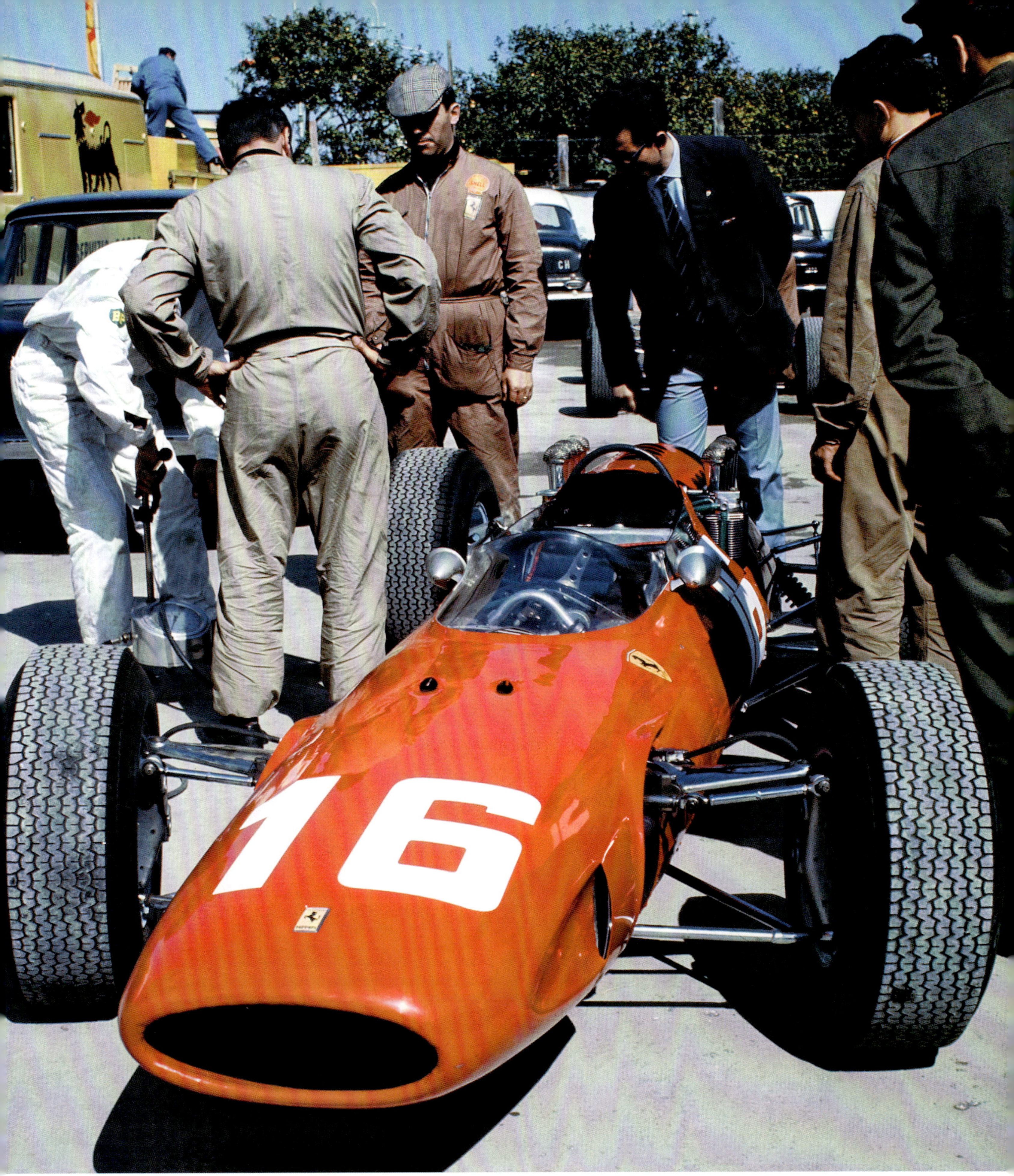
16
CH

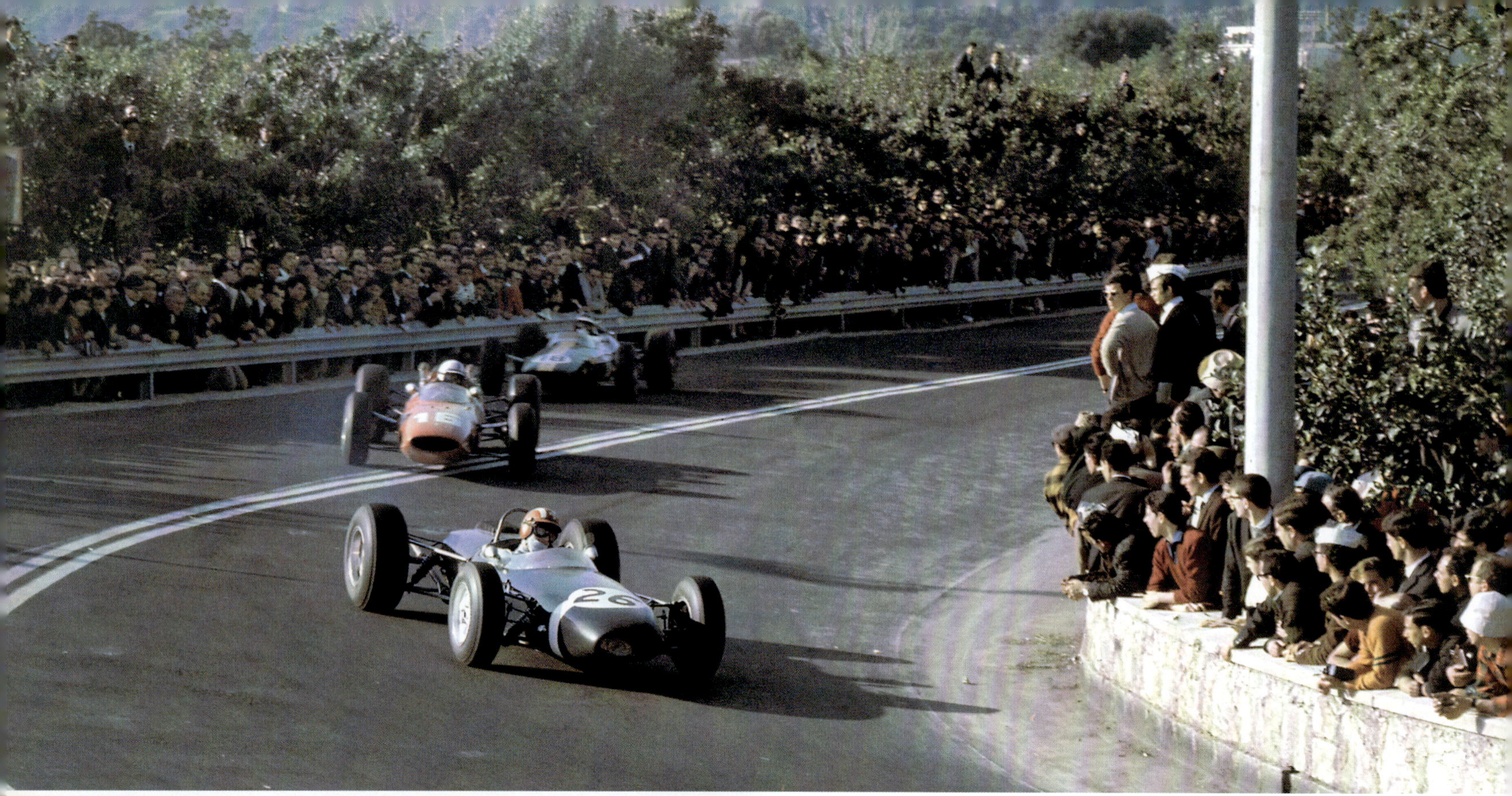

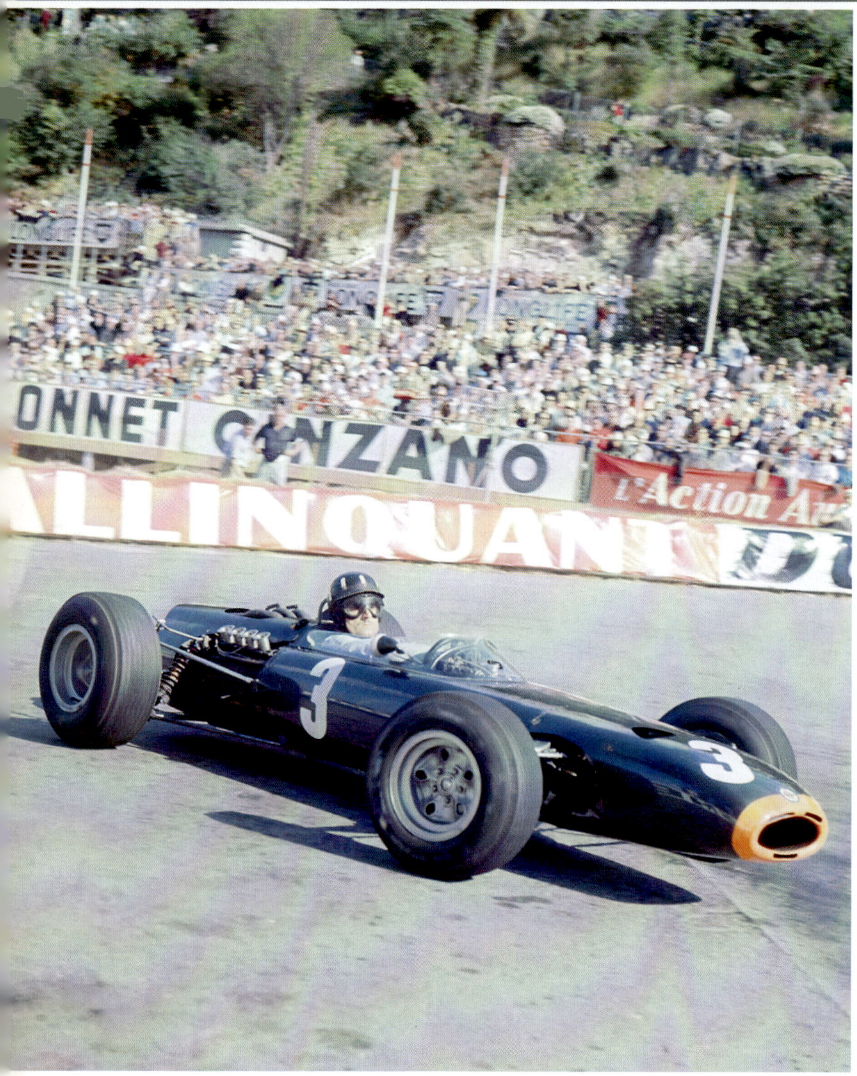

↑ Jo Siffert had famously won the 1964 Gran Premio de Mediterraneo at Enna in his Brabham BT11 BRM (F1-6-64) beating Clark's works Lotus (he would repeat the dose in 1965). Meanwhile, car and driver joined Rob Walker in 1965 and he led John Surtees and Jim Clark at Syracuse until he missed a gear and over-revved the engine leaving Clark to win from an ailing Ferrari.

← Still wearing his battered old helmet that dated back to 1960/61, a very determined Graham Hill exits Gasworks hairpin on opposite lock in his BRM P261 (2616). He started from pole and led until lap 25 then had to take to the chicane escape road to avoid Anderson's stricken Brabham. Reverse gear would not select so Graham got out of the car, pushed it back onto the track, jumped in and restarted using the starter motor. Thereafter he caught and passed the Ferraris of Bandini and Surtees, setting a new lap record 2.2 seconds under the 1964 mark to win convincingly in probably his best ever drive.

↗ Monaco 1965 was notable for the absence of Clark and Gurney, both at Indianapolis which Clark won (naturally). Jackie Stewart fresh from his Silverstone International Trophy triumph spun off and broke a wheel, but ultimately finished 3rd whilst Surtees finished 4th having stopped on lap 99. With the classic harbour scene in the background John Surtees rounds the Gasworks hairpin in the Ferrari 158 T car 0005 during practice.

→ Jack Brabham's BT11 (F1-4-64) chases Lorenzo Bandini's Ferrari 1512 Flat-12 (0007) around the Station hairpin at Monaco. However, the old station has gone leaving only the forlorn skeletal glass and metal awning against the Mediterranean backdrop. Bandini finished 2nd whilst Brabham who had scrubbed in three new tyres in the opening laps led until his new 32-valve Climax V8 failed due to an oil leak caused by part of the rev-counter drive jamming.

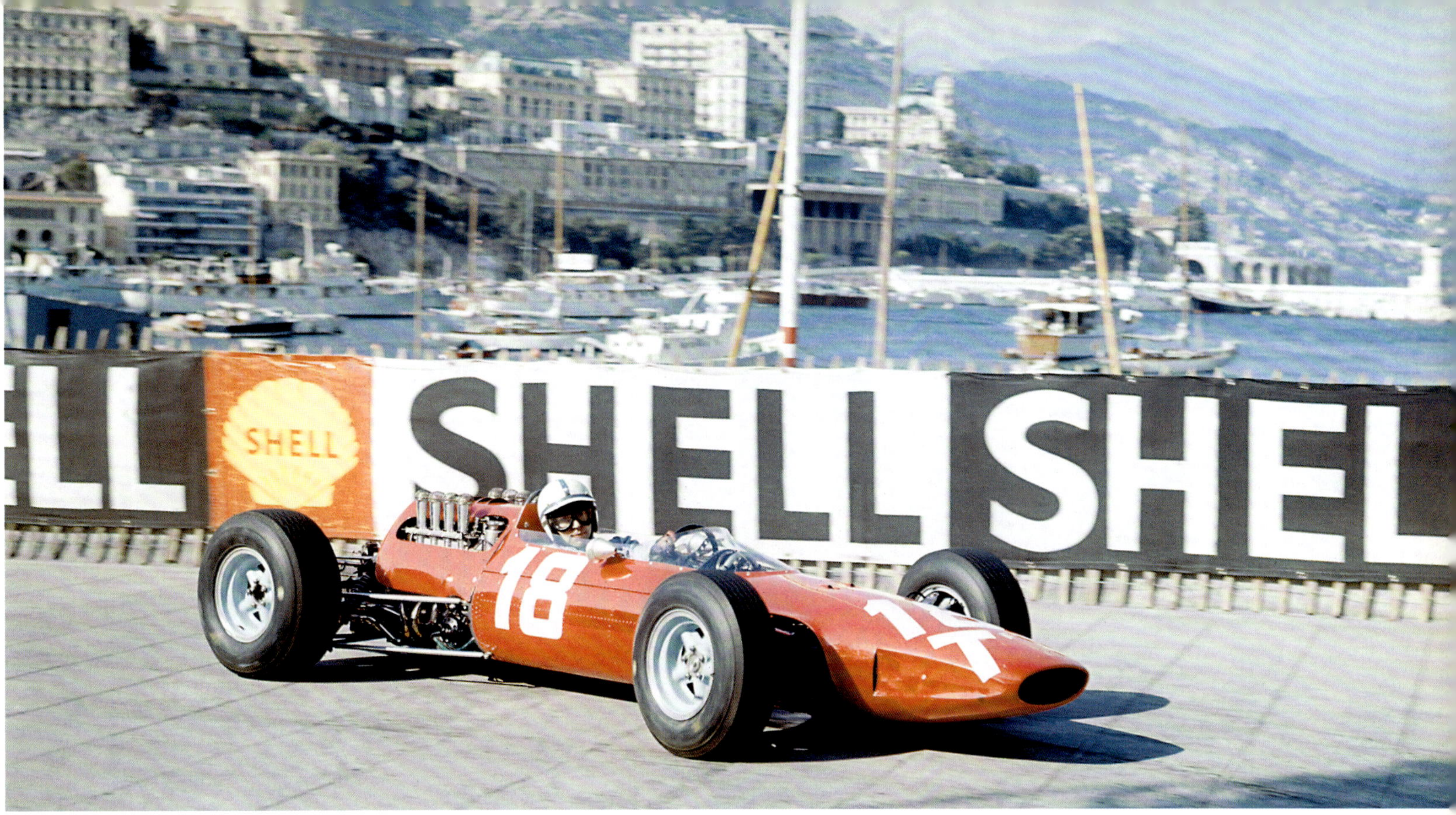
SHELL
SHELL
18

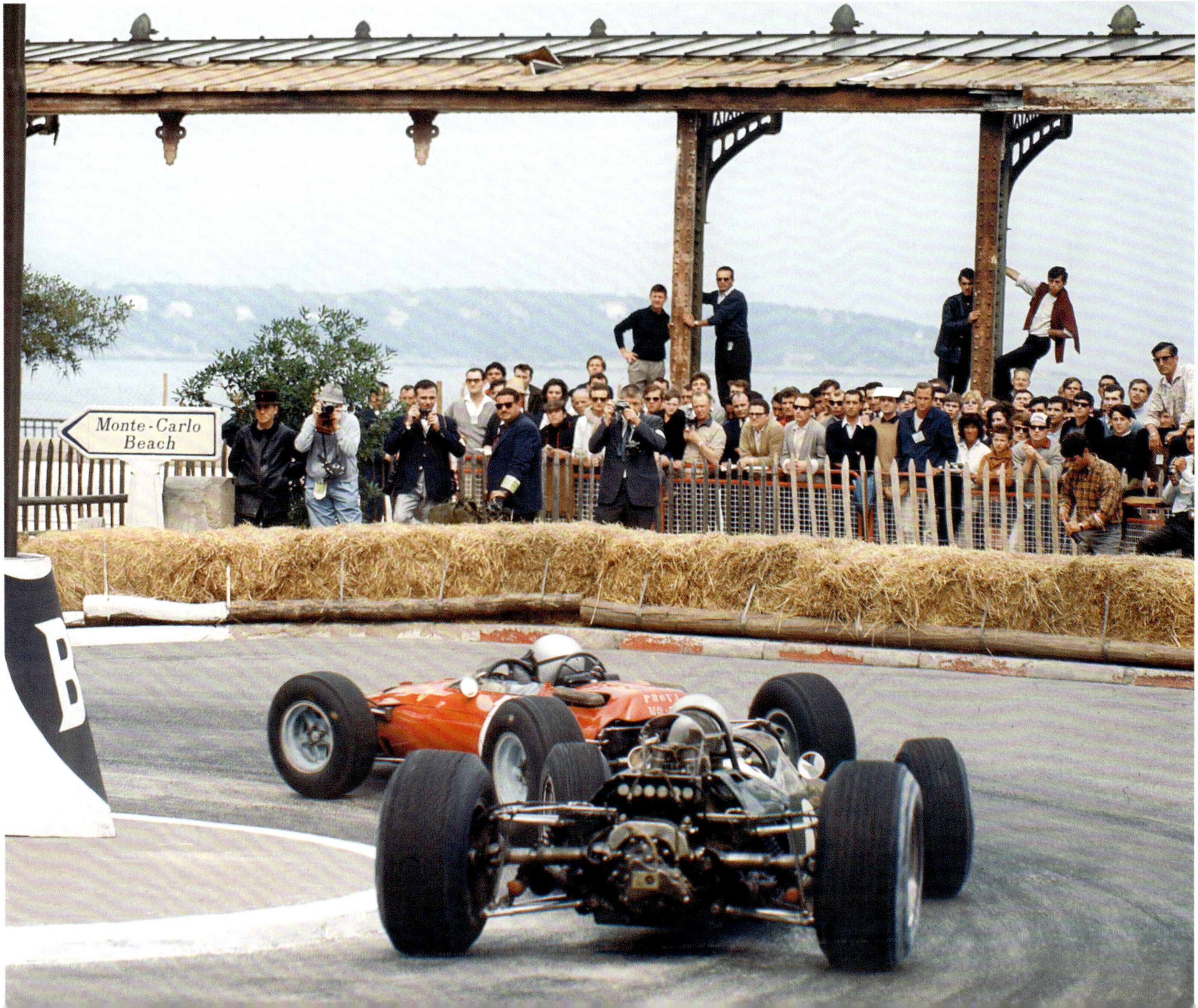
Monte-Carlo
Beach

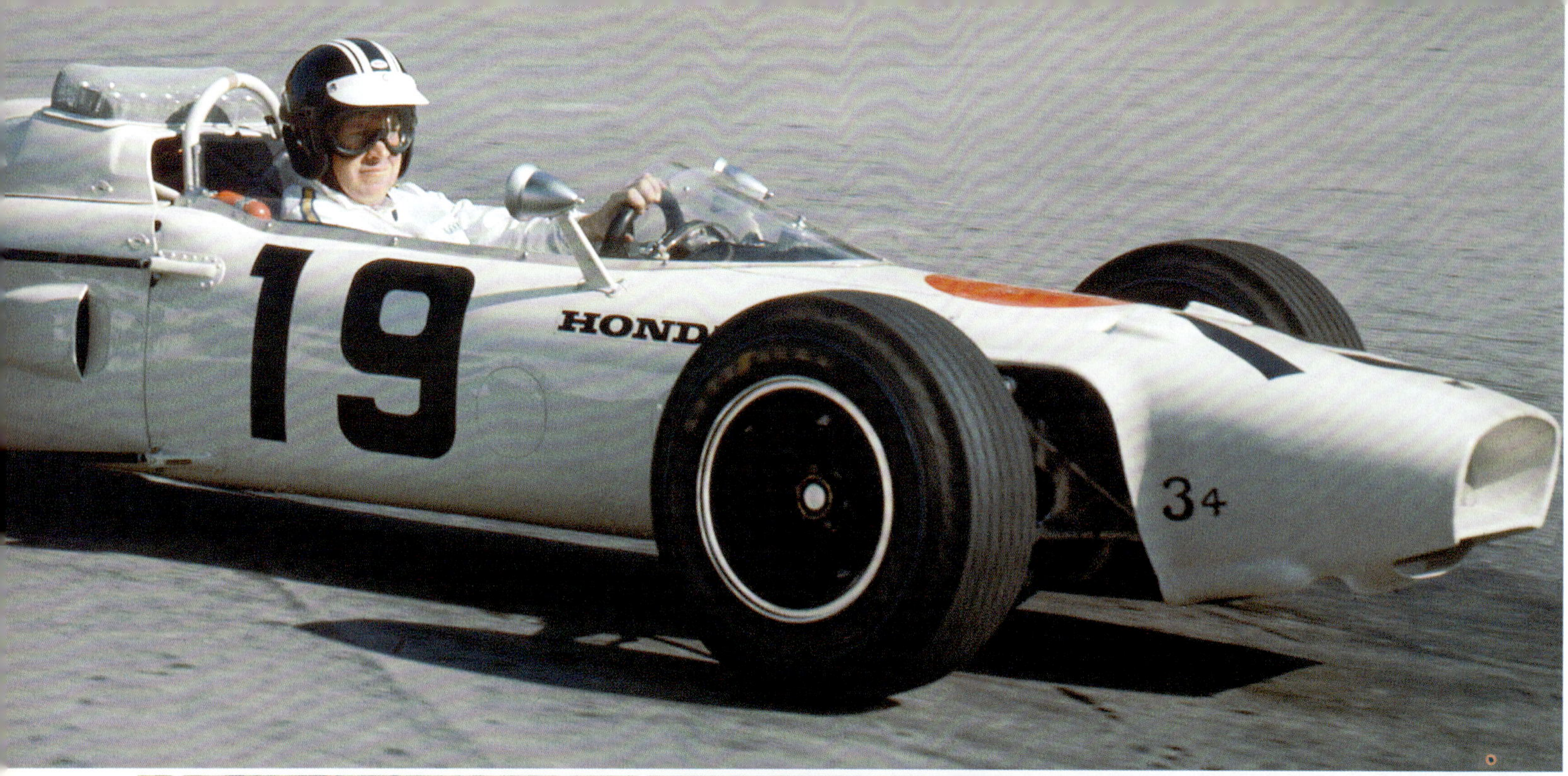
19
HOND
34

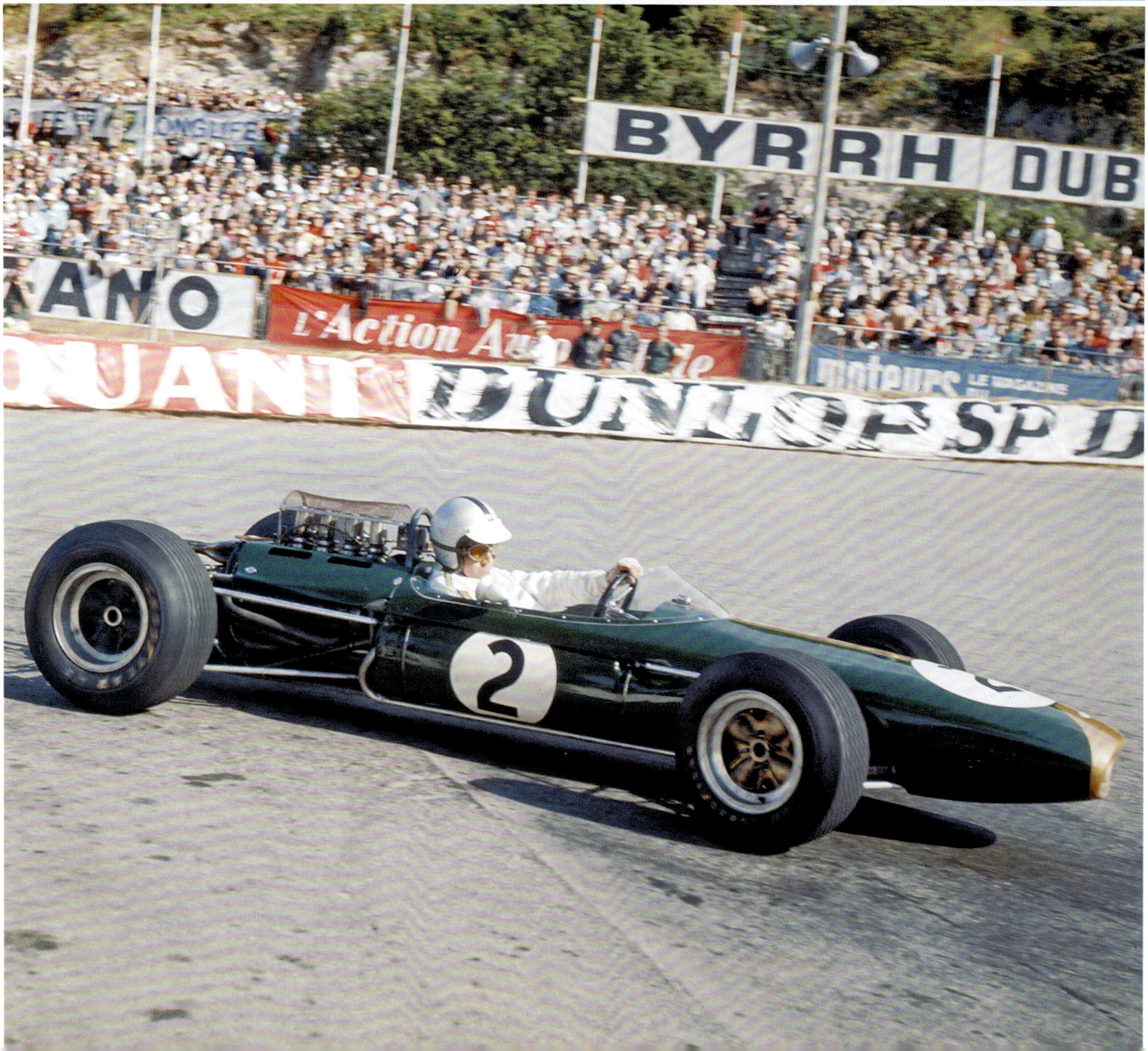
BYRRH DUB
ANO
2

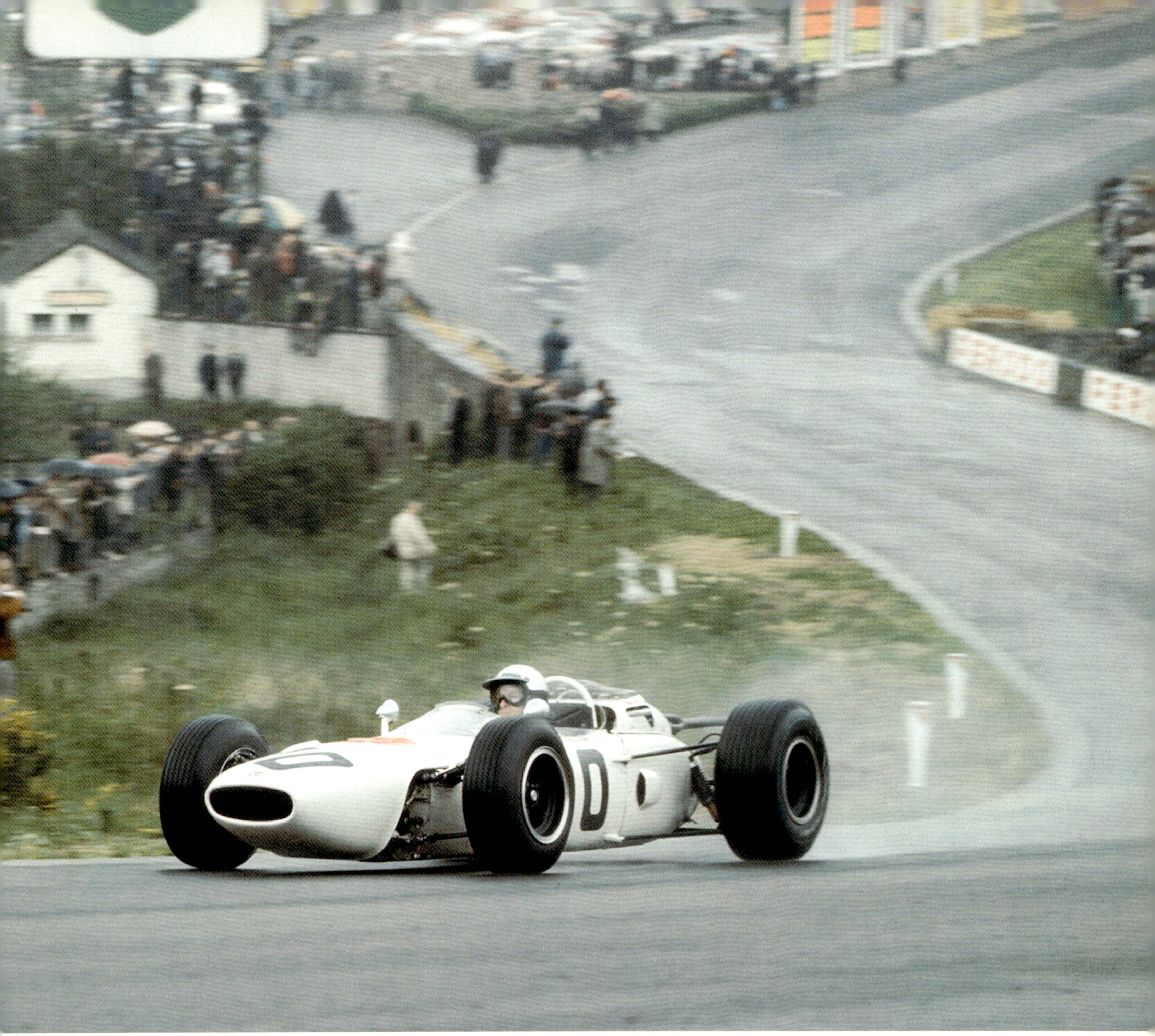

Following the Monaco débacle, Honda was in better shape at Spa, where Richie Ginther started on the second row of the grid and finished 6th with his new RA272-3 chassis. Here the car's front suspension is still showing signs of compression from the rising gradient on the exit of Eau Rouge.

Honda started their campaign at Monaco with Richie Ginther and retaining Ronnie Bucknum (here exiting the Gasworks hairpin in RA272-1). Both cars started from the back row, Ginther retiring immediately with a drive shaft failure and the other on lap 32 with gear linkage troubles. An ignominious beginning for the new cars. Note the truncated nose. Bucknum had abbreviated seasons with Honda during 1965 and 1966, ending his F1 career at the Mexican GP. He returned to sports car racing, Can-Am, USAC and Trans-Am during the 1970s and sadly died aged 57 from complications arising from diabetes in 1992.

With Dan Gurney away at Indianapolis, Denny Hulme took over the Brabham BT7 (F1-3-63) and finished 8th after a long pit stop. He had made his F1 debut at the Silverstone International Trophy but Monaco was his championship inauguration.

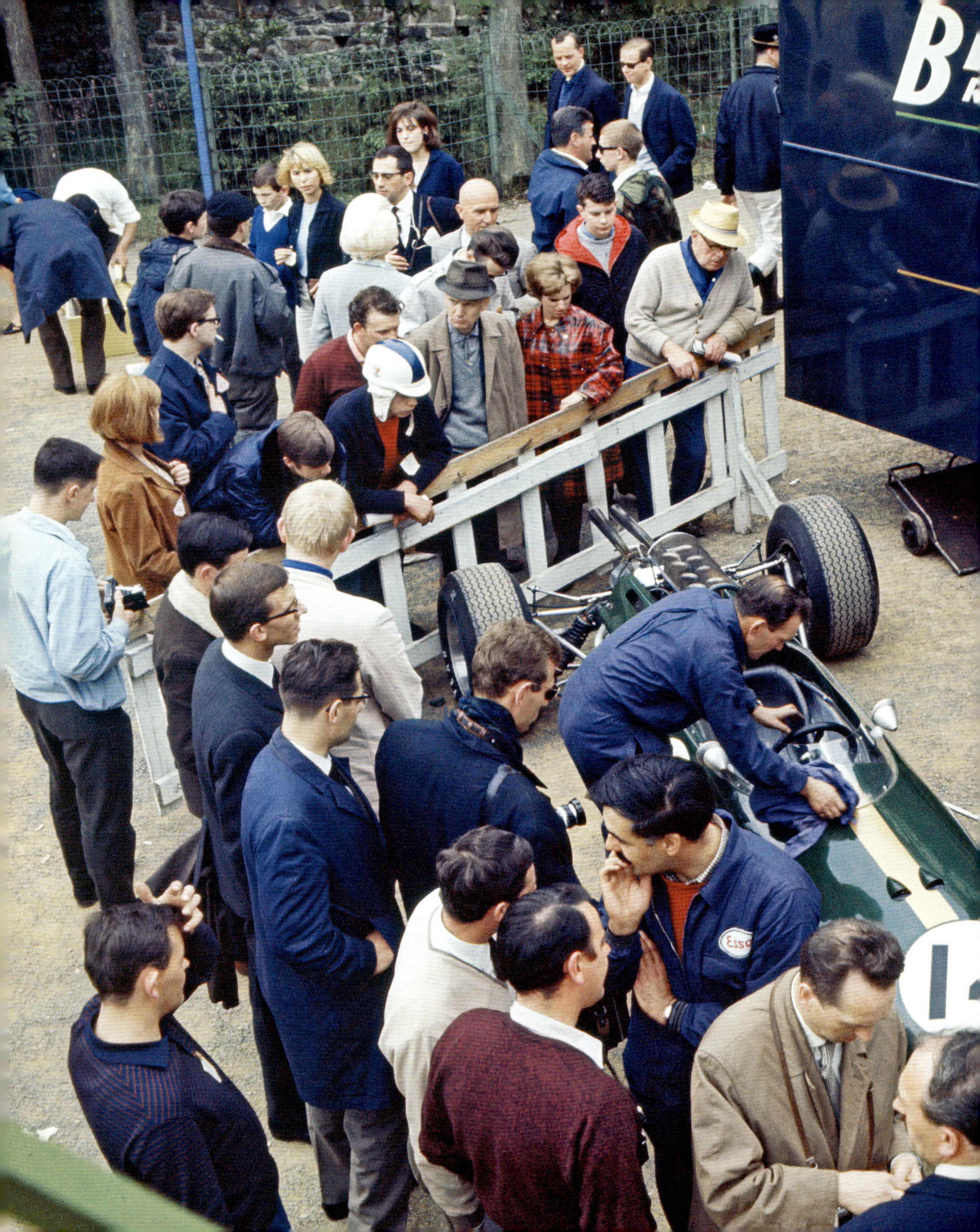
Esso

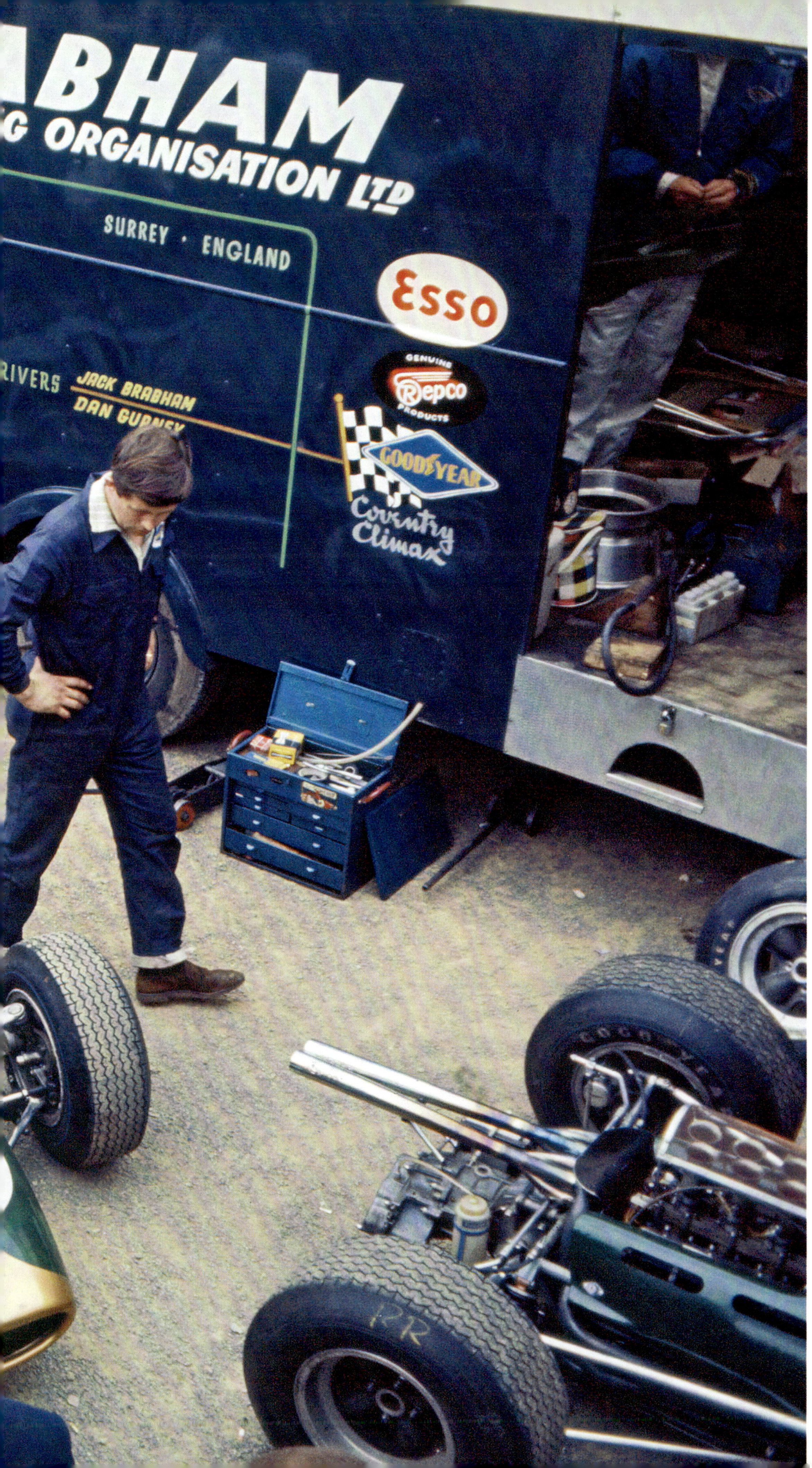

A scene of charming simplicity in the Spa paddock as the Brabham team prepare their charges. Number 14 is Brabham's BT11 (F1-1-64) that will finish 4th in the wet race. The lack of any real security and public access contrasts strongly with the military style hostility of latter day F1.

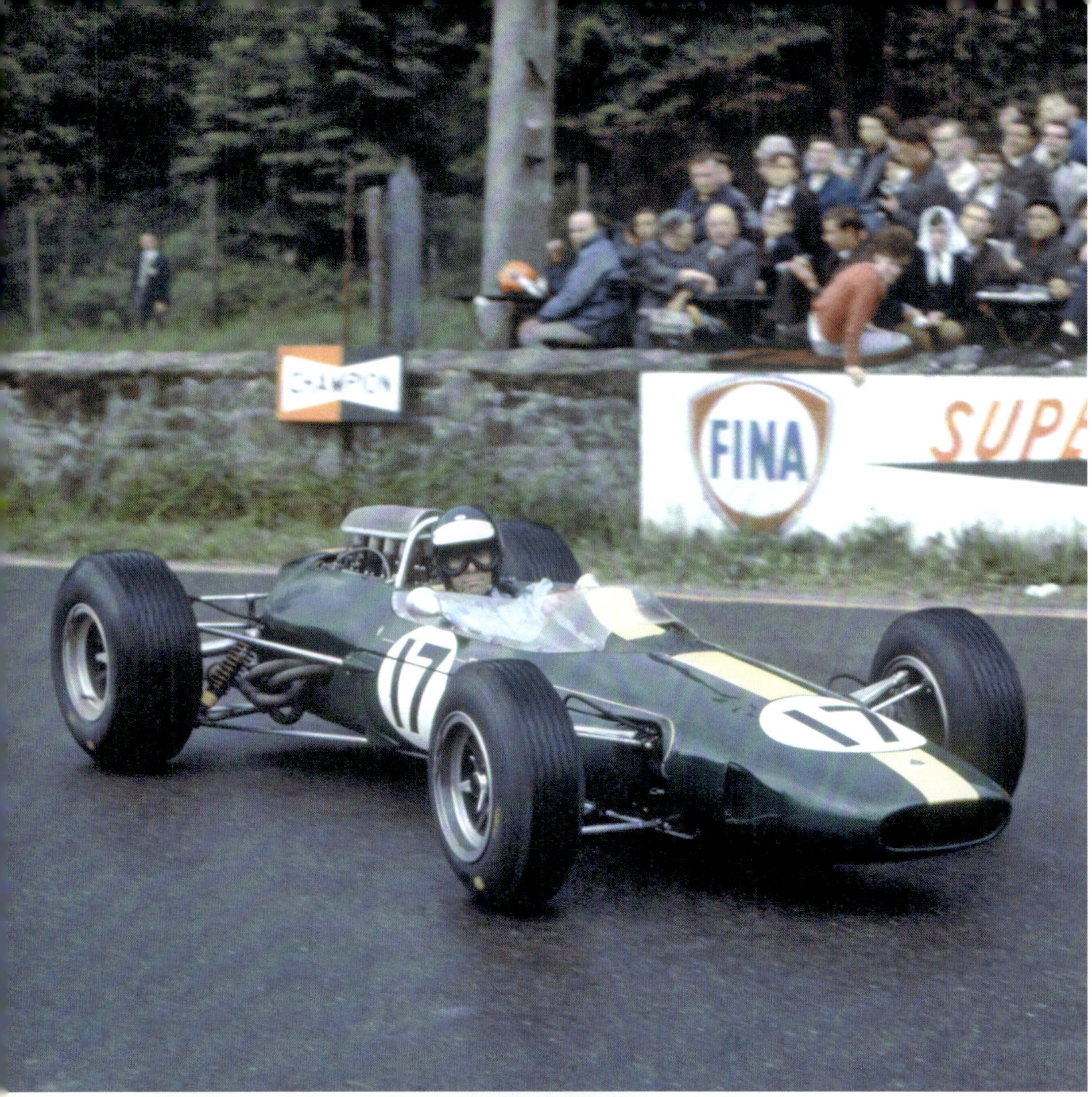

⇦ Normal service has been resumed. A wet Belgian GP so Jim Clark reigns supreme at Spa in the Lotus 33 (R11) winning by nearly 45 seconds from Jackie Stewart's BRM P261. Graham Hill had smashed the lap record during qualifying in dry conditions, 2.1 seconds quicker than Clark. However, the slippery conditions and Hill's usual rock hard suspension settings meant he could only finish a lapped 5th. Clark turns into La Source, apparently relaxed and at ease even though he never liked racing here, having witnessed Scott Brown's blazing Lister wreckage in 1958 and the carnage of the 1960 race. 1965 was his fourth consecutive Belgian GP victory.

⇩ Bruce McLaren was a proficient and thoughtful racing driver who preferred the technical and development side of motor racing. His smooth unruffled style really suited Spa and it was to be the scene of his fourth and final GP victory in 1968. This is the 1965 Cooper T77 (F1-2-65) that took him to 3rd place in the Belgian GP whilst new team mate Jochen Rindt finished 11th.

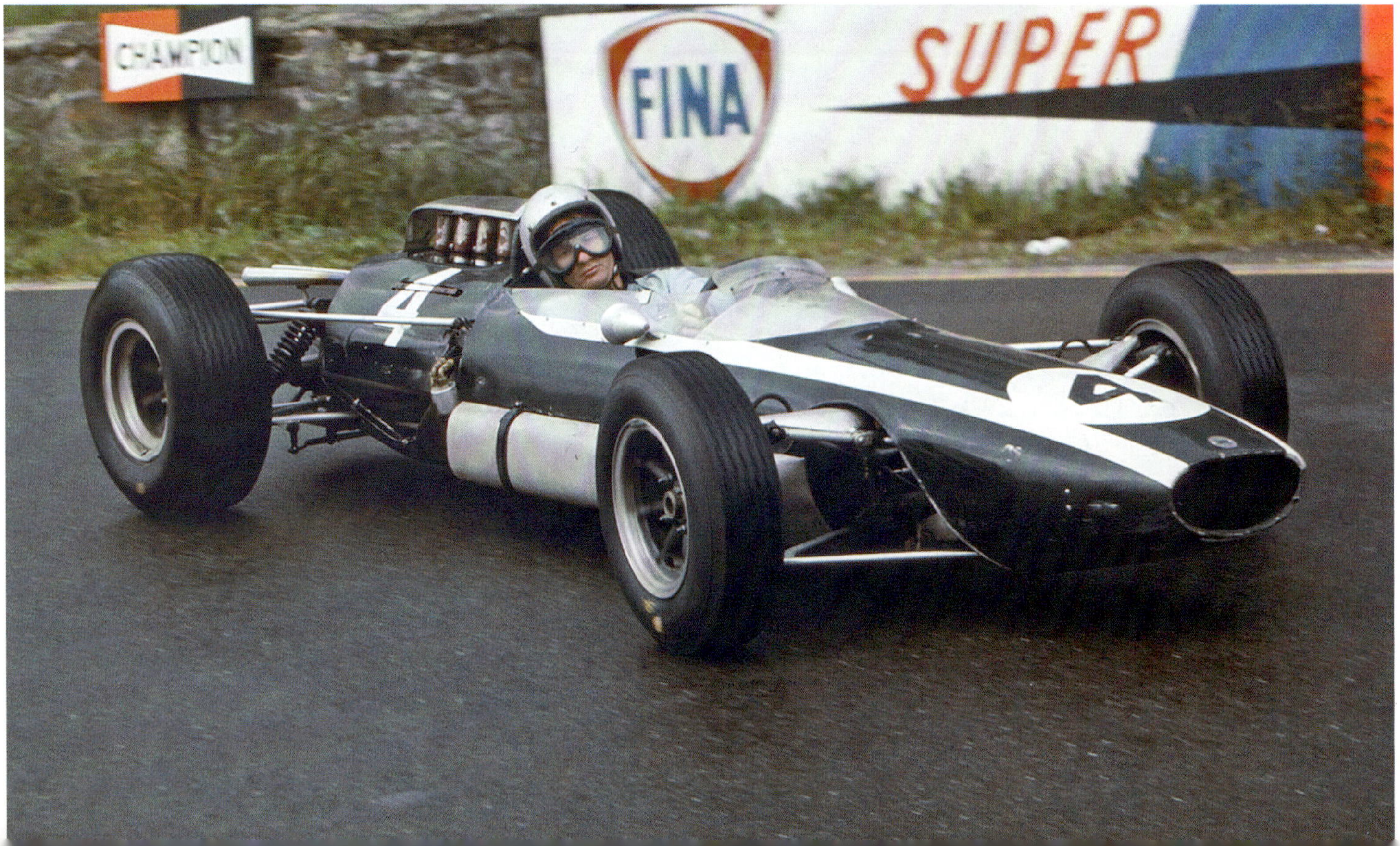

Jackie Stewart continued his Spa form to finish 2nd to Jim Clark in the French GP at Clermont-Ferrand. The 'Rocky Horror Show' that was the Charade circuit is amply illustrated here as Stewart races his BRM P261 (2617) around one of the interminable curves past age old bridges and abutments. Team leader Hill crashed in practice, straining his already damaged neck and was well off the pace but managed to finish 5th in the race.

Had somebody offered Jo Siffert a works drive earlier in his career the moustachioed Swiss would have achieved much more in single seaters. Instead he spent many years as a privateer and then with Rob Walker before winning the 1968 British GP. At Clermont-Ferrand he risks the dirt and stones of the rough verges that characterised the Charade circuit in the Rob Walker Brabham BT11 BRM (F1-6-64) on his way to 6th place. The French Grand Prix had changed venues yet again to this rugged setting in the Auvergne region of France.

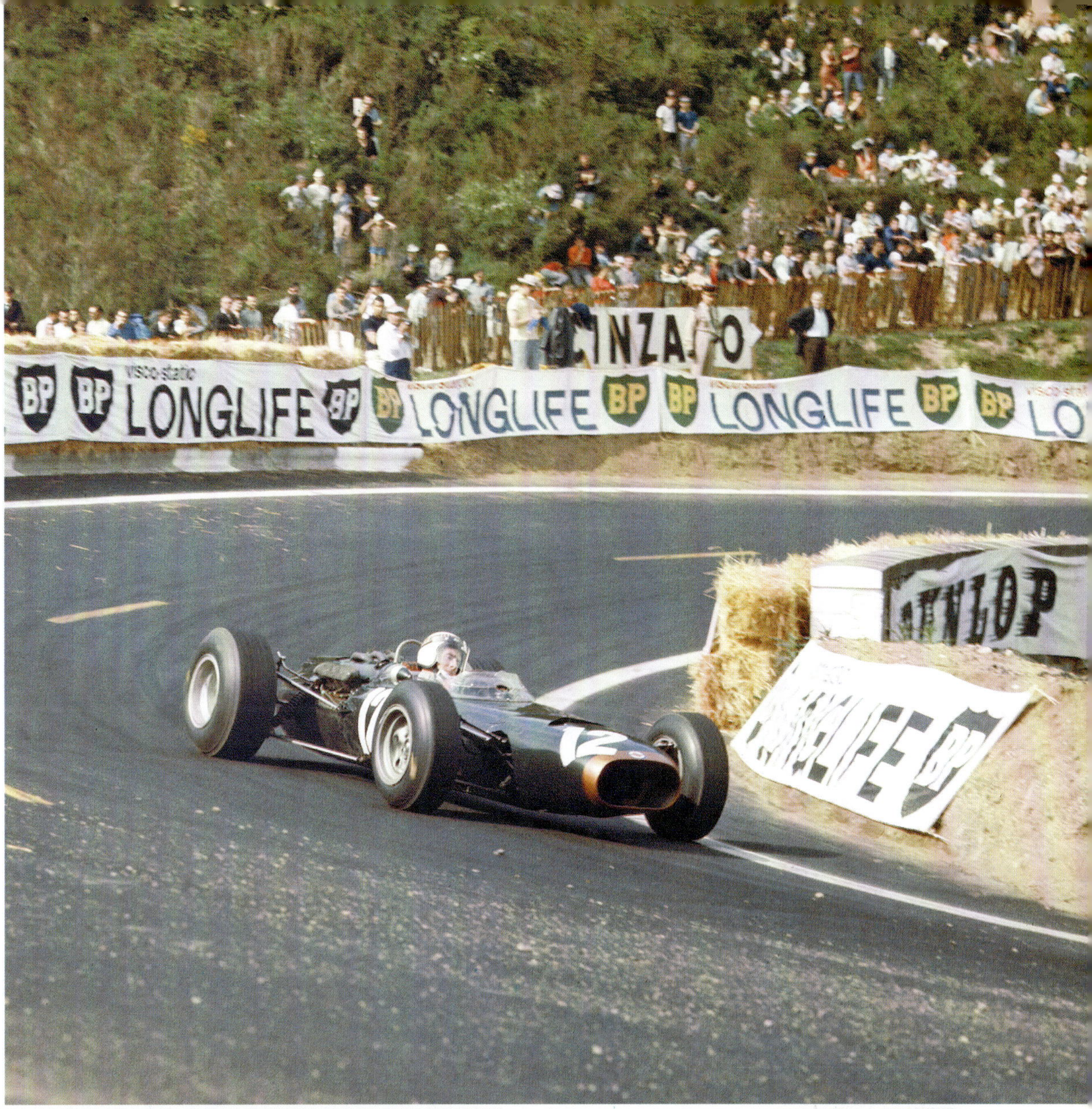

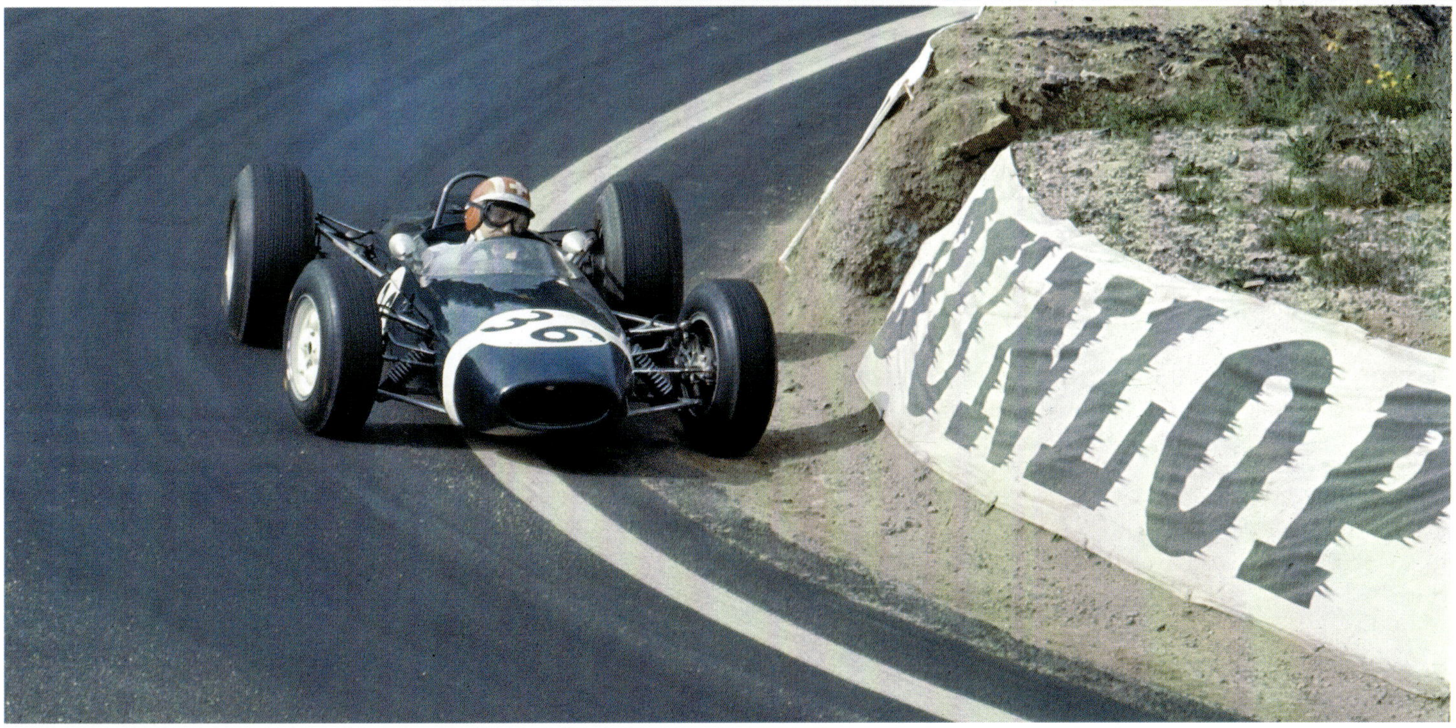

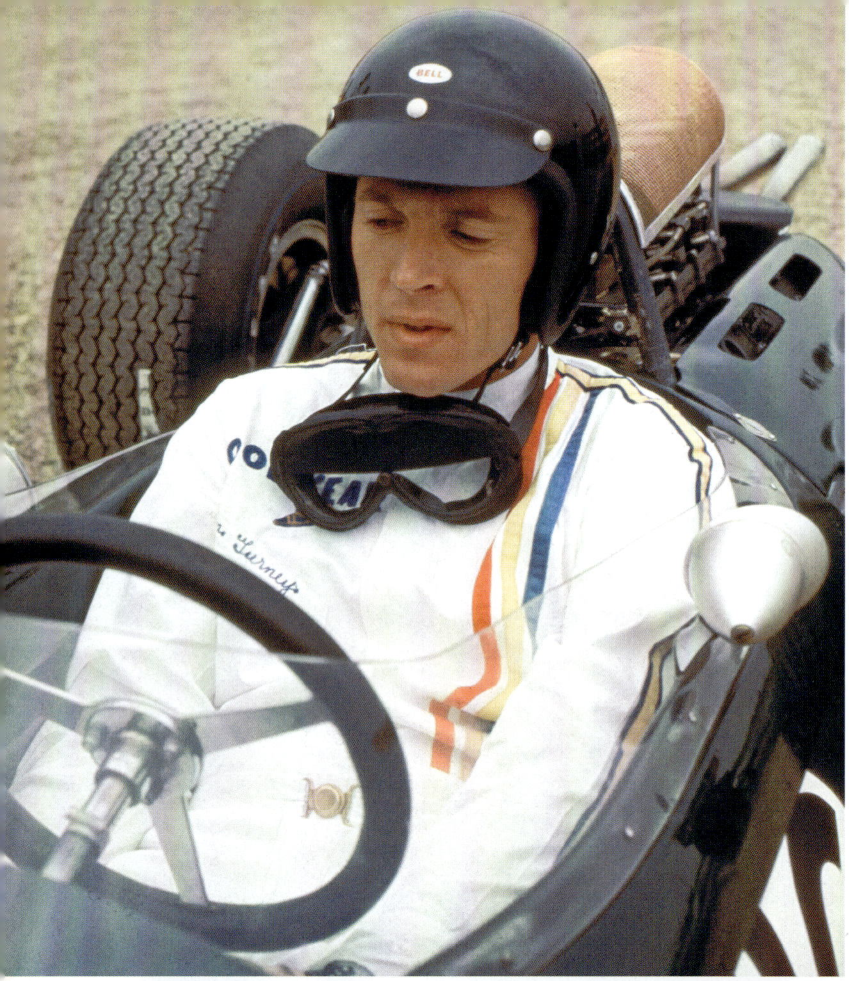

← Ron Tauranac recalled in 2005 that "Gurney used to like sitting quietly alone in the corner of the garage and prepare himself mentally before going out. His weight must have been a handicap in 1.5-litre cars". John Sismey, BRM engineer, recalls Dan Gurney as great and especially his comment about John's then newly grown moustache. "What's this then John?" "I'm growing a moustache Dan." "You know what they say in California about moustaches John." "What do they say Dan?" "Never cultivate on your face what grows wild around your arse!" This is the Dutch GP at Zandvoort and Dan sits in his BT11 (F1-2-64), seemingly too big for the cockpit. Note the absence of belts. He will finish 3rd behind that Scottish duo Clark and Stewart.

→ Bruce McLaren's Cooper T77 (F1-2-65) leads team mate Jochen Rindt (T77 F1-1-65) into the Karussel during practice for the German GP followed by Jim Clark's Lotus 33 (R11). The Cooper T77s are not in the same league as Lotus, BRM, Brabham, Ferrari and Honda, but Rindt will achieve a worthy 4th place in the race. McLaren retired with scrambled gear selectors.

↓ Just as Jim Clark never managed to win at Monaco thus Graham Hill at the British GP. Having led the race in 1960 before crashing and battling mightily with Clark at Brands Hatch in 1964 to finish 2nd 2.8 seconds behind, he was once again relegated to runner-up behind his Celtic nemesis. At Silverstone he was catching Clark's ailing car, but his own BRM P261 (2616) was hampered by failing brakes and despite setting the fastest race lap he lost by 3.2 seconds.

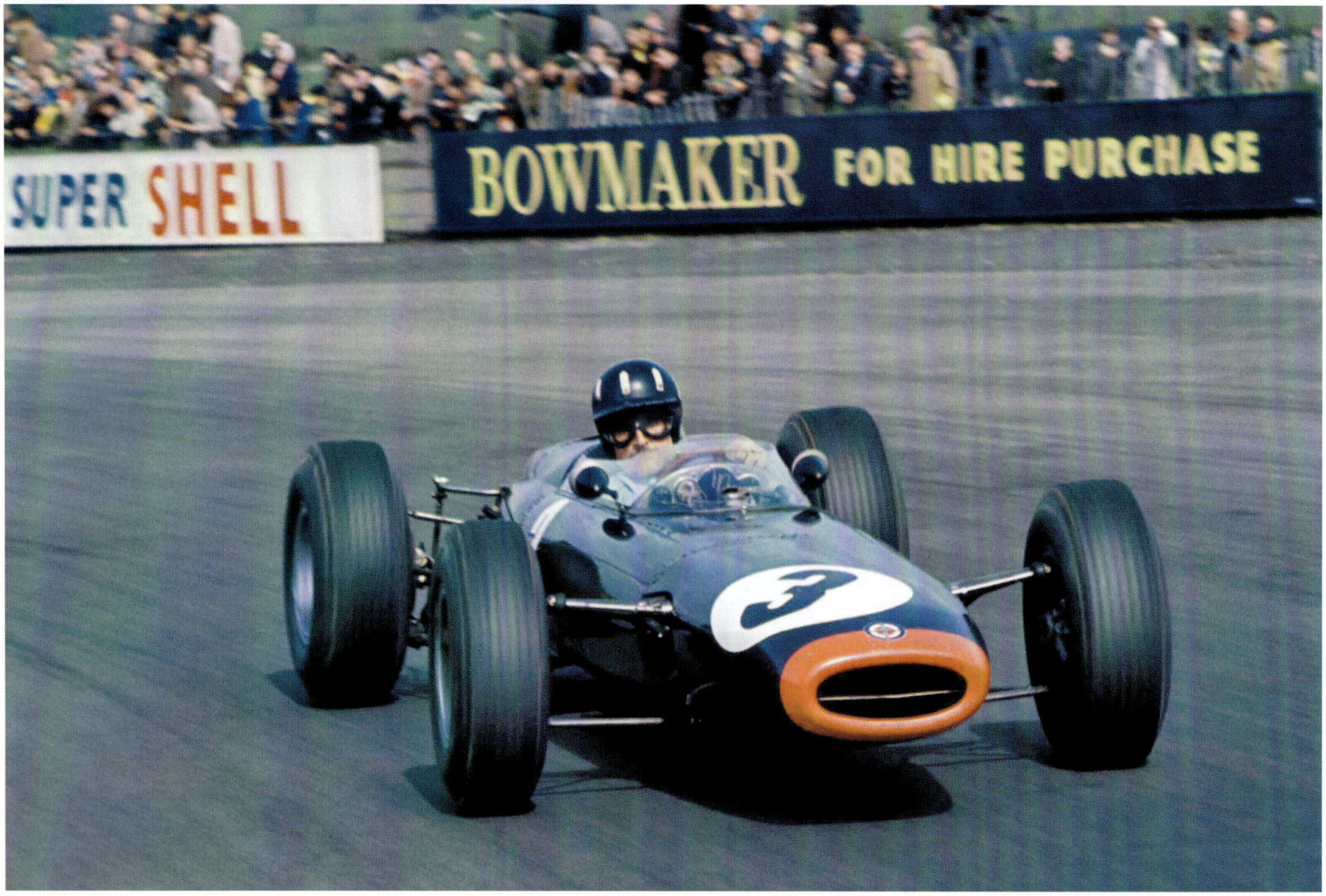

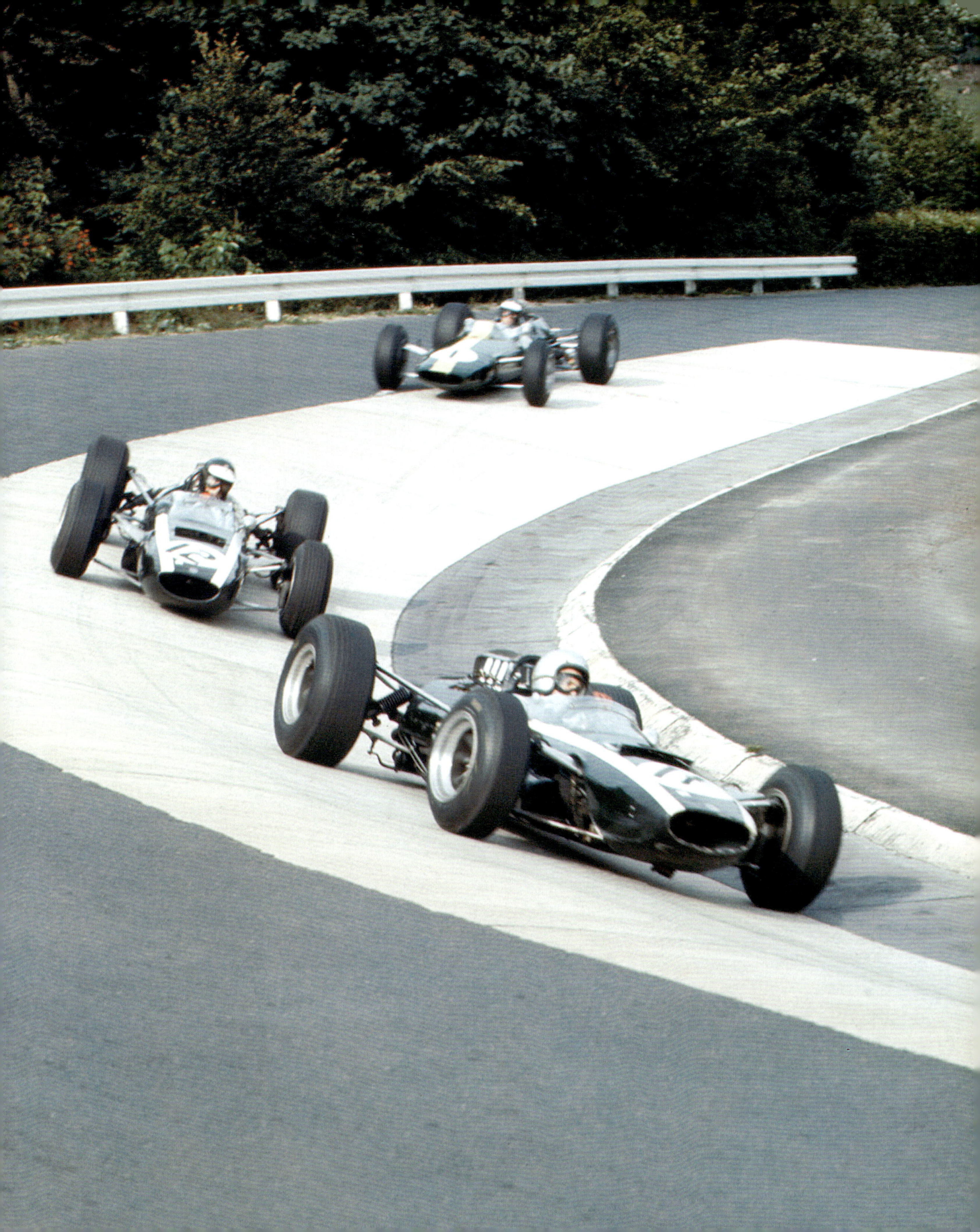

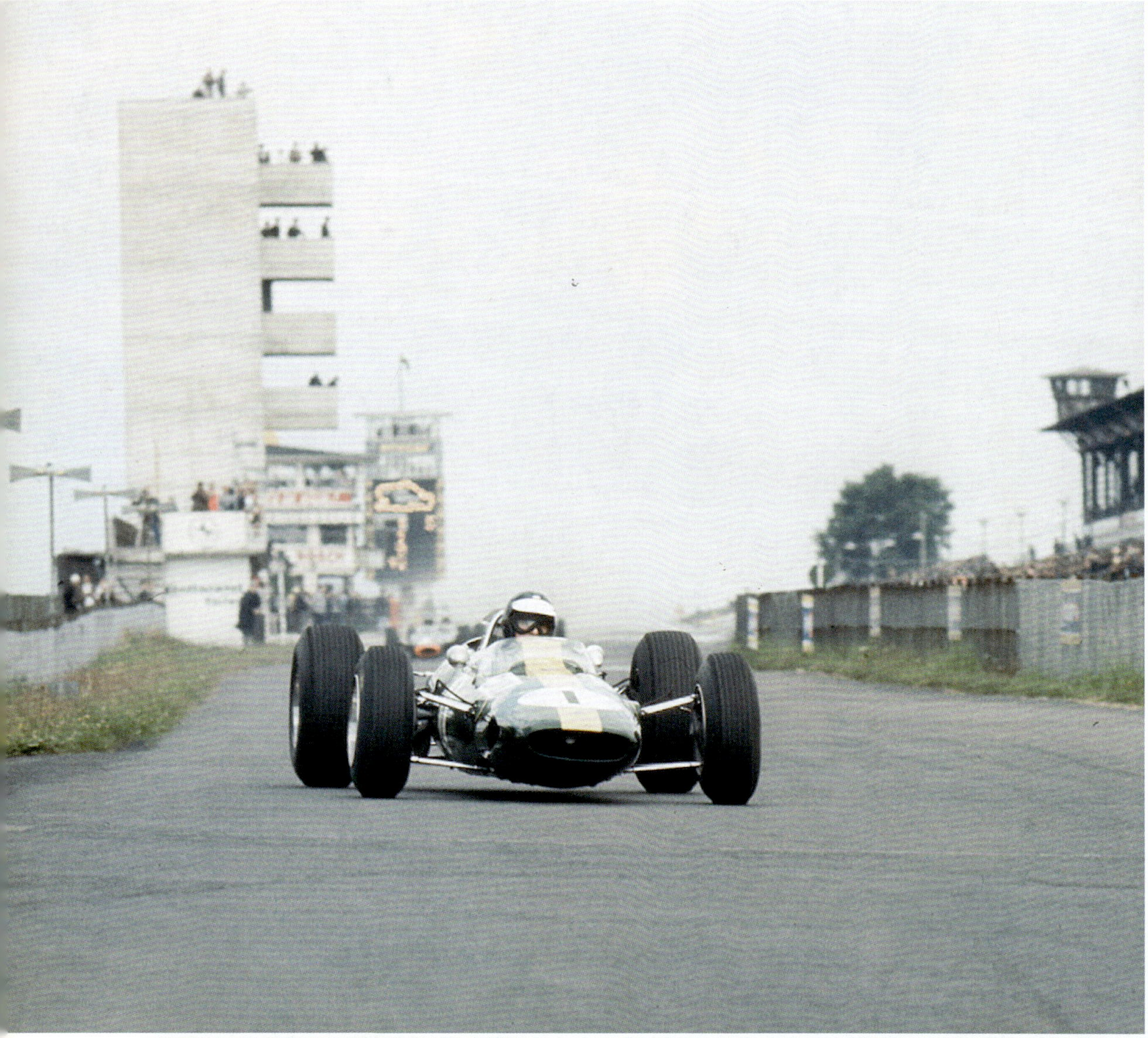

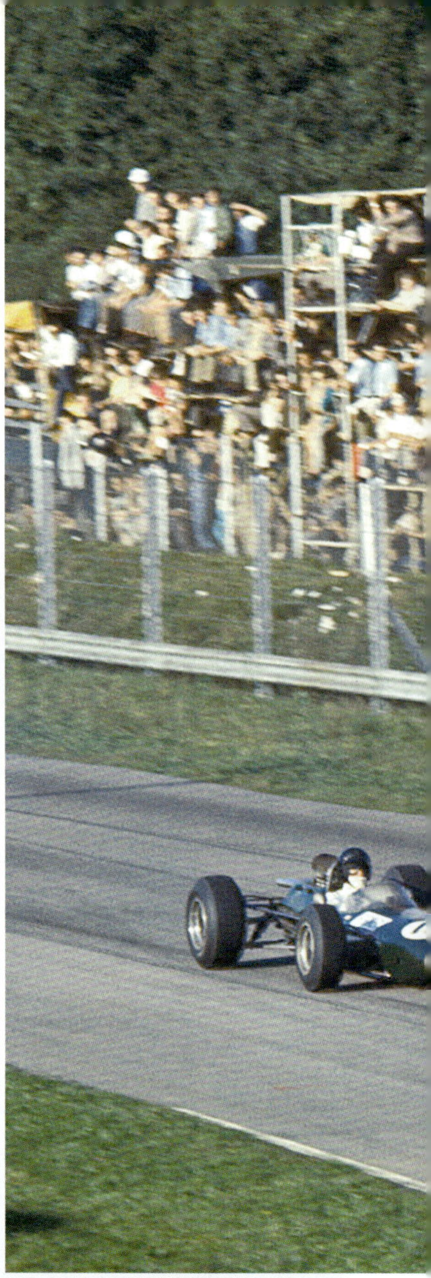

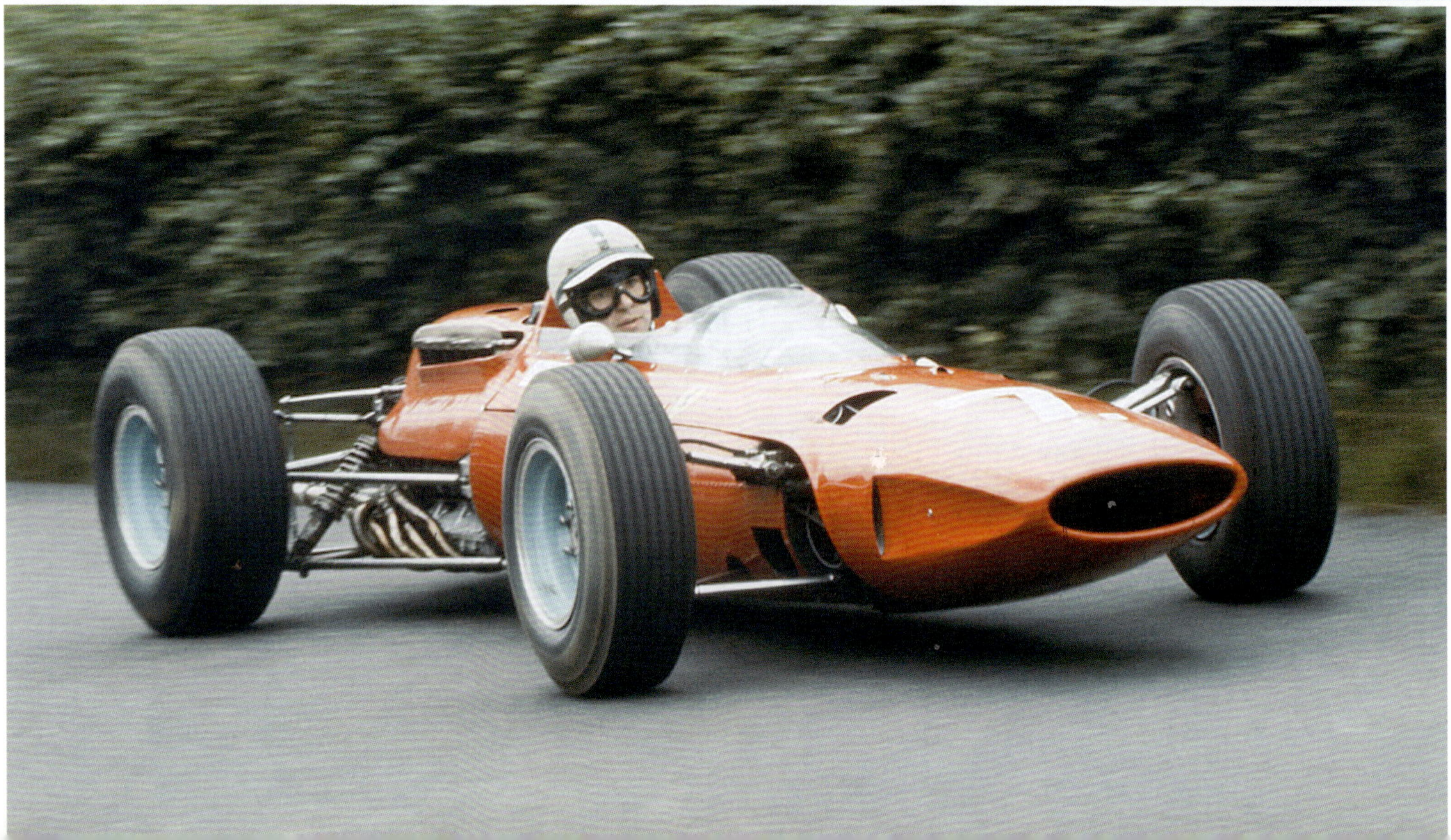

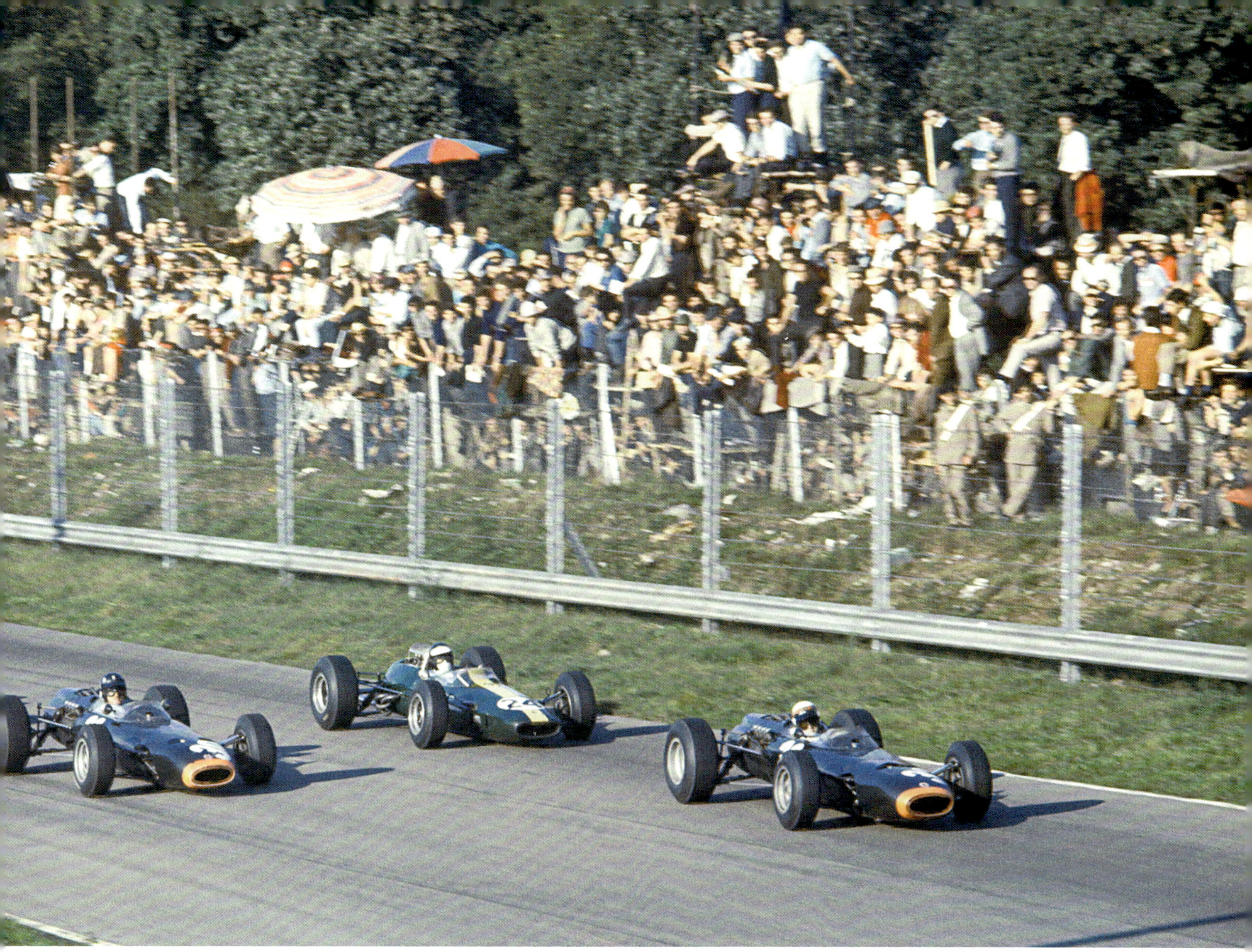

In the Italian GP at Monza, Stewart, BRM, Clark, Lotus, Hill, BRM, and Gurney, Brabham contest the lead late in the race. Earlier John Surtees had led in a new flat-12 Ferrari but stopped with clutch failure. Ultimately, Gurney lost the slipstream and fell behind whilst Tony Rudd gave his drivers a camouflaged pit signal to speed up. Clark was the meat in a BRM sandwich and the increased pace caused him to over-rev his engine and it blew up (officially fuel pump failure). This left Hill and Stewart contesting the lead and on the final lap at the Parabolica, Graham put a wheel in the dirt allowing Stewart to win by three seconds.

Jim Clark cannot be denied and wins his sixth Grand Prix of the season at the Nürburgring, and with it the Drivers' Championship. Look carefully and you can just see the BRMs of Graham Hill and Jackie Stewart in the distance behind the Lotus. This is the old track approaching the south loop that was obliterated by the new circuit in 1984. Compared with the circuit's latter-day clinical sterility, glass-fronted facilities, immaculate tarmac and corporate advertising, this setting seems positively antediluvian.

The reigning World Champion John Surtees was having a frustrating season in 1965. Having at last taken over the Flat-12 Ferrari 1512 (0008) from Lorenzo Bandini at Silverstone, John Surtees placed it 4th on the grid at the Nürburgring but experienced gear selection problems and retired on lap 11. This is just past the Adenau bridge and the blue wheeled Ferrari has noticeable front end lift. Later in the year after the Italian GP Surtees was badly injured driving a Lola T70, and missed the last two GPs.

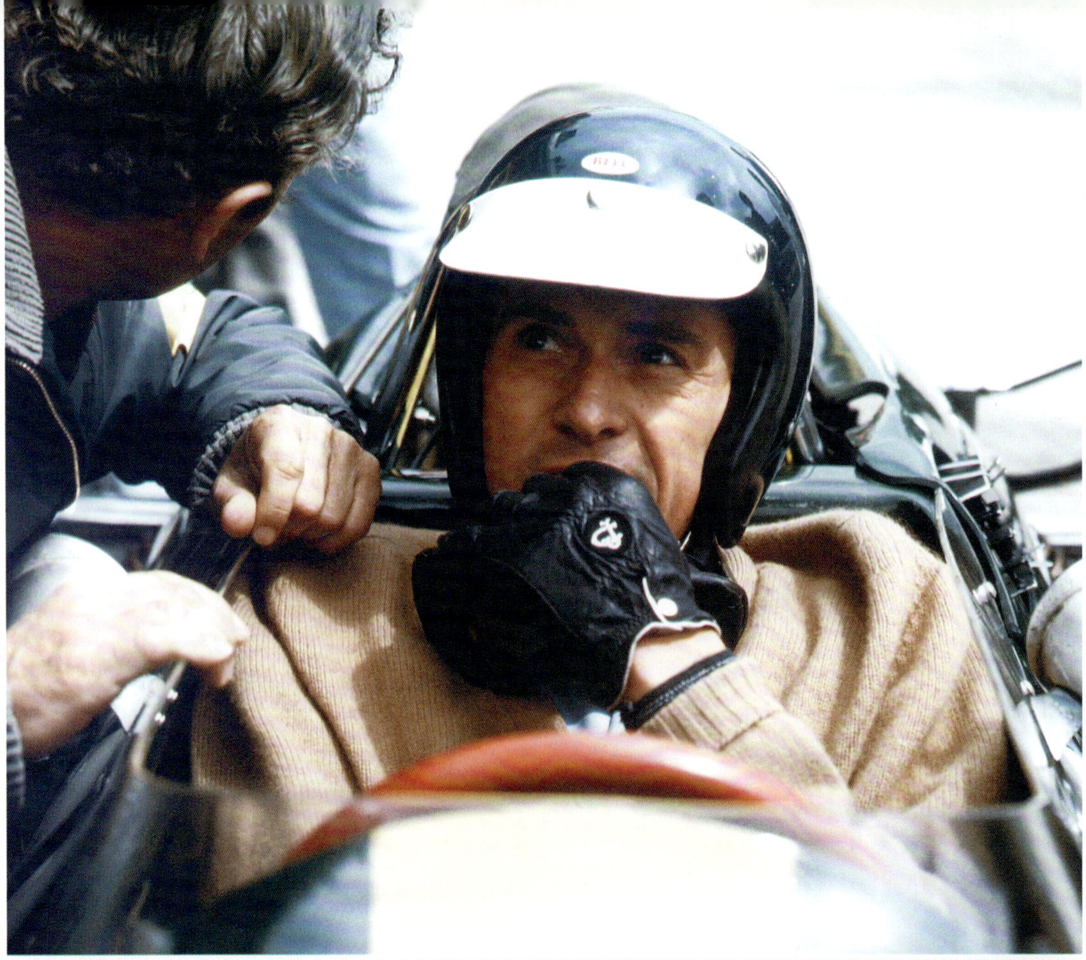

It could be chilly at Watkins Glen in October, hence the cardigan. Jim Clark confers with Colin Chapman during practice for the US GP. The golfer style gloves were marketed under Clark's name complete with a stylised JC monogram on the back, plainly visible here. They were available in black or tan and cost 3 guineas, £3.15 in modern currency, a lot of money at the time. Clark lined up second on the grid behind Graham Hill's BRM but the Lotus expired on lap 12 with piston failure. Hill won.

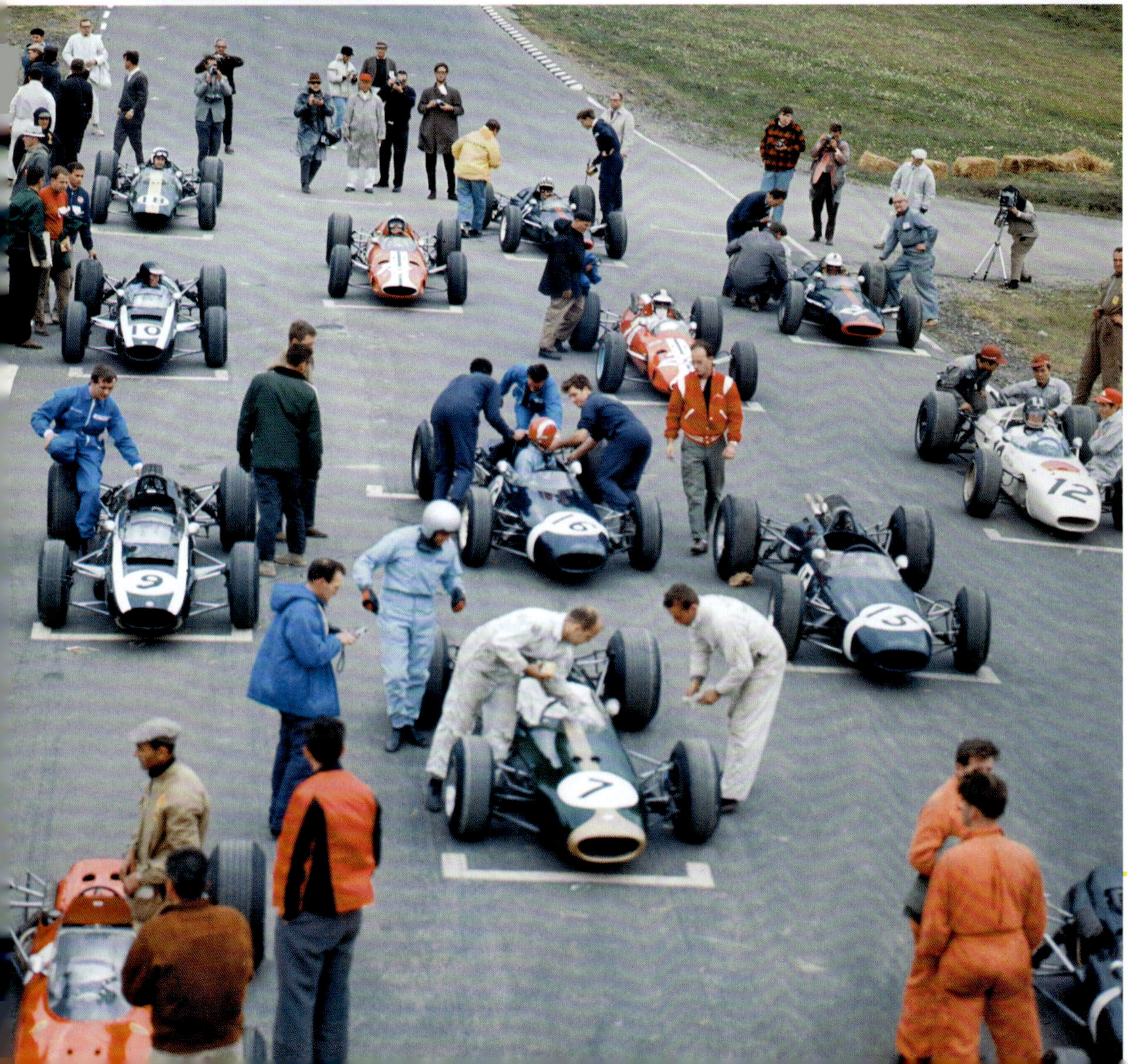

This view of part of the grid for the US Grand Prix at Watkins Glen conveys an almost relaxed atmosphere. The prominent cars are Jack Brabham's Brabham BT11 (No 7), the Rob Walker team Brabhams of Jo Bonnier (15) and Jo Siffert (16, looking over his shoulder), Bruce McLaren's Cooper (9) and Ronnie Bucknum's Honda (12). Behind them are Jochen Rindt's Cooper (10), the red and white striped NART Ferraris of Bob Bondurant (24) and Pedro Rodriguez(14), Richard Attwood's Lotus, Moises Solana's third works Lotus (with yellow stripe) and Innes Ireland's Parnell Lotus.

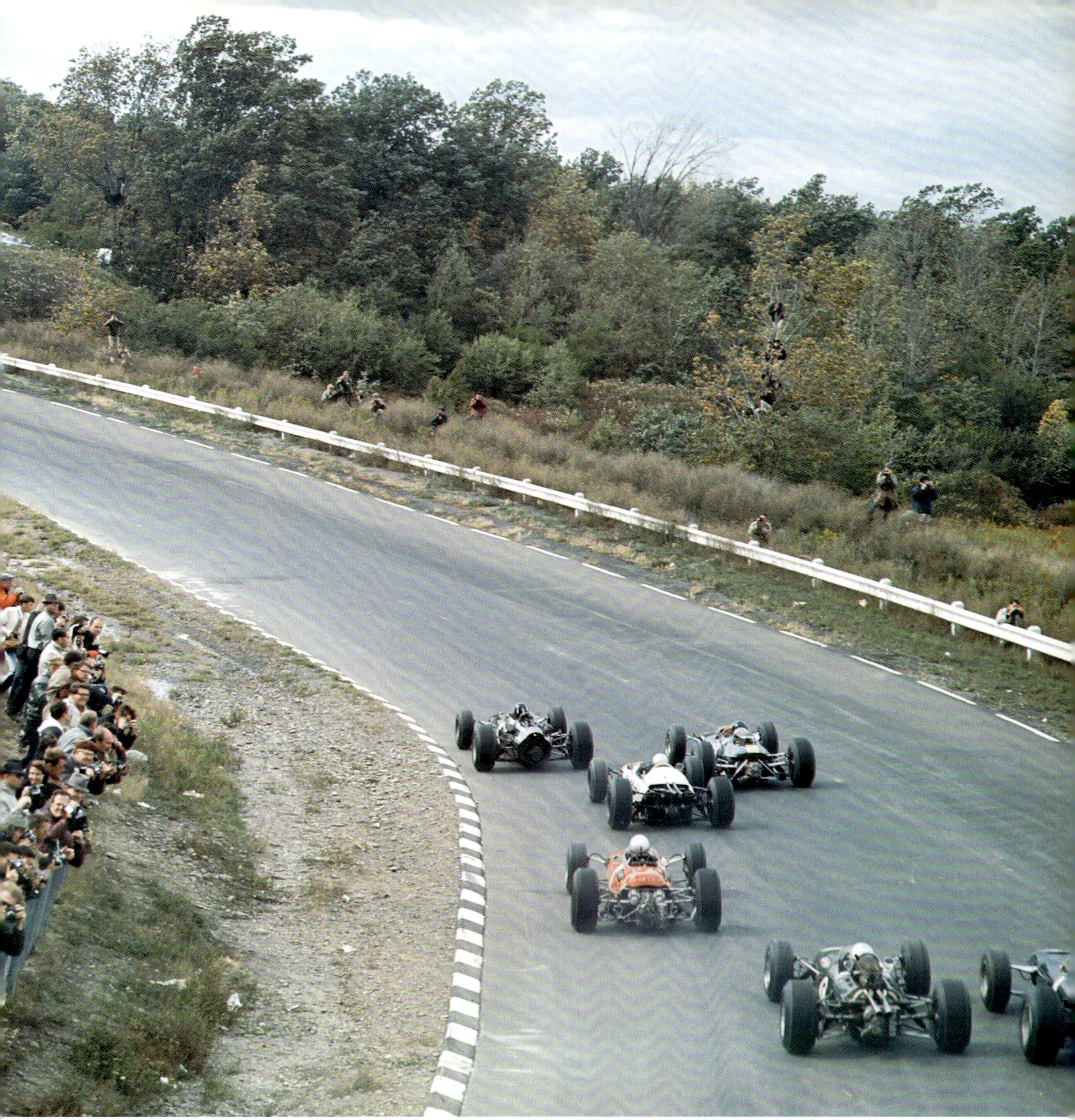

↑ First lap, first corner of the US GP at Watkins Glen and Hill (BRM) has taken the lead from Clark (Lotus) with Ginther's Honda right behind them followed by Bandini's Ferrari, Brabham's Brabham and Stewart's BRM. Hill and Clark disputed the lead until Clark retired, Ginther finished 7th, Bandini 4th, Brabham 3rd and Stewart stopped with suspension damage caused by a nudge from Ginther. Dan Gurney was 2nd in the other Brabham. The track is narrow, bordered by dirt verges and a single layer of early Armco. How things have changed.

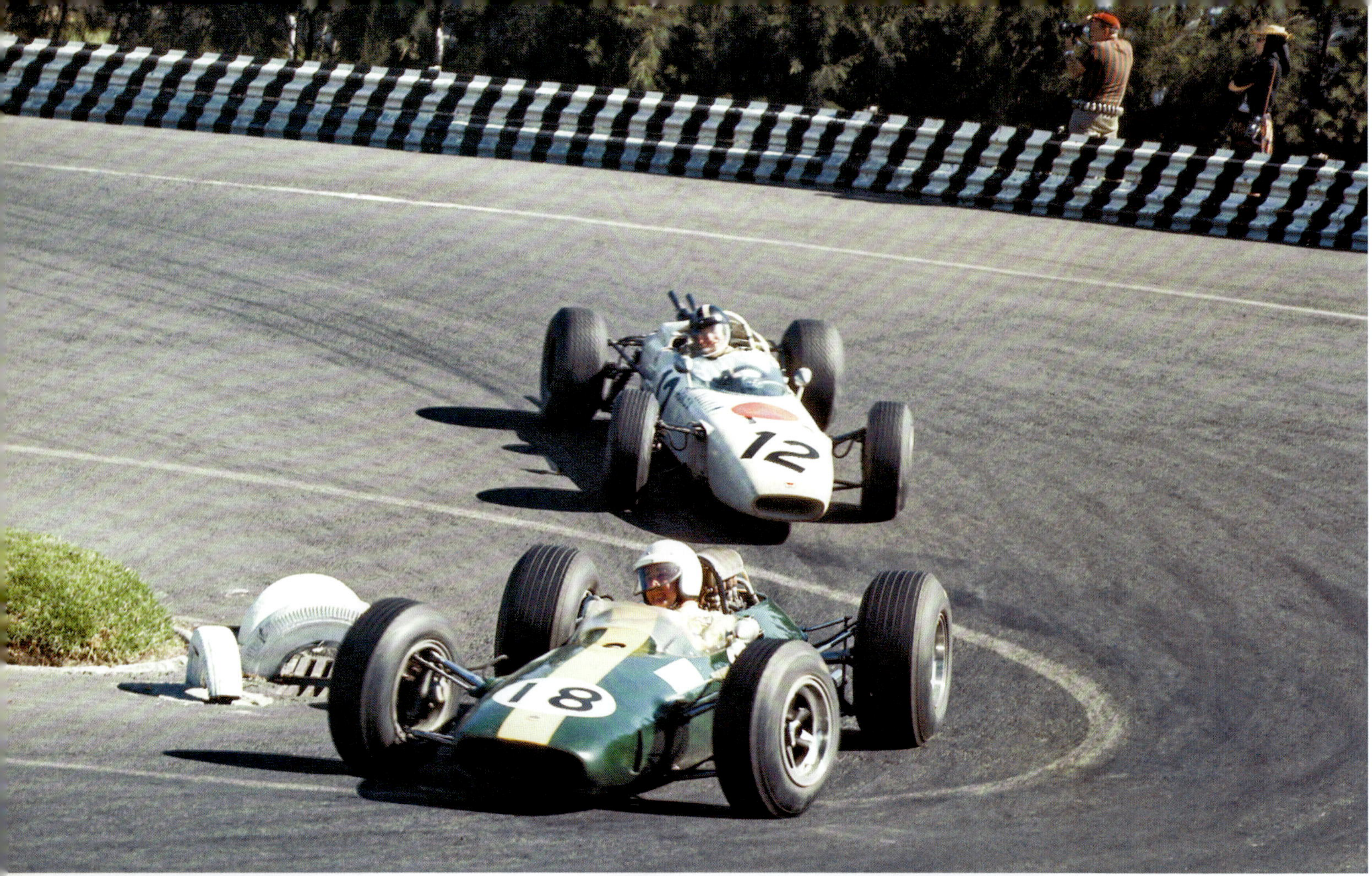

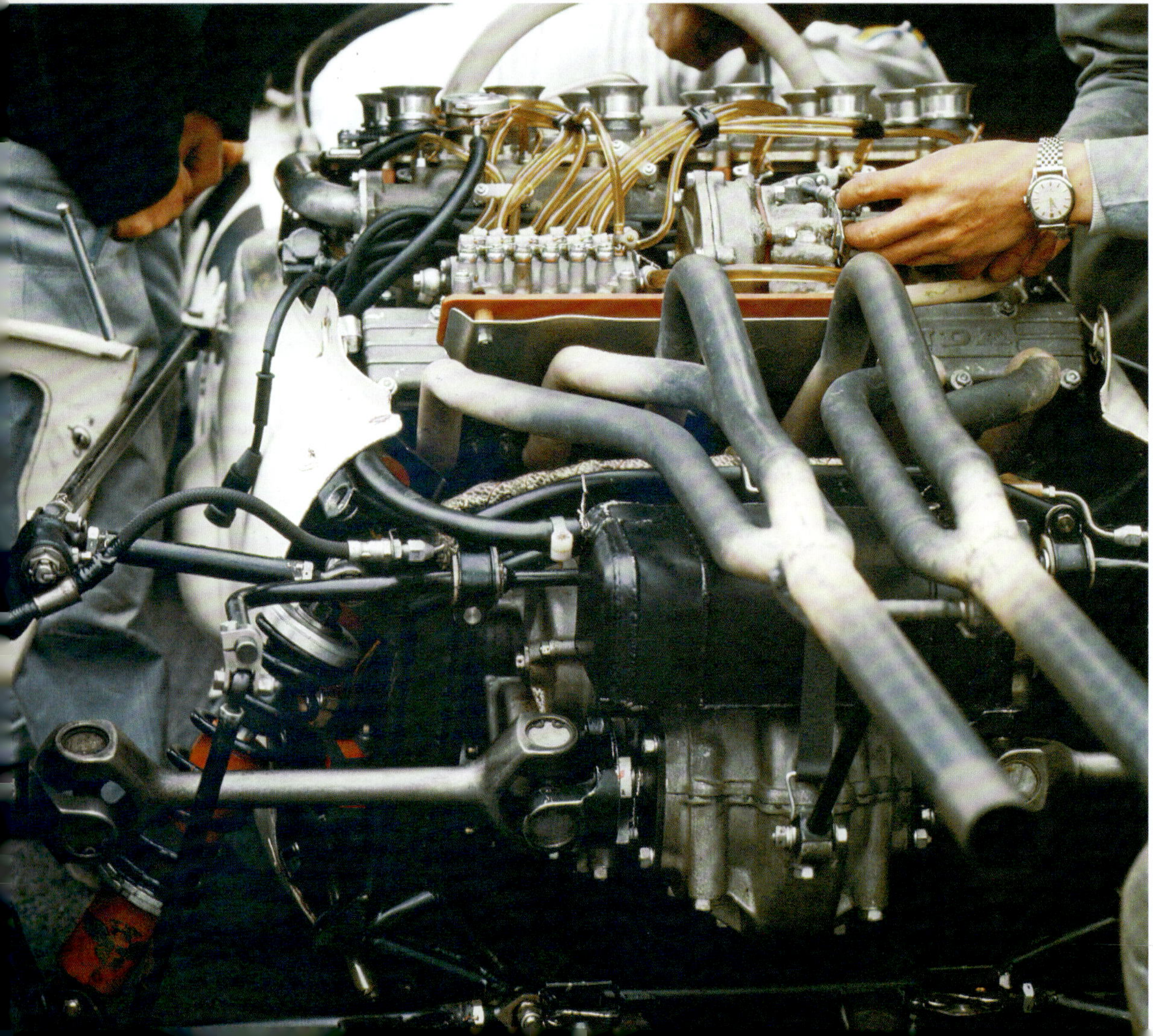

Moises Solana was one of the rare local 'rent a drivers' who were actually talented. He drove in his home GP at Mexico City from 1963 until 1968 plus two US GPs in 1965 and 1967, usually for Team Lotus excepting 1963 and 1966. This is the updated 1962 Lotus 25 (R6) and he is battling with Ronnie Bucknum's Honda RA 272-2. Solana retired with ignition problems whilst Bucknum finished 5th, his best ever GP result. Team mate Richie Ginther won the race, the last ever of the 1.5-litre formula.

Honda's uniquely transverse-mounted V12 developed about 230bhp at 12,000rpm, more than any of its rivals. Richie Ginther endured an inconsistent season as the car qualified well but often faded during racing because it had a tendency to overheat and lose power (but not in Mexico).

1965 Teams, drivers and results

Cooper Car Co. – Cooper T73 Climax V8 and T77 Climax V8
Bruce McLaren (NZ)
Jochen Rindt (A) (dnq Monaco GP)

Team Lotus – Lotus 25 Climax V8 and 33 Climax V8
Jim Clark (GB) (WORLD CHAMPION, missed Monaco GP, racing at Indianapolis 500)
Mike Spence (GB) (Missed Monaco GP due to starting money dispute)
Gerhard Mitter (D) (German GP only)
Giacomo Russo aka 'Geki' (I) (Italian GP only)
Pedro Rodriguez (MEX) (Entered but dns Monaco GP due to starting money dispute)
Moises Solana (MEX) (US and Mexican GPs only)

Owen Racing Organisation – BRM P261
Graham Hill (GB)
Jackie Stewart (GB)

Brabham Racing Organisation – Brabham BT7 Climax V8 and BT11 Climax V8
Jack Brabham (AUS) (dns British GP, car taken over by Gurney, missed Dutch, French and Italian GPs)
Dan Gurney (USA) (Missed Monaco GP, racing at Indianapolis 500, took over Brabham's car for British GP)
Denny Hulme (NZ) (Monaco, French, British, Dutch, German and Italian GPs only)

SEFAC Ferrari – Ferrari 158 and 1512 Flat 12
John Surtees (GB) (Missed US and Mexican GPs due to injuries from Can-Am crash)
Lorenzo Bandini (I)
Nino Vaccarella (I) (Italian GP only)

North American Racing Team – Ferrari 158 and 1512 Flat 12
Pedro Rodriguez (MEX) (US and Mexican GPs only)
Bob Bondurant (USA) (US GP only)

Honda R&D Co – Honda RA272
Richie Ginther (USA) (Missed South African and German GPs, won last ever Championship 1.5 F1 race Mexico)
Ronnie Bucknum (USA) (Missed South African and German GPs, Monaco, Belgian, French, Italian, US and Mexican GPs only)

R. R. C. Walker Racing Team – Brabham BT7 Climax V8 and BT11 BRM V8
Jo Siffert (CH)
Jo Bonnier (S)

DW Racing Enterprises – Brabham BT11 Climax V8 and Lotus 33 Climax V8
Bob Anderson (GB) (dns Belgian GP, dns German GP after practice accident and missed the rest of the season)
Paul Hawkins (AUS) (Monaco [crashed car into harbour] and German GPs only)

Reg Parnell (Racing) – Lotus 25 BRM V8 and 33 BRM V8
Tony Maggs (ZA) (South African GP only, last ever F1 race)
Richard Attwood (GB) (Missed South African and French GPs)
Mike Hailwood (GB) (Monaco GP only)
Innes Ireland (GB) (Missed South African, Monaco and German GPs, dns Mexican GP after being sacked by team for being late for practice)
Chris Amon (NZ) (French and German GPs only)
Bob Bondurant (USA) (Mexican GP only)

Scuderia Centro Sud – BRM P57
Lucien Bianchi (B) (Belgian GP only)
Masten Gregory (USA) (Belgian, British, German and Italian GPs only)
Roberto Bussinello (I) (dnq German GP, Italian GP only)
Giorgio Bassi (I) (Italian GP only)

John Love – Cooper T55 Climax FPF
John Love (RSR) (South African GP only)

Bob Gerard Racing – Cooper T60 Climax V8
John Rhodes (GB) (British GP only)

John Willment Automobiles – Brabham BT11 BRM V8, BT10 Ford 4
Frank Gardner (AUS) (Missed French, US and Mexican GPs)
Paul Hawkins (AUS) (South African GP in Brabham BT10 only)

Ian Raby (Racing) – Brabham BT3 BRM V8
Ian Raby (GB) (British GP only, dnq German GP)
Chris Amon (NZ) (dns British GP, Raby drove car)

David Prophet Racing – Brabham BT10 Ford 4
David Prophet (GB) (South African GP only)

Otelle Nucci – Alfa Special Alfa Romeo
Piet de Klerk (ZA) (South African GP only)

Sam Tingle – LDS Alfa Romeo
Sam Tingle (RSR) (South African GP only)

WORLD CHAMPIONSHIP VENUES AND WINNERS (ten rounds)

South African GP	East London	Jim Clark
Monaco GP	Monte Carlo	Graham Hill
Belgian GP	Spa-Francorchamps	Jim Clark
French GP	Clermont-Ferrand	Jim Clark
British GP	Silverstone	Jim Clark
Dutch GP	Zandvoort	Jim Clark
German GP	Nürburgring	Jim Clark
Italian GP	Monza	Jackie Stewart
United States GP	Watkins Glen	Graham Hill
Mexican GP	Mexico City	Richie Ginther

DRIVERS' CHAMPIONSHIP
Points: 9-6-4-3-2-1. Best 6 scores

1	Jim Clark	Lotus	54
2	Graham Hill	BRM	40
3	Jackie Stewart	BRM	33
4	Dan Gurney	Brabham	25
5	John Surtees	Ferrari	17
6	Lorenzo Bandini	Ferrari	13
7	Richie Ginther	Honda	11
8	Mike Spence	Lotus	10
9	Bruce McLaren	Cooper	10
11	Jack Brabham	Brabham	9
11	Denny Hulme	Brabham	5
12	Jo Siffert	Brabham	5
13	Jochen Rindt	Cooper	4
14	Pedro Rodriguez	Ferrari	2
15	Ronnie Bucknum	Honda	2
16	Richard Attwood	Lotus	2

CONSTRUCTORS' CHAMPIONSHIP
Points: 9-6-4-3-2-1, (awarded only to best-placed finisher).
Best 6 scores

1	Lotus-Climax	54
2	BRM	45
3	Brabham-Climax	27
4	Ferrari	26
5	Cooper-Climax	14
6	Honda	11
7	Brabham-BRM	5
8	Lotus-BRM	2

1966

THIRD TIME AROUND

On 21–22 November 1963 at the FIA headquarters in Paris a 3-litre F1 option beginning in 1966 was virtually nodded through, much to the approval of Ferrari's Mauro Forghieri. Minimum weight was to be 500kg using commercially available pump fuel.

1966 was hailed as the return to power, but some British teams had no race ready 3-litre engines. Instead they utilised oversized Coventry Climax and BRM V8s. Lotus were one but later used BRM's new H16 unit in the type 43 and Jim Clark won the US GP. He was partnered by the returning Peter Arundell, but sadly his former pace had gone. BRM's new P83 H16 however was a disaster and Jackie Stewart and Graham Hill raced the 1965 car for most of the year (Stewart won Monaco with a 2-litre version). Shortly afterwards his Spa crash had serious long-term repercussions for motor racing. Hill scored no wins but had several top three finishes and outscored his Scottish rivals.

Ferrari with a suitable V12 should have dominated, but internal politics generated by team manager Eugenio Dragoni caused John Surtees to leave the team at Le Mans after convincingly winning the Belgian GP. The Ferrari was initially underpowered, but the newly promoted Lorenzo Bandini together with Ludovico Scarfiotti and Mike Parkes were quite successful. Scarfiotti won at Monza while Parkes and Bandini produced a slew of 2nd and 3rd place finishes.

Eschewing mechanical complexity the ever canny Jack Brabham used a redesigned GM 3.5-litre Oldsmobile lightweight V8 production engine from Repco in Australia. With Denny Hulme he won the Championship achieving four GP victories for his third drivers' title. Meanwhile, Dan Gurney left Brabham to found Anglo American Racers and race his own Eagle cars to be powered by Weslake designed V12s. These were delayed so they began with a 2.7-litre version of the venerable Coventry Climax 4 cylinder FPF. Former Cooper driver Bruce McLaren tried two different V8s from Ford and Serenissima in his new McLaren M2B but neither was satisfactory.

Maserati's antique 1957 2.5-litre V12 enlarged to 3 litres turned up in the back of Cooper's new T81. John Surtees joined the team post Ferrari and resurrected their prospects by outdriving the highly rated Jochen Rindt and winning the season's finale in Mexico. Rindt finished 2nd at Spa and Watkins Glen to further enhance his reputation. Richie Ginther and Chris Amon also tried the cars but the privately entered T81s achieved nothing much. The cast of genuine privateers included such oddities as the Godiva Climax V8 Shannon. A frequent distraction was provided by the making of the John Frankenheimer film 'Grand Prix'. At Monza, Ginther was reunited with Honda and their new RA273 which he took to 4th place in Mexico.

The diminishing non-championship F1 events began at East London in South Africa on January 1st with a win for Spence's Lotus 33. Syracuse was an easy victory for Surtees's Ferrari 312 while the Silverstone and Oulton Park races were won by Jack Brabham.

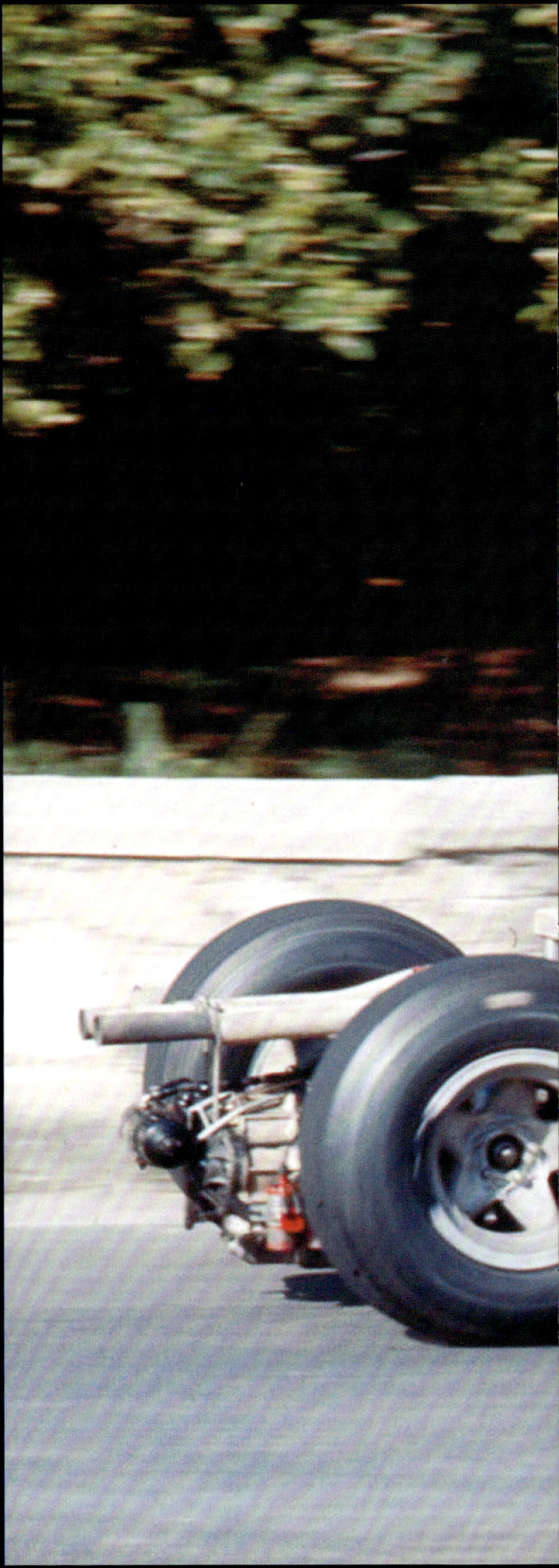

John Surtees drove the handsome Ferrari 312 (0010) to victory at the XV Gran Premio di Siracusa on 1 May 1966. At this stage the Prancing Horse looked set to clean up in the new 3-litre F1 but all was not well. It is noticeable that the crowds who always populated this corner are no longer in evidence.

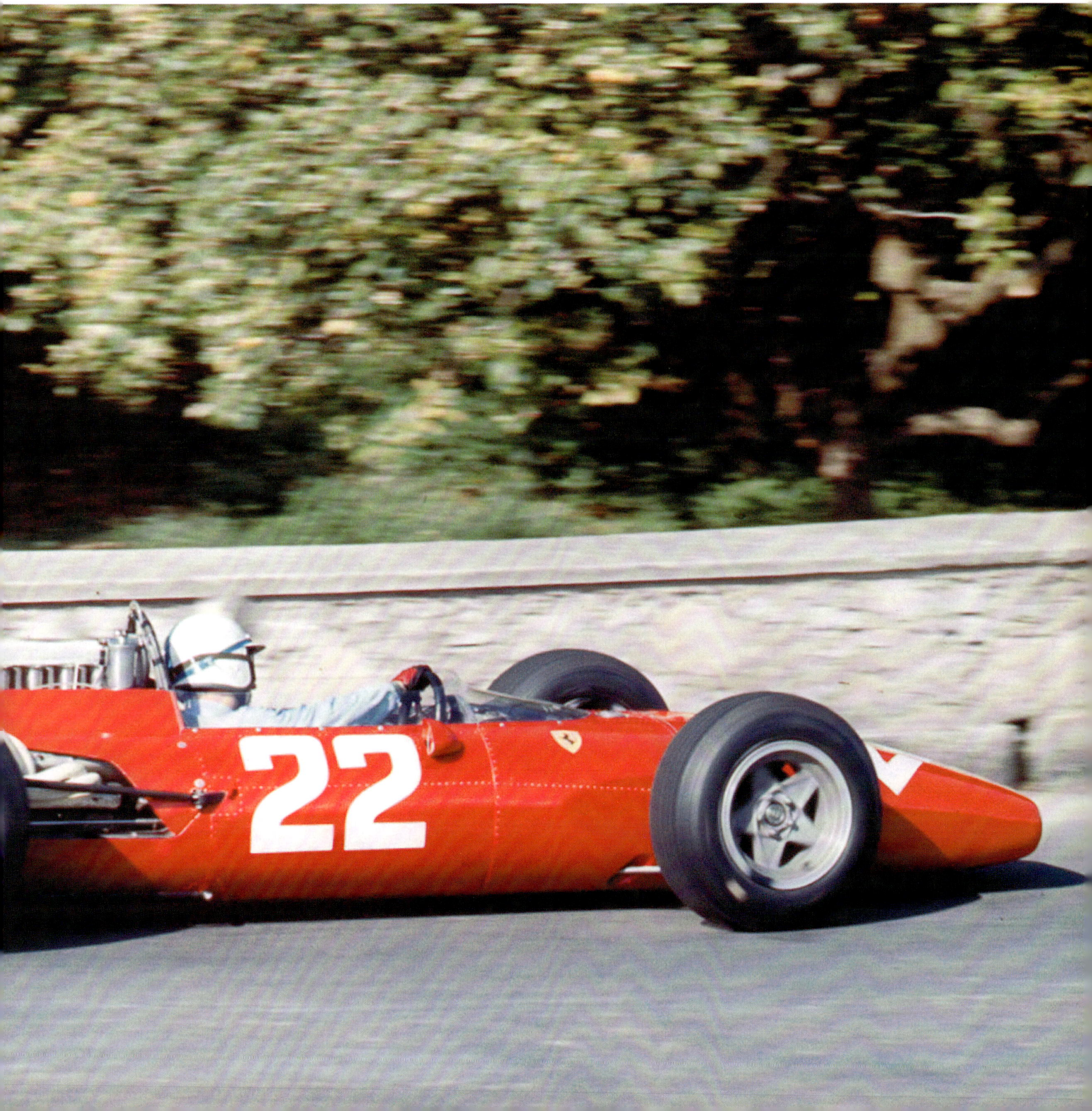

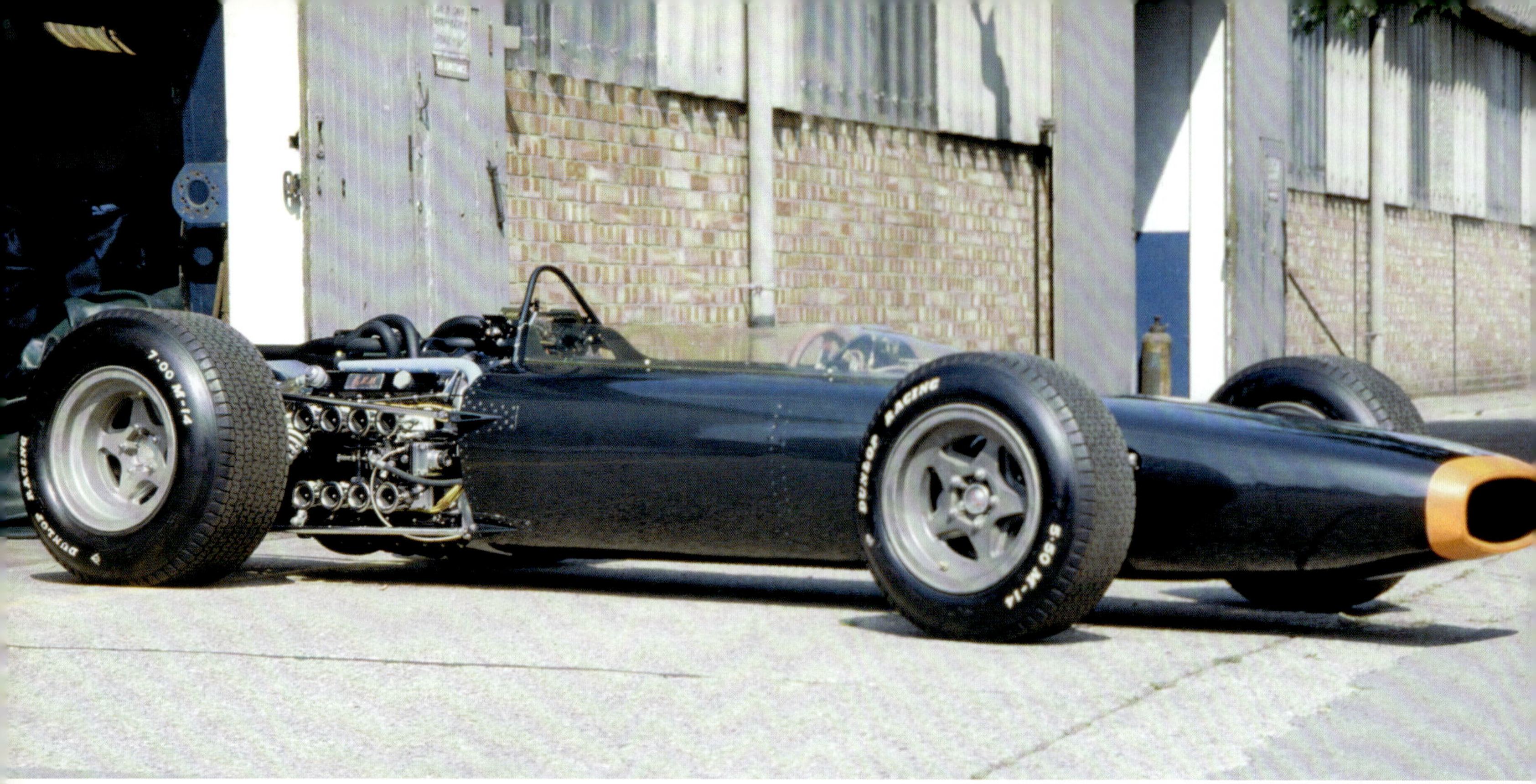

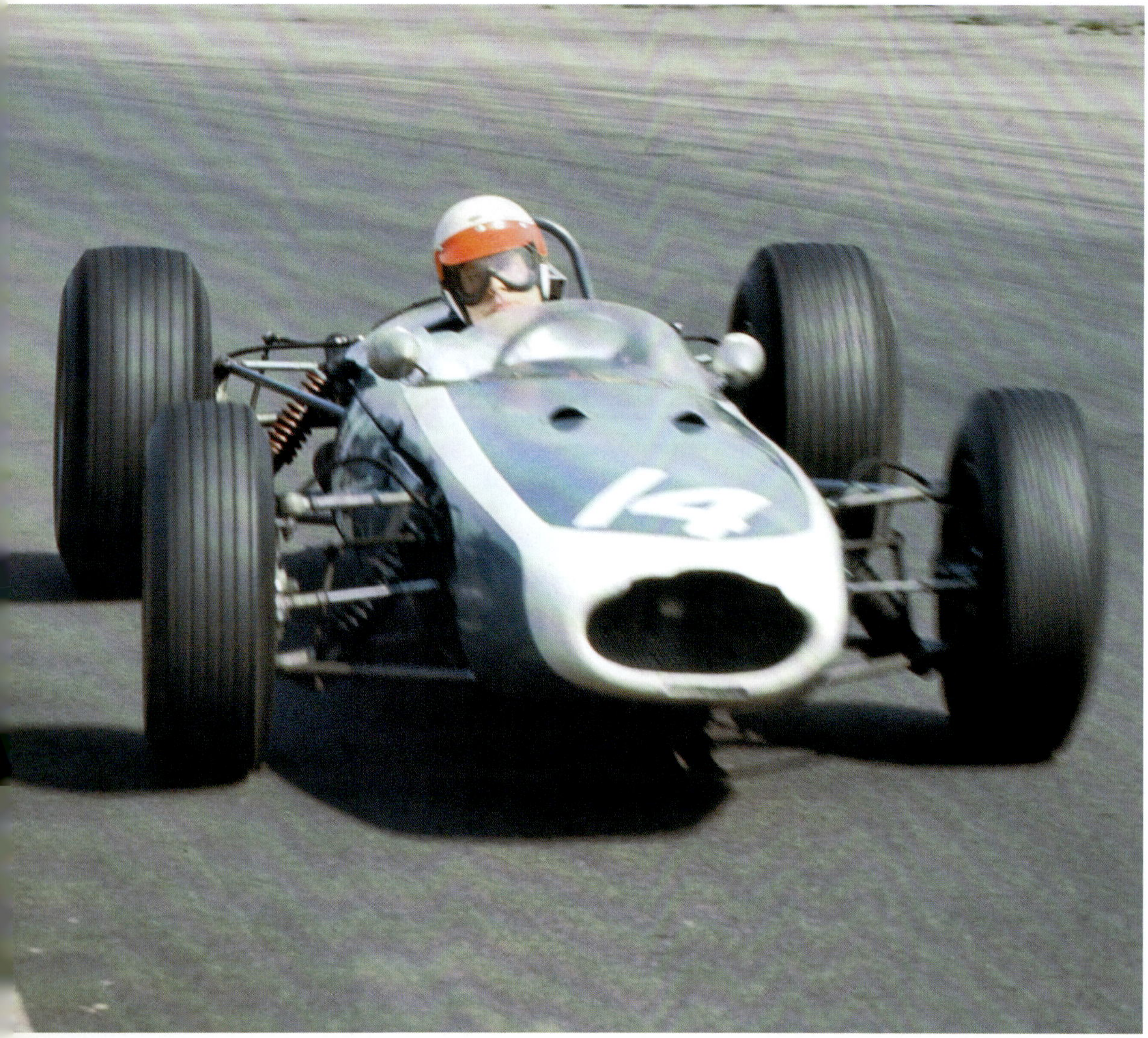

BRM's new 3-litre contender the P83, was another 16-cylinder folly, being overweight, underpowered (less than 400bhp in 1966), unreliable and too complex. The impressive looking but obese H16 engine weighed close to 265kg even after development in 1967 when power output peaked at 420bhp @ 10,500rpm on the test bed.

John Taylor was a competent single-seater racer who drove for Bob Gerard in the 1964 British GP. For 1966 he raced the ex-Willment/Frank Gardner Brabham BT11 BRM (F1-4-64). It was entered by David Bridges at the Silverstone International Trophy where Taylor finished 6th. Thereafter he was a worthy 6th at the French GP, 8th in the British and Dutch GPs but collided with Ickx's F2 Matra at the Nürburgring. The car caught fire and Taylor suffered serious burns but appeared to be stable until he suddenly deteriorated and died a month later.

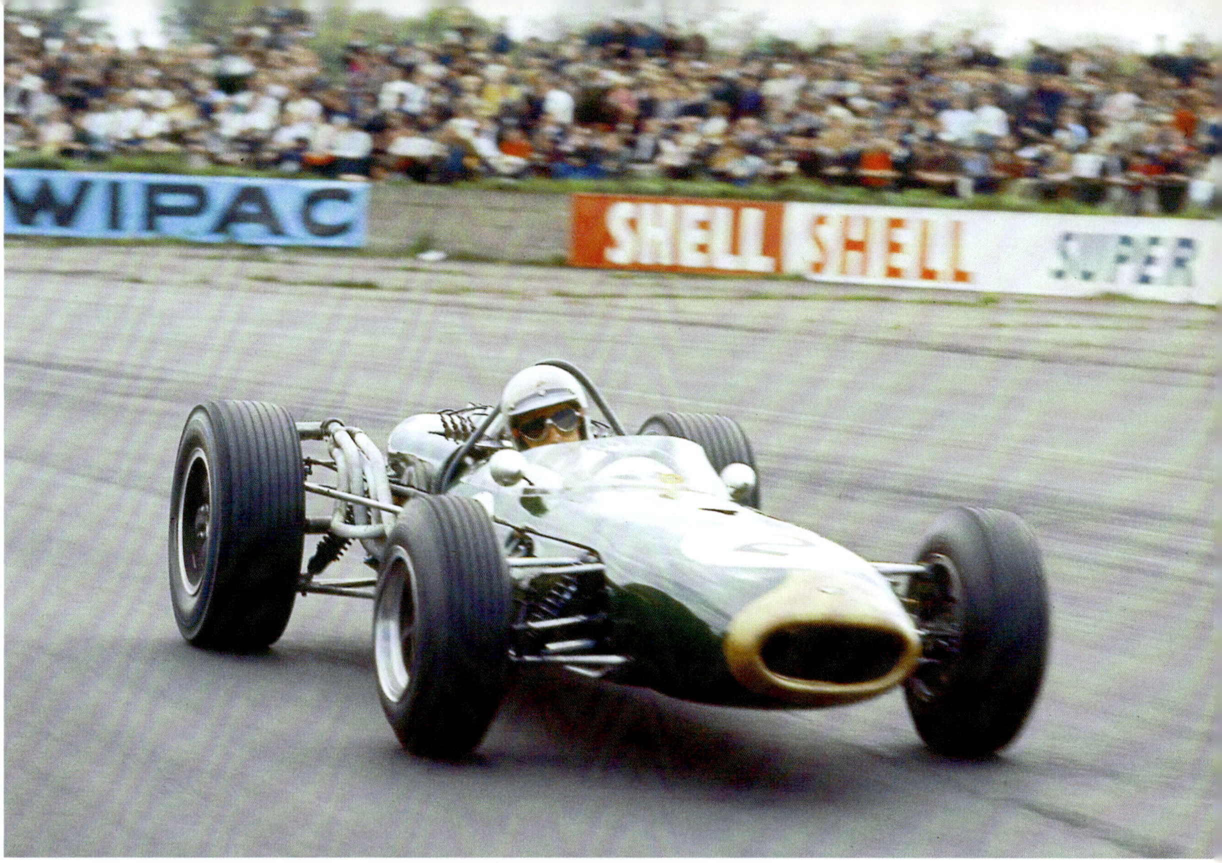

The new Repco powered Brabham BT19 (F1-1-65) was first seen at East London in January where it dominated the non-championship South African GP before retirement. Starting from pole in the International Trophy at Silverstone, Brabham won the race convincingly from the much fancied Ferrari 312 of Surtees, really pleasing Jack who always loved beating Ferraris. It was achieved with an engine that developed only 278bhp, which says much about the V12 Ferrari's lack of oomph and Brabham's consummate skill. Note the square shoulders of the rear Goodyear tyres and 'on tiptoes' stance of the car.

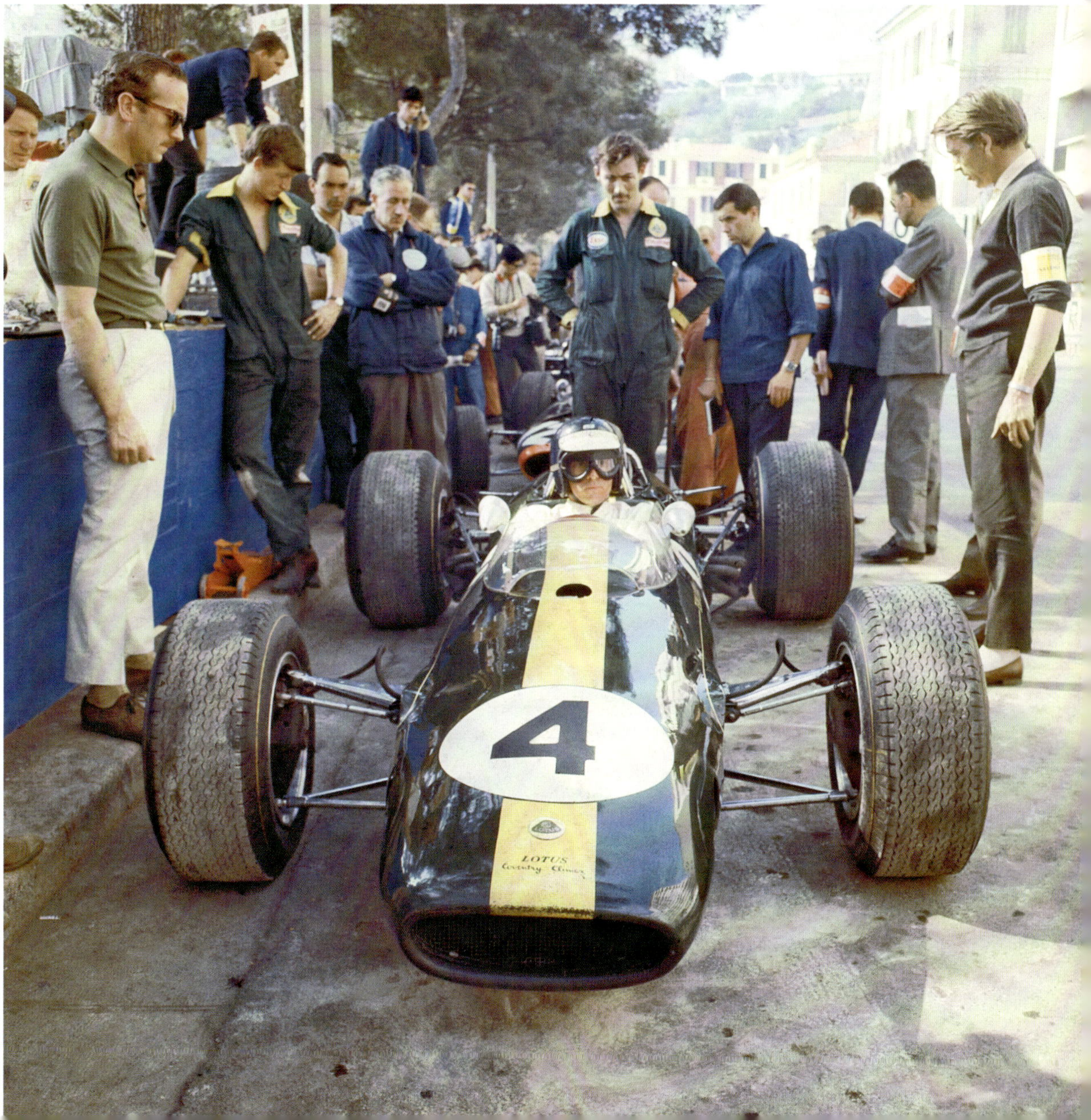

Eyes wide open. Jim Clark in his Lotus 33 (R11) on the streets of Monaco prior to his pole position lap. Colin Chapman (left) and crew chief Jim Endruweit appear concerned. The nose of the Lotus wears a tar and molten rubber lipstick whilst the filthy oil spattered road bears witness to the many incontinent racing cars. Unable to select his special 'start only' bottom gear in the race Clark was slow away and spent until lap 61 reaching 3rd place when a rear hub carrier failed ending his day.

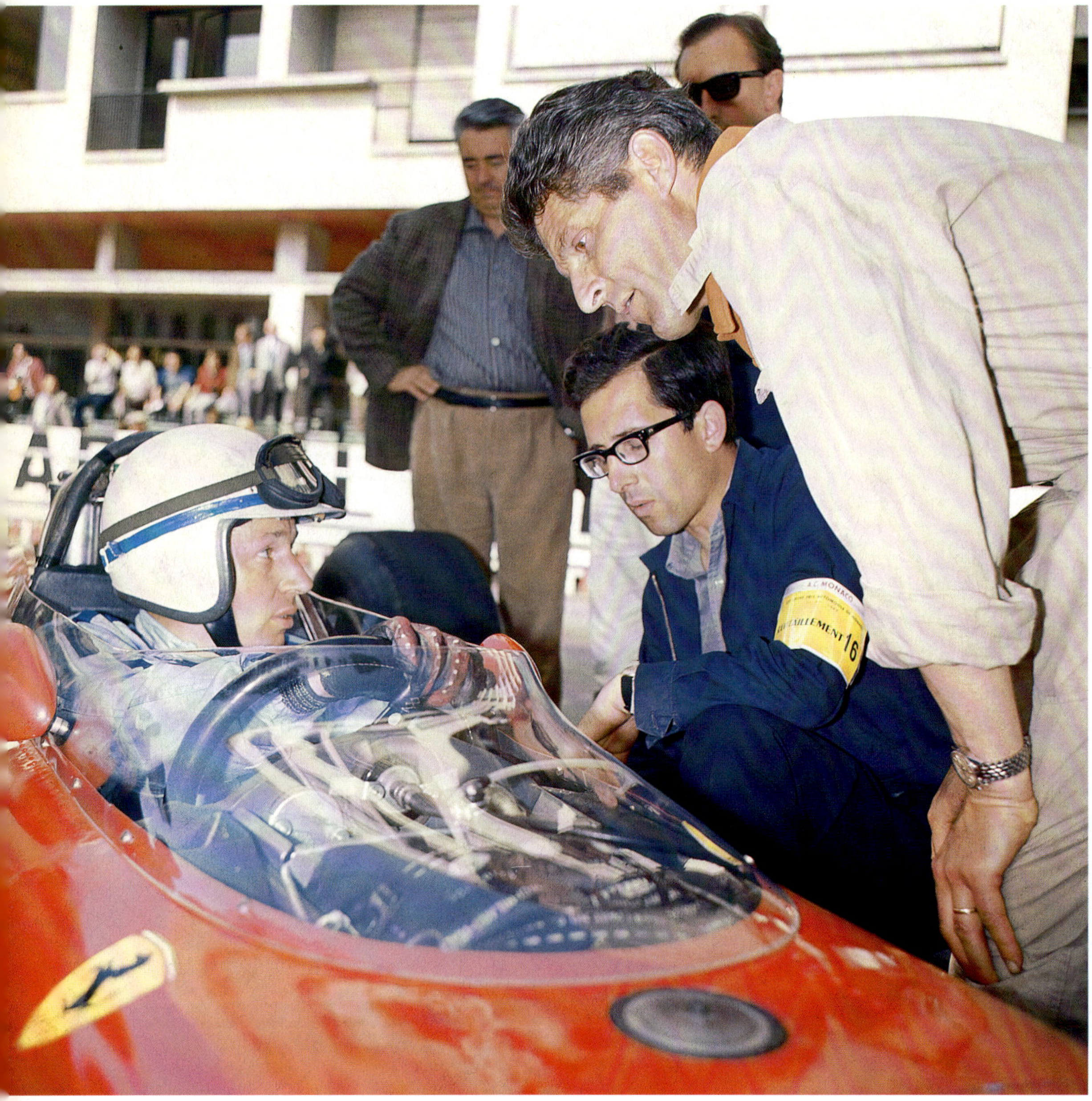

An increasingly unhappy John Surtees in the 312-0010 confers with Ferrari engineer Mauro Forghieri at Monaco. He should be driving the 2.4-litre Dino V6 158 (0006) that was far better suited for Monaco. This, however, was allocated to Lorenzo Bandini who still seemed to be favoured over Surtees by team manager Dragoni. Ferrari claimed 360bhp for the 24-valve V12 312 but Surtees reckoned it felt more like 270! He joined Clark on the front row and led the race for 16 laps until his differential broke. Note he is wearing his own brand of driving gloves.

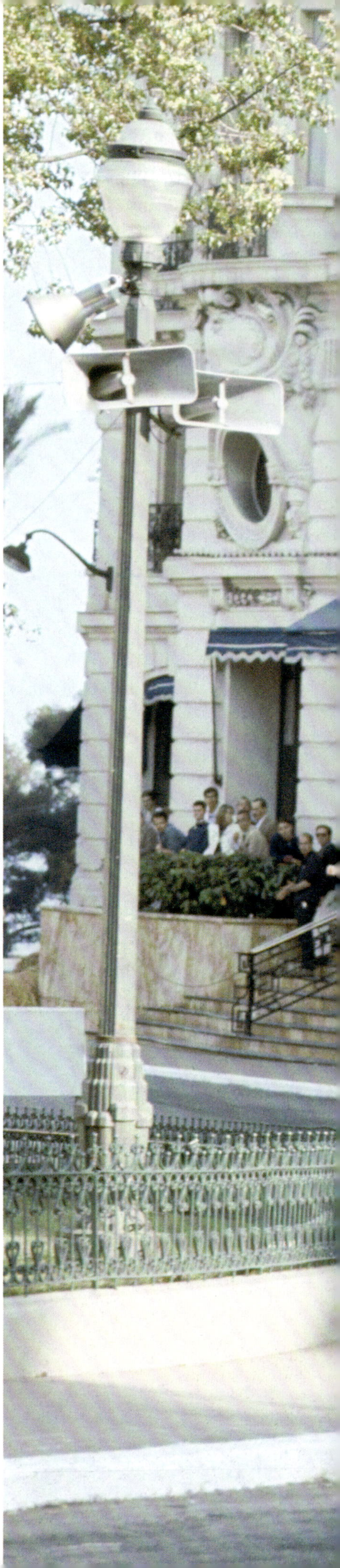

25 to go. Monaco was Jackie Stewart's second GP victory. His BRM P61/2 (2617) had an enlarged 1965 V8 of 1930cc giving 265bhp and was used in preference to the new but overweight P83. Stewart races through Casino Square with the Hotel de Paris in the background, apparently ignored by a casual bystander who is more interested in the crowd occupying the terrace. He beat a fading Lorenzo Bandini (Ferrari) by 40.1 seconds with Graham Hill 3rd in the sister BRM that was slowed by a slipping clutch.

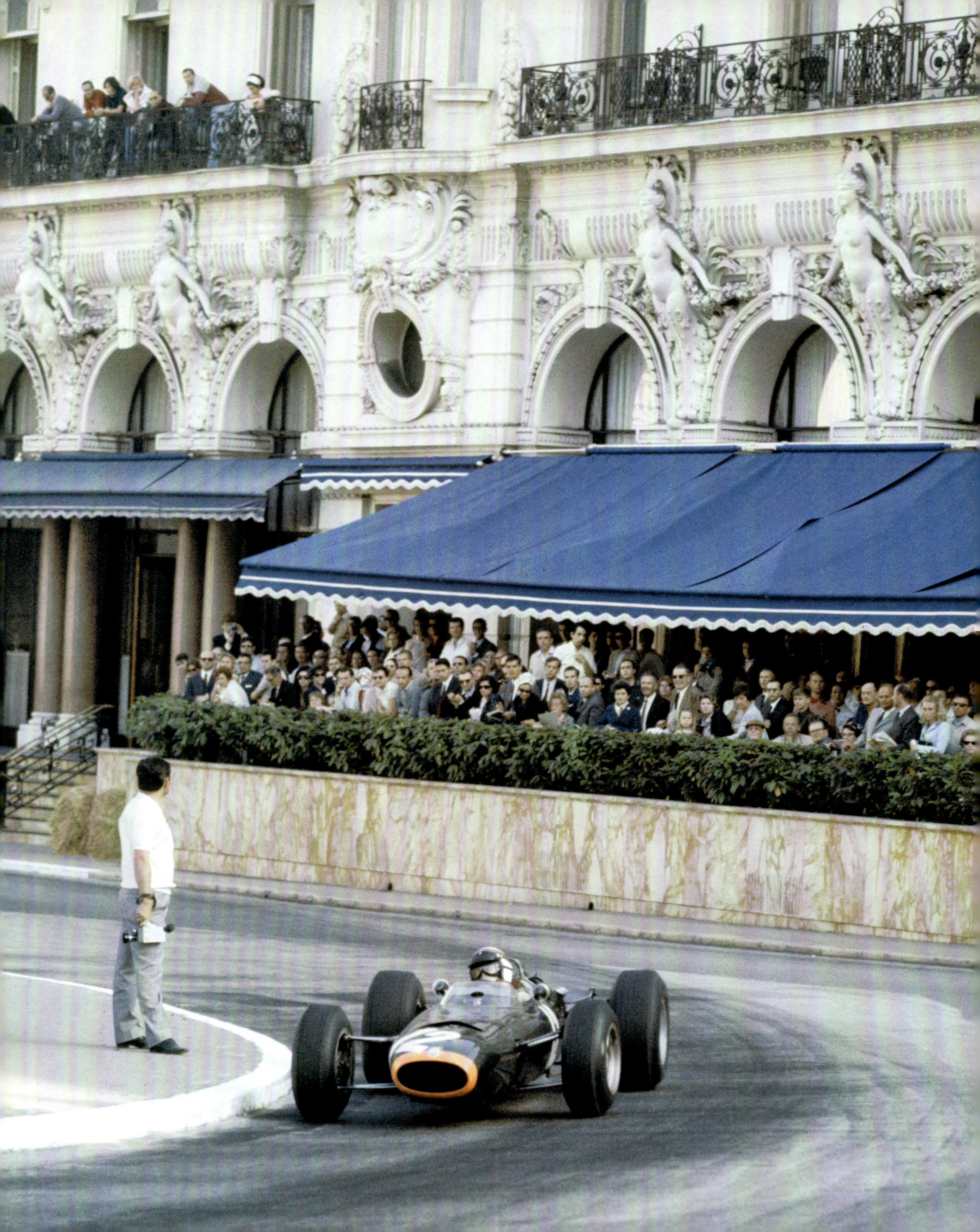

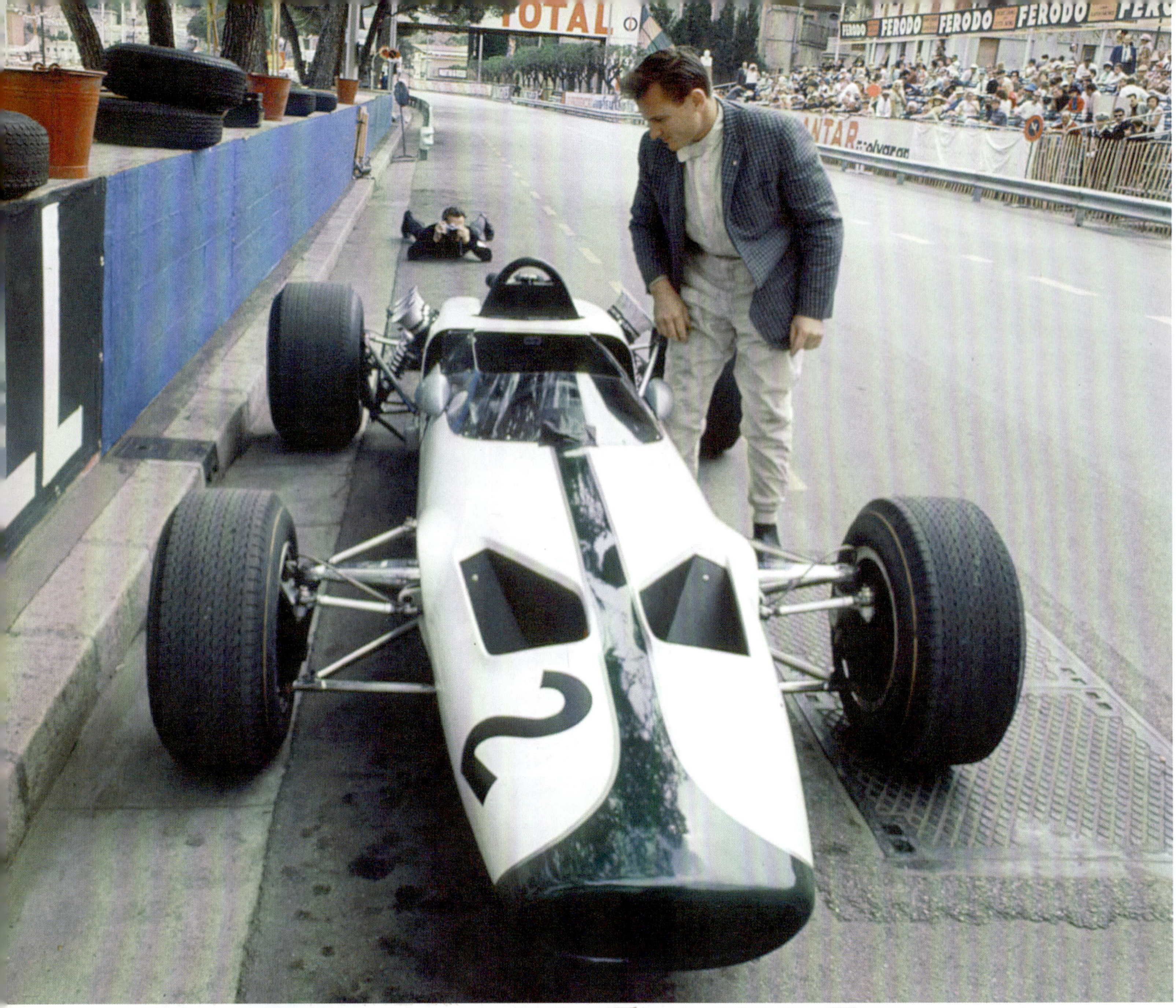
TOTAL
FERODO FERODO FERODO

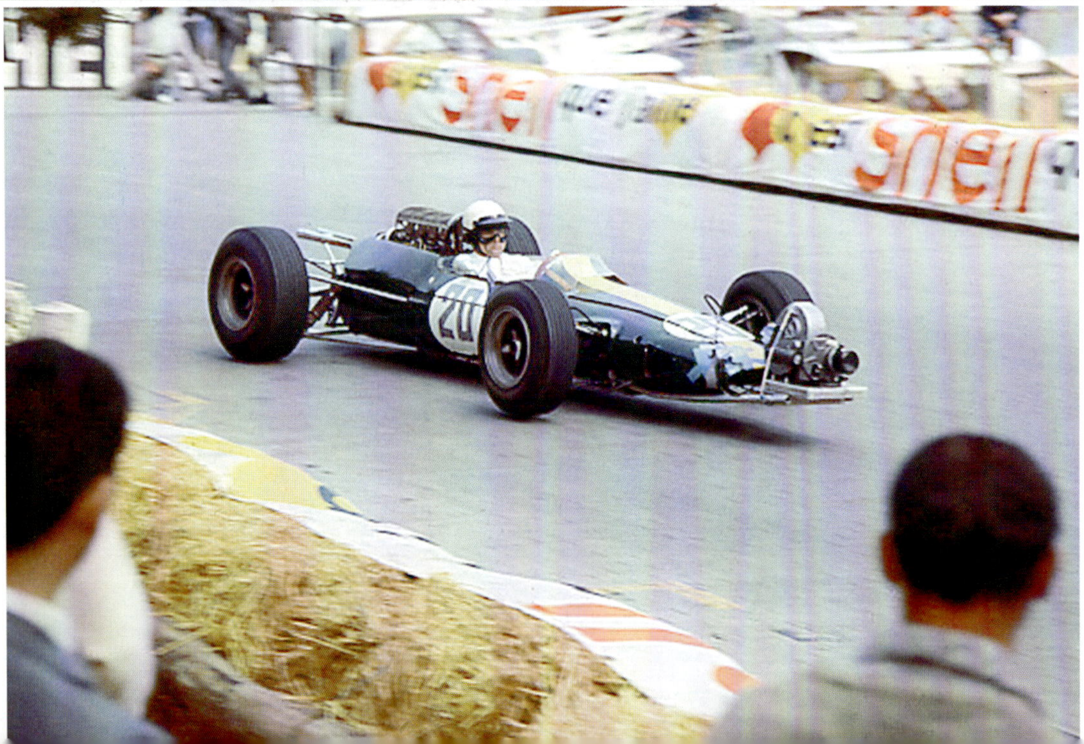
20

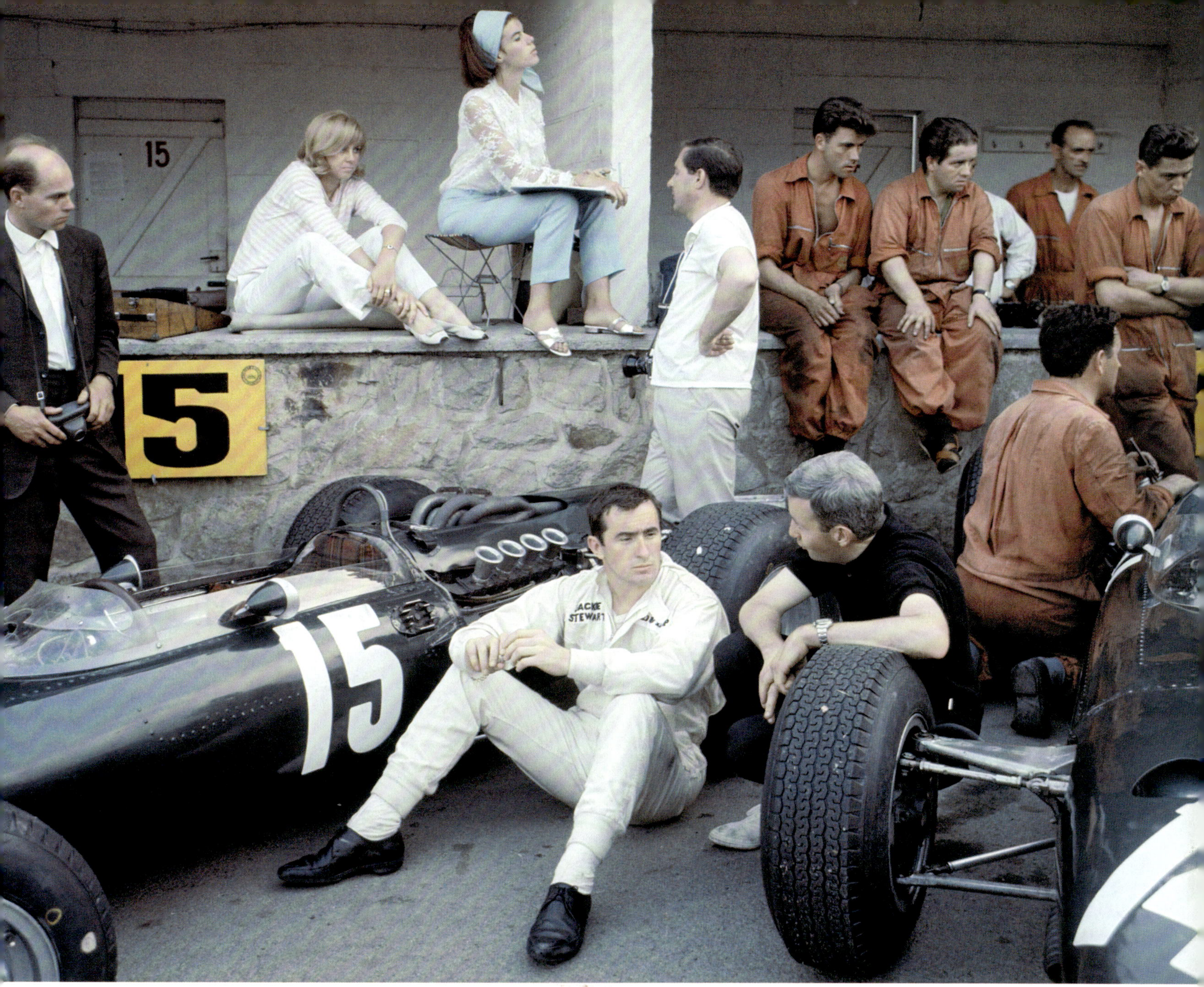

A short haired Jackie Stewart takes counsel from Teddy Meyer in the BRM pits at Spa. Sitting on the pit counter on a folding seat is wife Helen whilst rather glum looking Bourne mechanics occupy the adjacent pit. The brilliant Scot crashed on the wet opening lap of the Belgian GP and was rescued from the wreckage by team mate Graham Hill. The absence of safety measures, proper medical care, general facilities and back-up on one of the most dangerous tracks in use kickstarts Stewart's safety campaign. It will ultimately change motor sport irrevocably and make him very unpopular with the press, pundits, public and some drivers.

Bruce McLaren's first attempt at an F1 car was the Robin Herd designed M2B powered by a 3-litre version of Ford's 4.2-litre V8 Indy engine. It had too narrow a power band with oversized ports and valves offering only 300bhp @ 9000rpm. Bruce looks into the cockpit of the car during practice and is perhaps already regretting his choice of powerplant. He retired on lap 9 with an oil leak. Note the photographer lying prone behind the car.

A controversial feature of the 1966 season was the shooting of racing footage for John Frankenheimer's famous film 'Grand Prix'. Inevitably this caused some disruption and not everybody was happy to accommodate the activities. Phil Hill did a lot of the in car shots and is seen here at Monaco in an old Lotus 25 (R6) with a nose mounted movie camera. Sometimes he went off with the field from the back of the grid during the opening laps of a race! The past is a different country.

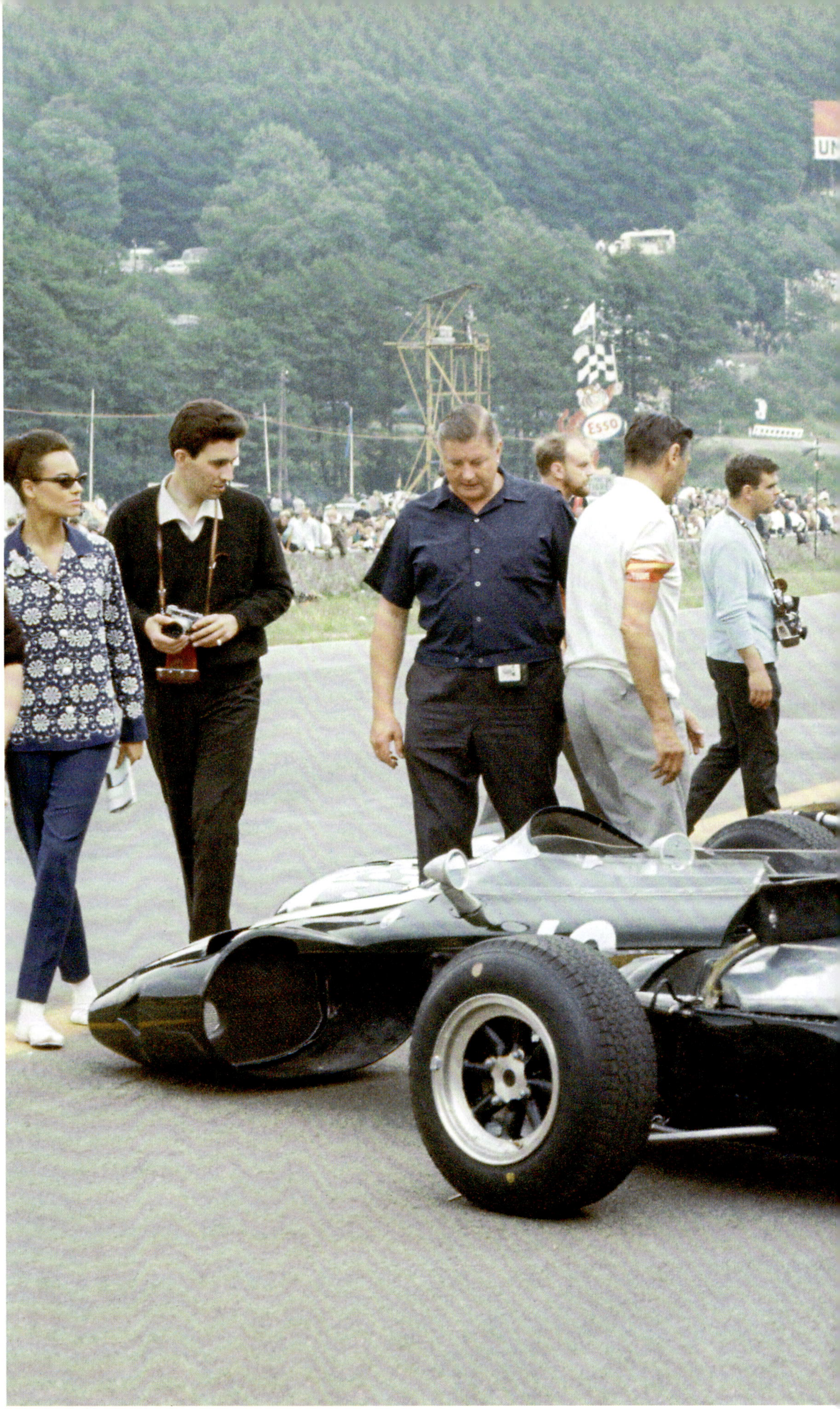

➔ Further along the Spa pit-lane, mechanics tend to the works Cooper-Maseratis during practice. No 19 is Jochen Rindt's T81 (F1-3-66) that will finish 2nd behind Surtees's Ferrari in the wet, accident blighted race, surviving a high speed spin at the Masta kink on the opening lap. In his autobiography 'The Jack Brabham Story' with Doug Nye, Brabham recalled that "I've never seen a car spin so violently, nor so many times. I had a grandstand seat. Amazingly, he kept tracking through the corners on line while actually spinning end-for-end. His head was snapping like a ballet dancer's to keep track of where he was."

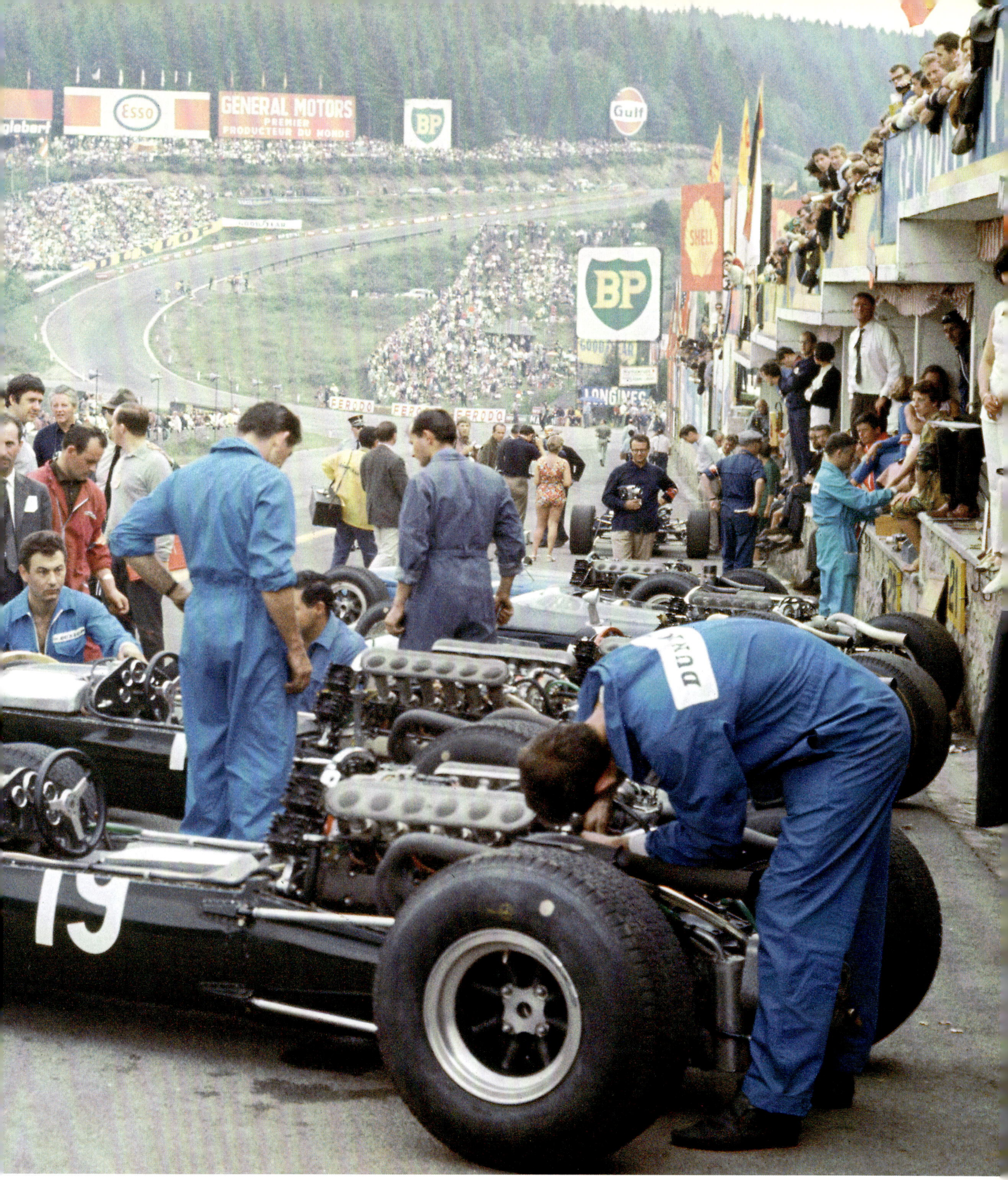
Esso
GENERAL MOTORS
PREMIER
PRODUCTEUR DU MONDE
BP
Gulf
SHELL
BP
LONGINES
FERODO
19

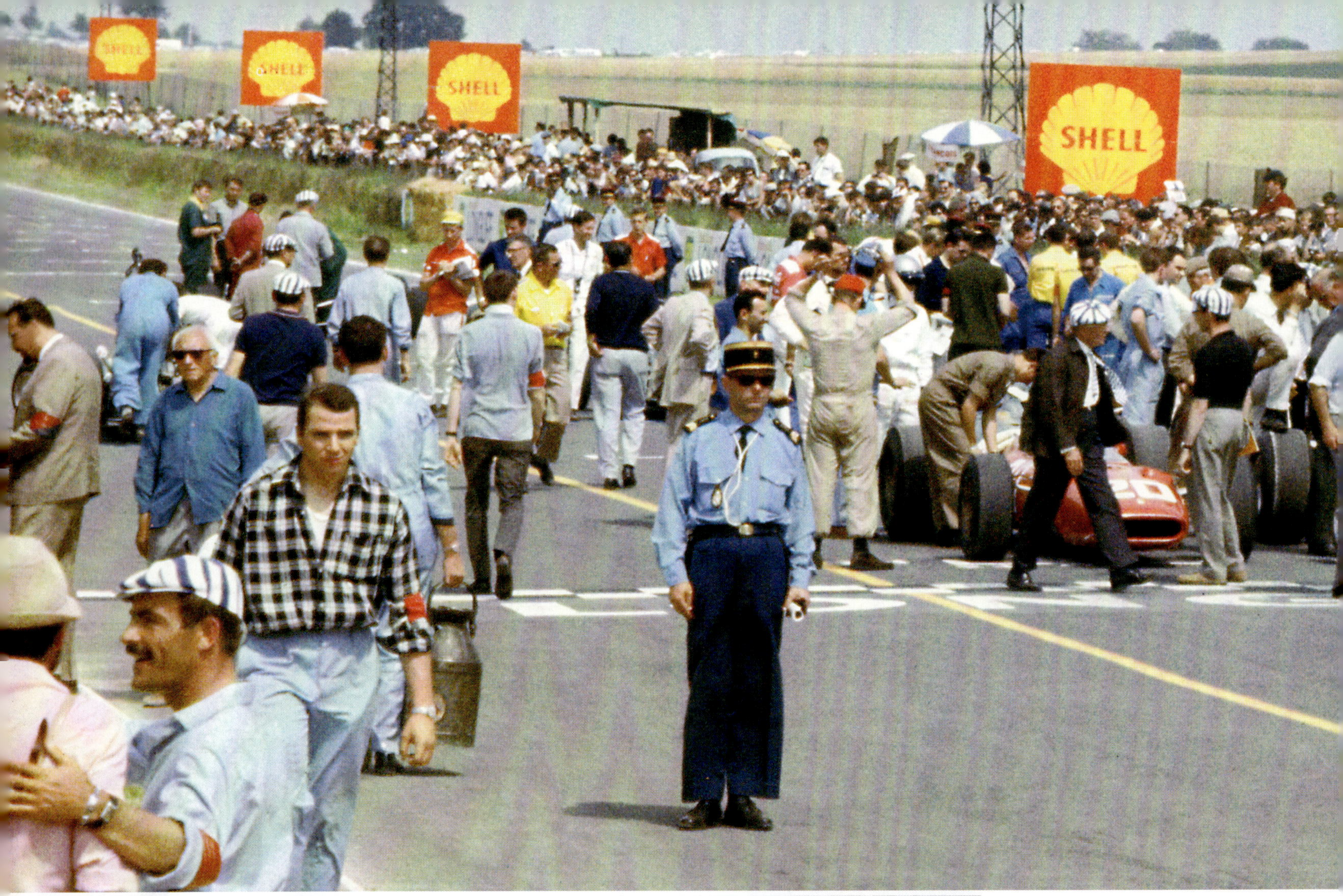
SHELL
SHELL
SHELL
SHELL

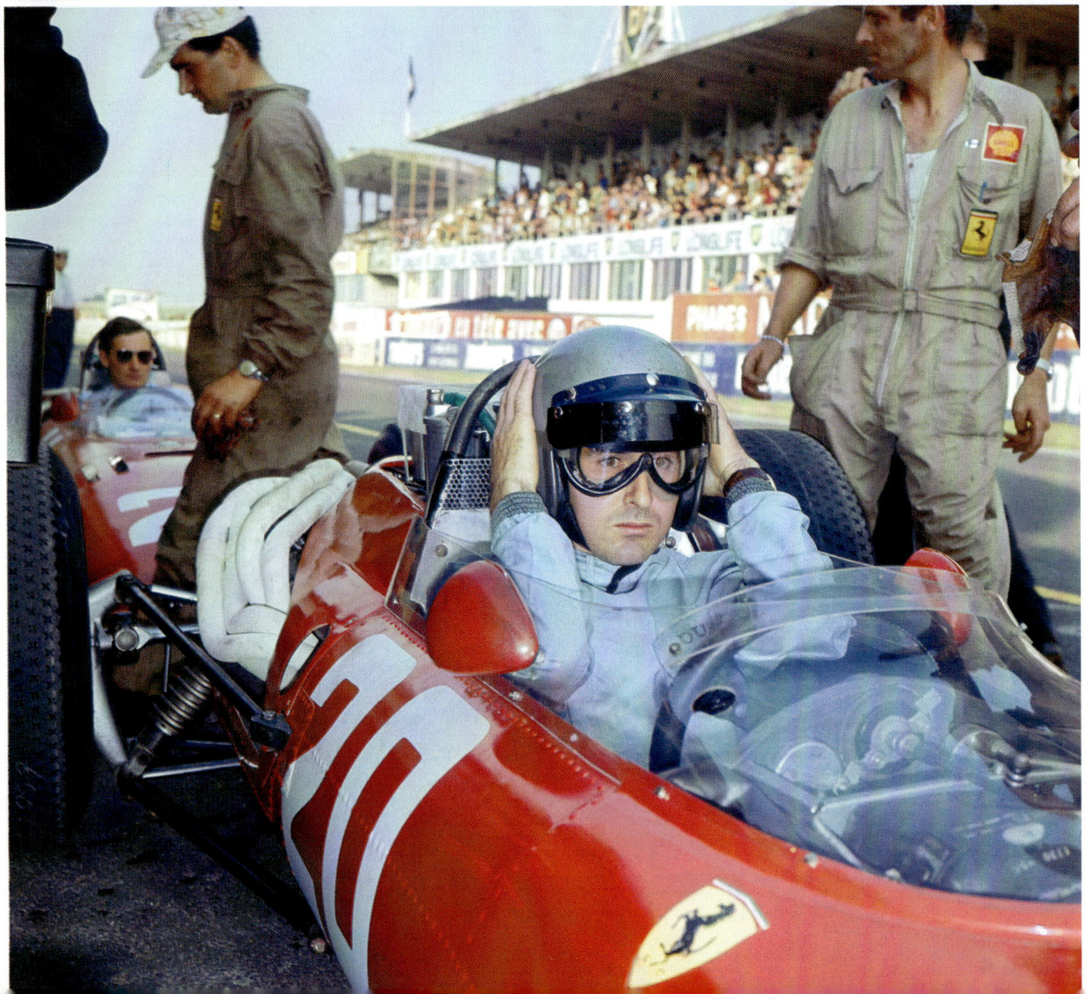
PHARES

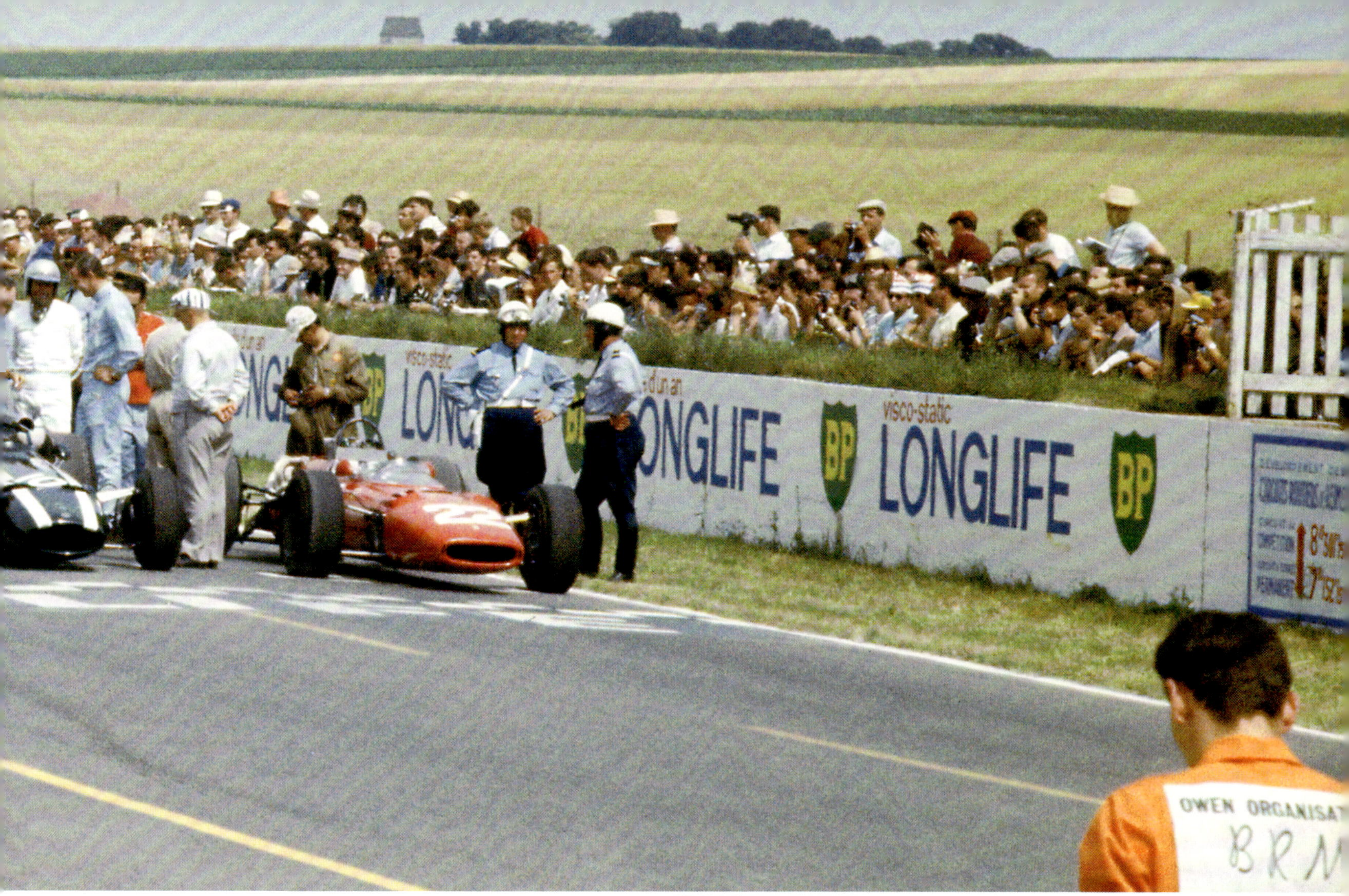

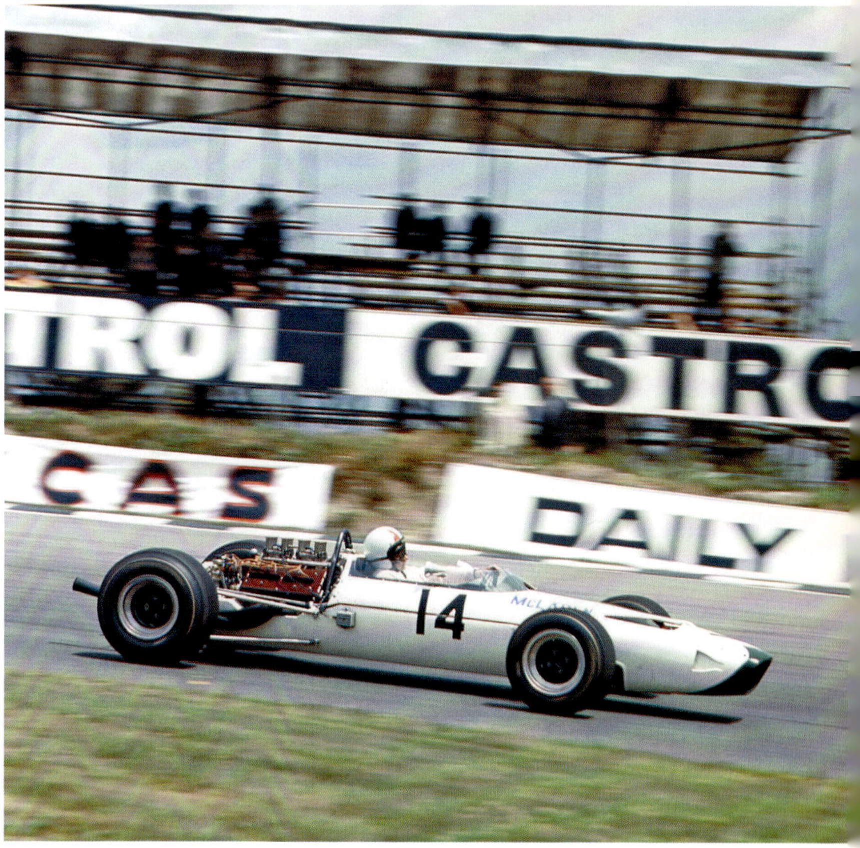

The very busy looking grid belies the fact that there were only 17 starters amidst the characteristically flat 'champagne country' landscape of Reims. This was the last French GP held here, the first being in 1932. Jack Brabham (white suit) can be seen standing between the helmetless John Surtees (left) and Mike Parkes (right) on the front row between the Parkes Ferrari and the Surtees Cooper with Bandini's Ferrari on the left. Jim Clark non-started after being hit in the face by a bird during practice. The gendarme (front left) is sporting this season's above the ankle look.

Following the departure of John Surtees from Ferrari, Lorenzo Bandini was promoted to *numero uno*. He responded by setting pole position from Surtees at Reims and led the race until a broken throttle cable intruded leaving a delighted Jack Brabham to win, the first time a car bearing the driver's name had won a World Championship race. Bandini with his staring eyes encapsulates the drama of the moment as he sits in the Ferrari 312 (0010) during practice at Reims. Behind is Ferrari team mate Mike Parkes who finished 2nd.

The dumpy profile of the McLaren M2B rounding Paddock Hill Bend at Brands Hatch during the British GP reveals the Serinissima V8 engine that had replaced the unsuccessful Ford Indy derivation seen at Monaco. It was a sports car engine supposedly giving 350bhp but probably offered about 260bhp. Nevertheless, Bruce McLaren finished 6th, thus scoring the constructor's first ever World Championship point.

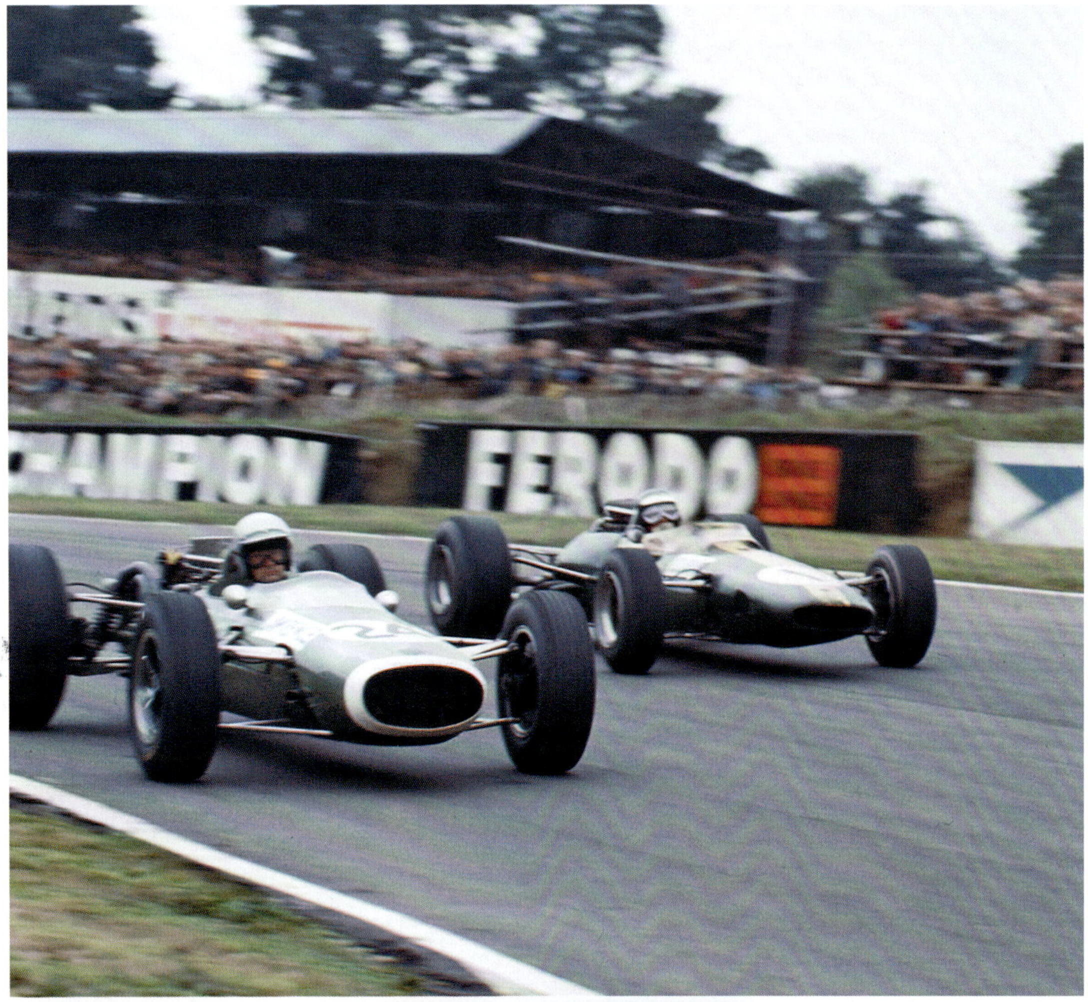

There were no Ferraris at the British GP due to industrial problems but a Ferrari powered car did race, the J.A. Pearce Engineering entered Cooper T73 Ferrari (F1-2-64) driven by renowned Morgan racer Chris Lawrence. It was powered by a Ferrari V12 engine from the 'breadvan' Ferrari and Lawrence was the last classified finisher in 11th place. Here he is lapped by Clark's Lotus 33 (R14). Elsewhere Lawrence retired from the German GP, finished 5th in the Oulton Park Gold Cup and 8th at the 1967 Brands Hatch Race of Champions.

Following a successful F3 campaign in 1964 and F2 experience in 1965, Chris Irwin began his F1 career at the British GP in the spare Brabham BT11 Climax FPF (F1-1-64) entered by Brabham. He finished a worthy 7th two laps behind his team mates Brabham and Hulme in the team's first 1–2 with the Repco powered cars.

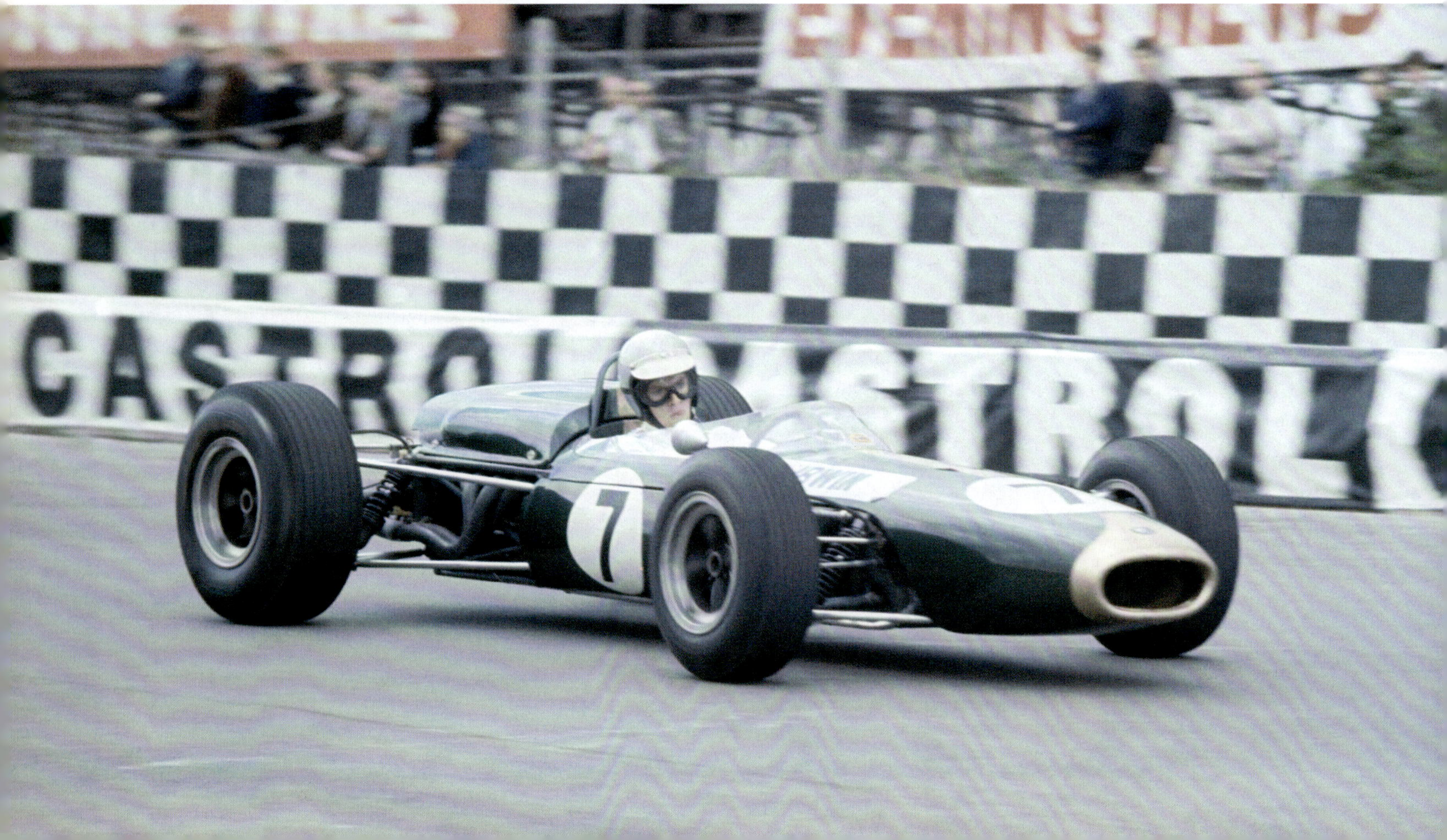

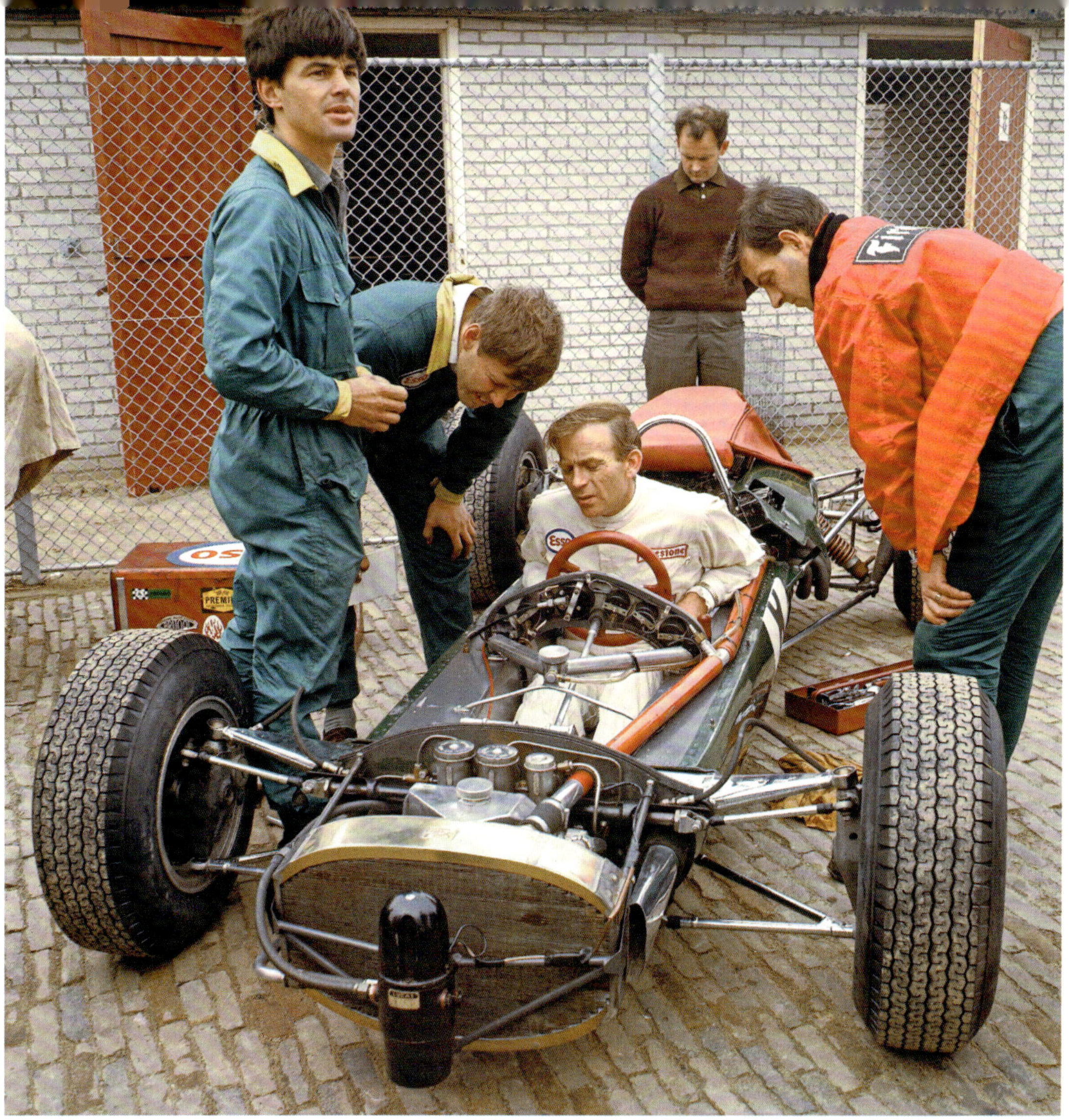

Colin Chapman had promised Peter Arundell his Lotus F1 drive back when he was fully recovered from his 1964 Reims F2 crash and kept his word. This displaced Mike Spence, who joined Reg Parnell Racing for 1966 whilst awaiting a BRM seat in 1967, but Arundell was unable to reproduce his former pace. From left to right Alan McCall, Dick Scammel, Arundell (in car) and Dougie Bridge in the Zandvoort paddock with the Lotus 33 BRM (R11).

Jack Brabham and Denny Hulme lead Jim Clark and Graham Hill at the Dutch GP. Jim Clark might have won in the Lotus 33 (R14), but a damaged water pump caused overheating and after stopping for water he finally finished 3rd with a cooked engine. Brabham walked to the grid wearing a false beard and brandishing a walking stick to celebrate his 40th birthday. He won with Hill's BRM 2nd but Hulme retired with ignition failure.

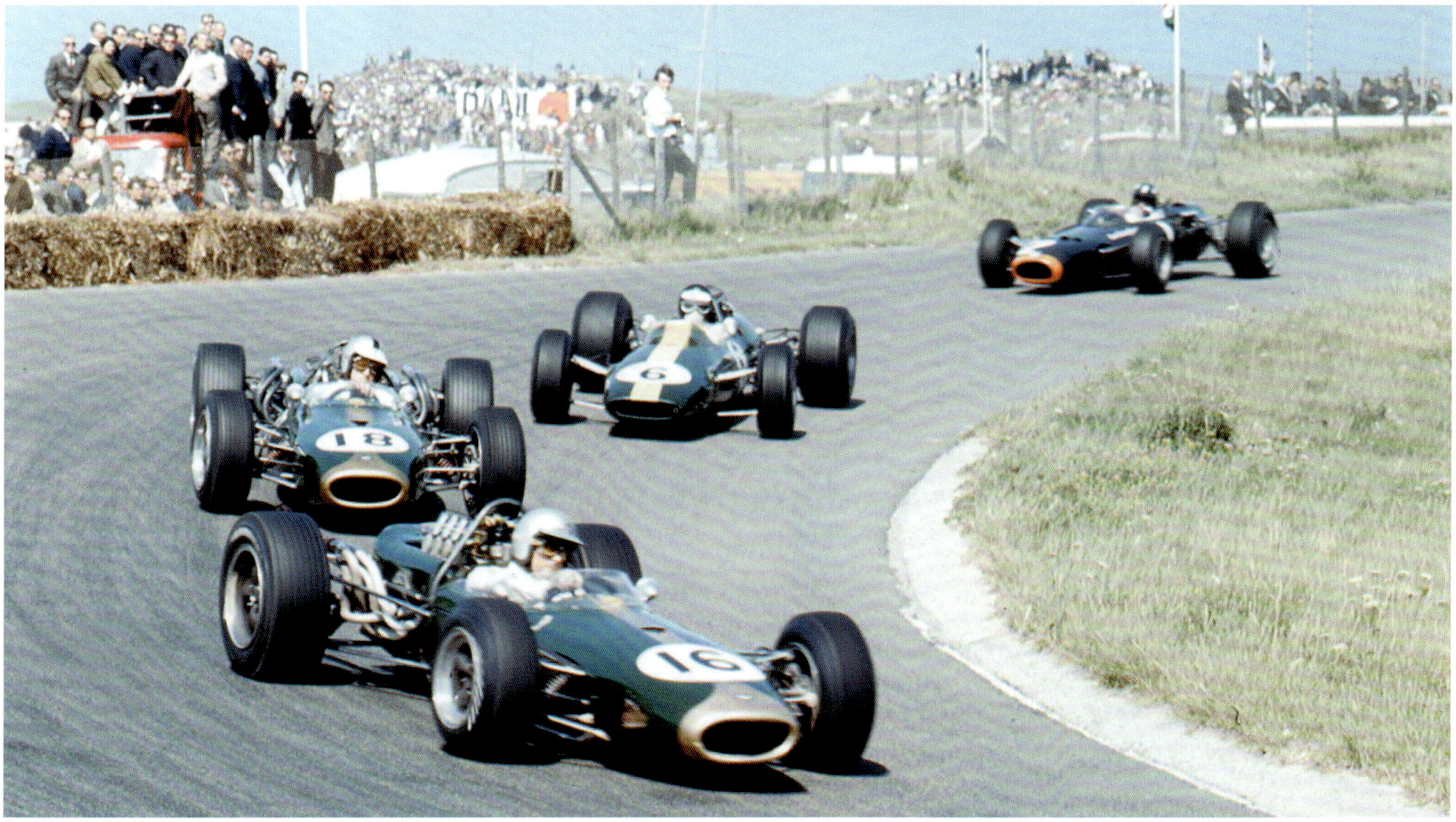

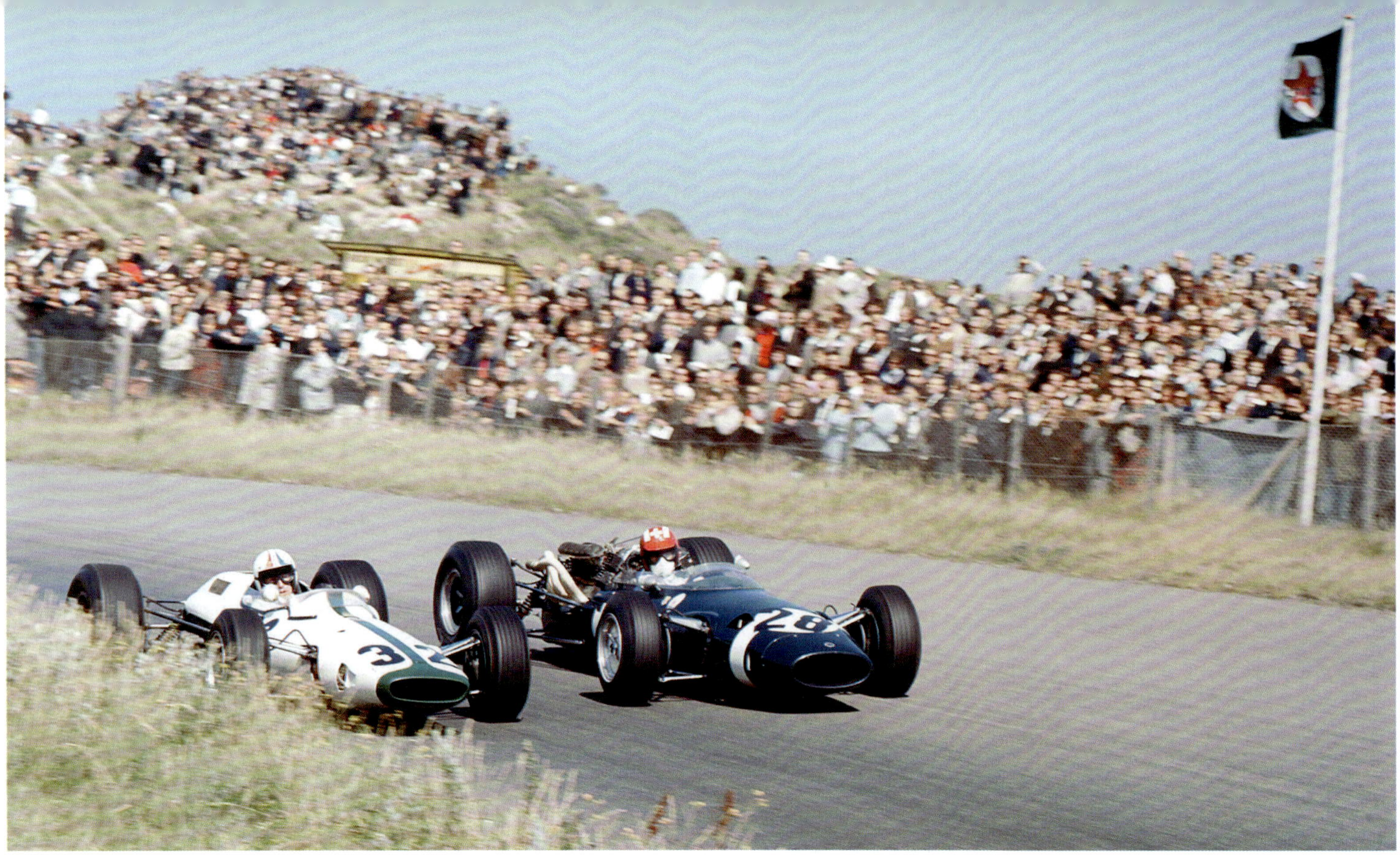

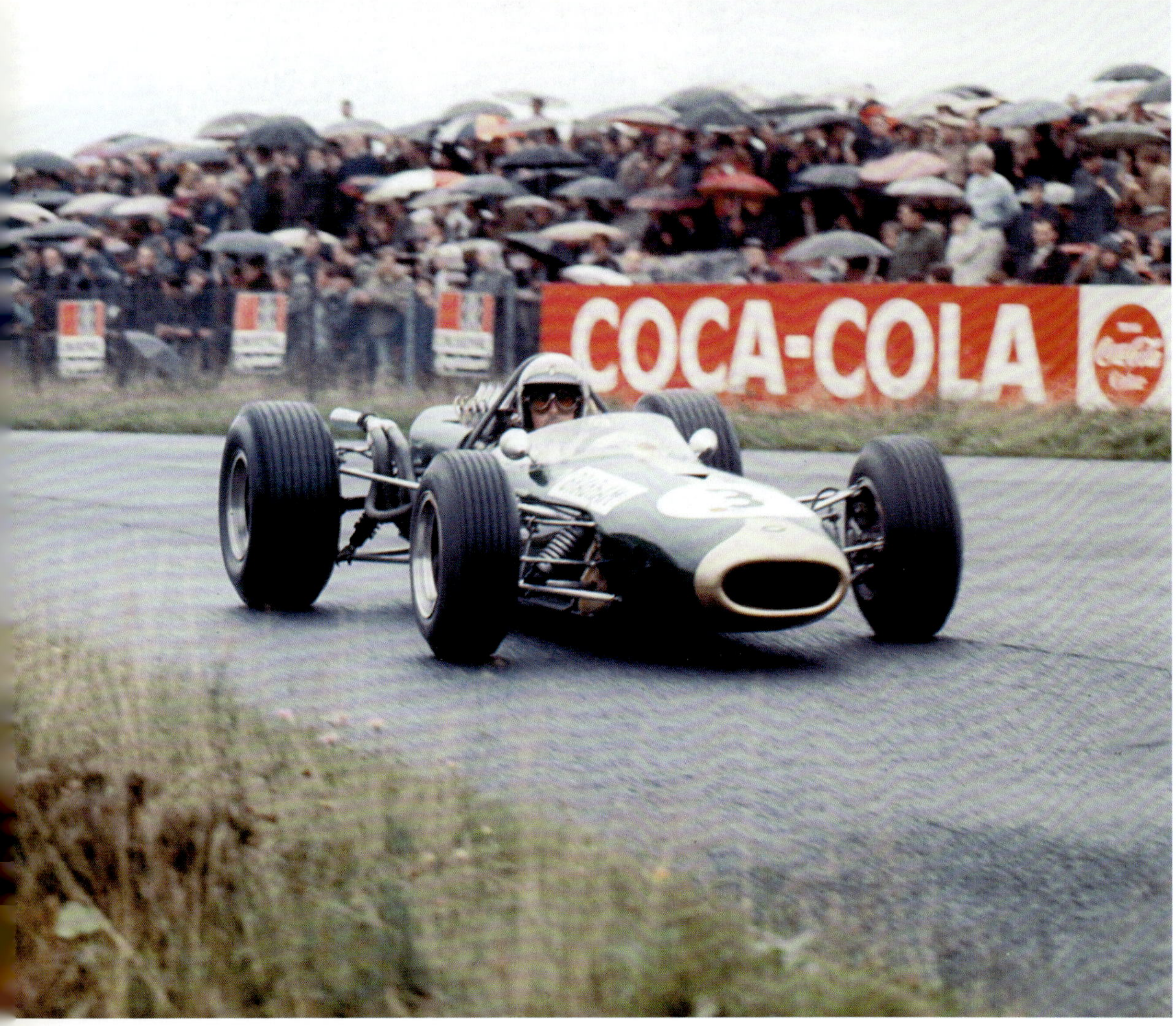

Jo Siffert in Rob Walker's Cooper-Maserati T81 (F1-2-66) battles with Mike Spence's Parnell Racing entered Lotus 33 BRM (R13) during the Dutch GP. Siffert retired on lap 79 while Spence finished 5th. The Cooper was nicknamed the *Torrey Canyon*, after the infamous wrecked oil tanker, for its propensity to leak lubricant. The Lotus is finished in the colours of the fictional Japanese Yamura team for the filming of 'Grand Prix' and Spence is wearing a Chris Amon helmet that was used by the character Pete Aaron played by James Garner. Nothing is ever simple.

Although he started from the second row Jack Brabham had no trouble in winning the German GP in his Brabham BT19 Repco (F1-1-65). This was his fourth consecutive GP win although Clark's Lotus had occupied pole but his Firestone tyres lacked grip in the wet and he crashed on lap 11. Compare the rounded rear tyre shoulders here with the square profile of the same car's Goodyear rear tyres at Silverstone.

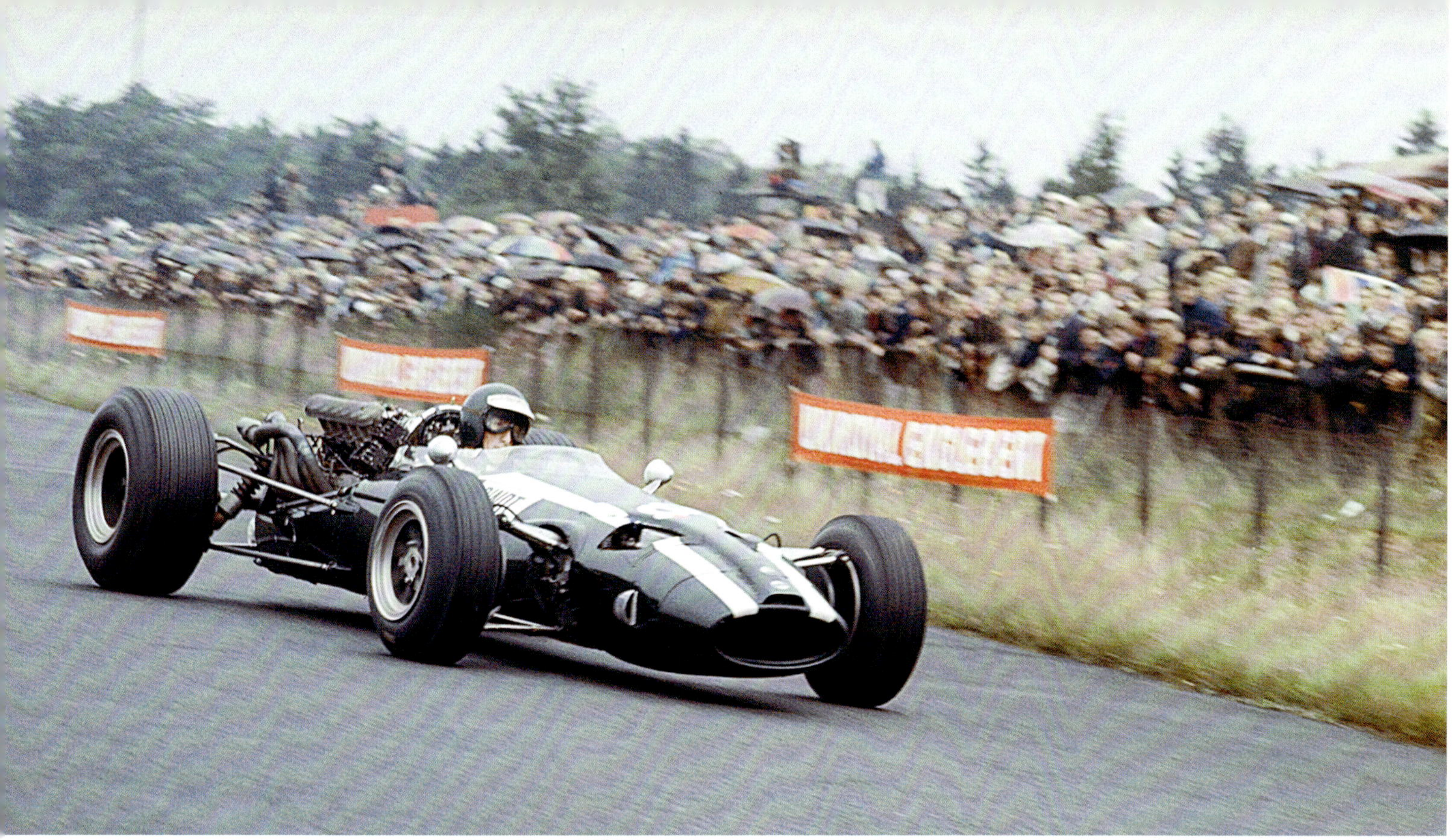

Jochen Rindt finished 3rd in the German GP in the works Cooper-Maserati T81 (F1-3-66) but he was comprehensively outdriven by team mate John Surtees who finished 2nd despite an inoperative clutch and handling problems.

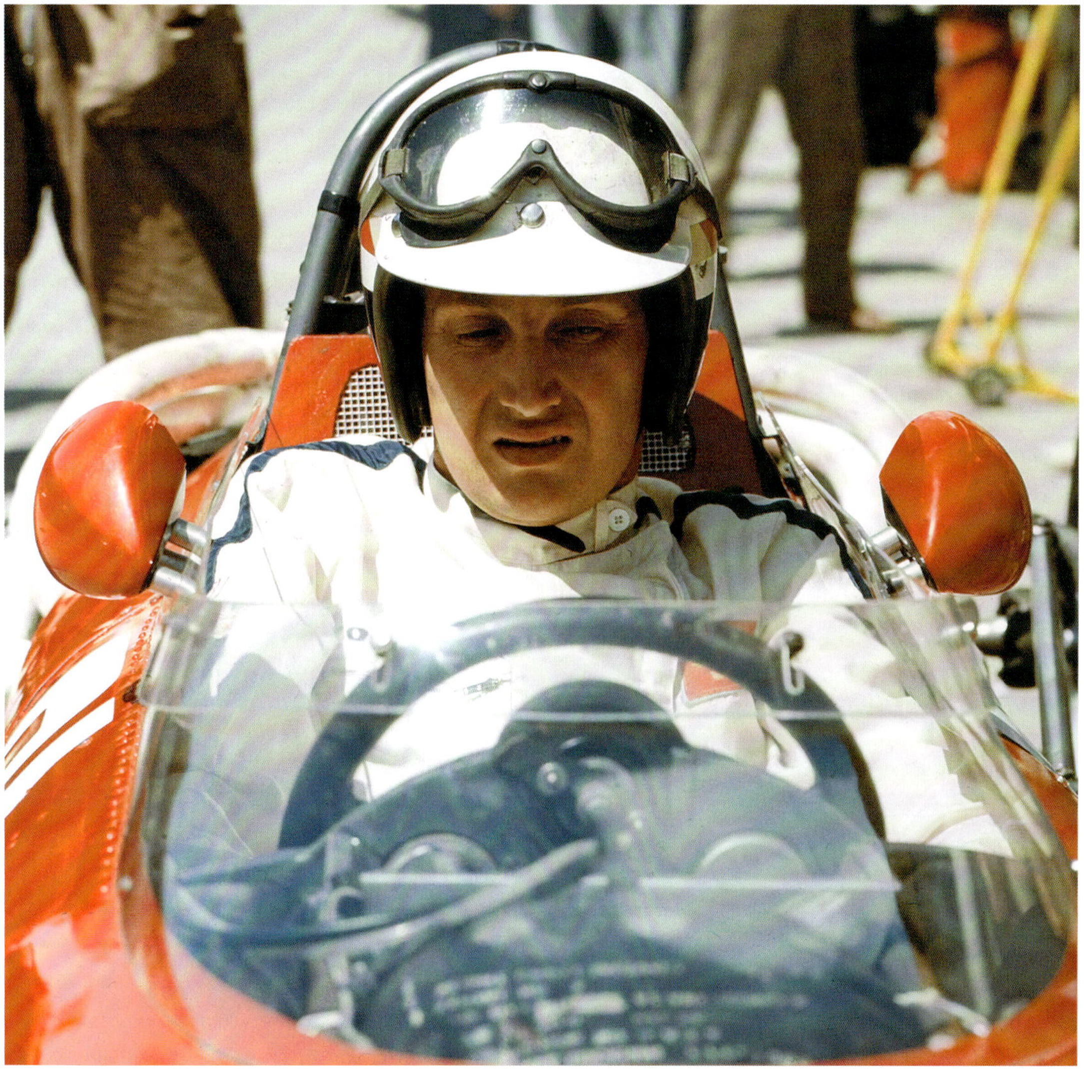

Mike Parkes helped develop the Hillman Imp but is best remembered as a formidable Ferrari GT and sports car racer. His height required a special lwb chassis and he started the German GP from row two in this Ferrari 312 (0012) but crashed during the wet race. In 1967, Parkes was badly injured at Spa which ended his F1 career. He resumed sports car racing in late 1969 and drove for NART and Scuderia Fillipinetti in 1970/71, but the speed was gone. Later on he joined Fiat and ultimately Lancia where he helped develop the Stratos, but sadly died in a road accident caused by fog near Turin on 28 August 1977.

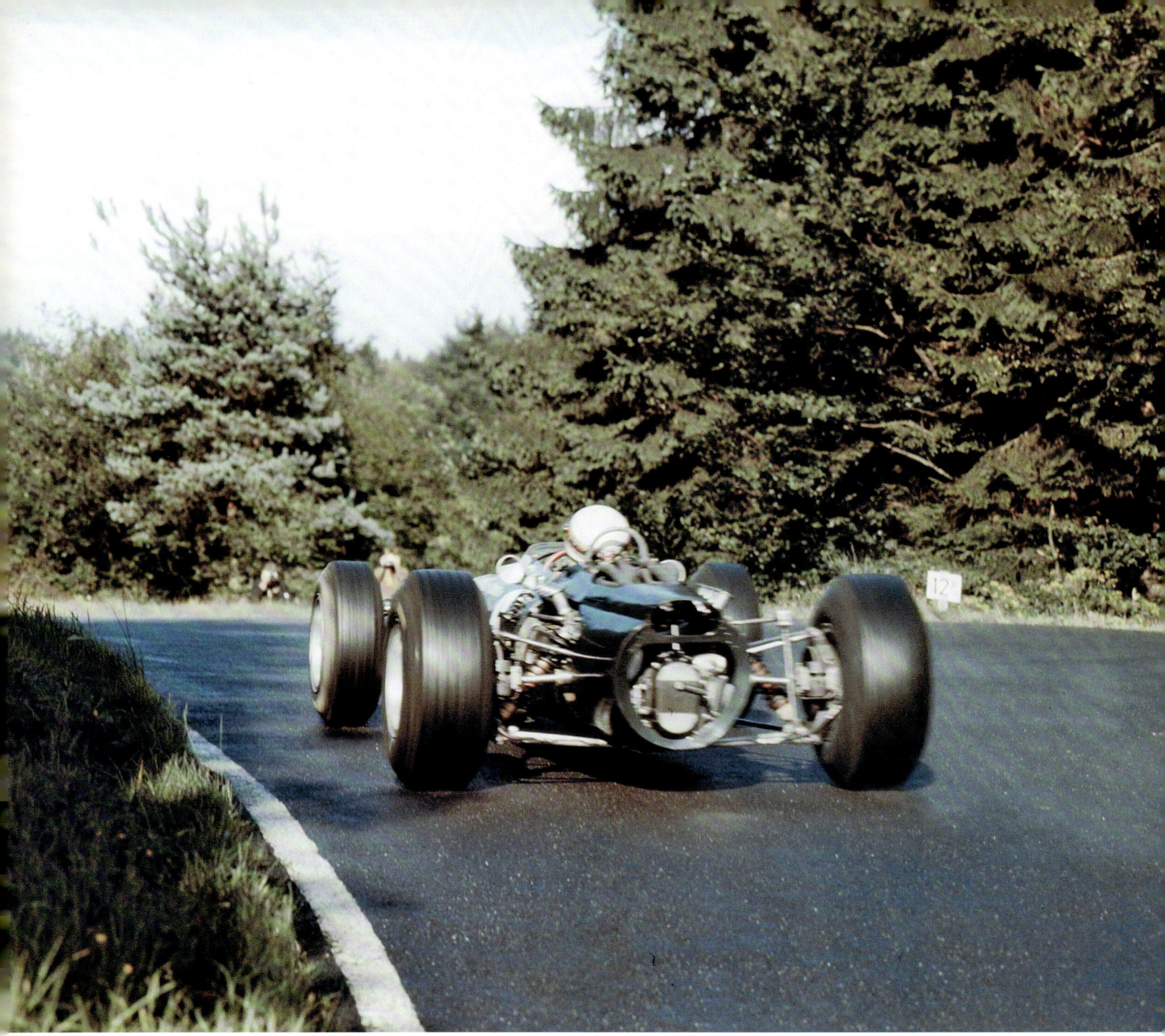

↑ Not for nothing was the Nürburgring known as 'green hell'. Despite his safety concerns Jackie Stewart always 'leant on it' to use the racing parlance. Stewart's BRM P261 (2614) braves the Nordschleife's interminable crests on his way to 5th place in the wet German GP.

↗ Displaying a certain insouciance Jo Bonnier reads a magazine whilst his Cooper-Maserati T81 (F1-5-66) is refuelled at Monza by the archetypal fuel churns. The T81 was designed by former Connaught and Jaguar chassis engineer Derrick White and constructed by ex-BRP chief mechanic Tony Robinson. This was Cooper's first monocoque, large, heavy and well built but not the most aesthetically pleasing. Bonnier started well down the grid as usual and retired on lap 2 of the Italian GP with a broken throttle linkage.

→ American Bob Bondurant, Cobra and Ferrari sports car racer, drove this ex-works BRM P261 (2615) for Bernard White (entered as Team Chamaco Collect) in 1966 finishing 4th at Monaco and 7th here at Monza. This was his last drive for the team, thereafter ending the season with Gurney's Anglo-American Racing.

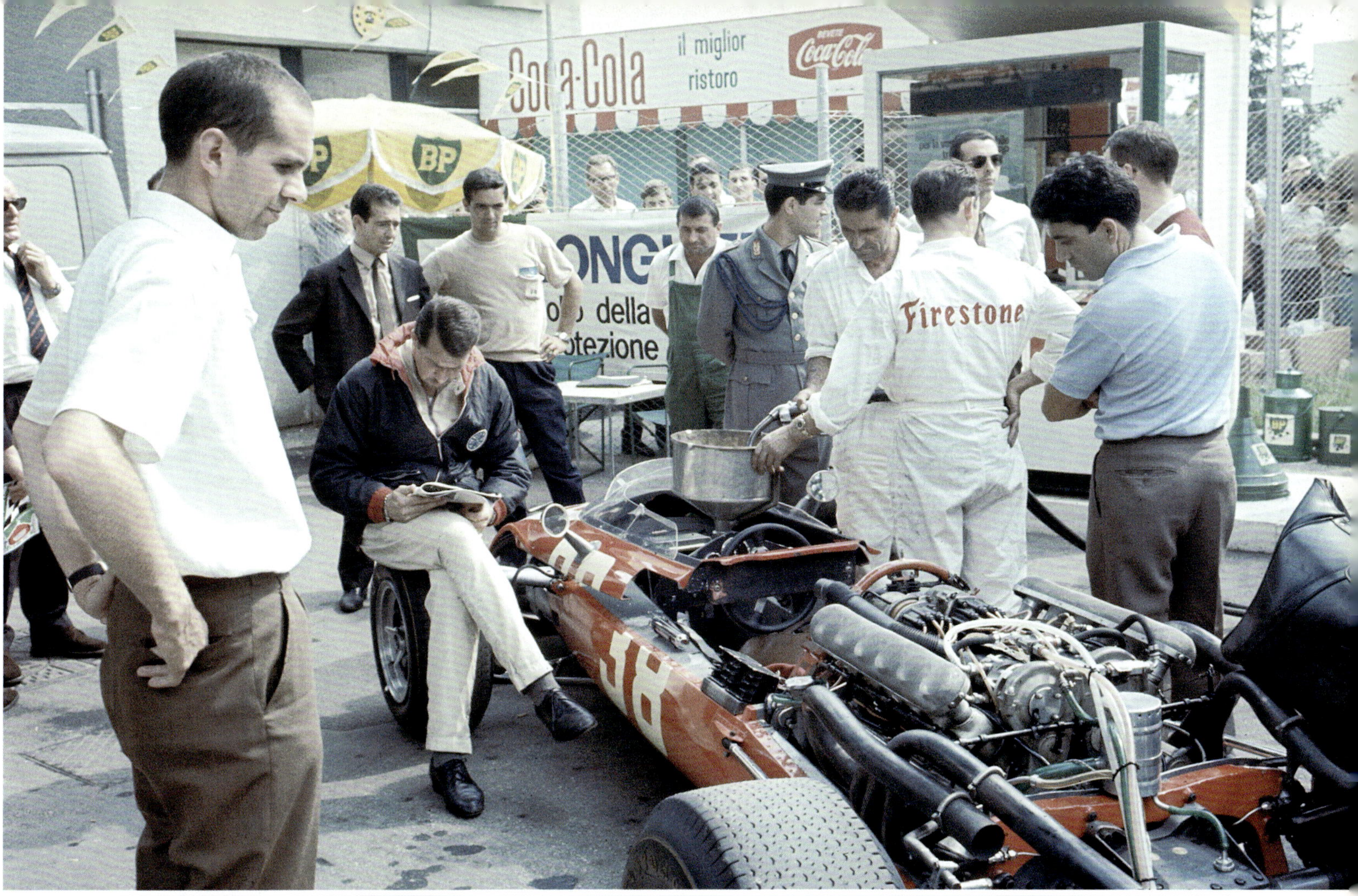
Coca-Cola
il miglior
ristoro
BP
Firestone
38

BEVETE

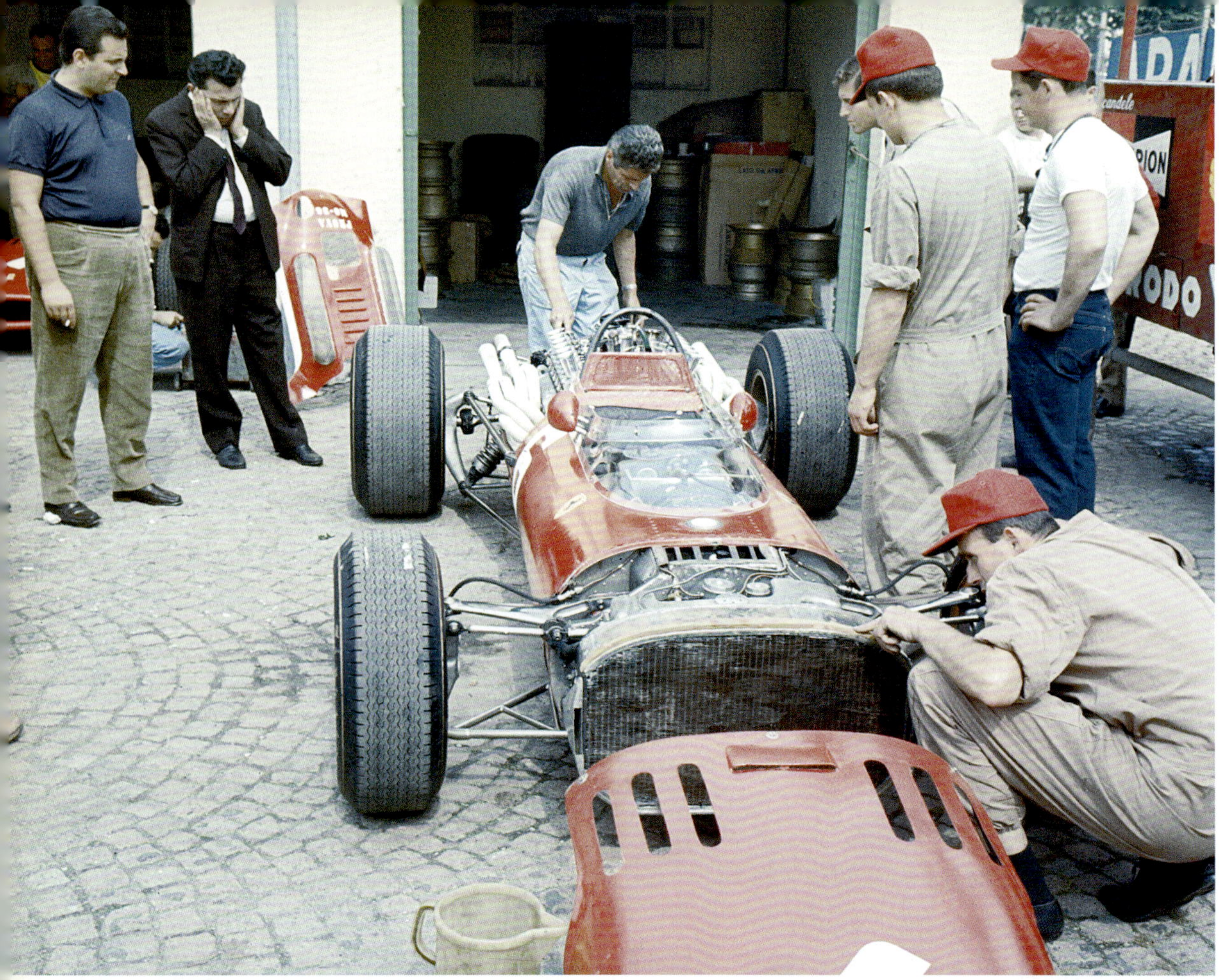

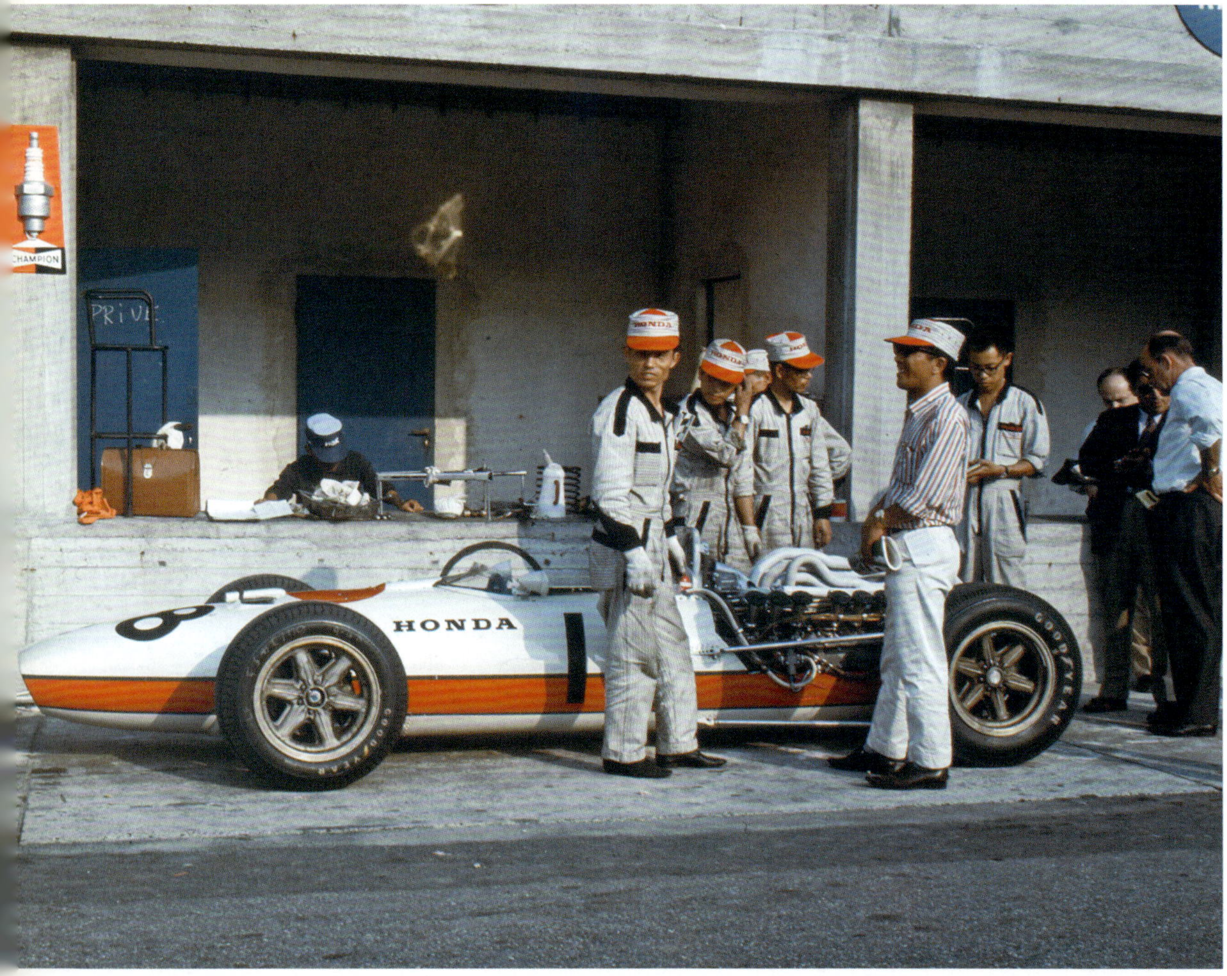

Mama mia! The noise from 'Lulu' Scarfiotti's Ferrari 312 (0011) at Monza is a trifle excessive. Note the enormous front mounted radiator. The three cars of Bandini (0010), Scarfiotti and Parkes (0012) are fitted with new 36-valve heads producing a claimed 370bhp and are quicker than the opposition. Parkes was on pole flanked by 'Lulu' with Bandini on row two. Scarfiotti won the Italian GP, Parkes finished 2nd and Bandini retired.

Given the trouble that BRM suffered with their H16 cars, it was serendipitous that Jim Clark would win the US GP in the H16 powered Indy based Lotus 43-1. Tyres smoking he blasts off the grid, but victory only came after Bandini's Ferrari and Brabham's BT20 suffered engine failures.

Honda's new 3-litre RA273 V12 finally appeared at Monza. The very wide and heavy 90-degree V12 contributed to the car's staggering 740kg weight, 240kg over the minimum! It allegedly developed a rather optimistic 420bhp @ 10,000rpm and Richie Ginther did well to qualify on the third row with chassis F101. In the race he did even better, reaching 2nd place before a puncture caused him to crash at the Curva Grande, destroying the car but fortunately emerging relatively unscathed.

Tony Rudd and an unhappy Graham Hill discussing the temperamental BRM P83 H16 (8302) at Watkins Glen. Hill outqualified team mate Jackie Stewart but the BRM's crown wheel and pinion failed on lap 52. Rudd joined BRM during the V16 era, an engineer and capable test driver who progressed to chief designer saving BRM from almost certain closure. He left in 1969 to work for Colin Chapman, retired in 1991 and passed away in 2003 aged 80.

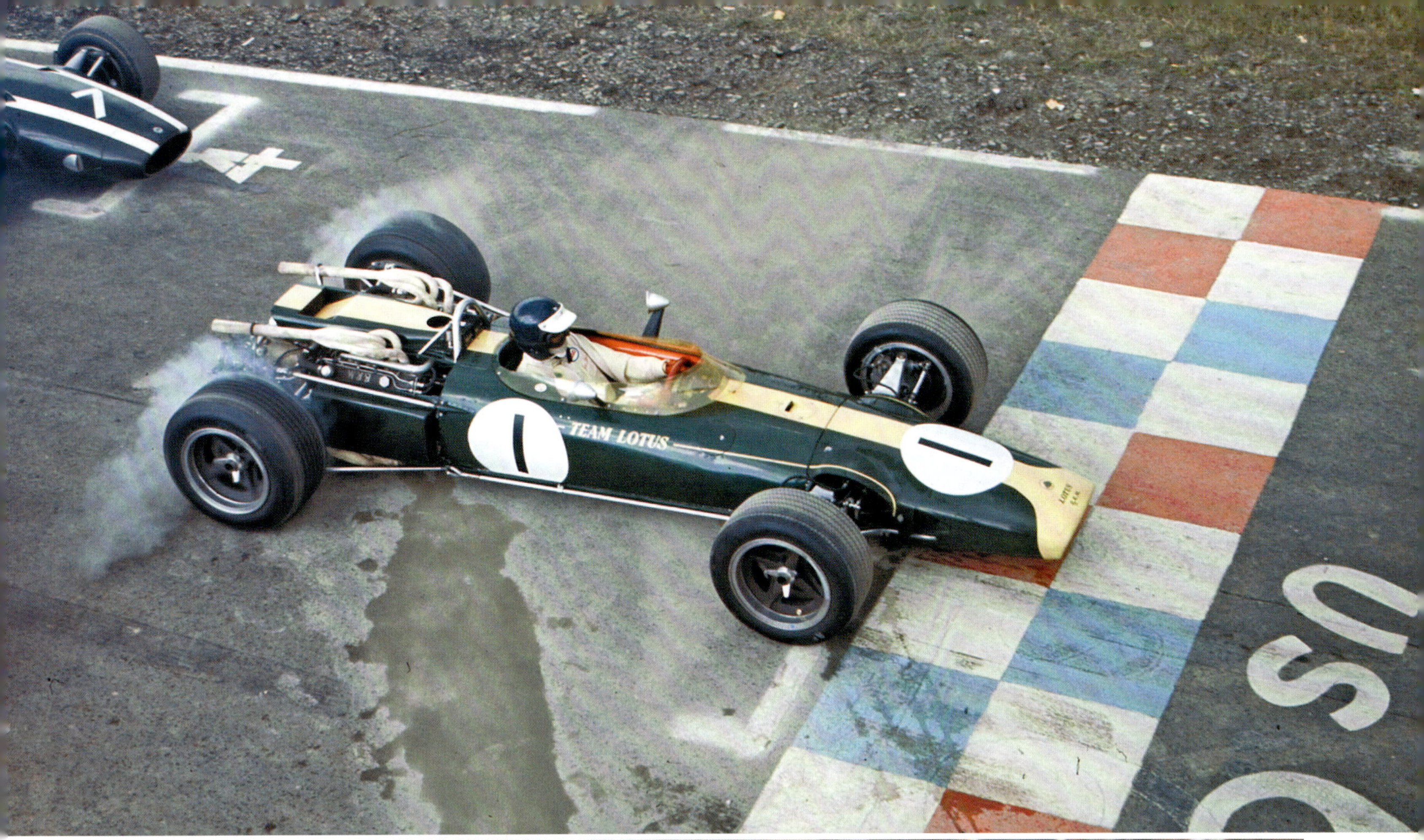
TEAM LOTUS

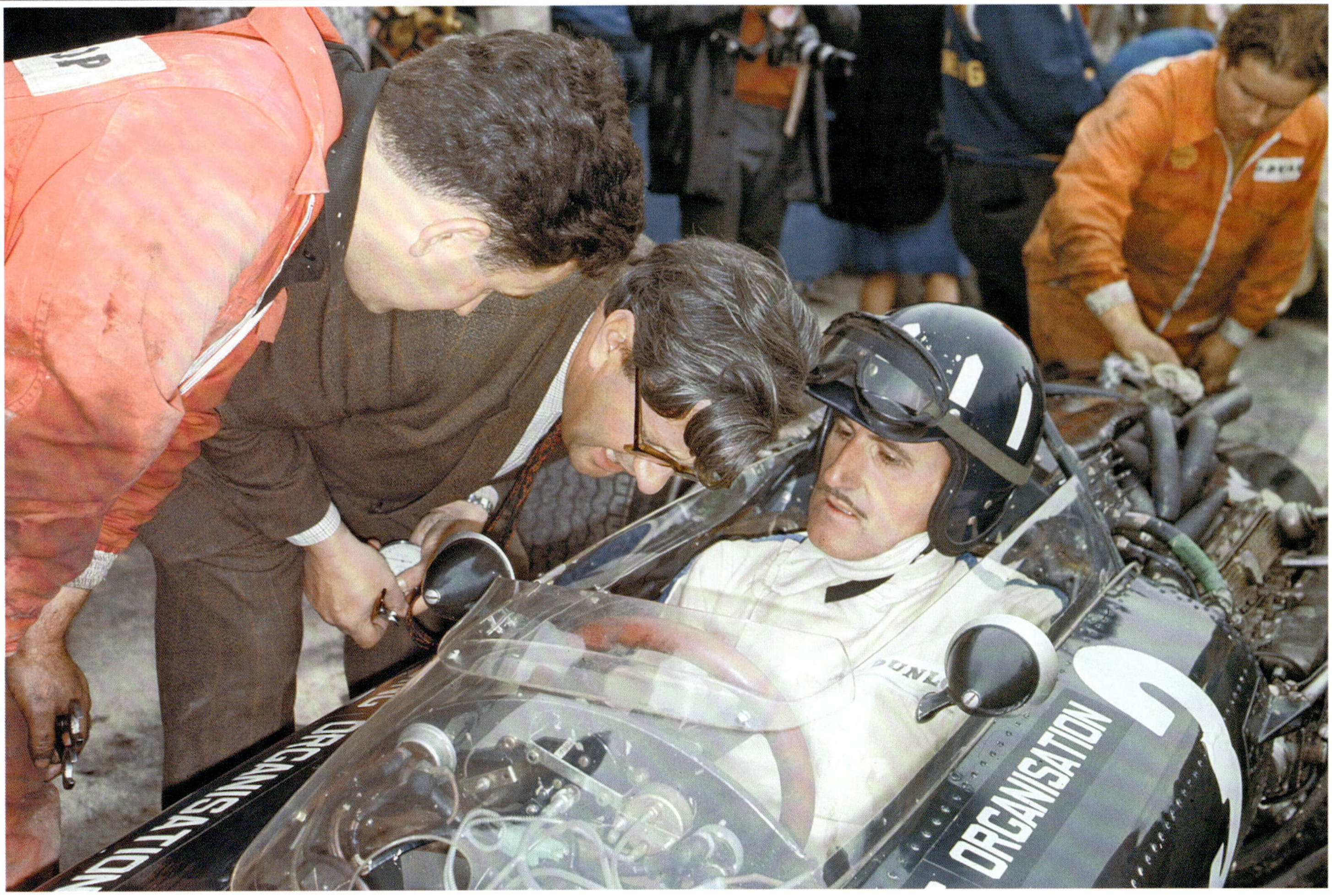
ORGANISATION
ORGANISATION

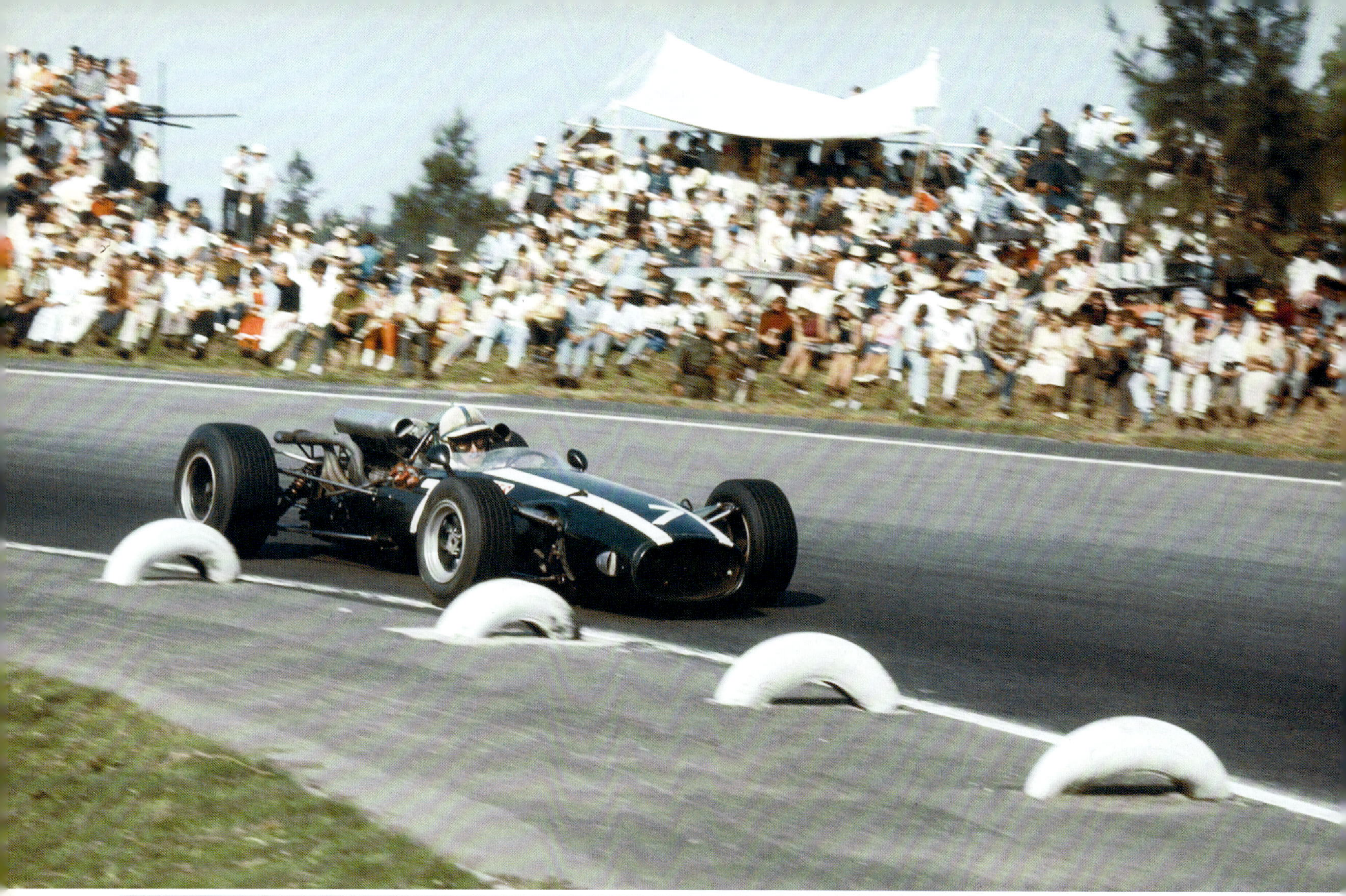

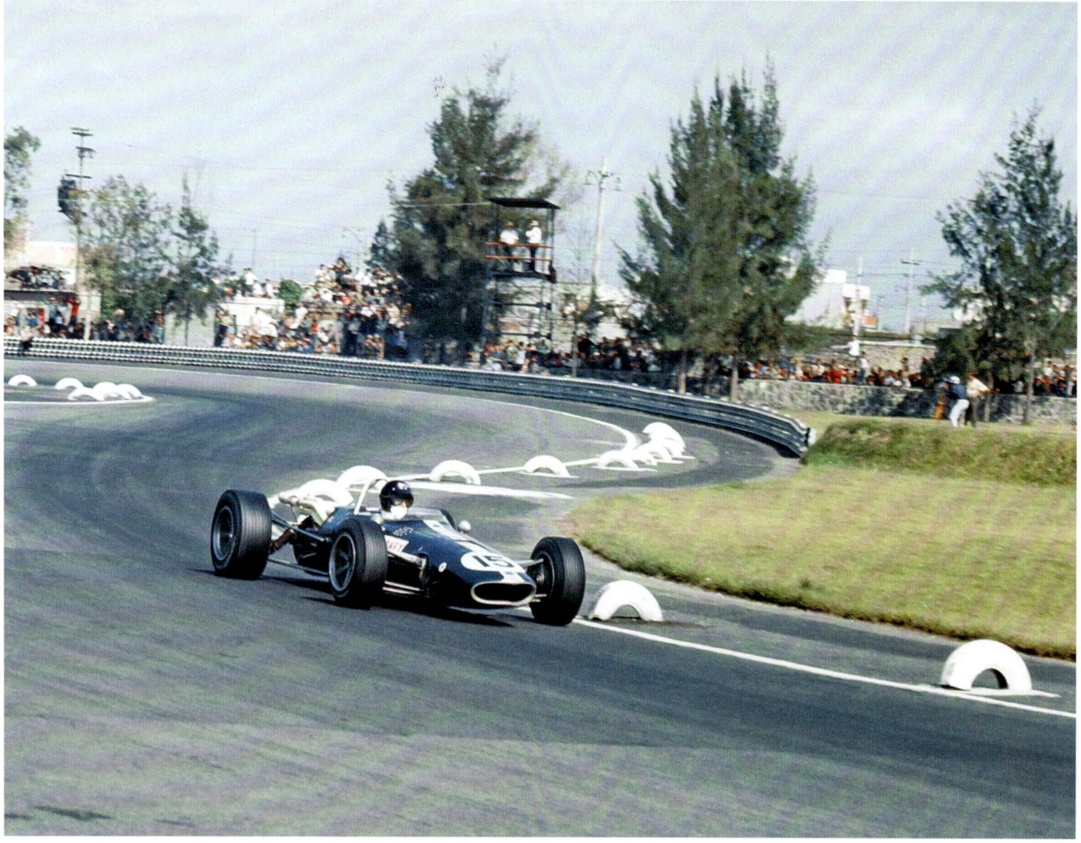

↑ Having been denied victory by unfavourable circumstances and bad luck, John Surtees finally achieved a win for Cooper at Mexico in his regular T81 (F1-6-66). Starting from pole he beat Brabham and Hulme to the flag in the first of only two GP victories for the Cooper-Maserati in its various forms.

← Dan Gurney's AAR Eagle-Climax T1F finished 5th in the Mexican GP, repeating its best result from the Reims race. The beautiful Len Terry designed car was handicapped in its debut season by the long delay in supply of the new Weslake V12 engines that finally arrived at Monza. However, Gurney raced the old Climax FPF engine thereafter leaving Bob Bondurant to carry out race development on the Weslake unit.

1966 Teams, drivers and results

Cooper Car Co – Cooper T81 Maserati V12
Jochen Rindt (A)
Richie Ginther (USA) (Monaco and Belgian GPs only)
Chris Amon (NZ) (French GP only)
John Surtees (GB) (French GP onwards)
Moises Solana (MEX) (Mexican GP only)

Team Lotus – Lotus 33 Climax V8 and 43 BRM H-16
Jim Clark (GB) (Missed French GP due to practice injury)
Peter Arundell (GB) (Missed Monaco and Belgian GPs)
Pedro Rodriguez (MEX) (French, US and Mexican GPs only)
Giacomo Russo aka 'Geki' (I) (Italian GP only)

Owen Racing Organisation – BRM P261 and P83 H-16
Graham Hill (GB)
Jackie Stewart (GB) (Missed French GP due to injuries received in accident at Belgian GP)

Brabham Racing Organisation – Brabham BT11 Climax FPF and Brabham Repco BT19 and BT20
Jack Brabham (AUS) (WORLD CHAMPION)
Denny Hulme (NZ)
Chris Irwin (GB) (British GP only)

SEFAC Ferrari – Ferrari 158 Dino 246 and 312
John Surtees (GB) (Left Ferrari after Le Mans and joined Cooper)
Lorenzo Bandini (I) (Ferrari did not attend British and Mexican GPs)
Mike Parkes (GB) (French, Dutch, German and Italian GPs only)
Lodovico Scarfiotti (I) (German and Italian GPs only)

Anglo-American Racers – Eagle 1F Climax FPF and 1G Gurney-Weslake V12
Dan Gurney (USA) (Missed Monaco GP)
Bob Bondurant (USA) (US and Mexican GPs only)

Honda Racing Team – Honda RA273
Richie Ginther (USA) (Italian, US and Mexican GPs only)
Ronnie Bucknum (USA) (US and Mexican GPs only)

Bruce McLaren Motor Racing – McLaren M2B Ford V8 and M2B Serenissima V8
Bruce McLaren (NZ) (dns Belgian and Dutch GPs, Monaco, British, US and Mexican GPs only)

Reg Parnell (Racing) – BRM 261/2, Lotus 33 BRM V8 and 25 BRM V8 and Ferrari 158 Dino 246
Mike Spence (GB) (dns Mexican GP due to practice accident)
Giancarlo Baghetti (I) (Ferrari loaned to Baghetti and entered under Reg Parnell Racing)

R. R. C. Walker Racing Team – Brabham BT11 BRM V8 and Cooper T81 Maserati V12
Jo Siffert (CH) (Car not entered at German GP)

Guy Ligier – Cooper T81 Maserati V12
Guy Ligier (F) (dns German GP due to practice accident and missed rest of F1 season)

Anglo-Suisse Racing Team – Cooper T81 Maserati V12
Jo Bonnier (S)

DW Racing Enterprises – Brabham BT11 Climax FPF
Bob Anderson (GB) (Missed Belgian, US and Mexican GPs)

Team Chamaco Collect/Bernard White Racing – BRM P261/2
Bob Bondurant (USA) (Missed French and Dutch GPs)
Innes Ireland (GB) (US and Mexican GPs only)

David Bridges – Brabham BT11 BRM V8
John Taylor (GB) (French, British, Dutch and German GPs only, fatally injured during German GP after collision with Ickx)

Aiden Jones/Paul Emery – Shannon Climax Godiva V8
Trevor Taylor (GB) (British GP only)

J.A. Pearce Engineering – Cooper T73 Ferrari V12
Chris Lawrence (GB) (British and German GPs only)

F2 ENTRIES RACED IN GERMAN GP

Caltex Racing Team – Brabham BT18 Cosworth SCA
Kurt Ahrens (D)

Tyrrell Racing Organisation – Matra MS5 Cosworth SCA
Hubert Hahne (D)
Jacky Ickx (B)

Roy Winklemann Racing – Brabham BT18 Cosworth SCA
Hans Herrmann (D)
Alan Rees (GB)

Ron Harris Team Lotus – Lotus 44 Cosworth SCA
Pedro Rodriguez (MEX)
Piers Courage (GB)

Matra Sports – Matra MS5 Cosworth SCA
Jean-Pierre Beltoise (F)
Jo Schlesser (F)

WORLD CHAMPIONSHIP VENUES AND WINNERS (nine rounds)

Monaco GP	Monte Carlo	Jackie Stewart
Belgian GP	Spa-Francorchamps	John Surtees
French GP	Reims	Jack Brabham
British GP	Brands Hatch	Jack Brabham
Dutch GP	Zandvoort	Jack Brabham
German GP	Nürburgring	Jack Brabham
Italian GP	Monza	Lodovico Scarfiotti
United States GP	Watkins Glen	Jim Clark
Mexican GP	Mexico City	John Surtees

DRIVERS' CHAMPIONSHIP
Points: 9-6-4-3-2-1. Best 5 scores

1	Jack Brabham	Brabham	42
2	John Surtees	Ferrari/Cooper	28
3	Jochen Rindt	Cooper	22
4	Denny Hulme	Brabham	18
5	Graham Hill	BRM	17
6	Jim Clark	Lotus	16
7	Jackie Stewart	BRM	14
8	Mike Parkes	Ferrari	12
9	Lorenzo Bandini	Ferrari	12
10	Lodovico Scarfiotti	Ferrari	9
11	Richie Ginther	Cooper/Honda	5
12	Dan Gurney	Eagle	4
13	Mike Spence	Lotus	4
14	Bob Bondurant	BRM/Eagle	3
15	Jo Siffert	Brabham/Cooper	3
16	Bruce McLaren	McLaren	3
17	John Taylor	Brabham	1
18	Bob Anderson	Brabham	1
19	Peter Arundell	Lotus	1
20	Jo Bonnier	Cooper/Brabham	1

CONSTRUCTORS' CHAMPIONSHIP
Points: 9-6-4-3-2-1, (awarded only to best-placed finisher).
Best 5 scores

1	Brabham-Repco	42
2	Ferrari	31
3	Cooper-Maserati	30
4	BRM	22
5	Lotus-BRM	13
6	Lotus-Climax	8
7	Eagle-Climax	4
8	Honda	3
9	McLaren-Ford	2
10	Brabham-BRM	1
11	McLaren-Serenissima	1
12	Brabham-Climax	1

1967

THE START OF SOMETHING BIG

There were many changes for the 1967 season. It was welcome back to the South African GP, hello to the Canadian GP and yet another change of venue for the French GP.

Graham Hill joined Lotus to partner Jim Clark, Mike Spence moved to BRM while a second string BRM team run by Tim Parnell employed newcomers Chris Irwin and Piers Courage. John Surtees moved to Honda, Pedro Rodriguez to Cooper with Jochen Rindt and also Alan Rees, Jacky Ickx and Richard Attwood on occasion. Ferrari began the year with Lorenzo Bandini and Chris Amon backed up by Ludovico Scarfiotti, Mike Parkes and ex-pat Englishman and Monza F3 ace Jonathan Williams. Dan Gurney's AAR also employed multiple drivers including Richie Ginther, Bruce McLaren mid-season and even Scarfiotti as well as Dan himself. The rest of the grid, typically old BRMs, Lotuses and 1966 Cooper-Maseratis simply made up the numbers.

The big news of the year was Keith Duckworth's masterpiece, the Cosworth DFV V8 that bolted straight onto the back of Lotus's new 49. It was significantly more powerful than the competition and Lotus had a monopoly of the engine for 1967. Clark won first time out at Zandvoort after Hill led but retired. He scored three more GP victories but Graham suffered seven retirements and only finished twice.

For Brabham it was another stellar year, but this time Denny Hulme took the title with JB backing up. Between them they won four races as well as a string of 2nds and 3rds that was enough to see off the uneven competition. In between, Rodriguez, Gurney and Surtees all won a race apiece. These were respectively the last GP win for Cooper, the only GP victory for an American driver in an American entered car (and for AAR) and the last GP victory for a Japanese car albeit one that was nicknamed 'Hondola' due to Surtees's collaboration with Eric Broadley of Lola.

BRM had more disappointing experiences with the problematical H16, although Stewart finished a brave 2nd at Spa, and were still using the old V8 cars at times. A fatigued Bandini crashed at Monaco trying to catch Hulme and was fatally burned as his car ignited the straw bales at the chicane. This resulted in the race distance being shortened from 100 laps to 80 laps in perpetuity. Ferrari also lost Parkes who was very badly injured at Spa, ending his F1 career. For Maranello it was a dreadful year with Amon's two 3rd places their best effort.

Despite a lucky win at Kyalami the Maserati-powered works Coopers were struggling, not helped by a disgruntled Rindt who was very unhappy with car and team.

The four domestic F1 events in England gave Gurney a convincing win at Brands Hatch with two for Brabham at Oulton Park. Mike Parkes won at Silverstone and also deadheated at Syracuse with Ferrari team mate Scarfiotti. Clark and Hill finished 1–2 in the inaugural Spanish GP at Jarama in anticipation of its championship status for 1968.

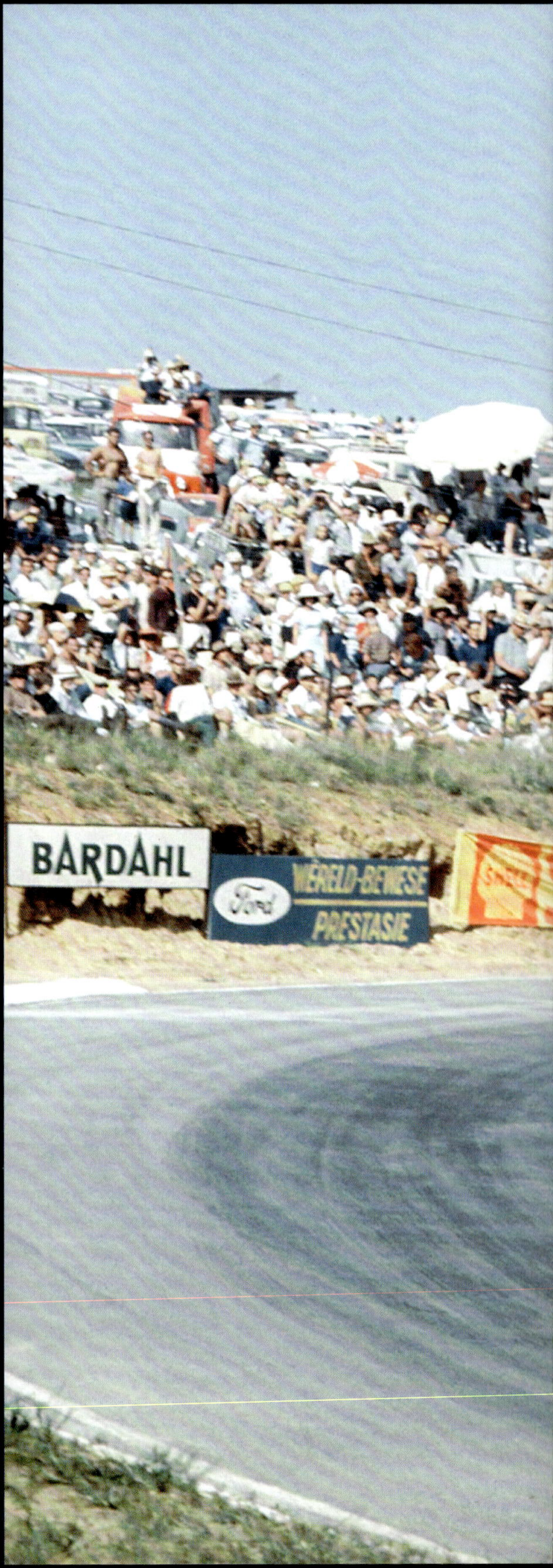

So near, yet so far. But for a few litres of fuel the 42-year-old Rhodesian John Love would have won the season-opening South African GP in his Cooper T79 Climax FPF (FL-1-65). Instead he finished 2nd behind the winning Cooper-Maserati of Pedro Rodriguez. Love passed away in 2005. Note the totally exposed infield, the stylised Shell 'lamp post' and Gurney's Eagle that is displaying considerable understeer.

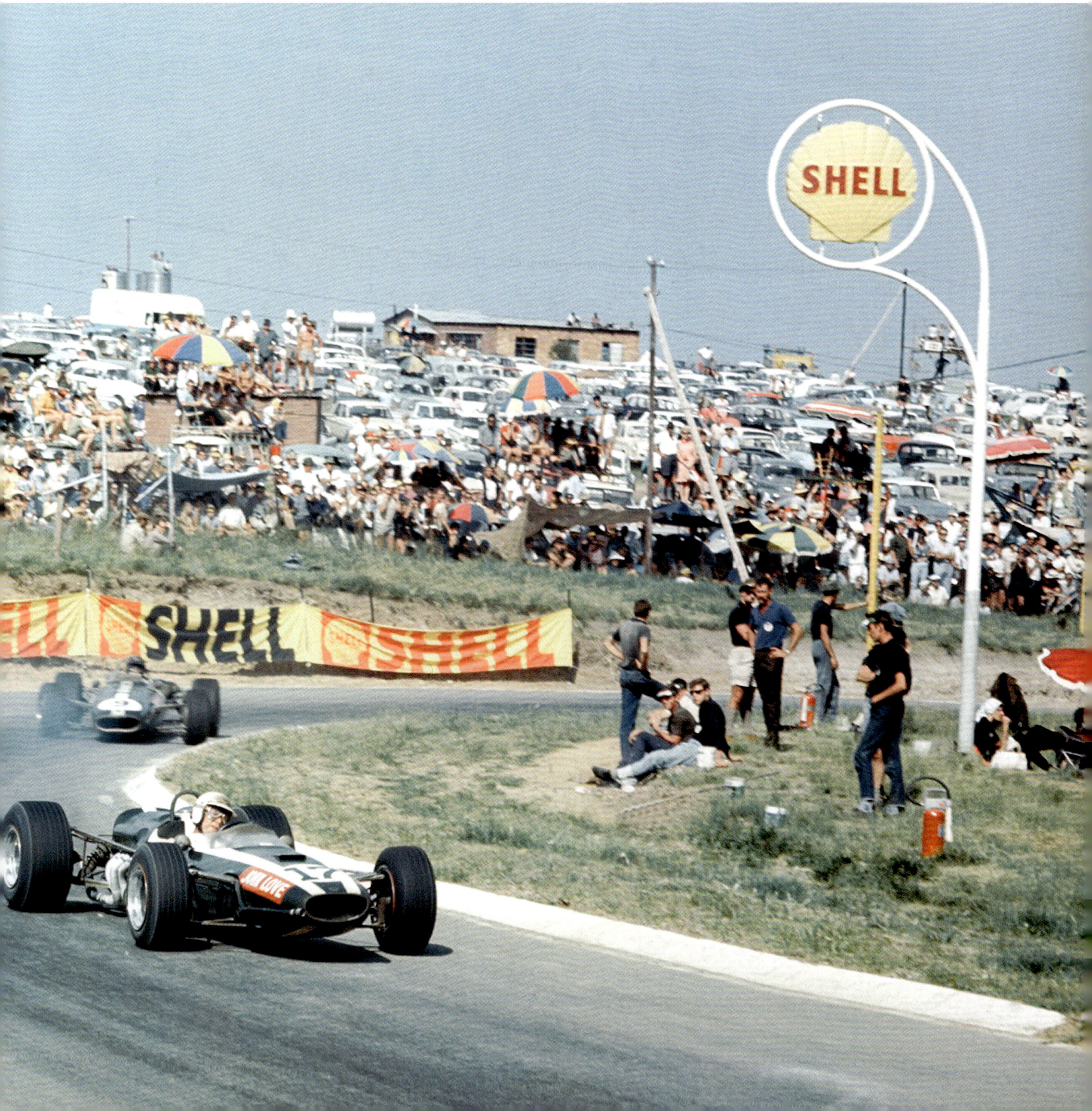

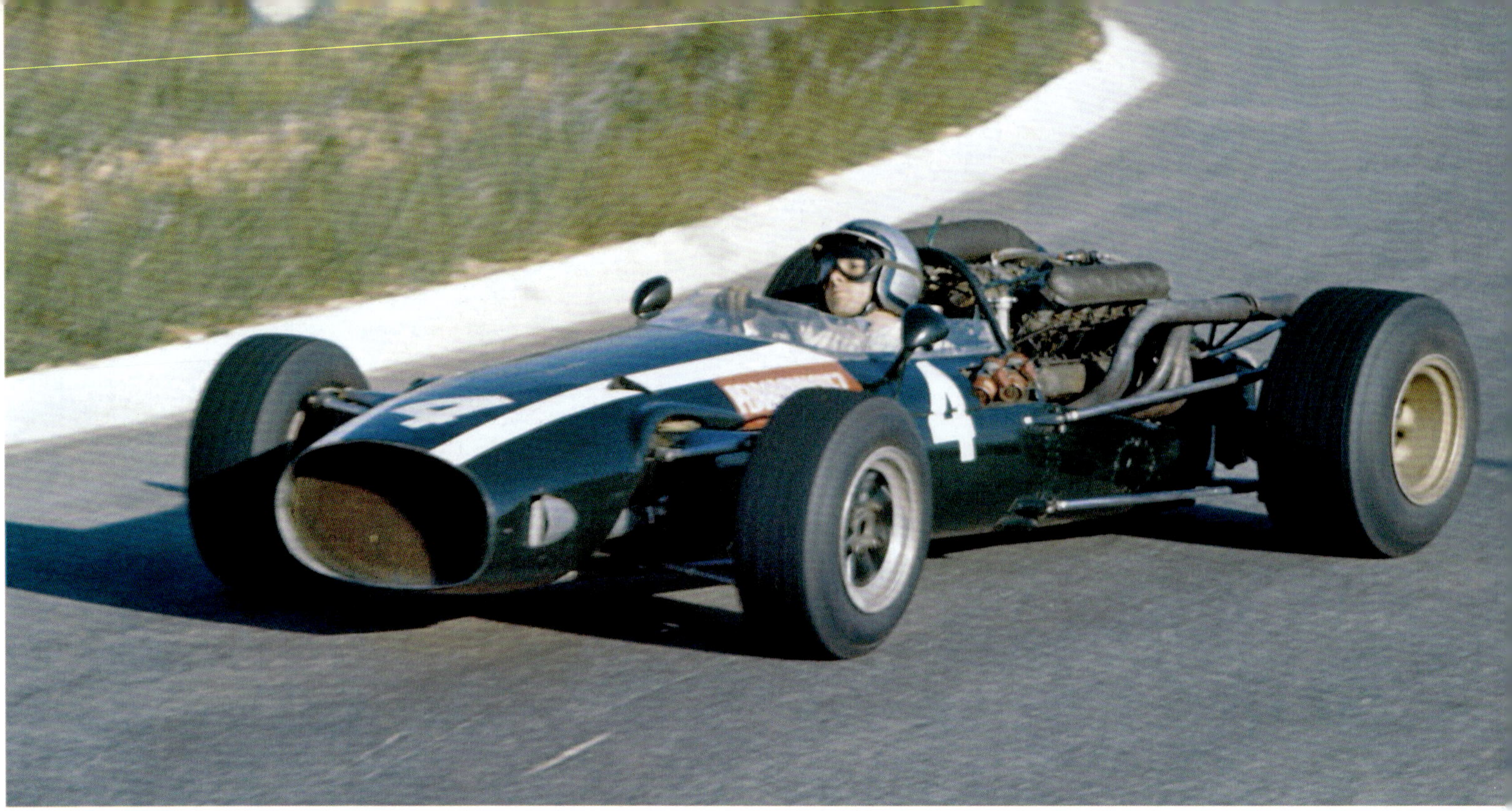

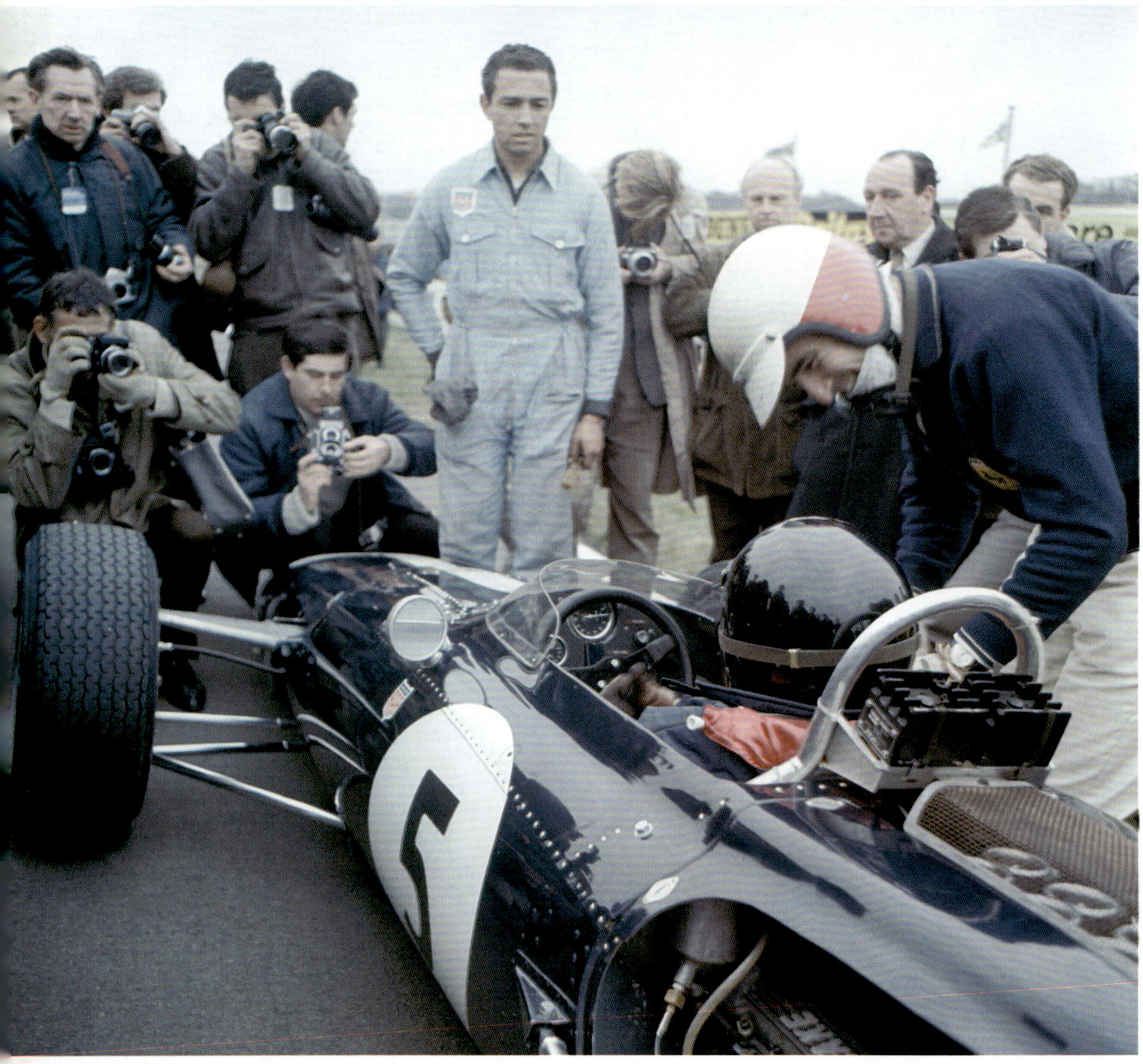

↑ One for the history books. Pedro Rodriguez was lucky to win the South African Grand Prix after John Love's Cooper T79 Climax had to stop for more fuel. His Cooper T81 Maserati (F1-6-66) has an oversteering moment as Pedro wins Cooper's last ever Grand Prix, nine years after Stirling Moss scored their first World Championship victory at the 1958 Argentinian Grand Prix in Rob Walker's tiny T43.

← Dan Gurney and Lorenzo Bandini share a moment on the grid for the Race of Champions at Brands Hatch. Gurney's victorious Eagle Weslake 1G (102) developed a claimed 413bhp. Note the twin Lucas 'black boxes' behind the roll over bar. AAR chief mechanic Jo Ramirez standing directly in front of the car began his F1 career as a Ferrari mechanic, later becoming team manager for Fittipaldi, Shadow, ATS and Theodore Racing. Ultimately he joined McLaren and finally retired in 2001.

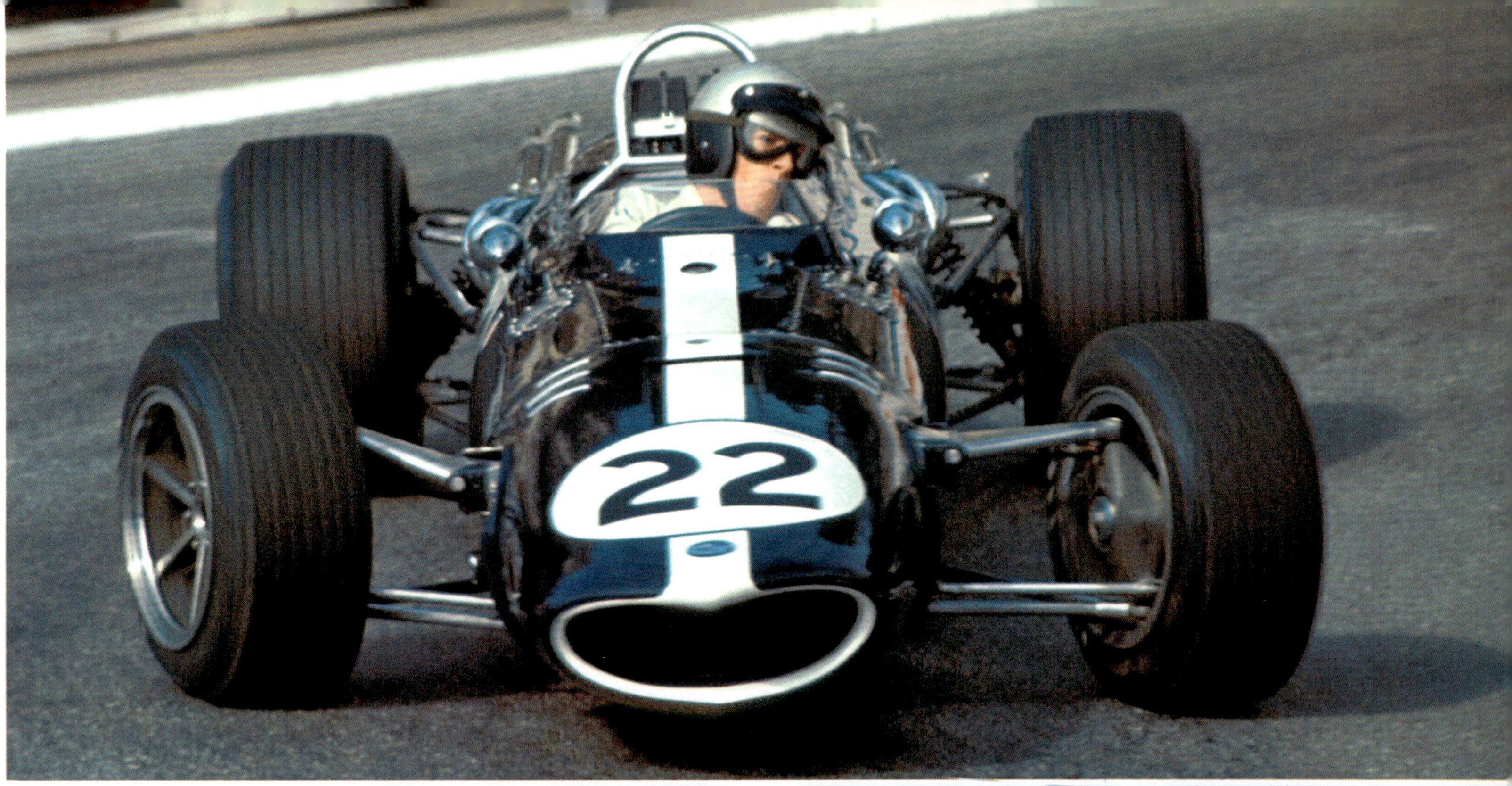

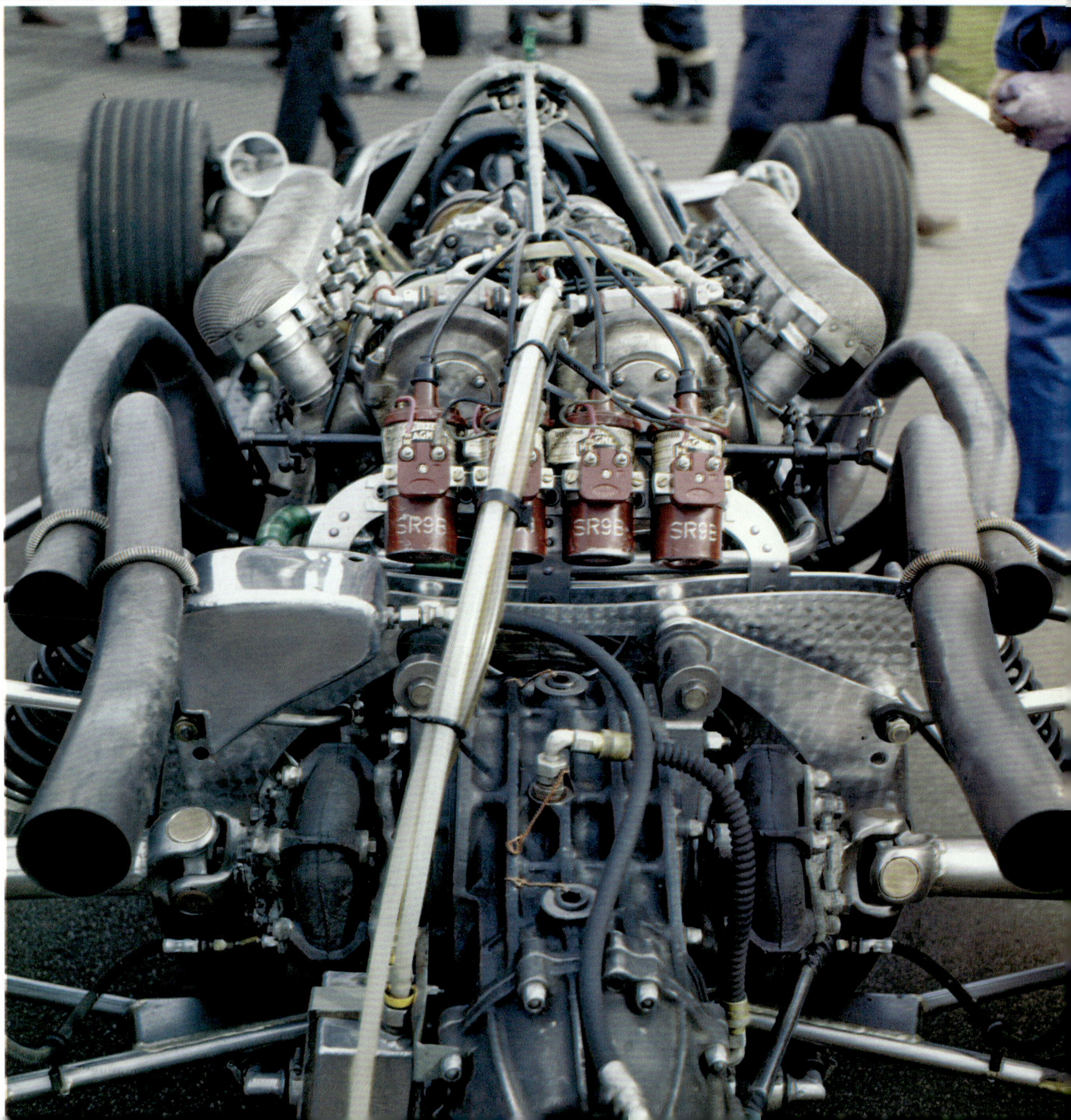

Richie Ginther failed to qualify the No 2 Eagle at Monaco and whilst practising for the Indianapolis 500 decided to retire from driving. In 1977, while holidaying in St. Tropez with former mentor John von Neumann and his wife Cleo, Richie was beaten up by British football hooligans. He required facial surgery and suffered pain for the rest of his life. Later Cleo divorced and lived with Ginther in Baja, Mexico. A frail looking Richie appeared at Donington in 1989 to celebrate BRM's 40th anniversary and Rick Hall remembers him being scared to death of driving the BRM P57. He died in France a few days after from heart failure.

The very busy rear end of Ing. Giulio Alfieri's Maserati V12 that began life as a 2.5-litre engine in the 1957 Maserati 250F. Redesigned and enlarged to 3 litres it gave a reputed 360bhp @ 9250rpm as supplied to Cooper. In 1967, a modified 36-valve heron head engine with a longer stroke offered 380/390 bhp, but neither Maserati or Cooper could afford to develop it further and Maserati's F1 involvement ended in early 1968.

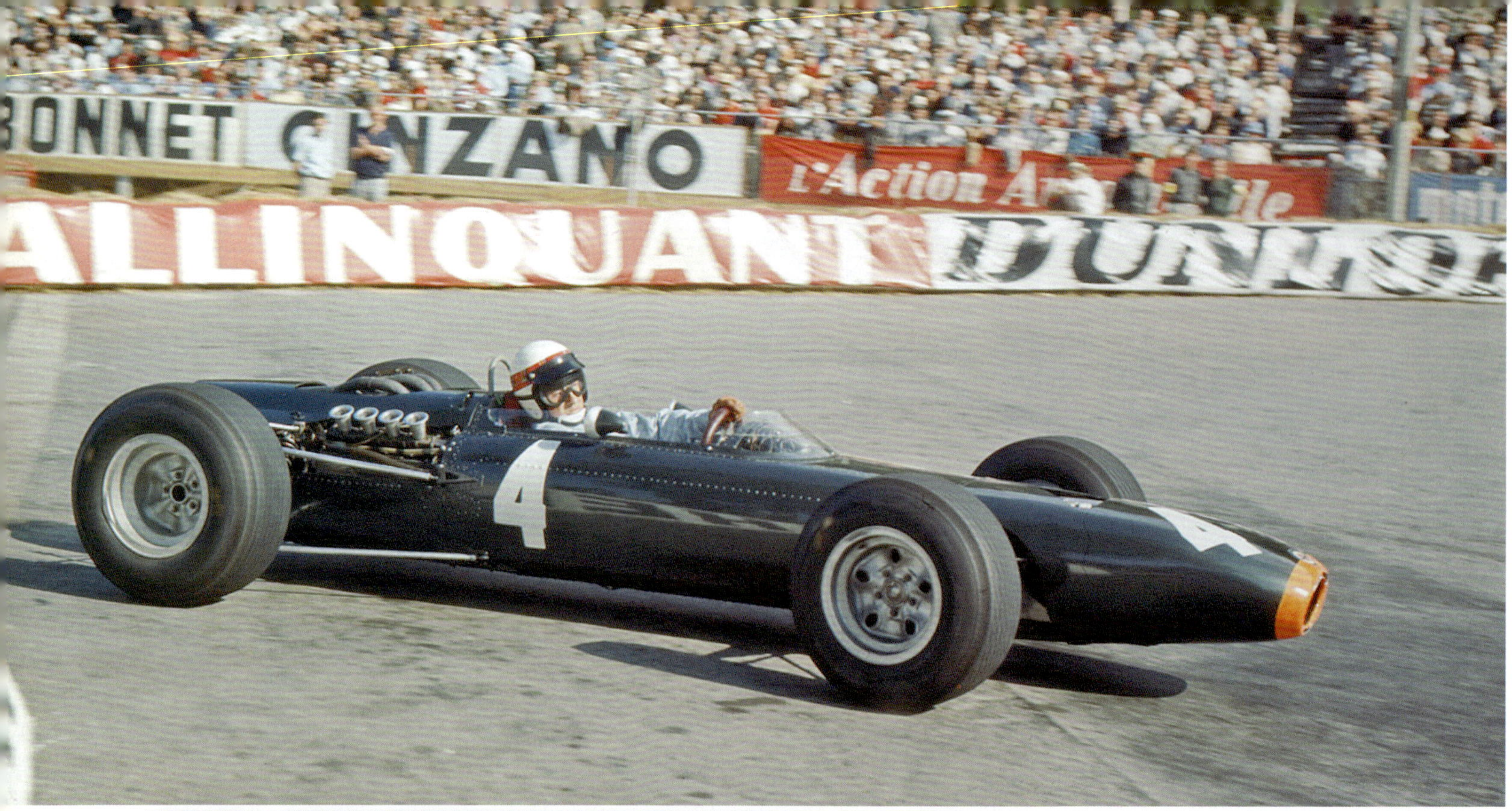
BONNET
ALLINQUANT
4

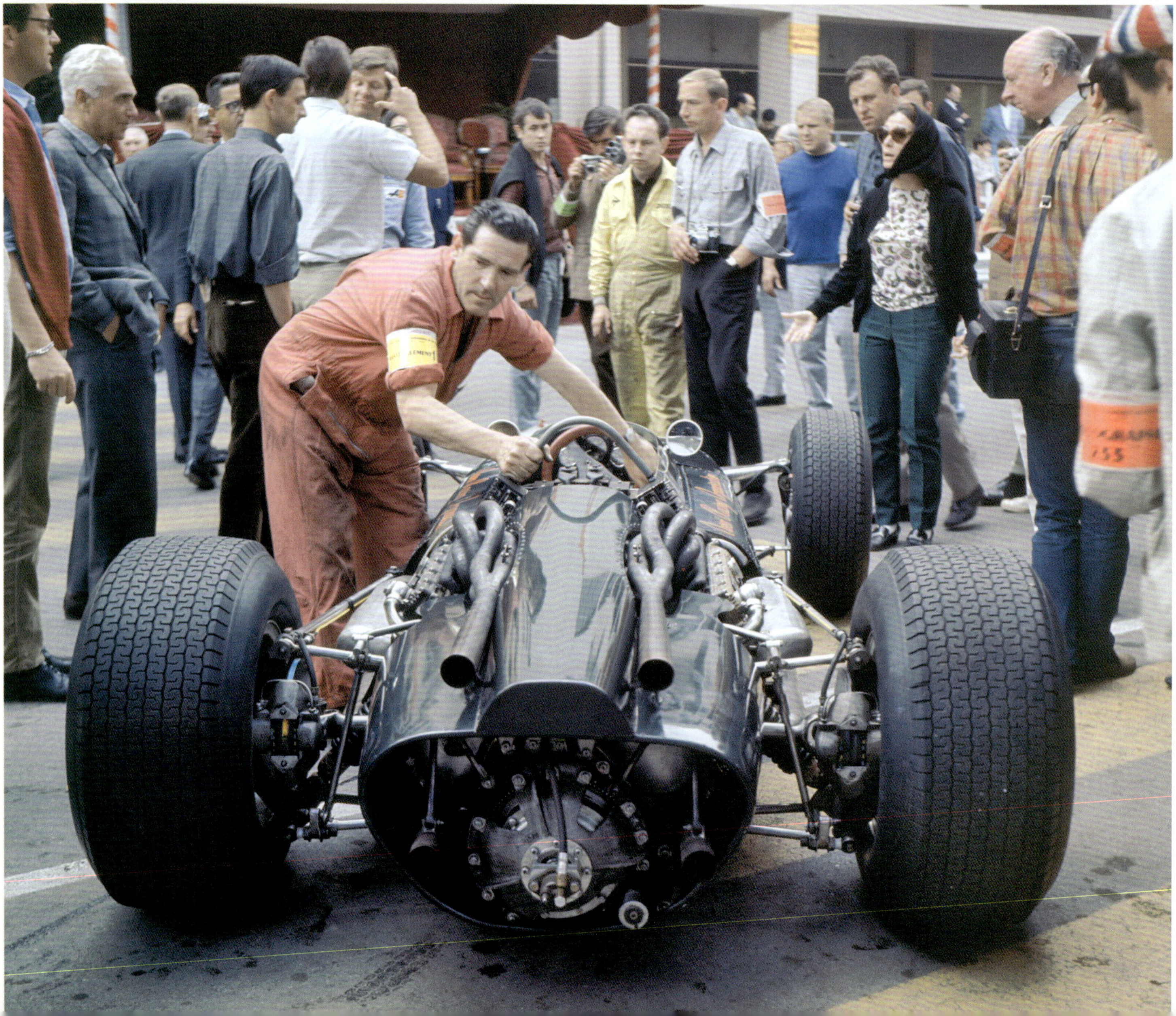

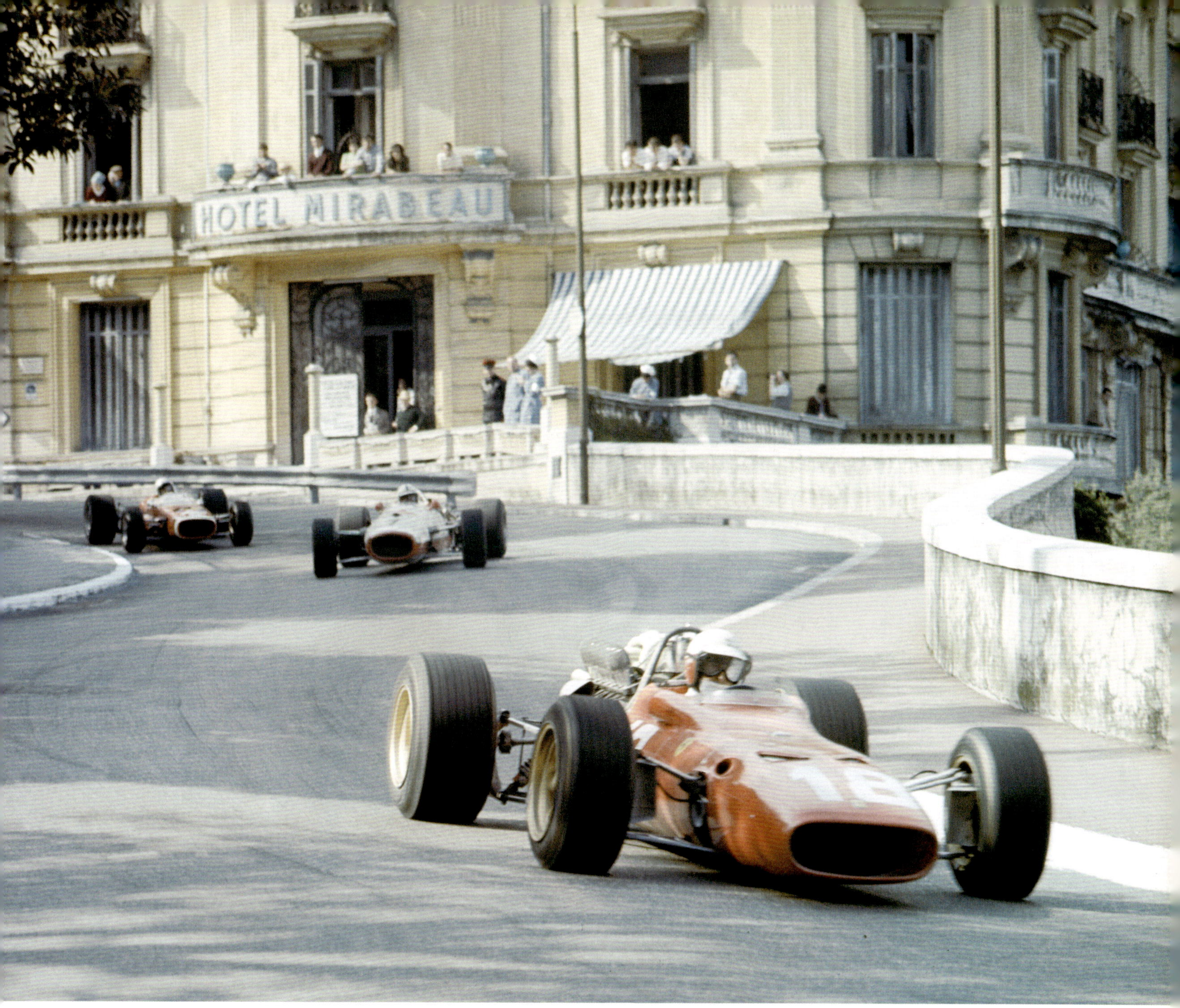

The Monaco GP had been 100 laps or more for many years but after 1967 the race was shortened to 80 laps. Chasing leader Denny Hulme's Brabham a fatigued Lorenzo Bandini crashed his Ferrari 312 (001) at the chicane on lap 82. It turned over and caught fire igniting the straw bales. Poor Bandini was horribly burned and died two days later. John Surtees in the Honda RA273 and Bruce McLaren's F2 based McLaren M4B BRM chase him earlier in the race. The lithe, shapely form of the Ferrari belies the fact that it is a mobile petrol bomb, as were most F1 cars of the period.

Jackie Stewart's career endured a brief hiatus in 1967 when BRM's H16 P83 continued to disappoint. At Monaco he drove the old 1965 P261 (2616) V8 and led the race until a broken cwp stopped him on lap 15. Unlike his Dunlop-shod team mates Stewart raced on Firestone rubber.

BRM's Cyril Atkins pushes one of the muscular H16s during Monaco practice. The sheer bulk and overflowing machinery barely contained by the bodywork emphasise its steroidal demeanour. A lightweight, slimmer version introduced at the French GP still weighed 609kg! On the left wearing a sports jacket with hand in pocket is Piero Taruffi, whose soubriquet was 'Silver Fox', winner of the last ever Mille Miglia in 1957. On the right can be observed the balding head of BRM team chief Louis Stanley.

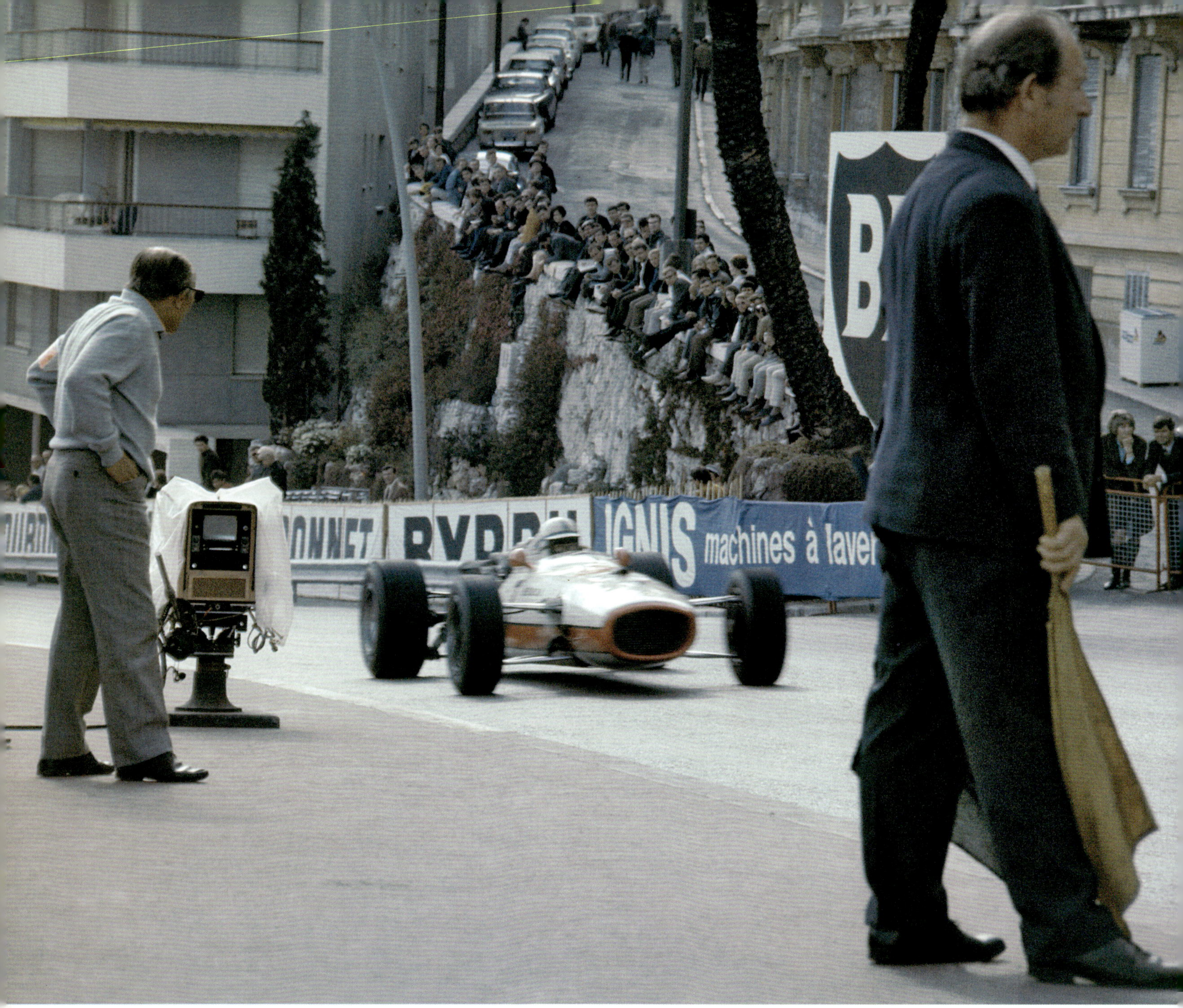

↑ Seeing is believing. John Surtees ascends the hill approaching Casino Square at over 140mph. The man with the flags is seemingly unconcerned or unaware of the Honda RA273's proximity. Appearing on the telly could have been literally an all too real possibility here, and who now would be brave (or stupid) enough to operate the pavement mounted TV camera?

↗ At a stroke Lotus and Cosworth raised the bar with their new 49 and its Ford financed Cosworth DFV 4 cam V8 engine as a stressed part of the chassis. The DFV (double four valve) 90-degree V8 engine was virtually two Cosworth FVA (four valve A series) F2 engines joined together and offered over 400 bhp from 2993cc. Cosworth (Mike Costin and Keith Duckworth) had signed the contract to build the new engine on June 23rd 1966. Graham Hill who had done most of the testing development rather than Jim Clark, who was now a tax exile, put his 49 (R1) on pole at its Zandvoort debut. He led the Dutch GP for 11 laps before stopping with cam gear failure.

→ Graham Hill suffered the inevitable engine problems at Zandvoort after starting from pole and leading in the Lotus 49 (R1) for 11 laps before retiring. This left Jim Clark to win in the sister car but only due to his gentle touch and a large dollop of luck as R2 was suffering from a similar cam gear problem that stopped Hill.

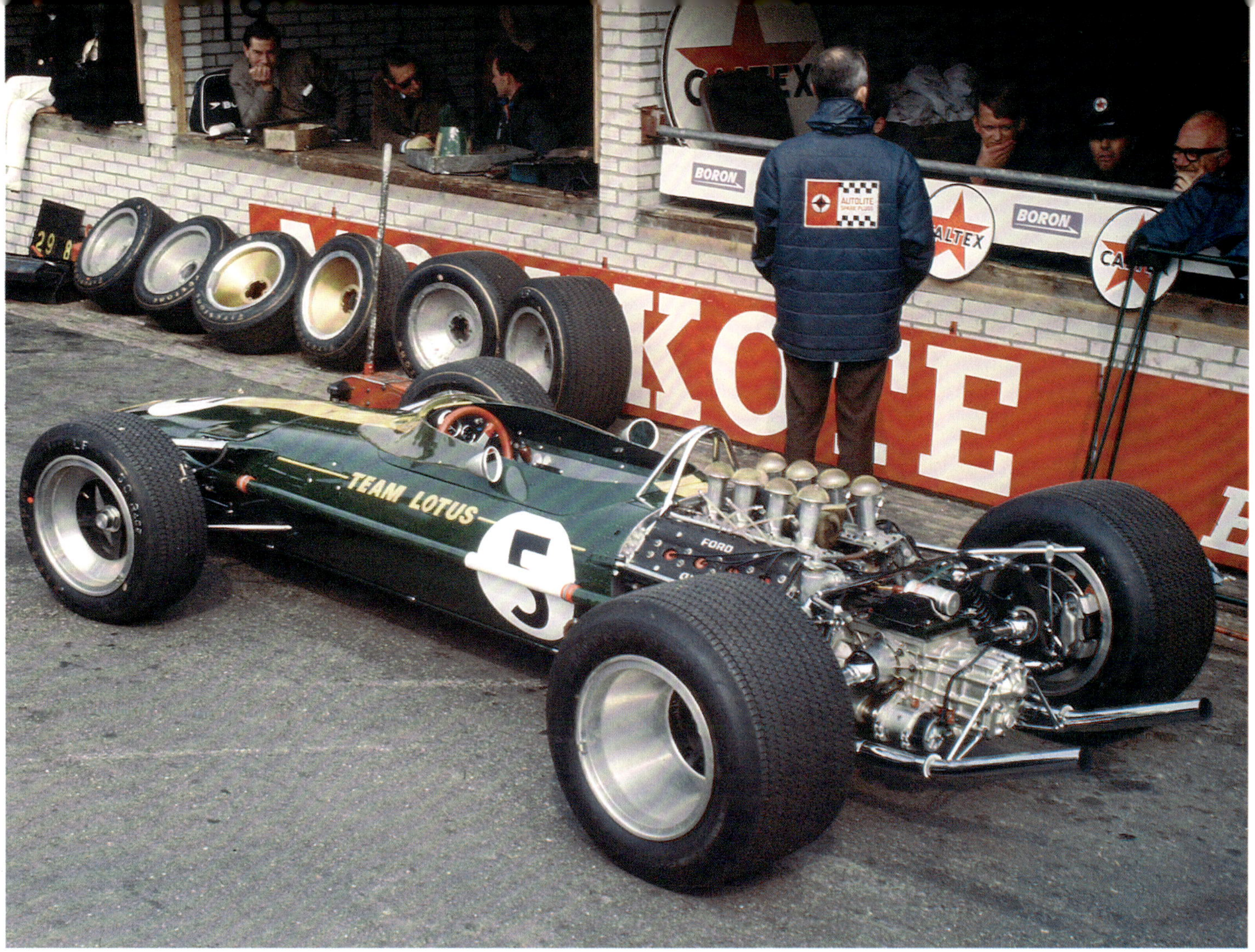
BORON
BORON
TEAM LOTUS
5
FORD

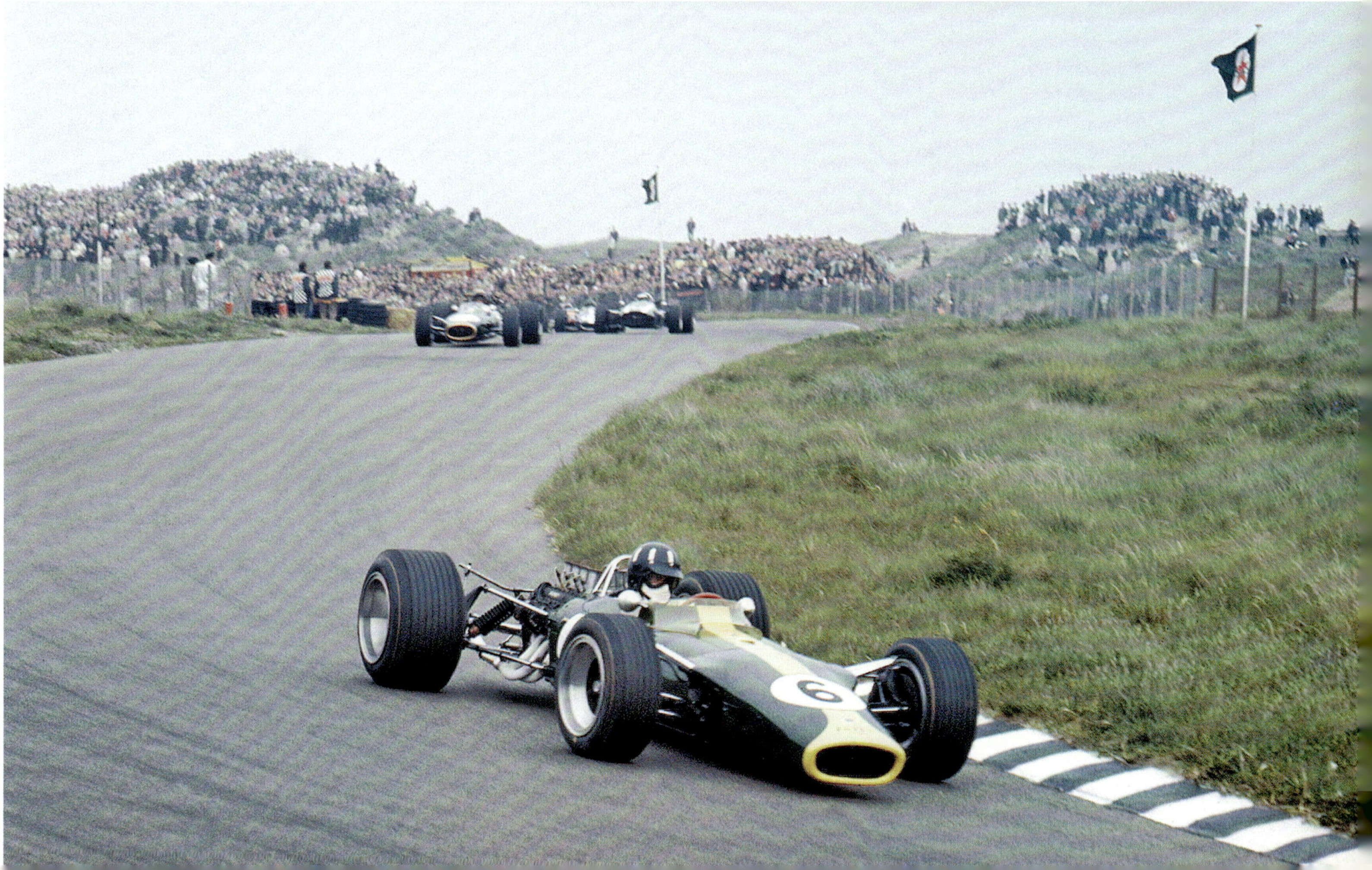
6

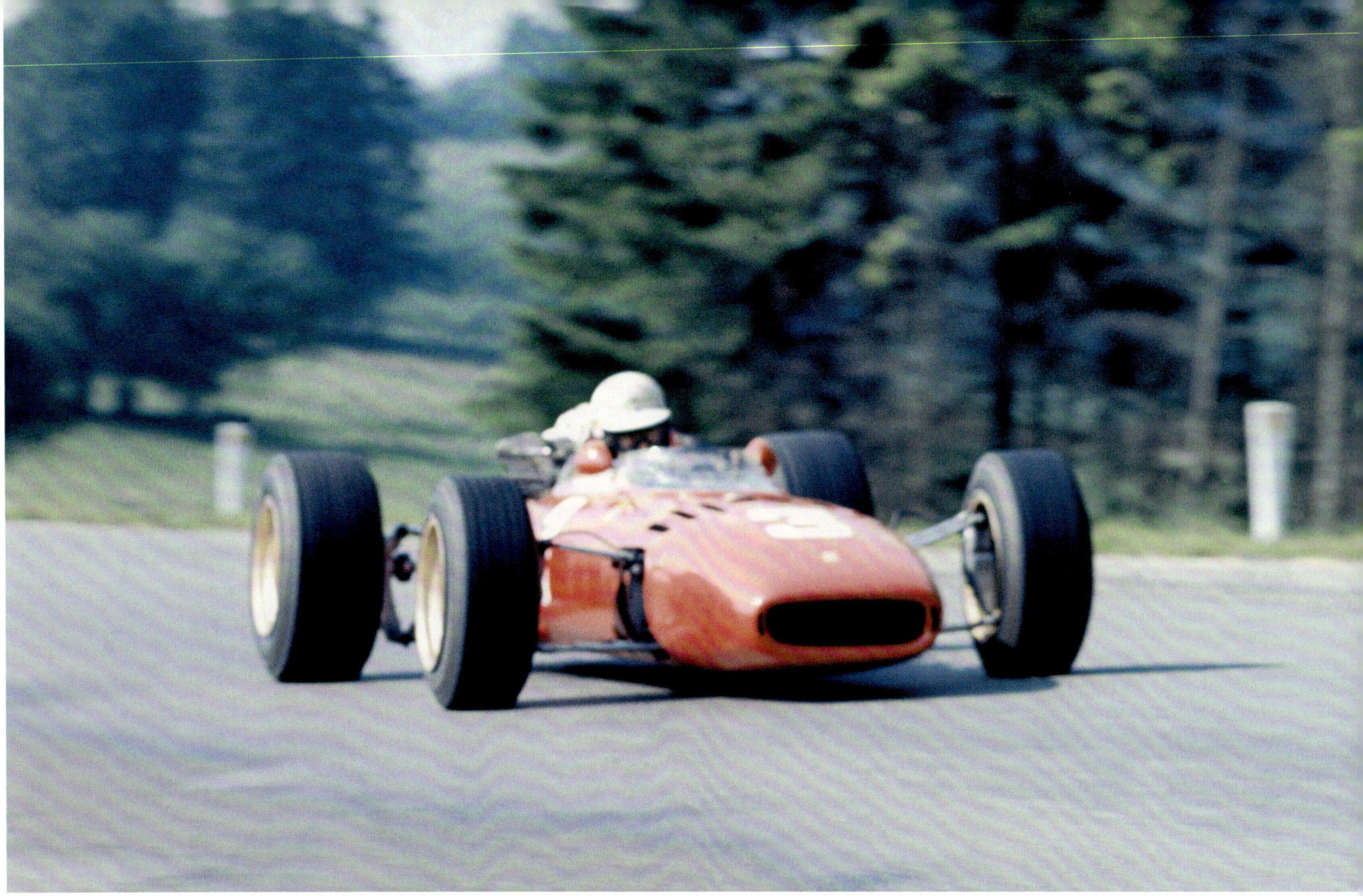

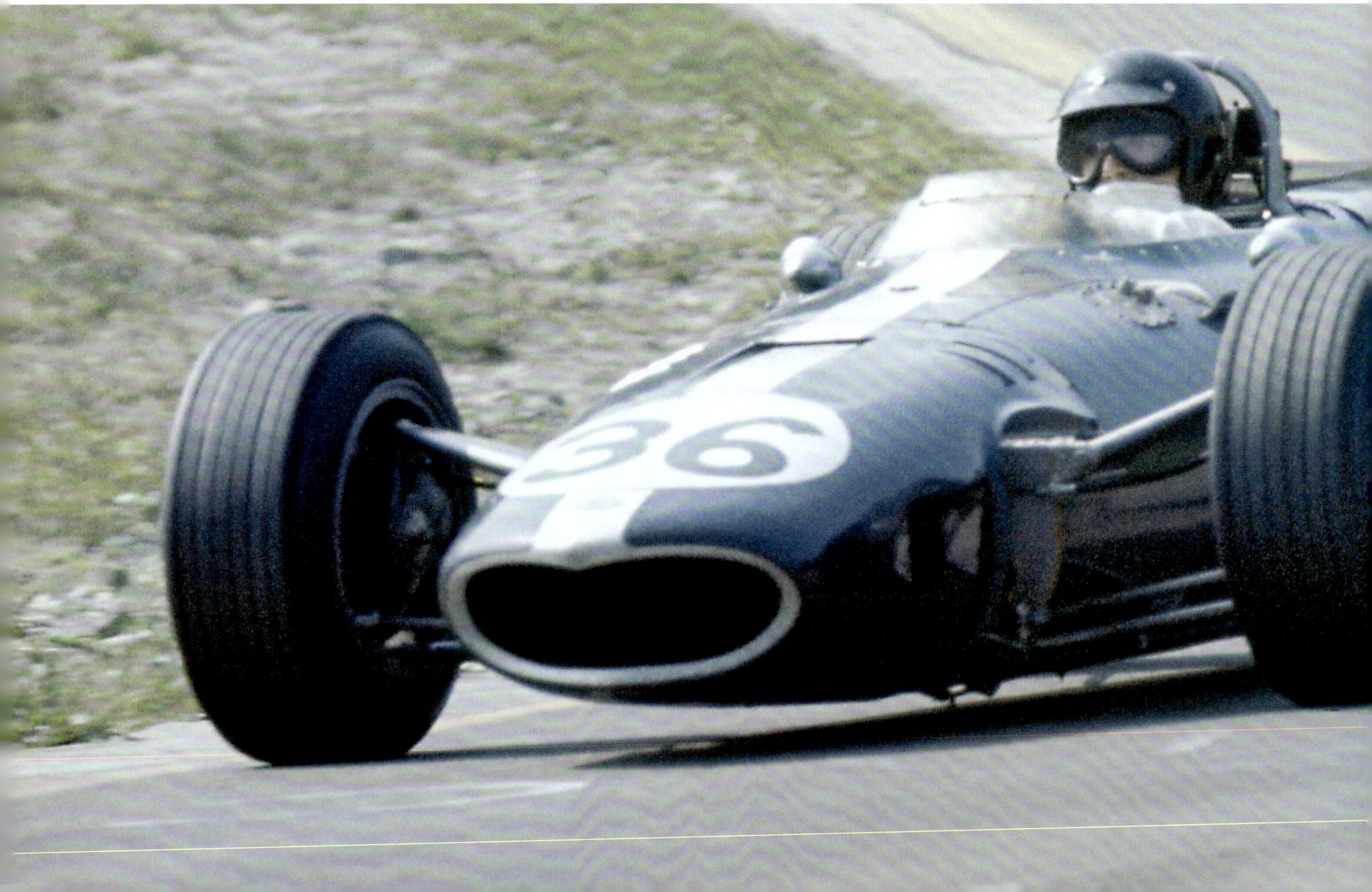

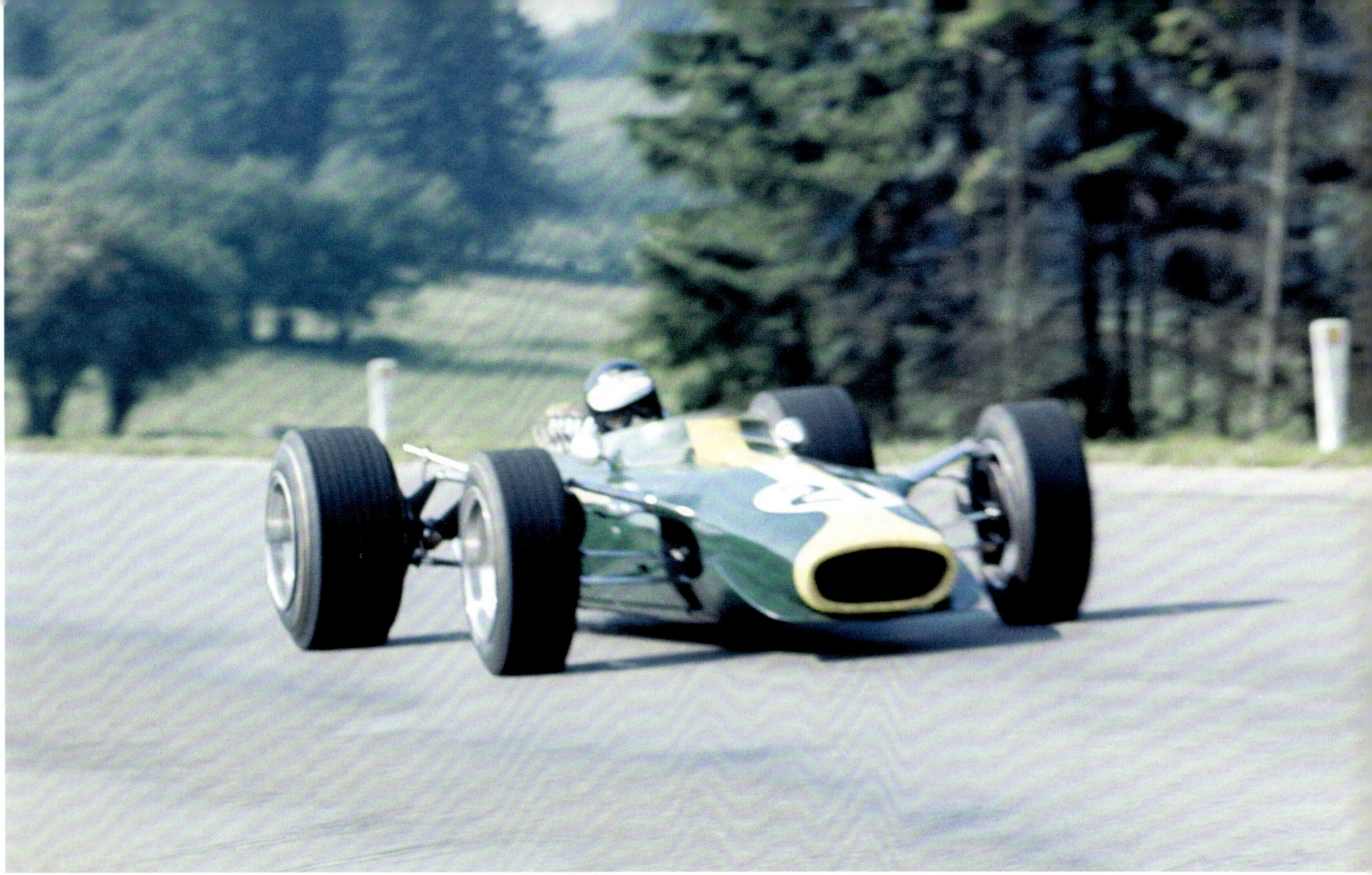

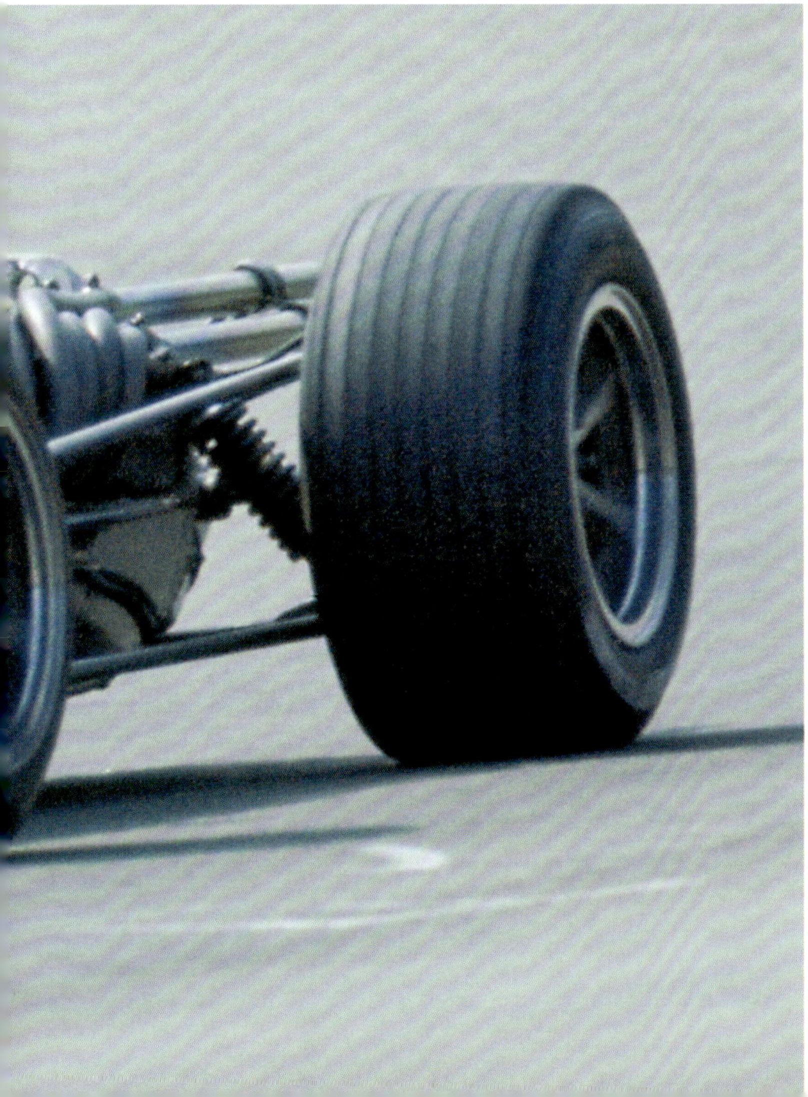

Full bore! Contrast Mike Parkes' Ferrari 312 (0012) above left and Jim Clark's Lotus 49 (R2) above, at Spa-Francorchamps. The Ferrari is totally compressed onto the road, the Lotus slightly higher, but look at the angle of its front wishbones! You had to be really brave at Spa, just imagine the consequences of going off here. Sadly Parkes crashed at 150mph at Blanchimont on the first lap, suffering serious head injuries, a broken leg and wrist that ended his frontline career. Clark led until plug problems intervened. The Ferrari, like BRM and Honda, suffered from excess *avoirdupois*, weighing in at 590kg.

Following his Le Mans triumph with A.J. Foyt for Ford, Dan Gurney won the Belgian GP in his beautifully finished Eagle Weslake T1G (104). The first and so far only time an American in an American car has won a World Championship Grand Prix. The new lighter Eagle had magnesium rather than alloy panels, magnesium engine castings and many steel engine and suspension components replaced by titanium equivalents. It weighed 542kg. Gurney won despite a top end misfire from a brave Jackie Stewart who had to hold his BRM H16 in 2nd gear, with Chris Amon's Ferrari 3rd.

The French GP's peripatetic existence continued in 1967 with yet another venue, the Bugatti circuit at Le Mans, its fourth consecutive change due to financial and political pressure. This utilised the start and finish area of the 24-hour track with an infield to produce a rather abbreviated 4.4km circuit that ran through two car parks. It was universally unpopular and not used again for F1. The two Team Lotus 49s are at the front with Jochen Rindt's Cooper-Maserati T81B (No 12), Bob Anderson's old Brabham BT11 Climax (No 17) and the Guy Ligier Cooper-Maserati T81 (No 16) alongside Jo Siffert's Rob Walker similar car. The Brabhams of winner Jack Brabham (No 3) and Denny Hulme (No 4) who finished 2nd occupy the pitlane.

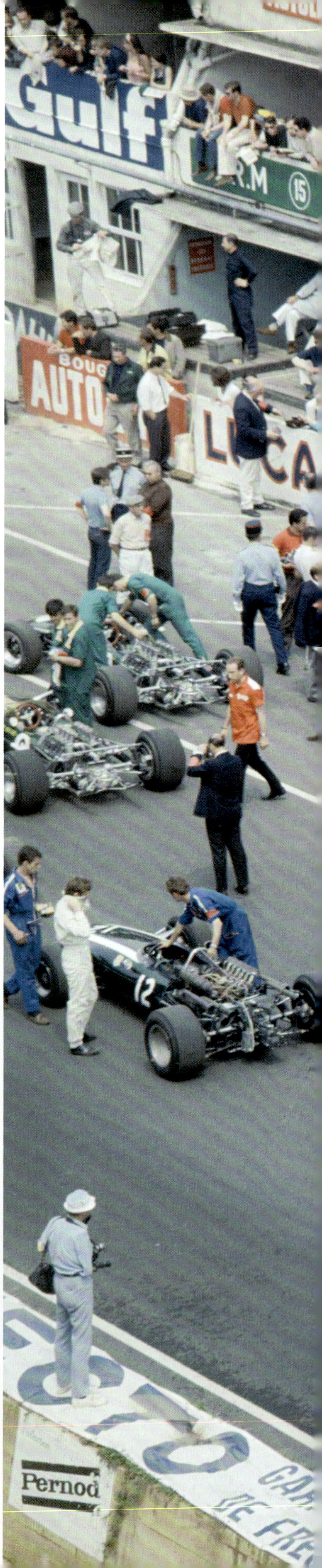

Poacher turned gamekeeper. Before he became a constructor former international rugby player Guy Ligier was an F1 privateer running this Cooper-Maserati T81 (F1-4-66) during 1966 and up to the 1967 French GP. He is pursued by Stewart's old P261 2614 (this would be the final GP outing for a works P261). Ligier was unclassified after a long pit stop but Stewart came 3rd albeit a lap behind Jack Brabham and Denny Hulme.

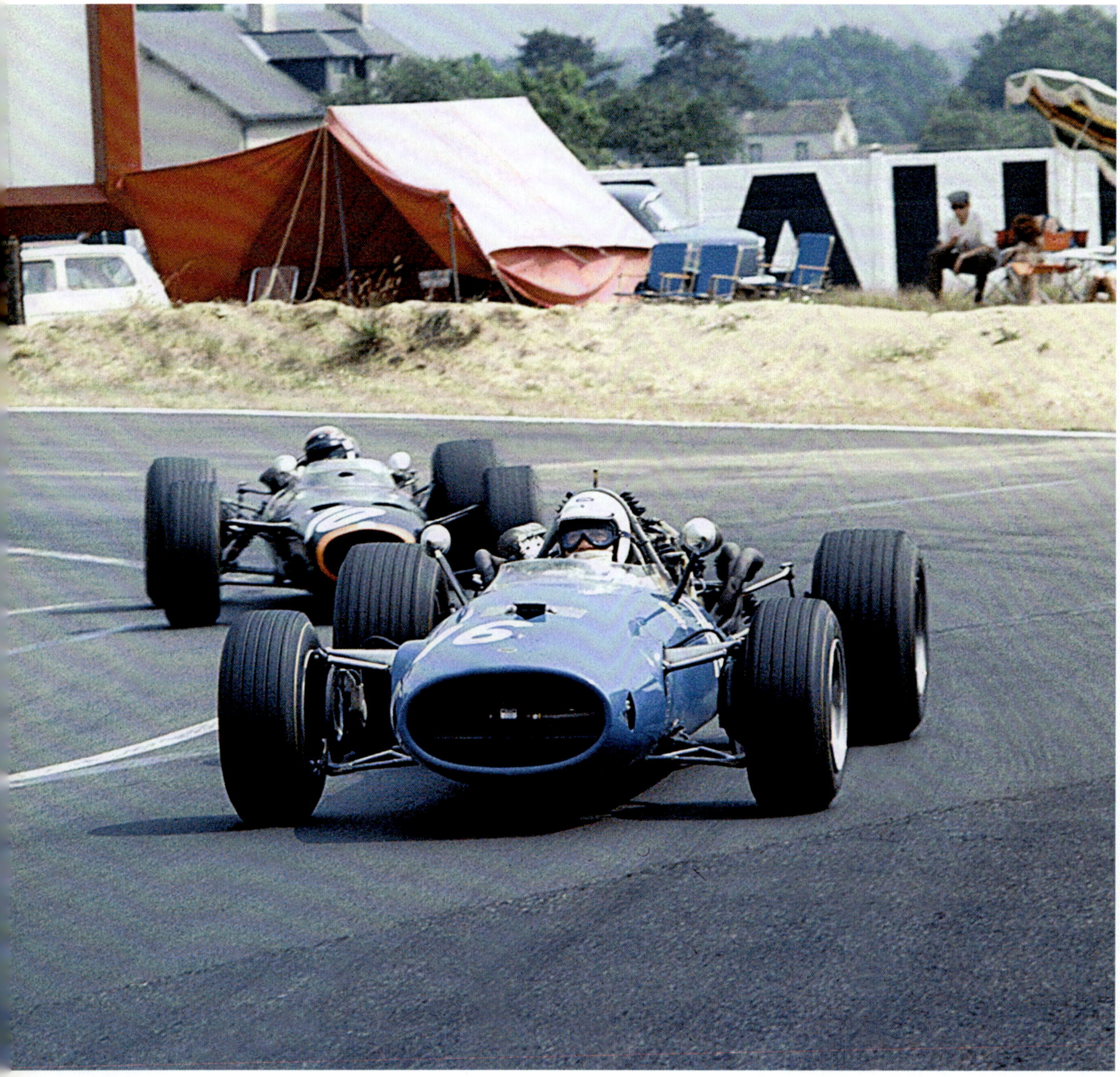

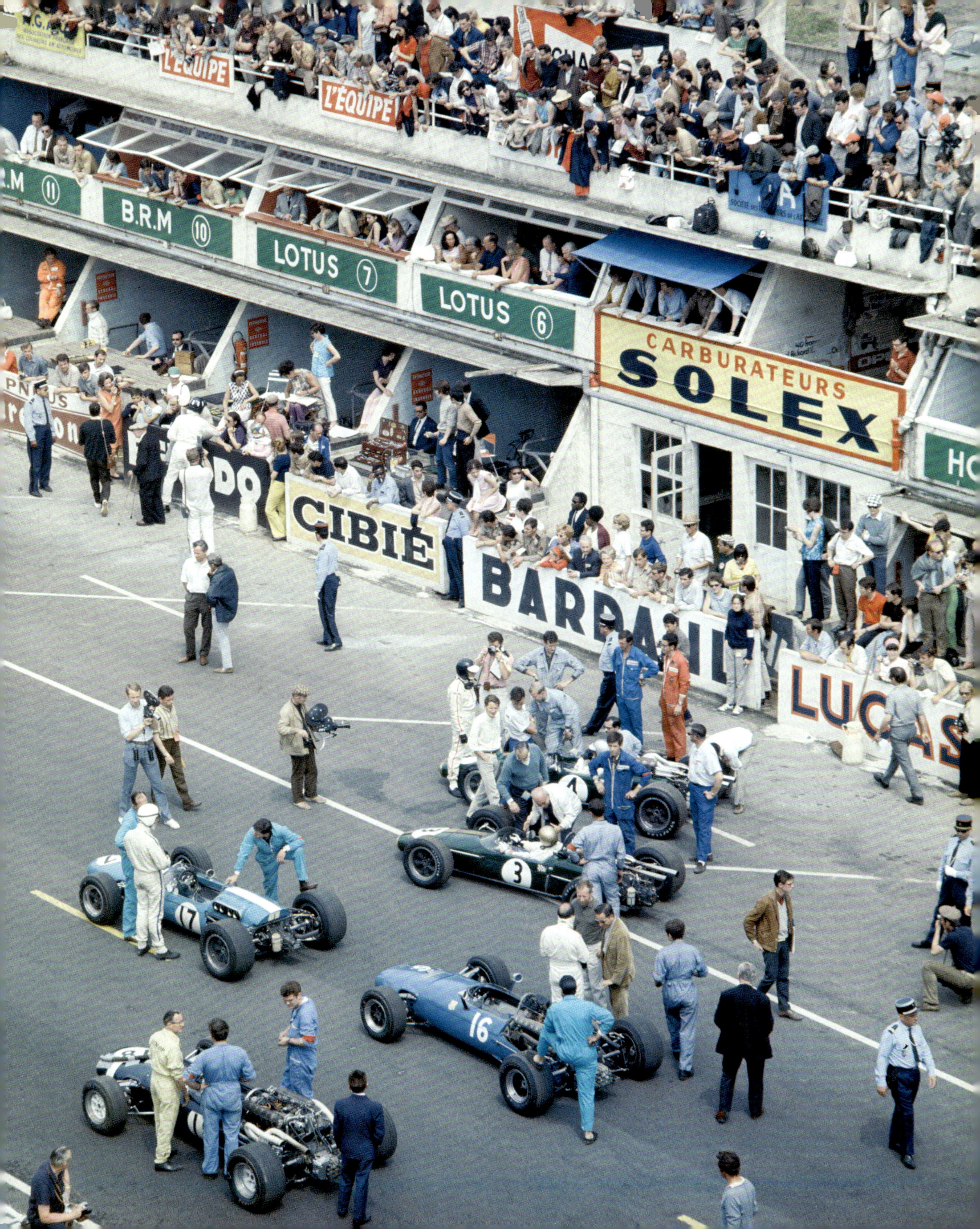

L'EQUIPE
L'EQUIPE
B.R.M 10
LOTUS 7
LOTUS 6
CARBURATEURS
SOLEX
CIBIÉ

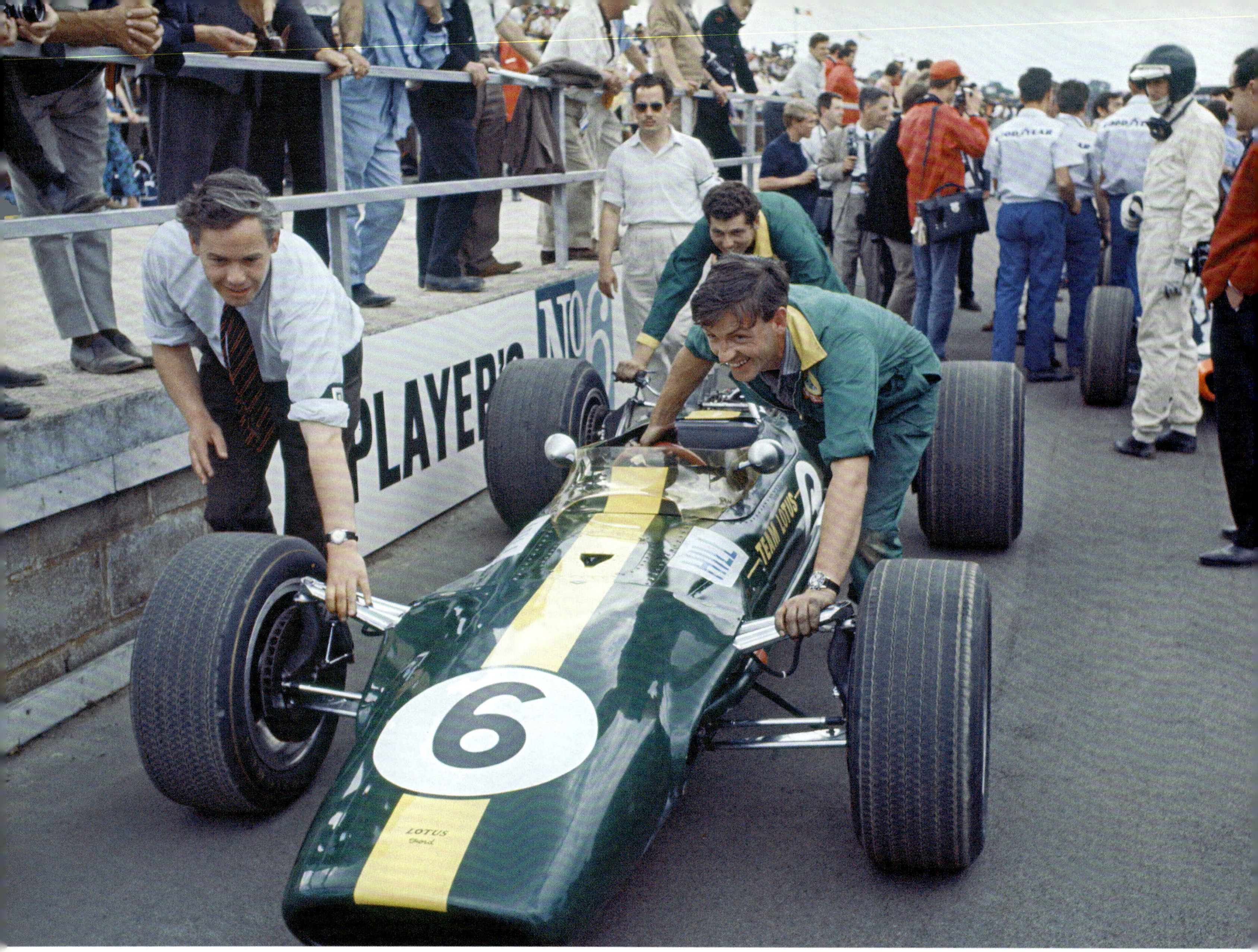

↑ Graham Hill had an adventurous time in the British GP at Silverstone. A faulty weld on a lower rear radius arm mounting plate on his 49 (R1) detached itself causing the Lotus to hit the pit retaining wall as Hill pulled in from practice. The car was too badly damaged to repair in time so a new chassis (R3) was completed using the pipework and ancillaries from R1 that had been transported back to Hethel that night. There was no spare fibreglass nose so an aluminium buck was used with an old 25/33 type air-deflector screen. Keith Duckworth (left who died in 2005), Dougie Bridge (right) and Dale Porteous at the rear push R3 to Hill's front row slot, still smiling despite working all night and driving to and fro! In the background Jochen Rindt looks on. In the race Hill took the lead from team mate Jim Clark on lap 5 and stayed there for 50 laps when an Allen screw fell out of the top left-hand rear suspension link. Graham made it back to the pits where the sagging rear wheel and link were reattached, but the Lotus retired on lap 64 with engine failure. This was typical of Hill's year, whilst Clark won.

↗ Chris Amon spent much of the British Grand Prix battling with Jack Brabham's Brabham BT24. The driving was quite robust, but eventually he found a way past to finish 3rd in the Ferrari 312/67 0003 five seconds ahead of Brabham.

→ Alan Rees, one of the founders of March, was a very fine driver having beaten Clark, Hill, Rindt *et al* in F2. He drove this works Cooper-Maserati T81 (F1-3-66) in the British GP at Silverstone to finish 9th, his only race in an F1 car. By the end of 1968 he decided that his racing career had peaked and retired. Following the March project he became team manager for Shadow and then the breakaway Arrows outfit with Jackie Oliver, Tony Southgate and Dave Wass during the 1970s.

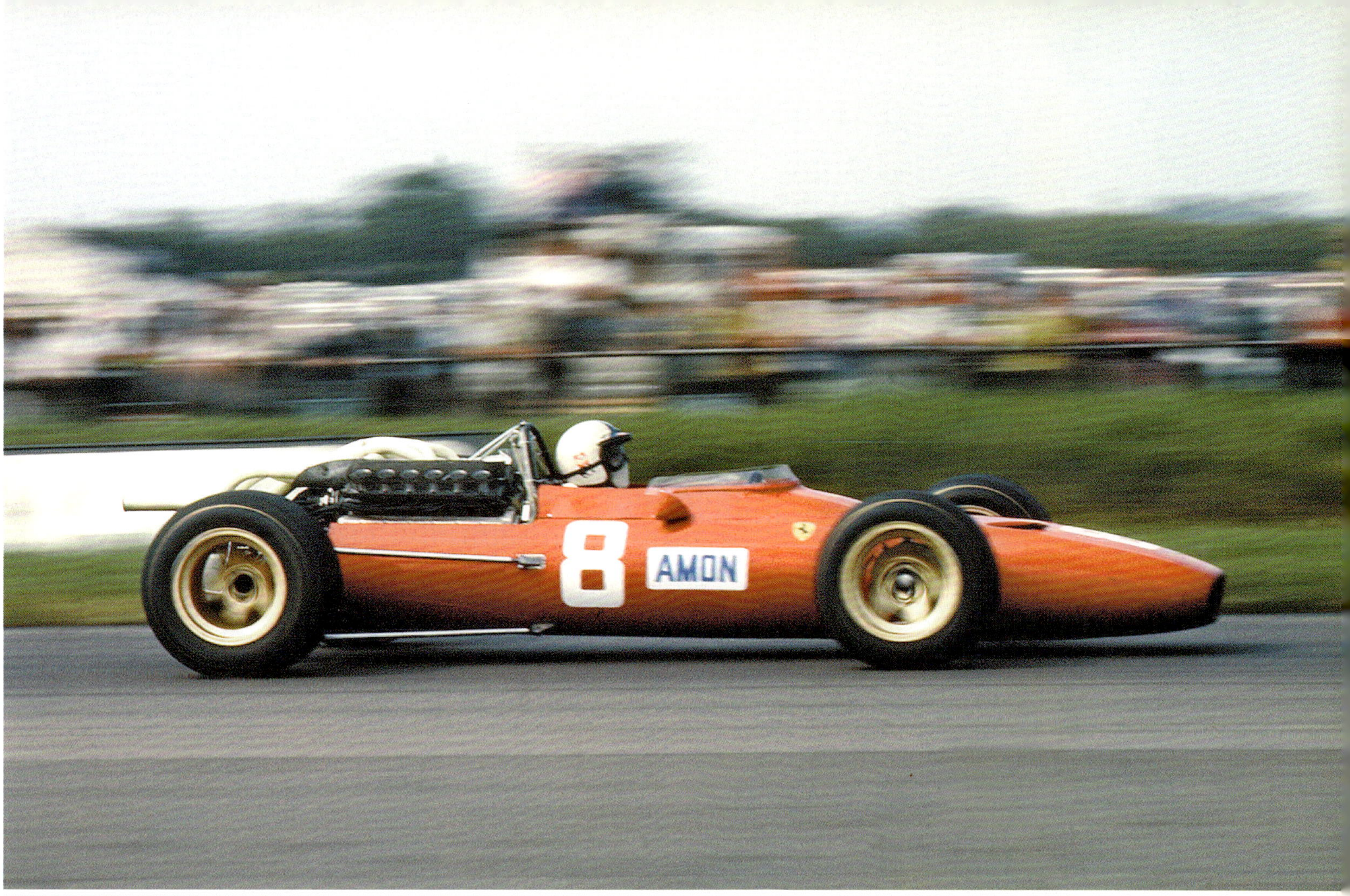
8
AMON

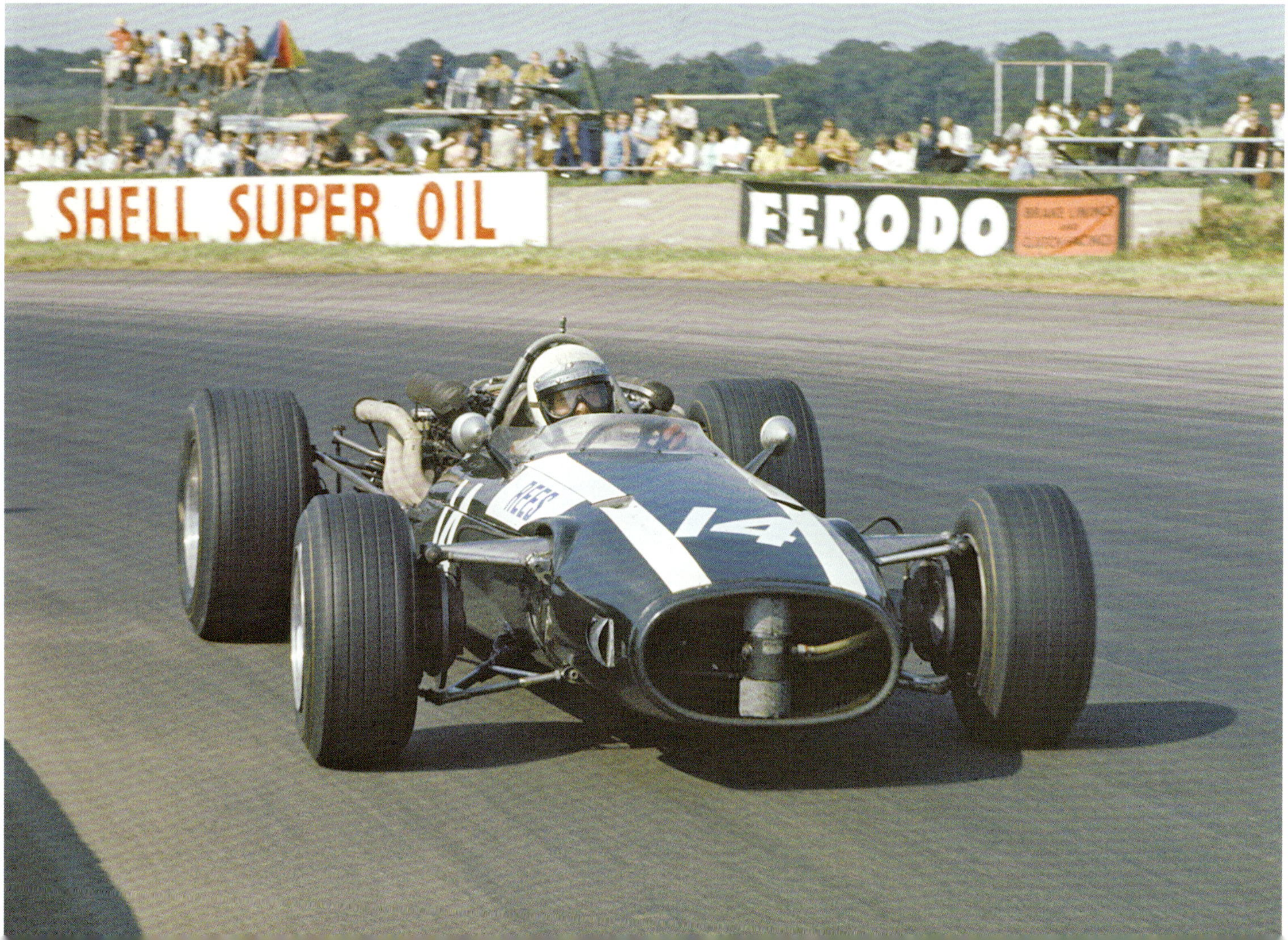
SHELL SUPER OIL
FERODO
REES
14

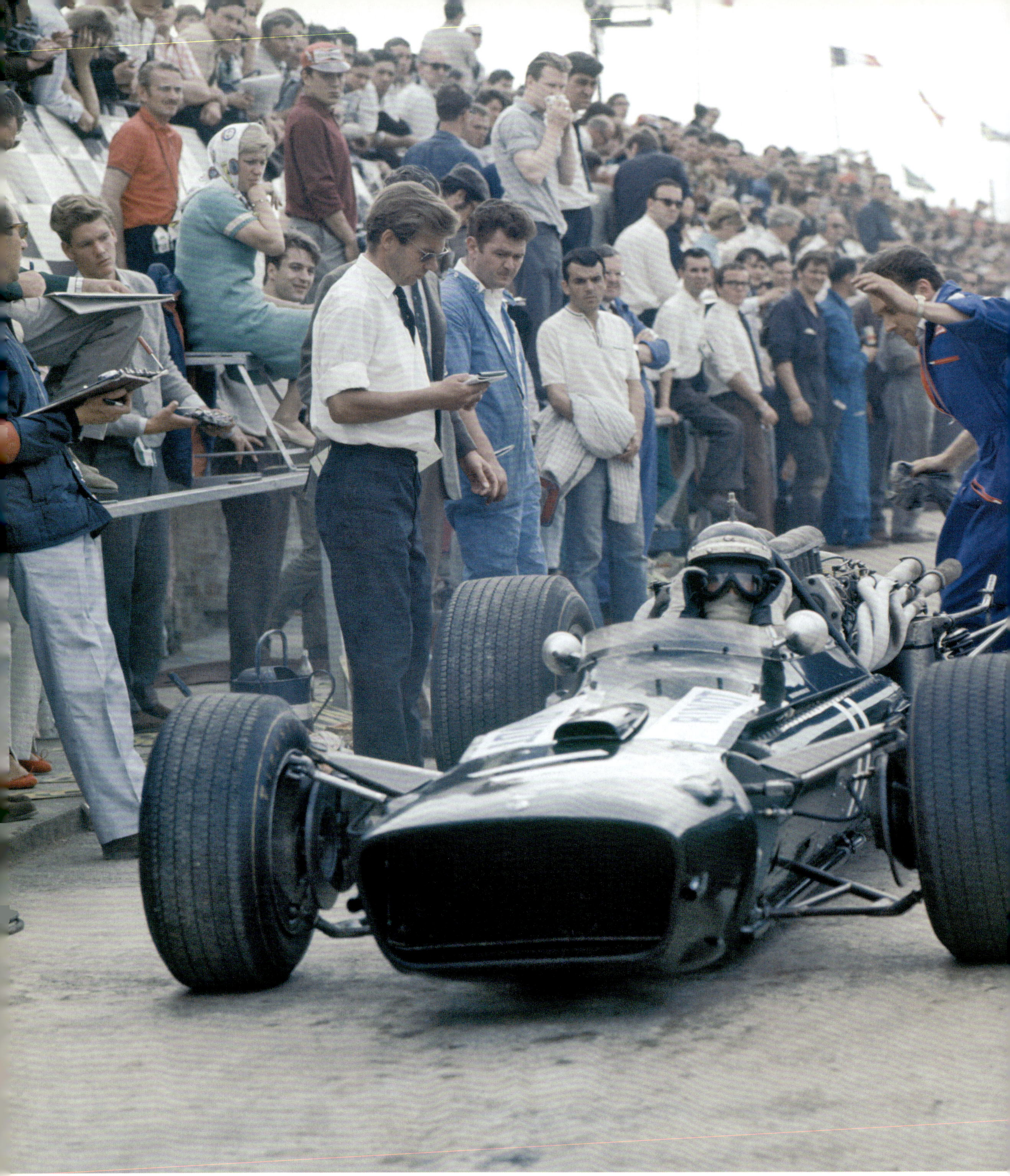

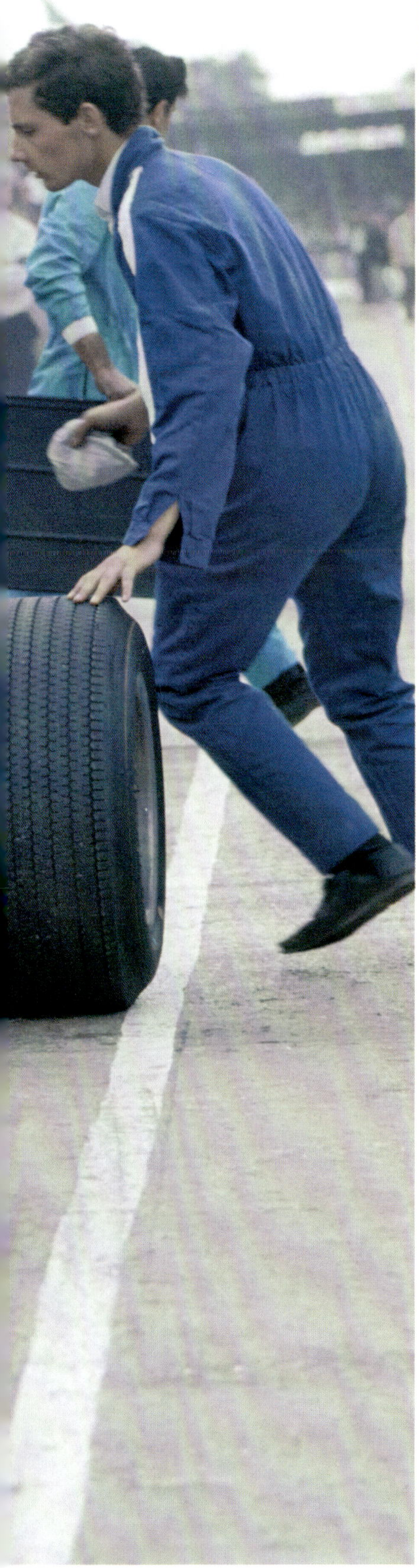

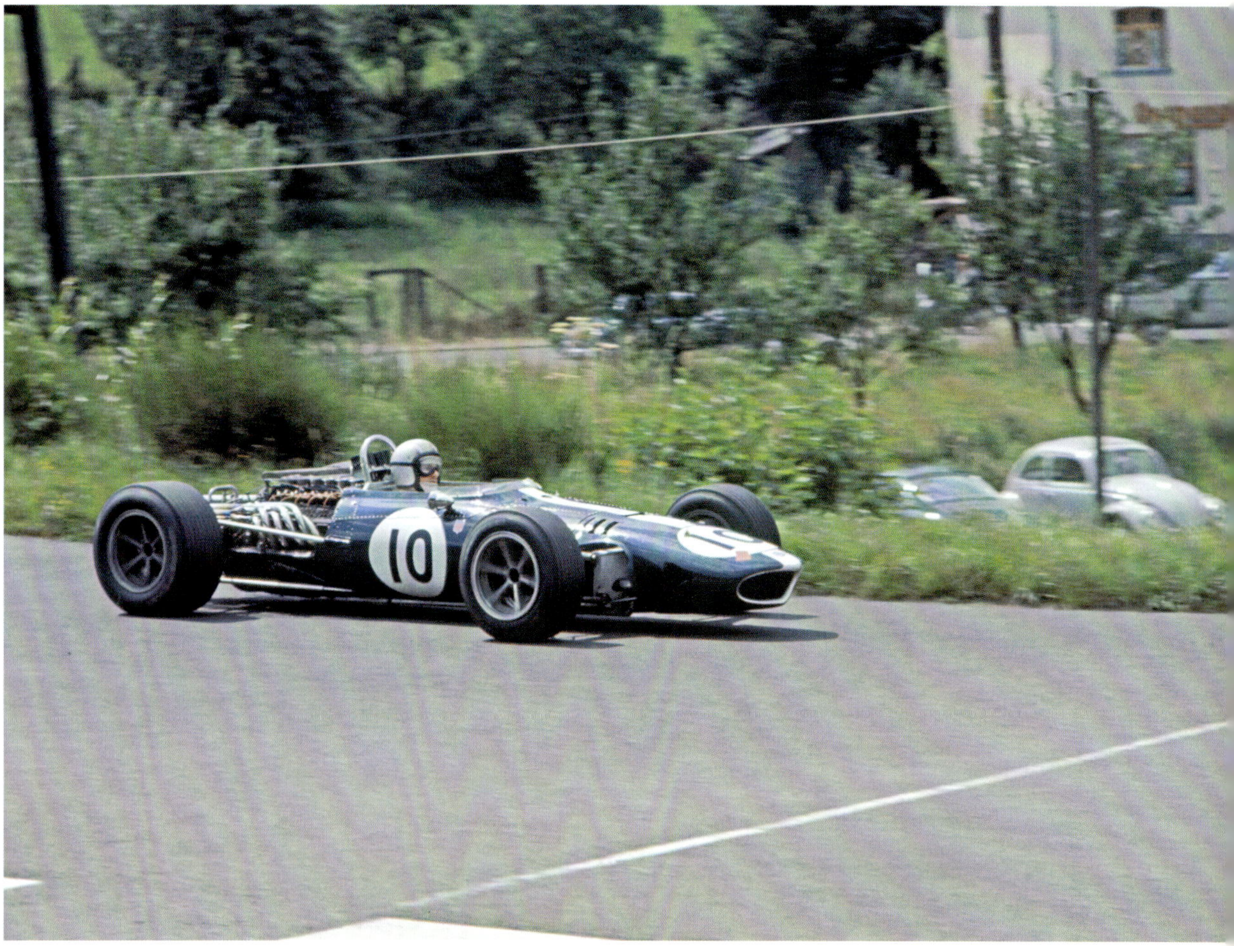

Bruce McLaren spent part of his season driving the second Eagle Weslake T1G (102) starting with the French GP, then the British round where he retired and now at the Nürburgring. McLaren started on row two but only lasted three laps before an oil pipe failed. The town of Adenau provides the civilian backdrop.

Jochen Rindt's new magnesium electron skinned monocoque Cooper T86 Maserati (F1-2-67) made its debut at Silverstone but retired with engine problems. The new construction saved 51kg over the older T81 version. The mechanic running round the rear wheel is *the* Ron Dennis.

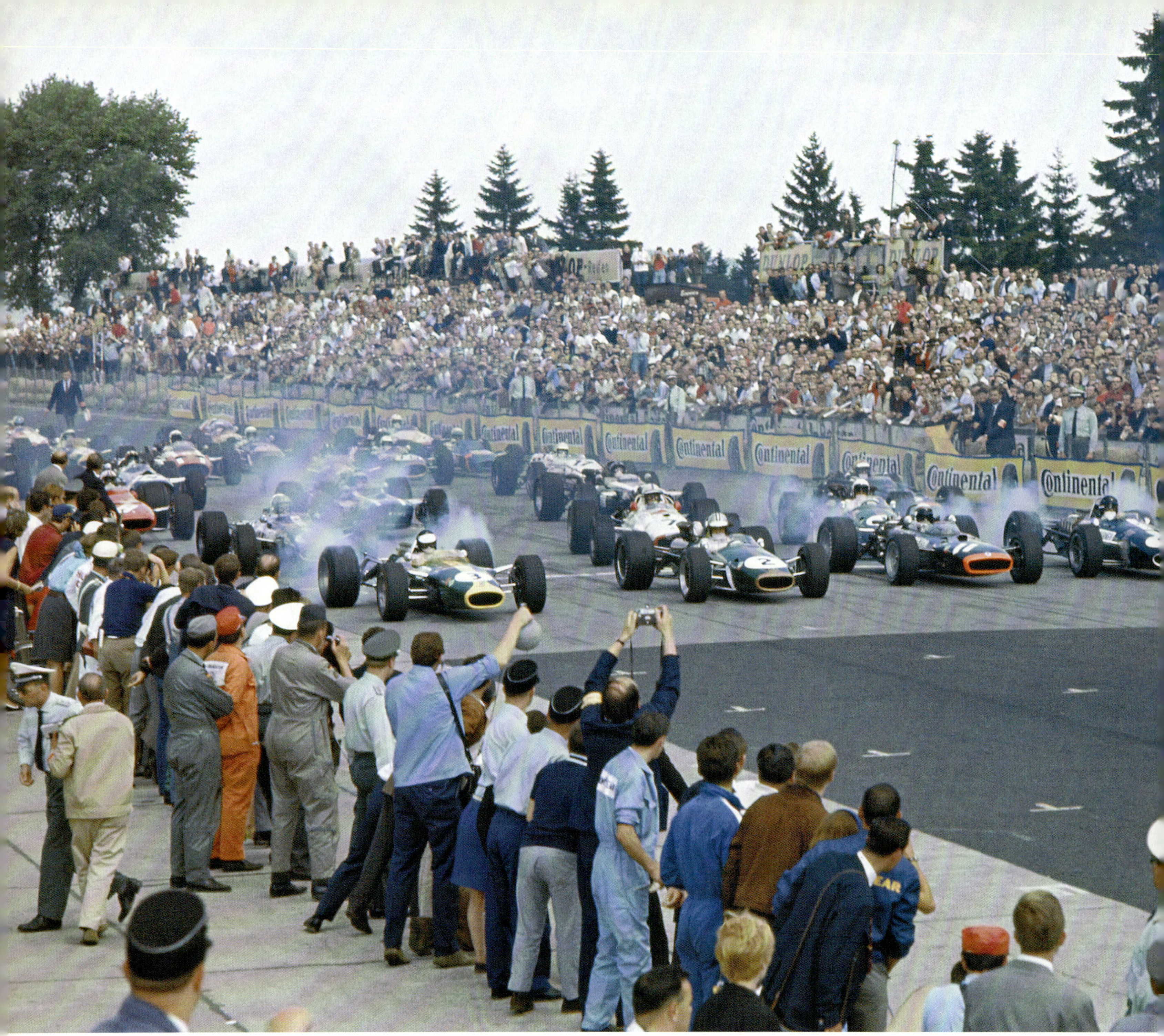

Lights, camera, action! The old Nürburgring employed a 4–3–4 grid formation and the front row, tyres smoking, of Clark, Lotus 49, Hulme, Brabham BT24, Stewart, BRM P115 and Gurney, Eagle Weslake T1G erupts into life.

The German GP was a race of high attrition. Jim Clark led until his Lotus front suspension collapsed, then moral victor Dan Gurney caught and passed Denny Hulme, setting a new lap record, but his Eagle broke a drive shaft late in the race. This left Denny in his Brabham BT24/2 Repco to win handsomely from his boss who just held off Amon's Ferrari in a repeat of their British GP duel.

1967 was BRM's worst season since 1961 and despite development the H16 cars continued to frustrate. Whilst team leader Jackie Stewart drove the latest P115 version, Mike Spence qualified 10th for the wet Canadian GP at Mosport Park one place behind Stewart in the P83. He finished 5th, albeit three laps behind, courtesy of the many retirements and mishaps that befell others in the miserable conditions.

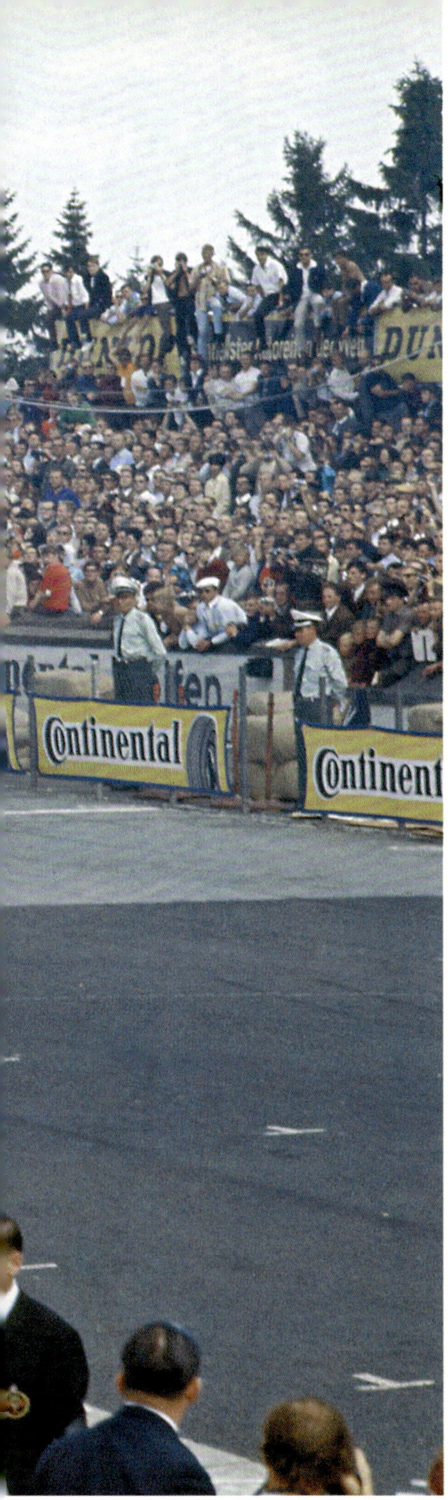
Continental

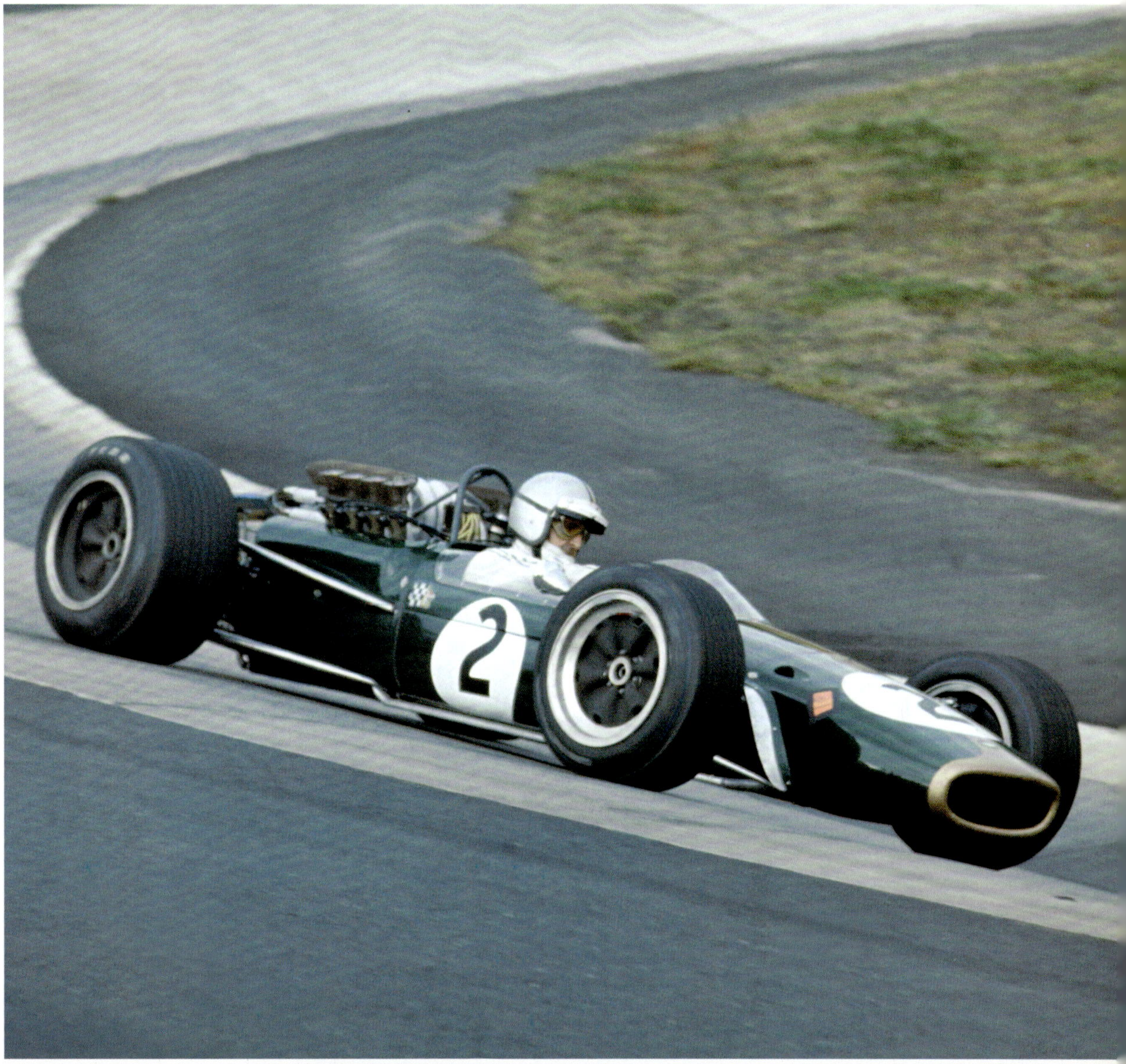

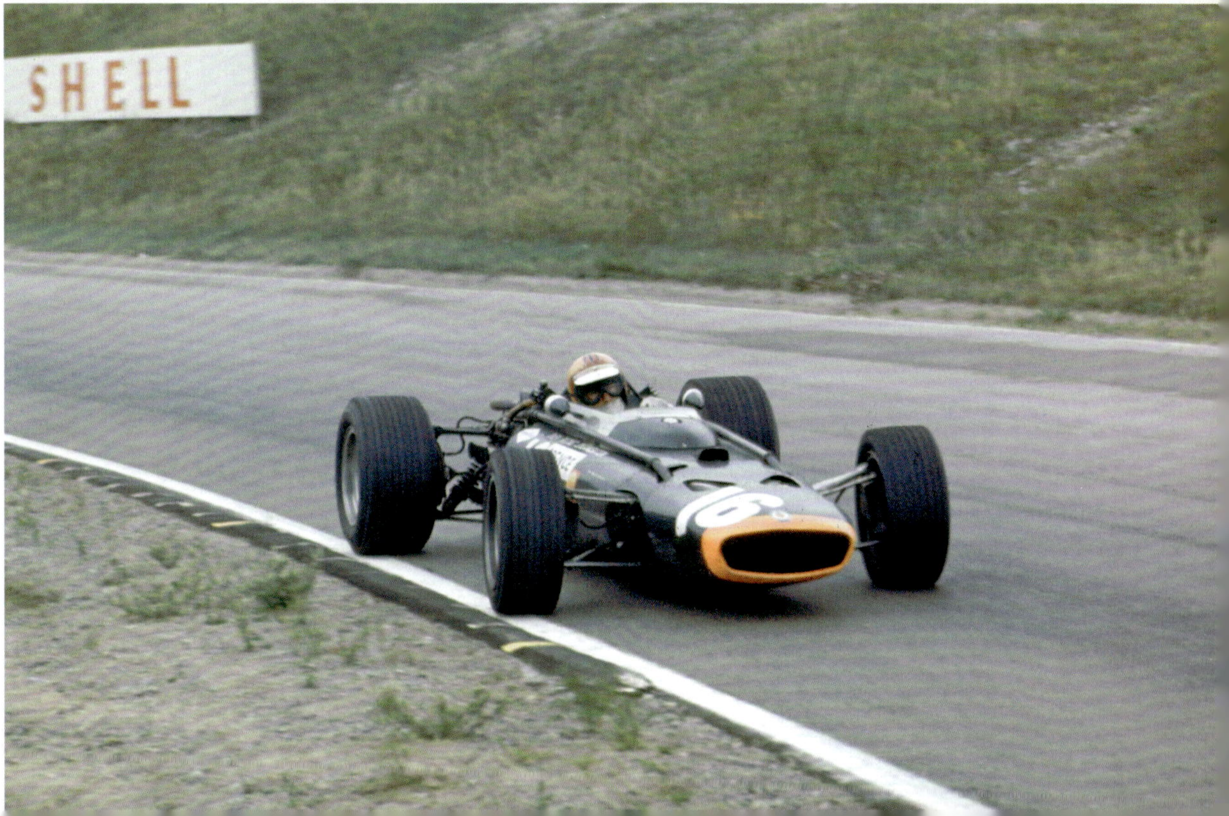
SHELL

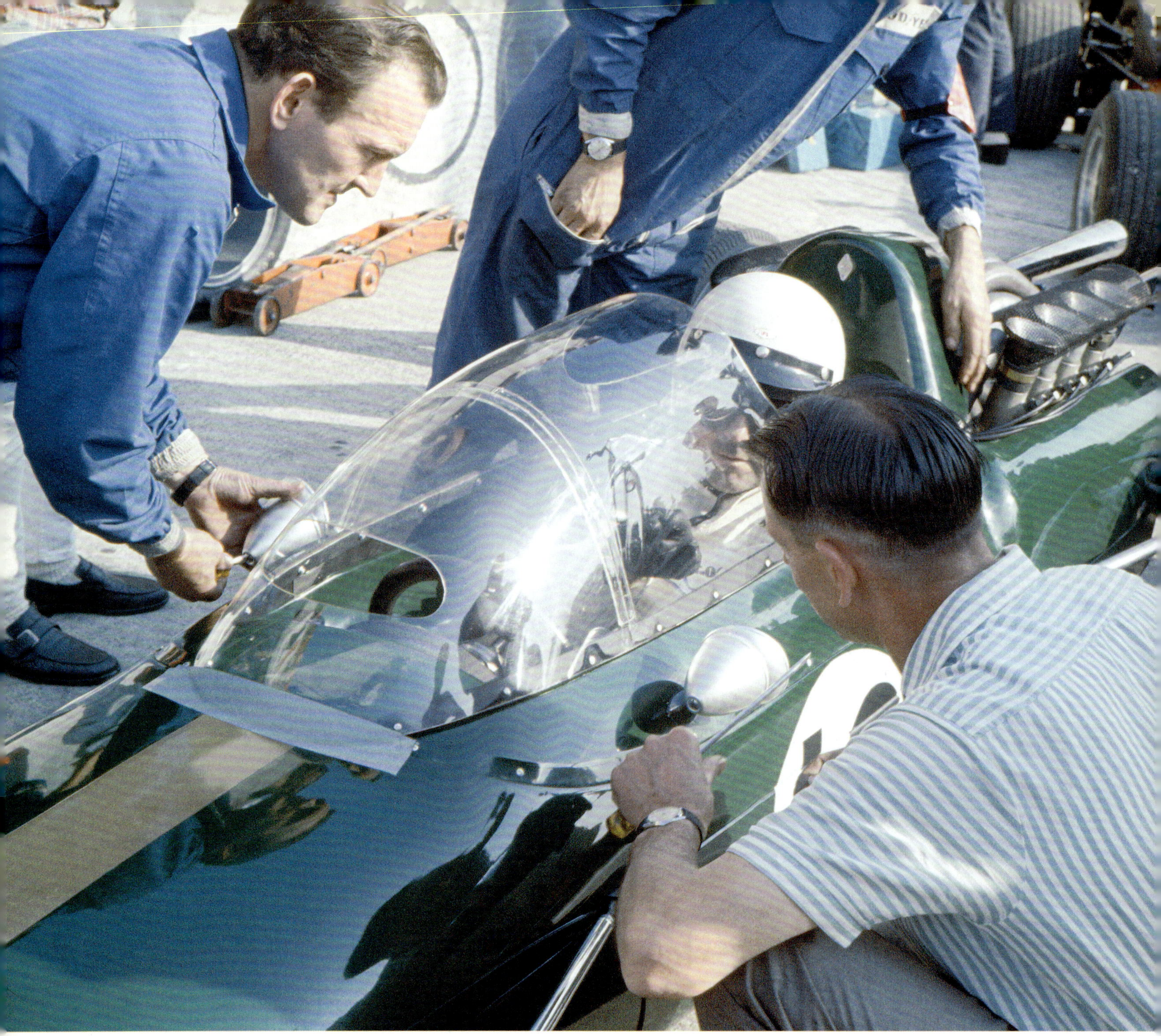

↑ After another team 1–2 in Canada, Jack Brabham tried a Perspex canopy during practice for the Italian GP at Monza in search of more straightline speed. However it caused vision distortion and was discarded while the special gearbox fairing overheated the gearbox oil. Ron Tauranac chats to Brabham during practice. In the race he famously lost the lead to John Surtees's Honda on the last corner (Parabolica) of the last lap. However, Hill's Lotus led conclusively before retiring whilst a delayed Clark (Lotus) unlapped himself, overtook the leaders but ran out of fuel on the final lap whilst leading.

↗ Dougie Bridge (back to camera), Gordon Huckle, an unknown girl with Jim Clark and famous French journalist 'Jabby' Crombac, who died in 2005, (in cap and glasses, festooned with cameras) enjoy a brief respite from the sound and fury at Monza.

→ Jacky Ickx had twice impressed with F2 Matras in the German GP (1966/67), but the Italian GP was his first race in a pukka GP car, the works Cooper-Maserati T81B (F1-1-67) in which he finished 6th at Monza despite a puncture on the last lap.

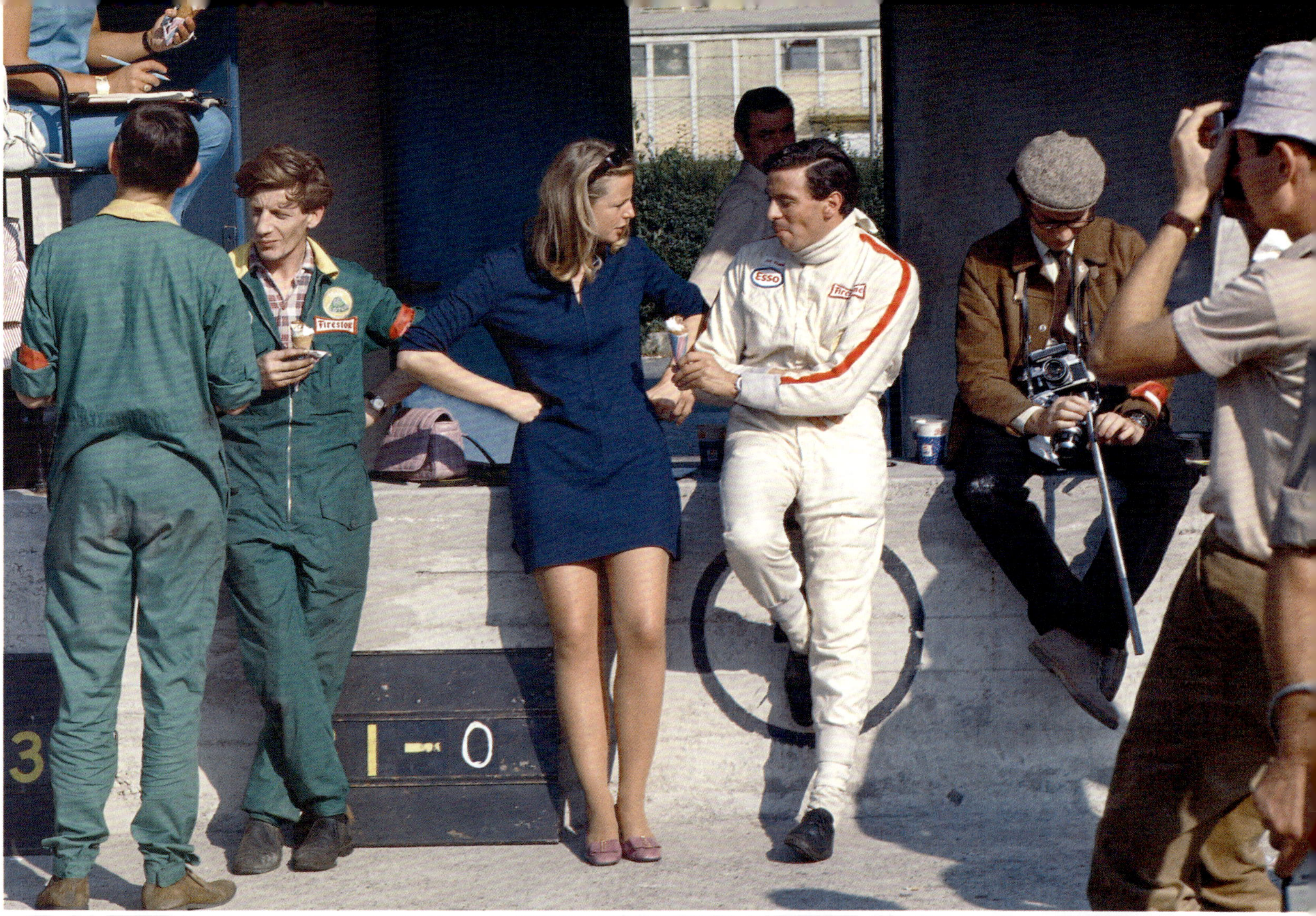
ESSO

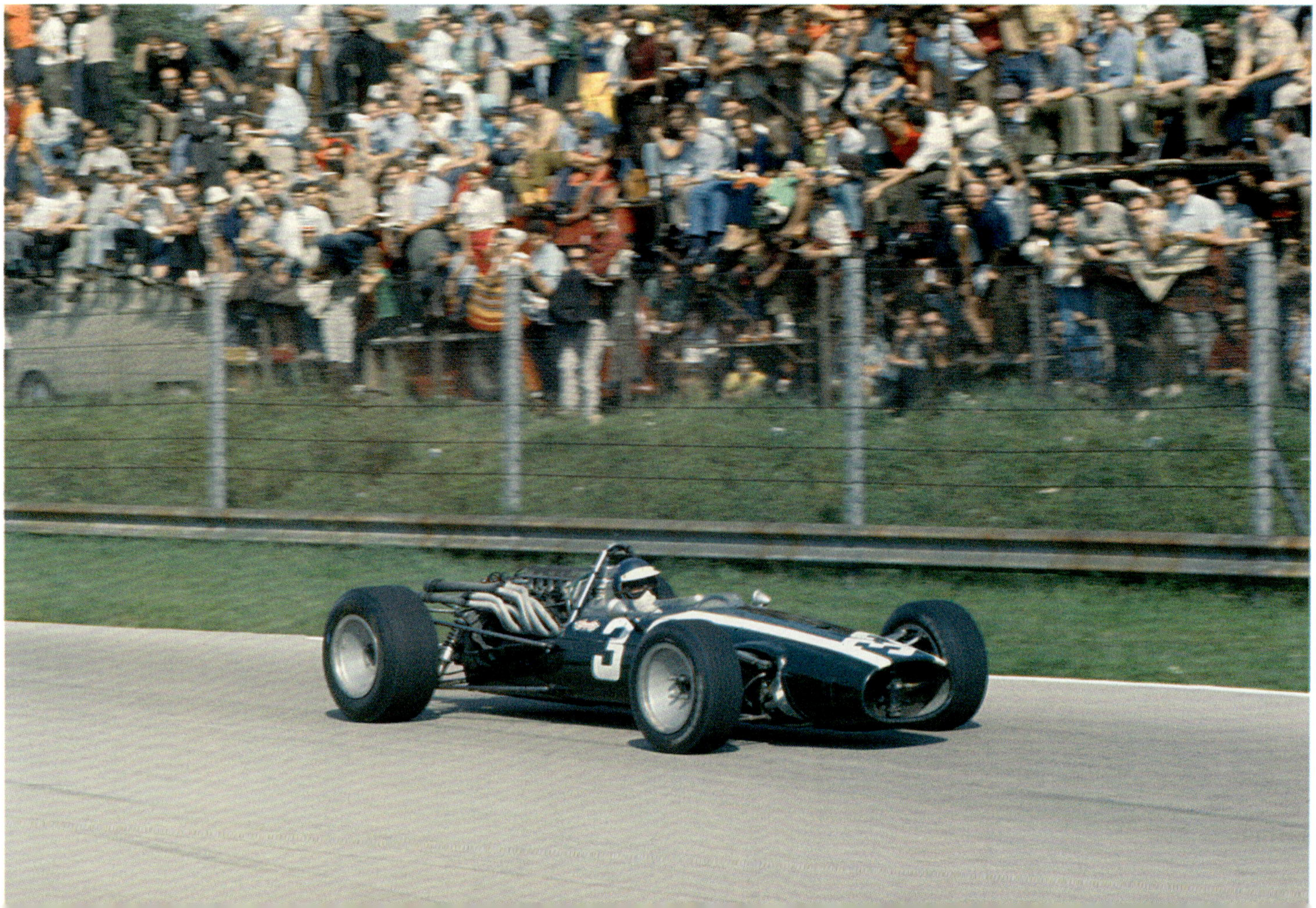

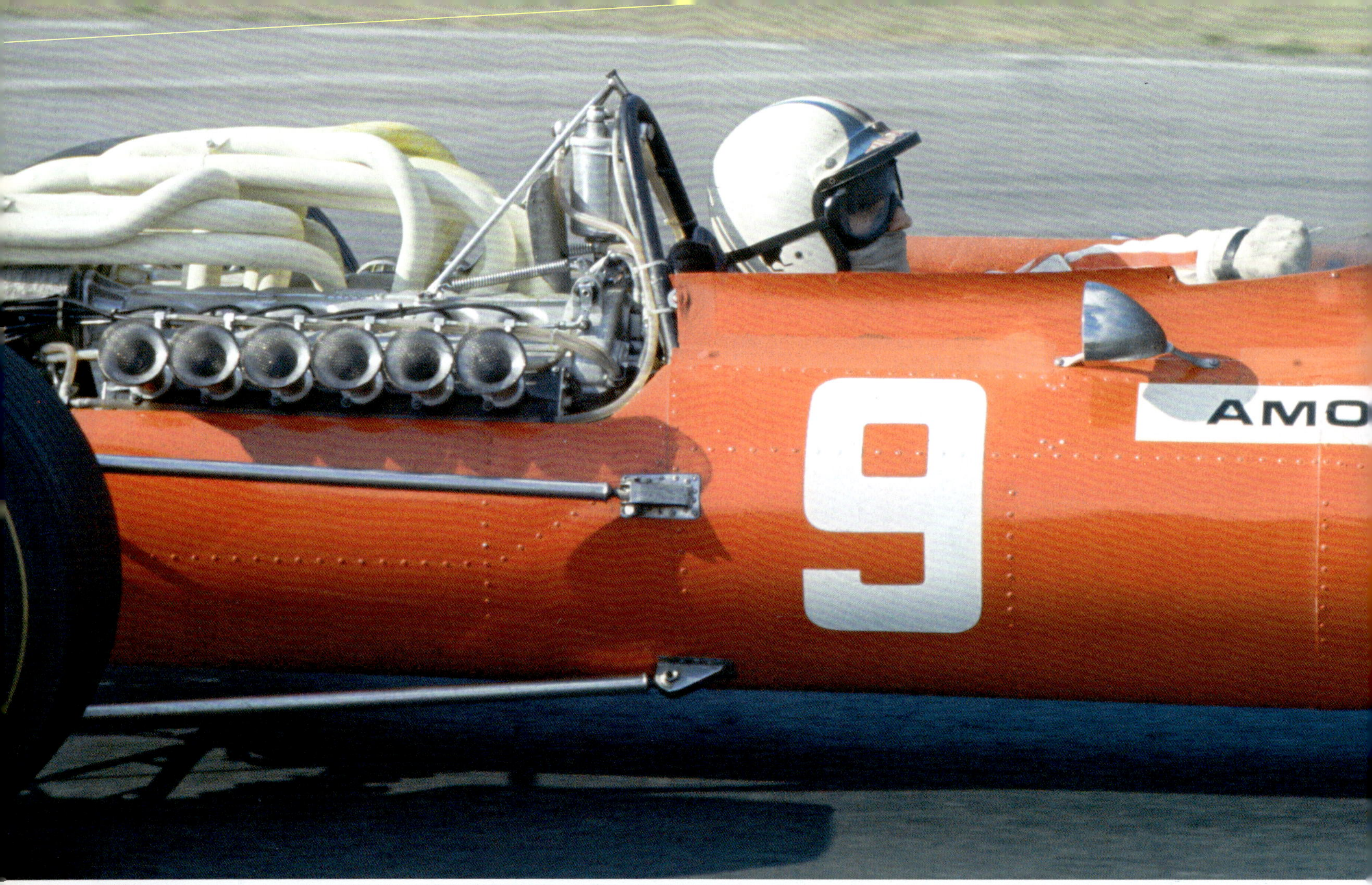
9
AMO

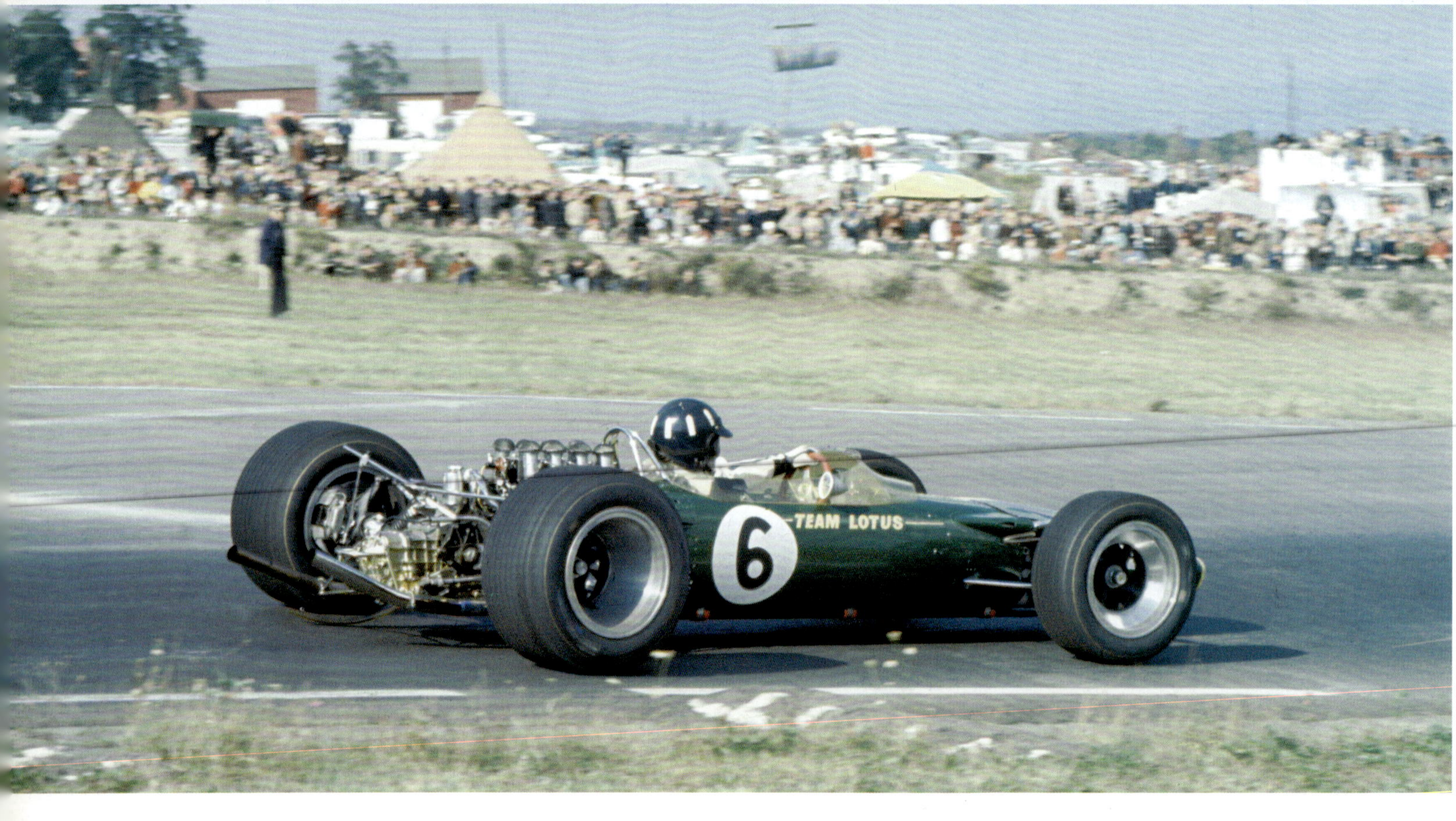
6
TEAM LOTUS

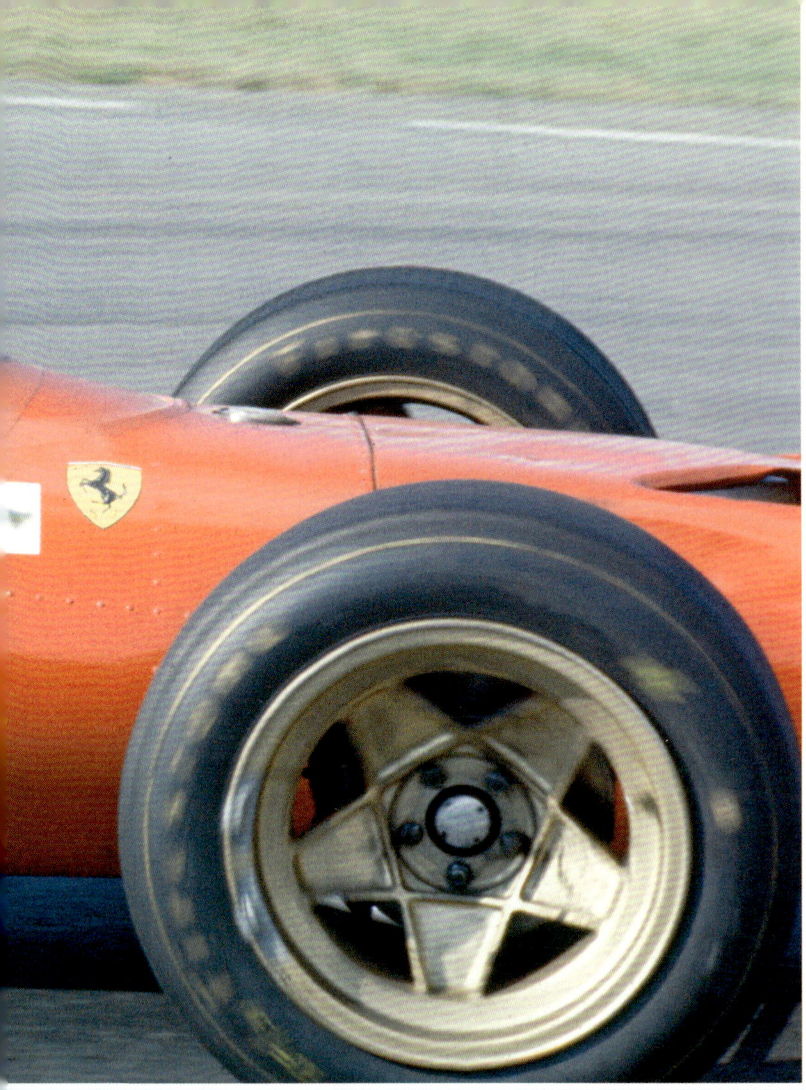

After the Spa accident to Mike Parkes, Ludovico Scarfiotti left Ferrari leaving Chris Amon to carry on alone for the next six races. Ferrari as ever were more bothered about their prototype sports cars and it showed. At Monza this new lightweight 312 (0007) appeared with a 48-valve head and the 390bhp they had claimed for the earlier 36-valve car. Amon had quite a tussle with Hill's handicapped Lotus at Watkins Glen but retired on lap 96 with falling oil pressure.

Lotus scored a 1–2 at Watkins Glen but were very lucky to do so. Graham Hill's pole sitting 49 R3 seen here suffered intermittent clutch problems after leading for 41 laps. Jim Clark took over, leaving Hill fighting Amon's Ferrari but also grappling with falling oil pressure and a broken flywheel. Then on lap 106 Clark's right rear suspension collapsed, but Lotus failed to signal Hill that Clark was in trouble. During practice, Walter Hayes of Ford, alarmed at the duo trading fastest laps, insisted that the drivers toss a coin to see who should win the race rather than risk breaking the cars. Hill had won the toss.

Just beyond the Esses at Watkins Glen is John Surtees in the Monza-winning Eric Broadley adapted Honda RA300/1 that became known as the 'Hondola'. Surtees had struggled all year with excessive weight, dodgy handling, narrow power bands and unnecessary complexity and the radically redesigned 395bhp RA300 was the response, but still weighed 609kg. The handsome car started on row six in the US GP but suffered fuel injection problems before retiring near the end with alternator failure.

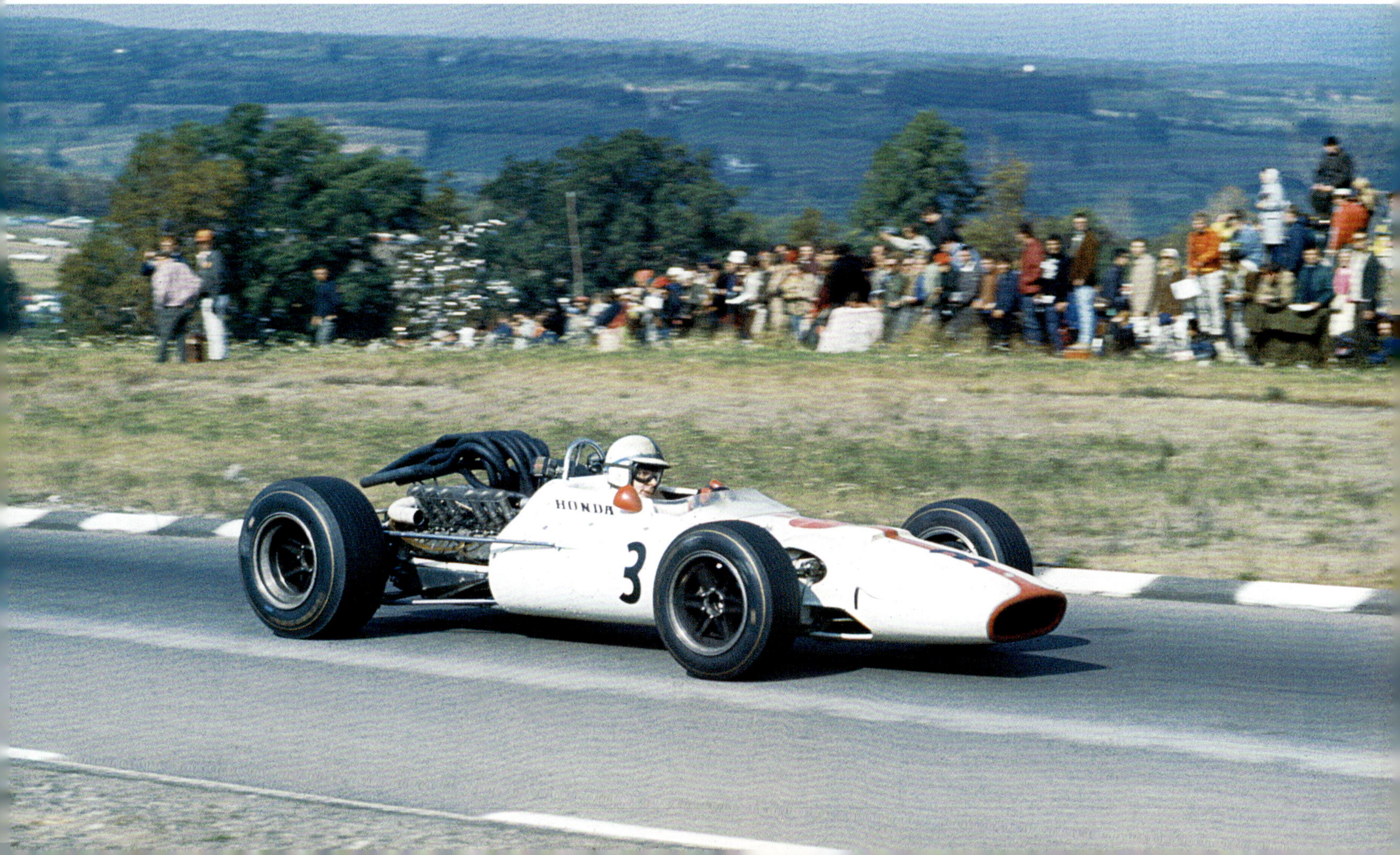

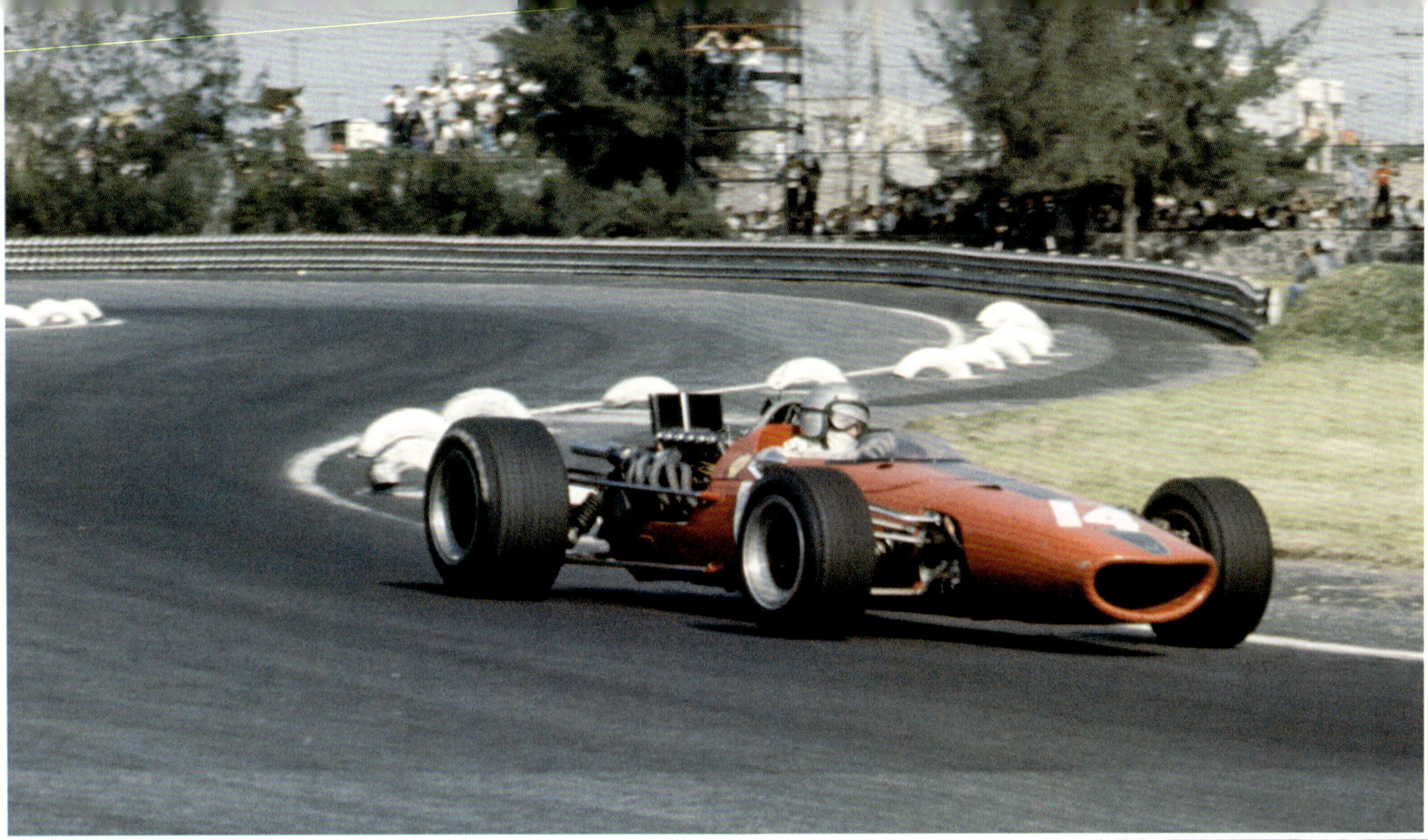

Bruce McLaren's brief sojourn at AAR ended after the German GP and he wheeled out a new 3.0-litre V12 BRM powered car, the M5A, that contested 3rd place at Monza until it blew up. It used BRM's prototype 24-valve 101 V12 that offered 365bhp (according to McLaren) or 390bhp @ 9750rpm (according to BRM's Tony Rudd). Alas it also broke down in America and Mexico.

Jackie Stewart effectively wasted a year of his F1 career at BRM with the recalcitrant H16 cars. He was outqualified at Mexico City by team mate Mike Spence in the older P83, both cars being seconds off the pace. This was his final BRM drive and after pitting early in the P115 (1151) running on 14 cylinders and, suffering a broken rev counter, he retired the 16-cylinder behemoth on lap 24. Note the shortened snout and enlarged intake in an effort to get more air and cooling to the engine due to the high altitude. Spence went on to finish 5th.

Moises Solana drove a works Lotus 49 (R2) in his home GP at Mexico City. He was 9th quickest in practice (Solana started with R1 but this was commandeered by Jim Clark leaving Moises with R2 and a tired engine), but stopped on lap 13 with front suspension failure. This tendency for suspension failures was causing considerable friction. When Clark's mechanic Allan McCall took it upon himself to beef up the car in Mexico following Clark's US travails, Colin Chapman was unappreciative. Hill's car also broke but of course Clark's did not and he won by a massive 86 seconds. Solana raced here again for Lotus before dying in a hillclimb accident in 1969.

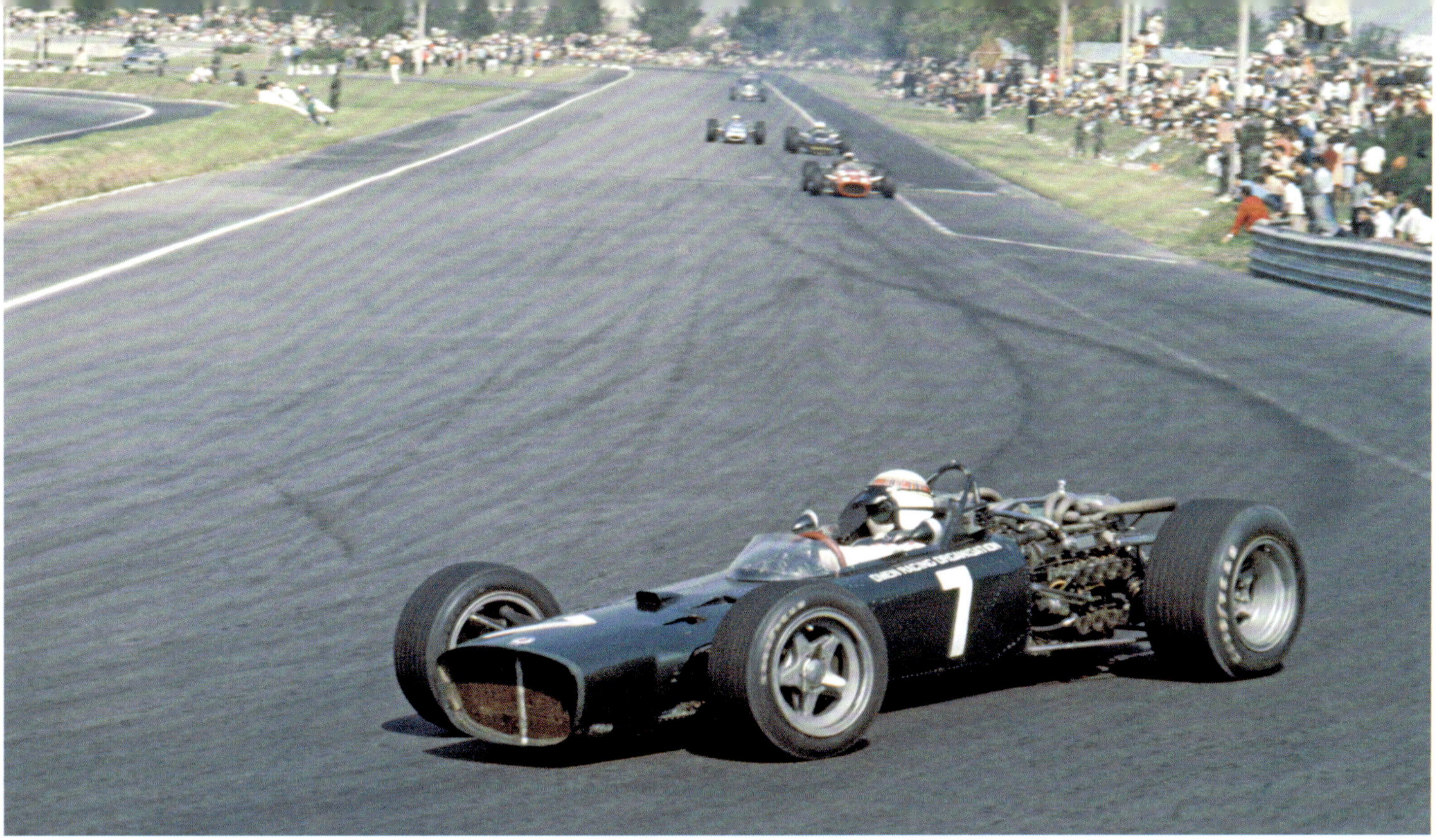
7

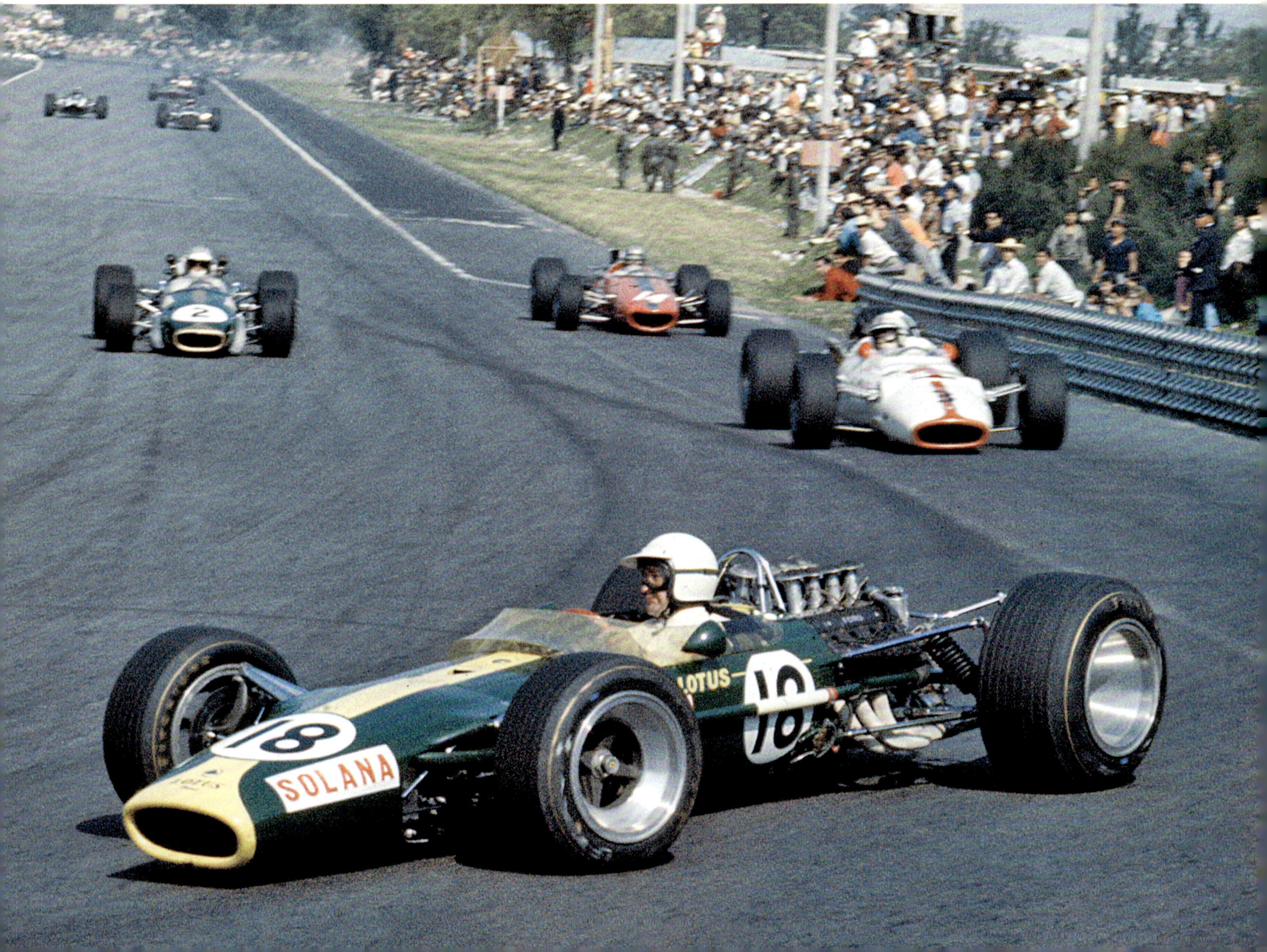
2
LOTUS
18
SOLANA

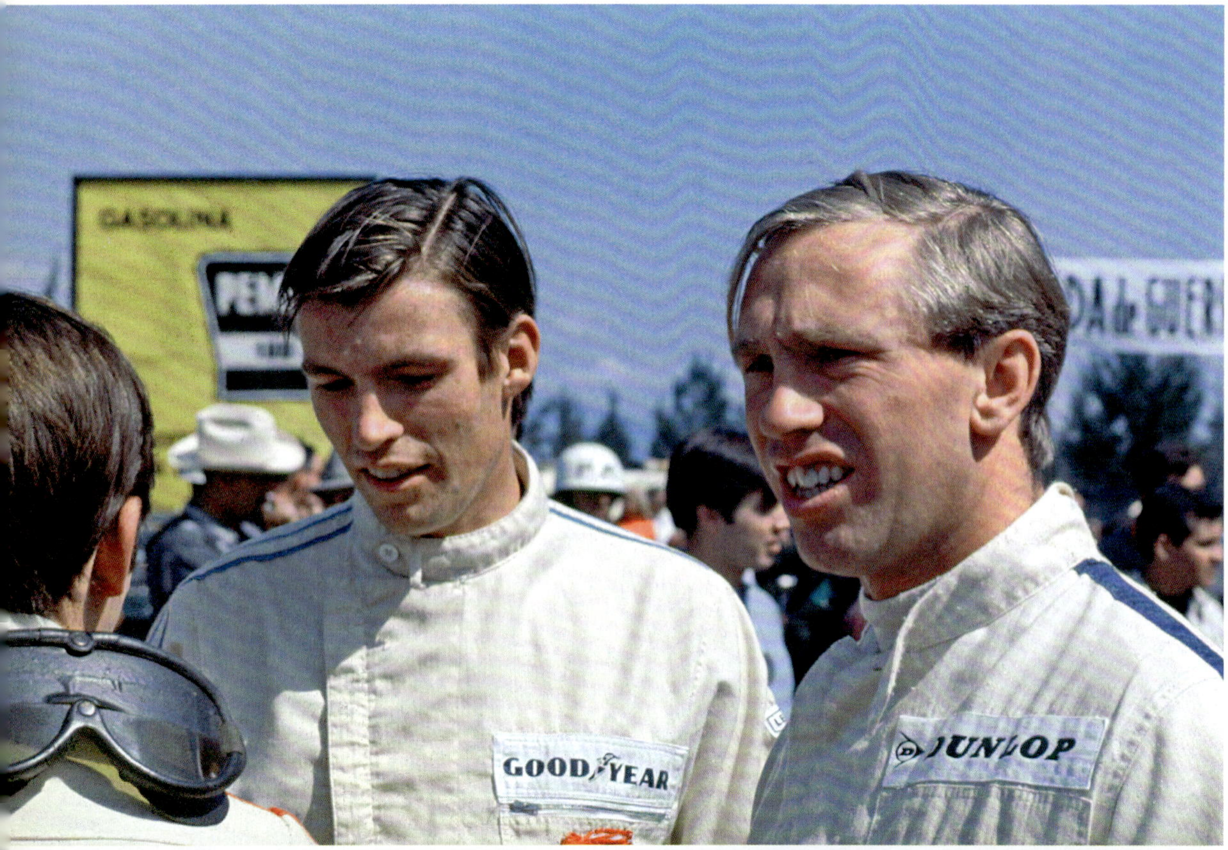

Kismet. Jackie Stewart converses with Chris Irwin (centre) and Mike Spence (right) at the Mexican GP. Stewart will join Tyrrell, and achieve a further 25 Grands Prix victories, three World Championships, future F1 team ownership and a knighthood. The aggressively brave Irwin, who drove the Parnell Racing BRMs, suffered dreadful head injuries after crashing the Ford PL3 prototype during practice for the 1968 Nürburgring 1000km that ended his career. Poor Spence showed tremendous pace with BRM's new P126 in 1968 but crashed during qualifying for the Indianapolis 500, receiving fatal head injuries.

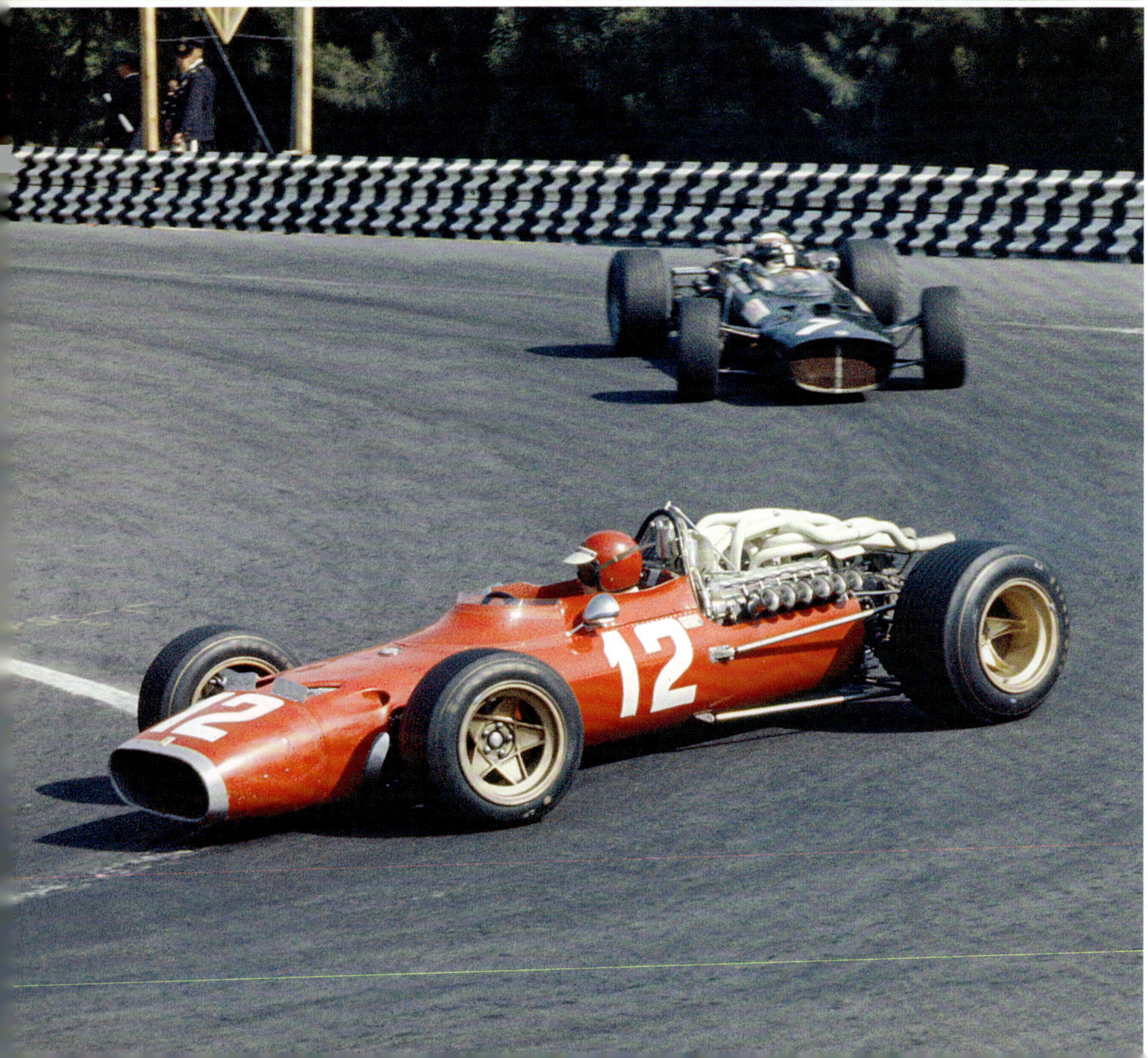

During this era Ferrari employed an eclectic choice of drivers including Italian based De Sanctis F3 star Jonathan Williams. He was contracted for 1967, but they only used him once in F1, once in F2 and in a handful of Can-Am and sports car drives before dropping him. For 1968, he raced in F2 with Frank Williams, and then sports cars until the early 1970s before retiring and turning to aviation. The Ferrari 312 (0003) took him to 8th place in the Mexican GP, followed here by Jackie Stewart's BRM P115.

1967 Teams, drivers and results

Cooper Car Co – Cooper T81/T81B Maserati V12, T86 Maserati V12
Pedro Rodriguez (MEX) (Missed Canadian, Italian and US GPs due to injury)
Jochen Rindt (A)
Jacky Ickx (B) (Italian and US GPs only)
Alan Rees (GB) (British GP only)
Richard Attwood (GB) (Canadian GP only, replacing injured Rodriguez)

Team Lotus – Lotus 43 BRM H16, 33 Climax V8, 33 BRM V8 and 49 Cosworth DFV
Jim Clark (GB)
Graham Hill (GB)
Eppie Wietzes (CDN) (Canadian GP only, entered jointly with Comstock Racing Team)
Giancarlo Baghetti (I) (Italian GP only)
Moises Solana (MEX) (US and Mexican GPs only)

Owen Racing Organisation – BRM P261, P83 H16 and P115 H16
Jackie Stewart (GB)
Mike Spence (GB)

Brabham Racing Organisation – Brabham BT19 Repco, BT20 Repco and BT24 Repco
Jack Brabham (AUS)
Denny Hulme (NZ) (WORLD CHAMPION)

SEFAC Ferrari – Ferrari 312/67
Lorenzo Bandini (I) (Fatally burned at Monaco GP)
Chris Amon (NZ) (No Ferraris entered for South African GP)
Mike Parkes (GB) (Dutch and Belgian GPs only, serious injuries at Spa end his F1 career)
Lodovico Scarfiotti (I) (Dutch and Belgian GPs only)
Jonathan Williams (GB) (Mexican GP only)

Anglo American Racers – Eagle T1G Climax 4 and T1G Weslake V12
Dan Gurney (USA)
Richie Ginther (USA) (dnq Monaco and end of Formula 1 career)
Bruce McLaren (NZ) (French, British and German GPs only)
Lodovico Scarfiotti (I) (Italian GP only)

Honda Racing – Honda RA273 and RA300
John Surtees (GB) (Missed French and Canadian GPs)

Matra Sports – Matra MS7 Cosworth (F2 car)
Johnny Servoz-Gavin (F) (Monaco GP only)
Jean-Pierre Beltoise (F) (dnq Monaco GP, US and Mexican GPs only)

Bruce McLaren Motor Racing – Mclaren M4B BRM V8 and M5A BRM V12
Bruce McLaren (NZ) (Missed South African and Belgian GPs)

Rob Walker/Jack Durlacher Racing – Cooper T81 Maserati V12
Jo Siffert (CH)

Reg Parnell Racing Ltd – Lotus 25 BRM V8, BRM P261 and BRM P83 H16
Piers Courage (GB) (South African and Monaco GPs only, dns British GP as Irwin drove car)
Chris Irwin (GB) (Missed South African and Monaco GPs, drove Courage's car at British GP)

DW Racing Enterprises – Brabham BT11 Climax 4
Bob Anderson (GB) (Fatally injured in testing accident at Silverstone in August)

Joakim Bonnier Racing Team – Cooper T81 Maserati V12
Jo Bonnier (S) (Missed Monaco, French and Dutch GPs)

Guy Ligier – Cooper T81 Maserati V12 and Brabham BT20 Repco V8
Guy Ligier (F) (Missed South African, Monaco, Dutch and Canadian GPs, used Brabham from British GP onwards)

Bernard White Racing – BRM P261
David Hobbs (GB) (British and Canadian GPs only)

Charles Vögele – Cooper T77 ATS V8
Silvio Moser (CH) (British GP only)

Castrol Oils Ltd – Eagle TG101 Climax FPF
Al Pease (CDN) (Canadian GP only)

Mike Fisher – Lotus 33 BRM V8
Mike Fisher (USA) (Canadian GP only, practised but dns Mexican GP)

John Love – Cooper T79 Climax 4
John Love (RSR) (South African GP only)

Scuderia Scribante – Brabham BT11 Climax 4
Dave Charlton (ZA) (South African GP only)

Sam Tingle – LDS Mk3 Climax 4
Sam Tingle (RSR) (South African GP only)

Luki Botha – Brabham BT7 Climax 4
Luki Botha (ZA) (South African GP only)

F2 ENTRIES RACED IN GERMAN GP

Bayerische Motoren Werke – Lola T100 BMW
Hubert Hahne (D) (This was accepted as an F1 entry by the AvD even though it was an F2 car)

Ken Tyrrell Racing – Matra MS7 Cosworth FVA
Jacky Ickx (B)

Lotus Components Ltd – Lotus 48 Cosworth FVA
Jackie Oliver (GB)

Roy Winkelmann Racing – Brabham BT18 Cosworth FVA
Alan Rees (GB)

Ecurie Ford-France – Matra MS5 Cosworth FVA
Jo Schlesser (F)

Lola Cars Ltd – Lola T100 BMW
David Hobbs (GB)

Ron Harris Racing Team – Protos Cosworth FVA
Kurt Ahrens Jnr. (D)
Brian Hart (GB)

Gerhard Mitter – Brabham BT23 Cosworth FVA
Gerhard Mitter (D)

WORLD CHAMPIONSHIP VENUES AND WINNERS (eleven rounds)

Part 1

South African GP	Kyalami	Pedro Rodriguez
Monaco GP	Monte Carlo	Denny Hulme
Dutch GP	Zandvoort	Jim Clark
Belgian GP	Spa-Francorchamps	Dan Gurney
French GP	Le Mans (Bugatti)	Jack Brabham
British GP	Silverstone	Jim Clark

Part 2

German GP	Nürburgring	Denny Hulme
Canadian GP	Mosport	Jack Brabham
Italian GP	Monza	John Surtees
United States GP	Watkins Glen	Jim Clark
Mexican GP	Mexico City	Jim Clark

DRIVERS' CHAMPIONSHIP

Points: 9-6-4-3-2-1 (awarded only to best-placed finisher). Best 5 scores counted from Part 1 (six races), plus best 4 scores from Part 2 (five races).

1	Denny Hulme	Brabham	51
2	Jack Brabham	Brabham	46
3	Jim Clark	Lotus	41
4	John Surtees	Honda	20
5	Chris Amon	Ferrari	20
6	Pedro Rodriguez	Cooper	15
7	Graham Hill	Lotus	15
8	Dan Gurney	Eagle	13
9	Jackie Stewart	BRM	10
10	Mike Spence	BRM	9
11	John Love	Cooper	6
12	Jochen Rindt	Cooper	6
13	Jo Siffert	Cooper	6
14	Bruce McLaren	Eagle/McLaren	3
15	Jo Bonnier	Cooper	3
16	Bob Anderson	Brabham	2
17	Mike Parkes	Ferrari	2
18	Chris Irwin	Lotus/BRM	2
19	Lodovico Scarfiotti	Ferrari/Eagle	1
20	Guy Ligier	Cooper	1
21	Jacky Ickx	Cooper	1

CONSTRUCTORS' CHAMPIONSHIP

Points: 9-6-4-3-2-1 (awarded only to best-placed finisher). Best 5 scores counted from Part 1 (six races), plus best 4 scores from Part 2 (five races).

1	Brabham-Repco	63
2	Lotus-Ford (Cosworth)	44
3	Cooper-Maserati	28
4	Honda	20
5	Ferrari	20
6	BRM	17
7	Eagle-Weslake	13
8	Cooper-Climax	6
9	Lotus-BRM	6
10	McLaren-BRM	3
11	Brabham-Climax	2

1968

ANNUS HORRIBILIS

1968 was a truly dreadful year even by the cruel standards of the day. The era's greatest driver Jim Clark together with Mike Spence, Ludovico Scarfiotti and Jo Schlesser all perished within a few months.

The year started off predictably with Clark winning the South African GP, the last time in the familiar Team Lotus colours. During the Tasman series Team Lotus metamorphosed into Gold Leaf Team Lotus, the first European F1 team to rebrand itself with a sponsor's identity.

Following Clark's demise Lotus looked vulnerable, but Graham Hill responded by winning the Spanish GP, the latest addition to the calendar, and went on to a second World Championship following mid-season woes. Jack Oliver was drafted in but experienced all sorts of mishaps most not of his own making. The team also employed the brilliant Mario Andretti at Watkins Glen where he posted pole position.

Jackie Stewart departed BRM to join his 1964 mentor and F1 newcomer Ken Tyrrell. The French manufacturer Matra provided the car(s) and Cosworth the engines. He won three GPs and was runner-up in the championship. Matra's official version with a V12 engine was handled by Jean-Pierre Beltoise and later Henri Pescarolo. It showed initial promise but had flattered only to deceive.

Bruce McLaren's new M7 was the other recipient of Cosworth's DFV, boasting Gulf Oil sponsorship and he was joined by reigning World Champion Denny Hulme who had left Brabham. Bruce won the Belgian GP whilst Denny took the Italian and Canadian rounds. They were championship contenders up to the final race.

The gap at Brabham was filled by Jochen Rindt who had been lured on board by the promise of a new four-cam Repco engine, but it was a mechanical disaster. Jack Brabham and Rindt won no races and scored just ten points between them. John Surtees had a new Honda, the RA301, but it proved to be unreliable, albeit quick at times. A second place in France, that was overshadowed by Schlesser's death in the air-cooled RA302, was the best result.

Ferrari retained Chris Amon to be partnered by the young Jacky Ickx who won the French GP, but once again no victories for Amon. Also briefly employed were Andrea de Adamich and Derek Bell. BRM hired Pedro Rodriguez to join the doomed Spence who was replaced by Richard Attwood (and briefly Bobby Unser), but their season fell apart after a promising start with the new V12 P126/133.

Coopers continued their decline despite new BRM V12 engines and a plethora of drivers including Ludovico Scarfiotti and Brian Redman who was badly injured at Spa. Also in decline were the woefully unreliable and underfinanced AAR Eagles and Gurney ended the year driving a McLaren. The only independent team of note was Rob Walker who bought a Lotus 49 (later replaced by a 49B) driven as ever by Jo Siffert. He won the British GP and enjoyed a late season rise in form.

The non-championship races at Brands Hatch and Silverstone fell to McLaren and Hulme, leaving the Oulton Park Gold Cup to Stewart's Matra.

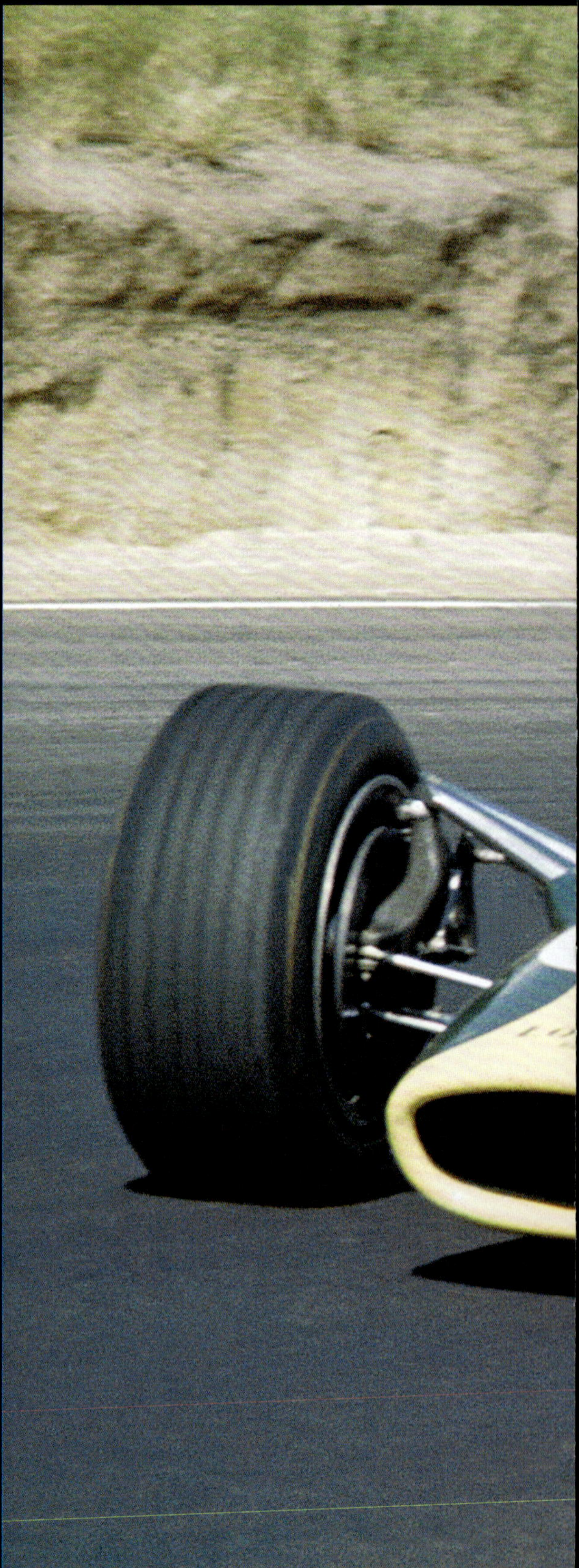

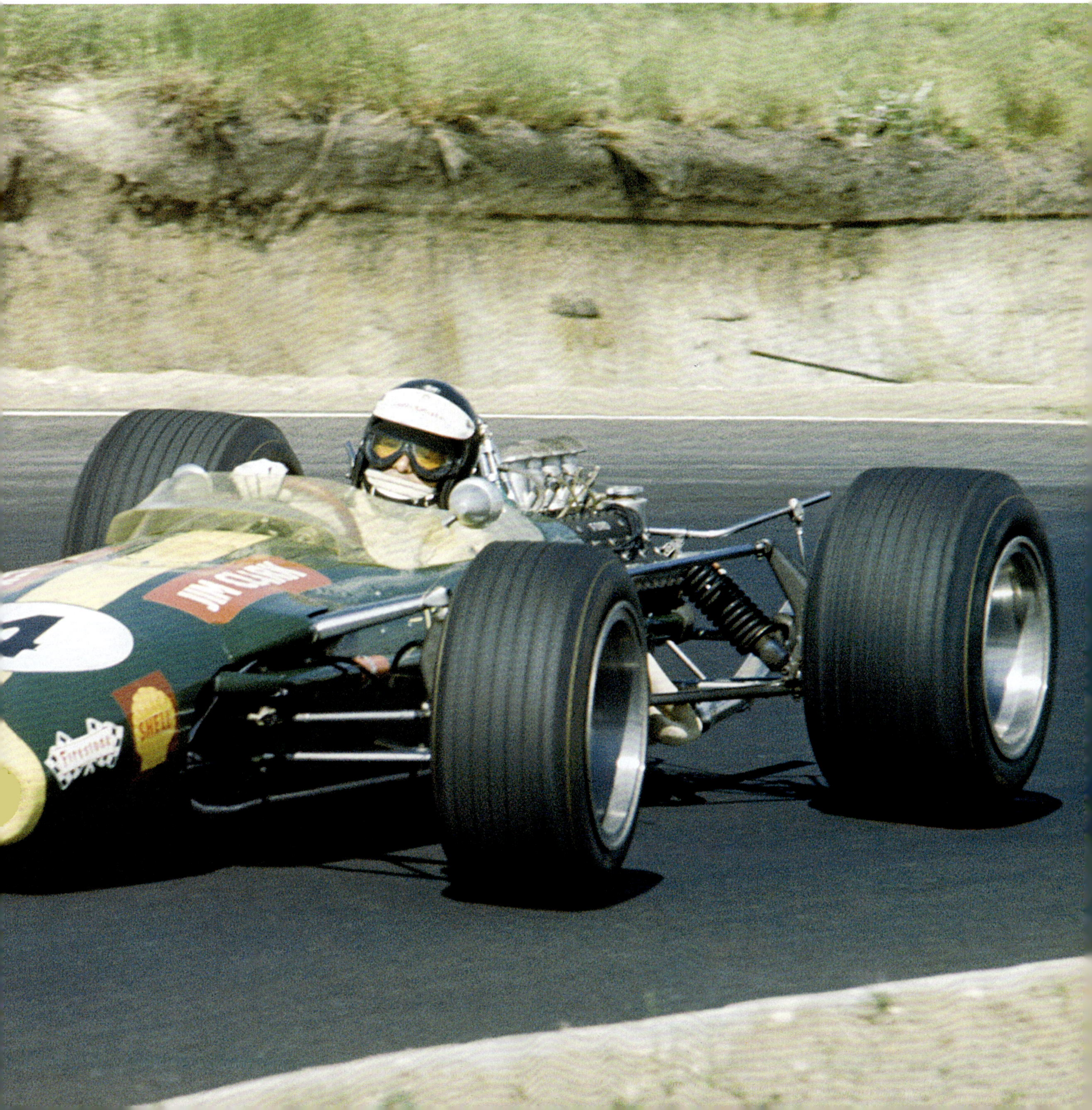

Its all over now. Jim Clark's final GP victory at Kyalami on 1 January 1968 was achieved in a new Lotus 49 (R4). He started from pole, led from lap two onwards, set fastest lap and beat team mate Graham Hill, whose car had an inoperative clutch for half the race, by 25.3 seconds. This was the final Grand Prix appearance of Team Lotus in their familiar green/yellow stripe colours.

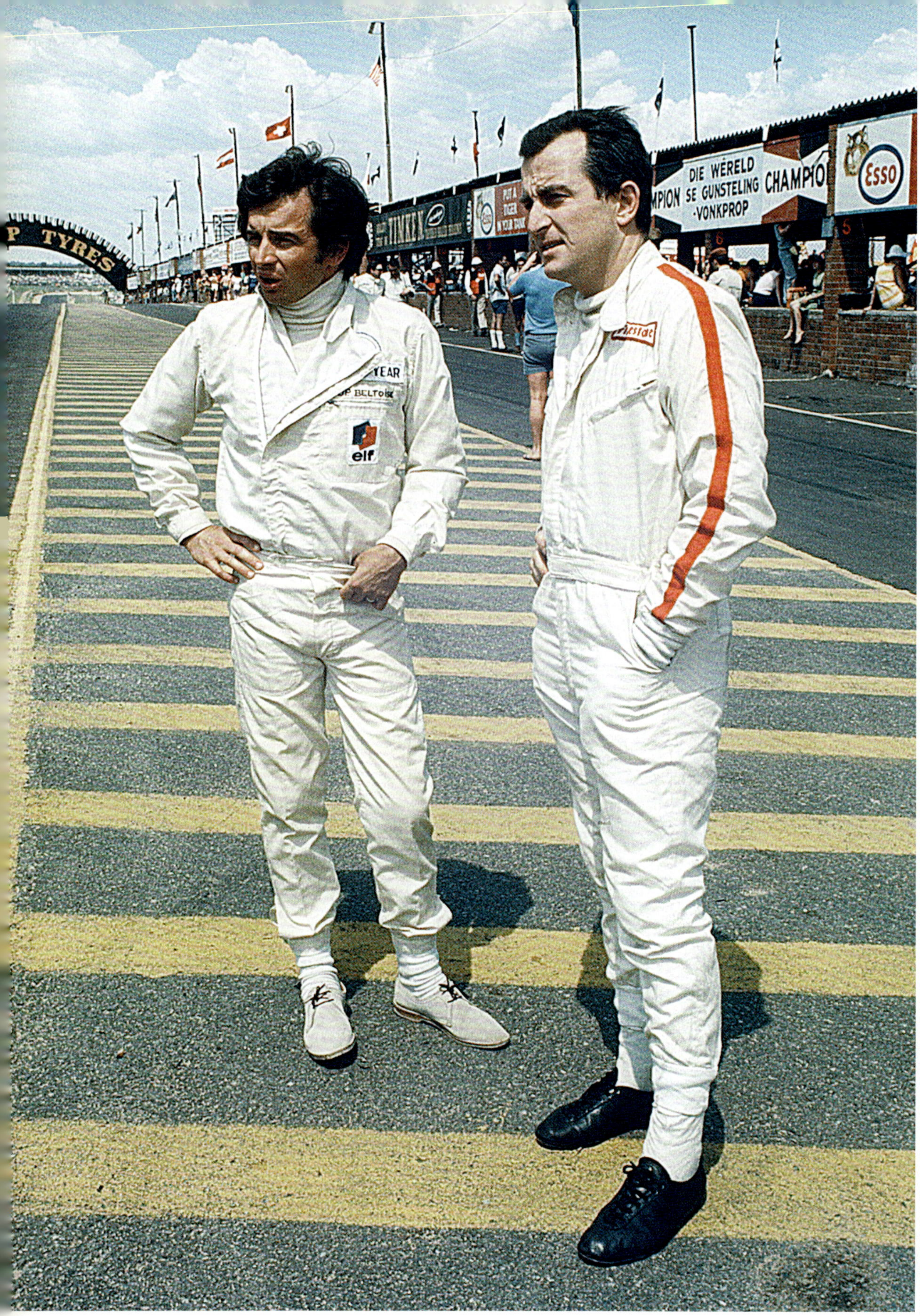

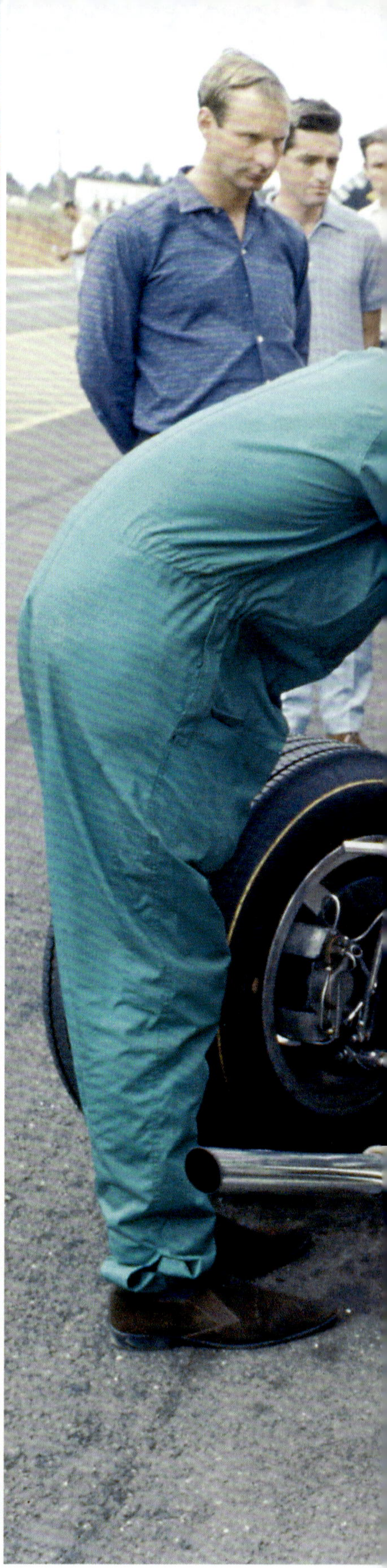

Jean-Pierre Beltoise (left) at the South African GP, Kyalami. His slightly awkward stance was the result of multiple injuries including a very badly smashed left arm that was permanently impaired after a crash at Reims in 1964. He raced a Matra F2 car here and finished 6th whilst awaiting the new V12 Matra MS11. Keeping him company is Ludovico Scarfiotti who had joined Cooper for 1968, but sadly perished in a hillclimb crash at Rossfeld in Germany in June driving a works Porsche.

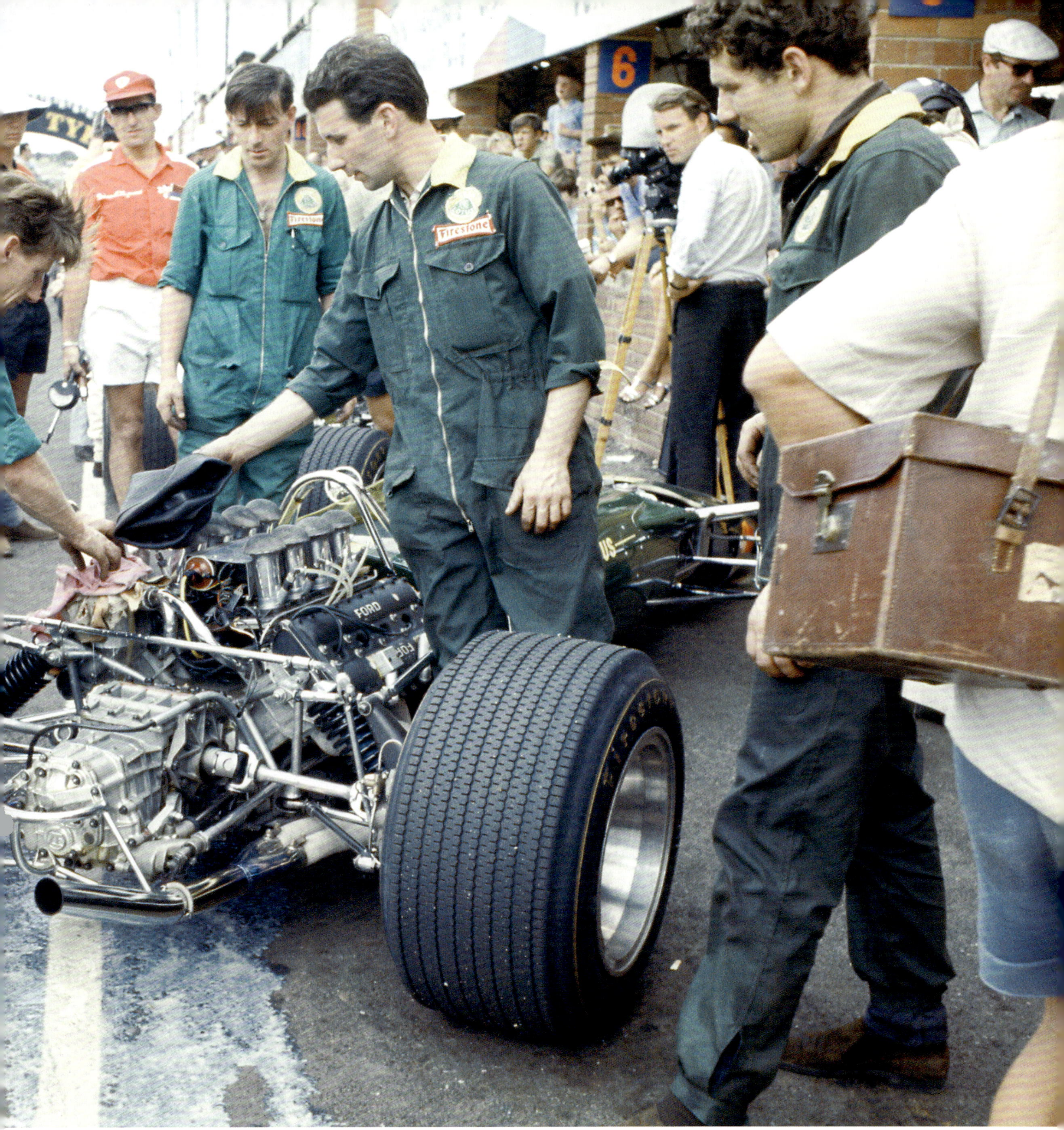

One of the Lotus 49s being prepared for practice by (left to right) Gordon Huckle, Dougie Bridge, Bob Dance and Dale Porteous. Team manager Andrew Ferguson wears the white shirt and slacks whilst 'Chunky' can be glimpsed, upper right, in the white flat cap.

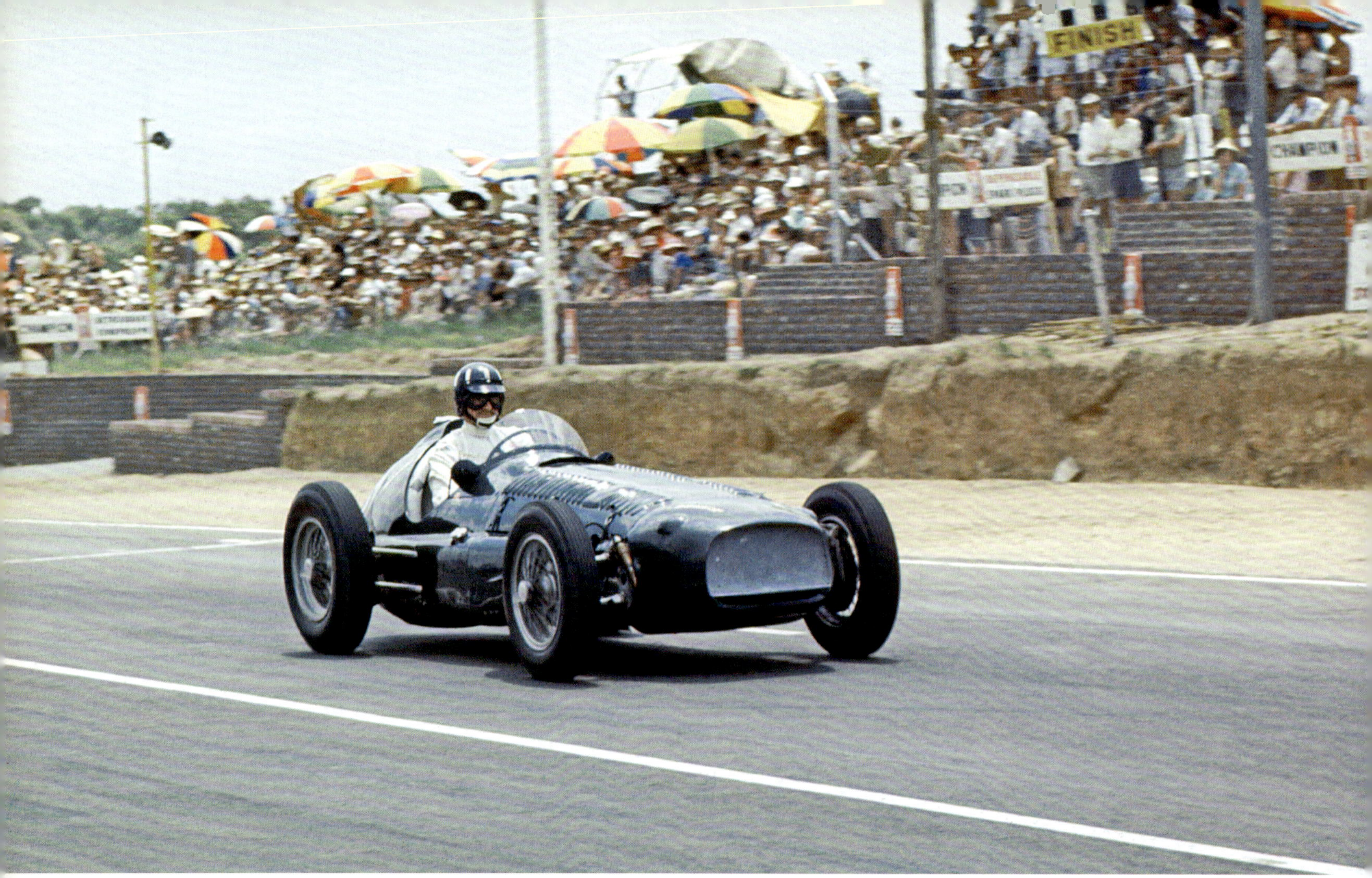
FINISH
CHAMPION

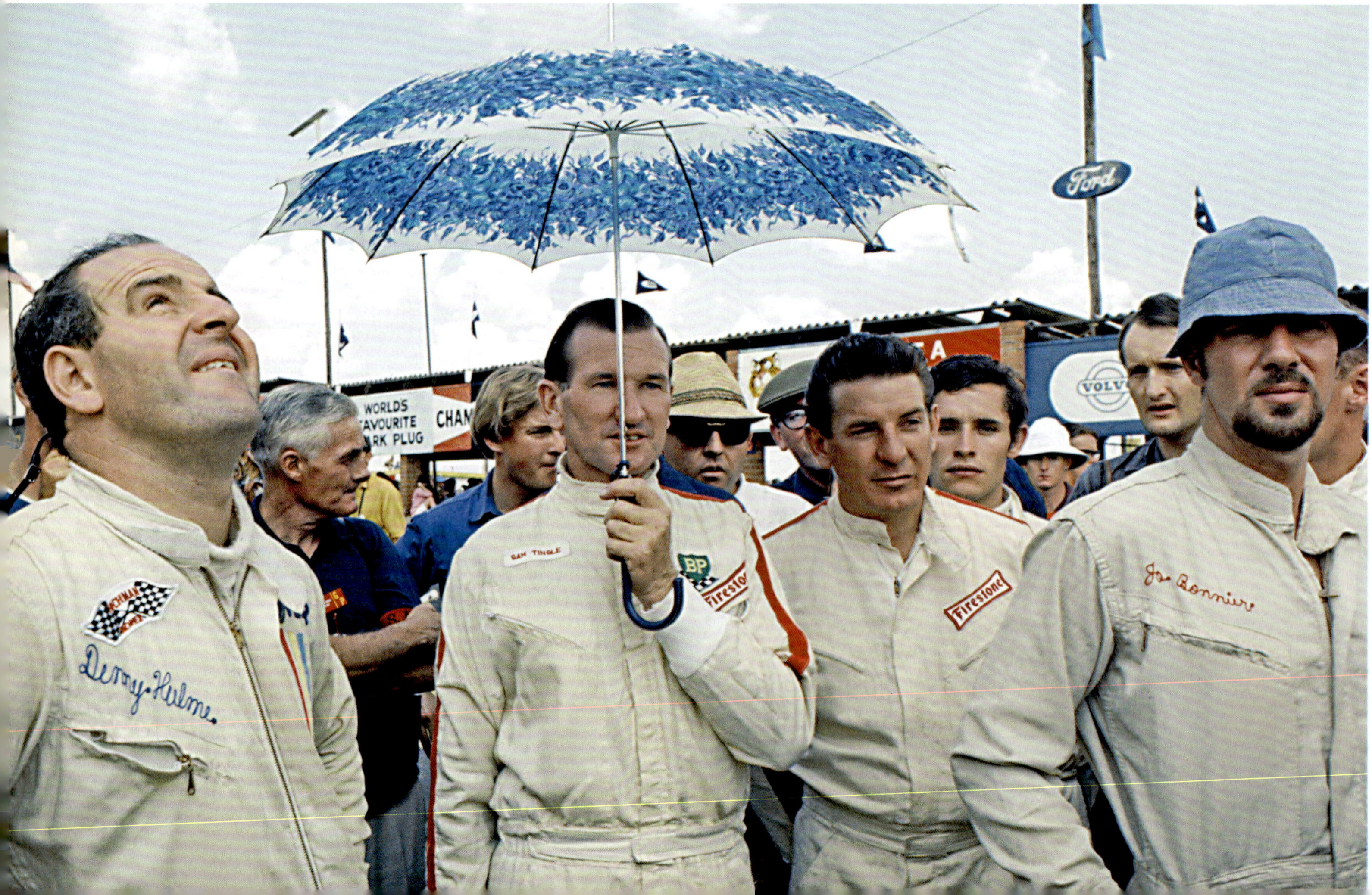
Ford
WORLDS
FAVOURITE
ARK PLUG
CHAM
VOLVO
Denny Hulme
SAM TINGLE
BP
Firestone
Firestone
Jo Bonnier

← 1962 BRM World Champion Graham Hill drove Rubery Owen's BRM V16 Mk2 at Kyalami as part of a public relations exercise for their locally owned subsidiaries on race morning. He was impressed by the power but his comments about the rest of the car were unrepeatable! I cannot under any circumstances envisage a latter day F1 star being allowed to demonstrate another team's historic car for PR purposes.

↙ The boys are back in town, for the South African GP. Denny Hulme keeps a wary eye open for the vultures while Sam Tingle (with brolly) who originally hailed from England, is taking no chances. Local Jackie Pretorious seems quizzical as Jacky Ickx peers over his shoulder and Jo Bonnier (blue hat) looks menacing.

→ Jackie Stewart's prototype F2 based Matra MS9 entered by Matra International (Ken Tyrrell) enjoyed an encouraging debut in South Africa lining up third quickest in practice. Stewart briefly led before Jim Clark and later Graham Hill swept by. Sporting a green undercoat the car's restricted fuel capacity would have necessitated a pit stop but the Cosworth DFV dropped a valve whilst running third in the car's only race.

↓ Robin Herd designed the handsome looking McLaren M7A with a 'bathtub' aluminium monocoque but then departed to Cosworth leaving Gordon Coppuck to complete construction of the new DFV powered cars (Gulf Oil sponsorship paid for five engines). They had a terrific debut with Bruce winning the 1968 Race of Champions at Brands Hatch in the first M7A/1 and newly joined Hulme 3rd in M7A/2. Five weeks later they finished 1st (Hulme) and 2nd (McLaren) at the Silverstone International Trophy. This is Druids hairpin on a typically chilly March day.

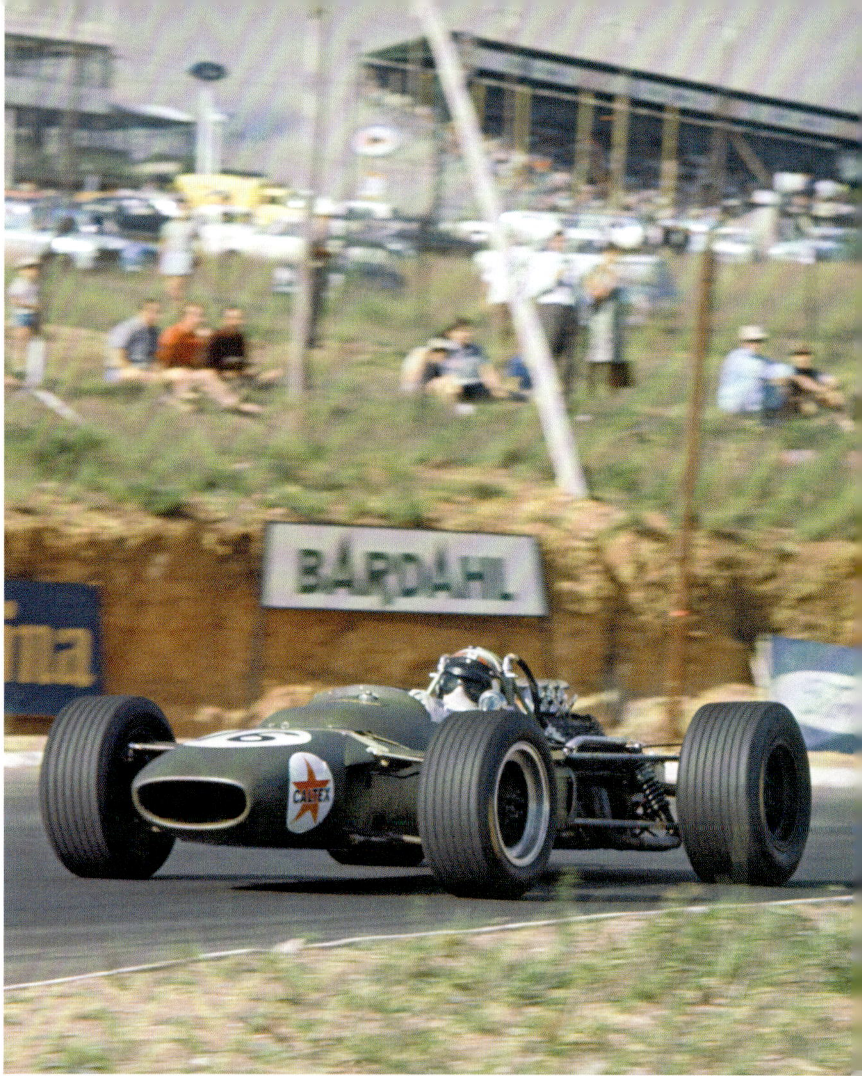

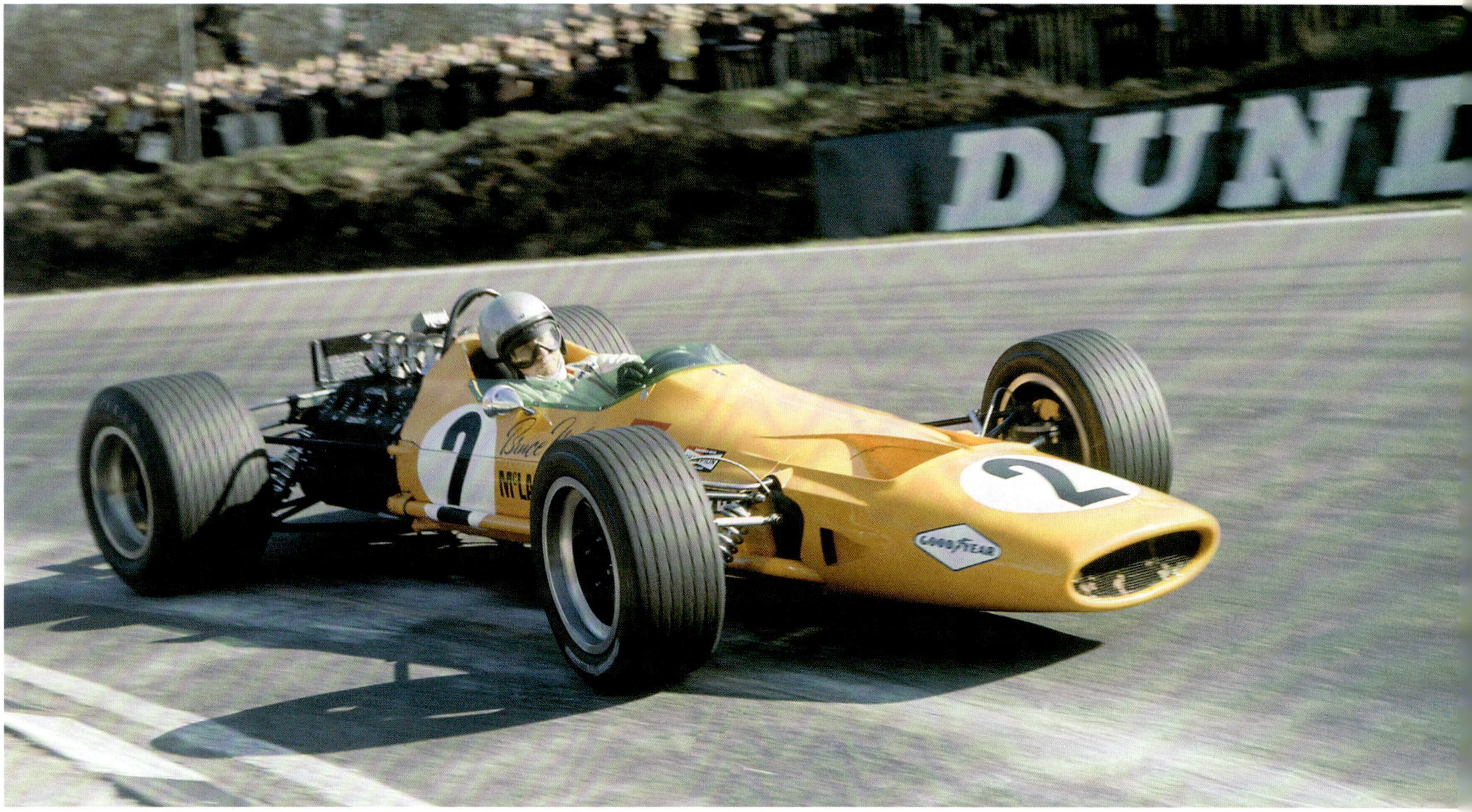

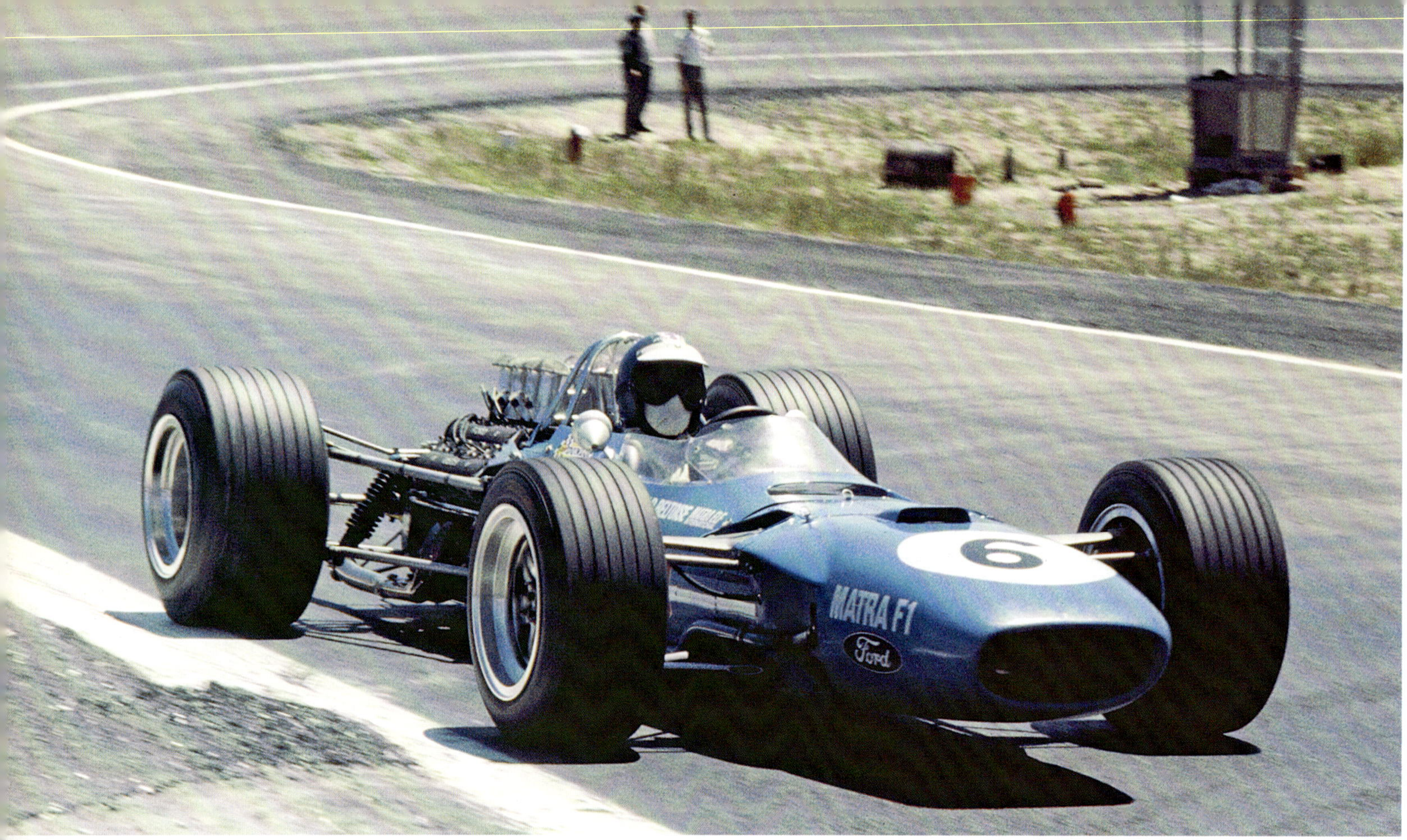

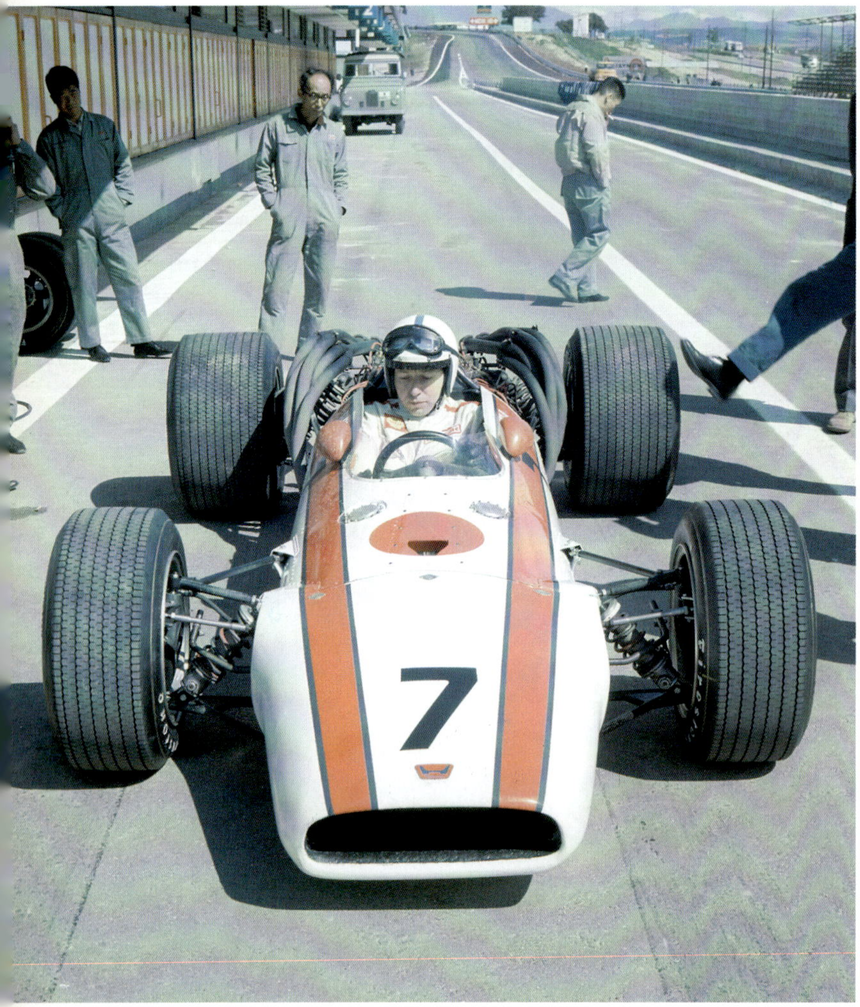

The Spanish GP at Jarama seemed distinctly odd without Jim Clark. Jackie Stewart was also absent after fracturing his wrist in an F2 race, so Jean-Pierre Beltoise stepped up to the plate to drive the Matra MS10-01 Cosworth first seen at Brands Hatch. This was the car that replaced the Kyalami 'mule' MS9 and weighed 560kg. He led the race until an oil leak delayed him, then rejoined to finish 5th and setting fastest lap. Pedro Rodriguez (BRM) and Chris Amon (Ferrari) also led but ultimately it was Graham Hill who gave the new Gold Leaf colours their first GP victory with the Lotus 49.

Cooper's new T86B was powered by a BRM 24 valve V12 originally intended for sports car racing, employing 'Lulu' Scarfiotti (front car F1-2-68) and Brian Redman (behind F1-1-68). They had lost their long standing BP support during 1967 and then their free Firestone tyre supply as well. There were only 13 starters at Jarama and many retirements so Redman finished 3rd in his T86B ahead of Scarfiotti whose 4th place was actually last. When Brian joined Hill and Hulme on the victory parade Graham turned to him and said "Christ almighty, don't tell me you were bloody third!" The spindly cranked lower front wishbones look very fragile (see Redman's Spa crash) and note the totally exposed disc brakes/pads. In June 1969 the team was auctioned off and one of the cars was bought for £1500 by John Scott-Davies whilst a 24 valve V12 BRM engine fetched £650!

Honda's new car the FA301 (F-801), an allegedly lightweight development was actually 41kg heavier than the superseded FA300. John Surtees ran as high as 3rd until gear selection trouble intervened, but the heavily revised V12 engine with resited exhausts still suffered fuel injection complications and the car's handling was inconsistent. At least one person wants to kick the recalcitrant machine in the Jarama pitlane.

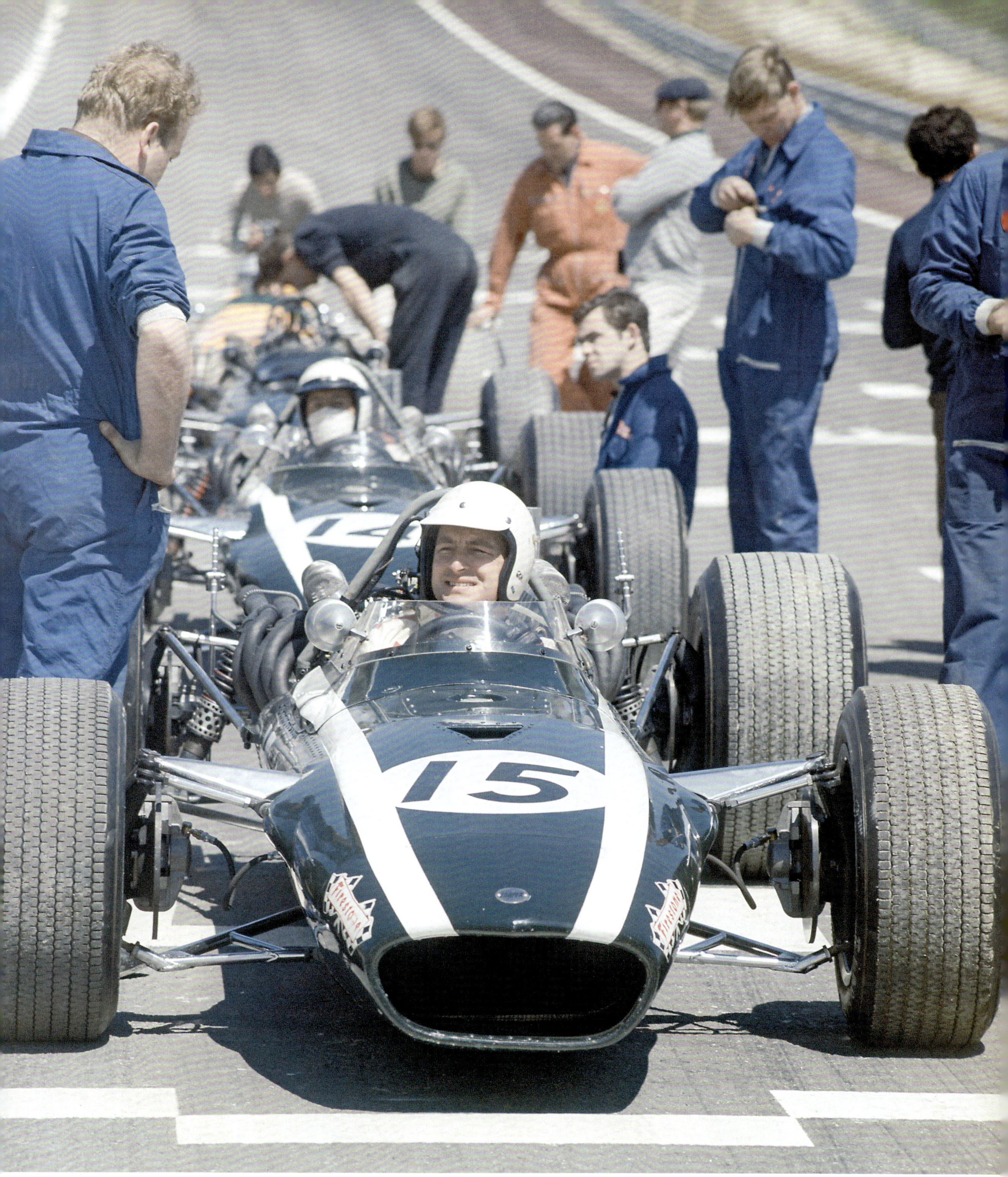
15
14

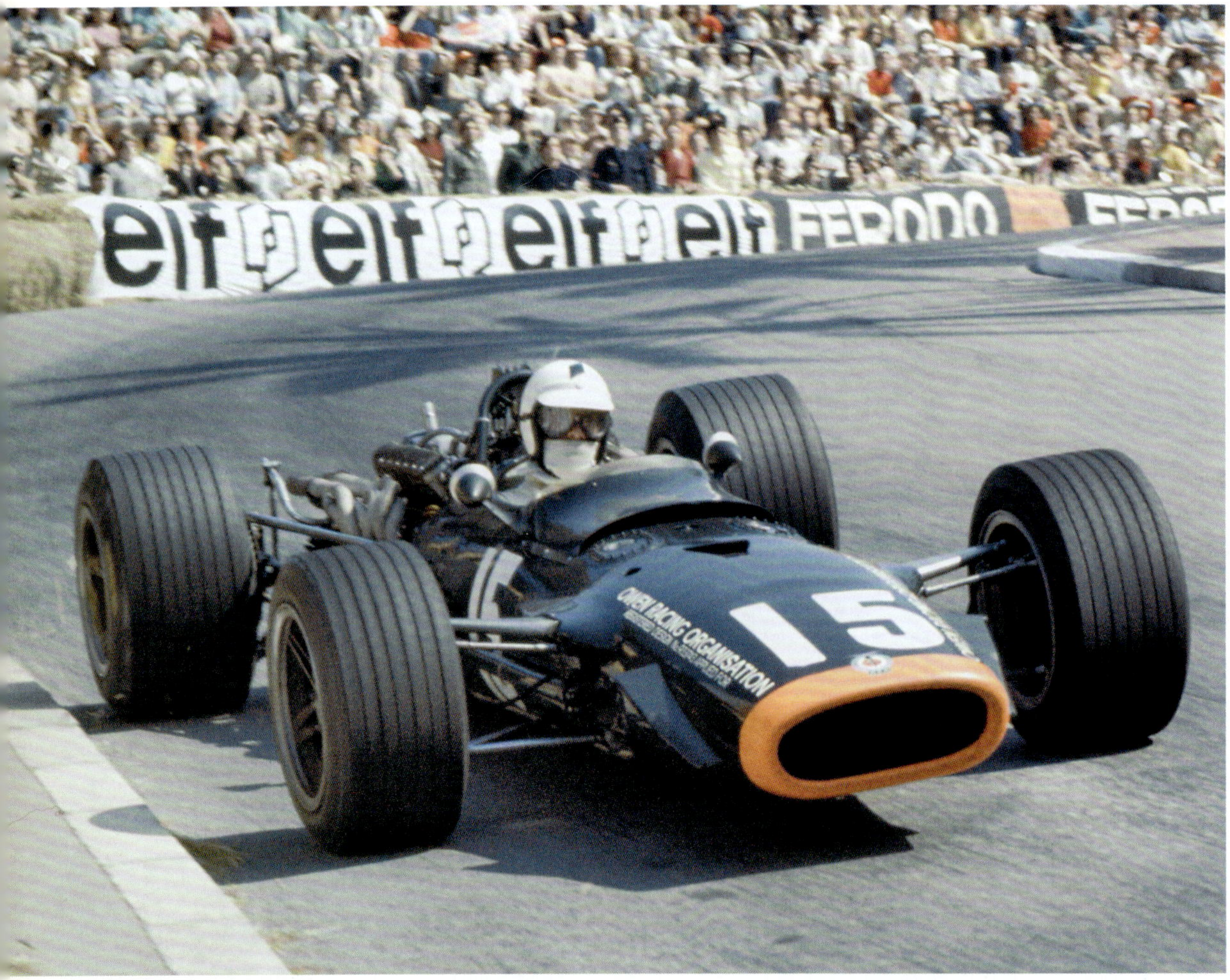

Following Mike Spence's fatal accident Richard Attwood impressed at Monaco. After all the early retirements he spent 63 laps in his BRM P126/03 (the P83/115 H16 replacement), chasing Graham Hill. The gap was closed to within 2.2 seconds at the flag and Attwood set the fastest lap, a tenth quicker than Hill's pole. A fantastic effort.

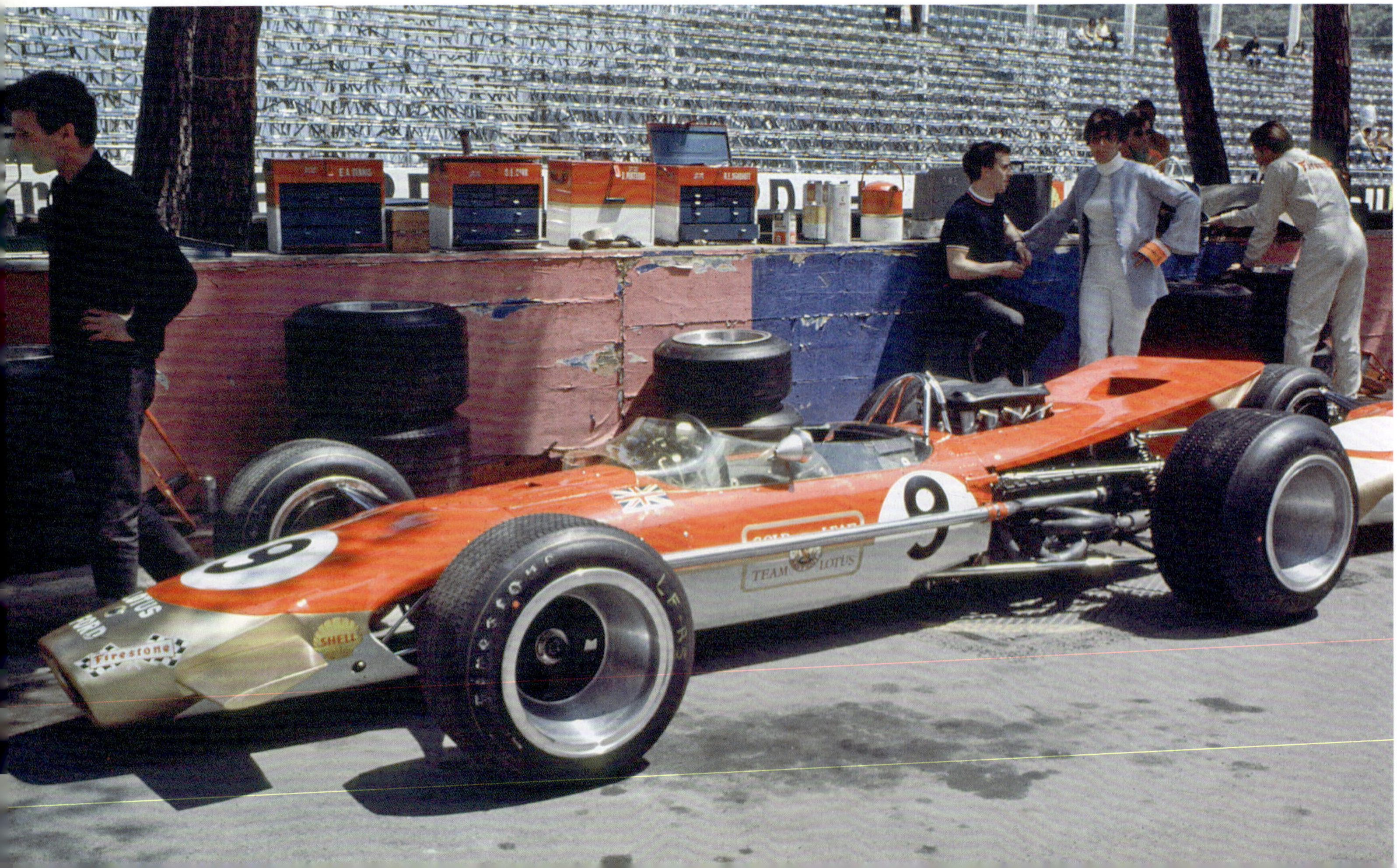

Graham Hill's fourth Monaco GP victory came despite, according to *Autosport*, sitting in a pool of petrol for some time. The new Lotus 49B (R5) featured a slightly narrower monocoque, improved suspension geometry, a Hewland gearbox and a new upswept tail body style. Its 15 inch rims were the widest yet seen in F1. New team mate Jack Oliver became involved in somebody else's accident and by lap 17 there were only five cars still racing!

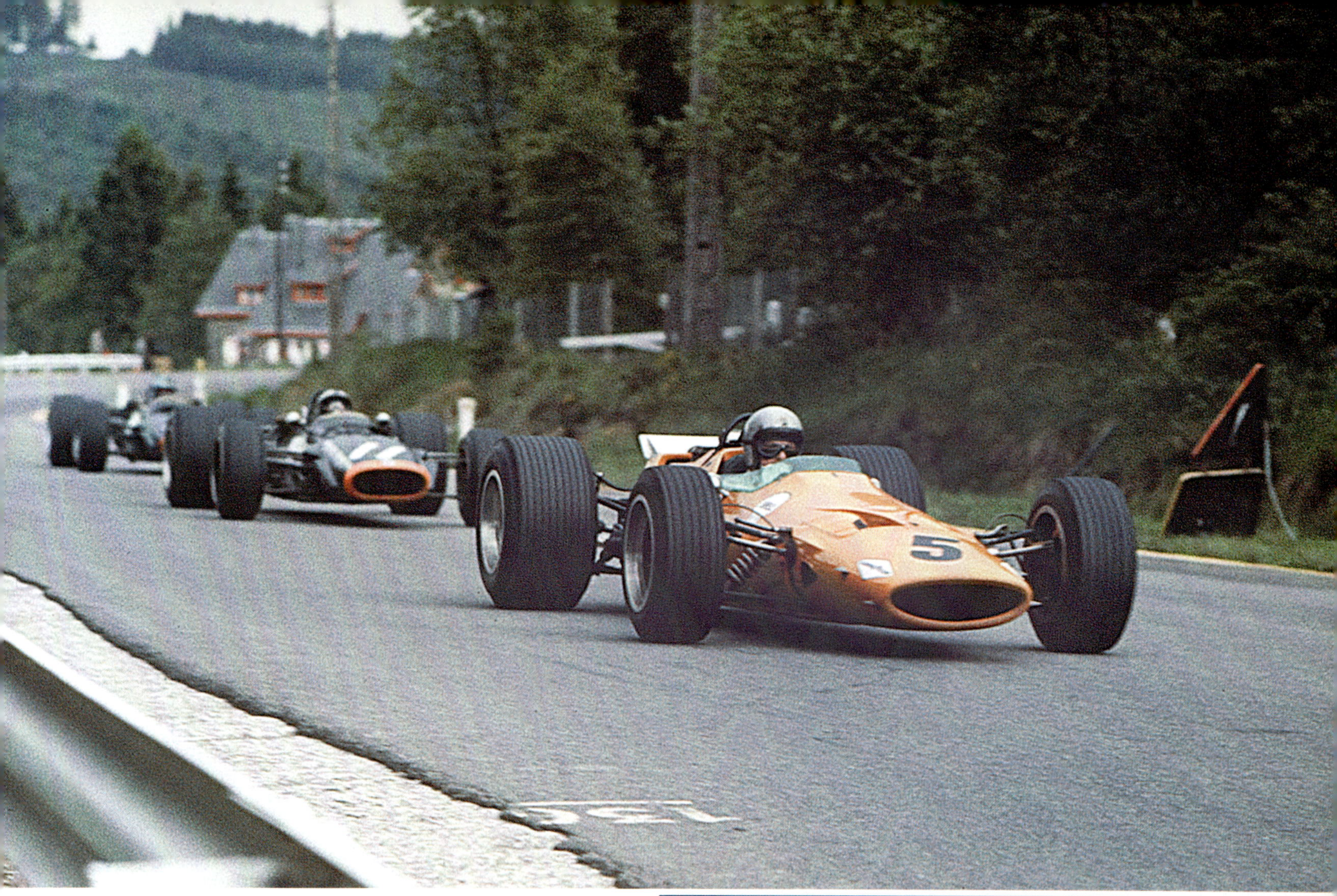

↑ The 1968 Belgian GP was the last of the decade and was also Bruce McLaren's final GP win. Early on the Ferraris of Chris Amon and Jacky Ickx battled with John Surtees's Honda, but Amon retired with a holed radiator and Surtees with suspension failure. The second half of the race was dominated by the returning Jackie Stewart, still with his injured wrist in a cast with McLaren running 3rd. However Stewart had to stop for fuel on the last lap (a Spa speciality) and was further delayed by a flat battery, dropping to 4th. Bruce won in his M7A-3 followed here by Pedro Rodriguez's 2nd place BRM P133-01 ahead of Jacky Ickx's Ferrari 312.

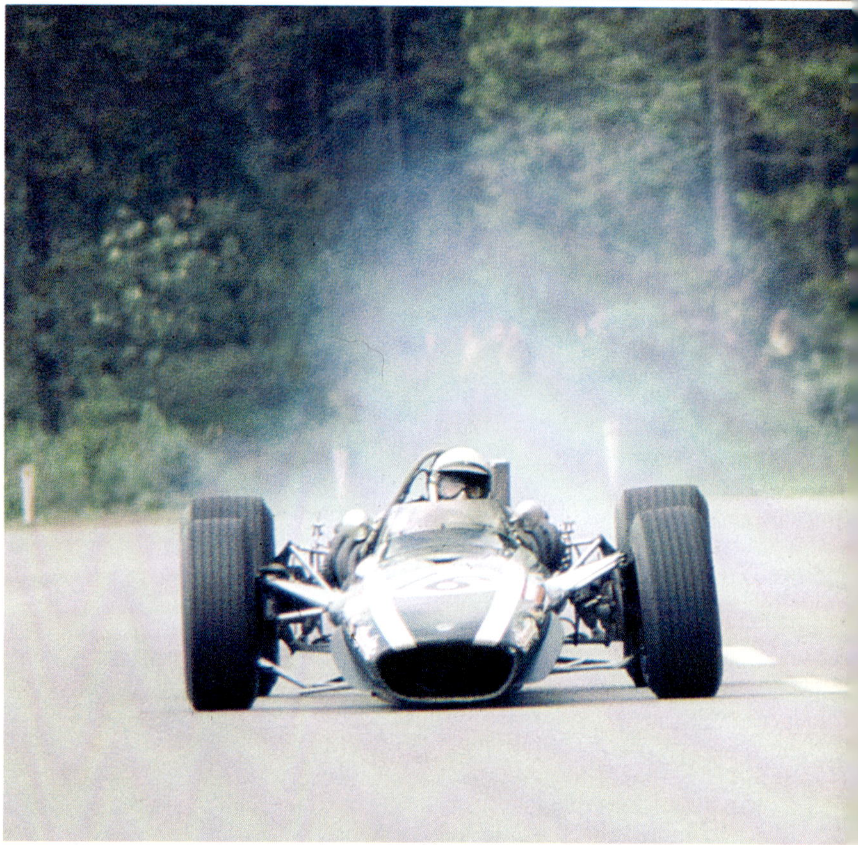

→ Brian Redman recalled in 2005 that John Cooper blamed him for his Spa crash. Fortunately Peter Burn's picture in *Autosport* showed the Cooper T86B's lower right front wishbone snapping under braking for Les Combes. It rolled over the barrier into a marshall's post, hit a parked car, caught fire and lost three wheels, one of which struck a marshall who suffered a heart attack and a ruptured spleen. Brian's crushed arm had compound fractures. It was a scene from hell. Redman's career was interrupted at a vital point and five months later he had to have another operation to reset the arm because the broken bones had not knitted together. Despite further serious injuries he became one of the world's greatest sports car drivers, a three times winner of the SCCA Formula 5000 series, the 1981 IMSA Camel GTP series and more.

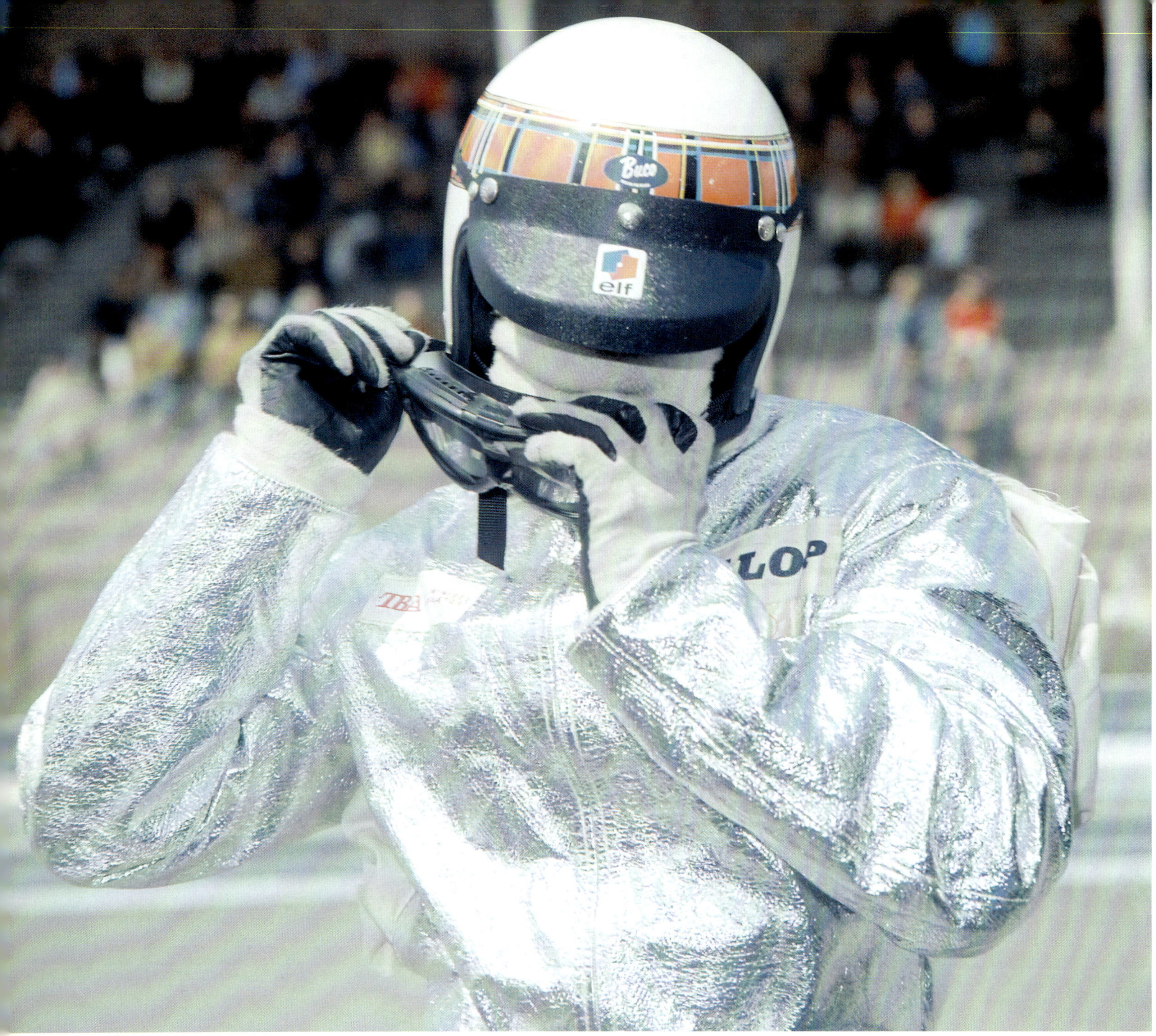

↑ Not suitable for a microwave. All of Jackie Stewart's driving suits post 1968 were made and supplied by Michel Finquel of NASA, not the American space agency but a French company. This aluminised asbestos apparel was tried during practice at Kyalami and Zandvoort whilst the Buco headgear was *de rigueur* until the Bell Star full face helmets took over in 1969.

↗ Displaying his phenomenal car control, Jochen Rindt presses on at a wet Dutch GP in his Brabham BT26-2 with its fragile four-cam Repco V8 (that was originally based on BMW's Apfelbeck F2 unit). He retired due to a damp ignition and then a flat battery. The engine had torsional vibration problems causing continual valvegear failure and was a disaster. Brabham designer Ron Tauranac's assessment of the Austrian rebuffs popular legend, "Rindt contrary to some opinions was easy to get along with, we shared a room at races, he probably did twice as many gear changes as Jack, keeping the engine at high revs continuously with little performance gain but wearing the engine out faster."

→ After disappointing at Monaco and Spa, Beltoise drove the V12 Matra MS11-01 to 2nd place behind Jackie Stewart at a wet Zandvoort, setting fastest lap despite a spin and a pitstop to clear his throttle slides. The Georges Martin designed 60-degree V12 developed 420bhp but with an unuseable power curve. A different exhaust system cured the problem but lost 30 bhp.

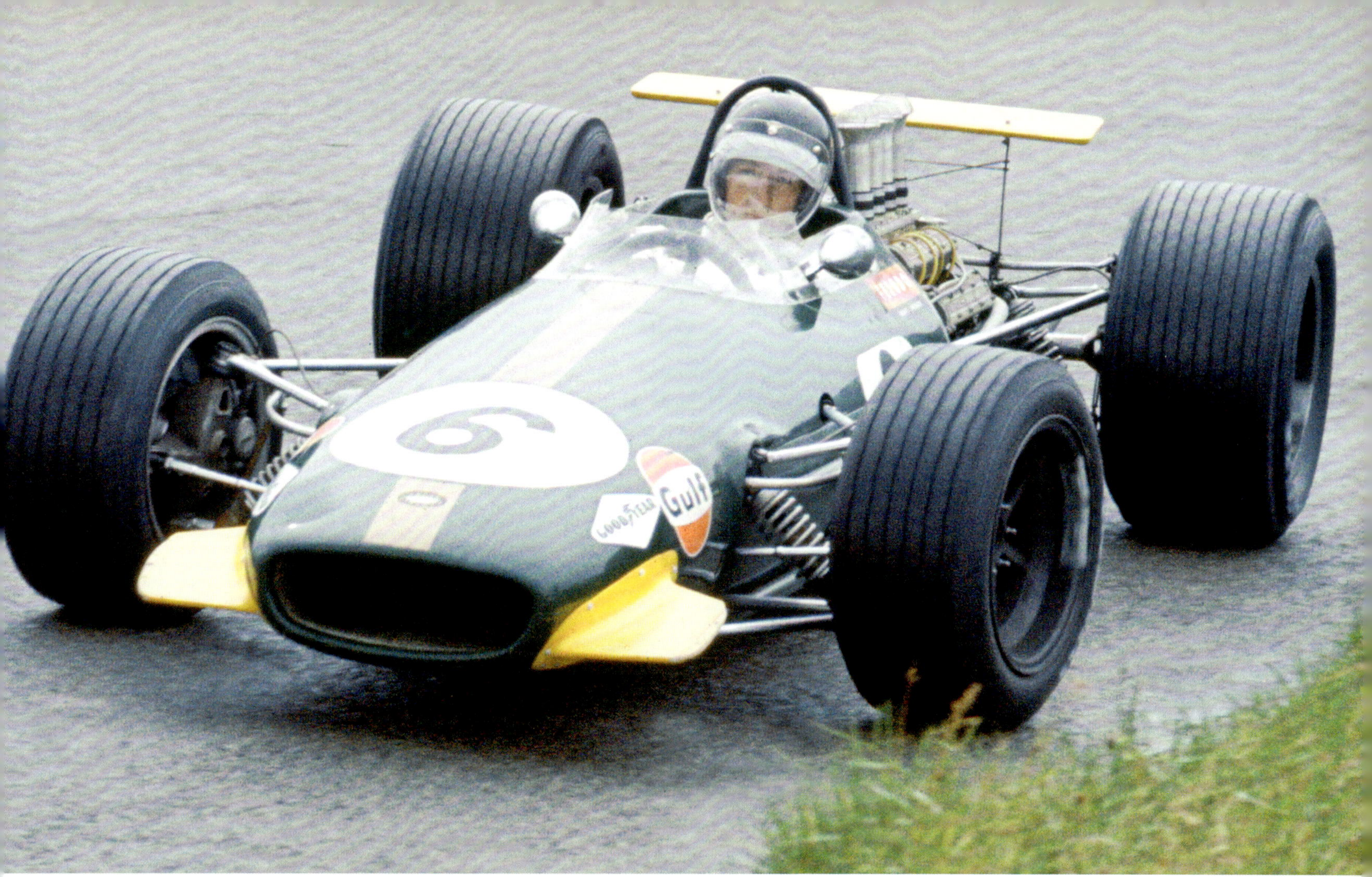
Gulf
GOODYEAR

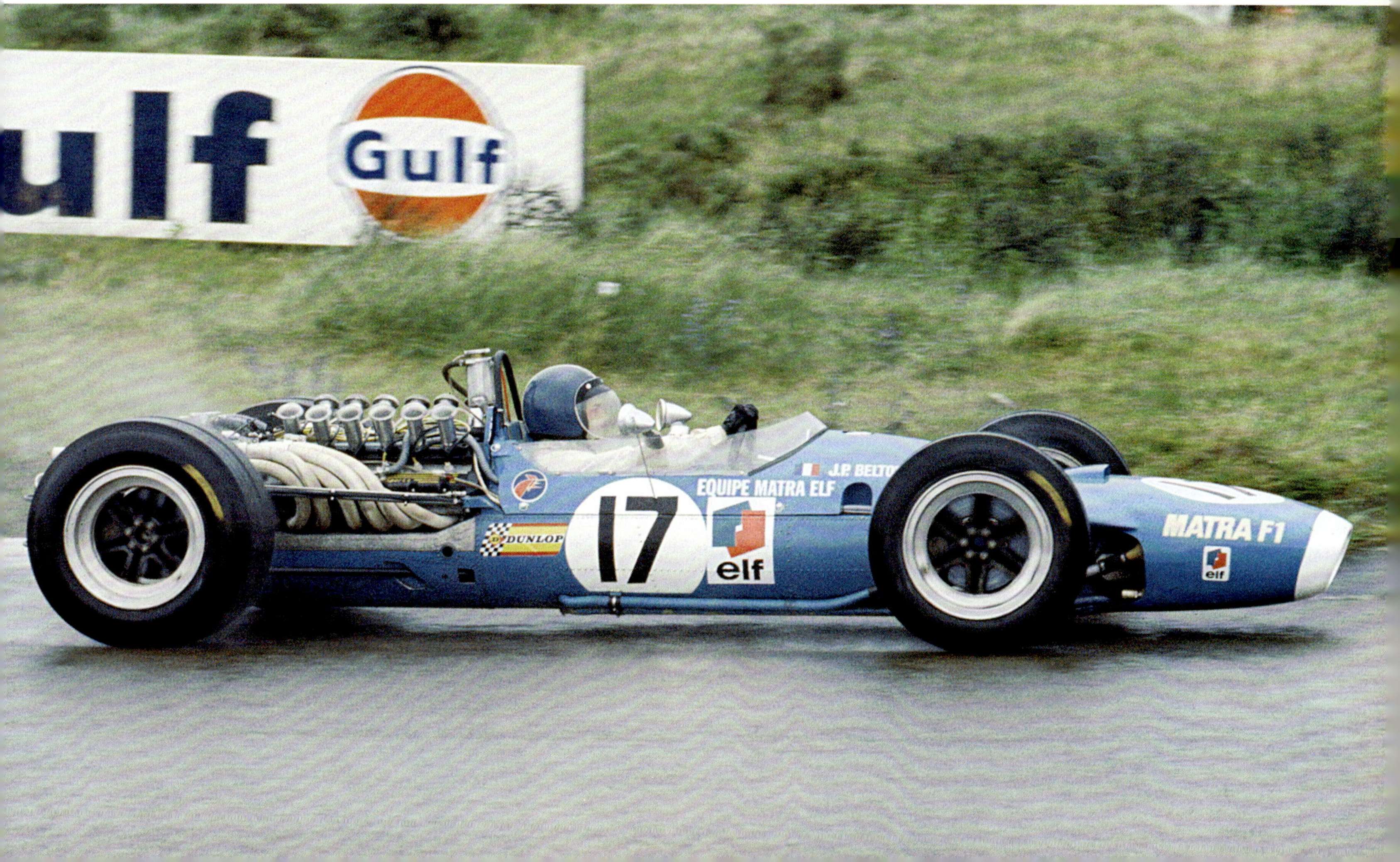
ulf
Gulf
J.P. BELTO
EQUIPE MATRA ELF
17
elf
DUNLOP
MATRA F1

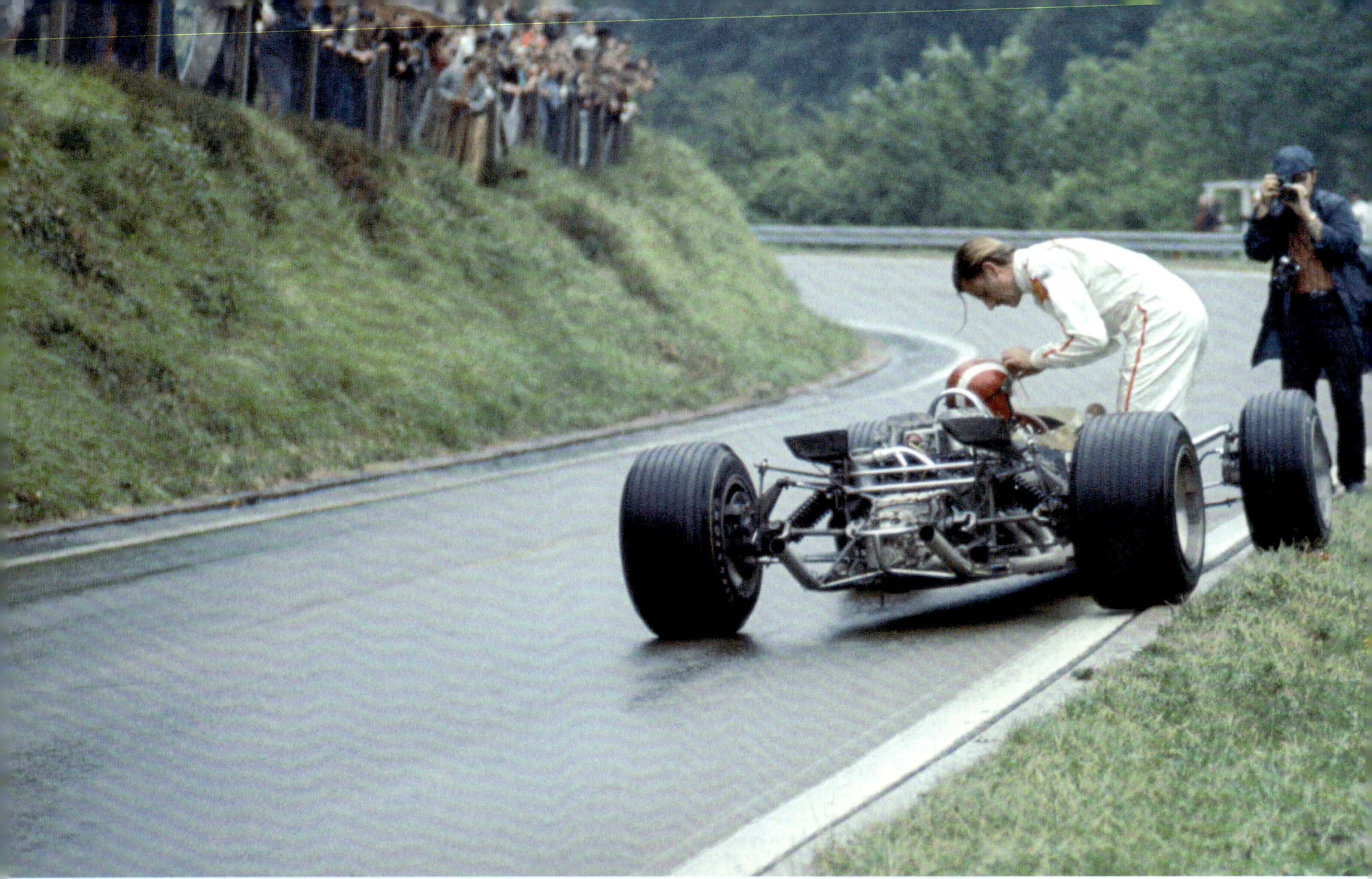

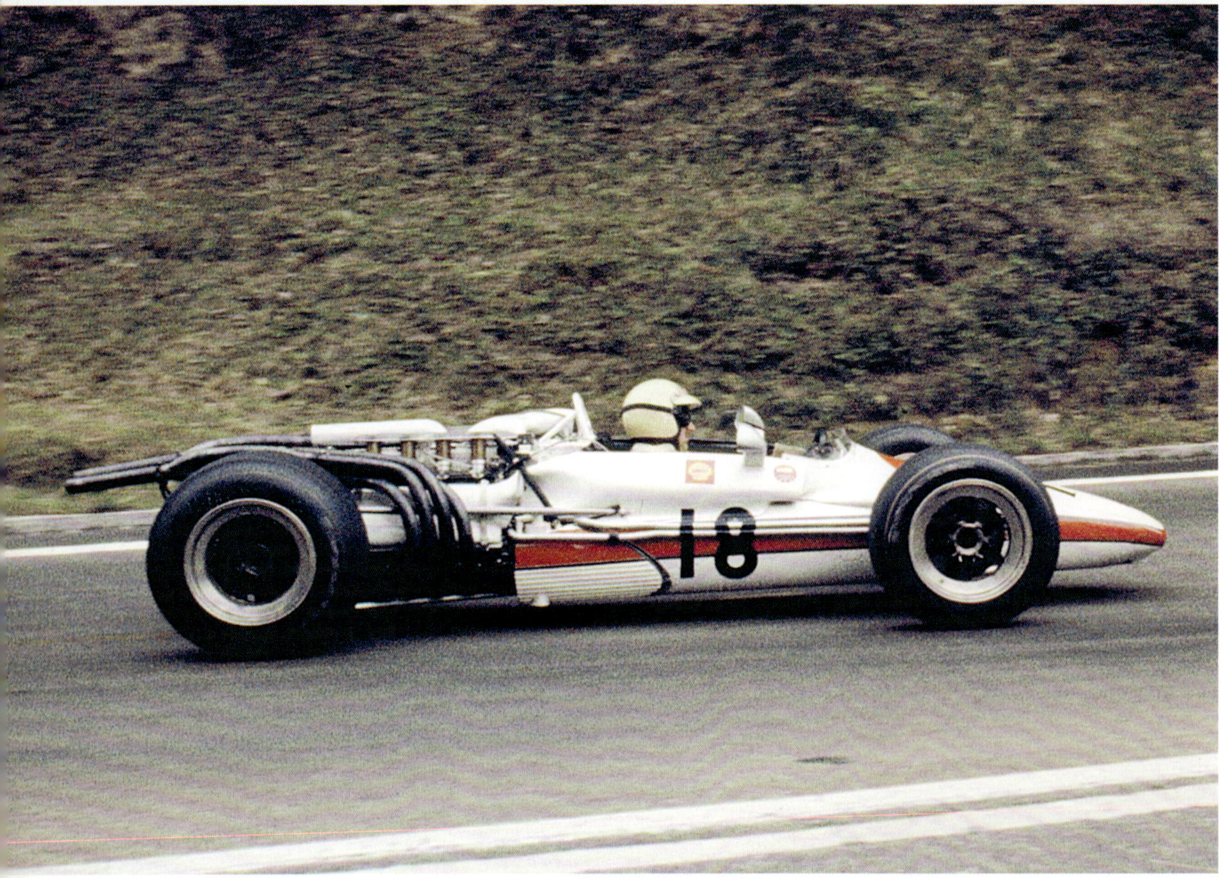

The air cooled largely magnesium Honda RA302 V8 that produced 380bhp @ 10,500rpm had no radiator so the driver sat further forward than was usual at the time. John Surtees had wanted to test it more thoroughly before any racing but instructions from Honda demanded otherwise. So they hired experienced French sports car racer Jo Schlesser to race it with tragic consequences. He started from the back row and crashed on lap three. The car, carrying 40 gallons of fuel, overturned and exploded into flames trapping poor Schlesser underneath for 20 minutes. Due to a lack of chemical fire extinguishers, water was used to try and damp down the magnesium inferno, making it worse and spreading burning fuel across the track. Afterwards there was very little left of anything and Surtees's 2nd place was completely overshadowed.

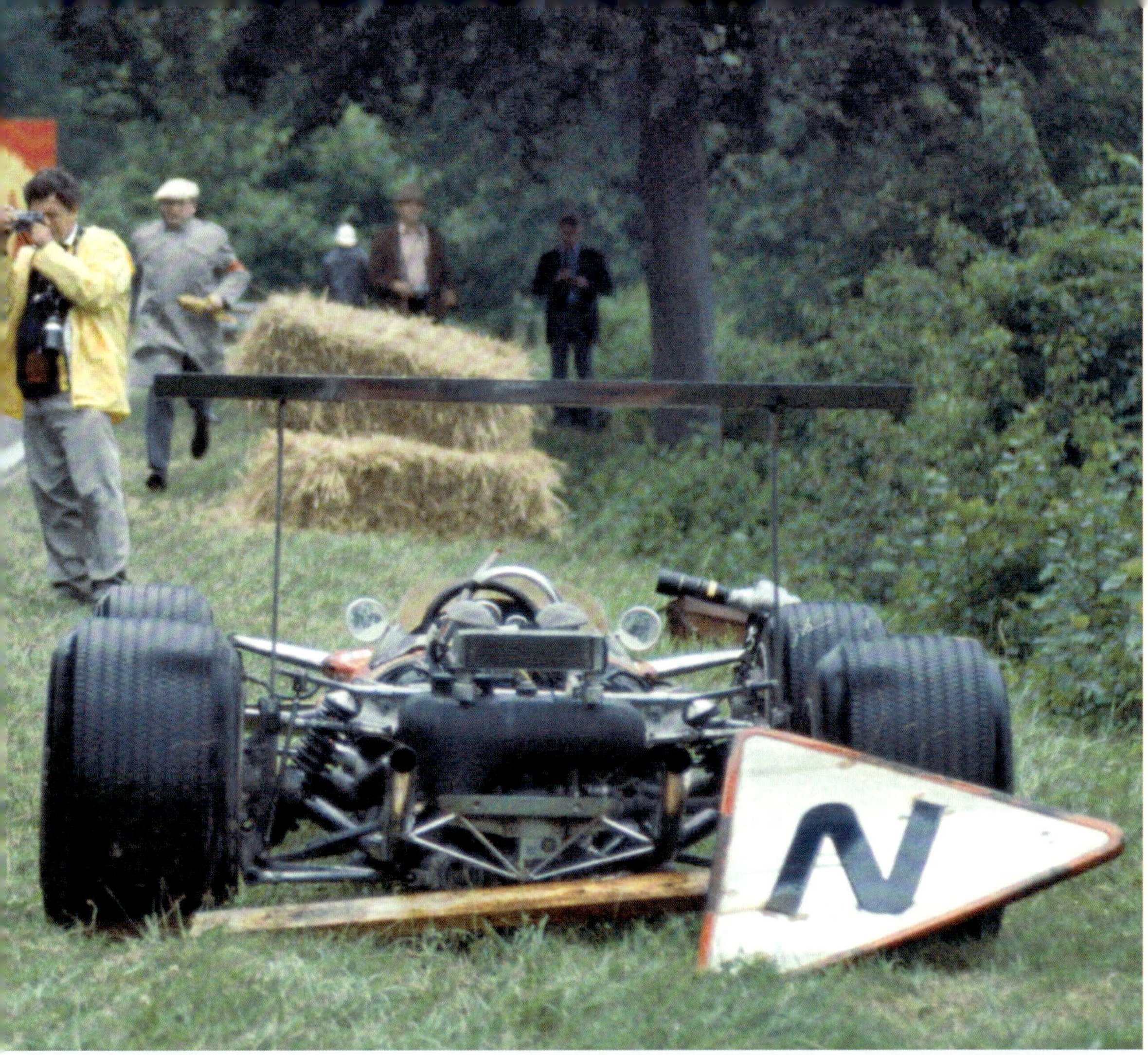

Gold Leaf Team Lotus suffered at Rouen with Oliver non-starting after a practice crash caused by wing failure and Graham Hill retiring from the race with drive shaft failure. A passing Jo Siffert in Rob Walker's Lotus 49 spotted Hill beside the track and stopped to borrow his visor! Today that would probably earn a hefty fine from the FIA and worse. Note the untrammelled track access and narrow road.

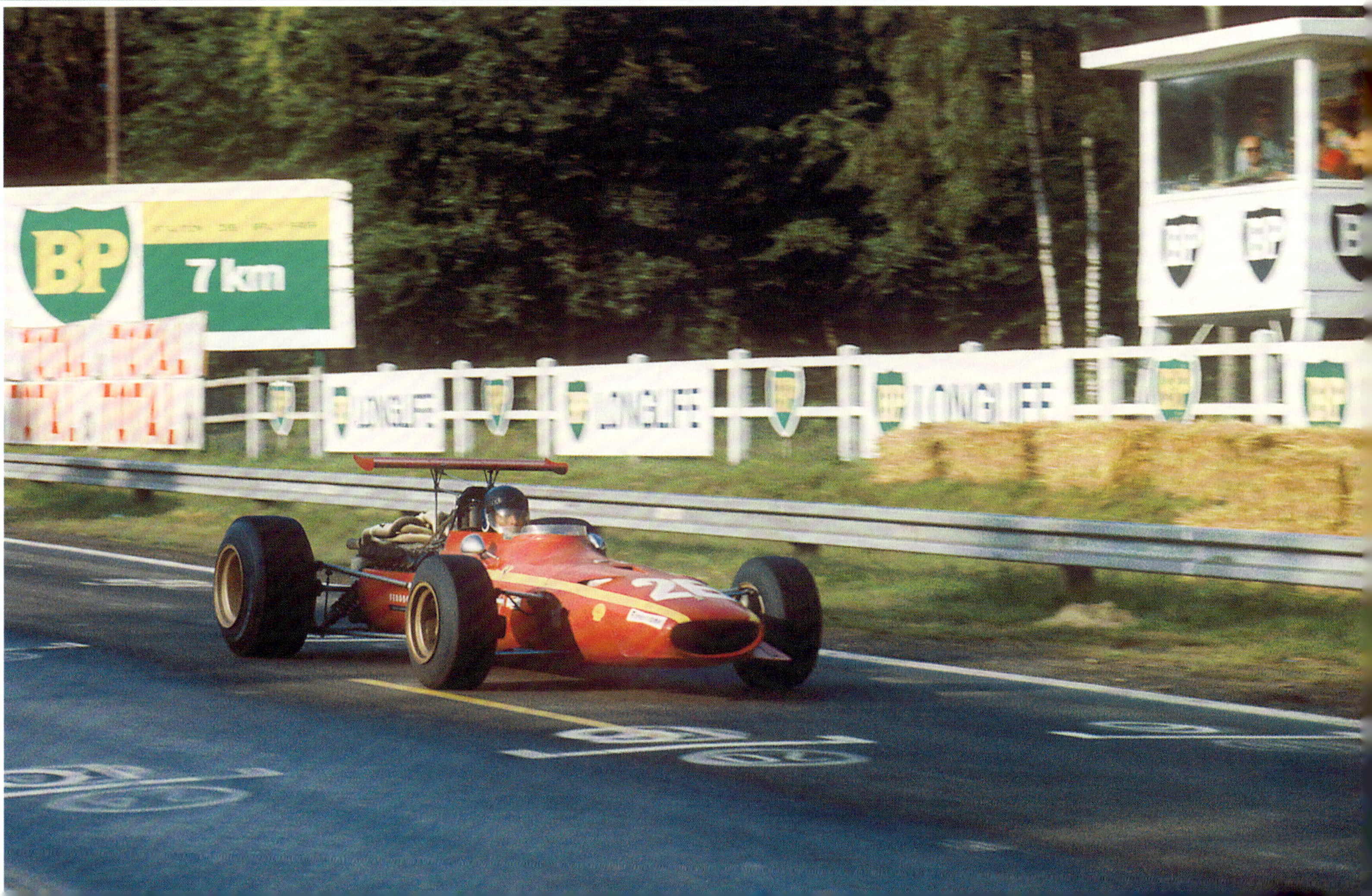

On a drying track Jacky Ickx won the French GP at Rouen-les Essart in the Ferrari 312 (0009) after a dominant performance in treacherous conditions, the first for a car with a rear wing. Team mate Chris Amon suffered his usual luck and spent the race with a mishandling Ferrari eventually finishing 10th, five laps behind. Ferrari's tyre supplier Firestone was very pleased having been so soundly trounced at the wet Dutch GP by the Dunlop users.

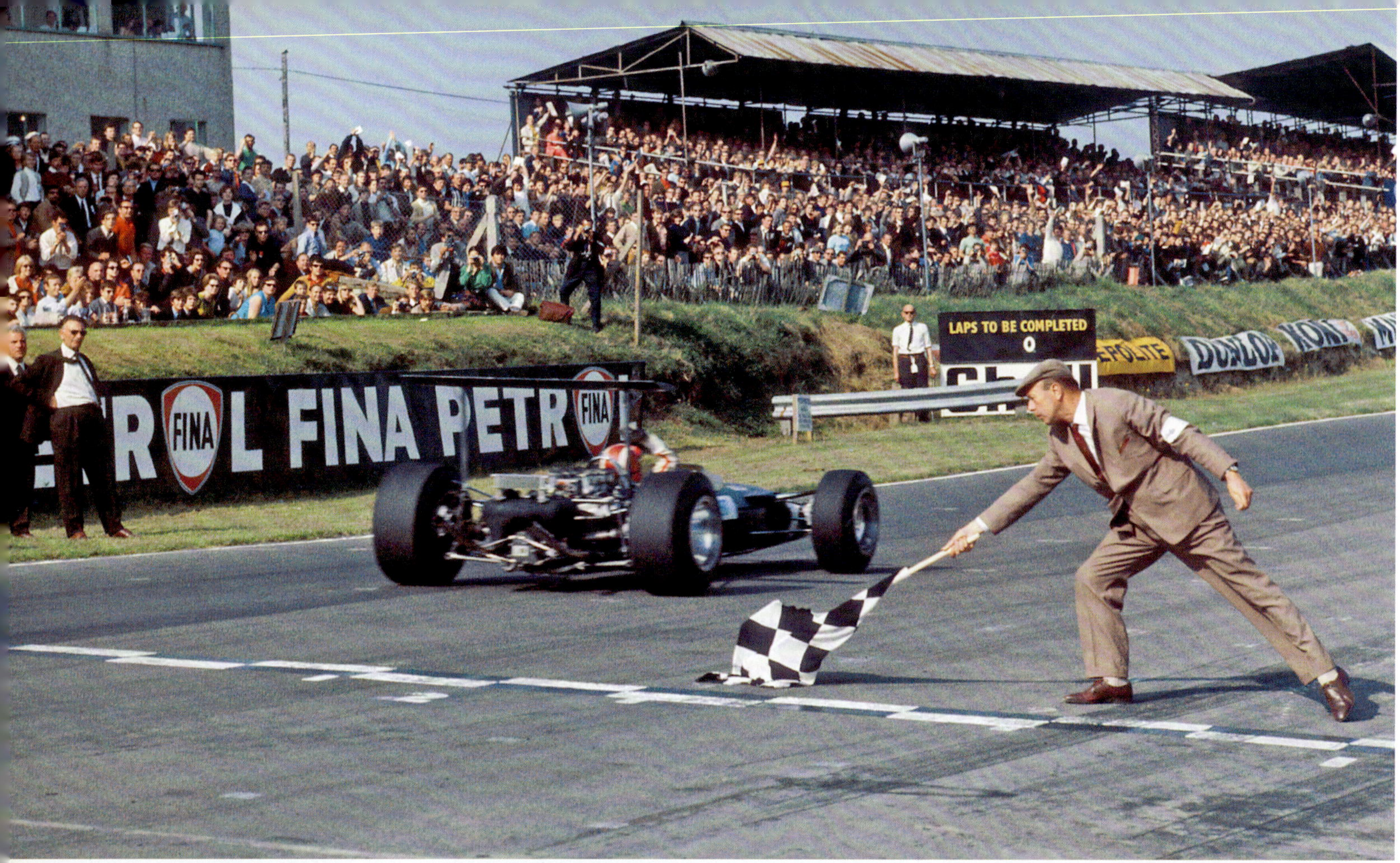
FINA PETR
FINA
LAPS TO BE COMPLETED
DUNLOP

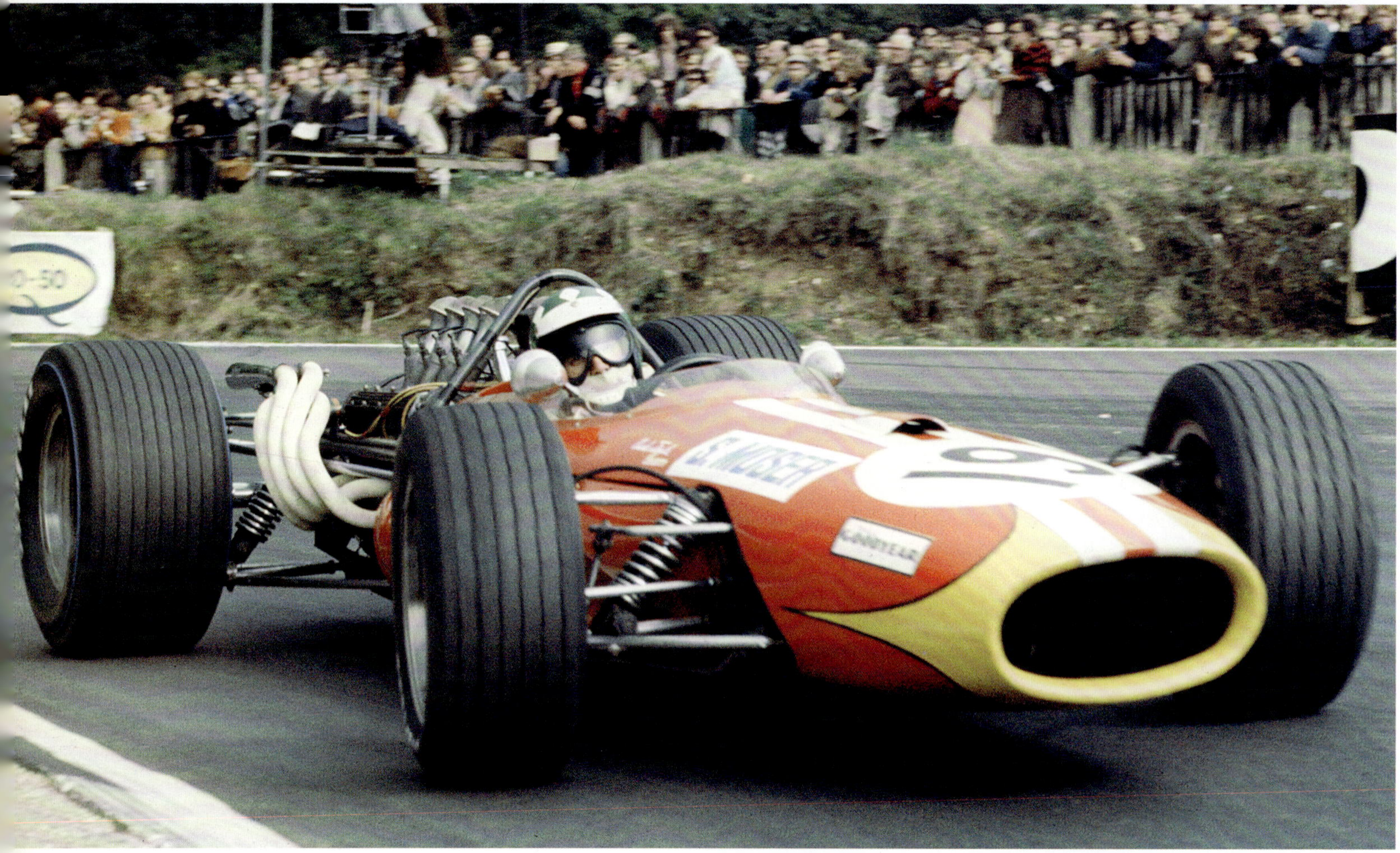
GOODYEAR

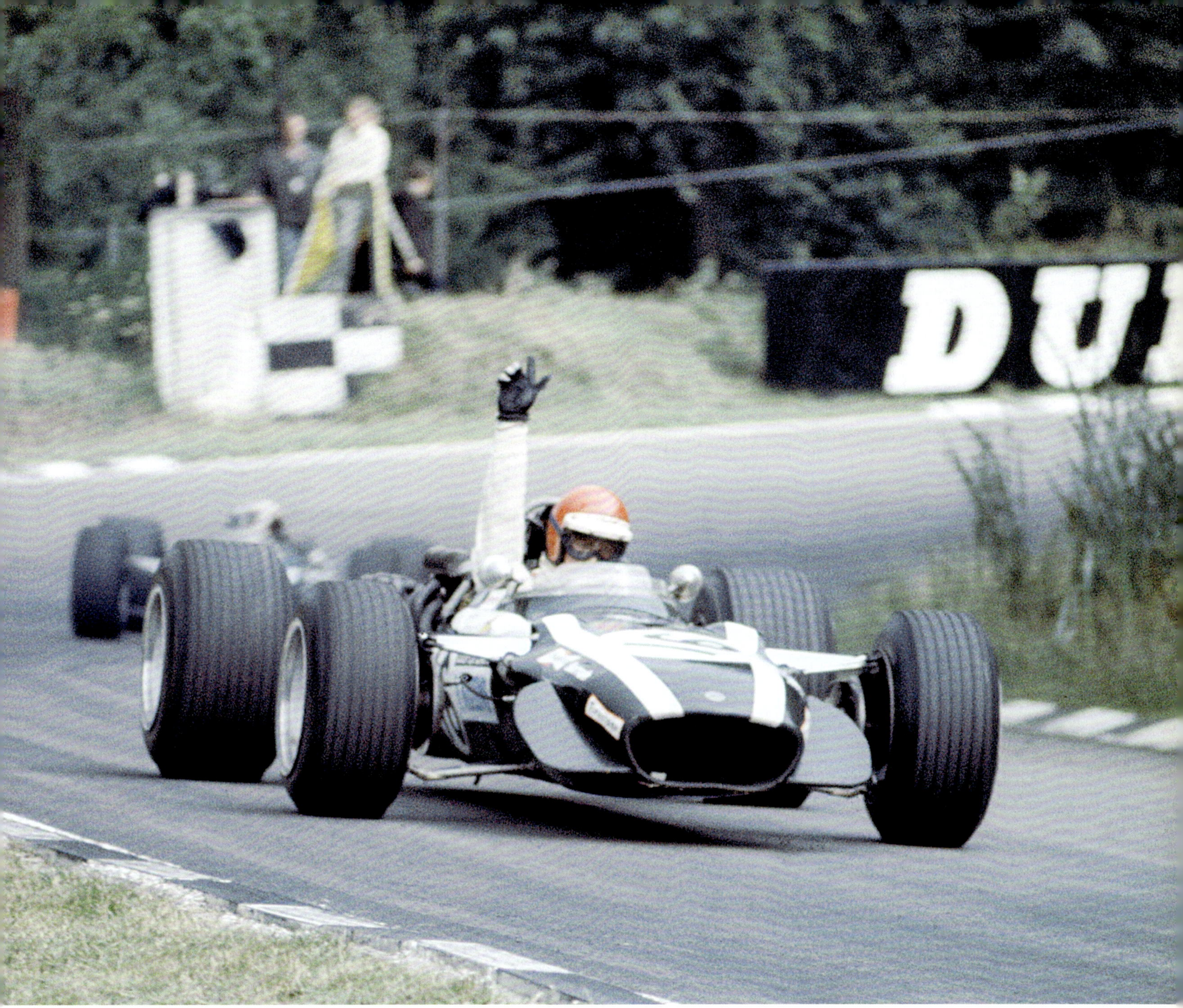

Cooper had a varied cast of drivers during the season and had used Lucien Bianchi, Johnny Servoz-Gavin and Vic Elford after Redman and Scarfiotti. This is former bobsleigh rider and F3 and F2 racer Rob Widdows who only drove in one GP, the 1968 British at Brands Hatch, in the works Cooper T86B BRM (F1-1-68). He retired on lap 36 with ignition failure. Thereafter he raced on in F2 but suddenly retired in 1970.

Howzat! Seven years after the last GP victory by a private team (also by Rob Walker, at the 1961 German GP) Jo Siffert (Lotus 49B R7) wins the British GP at Brands Hatch after a race-long battle with Chris Amon's Ferrari 312. The Gold Leaf Team Lotus cars should have won but both retired, the rising power levels and stickier tyres were causing transmission and driveshaft/hub failures. Seven years later James Hunt's Dutch GP win for Hesketh was to be the final hurrah for the independents.

There were independent teams and then there were independents. Silvio Moser's ancient Brabham BT20 (F1-2-66), Hulme's 1966 works car, entered by Charles Vögele was slowest but one at Brands Hatch and eventually finished an unclassified 9th with gearbox problems. Swiss Moser's shoestring F1 career began in 1969 and ended at Monza in 1971. Three years later with plans to return to F1 he was fatally injured at the Monza 1000km sports car race.

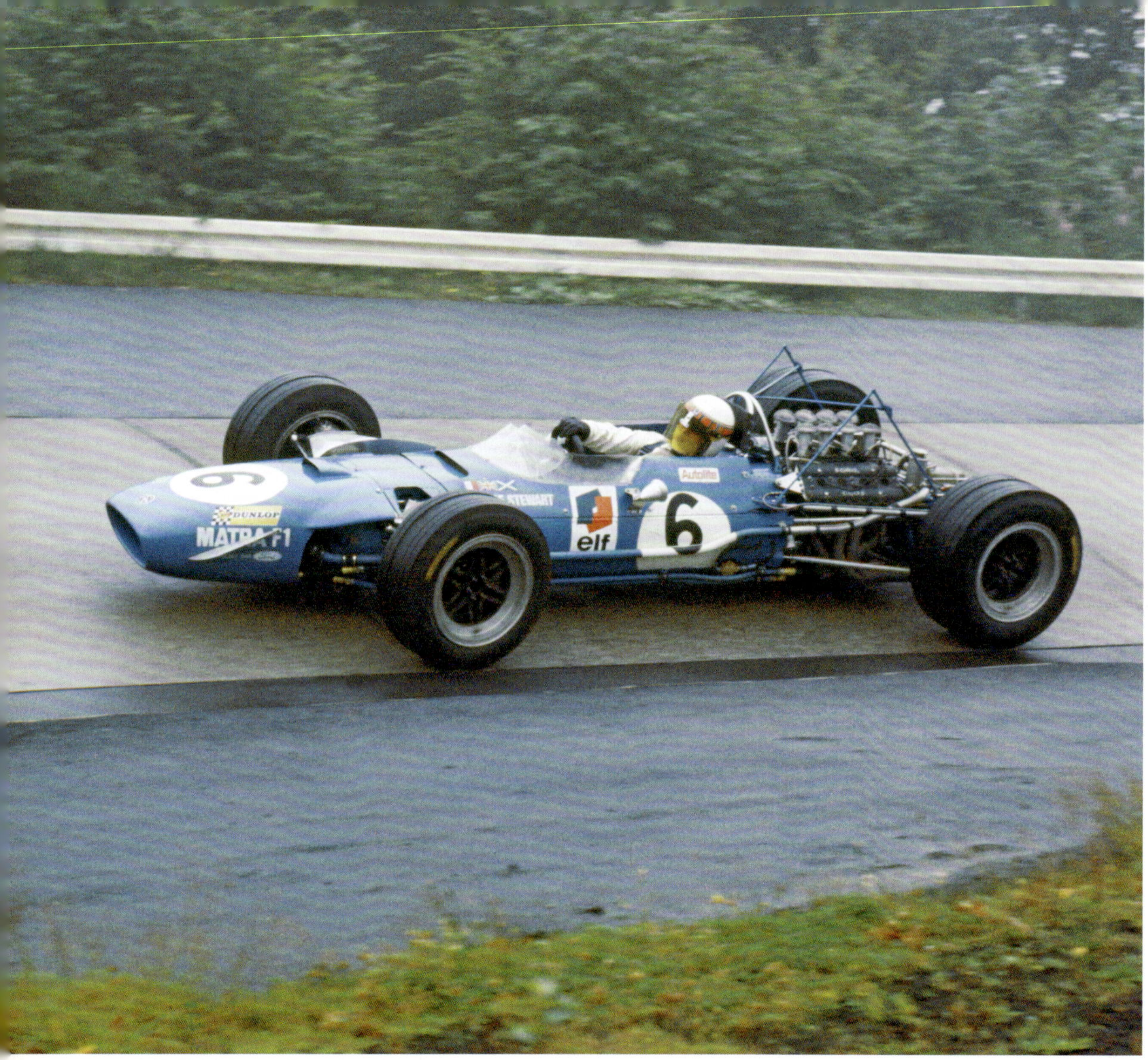

The first half of Stewart's 1968 season was compromised by a wrist injury acquired during an F2 race early in the year severely hampering his driving. Nevertheless he won the wet Dutch and German GPs, with fog making the Nürburgring even more daunting. At the Karussel he presses on in the gloom with the Matra MS10/2 on his way to winning by over four minutes from Hill's Lotus 49B. It was a *tour de force,* possibly the best performance of his entire career. The rest were always racing for 2nd place.

The motor racing paparazzi *en masse* in the Nürburgring pits. Kneeling down holding the medium format camera, is the moustachioed Rainer Schlegelmilch one of the best and most prolific photographers of the last 40 years. He still covers GP races today and many of his iconic images are used in the companion *F1 in Camera* books.

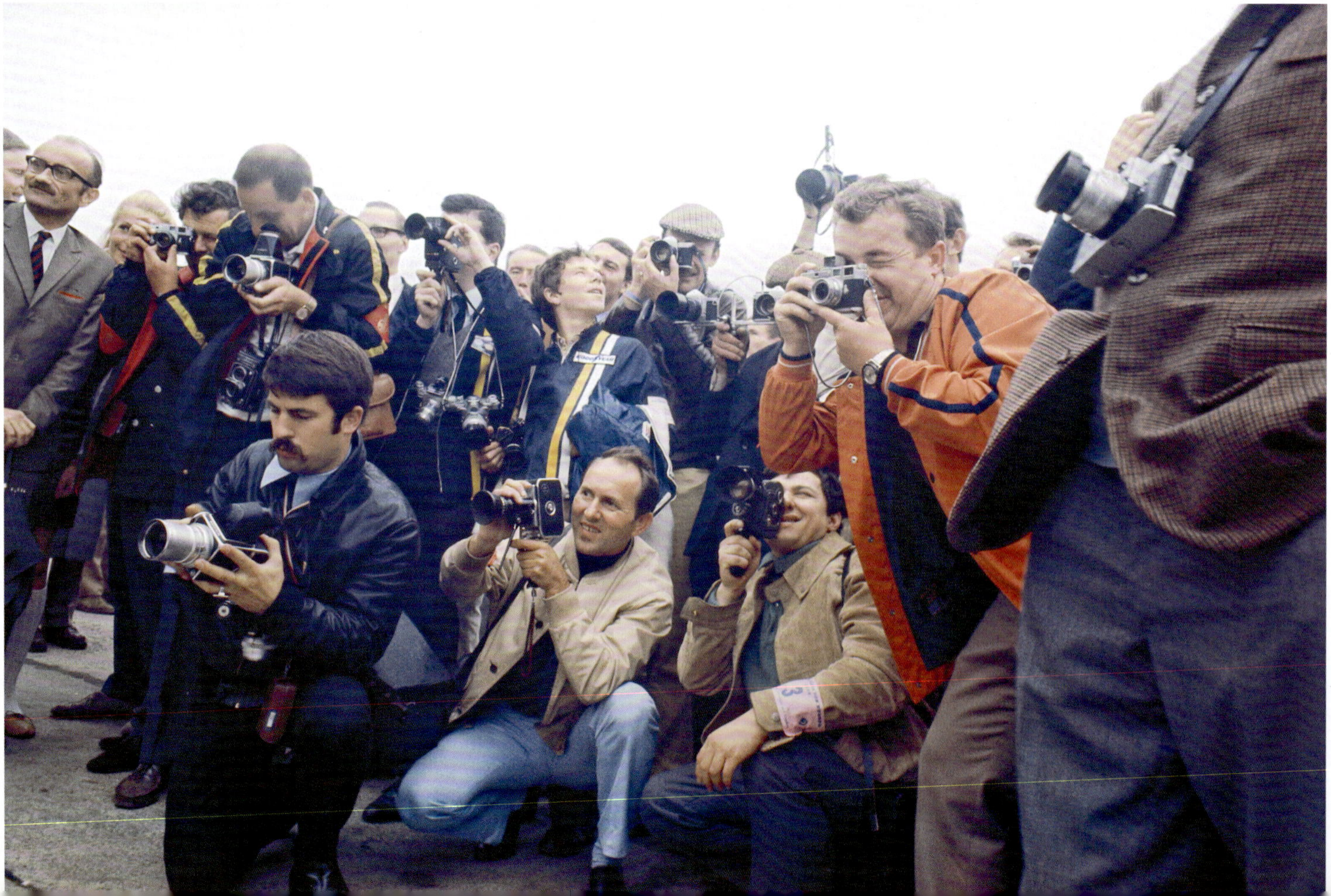

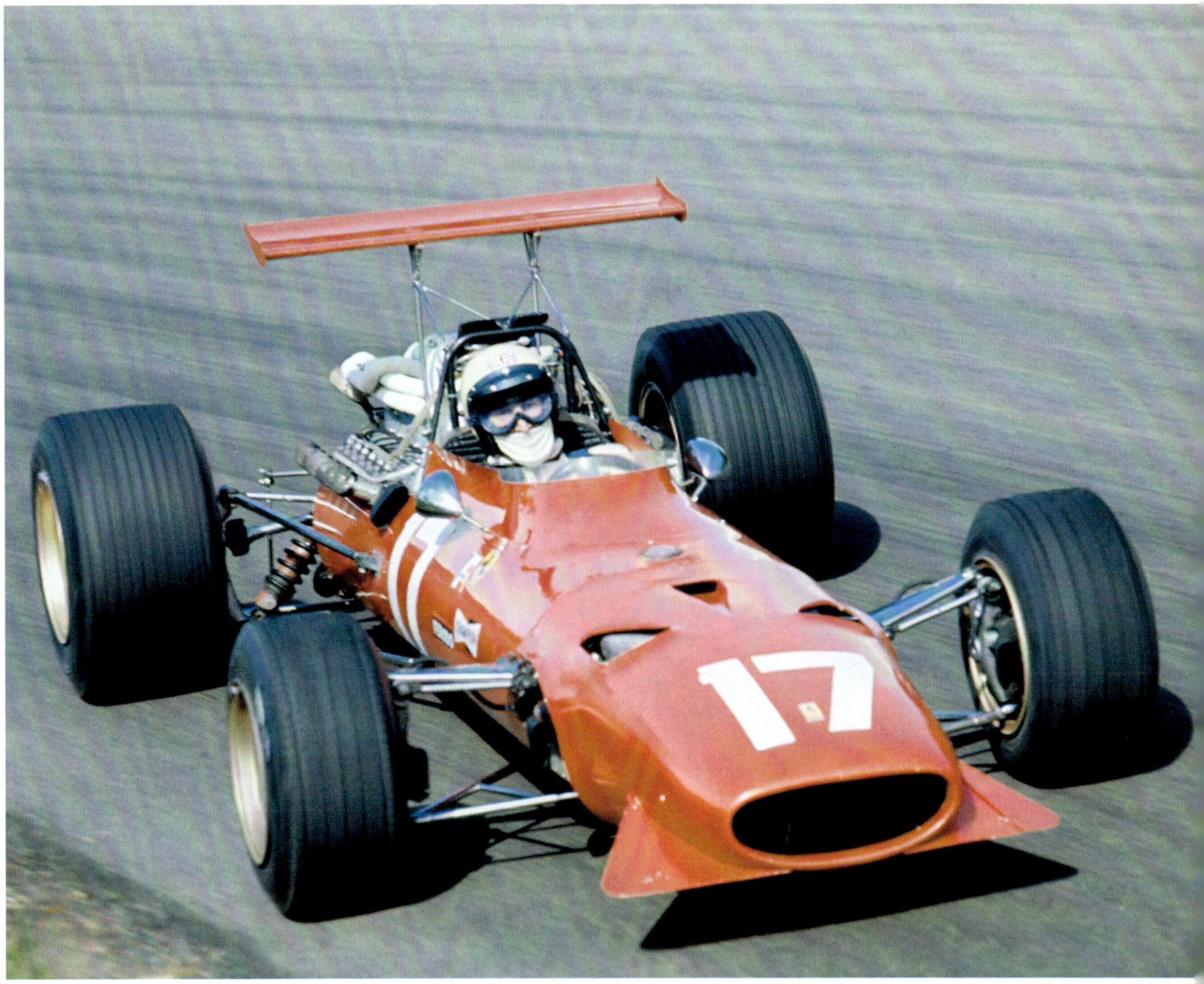

As with a number of British drivers of the era and beyond Derek Bell's F1 aspirations went largely unrewarded. 'Dinger' briefly enjoyed Ferrari F1 and F2 drives including this outing at the Oulton Park Gold Cup in the 312 0007, plus the Italian and US GPs, but retired in all three. As number three his tenure was always vulnerable and when Ferrari's F1 participation lessened in 1969 his drive disappeared.

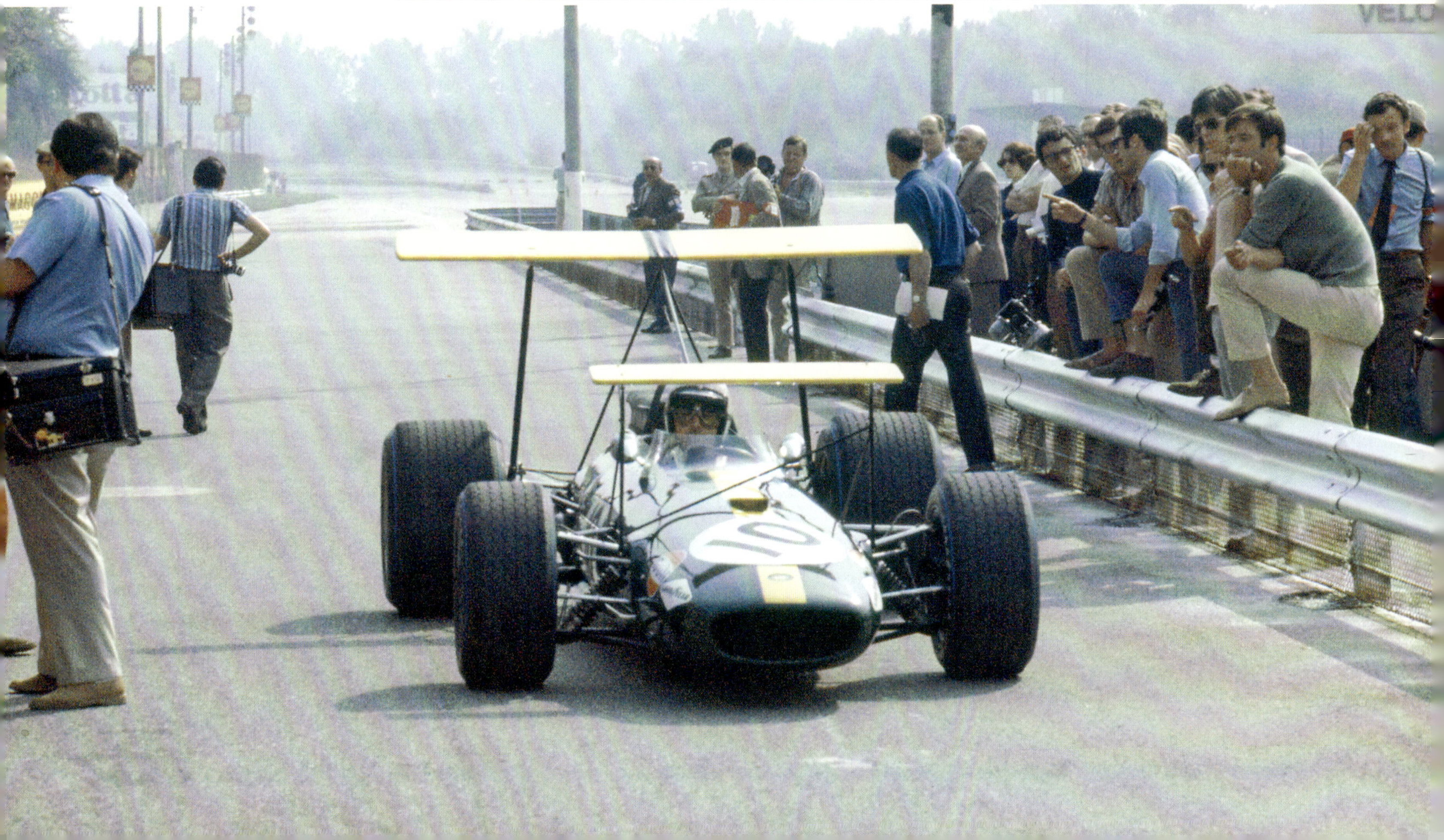

This season's daring new look, 'The bi-plane'. Messrs. Brabham and Tauranac were always very interested in aerodynamics despite their conservative car designs. This arrangement was tried during practice for the 1968 Italian GP but discarded when the adjustable rear wing developed the 'wobbles' according to Paddy McNally. The wings were designed by BAC aerodynamicist Ray Jessop in consultation with Ron Tauranac in an attempt to match Colin Chapman's innovations at Lotus.

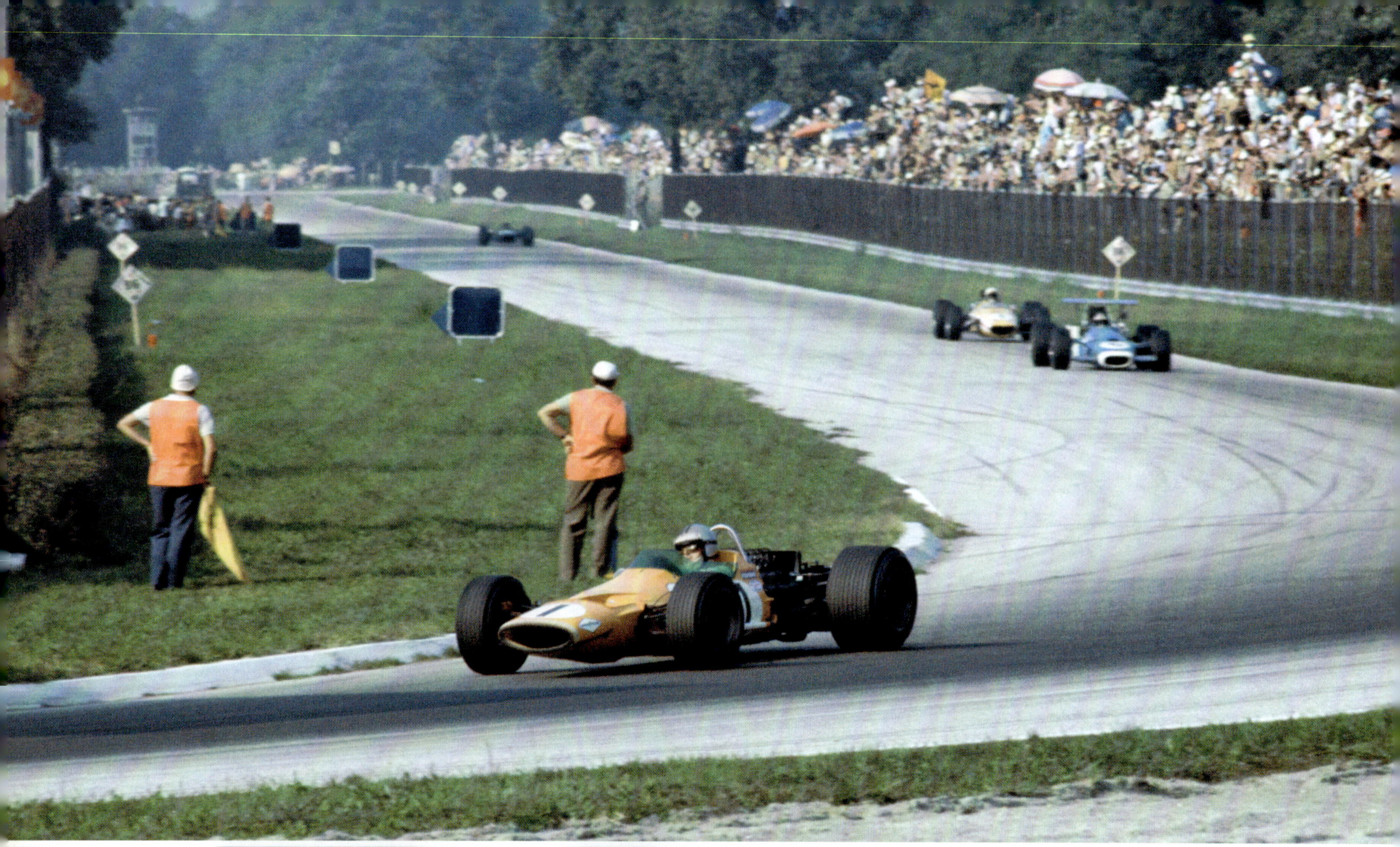

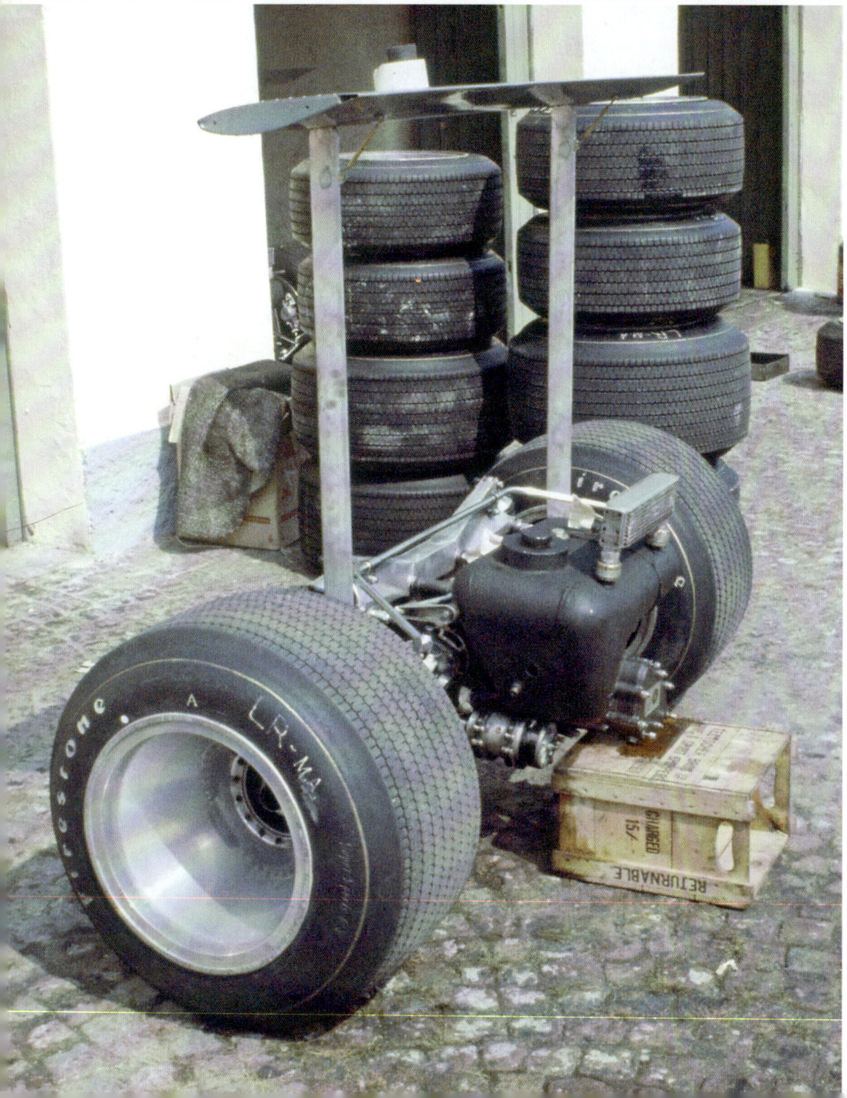

↑ Denny Hulme's consecutive victories in Italy and Canada brought him back into contention for the championship. His M7A/2 rounds the Parabolica, a classic Monza shot that is recognisably the same today. He beat Johnny Servoz-Gavin (Matra) and Jacky Ickx (Ferrari).

← For sale: Complete rear end, all matching numbers, one careful owner since new…. The suspension, gearbox, oil cooler/tank and rear wing of a Lotus 49B could be detached in one unit as demonstrated in the Monza paddock.

↗ Monza 1000km winner David Hobbs raced the second Honda RA301 (F802) at the Italian GP. He had driven Bernard White's old BRM P261 twice in 1967 but this was his only GP appearance in 1968. He only made three more GP starts but excelled on the American scene in Formula A, sports cars, Can-Am, touring cars, Indianapolis (5th in 1974) and much else, finally retiring in the 1990s. Today he is a race commentator on American television. At Monza he qualified impressively but retired with a dropped valve. He is chased by Rodriguez's BRM P138 (01), whose rear wing looks distinctly lopsided. Honda withdrew from F1 at the end of the season.

→ Dan Gurney founded his own engine workshop in May 1968 because of the inconsistency of his Weslake-built engines. He hired Aubrey Woods who had originally designed the V12 but the engines were still fragile and underpowered, (390bhp versus 413bhp in 1967) and Gurney missed several GPs. At Monza, the Eagle struggled in mid-field and stopped on lap 20 leaking oil and water, a sad finale to the AAR F1 project. Gurney raced a third works McLaren M7A (but entered by AAR) for the three remaining GPs.

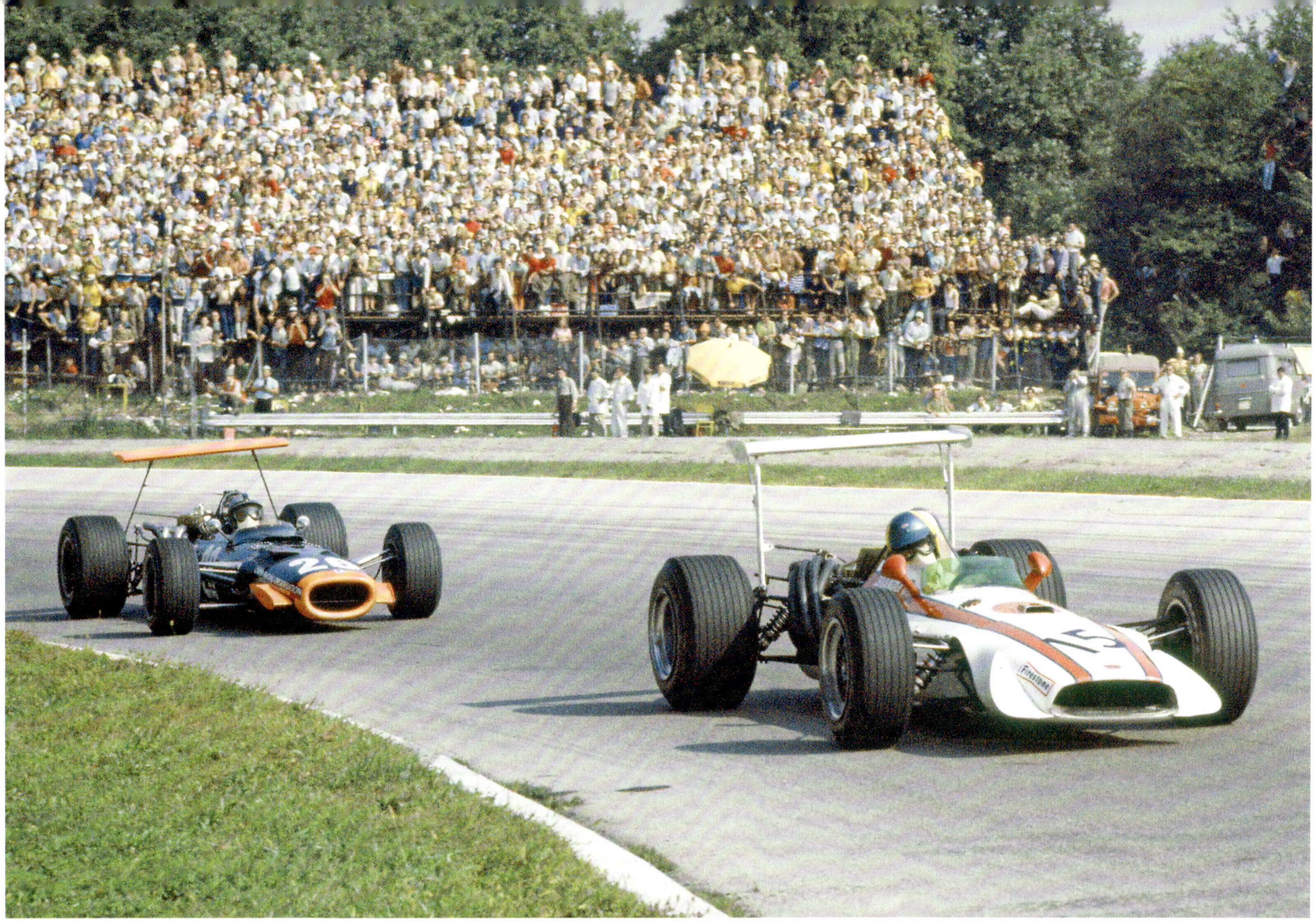
15

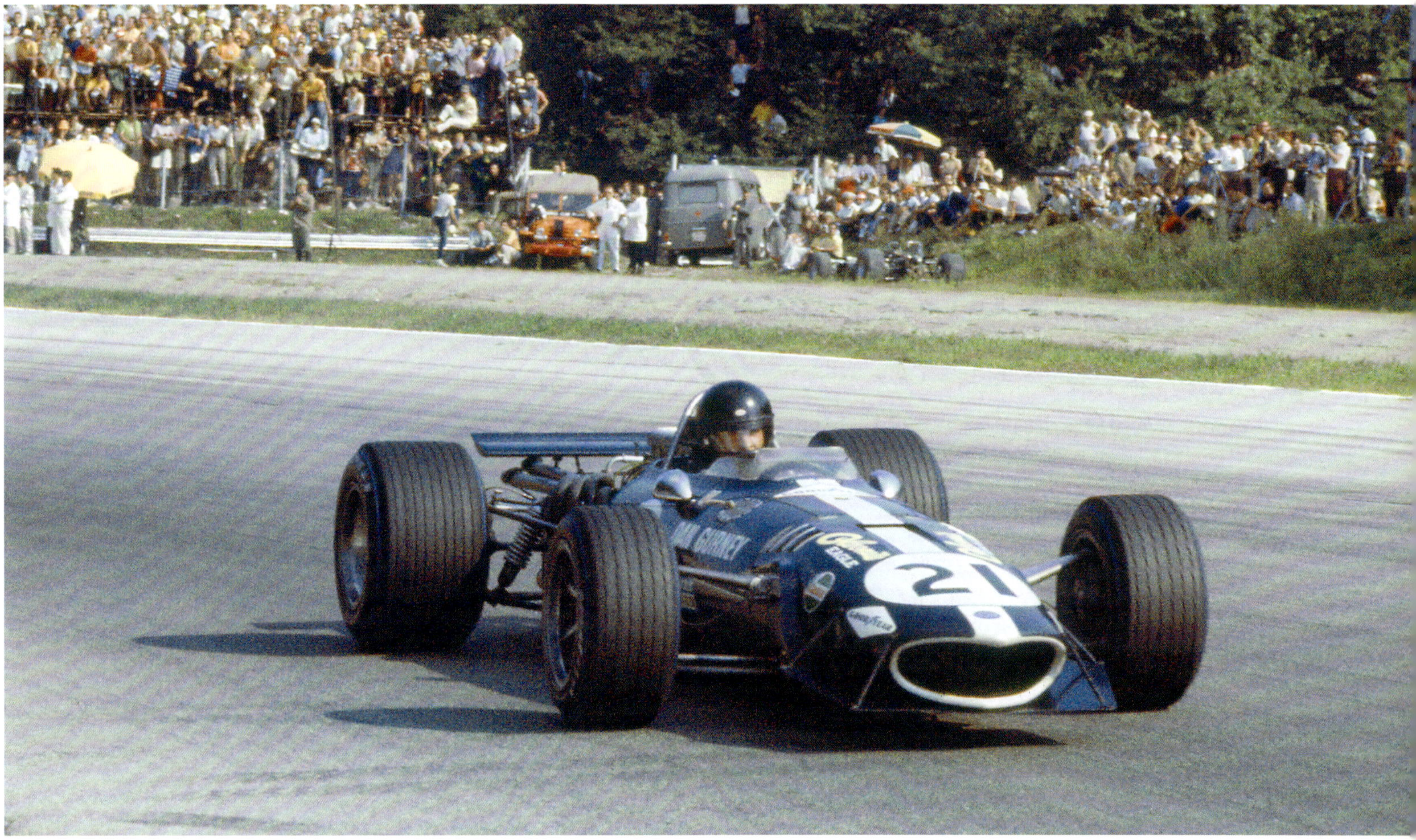
DAN GURNEY
21

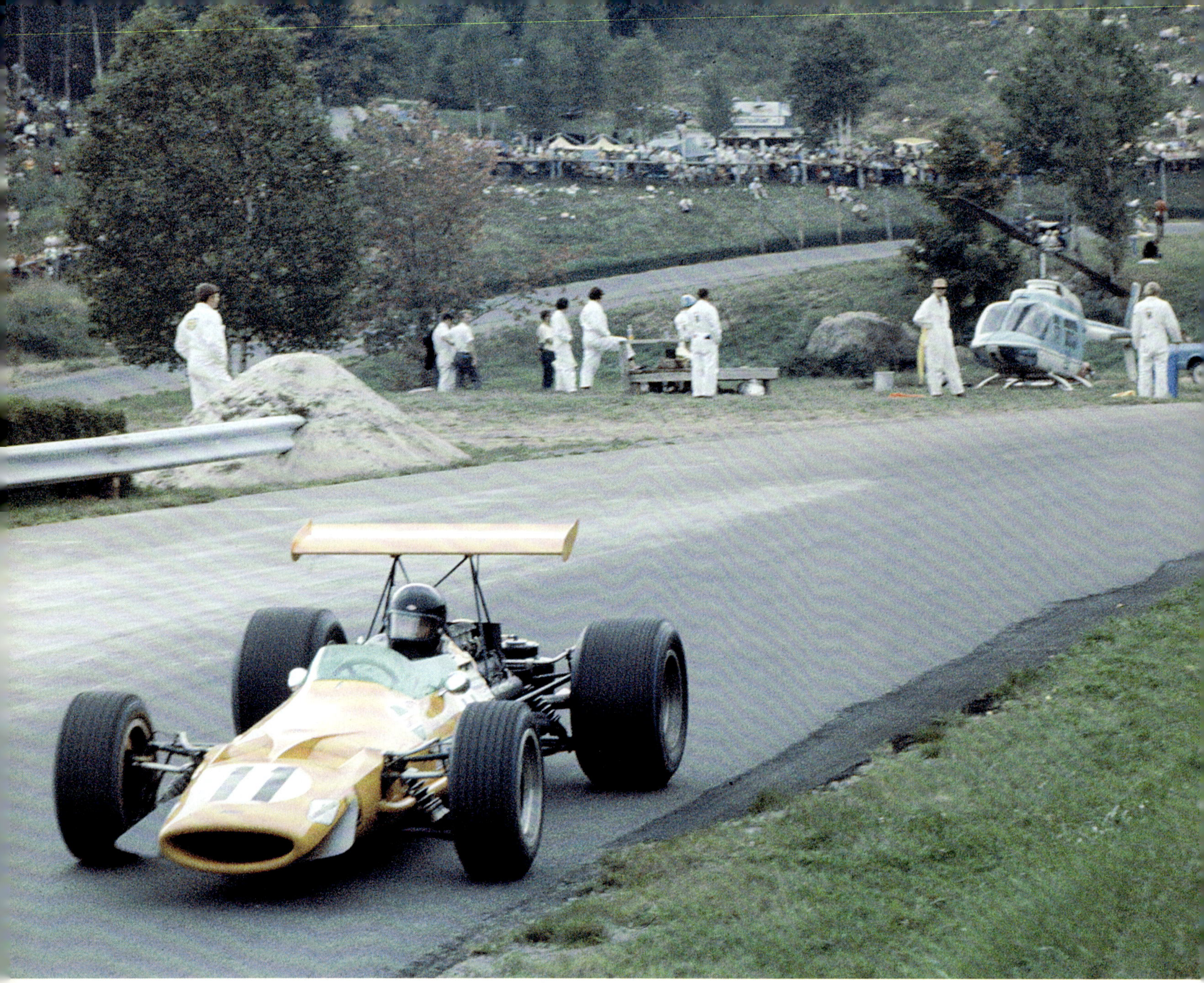

↑ The beautiful scenery of Mont Tremblant provided the setting for the 1968 Canadian GP on the narrow, undulating and bumpy 2.65-mile St. Jovite circuit. Jackie Stewart remarked that it looked like it had been designed by Walt Disney. It provided a 1–2 for Denny Hulme and Bruce McLaren after a dominant Chris Amon (Ferrari 312) retired. It was also the end of Jacky Ickx's championship bid as he crashed and broke a leg. Here Dan Gurney in the third McLaren M7A/3 leads Hulme before he retired. Note the exposed trackside vehicles and even a helicopter!

↗ Jo Siffert in the Walker/Durlacher Lotus 49B (R7) finished 5th at Watkins Glen for the US GP. The pits were rather basic and hardly well protected but at least the access road was wide rather than the usual narrow strip. Note the filthy floor, in stark contrast to the spotless conditions and ruthlessly applied protocols of the modern F1 scene.

→ At Monza, Mario Andretti (Lotus) and Bobby Unser (BRM) had been forbidden to race because of a rule forbidding anybody competing in two separate events within 24 hours (in this case the Hoosier 100 at Indianapolis and the Italian GP). No such nonsense attended Watkins Glen and Andretti started the GLTL Lotus 49B (R5) from pole, racing second to Jackie Stewart until the nose of the Lotus began to break up. He stopped to have it taped up, lost a lap but soon retired with clutch failure. Stewart won the US GP from Graham Hill and John Surtees.

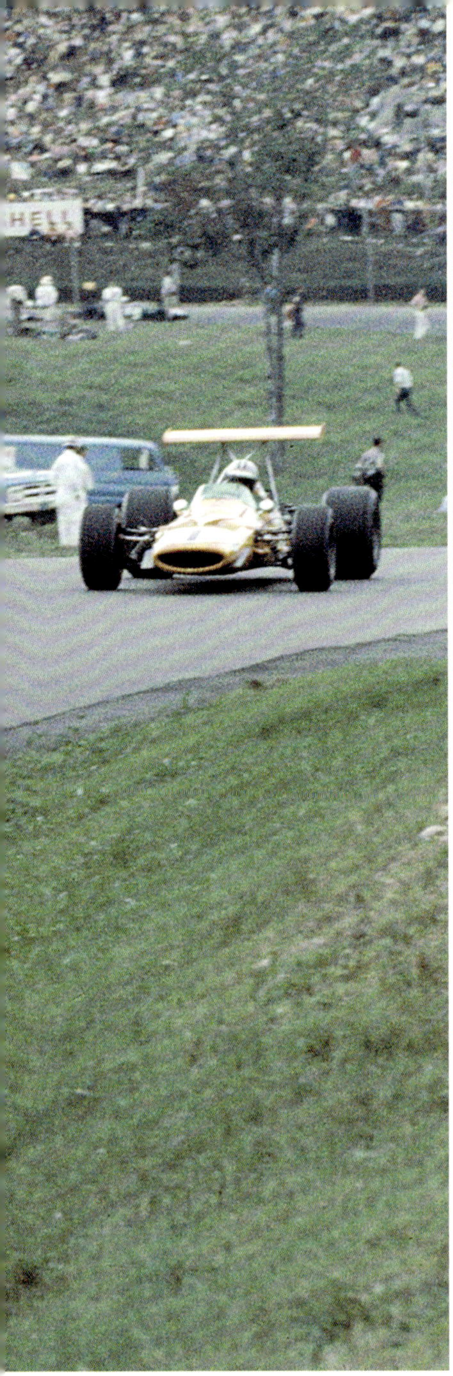

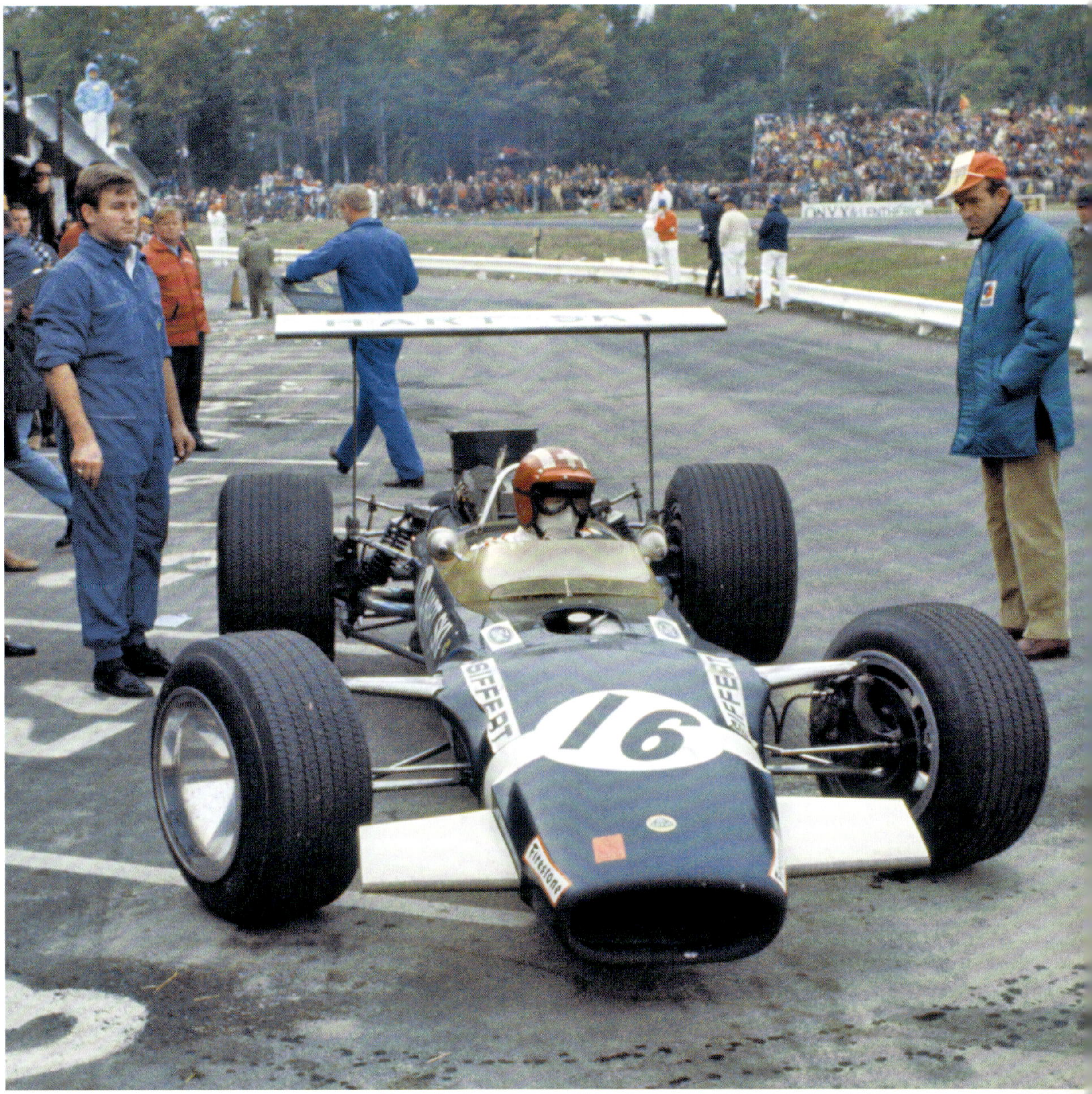
16
SIFFERT
SIFFERT

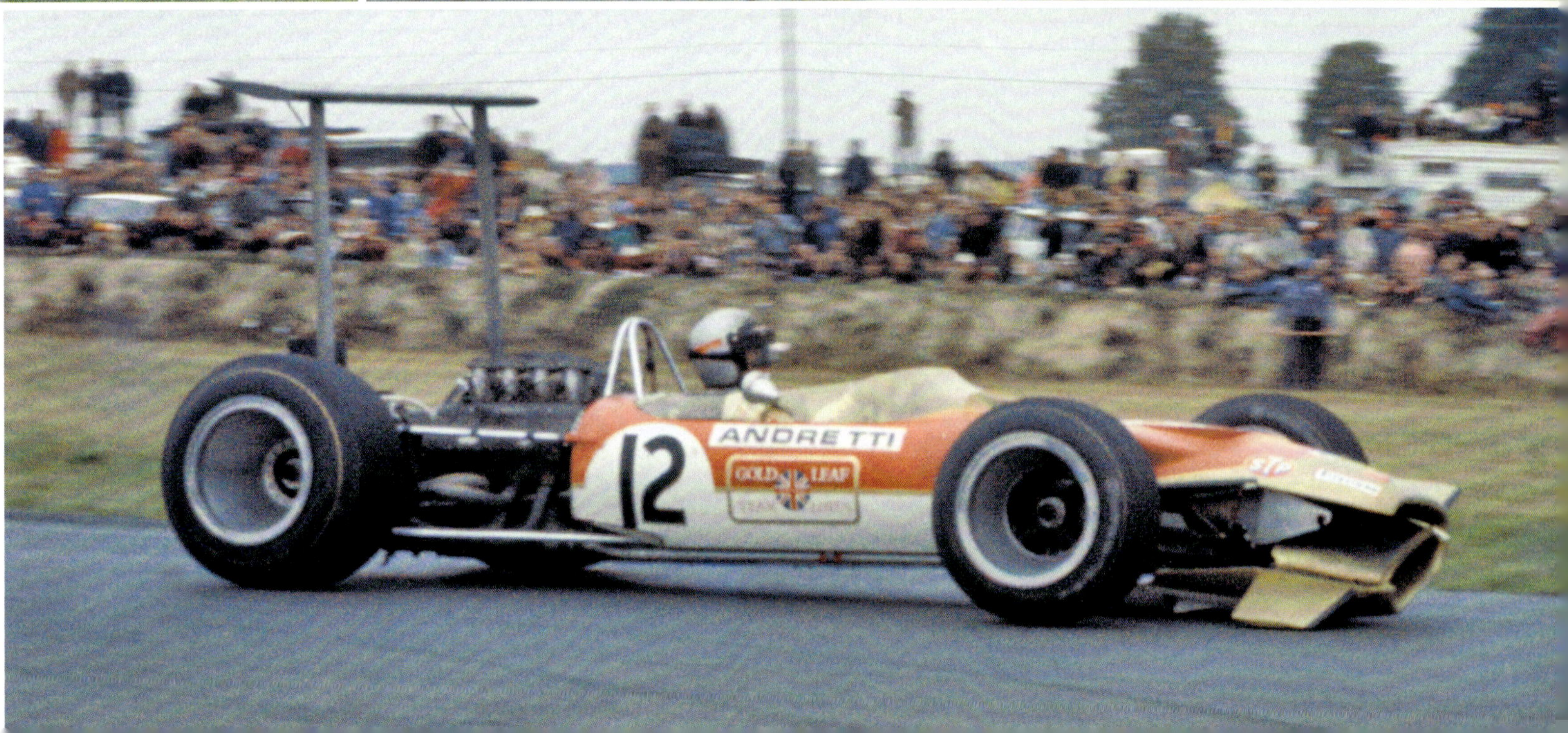
ANDRETTI
12
GOLD LEAF

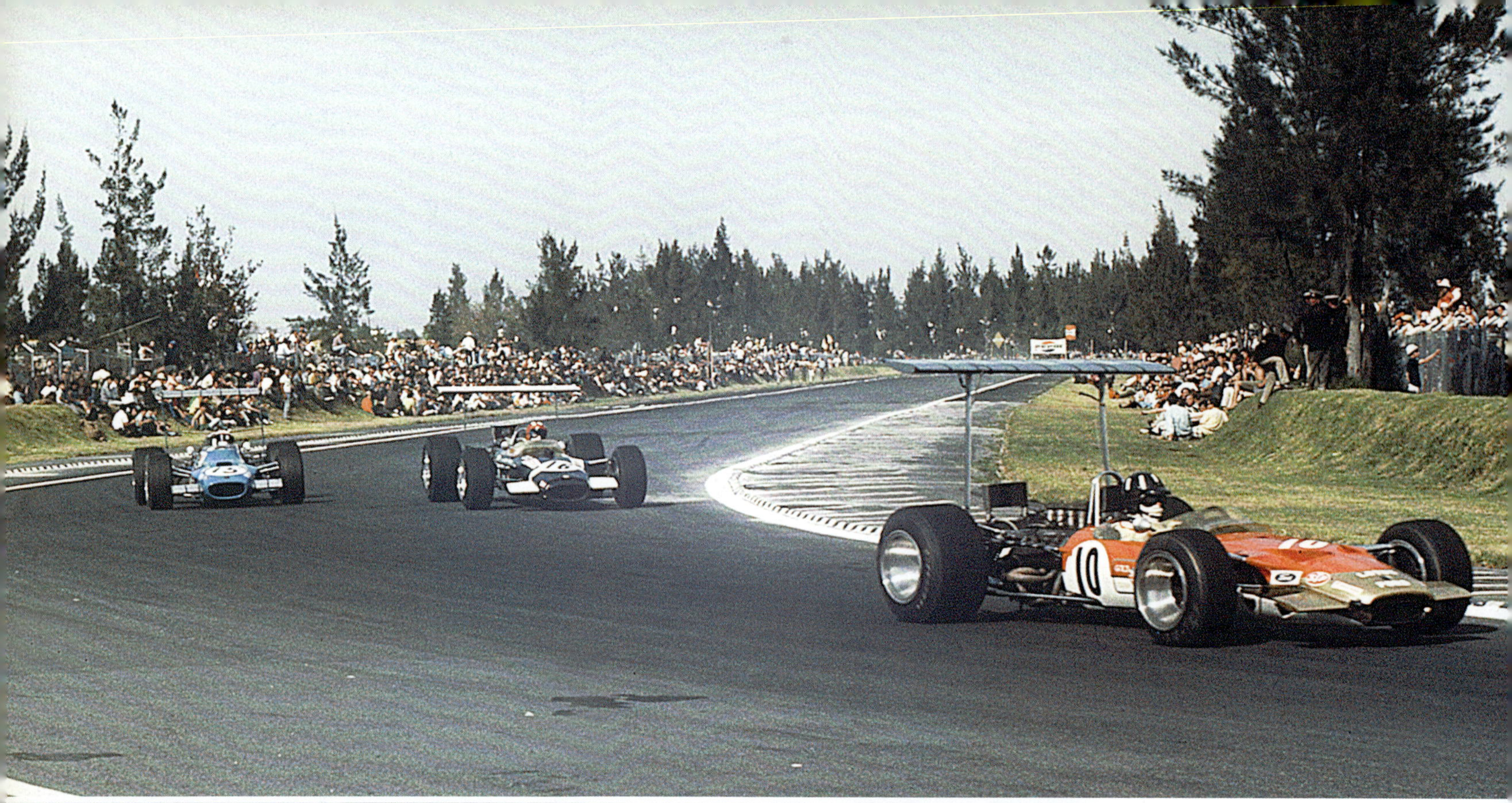

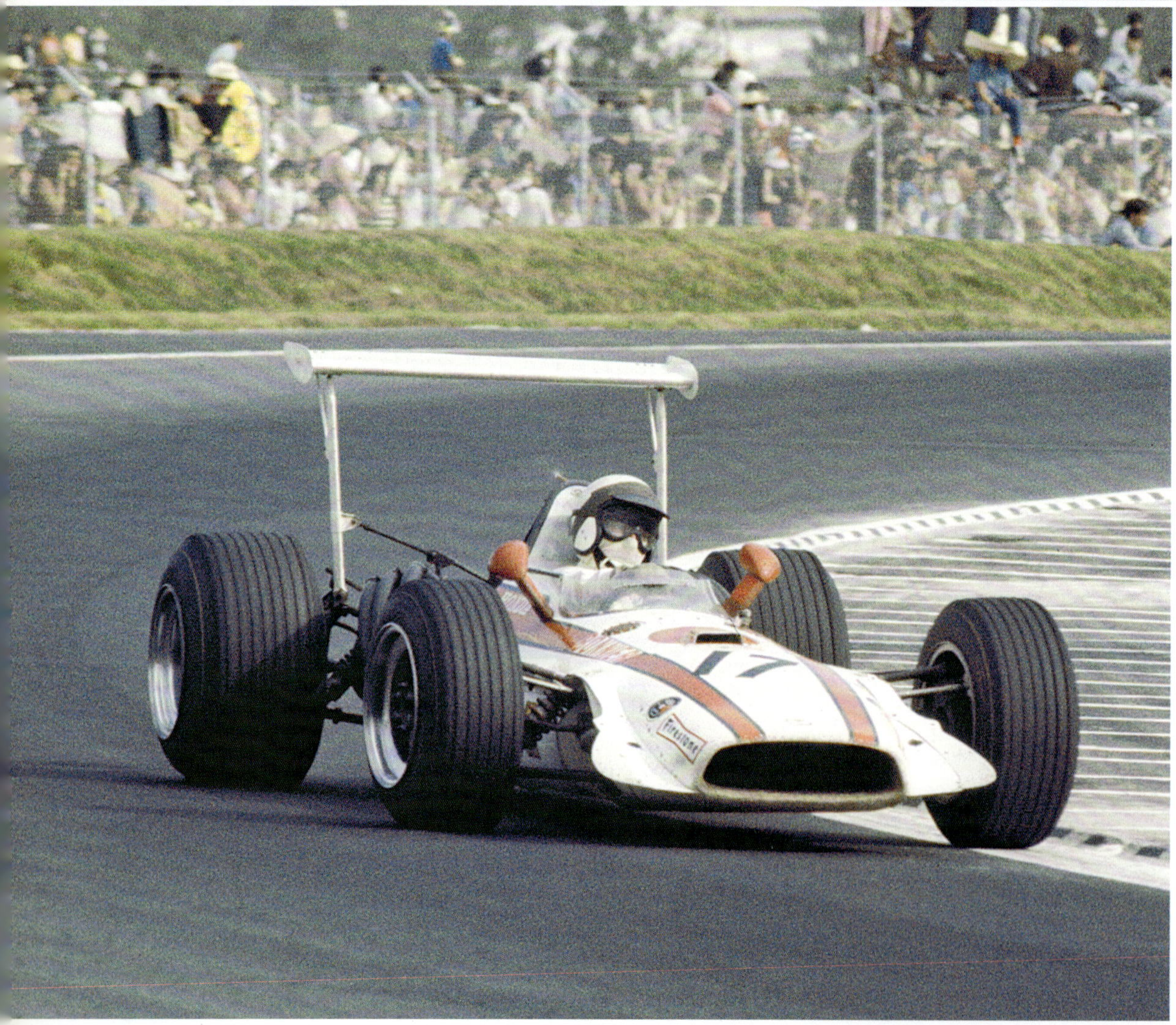

Coming to Mexico Graham Hill had 39 points, Jackie Stewart 36 and Denny Hulme 33. Hulme soon retired, but Hill, with an adjustable rear wing that could be feathered for less drag, swapped the lead with Stewart. Both were passed by Jo Siffert's pole sitting Walker/Durlacher Lotus 49B, seen here behind Hill's 49B (R6). However Siffert's throttle linkage broke and, after stopping for repairs, he finished 6th, breaking Clark's lap record by nearly four seconds! Meanwhile Stewart's Matra was misfiring and he fell to 7th. Hill won the race, his second World Championship and Lotus their third Constructors' title. He had overcome the team's demoralisation at the loss of Clark and his win in Mexico must have been consolation for losing the 1964 title here.

Who now remembers that Jo Bonnier raced the second Honda RA301 (F802) in Mexico? He started 18th on the grid but finished 5th one lap adrift. 'Jo Bo's GP career began at Monza in 1956 and ended at Watkins Glen in 1971.

1968 Teams, drivers and results

Cooper Car Co – Cooper T81B Maserati V12 and T86B BRM V12
Brian Redman (GB) (South African, Spanish and Belgian GPs only, crashed and injured at Spa and missed rest of season)
Lodovico Scarfiotti (I) (South African, Spanish and Monaco GPs only. Fatally injured at Rossfeld hillclimb in June)
Lucien Bianchi (B) (Monaco, Belgian, Dutch, German, Canadian, US and Mexican GPs only)
Vic Elford (GB) (French, British, German, Italian, Canadian, US and Mexican GPs only)
Johnny Servoz-Gavin (F) (French GP only)
Robin Widdows (GB) (British GP only)

Team Lotus and Gold Leaf Team Lotus (from Spanish GP onwards) – Lotus 49 Cosworth DFV and 49B Cosworth DFV
Jim Clark (GB) (South African GP only. Killed in F2 race at Hockenheim in April)
Graham Hill (GB) (WORLD CHAMPION)
Jack Oliver (GB) (Replaced Clark, missed South African and Spanish GPs, dns French and US GPs)
Mario Andretti (USA) (dns Italian GP, US GP only)
Bill Brack (CDN) (Canadian GP only)
Moises Solana (MEX) (Mexican GP only)

Owen Racing Organisation – BRM P115 H16, P125 V12 and P133 V12
Pedro Rodriguez (MEX)
Mike Spence (GB) (South African GP only, fatally injured during Indianapolis 500 qualifying)
Richard Attwood (GB) (Monaco, Belgian, Dutch, French, British and German GPs only)
Bobby Unser (USA) (dns Italian GP, US GP only)

Brabham Racing Organisation – Brabham BT24 Repco V8 and BT26 Repco V8
Jack Brabham (AUS)
Jochen Rindt (A)
Dan Gurney (USA) (Dutch GP only)

Bruce McLaren Motor Racing – McLaren M5A BRM V12 and M7A Cosworth DFV
Denny Hulme (NZ)
Bruce McLaren (NZ) (Missed South African GP)

Scuderia Ferrari SpA SEFAC – Ferrari 312/67 V12 and 312/68 V12
Chris Amon (NZ) (Missed Monaco GP)
Jacky Ickx (B) (Missed Monaco GP, dns Canadian and US GPs due to injuries received during practice for the Canadian GP)
Andrea de Adamich (I) (South African GP only)
Derek Bell (GB) (Italian and US GPs only)

Anglo American Racers – Eagle T1G Weslake V12 and McLaren M7A Cosworth DFV
Dan Gurney (USA) (Missed Spanish, Belgian and French GPs. Drove for Brabham at Dutch GP, bought spare McLaren from works and raced it in the Canadian, US and Mexican GPs)

Honda Racing – Honda RA300 V12, RA301 V12 and RA302 V8
John Surtees (GB)
Jo Schlesser (F) (French GP only, fatal crash, car destroyed)
David Hobbs (GB) (Italian GP only)

Matra International – Matra MS9 Cosworth DFV and MS10 Cosworth DFV
Jackie Stewart (GB) (Missed Spanish and Monaco GPs due to injury)
Jean-Pierre Beltoise (F) (Spanish GP only)
Johnny Servoz-Gavin (F) (Monaco, Italian, Canadian and Mexican GPs only)

Matra Sports – Matra MS7 Cosworth FVA (F2 car) and MS11 Matra V12
Jean-Pierre Beltoise (F)
Henri Pescarolo (F)

Rob Walker/Jack Durlacher Racing – Cooper T81 Maserati V12, Lotus 49 Cosworth DFV and 49B Cosworth DFV
Jo Siffert (CH)

Reg Parnell Racing – BRM P126 V12
Piers Courage (GB) (Missed South African GP)

Joakim Bonnier Racing Team – Cooper T81 Maserati V12, McLaren M5A BRM V12 and Honda RA301 V12
Jo Bonnier (S) (Missed Spanish, French and German GPs. Raced spare works Honda under his name at Mexican GP)

Charles Vögele Racing Team – Brabham BT20 Repco V8
Silvio Moser (CH) (dnq Monaco and Italian GPs, Dutch and British GPs only)

Caltex Racing Team Frankfurt – Brabham BT24 Repco V8
Kurt Ahrens Jnr. (D) (German GP only)

Bayerische Motoren Werke – Lola T102 BMW
Hubert Hahne (D) (German GP only)

Castrol Oils Ltd – Eagle T1G Climax FPF
Al Pease (CDN) (Canadian GP only)

Team Gunston – Brabham BT20 Repco V8 and LDS Mk3 Repco V8
John Love (RSR) (South African GP only in Brabham)
Sam Tingle (RSR) (South African GP only in LDS)

Scuderia Scribante – Brabham BT11 Repco V8
Dave Charlton (ZA) (South African GP only)

Team Pretoria – Brabham BT7 Climax FPF
Jackie Pretorious (ZA) (South African GP only)

John Love – Cooper T76 Climax FPF
Basil van Rooyen (ZA) (South African GP only)

WORLD CHAMPIONSHIP VENUES AND WINNERS (twelve rounds)

Part 1

South African GP	Kyalami	Jim Clark
Spanish GP	Jarama	Graham Hill
Monaco GP	Monte Carlo	Graham Hill
Belgian GP	Spa-Francorchamps	Bruce McLaren
Dutch GP	Zandvoort	Jackie Stewart
French GP	Rouen-les Essarts	Jacky Ickx

Part 2

British GP	Brands Hatch	Jo Siffert
German GP	Nürburgring	Jackie Stewart
Italian GP	Monza	Denny Hulme
Canadian GP	St Jovite	Denny Hulme
United States GP	Watkins Glen	Jackie Stewart
Mexican GP	Mexico City	Graham Hill

DRIVERS' CHAMPIONSHIP
Points: 9-6-4-3-2-1.
Best 5 scores counted from Part 1 (six races), plus best 5 scores from Part 2 (six races).

1	Graham Hill	Lotus	48
2	Jackie Stewart	Matra	36
3	Denny Hulme	McLaren	33
4	Jacky Ickx	Ferrari	27
5	Bruce McLaren	McLaren	22
6	Pedro Rodriguez	BRM	18
7	Jo Siffert	Cooper/Lotus	12
8	John Surtees	Honda	12
9	Jean-Pierre Beltoise	Matra	11
10	Chris Amon	Ferrari	10
11	Jim Clark	Lotus	9
12	Jochen Rindt	Brabham	8
13	Richard Attwood	BRM	6
14	Johnny Servoz-Gavin	Matra/Cooper	6
15	Jack Oliver	Lotus	6
16	Lodovico Scarfiotti	Cooper	6
17	Lucien Bianchi	Cooper	5
18	Vic Elford	Cooper	5
19	Brian Redman	Cooper	4
20	Piers Courage	BRM	4
21	Dan Gurney	Eagle/Brabham/McLaren	3
22	Jo Bonnier	Cooper/McLaren/Honda	3
23	Silvio Moser	Brabham	2
24	Jack Brabham	Brabham	2

CONSTRUCTORS' CHAMPIONSHIP
Points: 9-6-4-3-2-1 (awarded only to best-placed finisher).
Best 5 scores counted from Part 1 (six races), plus best 5 scores from Part 2 (six races).

1	Lotus-Ford (Cosworth)	62
2	McLaren-Ford (Cosworth)	49
3	Matra-Ford (Cosworth)	45
4	Ferrari	32
5	BRM	28
6	Honda	14
7	Cooper-BRM	14
8	Brabham-Repco	10
9	Matra	8
10	McLaren-BRM	3

1969

GREAT SCOT

Out with the old, in with the new. Cooper, despite the possibility of a Cosworth powered car, disappeared. Sponsorship negotiations with Wilkinson Sword failed, the loss of their BP backing in 1967 having already undermined them. On 11 June 1969 everything was auctioned off, an ignominious end to the pioneers of the modern rear-engined Grand Prix car.

Driver changes came thick and fast. Lotus replaced Jack Oliver with Jochen Rindt to partner Graham Hill. They also ran Mario Andretti in three races. Jackie Stewart and Jean-Pierre Beltoise represented Tyrrell (aka Matra International), the French manufacturer having withdrawn their factory V12 cars.

Brabham dropped Repco and joined the Cosworth DFV club and hired Jacky Ickx who had left Ferrari to partner Jack Brabham in his penultimate season.

After a promising 1968 season McLaren with Bruce McLaren and Denny Hulme were not so impressive. Hulme won the Mexican GP but the team's Can-Am campaign was far more rewarding.

Following Honda's withdrawal John Surtees arrived at BRM and was partnered by Jack Oliver whilst Canadian George Eaton did the North American events. Tony Rudd resigned from BRM (and went to Lotus) and was replaced by Aubrey Woods from the now defunct Anglo-American Racing (Dan Gurney missed the 1969 F1 season). Pedro Rodriguez started with the second string BRM equipped Reg Parnell Racing but later joined Ferrari.

Chris Amon was Ferrari's sole driver until the British GP when Rodriguez came aboard. However, no Ferraris raced in Germany and Amon departed Maranello after testing problems with the new 312B at Monza. It was to be the nadir of Ferrari's F1 participation. They raced under NART colours in Canada, America and Mexico.

Amongst the independent teams Rob Walker appeared for his twelfth season, again with Jo Siffert. Newcomer Frank Williams made an impressive F1 debut with a Brabham for Piers Courage and Colin Crabbe's Antique Automobiles progressed from Cooper-Maserati to McLaren M7A for driver Vic Elford.

Lotus, McLaren and Ferrari used updated 1968 machines, but Matra, BRM and Brabham all fielded new cars. Following the catastrophic failures at the Spanish GP the high mounted wings on tall struts were banned before the second practice session at Monaco. All aerodynamic devices now had to be part of the bodywork, not suspension mounted aerofoils.

4WD returned to F1, but it no longer offered any advantage due to the wider, stickier modern tyres. Lotus, McLaren, Matra and Cosworth built cars but they were all duds. A more successful innovation was the advent of the new Bell Star full face helmet, although some found them claustrophobic.

The season was dominated by Stewart who had taken over the mantle of Jim Clark. He won six races to achieve his first World Championship at Monza. The remaining GPs were won by Hill, Ickx, Hulme and Rindt. The Belgian GP at Spa-Francorchamps was cancelled; it returned in 1970 but this was the last time it was used for F1 in the 8.76-mile configuration.

The non-championship events in Britain fell to Stewart (Brands Hatch), Brabham (Silverstone) and Ickx (Oulton Park).

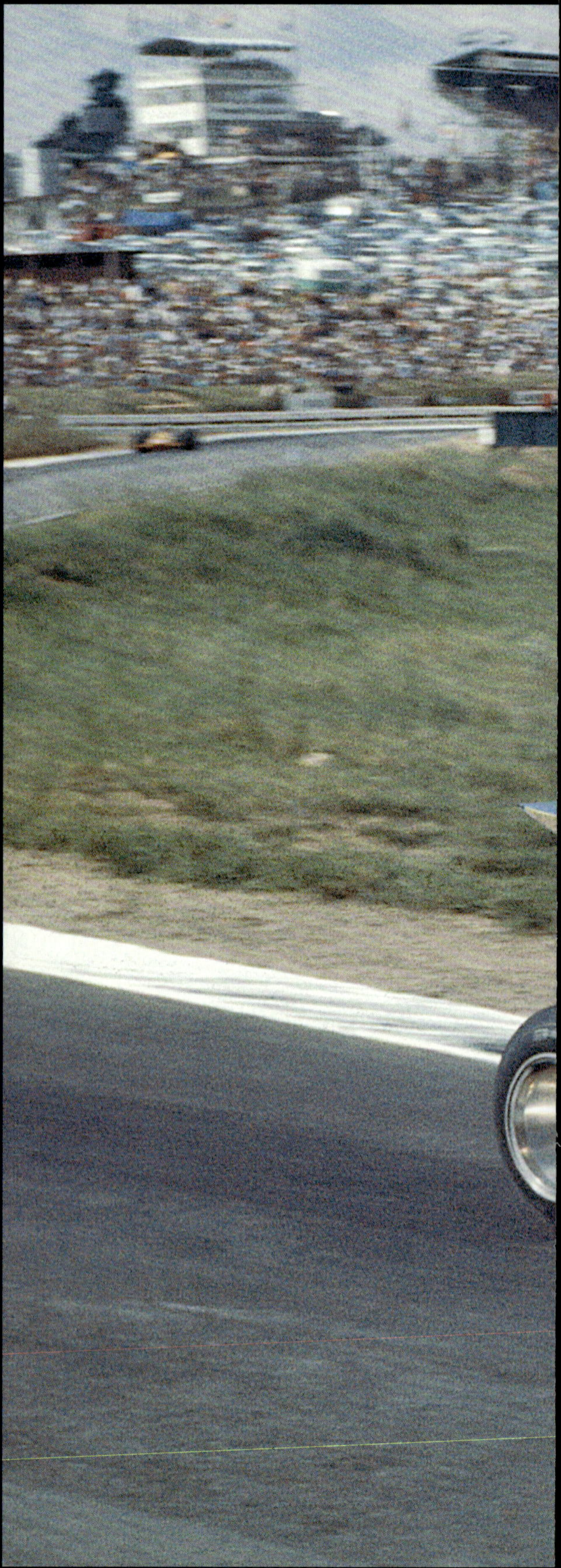

Lotus had a trio of stars at Kyalami with World Champion Graham Hill, Austrian Jochen Rindt and Mario Andretti in his second drive for the team. Andretti outqualified Hill but followed Rindt and Hill in the race. Eventually he reached 3rd after several retirements but then fell victim to transmission failure in the 49B (R11). Rindt also retired, but Hill finished 2nd behind Jackie Stewart's Matra with Denny Hulme's McLaren 3rd. The crowd meanwhile enjoy the warmth and sunshine and you can almost smell the barbecues and hear the popping of beer bottles.

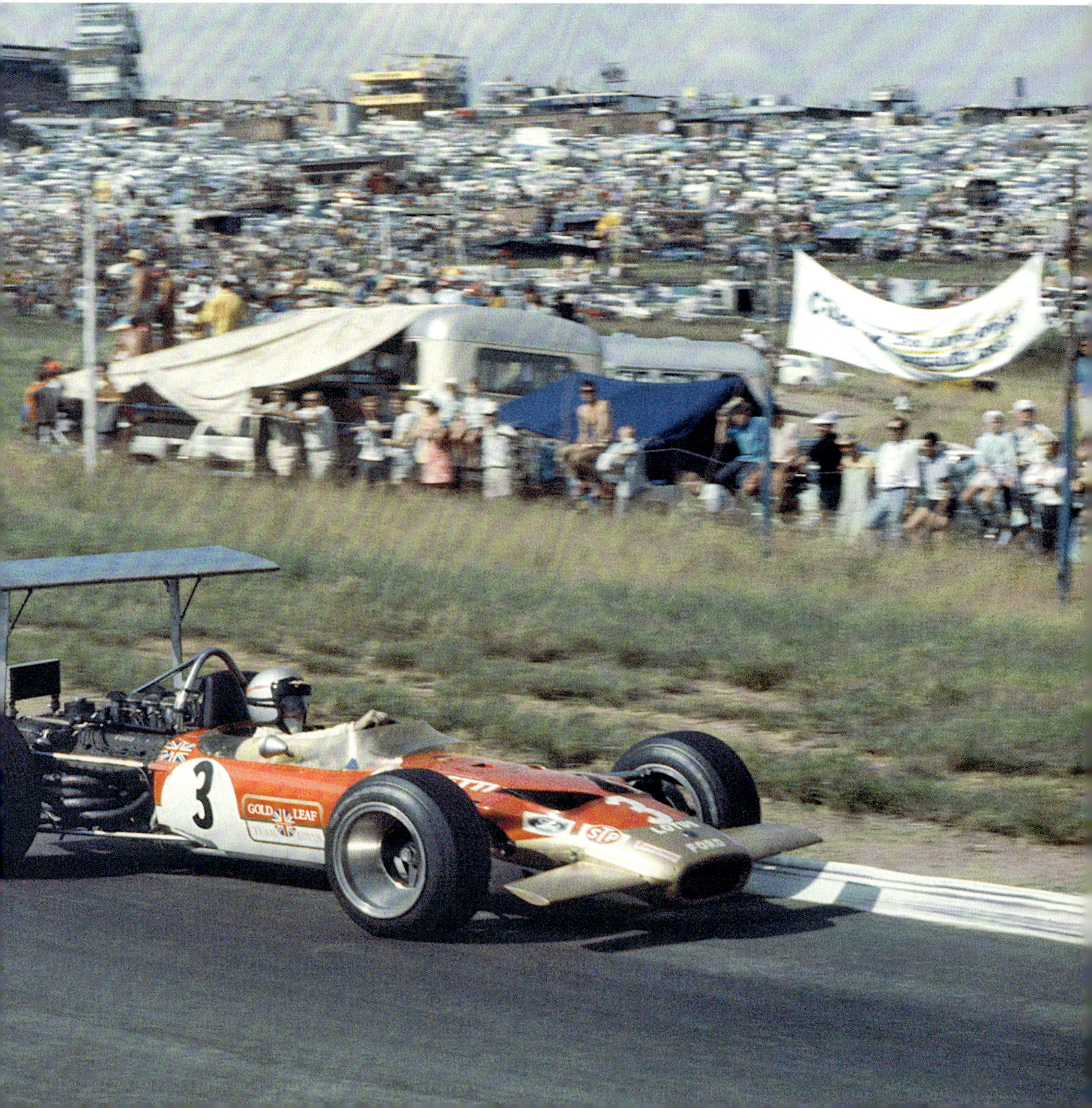

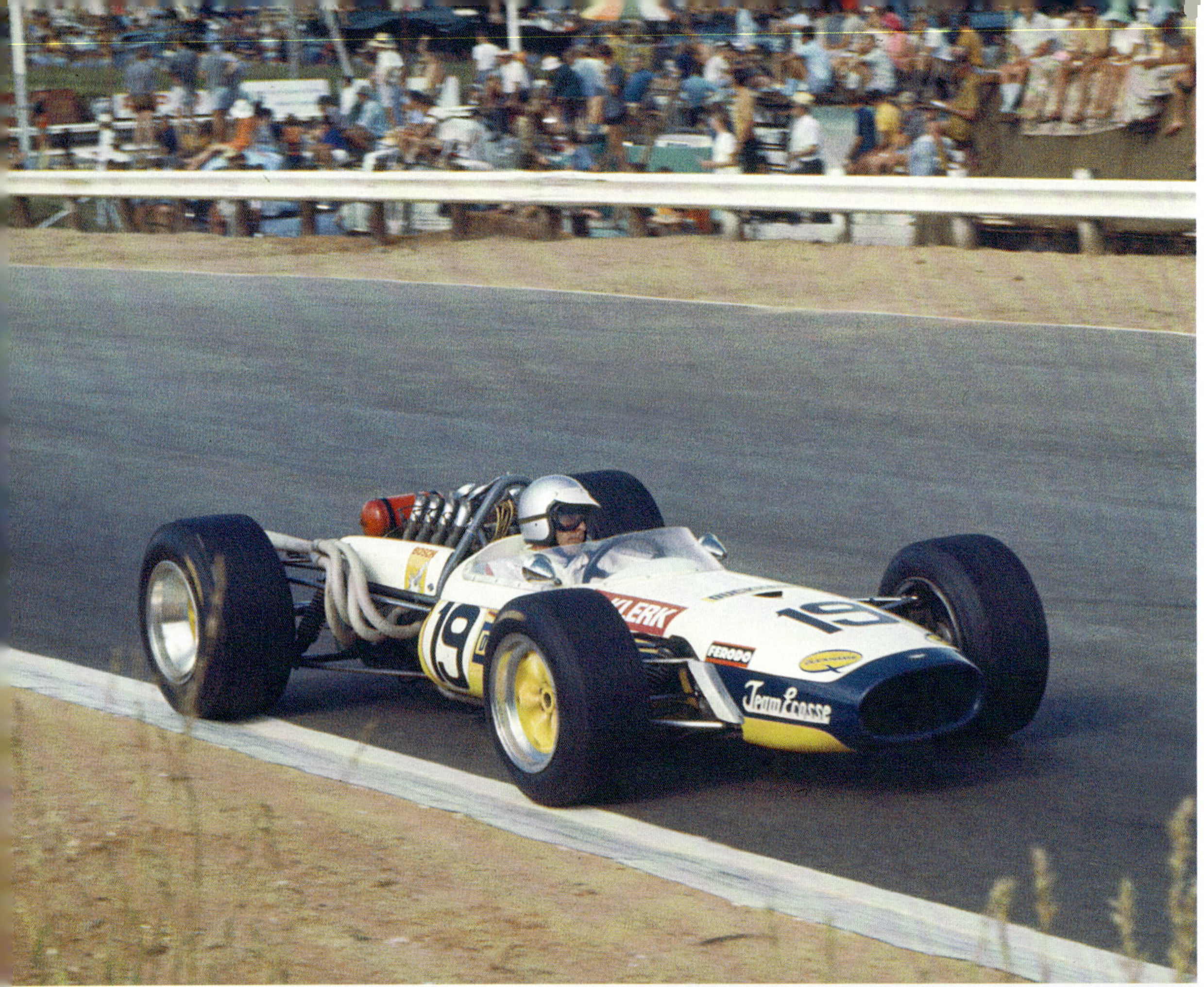

Peter de Klerk races the old Jack Holmes entered Brabham BT19 Repco (F1-1-66) at Kyalami. Every year the Europeans turned up in new cars and the local aces, driving obsolete machinery, found themselves relegated to the back of the grid. A talented driver, South African de Klerk only ever competed at World Championship level in his home race. He was an accomplished sports car driver and in 1967 drove one of the Surtees run Lola Aston Martin T70s at Le Mans.

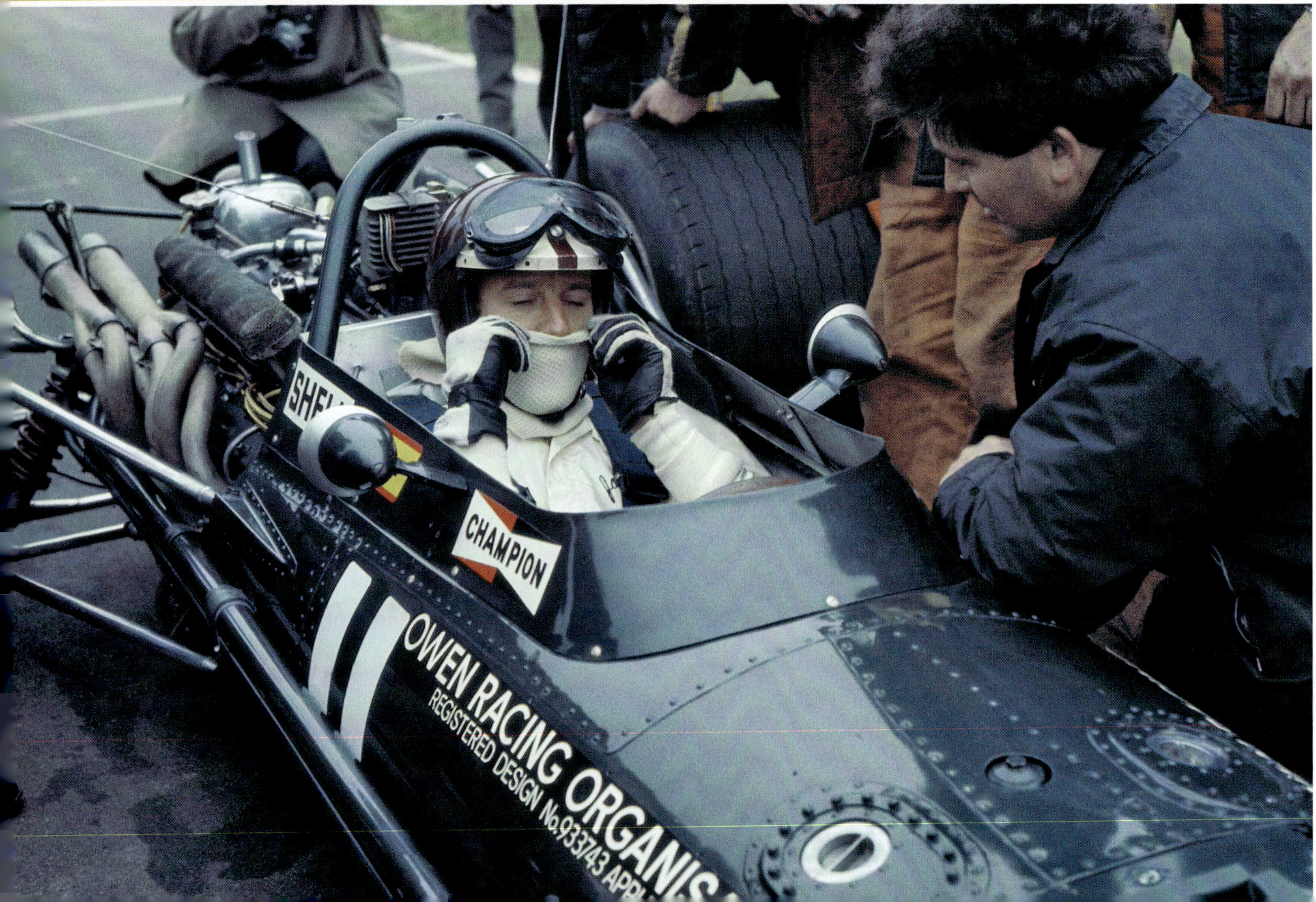

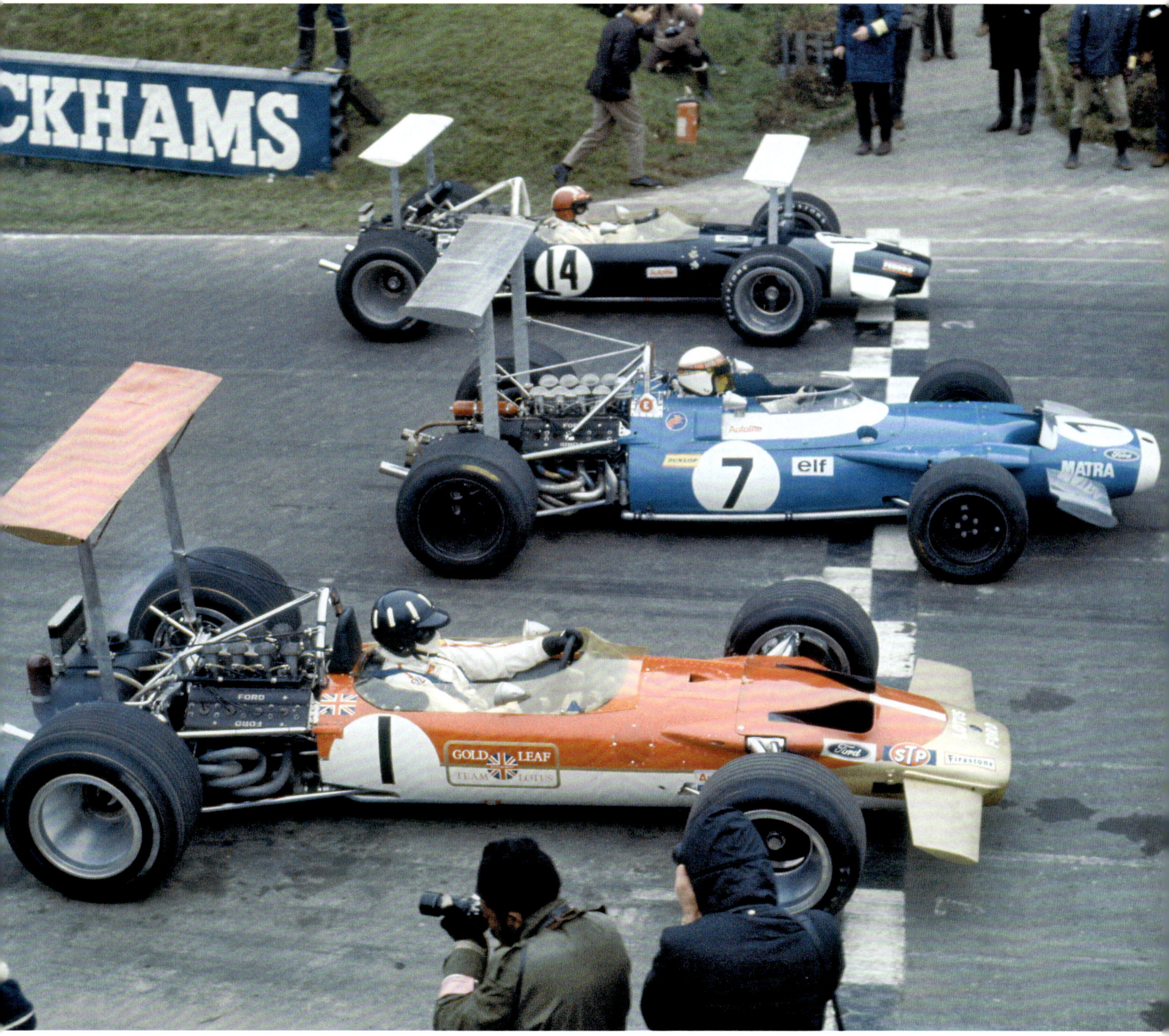

After Jackie Stewart's South African GP win in the Matra MS10 he used the new MS80-01 at the Brands Hatch Race of Champions, beating Hill's pole sitting Lotus 49B (R6) by 7 seconds. Denny Hulme's McLaren M7A was 3rd and Siffert's Rob Walker Lotus 49B (R7), seen here on the outside of the front row was 4th. However Hill's new team mate Jochen Rindt set fastest lap before retiring and is set to usurp the World Champion's position at Lotus.

Jack Oliver sitting in the Len Terry designed BRM P133 at the Brands Hatch Race of Champions. After a traumatic 1968 at Lotus, his contract was not renewed. This was unfair as most of the crashes and retirements had been caused by component failures rather than driver error. At BRM he had to face a team dominated by John Surtees and endured a dismal year, with uncompetitive and unreliable machinery.

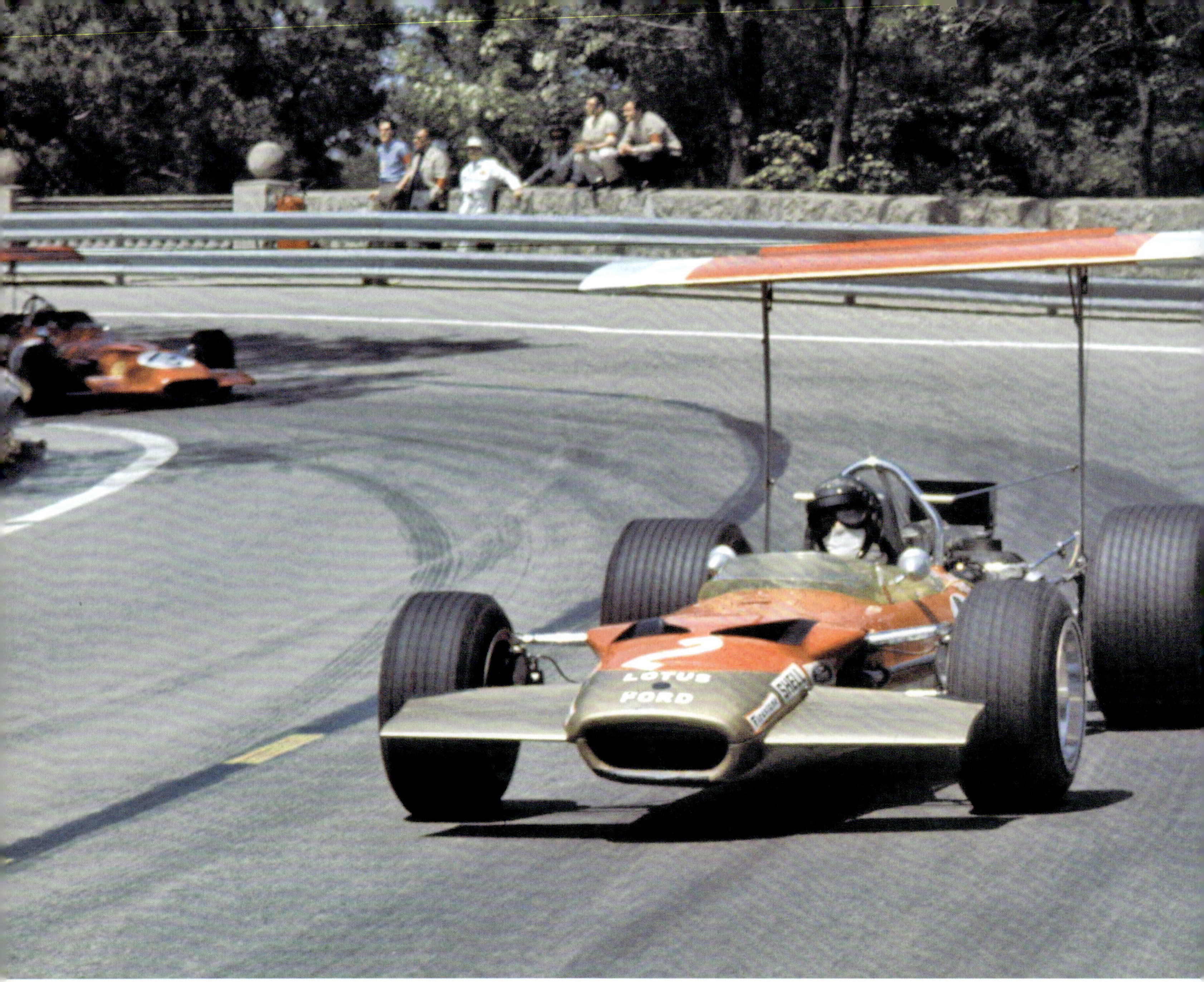

↑ Montjuich Park, Barcelona was rather like a lengthened, much faster Monaco. Jochen Rindt put his Lotus 49B (R9) on pole for the Spanish GP, leading the race ahead of Chris Amon's Ferrari. However, team mate Hill suffered a rear wing failure and crashed, fortunately without injury. During practice the rear wings were extended beyond the width of the rear wheels, (denoted by the white endpieces) and they had folded upwards causing the crash. The same fate befell Rindt who hit Hill's wrecked car, landing on top of the Armco and falling back onto the track. Rindt escaped with minor injuries from his smashed car.

↗ Yet again Chris Amon, who started alongside Jochen Rindt at Montjuich Park, convincingly led a GP only to have his engine seize on lap 57, handing victory to Jackie Stewart's Matra MS80. The Ferrari 312 (0017) was still an effective weapon in Amon's hands but the hugely gifted New Zealander was squandering his talent. Look at the angle of the front wishbones as Chris brakes as hard as he dares, and the puny single layer Armco barrier that barely protects the spectators from the speeding cars in such close confines.

→ John Surtees came to BRM in 1969 but they were in need of a sponsor. Surtees finished a delayed 5th in the Spanish GP in the P138-01 due to a defective ignition coil box. The BRM boasted a 48-valve V12 engine, but it was not giving the same power in the car as it had on the test bed.

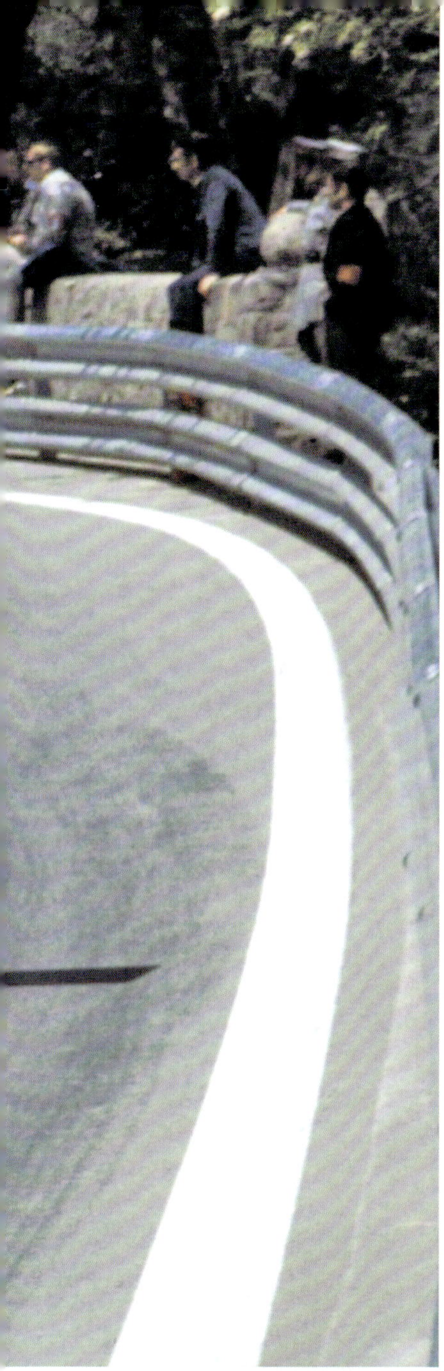

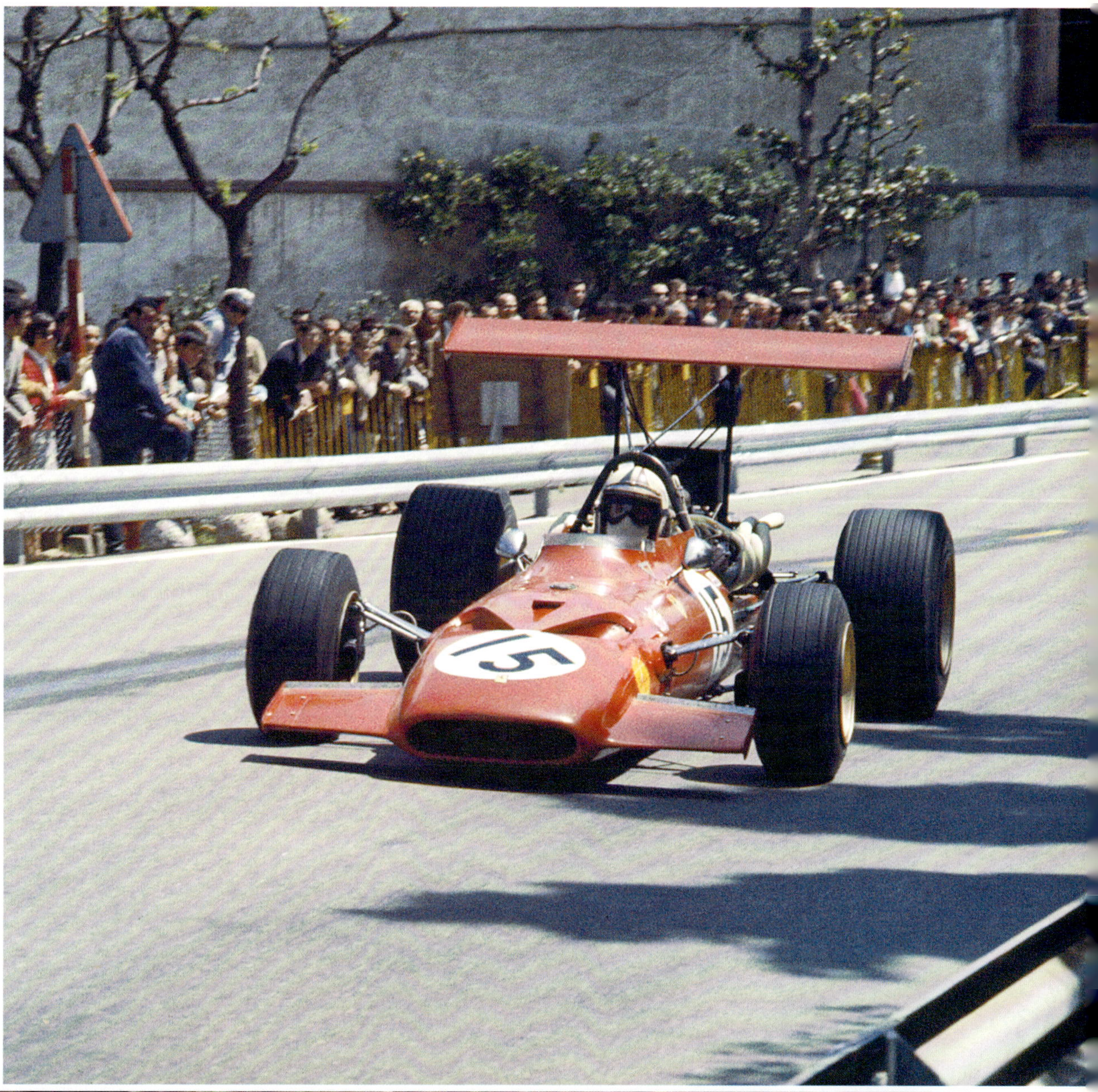
15

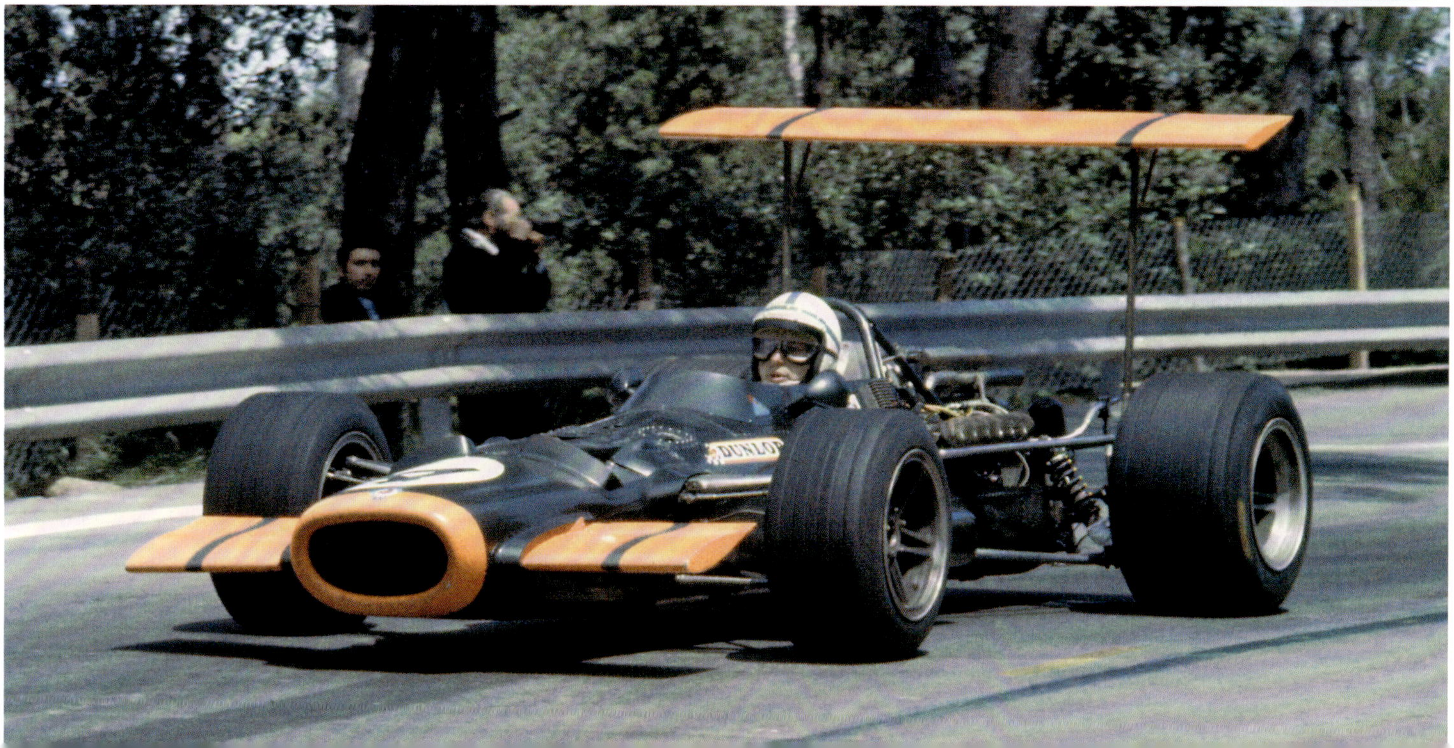
DUNLOP

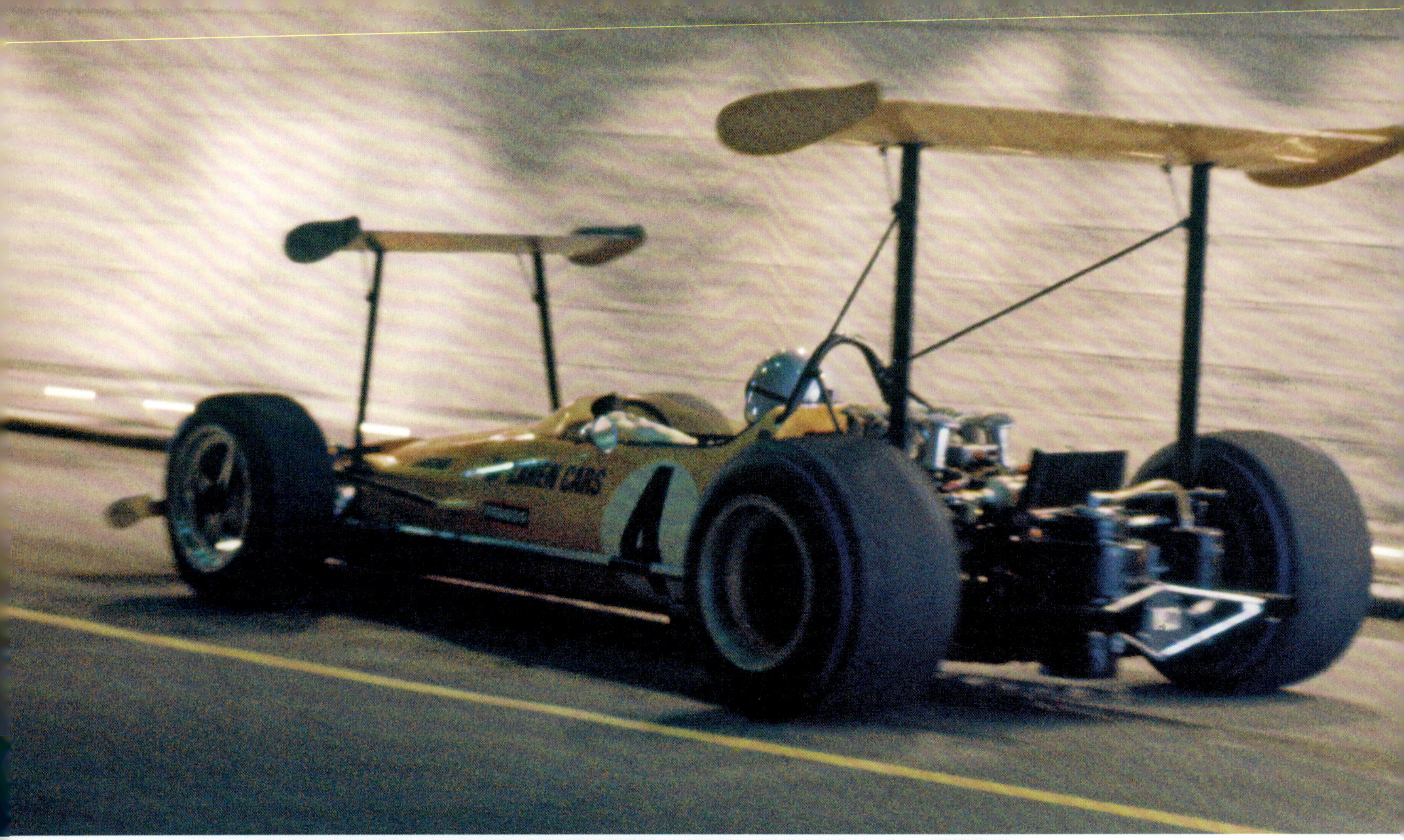

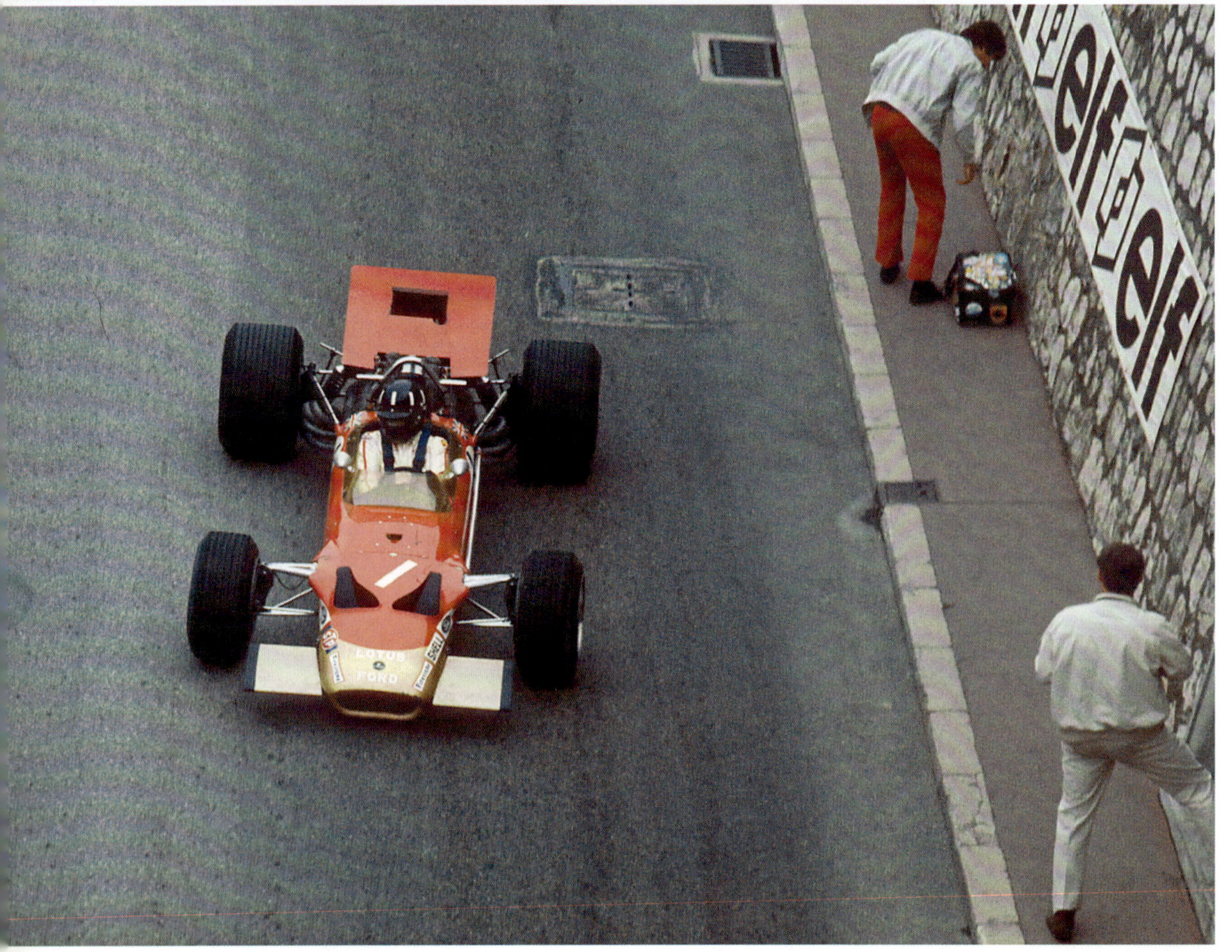

Following the accidents at Montjuich Park the Commission Sportive Internationale decided to ban wings after the first (Thursday) practice session at Monaco. It applied to all wings or aerodynamic panels that were not part of the bodywork, including suspension mounted aerofoils. Bruce McLaren, still bewinged, blasts through the tunnel in the McLaren M7C-1 on Thursday 16 May. Neither car was competitive and McLaren and Denny Hulme finished in 5th and 6th places respectively.

Nowhere to hide. Graham Hill, Lotus 49B (R10) races past the unconcerned photographers at Monaco. He was outpaced by Jackie Stewart's Matra and Chris Amon's Ferrari, but when they retired early in the race he won. This was Hill's fifth Monaco win and his final GP victory. The rear cowl of the 49B (R10) was made from aluminium sheeting removed from inside the team transporter, as Lotus had no spare alloy sheet after the Spanish crashes.

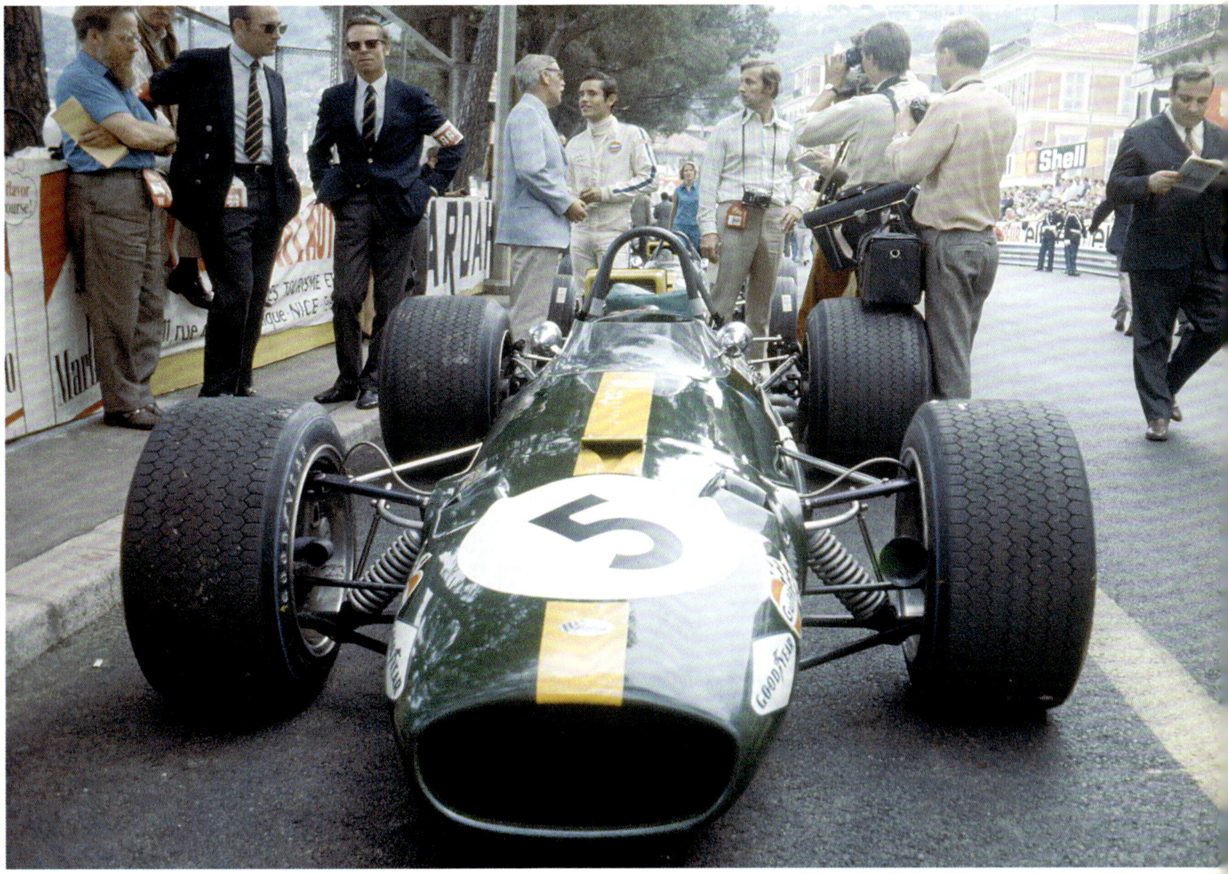

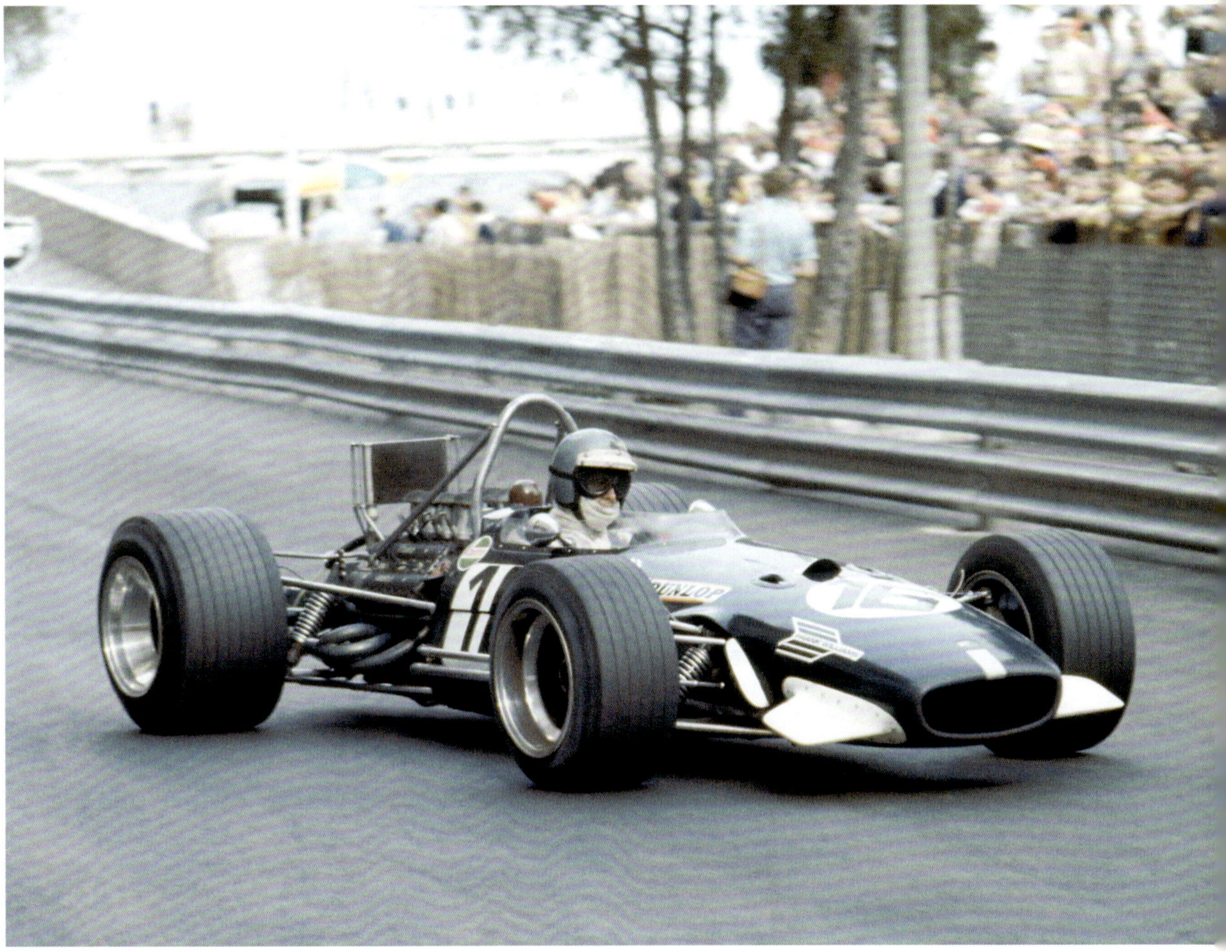

Jacky Ickx stands between famous Porsche team manager Husche von Hanstein and Paddy McNally of *Autosport* behind his Brabham BT26-3 Cosworth. Both Brabhams retired in the race. On the far left is the bearded figure of Denis Jenkinson (D.S.J. or 'Jenks') of *Motor Sport*, Mille Miglia and Eric Oliver sidecar racing fame. Wearing the second blazer from the left is 1960 Le Mans winner and famous motoring author Paul Frère who raced at Monaco in 1955.

With a proper car underneath him Piers Courage (seen here approaching the old chicane) raced to 2nd place at Monaco in the Frank Williams Brabham BT26-1 ahead of Jo Siffert's Rob Walker Lotus. Courage was offered a drive at Lotus in 1968 to replace Jim Clark, but he preferred to do F2 with Frank Williams whilst racing the Parnell BRMs in F1. 1969 was the first year of the Williams F1 team and for a long time thereafter its best.

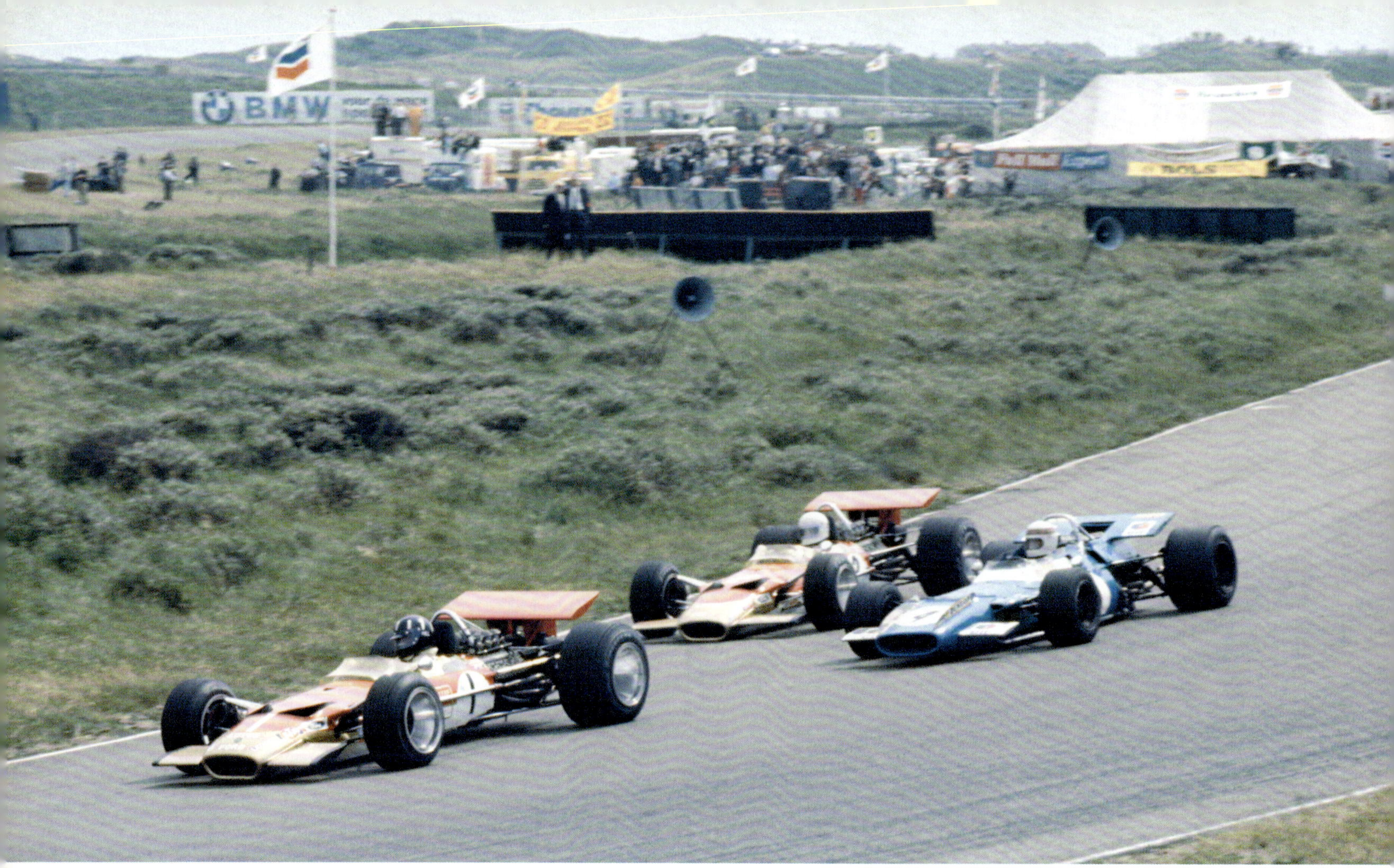

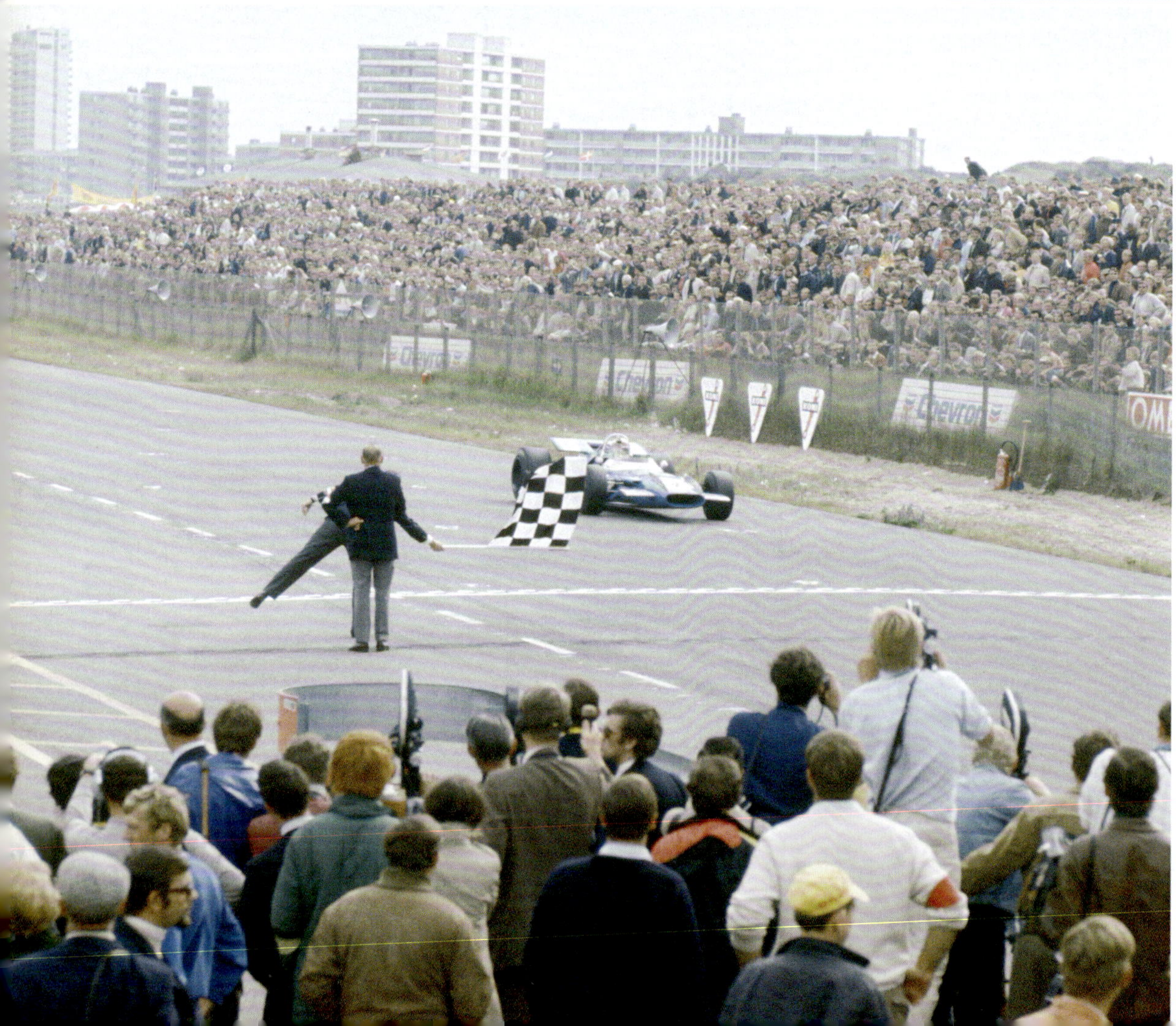

The GLTL Lotus 49Bs of Graham Hill and Jochen Rindt with Jackie Stewart in the Tyrrell Matra MS80 dive into Tarzan seconds after the start at Zandvoort. Hill briefly led, but his handling quickly deteriorated, then Rindt took over until a driveshaft velocity joint failed on lap 17, probably as a result of the wheelbanging between the Austrian and Hill in the opening laps. This left Jackie Stewart to win as he pleased, his third GP victory of the year.

Jackie Stewart crosses the line at the Dutch GP in the Tyrrell Matra MS80-02 in front of a huge crowd. The strange looking figure with three legs is in fact an observer standing behind the man waving the chequered flag. *Autosport*'s race report remarked that "One couldn't help thinking, though, that Zandvoort is not an ideal circuit, as there are so few places for people to pass." If only they had known what the future held in store.

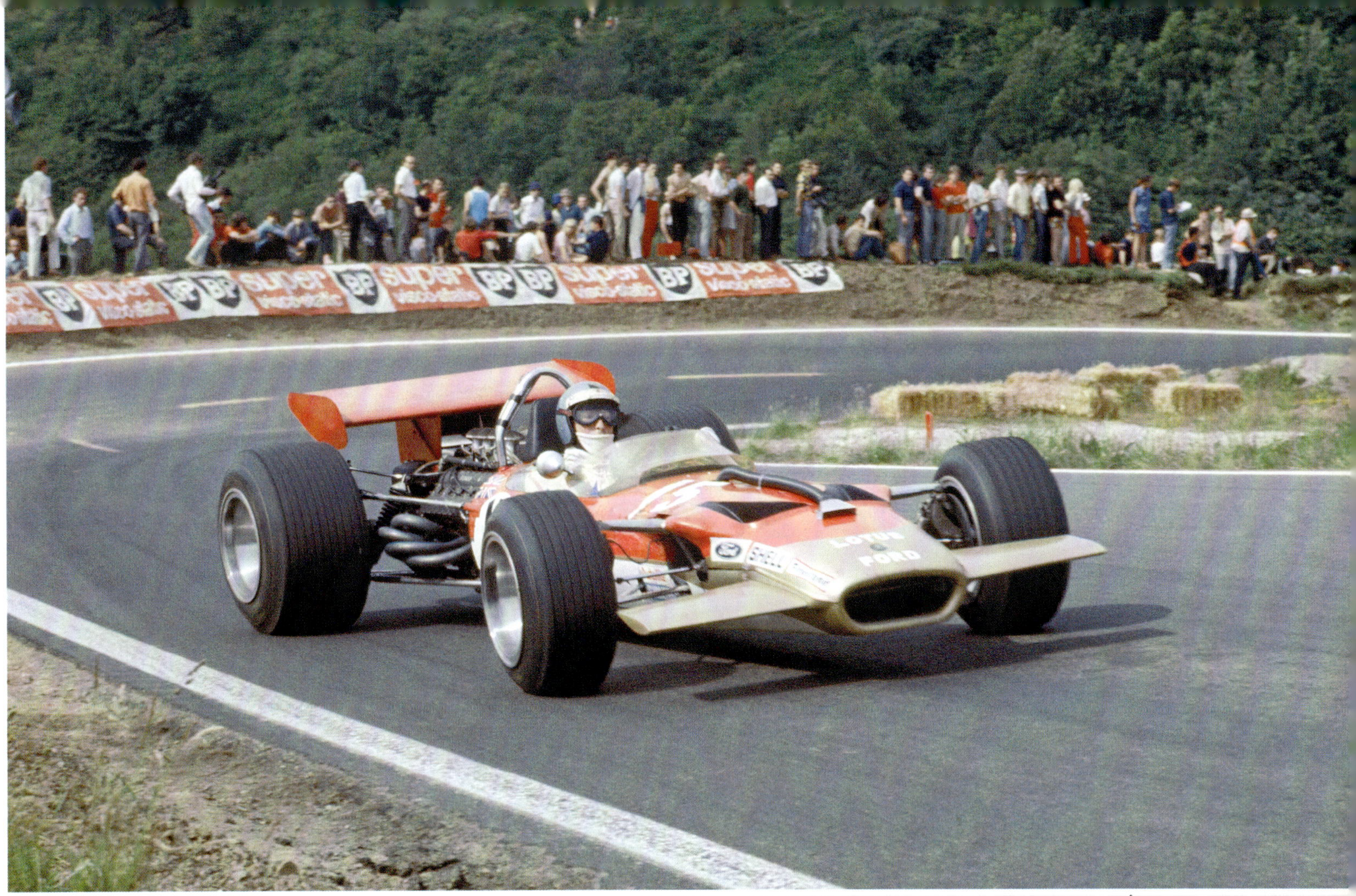

Thus far Jochen Rindt's Lotus sojourn was proving to be controversial. Rindt wrote an open letter to the FIA that appeared in the press demanding that wings be banned, infuriating Colin Chapman. During the French GP on the Charade circuit near Clermont-Ferrand another obstacle appeared, motion sickness, a legacy of his Spanish crash. To offset this he borrowed one of Piers Courage's open face helmets rather than use his full face Bell Star. Nevertheless the problem persisted, greatly exacerbated by the circuit's twisting, undulating nature and Rindt in the 49B (R6) had to stop with double vision and nausea on lap 23.

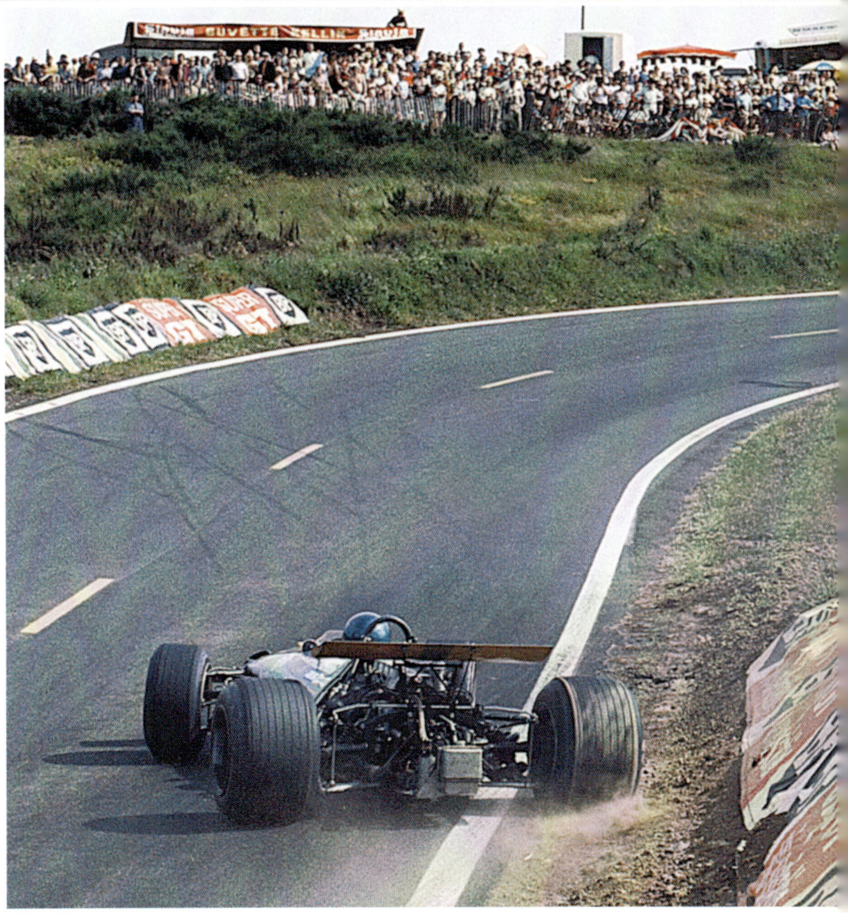

This is what you call putting a wheel in the dirt. Fortunately 1969 tyres were thick enough to take it. Jacky Ickx finished 3rd in the Brabham BT26A-2 behind the Matras of Jackie Stewart and Jean-Pierre Beltoise. Only 13 cars started the French GP on the 5-mile circuit and there were a lot of very big gaps and long silences. The works and Parnell Racing BRMs decided not to enter because of their lack of pace and Jack Brabham was out of action for several weeks after a nasty testing accident at Silverstone. Good old days? Not always.

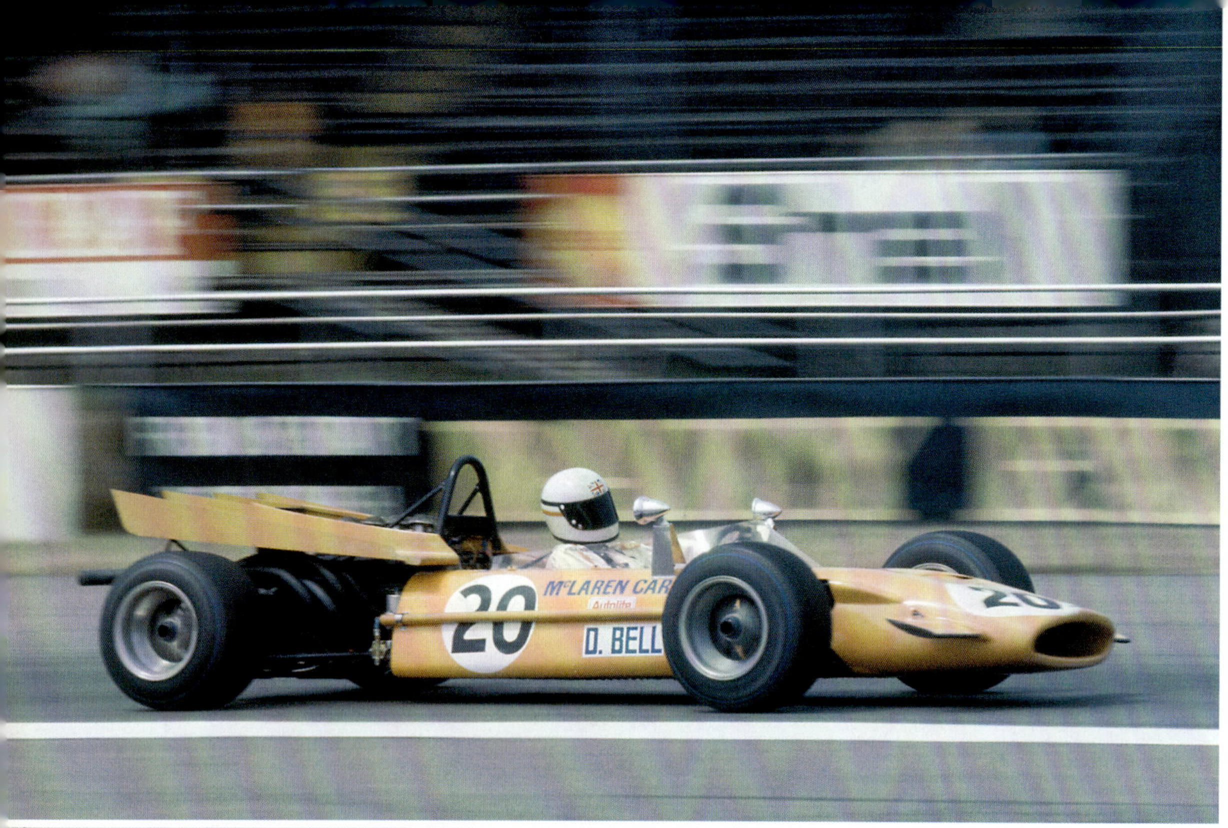

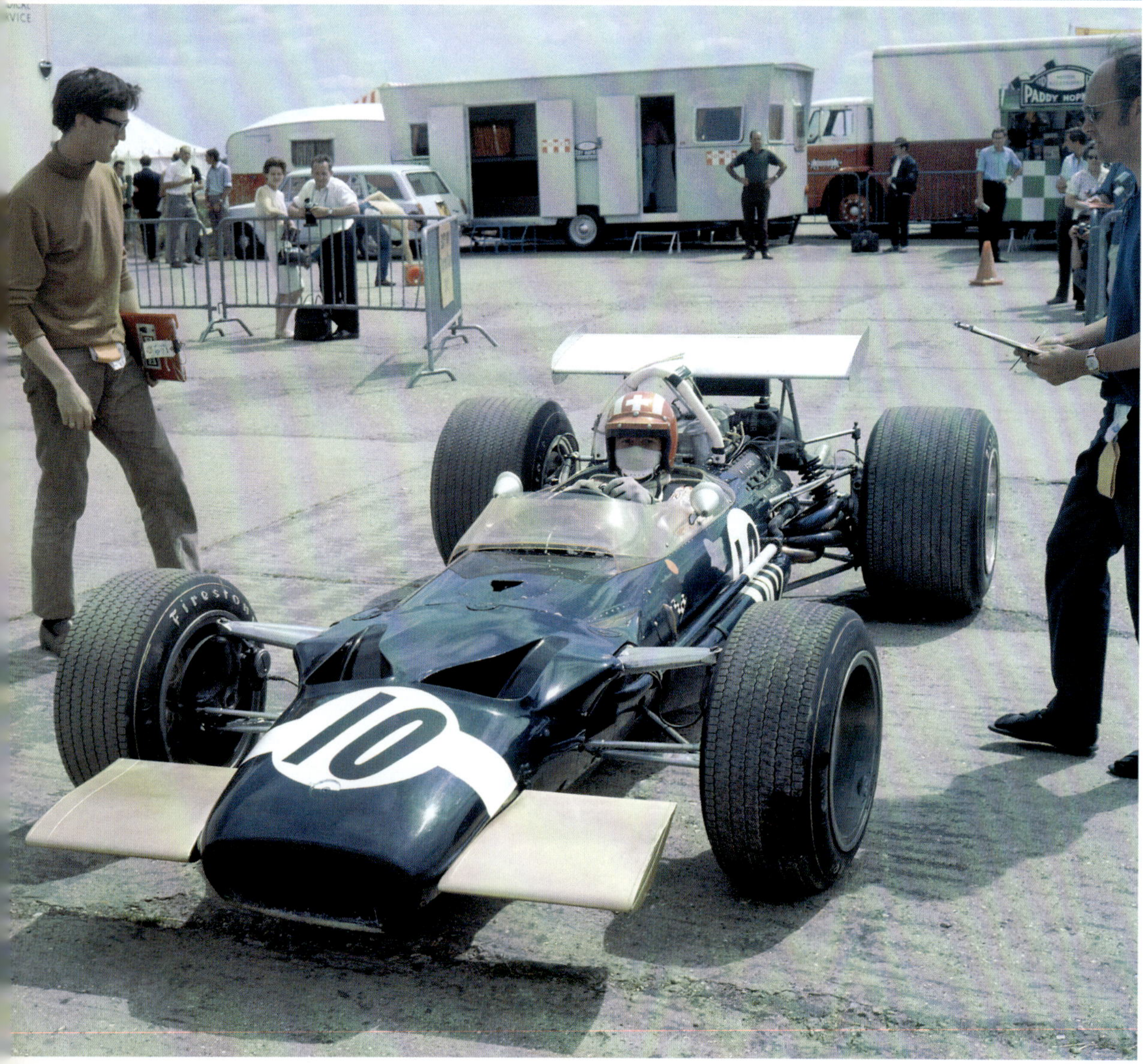

The 4WD McLaren M9A was designed by Swiss Jo Marquart who had been responsible for the very successful McLaren M8 Can-Am cars. Later he was involved with Huron, GRD, Modus and finally Argo. He died in 1993. It was a serious attempt, but the basic dynamics and packaging of 4WD were fundamentally flawed for F1 application by this time due to the advances in tyre and chassis technology in tandem with the use of aerodynamic devices. Derek Bell did his best at Silverstone, but the ungainly looking device languished on the penultimate row along with another 4WD turkey, the Lotus 63 of John Miles. The M9A retired on lap 5 with a broken rear suspension carrier.

Jo Siffert continued his inconsistent F1 form during 1969, sometimes fast as at Monaco and Zandvoort, sometimes average with the Rob Walker/Jack Durlacher Lotus 49B (R7) that was not as reliable as it should have been. At Silverstone the Lotus 49s had inadequate fuel capacity for what turned out to be a very rapid race and they all had to refuel during the last few laps. Siffert finished 8th having also experienced gearbox problems.

What are you doing in there? The versatile Pedro Rodriguez joined Ferrari at Silverstone and stayed until the end of the season. Pedro raced mid-field in the resurrected 1967 312 0009 but the engine failed on lap 61. Chris Amon's 1969 312 0017 race car (alongside) also broke and behind is his practice car 0019, both featuring oil coolers in nacelles mounted on the rear wings. Silverstone was Amon's last race for Ferrari despite the announcement of Fiat backing at the Dutch GP. Following repeated engine failures during testing with the new car he quit before the Italian GP. He should have waited; the new flat-12 312B turned out to be a winner in 1970.

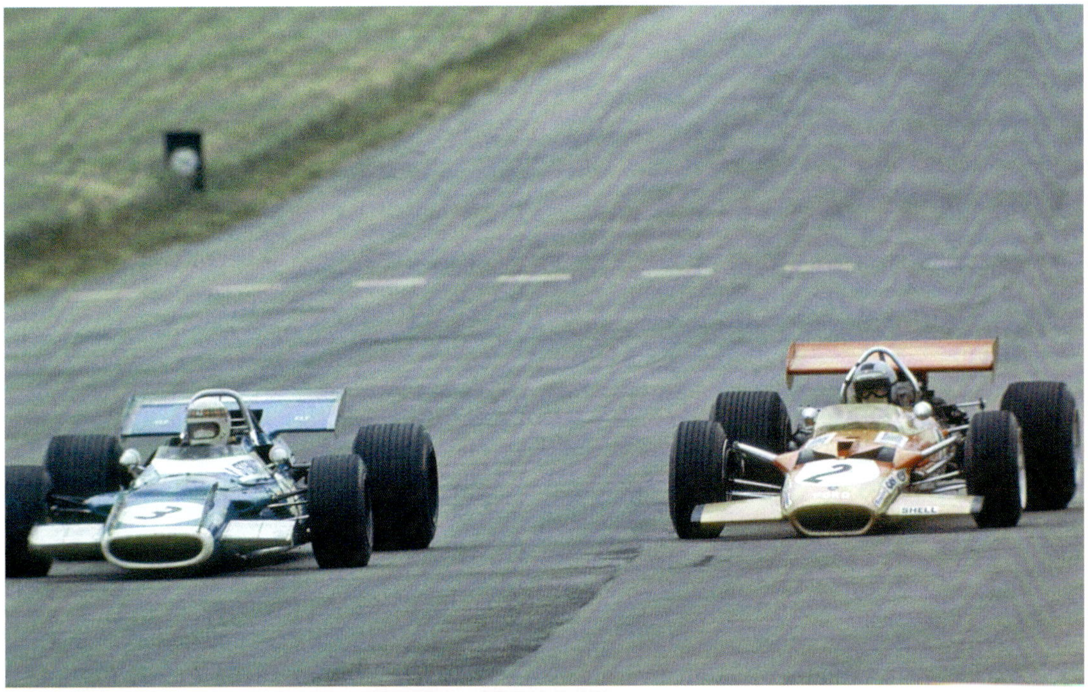

Jackie Stewart and Jochen Rindt had a tremendous set-to at Silverstone that was only ended by Rindt's problems. Heading into the braking area on Hangar Straight the Lotus nose is scraping the tarmac whilst Stewart's Matra MS80 seems less stressed. Unlike the other front runners including 2nd placed Jacky Ickx's Brabham, Stewart was not bothered by excessive fuel consumption because the Matra had a reserve tank. As in Spain he was running an older 8 series Cosworth DFV rather than the more powerful 9 series fitted to many other Cosworth users. Despite this and having to use team mate Beltoise's car after a practice mishap he set fastest lap on his way to victory.

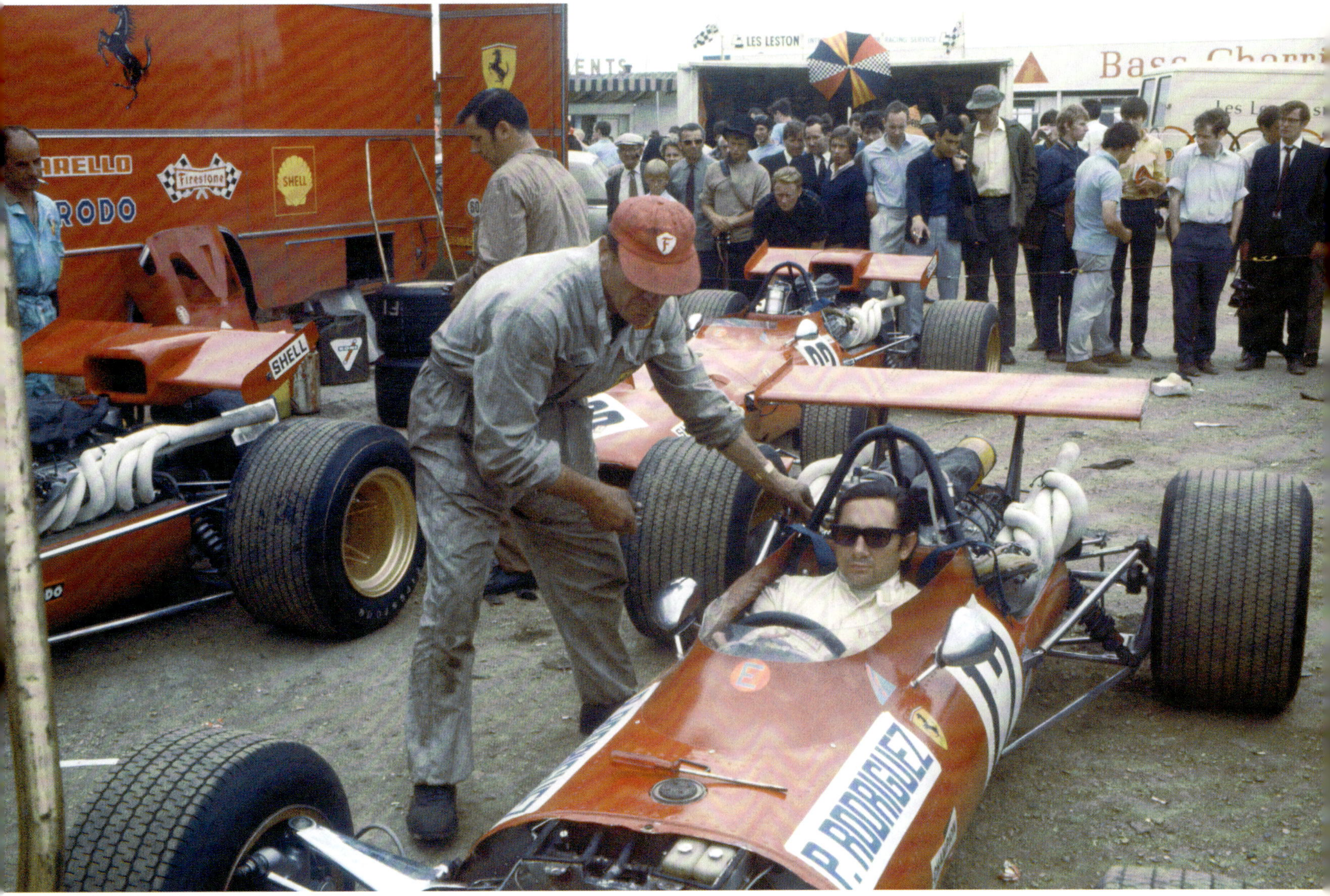

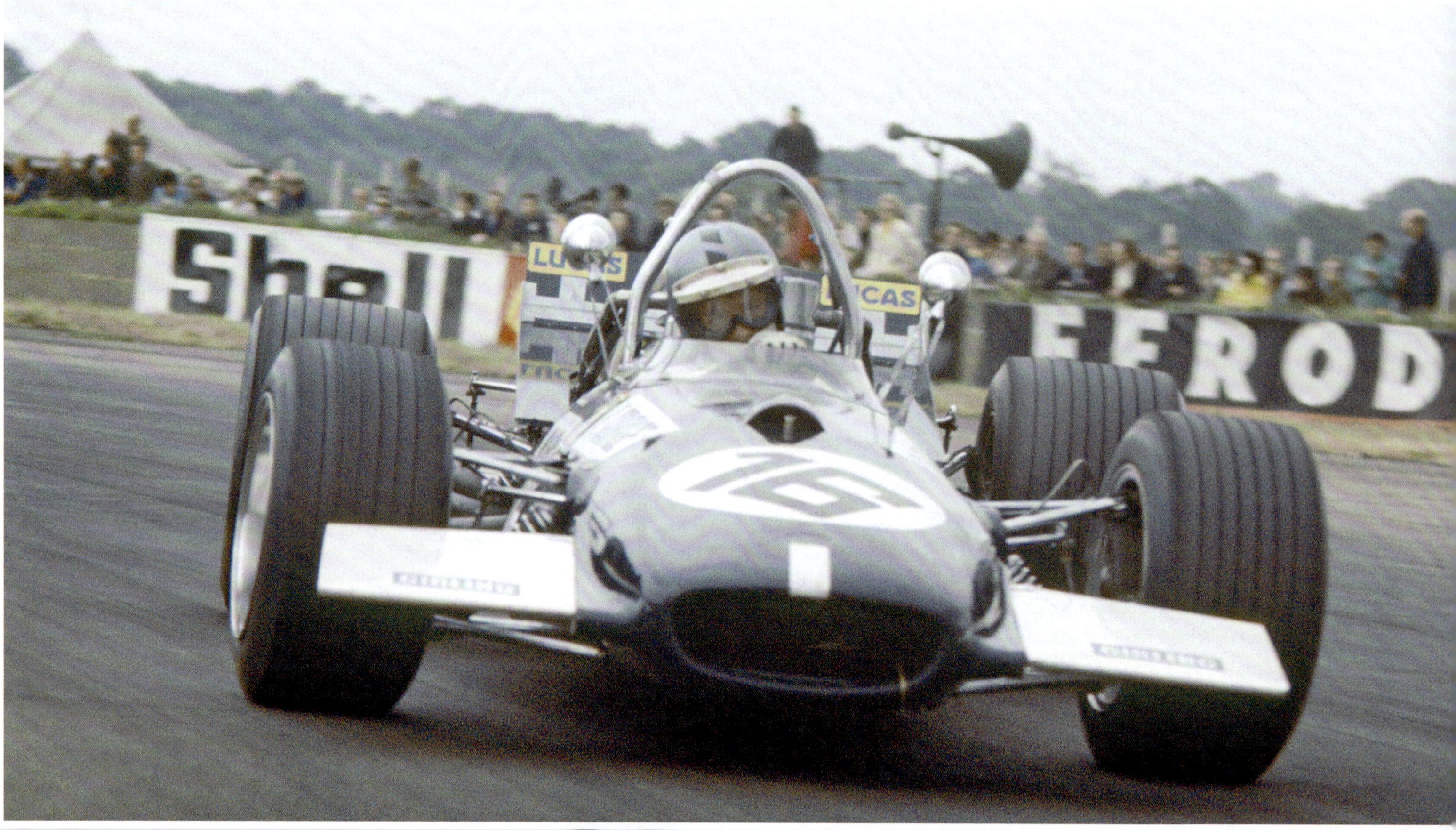
Shell
LUCAS
LUCAS

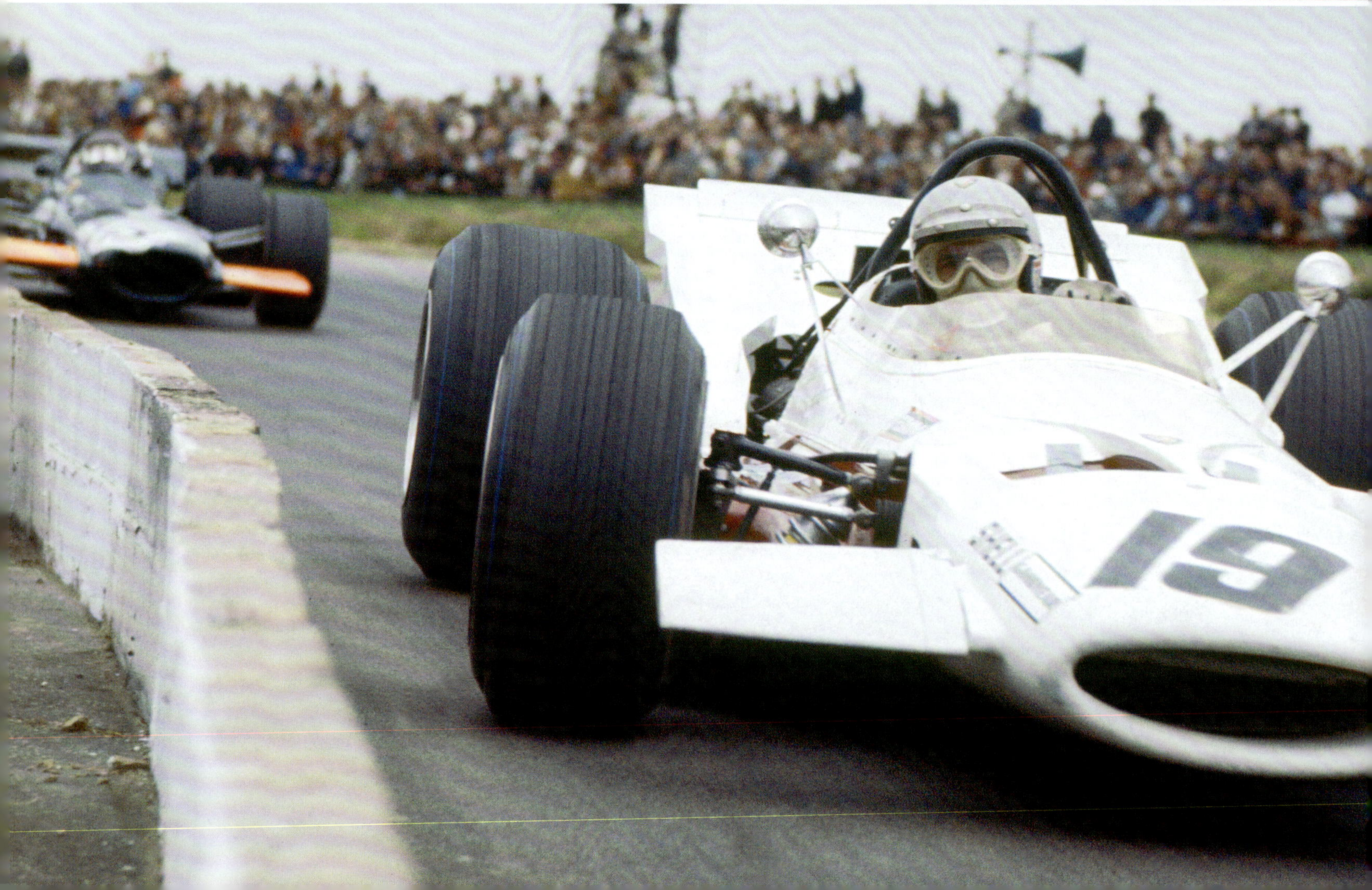
19

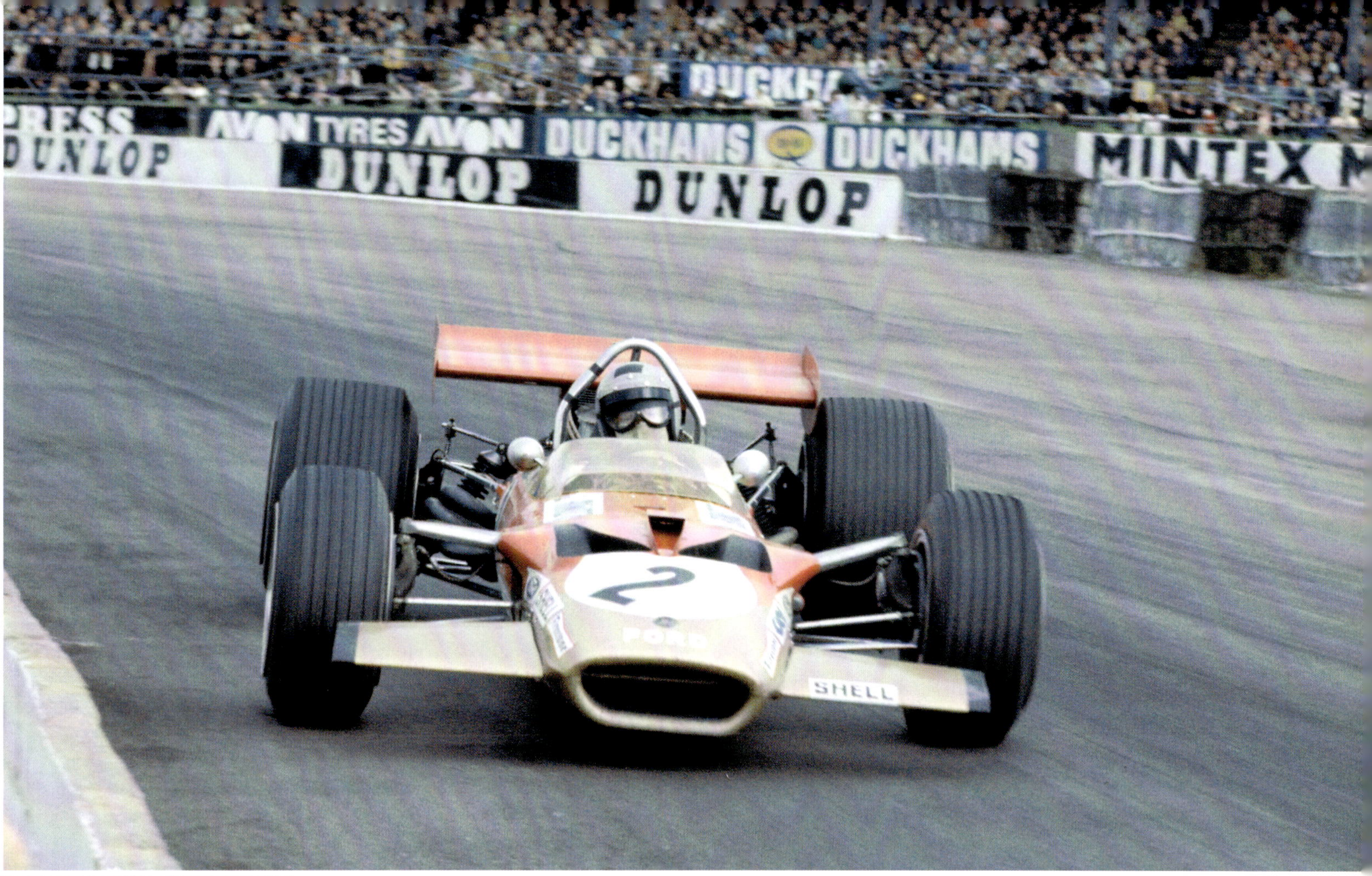

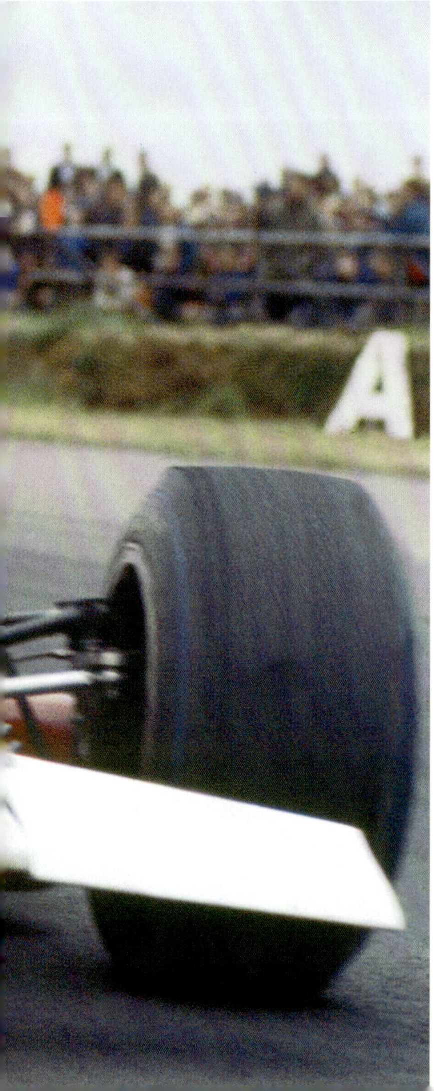

Starting from pole Jochen Rindt (still wearing Piers Courage's open face helmet) led the first six laps of the British GP. Then Jackie Stewart took over for the next nine with Rindt reasserting himself until lap 63 when he had to stop to remove the left rear wing end plate that was rubbing on a tyre. Rindt had to stop again as the Lotus began to run out of fuel eventually coming home 4th. The 49B (R6) has an impressive amount of body roll and suspension movement in this picture.

Get my drift. Many cars started to run out of fuel after the extreme pace and all-out battle between Stewart and Rindt during the British GP. Piers Courage also suffered and just lost 4th place to a delayed Rindt who had stopped twice. Displaying considerable *con brio* he slides the immaculate Frank Williams Racing Team Brabham BT26-1 to 5th place.

Up close and personal. 'Quick Vic' Elford raced for Colin Crabbe's Antique Automobiles in 1969 and they ran this McLaren M7A-3, the car raced by Dan Gurney at Mont Tremblant, Watkins Glen and Mexico City in 1968. He placed it 5th in the French GP and 6th at Silverstone. Jack Oliver follows in his BRM P133. If only we could take pictures like this today.

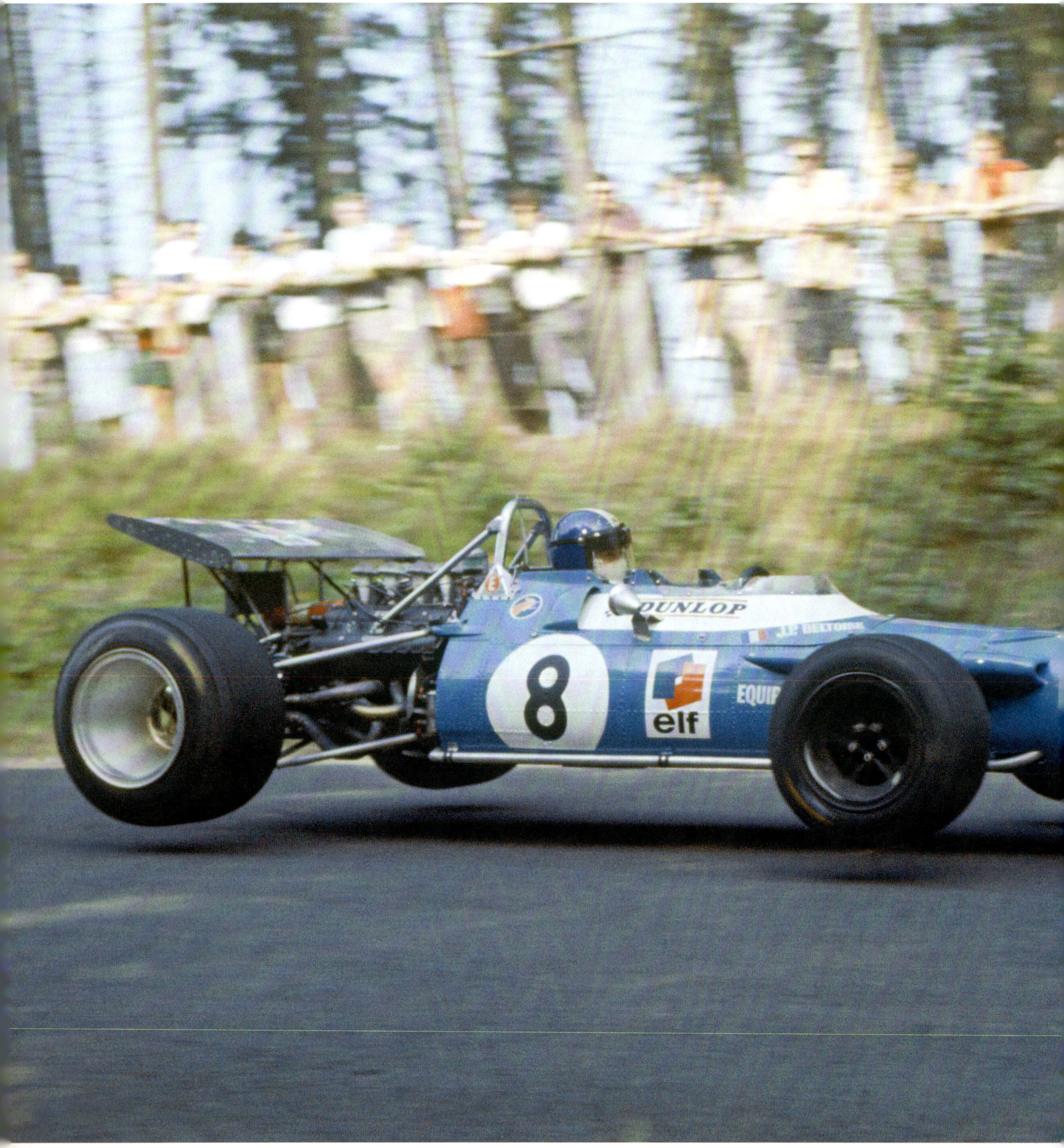
DUNLOP
8
elf

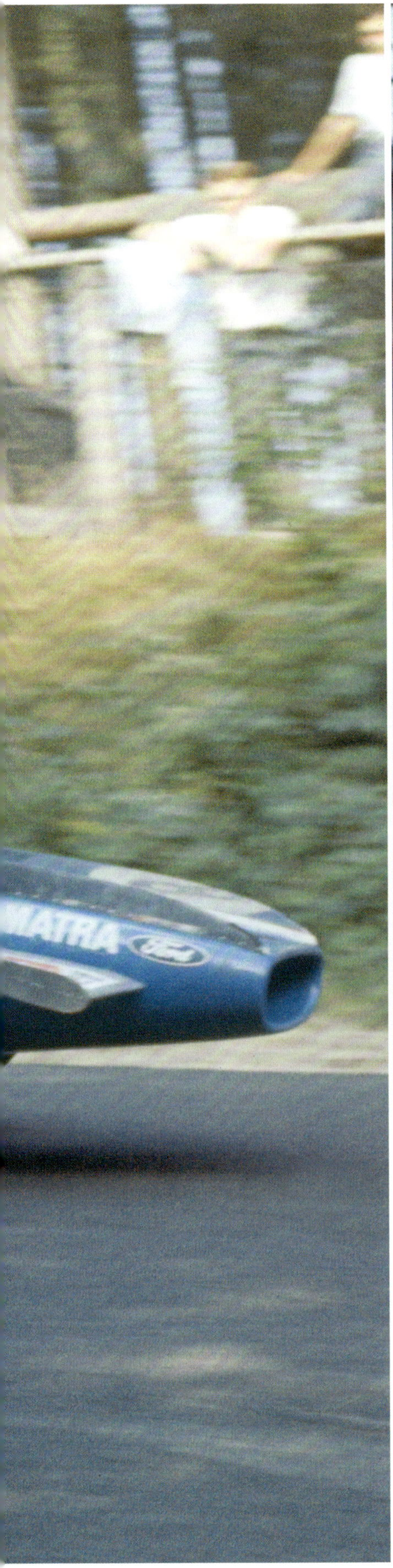

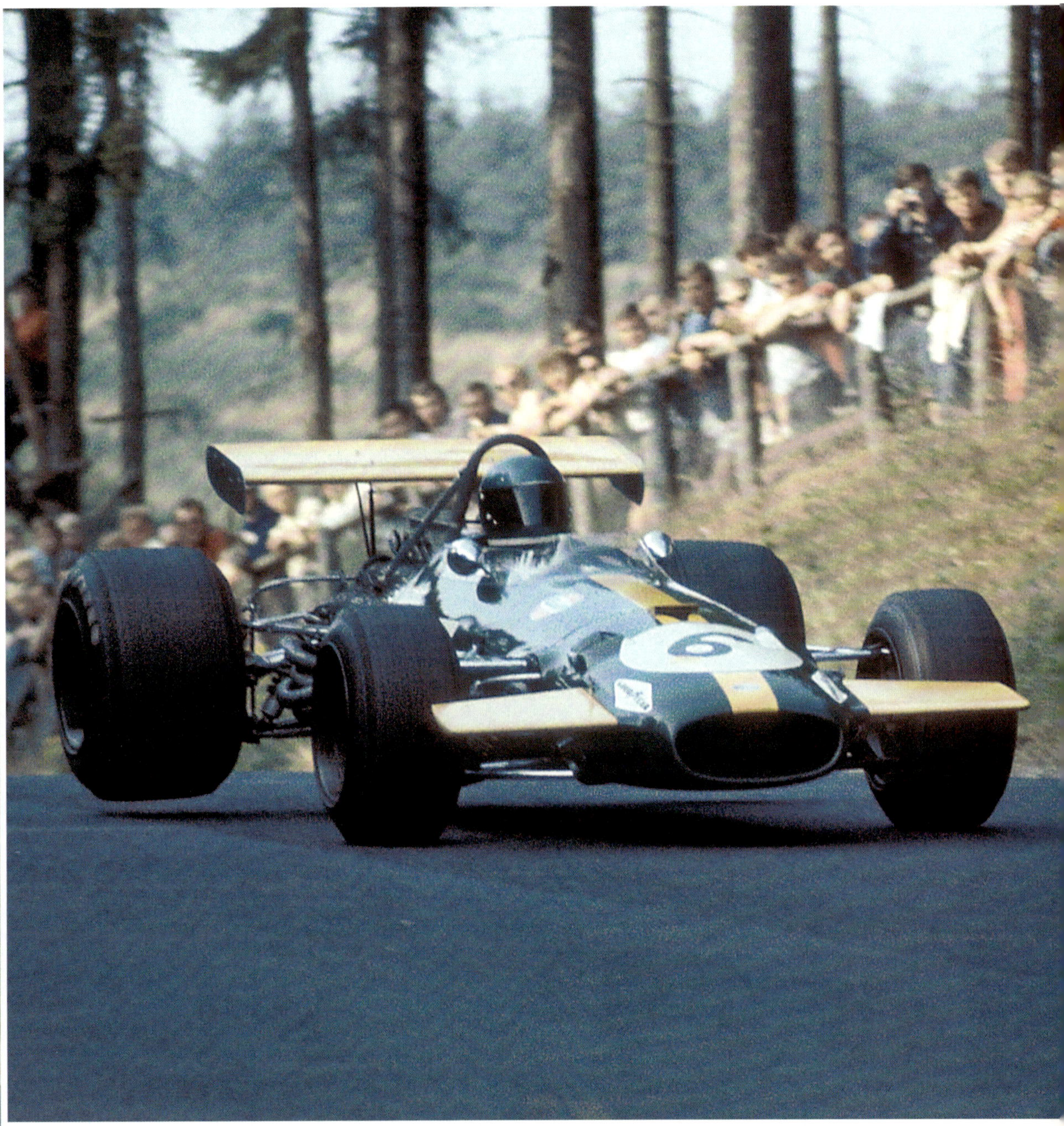

Just as François Cevert was to drive in the shadow of the master in later years, thus too Jean-Pierre Beltoise. When Matra briefly withdrew from F1, Beltoise joined Ken Tyrrell's Matra International but had a hard time trying to keep up with JYS. His six points-scoring finishes during the year included two 2nd places although the German GP ended in an accident when in 5th place with the Matra MS80-01 seen here flying at Brünchen.

The German GP suffered several absentees including Scuderia Ferrari leaving just 13 F1 starters. Twelve F2 cars (a race within a race) boosted the field and sadly Gerhard Mitter had a fatal accident in his BMW during practice. Jacky Ickx took pole position in the Brabham BT26A-4, a fraction quicker than Jackie Stewart's Matra. In the race Stewart led away whilst Ickx fluffed his start but he led by lap seven while Stewart lost 4th gear. Ultimately Ickx won easily from Stewart with Bruce McLaren 3rd. Only four F1 cars were classified as finishers.

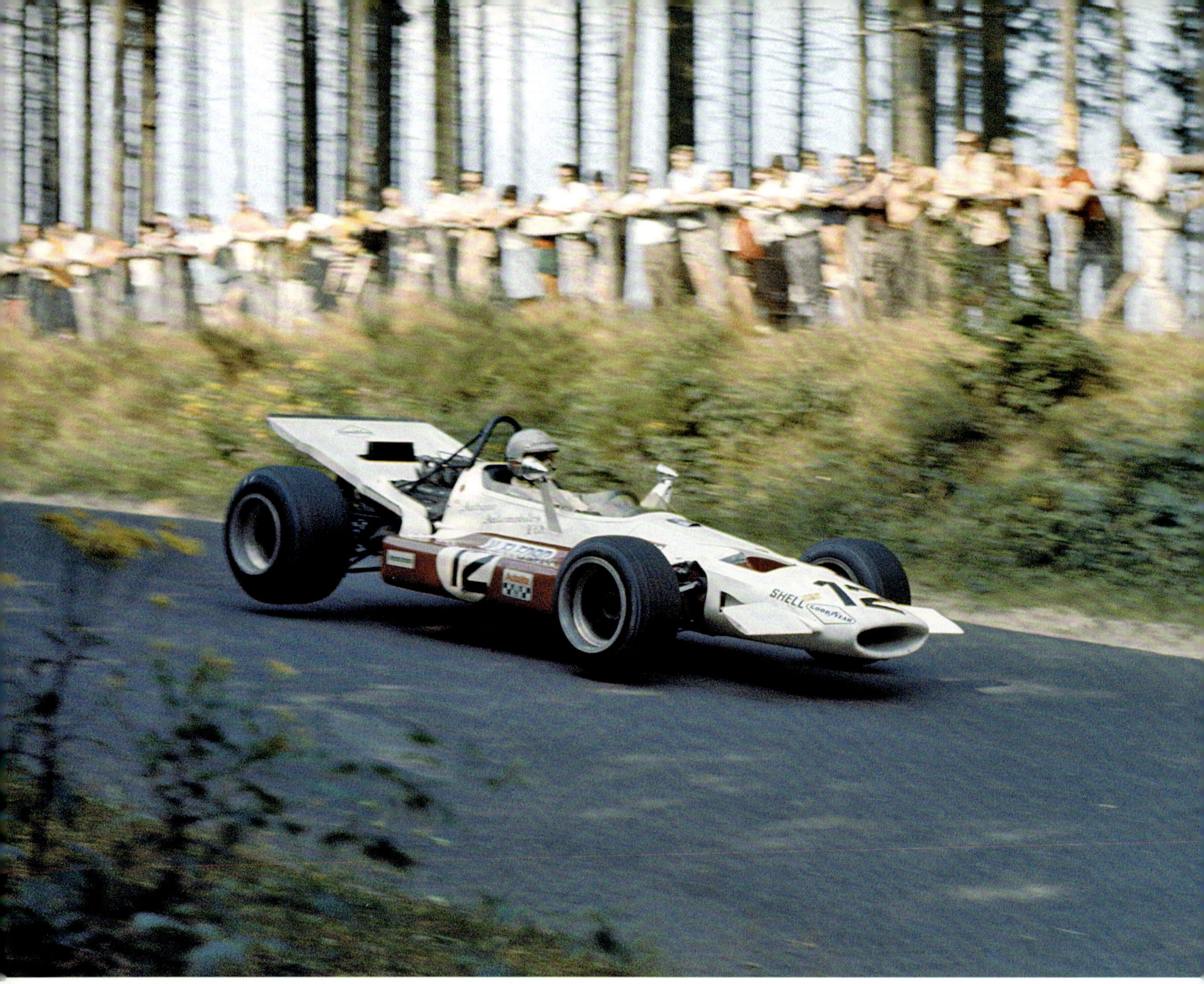

↑ Vic Elford lands the Antique Automobiles McLaren M7A-3 at the Nürburgring, setting 6th fastest practice time. On the first lap Elford ran over the debris from Mario Andretti's Lotus 63 accident at Wippermann. The McLaren took off and crashed down an embankment, turning over and trapping Elford who suffered a very badly broken arm, severely torn shoulder muscles and ligaments. The radiator ended up in the crushed car's cockpit. *Autosport* described this as "Vic's injuries were fortunately not severe". Elford only drove in one more GP, ironically at the 'Ring in 1971. 'Quick Vic' raced on in sports cars, F2 and Can-Am, winning a Trans-Am race before retiring in 1974.

↗ Jackie Stewart's Matra MS80-02 leads Graham Hill's Lotus 49B at Monza. Hill showed a return to form here after a lacklustre season and challenged for the lead but his car broke a driveshaft near the end. Note the absence of wings on both cars for boosting straight-line speed. In the closest GP finish ever, Stewart won the Italian GP from Jochen Rindt (Lotus), Beltoise and McLaren. Only 0.19sec separated 1st from 4th place and Stewart's victory made him the 1969 World Champion.

→ Colin Chapman was determined to make 4WD work and the Lotus 63 was the result. Hill tried it at Zandvoort and Rindt simply refused to even sit in it. 36 years later Bob Dance recalled that the gearbox was sited between the cockpit and the engine, the Cosworth DFV unit mounted back to front with the differentials being on the L/H side. John Miles had the pleasure of driving the beast at Clermont-Ferrand and Silverstone. Mario Andretti took over in Germany but crashed it and at Monza Miles started from the penultimate row but quickly retired.

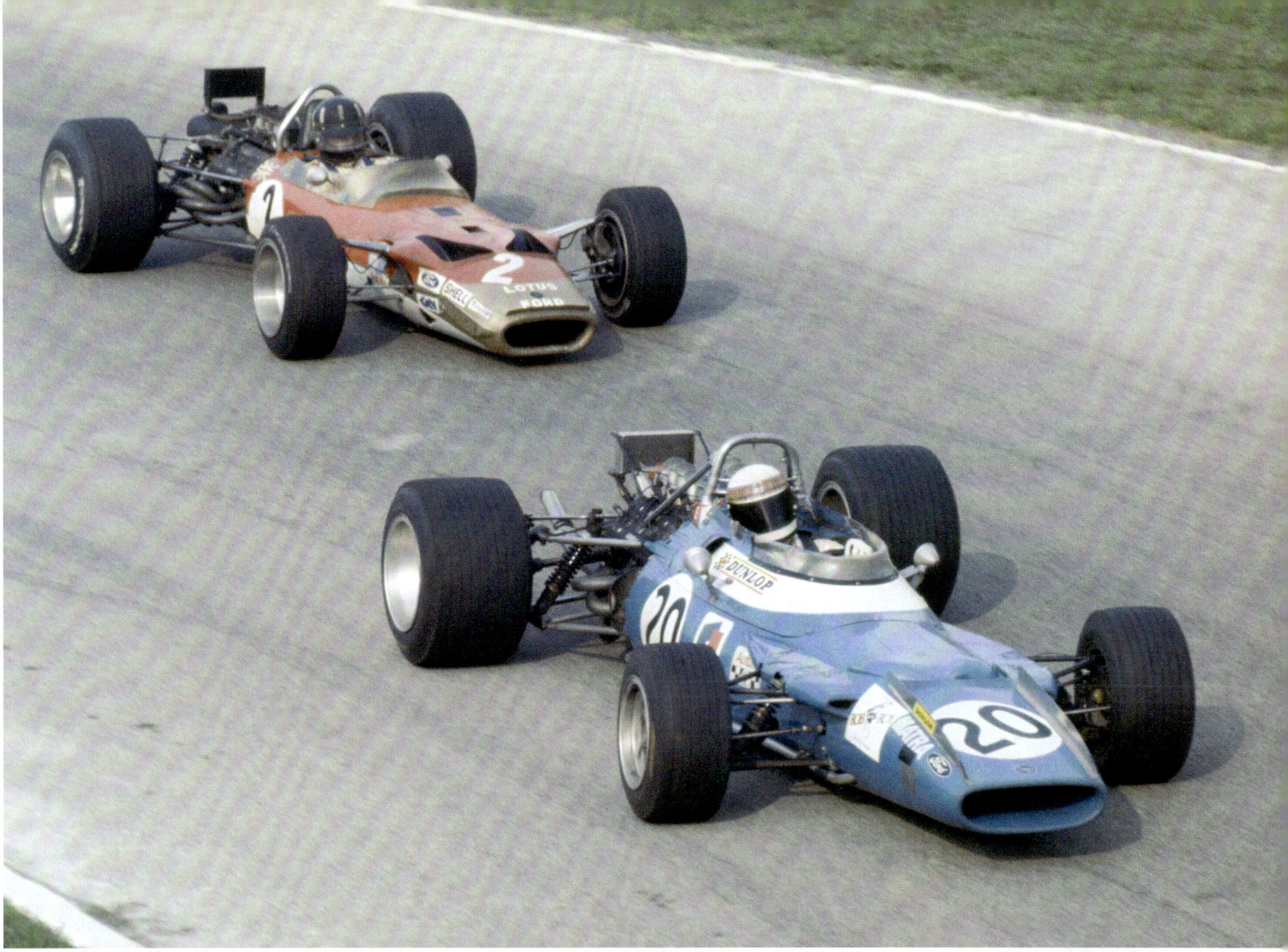
2
LOTUS
FORD
SHELL
DUNLOP
20

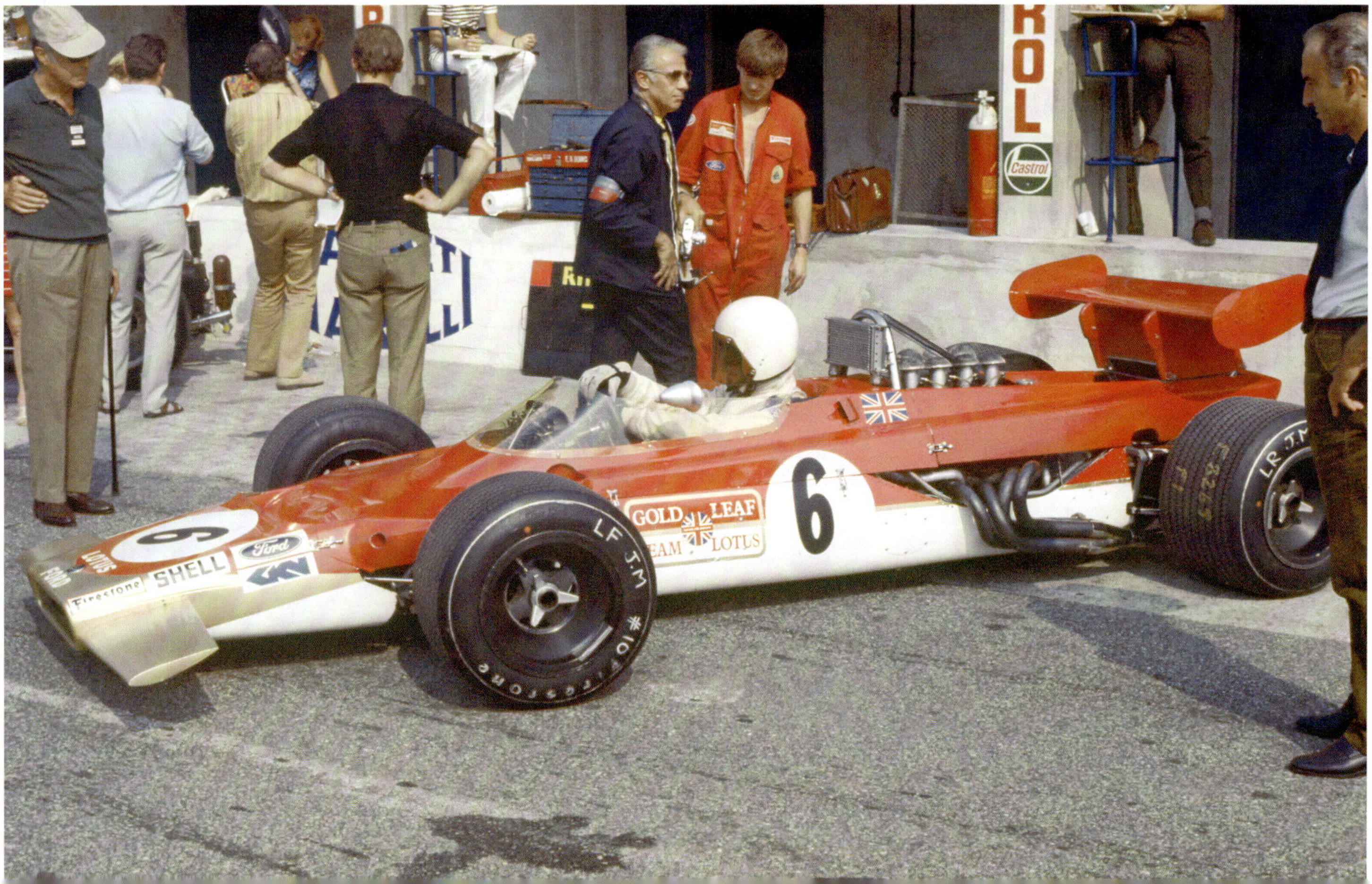
ROL
Castrol
GOLD LEAF
TEAM LOTUS
6
SHELL
Firestone

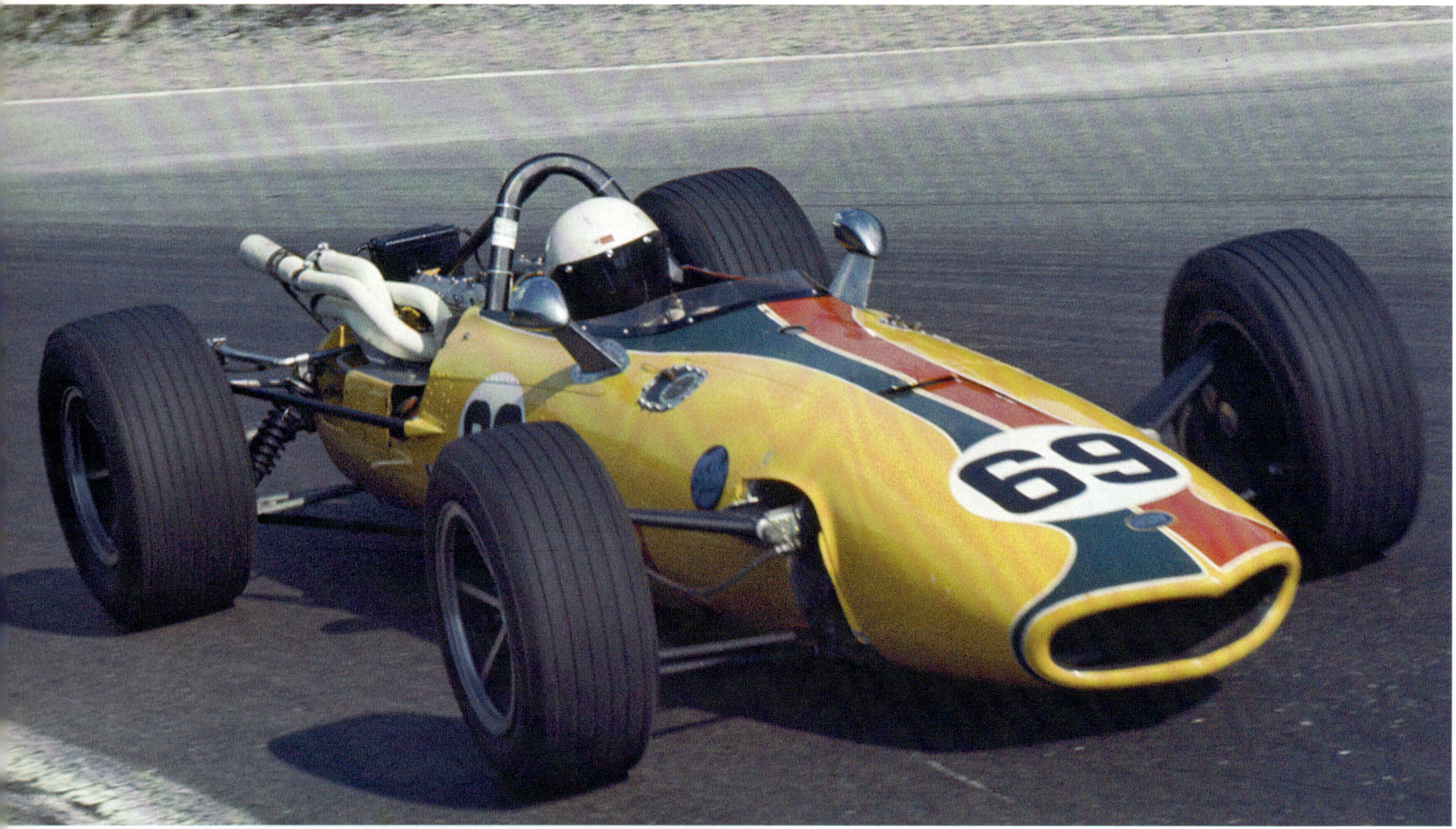

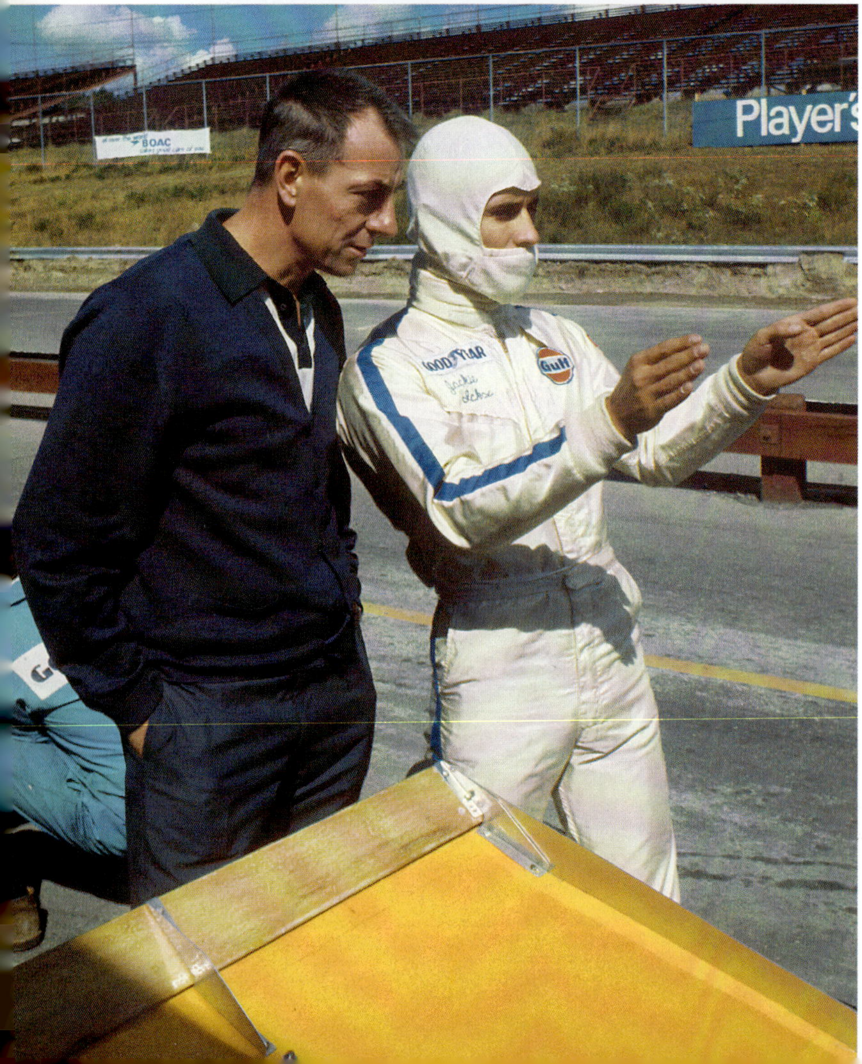

Al Pease raced the original Eagle Climax T1G 101 in three consecutive Canadian GPs. This was his last attempt and following a wheel banging incident that damaged Beltoise's Matra he was black flagged on lap 23 for being too slow. Even so he had out-qualified Bill Brack's BRM and the Brabhams of John Cordt and Silvio Moser. At least the car was immaculately turned out.

Ron Tauranac's impassive demeanour contrasts with Jacky Ickx's obvious conviction about the width of something. Ickx and Jochen Rindt were now major threats to Jackie Stewart's hegemony, in terms of performance if not the championship. According to the Brabham designer, "Ickx was never a team player with us, he arrived just in time for practice, stayed alone and never visited the factory. He performed very well when Jack was out of action with a broken ankle for a few races."

The Jackie and Jacky show in the Canadian GP on the short, bumpy Mosport Park circuit. Initially Jochen Rindt led but his Lotus 49B faded leaving Stewart ahead of 'Jackson'. Try as he might Ickx could not get past but on lap 33 after lapping Brack's BRM he clipped the Matra's L/H rear wheel at Turn 2. Stewart spun off, stalled and could not restart. So Ickx and Brabham won their second GP of the year and a happy Jack Brabham finished 2nd in the sister BT26A.

1969 was the peak of the great 4WD myth and Cosworth, Lotus, McLaren and Matra all produced complex machines of varying mediocrity. By far the best was Matra's unsophisticated space frame MS84-01 that Jackie Stewart tried at Zandvoort. Jean-Pierre Beltoise drove it to 9th at the British GP and Johnny Servoz-Gavin achieved 6th here in the Canadian GP and 8th in Mexico. Sadly he passed away in Grenoble in 2006.

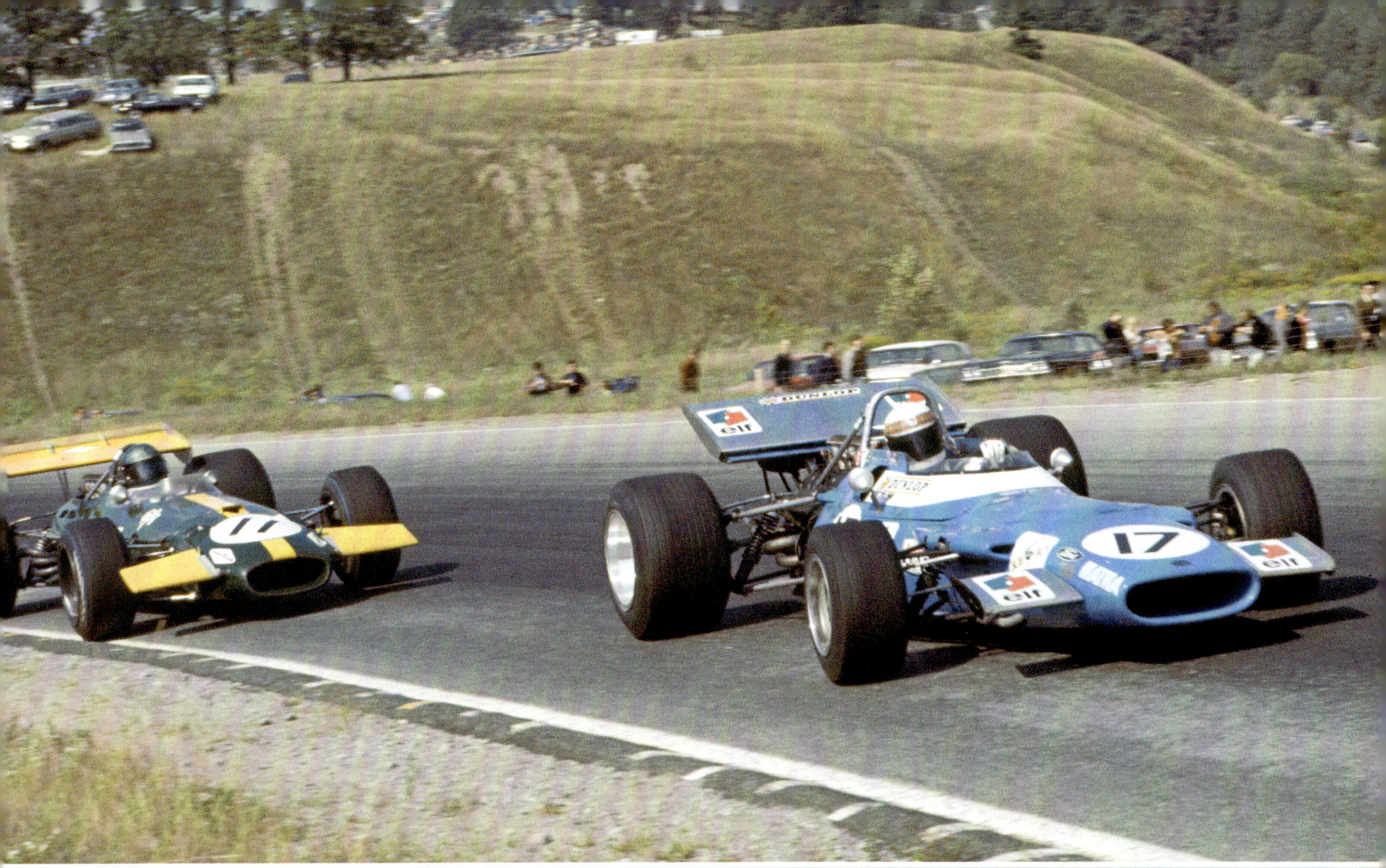
17
elf

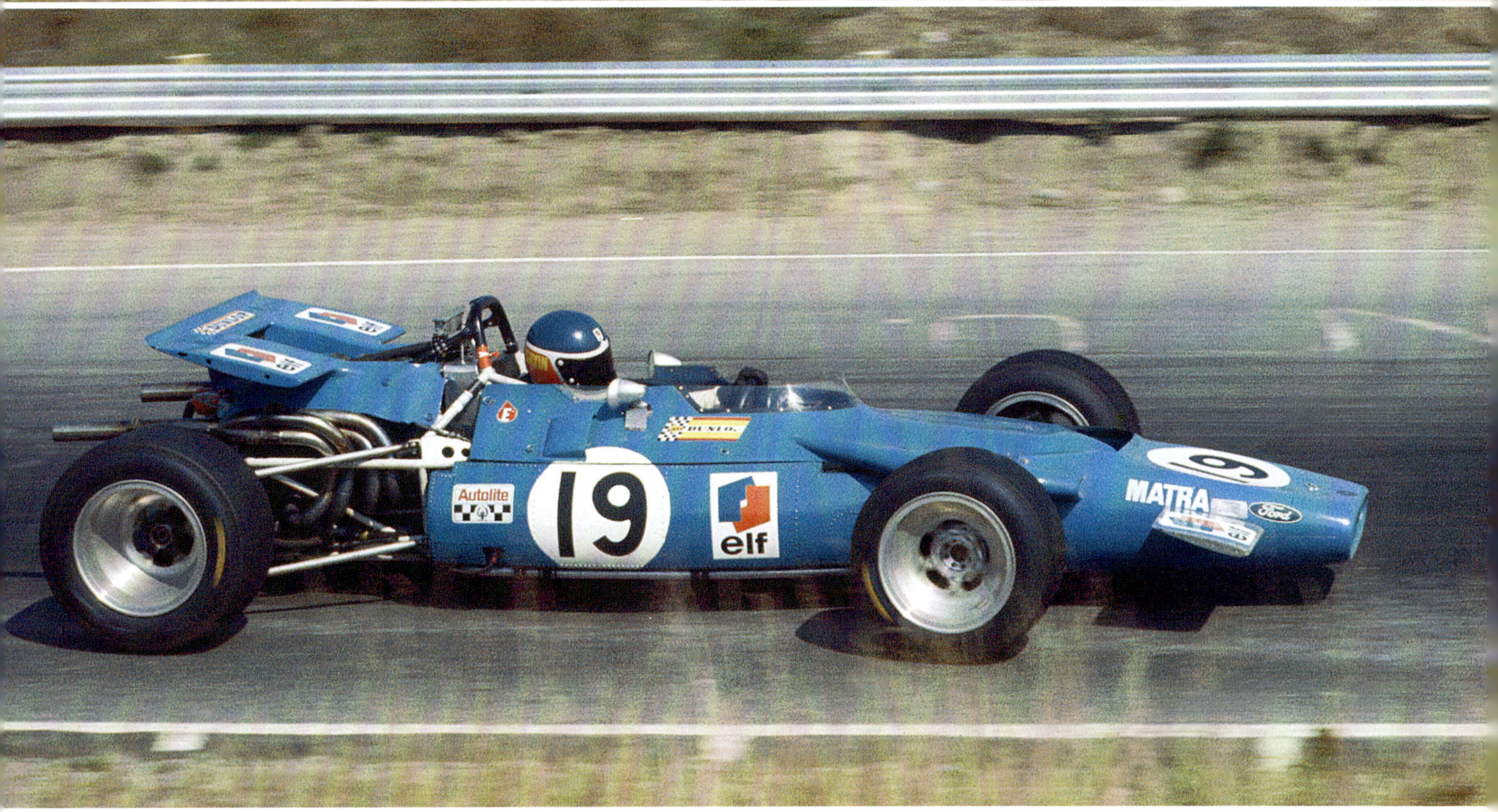
19
elf
Autolite
MATRA

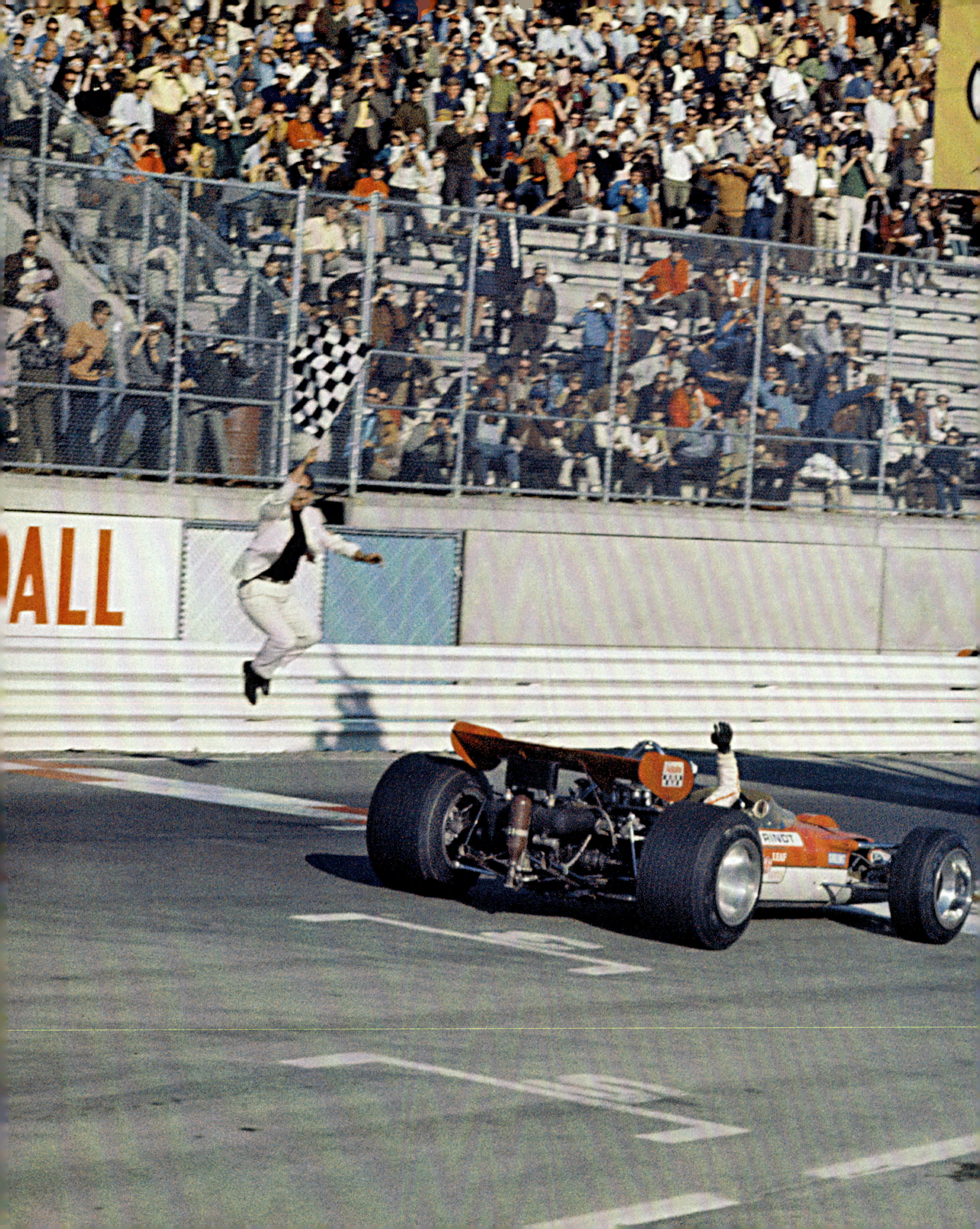

ALL

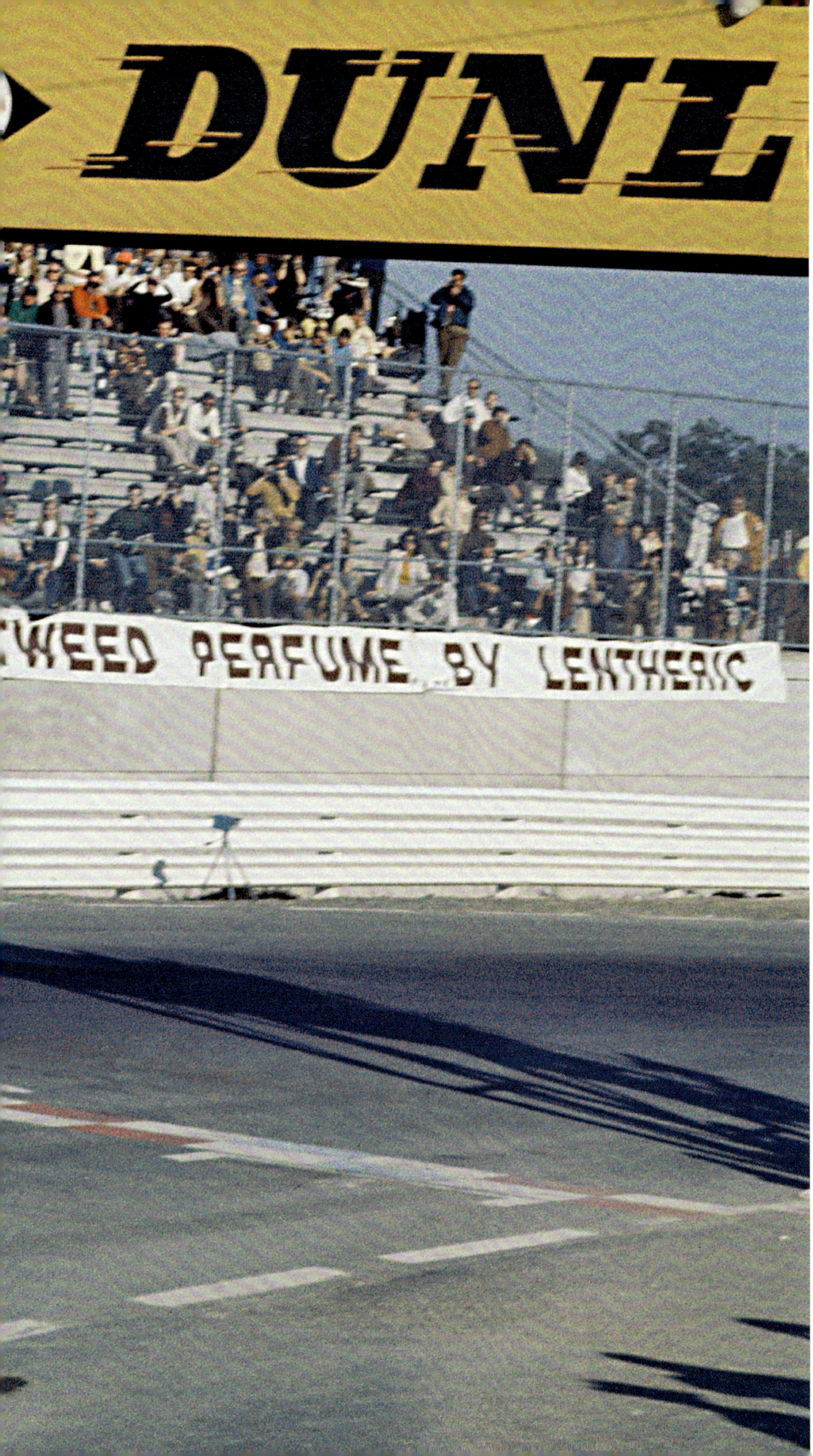

At long last Jochen Rindt achieved his maiden GP win at Watkins Glen, flagged across the line by the flamboyant Tex Hopkins. He drove the 49B (R6) and as a result of a rash bet that Rindt would not win a race that season, Denis Jenkinson had to shave off his beard. The win was clouded by team mate Graham Hill's misfortune when push starting his car after a spin he was unable to refasten his belts. He then crashed and was thrown out, badly smashing his legs, taking many months to recuperate and leaving him partially disabled. Following a meteoric rise via F2 to F1 in 1965 Rindt's career had stalled during 1967/68 with uncompetitive and then unreliable machinery. His failure to win a World Championship race was beginning to attract unfavourable comments, not least from the ever outspoken and trenchant 'Jenks'. Shades of a latter day 'star' perhaps. It is reasonable to assume that had Rindt survived then the outcome of the early to mid-1970s F1 championships might have been very different. The advertising banner for TWEED PERFUME BY LENTHERIC reminds us of how long some familiar consumer brands have been in existence.

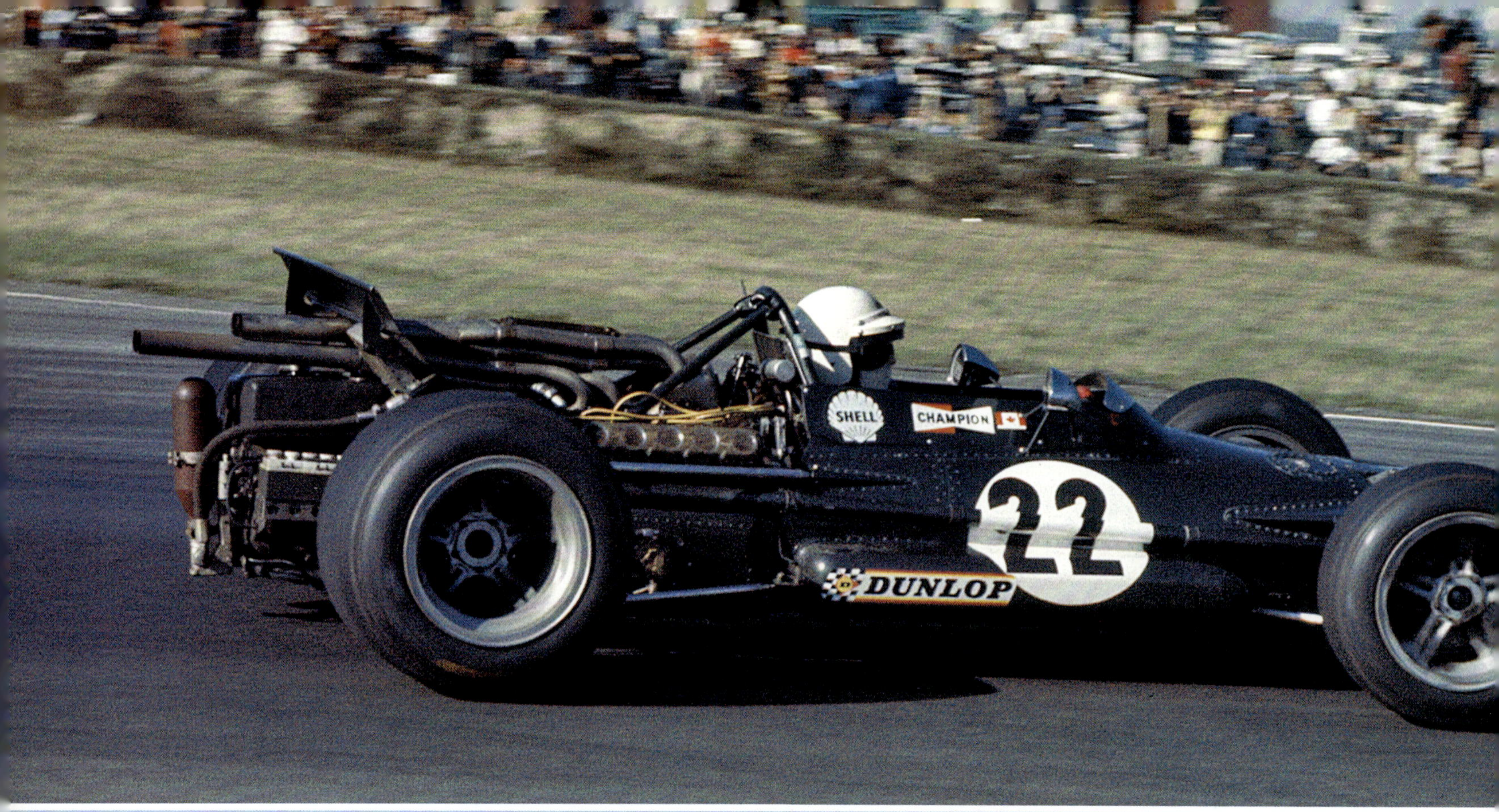
SHELL
CHAMPION
22
DUNLOP

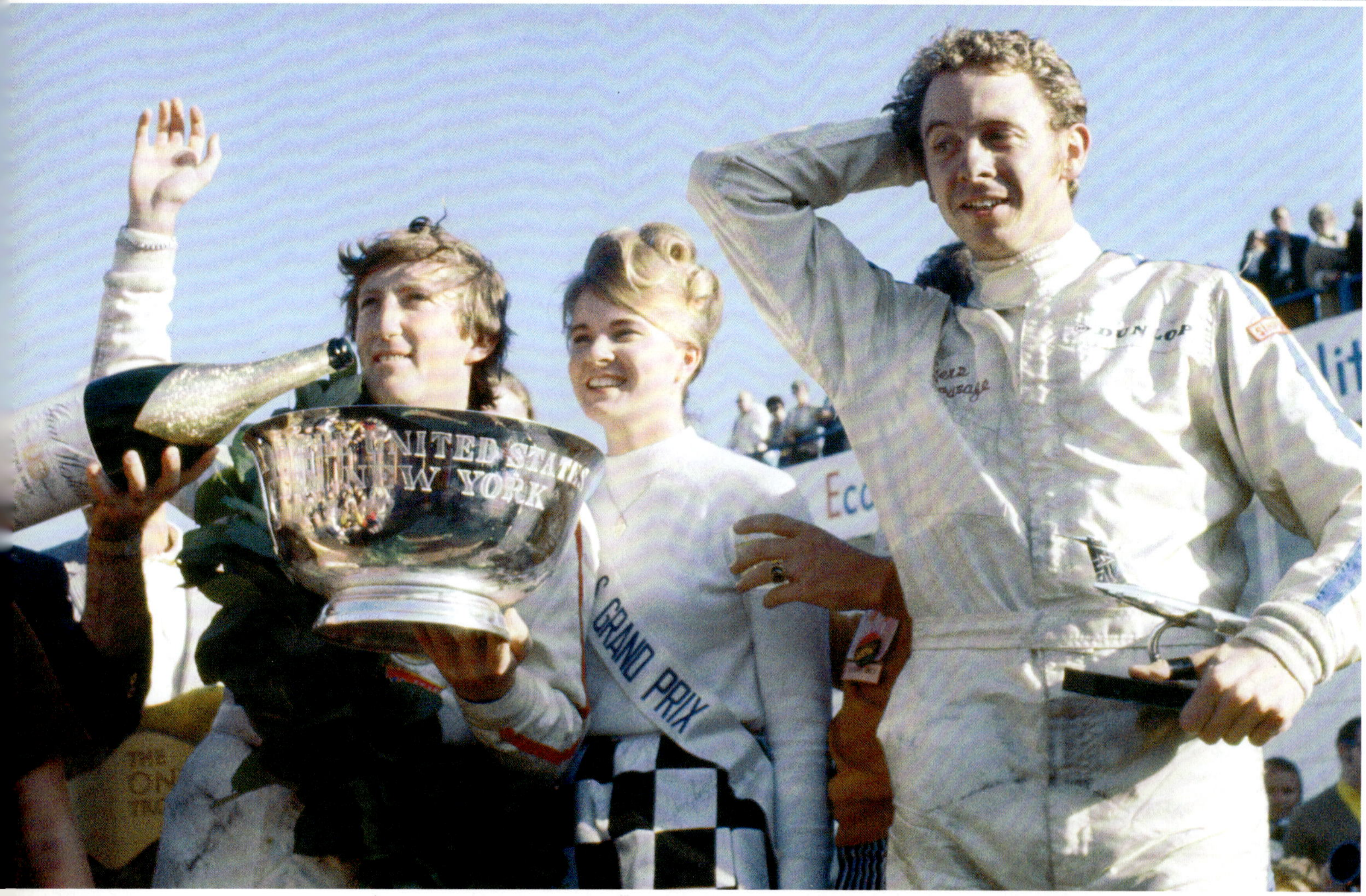
UNITED STATES
NEW YORK
GRAND PRIX
DUNLOP

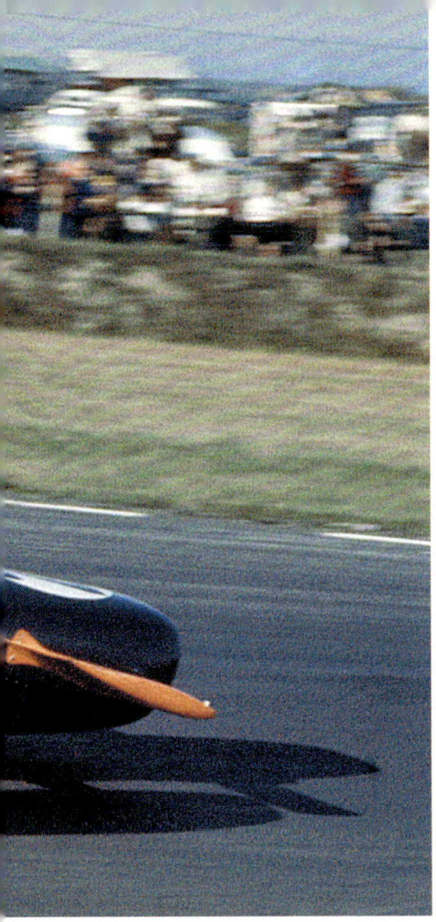

George Eaton in the BRM P138-01 at the 1969 US GP. He qualified last and retired on lap 77 with engine problems. His racing career included Can-Am and Formula A where he had acquitted himself well. The heir to a department store chain, Eaton did a full season with BRM in 1970 including racing their P54 Can-Am car. A single drive in 1971 at the Canadian GP ended his F1 aspirations.

Jochen Rindt looks underwhelmed by his victory whilst Piers Courage, who was awarded the BOAC Man of the Race Award for his 2nd place, seems suitably chuffed. Between them Miss United States Grand Prix smiles properly. John Surtees finished 3rd for BRM. The sad postscript to this picture is that both men were dead within 11 months, Courage perished at Zandvoort in June 1970 and Rindt at Monza that September.

That end-of-term feeling. Jack Brabham finished 3rd in Mexico having qualified fastest but he had given Jacky Ickx the only set of ultra-low gears and Brabham's BT26A was too highly geared for exiting the hairpin quickly. It also had an engine pick-up problem. Following is winner Denny Hulme's McLaren M7A-2 and Jochen Rindt's Lotus 49B (R6) that suffered broken suspension. Jochen Rindt had verbally agreed to return to Brabham in 1970 but Colin Chapman made Rindt an offer he couldn't refuse. Brabham let him go, something that haunts him to this day.

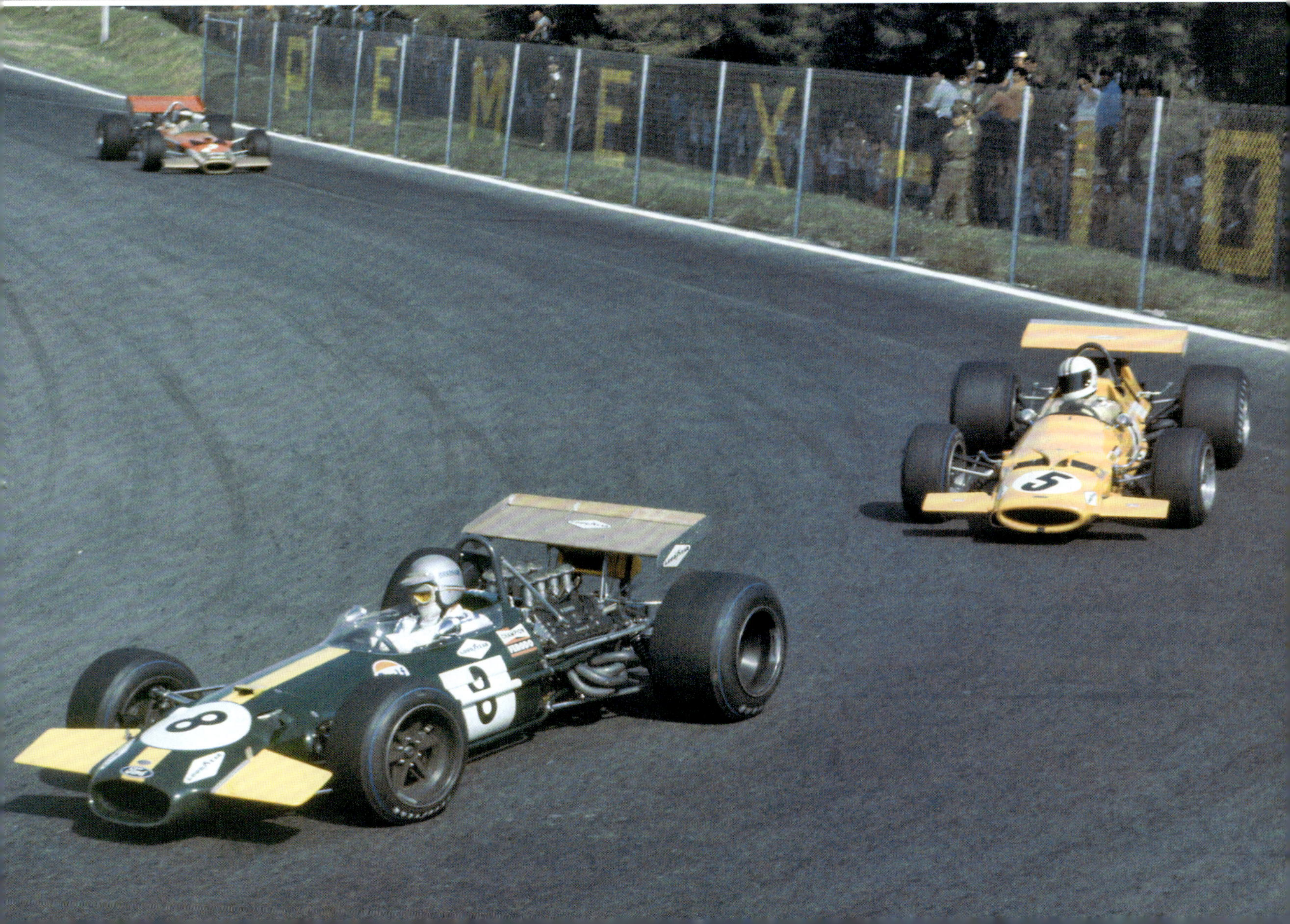

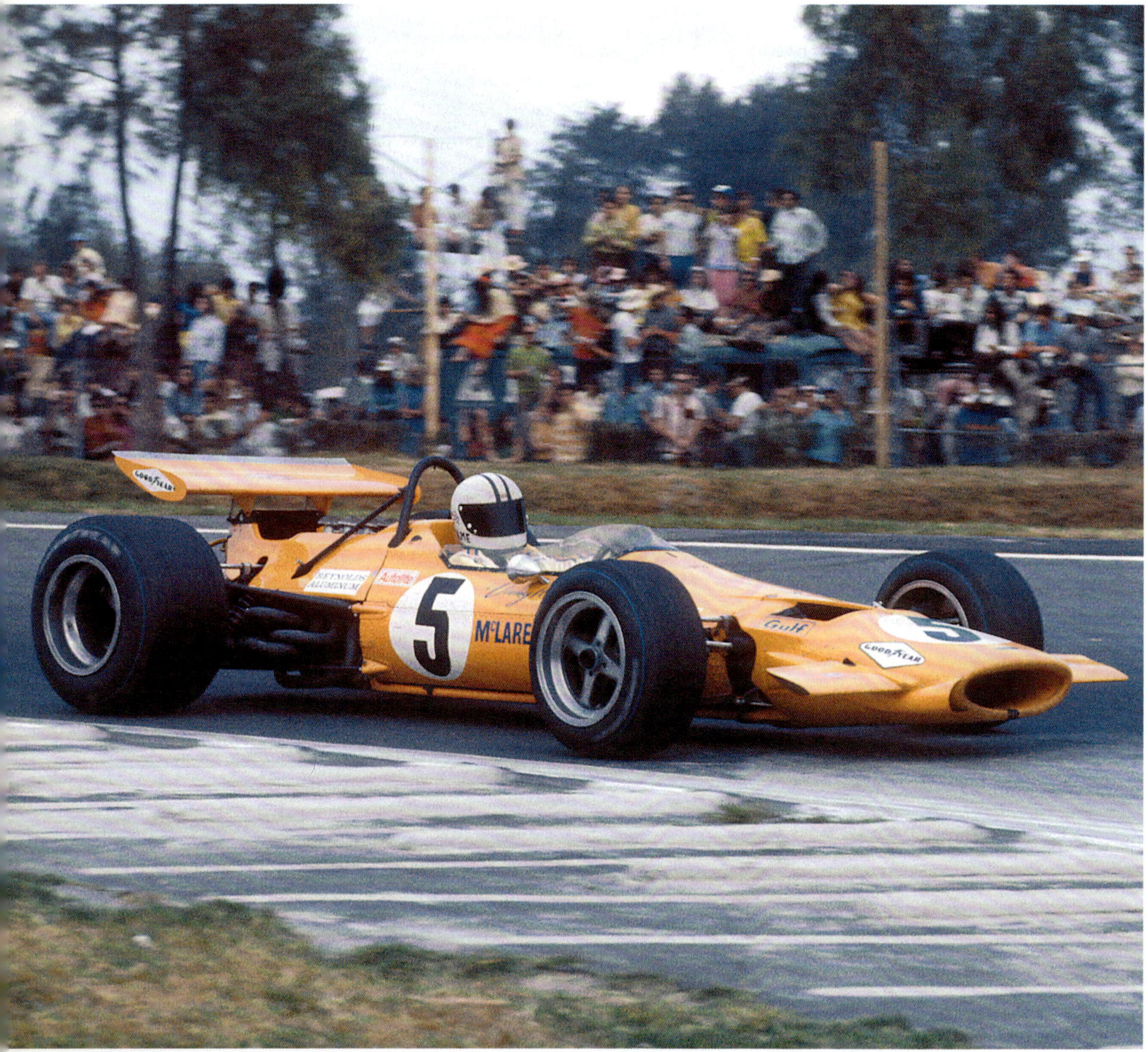

Denny Hulme's 1969 season had been disappointing, his best result so far being a 3rd at the first GP in South Africa. At Mexico City he started 4th on the grid, assumed the lead on lap ten and won the race. The Goodyear-shod McLarens and Brabhams had a tyre advantage whilst the Dunlop-shod Stewart fell to 4th. Denny stayed at McLaren until he retired at the end of 1974 and suffered a fatal heart attack whilst driving in the 1992 Bathurst 1000km aged 56.

American privateer Pete Lovely's F1 adventures began in 1959 at Monaco. The 1955 SCCA sports car champion raced a Cooper in the 1960 US GP but subsequently concentrated on his VW dealership in Seattle. In 1969 he purchased the Lotus 49B (R11) from Colin Chapman, repainting it white with a blue stripe, as seen here in Mexico, where it finished 9th. R11 was a reincarnation of Jim Clark's 1967 Dutch GP winning R2. Lovely sold it many years later, but the new owner died before he had fully paid for it. Lovely bought the car back from the deceased's estate in 1997 and still races it today.

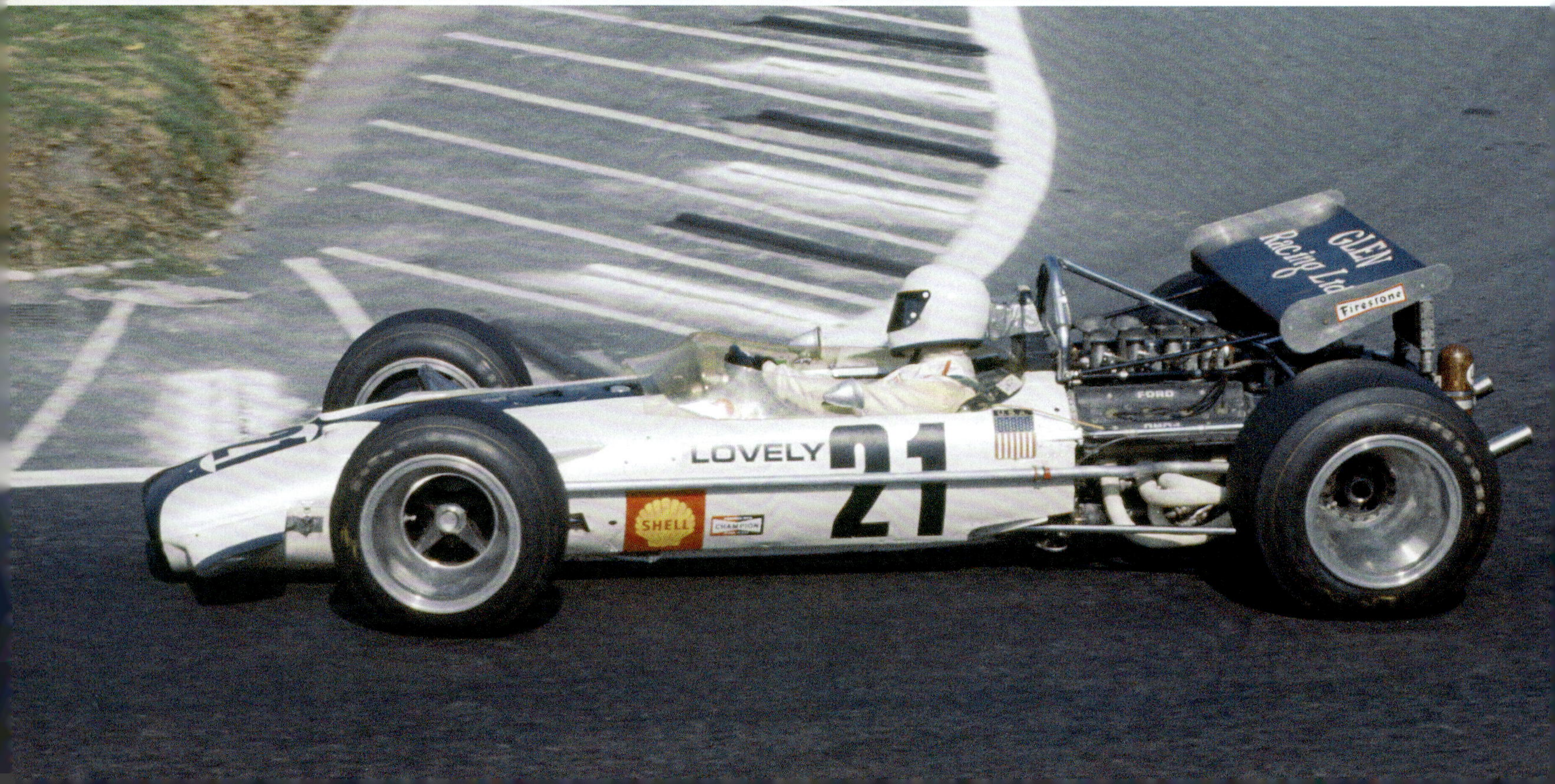

1969 Teams, drivers and results

Gold Leaf Team Lotus – Lotus 49B Cosworth DFV and 63 Cosworth DFV 4WD
Graham Hill (GB) (Missed Mexican GP due to injuries received at US GP)
Jochen Rindt (A) (Missed Monaco GP due to injuries received at Spanish GP)
Mario Andretti (USA) (South African, German and US GPs only, German and US in type 63)
Richard Attwood (GB) (Monaco GP only replacing injured Rindt)
John Miles (GB) (French, British, Italian, Canadian and Mexican GPs only, all in type 63)

Matra International – Matra MS10 Cosworth DFV and MS84 Cosworth DFV 4WD
Jackie Stewart (GB) (WORLD CHAMPION)
Jean-Pierre Beltoise (F) (British GP in MS84)
Johnny Servoz-Gavin (F) (Canadian, US and Mexican GPs only in MS84)

Owen Racing Organisation – BRM P133 V12, P138 V12 and P139 V12
John Surtees (GB) (Team withdrew from French GP)
Jack Oliver (GB)
Bill Brack (CDN) (Canadian GP only)
George Eaton (CDN) (US and Mexican GPs only)

Reg Parnell Racing – BRM P126 V12
Pedro Rodriguez (MEX) (South African, Spanish and Monaco GPs only)

Bruce McLaren Motor Racing – Mclaren M7A Cosworth DFV, M7C Cosworth DFV and M9A Cosworth DFV 4WD
Denny Hulme (NZ)
Bruce McLaren (NZ) (dns US GP, engine failure in warm-up)
Derek Bell (GB) (British GP only in M9A)

Motor Racing Developments – Brabham BT26 Cosworth DFV
Jack Brabham (AUS) (Missed French, British and German GPs due to testing accident)
Jacky Ickx (B)

Scuderia Ferrari SpA SEFAC – Ferrari 312/69 and 312/67
Chris Amon (NZ) (Stopped driving for team after the British GP, no cars at the German GP)
Pedro Rodriguez (MEX) (British and Italian GPs only, see NART below)

North American Racing Team – Ferrari 312/69
Pedro Rodriguez (MEX) (Canadian, US and Mexican GPs only)

Rob Walker-Jack Durlacher Racing – Lotus 49B Cosworth DFV
Jo Siffert (CH)

Frank Williams Racing Cars – Brabham BT26 Cosworth DFV
Piers Courage (GB) (Missed South African GP)

Antique Automobiles Racing Ltd – Cooper T86B Maserati V12 and McLaren M7A Cosworth
Vic Elford (GB) (Monaco, Dutch, French, British and German GPs only where he was injured and missed the rest of the season)

Silvio Moser Racing Team – Brabham BT24 Cosworth DFV
Silvio Moser (CH) (Missed South African, Spanish, British and German GPs)

Ecurie Bonnier – Lotus 63 Cosworth DFV 4WD and 49B Cosworth DFV
Jo Bonnier (S) (British and German GPs only)

Pete Lovely Volkswagen Inc – Lotus 49 Cosworth DFV
Pete Lovely (USA) (Canadian, US and Mexican GPs only)

Paul Seitz – Brabham BT23B Climax FPF
John Cordts (CDN) (Canadian GP only)

John Maryon – Eagle T1G Climax FPF
Al Pease (CDN) (Canadian GP only)

Team Gunston – Lotus 49 Cosworth DFV and Brabham BT24 Repco V8
John Love (RSR) (South African GP only)
Sam Tingle (RSR) (South African GP only)

Team Lawson – McLaren M7A Cosworth DFV
Basil van Rooyen (ZA) (South African GP only)

Jack Holme – Brabham BT20 Repco V8
Piet de Klerk (ZA) (South African GP only)

F2 ENTRIES RACED IN GERMAN GP

Ahrens Racing Team – Brabham BT30 Cosworth
Kurt Ahrens Jnr. (D)

Roy Winkelmann Racing – Lotus 59 Cosworth
Hans Herrmann (D)
Rolf Stommelen (D)

BMW AG – BMW 269
Hubert Hahne (D)
Gerhard Mitter (D) (Team withdrawn after fatal accident to Mitter during practice)
Diter Quester (A)

Matra-ELF – Matra MS7 Cosworth
Henri Pescarolo (F)

Matra International – Matra MS7 Cosworth
Johnny Servoz-Gavin (F)

Tecno Racing Team – Tecno Cosworth
François Cevert (F)

Frank Williams Racing Cars Ltd – Brabham BT30 Cosworth
Richard Attwood (GB)

Squadra Tartaruga – Brabham BT23C Cosworth
Xavier Perrot (CH)

Felday Engineering – Brabham BT30 Cosworth
Peter Westbury (GB)

WORLD CHAMPIONSHIP VENUES AND WINNERS (eleven rounds)

Part 1

South African GP	Kyalami	Jackie Stewart
Spanish GP	Montjuich Park	Jackie Stewart
Monaco GP	Monte Carlo	Graham Hill
Dutch GP	Zandvoort	Jackie Stewart
French GP	Clermont-Ferrand	Jackie Stewart
British GP	Silverstone	Jackie Stewart

Part 2

German GP	Nürburgring	Jacky Ickx
Italian GP	Monza	Jackie Stewart
Canadian GP	Mosport	Jacky Ickx
United States GP	Watkins Glen	Jochen Rindt
Mexican GP	Mexico City	Denny Hulme

DRIVERS' CHAMPIONSHIP

Points: 9-6-4-3-2-1.
Best 5 scores counted from Part 1 (six races), plus best 4 scores from Part 2 (five races).

1	Jackie Stewart	Matra	63
2	Jacky Ickx	Brabham	37
3	Bruce McLaren	McLaren	26
4	Jochen Rindt	Lotus	22
5	Jean-Pierre Beltoise	Matra	21
6	Denny Hulme	McLaren	20
7	Graham Hill	Lotus	19
8	Piers Courage	Brabham	16
9	Jo Siffert	Lotus	15
10	Jack Brabham	Brabham	14
11	John Surtees	BRM	6
12	Chris Amon	Ferrari	4
13	Richard Attwood	Lotus	3
14	Vic Elford	Cooper/McLaren	3
15	Pedro Rodriguez	BRM/Ferrari	3
16	Johnny Servoz-Gavin	Matra	1
17	Silvio Moser	Brabham	1
18	Jack Oliver	BRM	1

CONSTRUCTORS' CHAMPIONSHIP

Points: 9-6-4-3-2-1 (awarded only to best-placed finisher).
Best 5 scores counted from Part 1 (six races), plus best 4 scores from Part 2 (five races).

1	Matra-Ford (Cosworth)	66
2	Brabham-Ford (Cosworth)	49
3	Lotus-Ford (Cosworth)	47
4	McLaren-Ford (Cosworth)	38
5	BRM	7
6	Ferrari	7

FINAL THOUGHTS

Ah! The swinging sixties. All the clichés spring to mind, but they were in fact true. No other decade saw so much change across such a wide spectrum from social behaviour, politics and sport to personal aspirations.

Thus motor sport. The end of the classic front-engined GP car reign had begun in 1958 with the two Rob Walker/Cooper Climax wins in Argentina (Stirling Moss) and Monaco (Maurice Trintignant). By 1959, Ferrari, BRM and Aston Martin were fighting a losing battle against Cooper whilst Chapman wasted a year with his Lotus 16. Come 1960 only Ferrari fielded a serious front-engined GP car.

So the 'garagistes', as Enzo Ferrari dubbed Messrs. Chapman and Cooper and later Lola, Brabham and McLaren, took over. With the exception of 1961 and 1969 they more or less dominated the whole decade along with BRM. In 1966, Anglo-American Racing appeared with its Eagle but even this was British designed and built.

Of the other works teams Porsche quickly abandoned the F1 circus. They were rightly convinced that GT and sports car racing offered far better results in terms of marketing impact and sales than the enormous costs and minimal commercial returns of Grand Prix racing. The only major car manufacturer to enter the arena was Honda and overall this was a disappointment for a variety of reasons. They made their first appearance at the 1964 German GP and departed after the 1968 Mexican GP.

The arrival of French aerospace and niche car manufacturer Matra in 1968 was really another British success story. All the winning was done by the Cosworth powered cars run by the Tyrrell team. Matra's dedicated V12-engined MS11 only lasted a year and was then withdrawn, although they did return in 1970.

From a distant perspective it is strange to consider that at the beginning of the period that this book covers the F1 World Championship was only a decade old. Odder still is the public perception that there is and always has been Ferrari. In fact the Prancing Horse as a serious constructor barely pre-dated 1950 (although the origins lay in Enzo's pre-war Alfa Romeo based Scuderia Ferrari). Their almost legendary status was more due to their potent and multitudinous sports racing and GT cars, rather than the inconsistent single seaters.

A look at the tabulations makes the point. The Constructors' Championship was won by Cooper in 1960, Ferrari in 1961 and 1964, BRM in 1962, Lotus in 1963, 1965 and 1968 and Matra in 1969. However, without impugning the brilliance of John Surtees, Ferrari's 1964 championships owed a great deal to good fortune and Bandini's Mexican GP collision with Graham Hill rather than any true superiority. Surtees's talent in F1 post 1964 was frittered away by Ferrari when he could have seriously challenged Jim Clark's status as *numero uno*.

Analysis of the remaining years makes for mostly unhappy reading. Ferrari were 4th in 1960, 6th in 1962, 4th in 1963 and 1965, 2nd in 1966, 5th in 1967, 4th in 1968 and equal last with BRM in 1969. Between the 1960 Argentinian GP and the 1969 Mexican GP (a total of 99 races) they achieved 13 GP victories (Lotus recorded 36 during the decade) and in 1962, 1967 and 1969 won none at all. Additionally Ferrari regularly missed races apparently due to industrial action but probably also because of their discomfort over uncompetitive machinery.

Objectively speaking, Ferrari's F1 activities were handicapped by their endurance racing priorities and internal politics as John Surtees quickly discovered. An almost inevitable result of having a remote, patriarchal figure with Luddite tendencies at the helm who never travelled beyond Monza, and was dependent upon whosoever had his ear.

The remainder of the grid was the resting place of non-works teams and independents such as Rob Walker, UDT Laystall, Yeoman Credit, BRP (British Racing Partnership), Bowmaker Racing, Reg Parnell Racing, Scuderia Centro Sud and true privateers (Bob Anderson, Silvio Moser, Pete Lovely etc.) Several of these disappeared during the first half of the decade and only Rob Walker, who historically carried the Moss mantle, won anything of note.

This too highlights the relative isolation of F1 during the period in terms of the car industry, marketing, vehicle sales and associated commercial priorities. The classic endurance racing venues (especially Le Mans) probably had more impact and resonance with motorists and manufacturers than the highly specific and narrowly focused arena of F1 racing.

The Drivers' World Championship was another stronghold of Anglo Saxon influence and the English language. One Australian, one American, two Englishmen, two Scotsmen and one New Zealander won the drivers' titles and most of the races. Jim Clark alone accounted for 25 victories. It can be stated with some certainty that with one exception (1966), had Clark enjoyed better reliability at Lotus and survived the decade, he could have won every other championship from 1962 to 1968.

As ever sheer talent can go unrewarded and two of the very best, Dan Gurney and Chris Amon, suffered wretched luck. Gurney at least won four GPs unlike the eternally fated Amon who never broke his duck at GP level, almost entirely due to misfortune and unreliable machinery.

The relatively relaxed regimen of the first half of the 1960s led to an enormous variety of cars and drivers. It was possible to gain admittance to F1 simply by having a half decent car and/or driver, especially during the 1.5-litre formula. The diverse levels of driver potential and equipment did pose some problems, but for a while, it seemed, the more the merrier held sway.

Finally the crunch came from two directions: safety and cost. Driver fatalities and serious injuries, for so long tolerated as being unavoidable, slowly, very slowly, became less inevitable. Jackie Stewart's campaign was long overdue and the advent of the much faster 3-litre formula increased the hazards dramatically. Alas, it ultimately doomed the classic road circuits with their natural backdrops and aesthetic appeal, but the alternative was morally unacceptable and the consequences literally fatal.

The cost factor, which had always been paramount, escalated exponentially during the era and brought about the race to technology (and the necessity of ever greater external funding) that eventually distorted the entire *raison d'être* of motor racing.

Looking back it is possible to discern the gradual loss of the traditional racing genre and its associated personalities that finally became extinct during the 1970s.

ACKNOWLEDGEMENTS AND BIBLIOGRAPHY

Many thanks to all those who have helped in researching this book, but especially to Doug Nye, Paul Vestey, Liz Cooper, Len Terry, Clive Chapman, Bob Dance, Jim Endruweit, John Sismey, Rick Hall, Ron Tauranac, Sir Jack Brabham, Brian Redman, Vic Elford, Richard Heseltine, Helga Oates, Sir Jackie Stewart, Sutton Images, Ron Easton, Marcus Pye, Ted Walker of Ferret Photographic, Kevin Wood and Alexandra Goodchild of LAT and of course Mark Hughes, Christine Smith and Derek Smith of Haynes Publishing.

I have also consulted various sources including:

Autocourse History of the Grand Prix Car 1945–65 (Hazelton Publishing 1993) Doug Nye

Autocourse History of the Grand Prix Car 1966–85 (Hazelton Publishing 1986) Doug Nye

Grand Prix Who's Who, third edition (Travel Publishing 2000) Steve Small

It was Fun! (Patrick Stephens Ltd 1993) Tony Rudd

BRM – The Saga of British Racing Motors Volume 2 – Spaceframe Cars 1959–65 (MRP Publishing 2003) Doug Nye with Tony Rudd

Formula 1 Register Record Book 1966 (St. Leonards Press 1990) Paul Sheldon with Duncan Rabagliati and Yves de la Gorce

DINO The little Ferrari (Osprey Publishing 1979) Doug Nye

Grand Prix Volume 1 1950–65 (Haynes Publishing 1981) Mike Lang

Lotus 49: The story of a legend (Veloce Publishing 1999) Mike Oliver

The Formula One Record Book (Leslie Frewin Publishers 1974) John Thompson with Duncan Rabagliati and Dr. K. Paul Sheldon

Additionally I referred to issues of *Autosport* magazine 1960–69 and *Motor Sport* from the same period.

INDEX